Tales of
ALASKA
AND THE
YUKON

Compiled by
Frank Oppel

CASTLE

CONTENTS

1
News From
the Klondike

NEWS FROM THE KLONDIKE.

LETTER AND ILLUSTRATIONS FROM TAPPAN ADNEY,
SPECIAL CORRESPONDENT OF "HARPER'S WEEKLY."

LAKE BENNETT TO DAWSON.

AT the date we left Lake Bennett, the 9th day of October, we had no right to expect that a boat could reach Dawon before the closing of the river. We did not realize this truth then. The 7th had been clear, and we packed ur stuff across from the foot of Liudeman. A large outfit also arrived on Indians' backs, over the Dyea trail, three days out. In contrast to this, nineteen mules and horses were sent back from Bennett to find an outfit delayed at some point unknown on the Skaguay trail. A number of boats got under way down the lake, which lies between lofty snow-capped mountains, a narrow passage-way stretching into the distance as far as one can see. Eight or ten boats from Lindeman had been getting started to one with Skaguay outfits. Next day it rained, then turned into snow, in the midst of which we had to repitch the boat where the warm sun had lately melted the coating off.

On the 9th a gale is roaring down the gap, kicking up a great sea down the lake; but we ventured to start, not daring to wait longer. We rig the little spritsail; Brown tends sheet, while I take a big steering-oar in the stern. In a few moments we are among the white-caps, and the seas are boarding us, so we promptly run under the lee of a rocky point a mile from the starting-place. Half a dozen big boats with huge square sails go by us at railroad speed. We wait an hour or so, pick berries, which are very plentiful in patches among the rocks, and then push off again. We square away in great shape. There is so little freeboard amidships that if we should get in the trough of the sea we would swamp instantly. Our mast is tough pine, but when the wind snatches the rag of a sail it bends as if it would break.

Now begins the fight. The little sail, small though it is, begins to pull us to one side, and it takes all the strength of one pair of arms on a twelve-foot ash steering-oar to keep her head on. Now and then a big comber comes over the stern. In a few moments we have to bail out. There is not a cove or shelter in sight, and the sea keeps getting worse. Fresh water, being lighter, kicks up higher than salt, and we have every bit we want.

A little way on we pass a camp on shore where they are drying goods—a capsize, no doubt. Pretty soon, under the lee of little rocky capes, boats are drawn out on shore and parties are camped, driven in by the storm. The raw wind and the spray begin to make the fingers cold, but it is impossible to let go and

WHITE HORSE RAPIDS—LOOKING DOWN RIVER.

put mitters on. We are ovrhauling the little boats, and pass three or four, but the big ones show us clean heels.

About twelve miles down, the lake narrows to about half a mile, and here the waves are terrific, and the cross-wave break over the tarpaulin covering the goods amidships. In the midst of it all the mast goes overboard with a snap. Brown gathers inthe sail, and still scudding, we drop in behind a point fortunately close at hand. Here we are able to get a new and larger mast. One of the boats we had passed follows us in. It contains a New York party of two. When we start again they will not follow, on account of their heavy boatload.

At evening we run into a little cove opposite the west arm of Bennett, with a smooth sandy beach, where there are other boats. A few minutes later a big Peterboro canoe containing two men in yellow mackinaws runs in under a small sail. It is the United States mail for Circle City. Around the camp fire that night eager questions are plied these two men to know just what is going on at Dawson; for they had left Dawson only thirty-odd days before!

The boats had not get up when they left, and flour was six dollars a sack.

"Would there be starvation?"

We get this reply, spoken slowly and deliberately: "I have been eleven years in Alaska, and there hasn't been a year yet when everybody wasn't going to starve, but no one has starved yet."

"How cold is it?"

"Cold, but not so cold but that a man can stand it. I spent one winter in a tent."

All of which is comforting. The mailcarriers put up no tent, but lie down on a tarpaulin, with one over them, and are off at daylight. They have oars rigged to the canoe, and expect to reach Dawson in six or seven days.

We ourselves get under way not long after. The wind has moderated, but a heavy sea is still on. The lake is wide now, and we run along easily; we pass one boat that had got out ahead of us, and are making every inch of the little sail pull in order to overtake another. The lines of the bateau give it a tremendous advantage over the clumsy whipsawed boats built at the lakes.

We are running along about a quarter of a mile from the right-hand bank, which rises high and steep into the clouds, when we see a tent pitched on the shelving beach, with blankets and goods spread out in the sun. There are a black dog and a man, and a smallish boat drawn up on the shore. As we draw near, the man runs down to the edge of the water and fires off a gun, and then gets into the boat. We run in closer; and as we draw near, the man comes out, rowing frantically, and when we get near enough he calls out:

"Brown! Brown!"

We put the bateau around bow into the wind, and wait. When he gets within fifty yards we can see that he is much excited.

"My partners!" says he; "I haven't seen them—it was blowing too hard—and Pete went to take it out—and fell overboard—and McManus went after him!"

It is John, a Russian from San Francisco, who, with another Russian and poor McManus, had worked so hard on the trail. We had seen them all often, but did not know their full names. We gather bit by bit from his incoherent talk that their sail had been nailed fast. The yard would not lower, and in trying to unstep the mast during the hard blow of two days before, Pete had been carried overboard, and McManus had gone into the icy water to rescue him. It was nearly or quite dark at the time of this accident, and they were never seen again.

How the Russian managed to get ashore is a wonder. He had stopped several parties. They had advised him to go home, but he is anxious to get to Dawson. He offers Brown half the outfit to leave me and go with him. Brown refuses. The outfit consists of 3500 pounds of grub, and there are valuable furs and clothing. Finally, being able to do him no good, we turn on down the lake, and last see him awkwardly trying to row his ungainly craft ashore. He reported at the Canadian custom-house later, and it was rumored, thought with what truth we cannot determine, that in the endeavor to get down in the ice he had frozen his hands and feet.

By noon we are at the foot of Bennett, where, in gentler currents, between low banks a few rods apart, the green waters of the lake start again on their journey. This is Caribou Crossing, so called from its being a crossingplace for the caribou. About a mile, and the stream turns to the right into a very shallow muddy lake, two or three miles long, called Lake Nares, and then through another thoroughfare into Tagish Lake.

Tagish Lake is the name given to what is almost a group of lakes, or long arms, deep-set amid high mountains. The scenery in these lakes is magnificent. The wind, what there is, is now dead ahead. We put a trolling-line out, while Brown takes the oars. As we approach the junction of Windy Arm, which enters

BOAT IN EDDY BELOW WHITE HORSE RAPIDS.

Tagish from the southward, we expect a blow, and a battle with the cross-seas, that are said never to be absent. Extraordingary fortune is with us, for we row across the mouth of Windy Arm as on a looking-glass, in which the tall hills are doubled.

There is a tug at the trolling-line—a large salmon-troll, such as is used on Vancouver Island—and when we pull it is we have a fine large trout, in length about twenty inches, belly milk white, sides a drab gray, with large irregular, often triangular, spots of light; pectoral fines blue, ventrals tipped with light yellow—a strikingly handsome fish. We only hook this one, but get several bites. Where we camp that night, with several other boats, near the end of the lake, past the Taku Arm, one party had caught seven trout, weighting two or three pounds apiece. My own trout had a six-inch white-fish inside of it.

We are later than the others breaking camp next morning. We not only have a faculty for late rising, but have to reload the whole outfit on account of the leaking. All the boats are leaking badly. But our boat runs so easily that when we have what Brown facetiously terms a good "ash breeze" we can overtake and pass them all. The other boats are clumsy, and though they have often four oars to a boat, the oars are so heavy that they can only take short dips, and with a head-wind make no headway whatever. The lower end of the lake is full of ducks on their southward migration— hundreds of them. Having only a rifle, we miss a good opportunity. However, by a lucky shot, one drops while on the wing, to the little

30–30. We pass all the five boats we were with last night. The lake suddenly narrows, and we find ourselves in a slack current, and drifting about two miles, with flock after flock of ducks getting up.

We can see ahead, against a bank of evergreen on the right, the red flag of Britain and some tents, and make landing in shallow water at the Canadian customs office. We make camp, and before dark the others drop in and camp. There is a squad of North western Mounted Police here, under Inspector Strickland, who is also postmaster. There are, besides, John Godson, the customs officer, and several assistants. The police are building a large log barracks, and the scene reminds one of the timber woods of the East; for we have reached a region of small but plentiful timber and varied animal life. The timber grows littler as one goes down river; elevation affects growth more than latitude. It is a pretty spot they have chosen, comanding a view of the river both ways. The police have taken some huge white-fish in a weir. They caught on a troll one nineteen-and-a-half-pound trout at the outlet of Tagish. They tell me that a twenty-five-pounder has been taken on Touchi (or Too-tschai) Lake.

Mr. Godson explains why they have selected a point so far from the end of the trail. The first exploration party had come over the Skaguay Trail, had proceeded down Shallow Lake, thence over to Touchi, and down to Taku Arm. This they supposed to be the end of the trail. It happened, indeed, that there was no trail at all over the summit, and

TRADING WITH INDIANS AT LITTLE SALMON RIVER.

one was free to wander whither he listed from that point on. The trail was finally made to Bennett; but thinking Taku Arm would be the route taken, they had settled on foot of Tagish.

In regard to collection of duty on Canadian horses by the United States customs officials, Godson says he could have stationed men at the summits and taken duty on every American horse as it arrived, and done so every time it arrived. But his instructions were to use his own judgment in every particular, and, beyond asserting Canada's right to collect duty, as at Montreal or Victoria, to inflict no needless hardship on the miners. Having this in mind, he knows that man coming through are short of money, and it is his intention only to make those pay who can pay. Godson goes around in the evening by the light of the camp fires and takes the inventories of all Americans with dutiable goods, in order not to delay them in the morning.

An old-timer, familiar with the river, tells us all that he doubts if we will get through.

"You will get through Lake Marsh, then the White Horse; and if you get through Lake Labarge before it freezes, you will make Thirty Mile River, and possibly Pelly River, and if you get that far you may get down with the mush ice."

What is the mush ice?

He urges us all to "hurry! hurry!" So do all the officers—to start to-night if possible, before

LANDING AT CUSTOM-HOUSE, TAGISH.

the wind changes. The other boys, therefore, after some discussion, get their stuff aboard and start at midnight. We wait, however, until afternoon the next day, in the hope that Burnham and his flotilla of canoes may turn up, and then we too get under way. We think a good deal over what Inspector Strickland tells us—that on the 13th of October for the past three years the Klondike was frozen tight. It is now the 12th.

Marsh Lake, at whose head we virtually are now, is about nineteen miles long, narrow, like the rest, and shallow. The sky is clear, and we row on until dark sets in. It grows cold, and we have to bundle up to keep warm, except the one who rows. About nine o'clock we put inshore, and find the shore ice out twenty feet; but we discover a place where there is dry land, build a big camp fire, and cook supper. The shore ice, as it rises and falls in the gently undulating surface of the water, creaks and cries for all the world like a hundred frogs in spring-time, and it is indeed a dismal sound that bodes us no good.

"If you get through Labarge before it freezes!"

Waiting only to finish eating, we put out into the lake, whose shores we can dimly make out. We head for a point about two miles off, and are about half-way there, when the bow of the boat crashes into thin ice. Thinking we are running ashore, we turn out, and come clear of the ice. Judge our dismay when again we crash into ice! We cut through this, and turn still further out, until we are cross-wise of the lake. Again we strike into ice. I am at the oars now, and keep on pulling with difficulty, each time cutting the blades into the ice for a hold, and we pass through two or three distinct belts

of ice that extend far out into the lake. We are now almost in a panic, for it seems as if the outlet must be frozen up tight. When we get to clear water we head north again, keeping out from the shore, and towards morning we land and spread our blankets on the ground among some small spruces on a low bank. There are several inches of snow on the ground. After a short nap we start again, at an early hour. There are no other boats in sight. It is not a great way to the outlet, which we know by the current that begins to carry us along while yet well within the lake, and we are soon floating down a black stream several hundred feet across, with low wooded banks.

An odd thing occurs here. I fire at a teal that is hugging the shore, and miss. I fire again as it rises up stream, and the bullet drops back of it. By this time it has gone thirty feet, and the third bullet also falls back of it. The fourth knocks it into the water, and as the feathers float down, a mink runs out and attempts to get it. I go ashore, and find nothing but feathers—the effect of the soft-nosed bullet. Chancing to look backward, I see the mink on its haunches, looking and smelling. A shot under the chin gets him too.

Snow is on the ground everywhere. The current is easy, the river winding about among banks of sand some two hundred feet high. Along these are the holes of countless thousands of swallows, which, as Schwatka writes, are a notable feature of the river when they are back at their nesting-sites in summer.

For a day we go on thus, the river winding more and more. We do not know how far the canyon is away, so we camp on the ground

CUSTOM-HOUSE AT TAGISH.

FIVE-FINGER RAPIDS.

under a big spruce two feet in diameter; awake wet with soft snow, and after an hour's run in swift current, during which we pass a fine boat smashed on a rock in mid-stream, we hear a shout, and see boats lined up in a large eddy on the right hand, below which is a wall of dark rock and an insignificant opening, which we are persuaded is the entrance to the canyon. The shout warns us that we will be into the eddy. These are some of the boats which left us at Tagish, and some new ones. They are taking in the situation, and most of them are unloading part of their good and packing it around, a distance of three-quarters of a mile. We go up the trail to a spot where we can stand on the brink of the canyon and look directly down into its seething waters.

It is about a hundred feet wide and fifty or sixty feet deep, the whole body of the Lewes River pouring at a high rate of speed between the steep perpendicular walls of the gorge. The rock is basaltic, and takes the original formation that is familiar to those who have seen pictures of the famous Fingal's Cave. Half-way down the canyon widens, and there is a large eddy which the boats are told to avoid by keeping the crest of the waves, and then continuing as before. A boat starts in as we are looking, manned by two men at the oars, and with a bow and a stern steering oar.

After our trip through Lake Bennett in the storm we feel pretty sure of our boat, so we conclude not to carry any of our stuff around. We tuck the tarpaulin down close and make everything snug, and when Brown has seated himself at the oar, and said "All ready," we push off and head for the gateway. I think I notice a slight tightening of Brown's mouth, but that is all, as he dips the oars and begins to make the long stroke; but he might retaliate by saying some unkind thing of me at this time. As soon as we are at the very brink we know it is too late to turn back, so when we drop down the first pitch I head her for the very seething crest. At the first leap she takes into the soapsuds the spray flies several feet off the flaring sides, and we know then we shall ride it. A dozen or two huge lunges and we land in the crest of the wave and send the water flying. All at once—it must be we are not exactly in the middle—the boat's nose catches in an eddy and we are swung around, head up stream. It is a simple matter turn her nose again into the torrent, and then we go on again, leaping and jumping with terrific force. Brown, who manages the oars splendidly, keeps dipping them, and in a few moments we emerge from between the narrow walls into an open basin.

There are a number of boats here too, but we have nothing to stop for, so we keep on; but suddenly remembering that the White Horse Rapids is only one and a half miles below the canyon, we drop ashore above what is called Squaw Rapids. There are at least two dozen boats in all ashore. The White Horse is just beyond the turn where the river goes to the left along the steep hill. It will be necessary to cross to the other side. We start again into the quick water, and then, cutting across a low bar at the head of the White Horse, make a landing on a low point, from which goods are carried around below these very dangerous rapids.

A view of the rapids is the first thing to be had. The river has made a quick bend to the left and then turning to the right, goes down through basaltic walls twenty to thirty feet high and several times the width of the canyon. Lashing itself into a purple fury, it narrows into a gorge a span wide, when, with a jumping and tossing, it bursts through, and then spreads out serene, once more the wide, generous river. From a vantage-point we can see it all, the foaming crest of the final and worst pitch half a mile away. A boat is just going through, and we watch it until it emerges into the quiet water and makes a landing.

IN CARIBOU CROSSING.

We resolve to take out part of our cargo here, so as to give us more freeboard, but undertake to drop below into a sort of eddy at the very brink of the rapids, so as to have a shorter carry. I get into the boat, while Brown drops it down with the painter. We have to go outside a reef of rock thirty feet off shore, and when we are out there the rope pulls out of Brown's hands, leaving me and the loaded boat in the fast water. I quarter the boat inshore, and then, by the hardest sort of paddling, the current swings the boat in, until I can get out into the water and take it ashore. We have taken only an inch of water in the canoe. It is an exceedingly close call.

We put all our personal baggage ashore, leaving an even thousand pounds in the boat, which gives us six inches or more of freeboard, and then turn her nose into the current.

Following the roughest water, to avoid the rocks, we are pitched into the dancing waves. The waves grow bigger, and we begin to pitch worse by far than in the canyon. We go up the sides of the waves, and when we drop it seems positively as if boat and all would keep right on through to the bottom of the river. The water begins to pour in, and it is plain that the boat will never live through. But one thought for a moment comes to comfort us: even if we are chock full of water, the fearful impetus with which we are moving must surely take us bodily through and out, and then—we can make the shore somehow. I begin to count the seconds we will be going through that last and worst part into which we now driving.

Forced from both sides, the river enters the gorge; and the effect to the eye, as one goes into the great white-caps, is that of a jumping, not only up and down, but from the sides to the middle.

PAYING CUSTOMS DUTIES.

Now we are into the waves. From all sides and ends a sheet of water pours over, drenching Brown and filling the boat; the same instant, it seems, a big side-wave takes the little craft, spins her like a top, quick as a wink, throws her into a boiling eddy on the left—and we are through and safe, with a little more work to get ashore.

Men who were watching us from the bank said that we disappeared from sight in the trough. Brown is wet up to his waist.

Everything is afloat. We land here, and when we have bailed out some of the water, drop the boat down to the usual landing-place, a little sandy cove, where we unload, pitch tent, and while tripping back for our five hundred punds of goods, watch the other boats come through. They are all big ones, and all get through without mishap.

We hear of pilots, both here and at the canyon, but every man takes his own boat through. The pilots take boats through the canyon for from ten to twenty dollars, and through the White Horse for twenty dollars. Two partners stopped two weeks earlies in the season and made enough to buy in on a claim on Bonanza. Those who unload have the worst of it. The heavy boats go through best. The double-ender swings so easily that it is hard to steer, and is rather small for the business.

The White Horse is a bit of water I have considerable respect for. I ask the imperturbable Brown how he felt—if he was scared.

"Why, no," he replies. "You said it was all right; I suppose you know—it's your boat and your outfit."

The compliment is altogether too extravagant. I believe that if a charge of dynamite were to explode under Brown, he would not wink an eyelash. Many say they took more water abroad in the canyon than in the White Horse, while Squaw Rapids is worse than the canyon. There is a dog in Dawson that swam the canyon. He probably tried to follow his master's boat, instead of walking around. He is a water-spaniel, though; but he must have had more ups and downs than he dreamed of when he started in the quiet water above.

There have been no drownings in the White Horse so far as known this year, and nearly every boat was run through. The trail around the rapids is lined with trees blazed and inscribed with the heroic deeds of those gone before. They are written on trees, on scraps of paper tacked on broken oar-blades, etc. Here is one: "Sept. 8, 1897. Boat Cora and Meda. 20 ft long. 8 ft 3 in beam. 26 in deep. safety shot the White Horse Rapids loaded with 4000 pounds," And this:

Gudmond Jensen
G. G. Tripp
Tom
Mike went
threw all right.

It is a great load off our minds when we are at last safely through. We care not how swift the river runs now; there is only Five Fingers, a long way off yet.

Another day brings us at dark to the head of Lake Labarge, up which a wind is blowing, with a big head-sea. Lights show up at a place on the left, and we steer towards this. It is totally dark when we get there, but when close inshore we run into fish-weirs, and hear the laughter and crying of children and the barking of dogs, and then we know that it is an Indian village, so we turn up shore, and after a mile, off around a turn, land on a beach by a huge pile of drift-wood. Attracted by our big fire, two or three other boats drop in, and we have a merry time. In an hour four Indians come over with furs to sell or trade for sugar. These Indians are Tinné They hunt moose, mountain-sheep, bears and fur-bearing animals. After hanging around a while they go away. I should not care to leave a boat-load of provisions in the neighborhood of these Siwashes. Experiences later with the same breed down-river justify the precautions we take.

Lake Labarge, named for Labarge, one of the explorers for the long-ago projected Russo-American telegraph line, is about thirty miles in length, and it is rare that a strong wind is not blowing there, so fiercely that the miners are often delayed, as at Windy Arm. It is as smooth as glass next morning. The shores are of moderate height, of a diversified rounded form of gray stone. Seen as we see it, is is a most picturesque body of water, and very clear. As we near the end a wind catches us, and as there is no shelter we have to keep on in the darkness. For several hours we see friendly beacons, and when we get to them we find a camp of friends who had left several days ahead of us. Next morning finds us near the outlet of the lake, and a short pull brings us in to Thirty Mile River, as the Lewes is known

until it joins the Teslintoo, or Hootalinqua of the miners. The latter stream follows the structural valley of he river. The Lewes has a much smaller sectional are, but discharges more water. The Teslintoo is the larger, and the true source of the Yukon. Schwatka is responsible for the prevailing notion that Lindeman is the source of the Yukon, because he stated that, starting at Lindeman, he had followed the Yukon "to its mouth." The Lewes breaks through a barrier of hills at right angles. Looking up river, any one would say the Teslintoo was the main river. The country seems different. The water, no longer clear, is tinged with the mud of the latter river. White birches now appear.

Big Salmon, Little Salmon, are successively passed, the latter 285 miles from Dyea. We take no account of this. Our chief diversion is in seeing how quick we can overtake a boat when once we get a sight of it, and also in keeping up with a certain other boat, whose occupants cook on board, rise earlier, and go into camp later than we do. There is now about eight inches of snow, and we have to scrape a hole and line it well with boughs when we camp.

A very short way below the Little Salmon we see (and it should be observed that we *hear* at the same time) a number of people beckoning and signalling from the shore. We stop at a platform of hewn boards built out in the water, and are at once surrounded by a horde of dirty, uncouth, wild-looking savages, of all sizes and shapes, each with something to trade. They want to buy everything in sight. We have left some things uncovered; they seize on these things, and shove into our faces a dirty fur cap or a moose-hide or a bear-skin. I haven't the smallest notion what they want

THE MAIN CHANNEL—FIVE FINGER RAPIDS.

CHARACTERISTIC VIEW ON YUKON RIVER.

with my camera. I have to push them off my end of the boat, but they hang on front, back, and sides, pulling and tugging to draw attention to their wares. I have never seen such fierce trading in my life. We know nothing like it in civilized life. A person could keep himself warm at 60 degrees below, trading as they do. I try to get away, but Brown has opened up some tobacco he had, so we are in for it. There are about twenty aboard our little boat. I buy a pair of fur-trimmed mittens; and then, with astonishing finesse, the fellow tries to beat me out of the mittens, pretending he has given them to me. So I get out on the platform, take him by the arm, and forcibly extract the two silver dollars from his fist. While this is going on another boat stops, and shortly there is a hubbub; the Indians run up, and a crowd rushes down from the village on the bank beyond. I ask the trouble.

"Just Injun talk," an Indian replies.

That night I learn the cause. An Indian had showed a watch, and had himself dropped it and broken the crystal. With great wit, he handed it to one of the white boys, and then raising the cry that they had broken it, demanded $5. The boys not having arms handy, and the Indian having two shot-guns, they paid the five dollars.

As we are leaving, the Indian who had tried to cheat me comes running to the boat, tosses the lost mittens aboard, and I give him the money. But on taking stock I find myself out a pair of scissors, a box of tobacco, and a candle.

Five Finger Rapids, 344 miles frm Dyea, is reached in company with a small fleet of boats. We are all distinctly apprehensive, not knowing whether we are five or fifty miles from the rapids. When they come into view, the row of huge square blocks of rock standing like the piers of a bridge across the steam, they are unmistakable.

We run our boat into the eddy above the right-hand entrance, while the other boats line down from above. There is a short sudden drop and a nasty upward swirl, it is true, but nothing to care about, so we shoot in, all the rest, I suppose, following. We take a little water, and then enter a series of rapids, which shortly brings us to another object of apprehension, Rink Rapids. There is nothing here but a reef, with good easy current on the right hand. Just below, a great congregation of ravens indicates where the cattle have been driven in and butchered and rafted down.

The river is full of islands, and it is the hardest sort of work keeping off he bars. More than once we get into an inside channel, and have to wade out and tow up and around. When at length we reach the mouth of the Pelly River, it looks as if we shall reach Dawson. We have been cautioned about Pelly. On the left, below the mouth of Pelly, are an Indian village, a mission, and the house and store of Mr. Harper. We land here to camp. The camping-place is really several miles below; but Mr. Pitts, the storekeeper in charge, will have nothing of the kind. He puts us into one of Mr. Harper's houses, with a stove, and a good dry floor to lie on, and his own kerosene-lamp, all of them luxuries. He treats us handsomely, as well as giving us the first authentic information of the country to

MAKING A LANDING BELOW WHITE HORSE RAPIDS.

which we are going.

We relate our experience with the Indians at Little Salmon. He tells us that those on the Yukon proper are different altogether; they are honest, and in a degree virtuous, whereas those further up river have been mistreated so long by the Chilkats that whenever opportunity offers they treat others the same way.

There is nothing left of the old Hudson Bay Fort, burned down in that raid of the Chilkats in 1852. The post, supplied at great cost and hazard *viá* Upper Pelly and the Liard River, was never re-established. The spot is still called Fort Selkirk.

In the store there are a dozen silver-gray fox-skins and one black fox, which in this country are more plentiful than anywhere else in comparison with the red fox, of which they are varieties. Formerly one could by snowshoes and fur robes here, but this year the rush has cleaned out all but a few moose-hides, some of which Mr. Pitts is for sending to Dawson by us; but he does not, fearing we may not get there. The thermometer registers two above zero at seven o'clock in the morning.

What do we see when we look out?

On the far side of the river, a procession of blocks of something white—the mush, or slush, ice!

It is coming out of Pelly. We take the left side of the river, where it is clear, and at night find a good camping-place. The timber seems to grow better and better on the flats and islands. The nights and days are cold.

The first night out from Pelly we make the boat fast on the side free from ice. The bank here is about twelve feet high, and the tent is several yards back. We are lying before an open fire, about to go to sleep. The air is still, and we can hear the ominous "s-s-sh" of the ice in the river.

Suddenly there is a dull prolonged roar under the bank. I jump up, and down the bank, in time to see a floe forty feet long go by, having scraped the entire length of the boat; and the river is full of floes, large and small, rushing and grinding against one another. Calling for Brown, it is but a few moments' work to unload the boat and haul it out. Next morning the whole river is full of ice, rushing along like a mill-race. This is the mush ice—ice formed on the bottom, soft and slushy. It hardens into floes, and floe freezes to floe to make larger ones.

We put out into the ice, getting into the current, keeping barely clear with the paddles, and whenever a lead opens up we make the most of it with oars, and soon find that by reason of her double end we can work her about where we choose. There is no stopping at noon now; we eat a bite of cold beans and hardlack. After noon we come upon six boats ranged on the shore of a wooded island. It seems time to land, which we do at considerable risk, for the ice is setting hard against the shore.

Around a camp fire in the woods are about twenty men, some of them friends who had left a week ahead of us. They are prepared to stay,

DOG-TRAINS LEAVING DAWSON FOR DYEA.

RUNNING THE WHITE HORSE RAPIDS.

Captain Kinsey, Dawson 1896

SAILING DOWN LAKE BENNETT.

they said, until the ice runs out. I tell them that they will wait till spring; that I am going on. It is a sore temptation to stop by their cheerful fire, but I reason that the camp fire is an accidental circumstance; had the boats not been there I should have kept on. So we do. None of them followed for three or four days, when they saw other boats passing, and realized their folly. Some of the men were eager to start, but in nearly every boat was some nervous partner, That night we find a safe camping-place in an eddy free of ice, and cut a channel for the boat into the ice, which now extends a number of feet from shore.

Camp-making is now reduced to the simplest method. At first we would carefully pitch the wall-tent. Now all we do is to take the two oars and three pine poles, tie the ends together tight and fast with a rope, walk around them with the tent, and build an open fire in front. Often we dispense with the tent entirely. Bread, salt, and beans are frozen hard as rocks. We meet several parties with hand-sleds and canoes working up against the ice, along the shore, going out.

"No grub in Dawson."

So that is the truth!

There is nothing to do but to drift with the ice, keeping the channel and opens, avoiding the places where it sets against the shore. The thermometer registers from 10 to 5 degrees above zero. Even at this we find six to ten feet of thick ice frozen around the boat each morning, and our first task is to chop it out, but still much sticks to the sides, the water near by freeze, and the boat sinks lower an lower in the water. We are practically in winter clothes, and even then it is hard to keep

warm facing a wind in the cold. We get fifteen or twenty miles in a day. Nervousness is disappearing. We no longer mind the crunching and punching of the floes. There is nearly always a boat in sight now.

When about twenty miles, we judge, above White River, which we look for on the left, and which we expect will put a lot more ice into the Yukon, we see a boat on the right-hand shore—a large boat with a stove cooking. As we draw near, it proves to be a party known as the "Christie" party, from the Skaguay trail. They have a Japanese cook and two ladies aboard. The Indians on Lake Labarge would not believe the Jap was not an Indian. "You Injun?" "No!" "You mamma Injun?" "No!" "You papa Injun?" "No! no!" protested the Jap; "me odder country."

With the Christie party is the New York *Times* correspondent, Pelletier. They are eating lunch, and at the same time trying to fend off the floes. They have been having trouble all the way down. They have only just come off an island where they have been three days. After this we keep them company, with this difference, that they hug the shore, while we keep out. It was easy for them to step out, but the boat is in imminent risk of being crushed by the heavy ice.

We pass White River without knowing it, and ten miles on we come to a straight reach, where on the right are thirty or forty boats drawn out on the ice, and tents set up, and cabins.

This is Stewart River. It seems as if every one is stopping here, except some who cannot get through the ice in time. They have stopped either to remain and prospect, or from fear of

ice, and also to hear whether it is safe to take their outfits to Dawson. Wild stories ae coming up river, and we know not what to expect.

We go on at noon the next day. One thing the ice does. It piles up on the heads of the bars, and now it is easy to avoid them, and to see the set of the water. We keep to the right-hand channel, among the many islands. Several miles below Stewart a bar with ice as usual piled up on the head of it, looms up. For our lives we cannot see, even by standing up, which way the water runs. While hesitating, we are borne directly on the island, and when we try to avóid that, we are carried directly towards the great mass of ice. Only one thing saves us: a floe happens to be between us when we strike. It crushes, and we slip along the side and slide out into deep water. Nothing else under heaven could have kept us from going under the ice.

We make shore quickly after this by a big pile of drift-wood, and have hardly got our tent up and a place chopped for the boat when another boat heaves in sight, and calls to us to take a line. It is the Christie party, and they have met with an accident.

Hugging the shore, as usual, they had run upon some sweepers hanging over the water. All hands jumped for the bottom. The boat was stern down stream when it struck. The sweeper caught the steering-sweep and swept the boat clear, stove-pipe and all. Christie had failed to find a point of safety, and had been doubled up and nearly killed.

We take their line, and they camp with us. After that, at last, that boat keeps clear of the shore.

Navigation is getting more difficult; the channels are growing so narrow that a boat can hardly go through. We can only drift and keep the sides of the boat clear. We have been told to keep to the right from Sixty Mile Creek down. On that side we can see scores of parties going out with sleds. By this time we have discovered one thing—that we are better off taking nobody's advice about camping-places, so we have taken the other side, and do not know how near Dawson we are.

On the 29th of October, judging ourselves to be about ten miles away, we make camp and set about fixing up a sled, stay there two days, then start once more. When we have the covers nicely tucked around for a big trip we turn suddenly to the left, and see on the right bank ahead a large number of tents, houses, and boats, some of them in the water, others drawn out.

"How far to Dawson?" we ask.

"This is Dawson," is the reply; "you'd better hurry, or you'll be carried past."

We make a landing in good order, and tie fast to the shore. We are not yet in Dawson proper. This is but a suburb, on the site of the old Indian village, and known as Klondike City, or Lousetown.

Four days later the river jammed, then it moved on again, and closed for good on the 7th of November. It had closed in front of Dawson on about the 15th of the month of October, but had broken again—a most fortunate circumstance for us. Little did we realize the danger we had been in, for we knew not then how the Yukon closed. Burnham's party with the four canoes, got no farther than Selkirk. Major Walsh's party lost three boats, one after another, under the ice. The last parties to reach Dawson had miraculous escapes, which have been detailed before. Yet there was only one death in the ice, so far as is known. When it is remembered how through the length of the upper river there were hundreds taking the greatest chances, first with water, then with ice, it would almost seem true, as has been said, that a guarding Providence watched over the new comers on the Yukon this year.

HOW ADNEY GOT THROUGH.

The "man leding the horses," mentioned by Tappan Adney in one of his late letters (June 4, 1898) from Dawson, has a vivid recollection of the chance meeting referred to, at the foot of Lake Lindeman, where the Skaguay trail of agony and mud joins the original thoroughfare to the gold-fields, viá Chilkoot Pass.

As I came down the sandy hill-side to the lake, I saw at the landing two men unloading a trim-looking double-ender boat of distinct individuality that it needed only a glance to show was vastly superior to the ordinary Yukon type. One of the men was a slender six-footer, with a face wind-tanned the color of sole-leather.

He wore weather-stained clothes, that, judging from the general suggestion, no doubt still carried a little of the smoky smell and balsam aroma from camps in the green woods of New Brunswick. His feet were moccasined, and his black hair straggled from under a red toboggan cap. Not only was his rig suggestive of the aborigine, but his every action proved him to be so thoroughly at home in his untamed environment that it is little wonder at first glance I took him to be an Indian, and that it required several minutes after his jolly

MINERS LEAVING DAWSON BECAUSE OF FOOD SHORTAGE.

smile and voluble greting to dispel the illusion.

Adney was a hustler of the most advanced type. Though just recovering from an attack of the prevailing malady of the trail, he carried across the portage packs weighing as much as 125 pounds that evening and the following days, and in an extremely short time had his boat emptied of her cargo and ready for the trip from Lindeman to Bennett. These lakes are connected by a rapid stream, with a rocky, obstructed channel. White men let their boats down by ropes—a process known as "lining." The Indians, who are familiar with the stream, shoot a portion of the rapids, but near the lower end they land, and make a short portage past a particularly dangerous place, where the current dashes tumultuously over and around a number of large bowlders lying in the bed of the stream. Above on the bank is the grave of a man who lost his outfit and in his despair committed suicide.

Adney was an expert at river navigation; and his companion, though inexperienced in this kind of work, was a champion oarsman, cool-headed, and gritty. On a later occasion I happened to be on the trail near the point referred to when I heard some men calling out from the top of the canyonlike bank that the HARPER'S WEEKLY man was shooting the rapids . I ran across just in time to see the boat swept by with the speed of a bolt from a crossbow, leaping from wave-crest to wave-creat, and drenching its occupants with sheets of spray. Adney and Brown were standing erect in bow and stern, each wielding a single oar used as a paddle, and from their masterly course it was evident that they had their boat well under control. It was all over in a very small fraction of time. They had avoided by the narrowest margin jagged bowlders that it seemed impossible to pass, and in a slather of foam shot out into the smooth water below.

I overheard one man remark on the daredevil skill of the newspaper man, to which his companion replied: "Oh, that's the kind of a fellow Andey is. I knew him at Sheep Camp."

J. B. BURNHAM.

2
The Great River
of Alaska

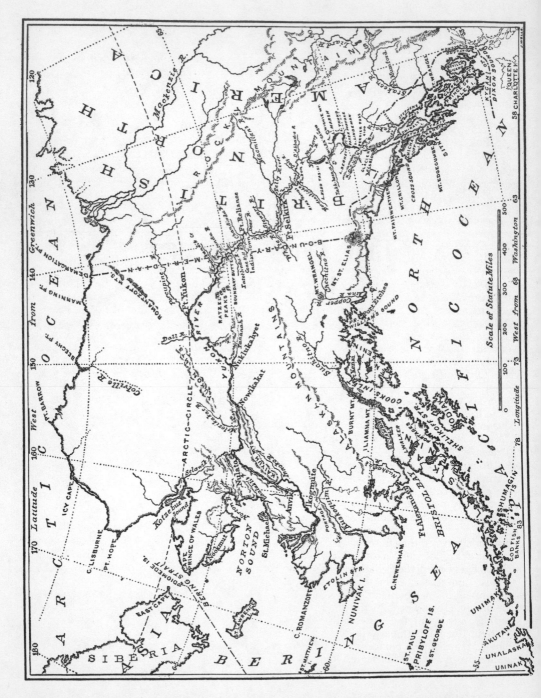

MAP OF ALASKA AND PART OF BRITISH COLUMBIA, SHOWING THE YUKON RIVER FROM ITS SOURCE IN BRITISH COLUMBIA
TO ITS MOUTH IN ALASKA, BEING THE COURSE OF LIEUTENANT SCHWATKA'S RAFT-JOURNEY IN 1883.

THE GREAT RIVER OF ALASKA.

EXPLORING THE UPPER YUKON.[*]

THE Yukon River naturally divides itself into three portions: the Upper Yukon, measuring about five hundred miles, and reaching from its source to Fort Selkirk, where it is joined by the Pelly; the Middle Yukon, extending from Fort Selkirk for another five hundred miles to Fort Yukon, at the junction of the Porcupine or Rat River; and the Lower Yukon, nearly a thousand miles in length, reaching from Fort Yukon to the river's many mouths in Bering Sea and Norton Sound. The middle and lower rivers had been traversed by Russian navigators or in the interest of the Hudson's Bay Company, thus completing the exploration of three-fourths of the Nile of Alaska; but the upper river was still unknown till the early summer of 1883. To describe briefly the Yukon and its exploration from Selkirk to its source, thus completing the chain, is the object of this article. Or, speaking more correctly, from its source to Fort Selkirk; for it was with the current that my little party floated on a raft over this part of the river. That Alaskan Indians of various tribes had broken through the different passes in the glacier-clad mountains which separate the Pacific from the head-waters of the Yukon, in order to trade with the Indians there, has been known for over a century. Why this route had not been picked out long ago by some explorer, who could thereby traverse the whole river in a single summer instead of combating its swift current from its mouth, seems singular, and can only be explained by supposing that those who would place sufficient reliance on the Indian reports to put in their maps the gross inaccuracies that fill even all our Government charts of the Yukon's source, would be very likely to place reliance on the same Indians; and these, from time immemorial, have united in pronouncing this part of the river unnavigable even by canoes, filled as it is with rapids, whirlpools, and cascades.

Arriving in Chilkat early in June, 1883, I found that miners had pioneered the way some distance down the river in search of gold, but no white person had as yet explored this part of the river; and when I humbly suggested a raft as my future conveyance, and hoped to make the whole river in a summer's dash, I was hooted at and ridiculed by natives and white men alike.

There are four passes known to the Indians leading over from salt water to the sources of the Yukon. The one by way of Lynn Channel and Chilkoot Inlet is the best of all, and is the one that was undertaken by my party. For many years this pass had been monopolized by the Chilkoot Indians, who did not even allow their half-brothers, the Chilkats, to use it. Both bands united in opposing the migration of the interior tribes to the coast for trading purposes, wholly monopolizing this Alpine commerce. I used numbers of each of these three bands of Indians in packing my effects over the mountains. As I have intimated, the journey began on the 7th of June, when we left Chilkat with thirteen canoes, I believe, towed in a long, continuous string by a little steam-launch kindly placed at my disposal by Mr. Spuhn, the manager of the Northwest Trading Company. They formed a pretty sight as they were towed down the Lynn Channel and up the Chilkoot Inlet, some twenty miles to the Chilkoot mission, where four or five canoes full of the latter tribe of Indians were added to the already long chain. Leaving the Chilkoot Inlet and entering another that the Indians called the Dayay, we could fairly say that our explorations had begun.

This inlet, like so many in Alaska, has more the appearance of a large river than a salt-water estuary,—flanked on either side by immense precipitous mountains, covered nearly to their tops with a dense growth of spruce and pine and capped with snow-white glacier ice, which feeds a thousand silvery waterfalls, whose gleaming stripes down the shaggy mountainside give a beautiful relief to the deep, somber green of the foliage. The mouth of the Dayay was reached that evening, and our effects of some three or four tons were lightered ashore by means of the Indian canoes;

* Lieutenant Schwatka's expedition to Alaska and the British Northwest Territory in 1883 had for its object the seeking of military information regarding the Indian tribes of those regions. A subordinate purpose was geographical exploration. The party consisted of seven white men — two officers, four soldiers, and one citizen (Lieutenant Schwatka, Dr. Wilson, Topographical Assistant Homan, Sergeant Gloster, Corporal Shircliff, Private Roth, and Mr. McIntosh) — and such Indians as were added from time to time during the journey.

the launch steamed out of sight, and my little party of seven white men were left alone with nearly ten times that number of Indian allies, to fight our way over the mountain range whose eastern slopes feed the great river that we desired to explore. Up the swift current of the Dayay, only thirty to forty yards in width, the Indians transport-

CANOEING UP THE DAYAY RIVER.

ed the load in canoes, two to each canoe, one pulling by a rope fastened to the bow and the other keeping the craft out in the stream by a long stiff pole reeved into the rope. Reaching the head of navigation at the foot of a boiling cascade, the canoes were unloaded and drawn out of water, and placed under cover of the dense willows that line the banks of this stream. Each human pack-mule now adjusted his load for the struggle ahead, the average weight of a pack being over a hundred pounds for the adults, one Indian carrying as much as one hundred and thirty-seven pounds; boys of fourteen or fifteen, who had eagerly solicited "a pack," carried from thirty to seventy pounds.

We followed the trail which led to the very head of the Dayay, where its waters poured beneath bridges and banks of snow, until we stood at the base of the pass, towering some three thousand to three thousand five hundred feet above us, capped with snow, and with long finger-like glaciers of clear blue ice extending down the granite gulches to our very level. Early on the morning of the 11th the pass was essayed, and it was an interesting sight to see our sixty odd packers strung out along the steep snow-covered mountain-side. In many places the ascent seemed almost perpendicular, the Indians using their hands and knees, and laying hold of the stunted juniper and spruce roots that stuck through the thin covering of snow. Along the steep drifts, where a misstep would have hurled them down the mountain-side, the foot-tracks of the leaders were made deep and inclining inward so as to give a firm foothold, and many of the party used rough alpenstocks to aid them. At the top of the pass, four thousand feet and more above the level of the sea, we were in the drifting fog that forever hangs over these vast fields of elevated ice, and which cut off the fine view

that we had anticipated from such a favorable height. The descent from Perrier Pass, as I called it, is very rapid for a few hundred yards, but it is a pleasant walk compared with the toilsome struggle to its summit. I noticed that the Indians in following a course on the snow, up-hill or on a level, or even on a slight descent, always step in each other's tracks, so that my sixty odd Indians made a trail that looked as if only five or six had passed that way; when going down a steep descent, however, each one would follow a separate course, and they would scatter out over many yards. I could not help being impressed with the idea that this would be worth remembering if one ever had occasion to estimate the number of a party of Indians that had traveled over a fresh trail.

Passing by a number of small lakes on our left, some few of which yet contained floating ice in small quantities, we sighted the main lake late in the afternoon, and in a couple of hours found ourselves upon its banks at the mouth of a beautiful clear stream, boiling down from the mountain-sides. This lake, which I named Lake Lindeman, was a beautiful sheet of water, some ten or twelve miles long, and looked not unlike a limited area of one of the broad inland passages traversed by the steamers plying to Alaskan ports farther south. Fish were very scarce in these cold glacier-fed streams and lakes, but we managed to vary the stereotyped fare of Government bacon with a few dusky grouse and equally tough ducks, for it was now getting to be the breeding season of all the feathered tribe. Flowers were in bloom on all sides, and the deciduous trees had long since put on their spring and summer fashions, and robins and many other singing birds fluttered through the foliage, while gulls and tern hovered over the waters of the lake.

boiling cascade, but a few minutes' hard work sufficed to pry the raft off; and as we brought up on the gravelly beach in the still waters of Lake Bennett, we all felt grateful that the

PERRIER PASS.

Here we commenced building our raft. The logs were of the smallest kind, consisting of dwarfed spruce and contorted pine, and it was a question whether a raft 15 x 30 would carry our effects and all our party, white and Indian,—a question which was finally settled in the negative, by sending only three persons and a little over half the material on the first voyage of the raft, a Government tent serving the purpose of a sail, which was amply filled by a southern gale that in other respects made navigation quite hazardous.

On the 16th we steered the raft through the mile of rapids and cascades that make up the short river that connects Lake Lindeman with the lake to the north, called by me Lake Bennett. Once we were jammed between a protruding rock and the shore in a narrow

safe passage had saved us a few days' hard work. But it was a necessity to remodel the raft on a larger plan in order to carry all that must find passage on its corduroy decks. Larger logs were found near the Payer Portage, and our raft was built on the plan of 15 x 40, although really nearer 16 x 42. Two decks were built up, fore and aft, leaving spaces at the ends for bow and stern oars, while the central part of the raft between the decks gave working-room for two side oars, with which the unwieldy craft could be rowed on still water at the rate of about three-quarters of a mile an hour. Behind the forward decks was a strong nine-foot mast, and the sail was a wall-tent with its ridge-pole for a yard, and the projecting poles of the deck gave lashing-points for the ends of the tent as we trimmed sail to vary our course before the wind; for, rude as our raft was, we could sail her for two or three points (about 40°) to the right or left from a straight-away course before the wind. Not one of the smallest discomforts of the trip was the necessity of standing all day in the water while building the raft. The water in the lake was icy, having just poured down from the glaciers and snow-fields that crown the surrounding mountains; ice-water and mosquitoes were a singular combination of discomforts. Caribou and bear tracks were found not far from the shores, but the animals themselves were never seen.

The morning of the 19th of June the new craft cast off bow and stern lines, and rowing a few hundred yards we set our primitive sail; and as the never-ceasing southern wind grew with the sun, we soon found ourselves lubbering over the beautiful lake at a speed of from two to two and a half miles an hour. Through the ice-fields capping the timbered mountains to the east protruded many a dull red rock and ridge surmounted again by the everlasting white fog. Specimens of this rock found in the terminal moraines of the little glaciers showed iron, and I named this bold range after that metal. By three in the afternoon the wind had increased to a gale, and the huge waves of the lake were sweeping the rear space of the stern oarsmen, and even at times breaking over the pole-deck itself; but still our faith in the queer sailer was sufficient to hold her head straight for the north. For two long hours we held our course, for a favorable wind over the lakes must be utilized to the last second possible; but the gale increased to a cyclone and threatened to carry away our mast; the white-capped seas swept both decks and deluged between so as to make rowing impossible; and the two ends of the craft worked like a hinged gate in the huge waves, for there was not a single log that extended much farther than half-way of the raft. When a few of the pins commenced snapping and a little sheltered cove was seen to our right, we turned the raft's head to the eastern shore, and in a little while were threatened with destruction in the seething breakers that broke upon the rough granite beach. A line was carried ashore by the Indians in a canoe, and with some to hold her off by means of stiff poles, the rest of us " tracked " or towed her back to the shelter of the cove. Here we remained a day and repaired the raft; four fine logs were found which would reach her whole length, and by their size so increased her strength and buoyancy that we thought she might be able to carry a name, and so dubbed her the *Resolute*, though I doubt if the name was heard half a dozen times afterwards.

The next afternoon by five o'clock we had

CREEPING THROUGH
THE FOG.

reached the north end of Lake Bennett, thirty miles long, and entered a short river that gave us a taste of the fact that drifting with the current also had its difficulties, for we were two hours prying the *Resolute* off a sand-bar at the mouth of this short river. This limited stream is known to the Tahk-heesh Indians as " the place where the caribou cross," and in certain seasons of the year many of these animals ford its wide, shallow current. The general trend of the new lake into which the river emptied was towards the east, and our old friend the south wind was of but little use; and though there were only three or four miles to traverse, it was three days before we got a favorable wind that carried us across. This little lake (Lake Nares), whose entire outline could be viewed from the high hills on the north, was the prettiest one we found nestling in these northern hills. The country was perceptibly opening, many level places could be seen, the hills were less steep, and the snow was disappearing from their crests. Many roses and wild violets were in bloom, and wild onions lined the lake shore in profusion and gave us a fair substitute for the vegetable diet that we had left behind; and everywhere there was a general change of verdure for the better. Grand terraces that looked like stairways for giants, symmetrical on opposite sides of the lake, showed its ancient and subsiding levels. These, too, in a less conspicuous manner, had been noticed on the northern shores of Lake Bennett. Grouse abounded everywhere, and the little broods were met every few yards in walking over the hills, the tiny ones scampering off in the weeds while the mothers walked along, clucking anxiously, often only a few feet ahead of the intruder. Once out of the little lake through a short river of a hundred yards, we entered another lake, still trending to the east, and eight or nine miles long, which I called Lake Bove, and on whose limited shore-line I was compelled to make two camps and half a dozen landings, so baffling was our motive power, the wind.

At one time, when we had rowed ashore to avoid a sudden head-breeze, our Indians carelessly set fire to some of the dry dead spruce timber, and the flames, enveloping the living trees for hours afterwards, sent upward dense volumes of smoke that we saw from many miles beyond. Toward evening, some fifteen or twenty miles ahead, a smoke was seen curling upward, and our Indians told us that it was an answer to the one we had accidentally made on Lake Bove. These signal-smokes were quite common between the Chilkats and Tahk-heesh Indians, the former thus announcing to the latter that they had crossed the mountains and were in their country for trading purposes. An old trader on the Middle and Lower Yukon told me that this Chilkat-Tahk-heesh traffic was so great some years ago, that as many as eighty of the former tribe have been known to cross the Kotusk mountains by the Chilkat and Chilkoot trails twice a year; or, in brief, eight tons of trading material found its way over Perrier Pass and, ramifying from this as a center, spread over the whole north-west. Fort Selkirk, for a brief period a Hudson's Bay Company post, interfered with this commerce; but a war party of Chilkats in 1851 extended their trading tour five hundred miles in order to burn it to the ground, and the blackened chimneys still standing in a thick grove of poplars are monuments that attest how well they did their work. We had an immense volume with us purporting to be an authority on Alaskan matters, and as we read that it was but two days' journey ("nay, hardly a day and a half") for the Indians from here to Selkirk in their swift birch canoes, we thought that possibly the worst of our journey was behind us; until our Indians, some of whom had grown gray-headed traveling this country as traders, dashed our hopes with the information that there were three rapids aggregating five or six miles in length ahead of us, that the Indians here never used birch-bark canoes, and that the journey took them nearly two weeks in their cottonwood ones and would take us three,

if we ever got through with the raft at all; for though their wavering faith had been strengthened by the actions of the *Resolute* in the past, they were not yet perfectly settled. Instead of being one hundred and twenty miles from Tah-ko to Selkirk, as guessed at, it was four hundred and thirty-three. A roughly built Tahk-heesh house stood upon the banks, and is the only one on this part of the Yukon River for hundreds of miles on either side. The next lake is nearly thirty miles in length, and proportionally much broader than any we had passed. I called it Lake Marsh, after the well-known scientist of our country. The waters of this lake were much warmer than those we had passed, and we all refreshed ourselves with a few minutes' bathing on its shores. Nearing the beach at Lake Marsh during the two or three camps we made on it, we found it impossible to get much closer than fifty to one hundred yards, owing to the huge deposits of "glacier-mud" that had been brought down by the streams whose waters at their sources came out from under these colossal pulverizers of the mountain flanks. The *Resolute* drew about twenty inches, and the stage of water was just such that we were compelled to pack our camping material this distance through a species of mud that almost pulled our rubber boots from our feet as we floundered through its tenacious mass.

We were now having our longest days, and so close were we to the arctic circle that type like that of THE CENTURY Magazine could easily be read at midnight. On the night of the 28th of June we sailed till after midnight, so imperative was it to take advantage of every favorable breeze, and at that time but one star in the cloudless sky could be seen, which was made out to be Venus. Faint signs of terraces were still observable on the hillsides, but they were lower, nearer together, and not so well marked. The trees on Lake Marsh, as had been often noticed before on the upper waters of the Yukon, all leaned, in more or less conspicuous inclinations, toward the north, or down-stream, thus plainly showing the prevailing direction of the stronger winds. About noon on the 28th, while sailing on Lake Marsh, we had an energetic thunder-shower, which lasted till past two in the afternoon, and which is worth noticing as the first thunder-shower ever recorded on the Yukon, they being unknown on the lower river. Many of the flat, level places on the eastern hills were still covered with last year's dense growth of dead yellow grass, that from the lake, as we slowly sailed by, looked strangely like stubble-fields of oats or wheat. The outlet from Lake Marsh was very annoying to our mode of navigation with its endless banks of "glacier-mud," most

THE GRAND CAÑON, UPPER YUKON.

of which was probably brought down by a large river—the McClintock—that here comes in from the east; a river so large that we were in some doubt as to its being the outlet, until its swift current settled all conjectures by swinging us around into the proper stream. This new river that we entered was much more picturesque than any we had so far met on this journey, and strongly resembled many of the streams of more favored climes. Its hillsides were covered with pine, hemlock, and spruce, with here and there little grass-covered prairies, while the valley was fringed with poplars and willows in the densest profusion. In fact these latter were so impenetrable and grew so close to the very water's edge that we were often baffled in finding good camping-places, unless some friendly ridge from the hills threw

out a pine-covered spur to the river-bank, that would allow a tent or two to be pitched under the evergreens, or at least give us room to bivouac and spread our blankets. The deck of the raft itself was preferred by many to the variety of uncomfortable beds that this country can offer to the traveler.

The exact location of the great rapids ahead of us was not known to our Indians, and we were in a nervous state of anxiety caused by watching for them in a craft that we could not get to shore for a landing in less than three hundred or four hundred yards run, and possibly a mile, if combinations should be unfavorable. The persistent fishing of the doctor and some of the men had occasionally been rewarded with success, and a few lake trout and graylings had been added to our slim fare. On the last

CASCADE NEAR THE END OF THE GRAND RAPIDS.

day of June, as we rounded a high bold bluff, we heard rapids ahead and saw that the current was getting swifter and the water much more shallow; and we ran our raft on shore with more haste than discretion, for an examination showed the rapids to be of the lightest character, with the worst part of them in the shape of a rocky reef some thirty or forty yards directly in front of the raft. It was, of course, impossible to clear this impediment when we cast loose, and so we floated against it, depending on a series of swingings outward until its end was reached and passed. As the raft brought up on the reef and the water was seething through the logs and the men preparing to get overboard to pry her around, a most energetic splashing was heard on the farther side of the craft, and much to our astonishment a large grayling was seen floundering on the end of a fish-line that some one had left hanging over the raft in the hurry of more important duties. This was our initiation into the grayling fishing-grounds that gave us some four or five hundred of these delicious and "gamy" fellows in the next few days, until we actually tired of them. The fish caught that evening in the ripples along the river-banks were of two distinct sizes, with very few that could be called intermediate, the larger weighing about a pound and a quarter to a pound and a half and the smaller about one-fourth as much. The next day, the

1st of July, with a Tahk-heesh Indian whom we had picked up as a guide, we approached the great rapids of which we had heard so much. Our guide in his canoe had told us that he would inform us of their proximity in time enough to reach the shore, but we could not help fearing that he considered our craft about as easy to handle as one of their canoes and would give his information accordingly,— a supposition that we found to be correct, for had we not closely followed at considerable labor the eastern bank, which we knew to be the one on which we must camp, it is more than probable we would have gone through the cañon without warning and been wrecked. Even when the conspicuous mouth of the cañon was descried but a little distance ahead, our fate hung on a quarter-inch halliard with which we suddenly fastened our craft to a poplar-tree on the bank. The line fairly sang like a harp-string as the swift water poured over the logs and the huge craft swung slowly into the bank, where we were a very few seconds in making it snug and secure.

An inspection of the rapids showed them to be nearly five miles long, in places narrow and deep, then shoaling out and exposing dangerous rocks. The first quarter of a mile the swift river pours in boiling foam through a cañon fifty or sixty feet deep, and but little greater in width, the sides of the chute being regularly laid basaltic columns that in places rival human workmanship. It then widens out into a large basaltic basin full of seething whirlpools and curling eddies, and then again for a third of a mile passes through another cañon the exact duplicate of the first. The current again spreads out some quarter of a mile into shallow rapids, looking much less dangerous than the cañon, but being really much more so with its countless bowlders and swift-dancing current. After running along for three or four miles in this manner, it again courses through basaltic columns hardly twenty feet high and narrowed to a cascade not over thirty feet wide, with waves running four or five feet high. As we descended through this chute the banks grew higher, and so swift was the current and so narrow the passage that the water would run up these banks for a long distance on either side and pour back in solid sheets into the foaming current below, making veritable horse-shoe falls. A rafting party of three were sent ahead next morning to be stationed below the cascade and give assistance when the raft came by; and at 11:25 that morning we turned the *Resolute's* head toward the upper end of the Grand Cañon of the Yukon. After spinning around four or five minutes in an eddy, as if fully comprehending

and dreading the dangerous trip, she at last swung slowly into the current and then shot forward with its swift waters. We soon entered the narrow cañon, going at a rate and urged by a power that a dozen giants could not have controlled had they been aboard. The raft's first encounter was with the perpendicular western wall, striking a fearful blow that tore the inner log from the side; and like the philosophical experiment with the suspended ivory balls, the outer log shot far away with an echoing snap. It took the craft but a mere moment to swing on her basaltic pivot, and down again she started in the race. Nearly down to the fearful chute a couple of my Indians jumped on the flying raft from a canoe in which they had paddled out from the shore, and in a few seconds more the cascade was reached. First the clumsy bow was buried in the boiling foam and waves, and the next instant it was reared high in the air, the whole body of the craft standing at the angle of a fixed bayonet as it shot through the narrow neck and slowly subsided in the bubbling waters beyond. A rope was soon gotten to the shore, and although the first time it was fastened it snapped with a twang, the second effort was successful. For two days we were repairing and strengthening the raft, and putting on a couple of new decks made from the fine slender pine poles that were here abundant, and dry and light as pipe-stems, the result of a fire that had swept through them probably two or three years before. Like all the coniferæ growing in dense masses, these timber districts have their periodical devastations of fire that feed on their resinous foliage, burning the bark to a blackened crisp; and when the first severe gale comes from the south, the roots having been weakened by rotting, they are thrown prostrate, making a perfect labyrinth of matted limbs and tempest-torn trunks that have not half decayed nor ceased to be impassable *chevaux-de-frise* before the next generation has sprung up and grown sufficiently high to add confusion to disorder. A sort of poplar chaparral borders the ravines that cut across the trails, to vary the misery and keep it from getting monotonous. In and around the Grand Rapids the grayling are numerous beyond computation, and it was but the work of a few minutes to catch a plentiful mess for even our party of over twenty whites and Indians; and most singular of all, this was done despite the fact that myriads of small brown moths or millers filled the air during our fishing-days, while their bodies often floated by thousands down the river, to be food for the graylings. The trout flies we used were often the "brown miller" and "brown hackle." While the graylings could be caught at any time, they would bite more freely during cloudy weather.

We had employed a few Tahk-heesh Indians to carry over the portage our valuable effects that we had taken from the raft to lighten it, and for safety in such a dangerous rapid. I could not but contrast the kindness they showed each other, and especially their women, with the ungenerous conduct of the more warlike Chilkats in their mutual intercourse. The latter when canoeing on the Dayay, after having left the launch and before reaching the head of canoe navigation, had a certain number, including even the boys, who were not provided with canoes; and although it would have added little to the labor of the canoemen to take the burdens of the others into their boats, they refused to do so. Those without canoes had to carry their loads on their backs, some ten or eleven miles. Nay, they would not ferry the porters across the rushing river in its serpentine windings from bluff to bluff, but forced them to wade the streams, often up to their middle, or make extended detours that would lengthen the direct ten miles to double that distance. Many other similar acts, shown even in cases of sickness, did much to strengthen this unfavorable impression. The mosquitoes were now thick beyond anything I have ever seen. As we crossed boggy places or the marshy rims of the numerous inland lakes, they rose in dense swarms. Hunting, the only object one could have in inland excursions, became impossible on account of these insects. Their stings could not be endured, and in looking through such swarms it was not possible to take sure sight at the game. The vigorous exercise needed to defend oneself was enough to fatigue the strongest to the verge of exhaustion; besides, these gesticulations would frighten the game. I believe this part of the Yukon country to be scarcely habitable in the summer on account of these pests, and think their numbers to be sufficient reason for the complete absence of game during that part of the year. On the lower river, beyond Fort Yukon, their numbers appreciably decrease; but as they are reënforced by the little black gnats and sand-flies, life for the traveler even there is not pleasant. It is not until the first severe frost comes, about the first of September, that this annoyance is abated completely, although for a short time before this the hopeful wanderer in these wilds thinks he notices a falling off in the census. Captain Petersen, a trader on the lower river, a person whom I found not given to exaggeration in any particular, says he has known Eskimo dogs to be killed by mosquitoes; and the Indians tell him, and he says he has no reason to doubt

them, that even the brown bear of Alaska, almost the peer of the grizzly, has been known in rare instances to be slain by them when he ventured into their swampy haunts. Captain Petersen and the Indians account for this by supposing, as the bodies show, that the bear, instead of securing safety by precipitate retreat from such places, fights them, bear style, reared up on his hind-quarters, until the stings near his eyes close them, and he is kept in this condition until starvation eventually causes death.

About eight o'clock in the evening, while camped a quarter of a mile below the cascades in the Grand Rapids, we could hear heavy concussions in single blows at two and three minute intervals. It was noticed by more than one, and thought by some to be distant thunder, although it sounded strangely unlike that noisy element in other climes, and there were no signs of a storm in the sky. A very light series of earthquakes also seemed a poor theory, and there was little or nothing else to which it could be attributed except the cascades, which I believe have been known to cause earth-tremblings and analogous phenomena.

The 5th of July we bade adieu to the worst cañon and rapids on the Yukon River. About noon we passed the mouth of the Tahk River (the Tahk-heen'-ah of the Chilkats), which measured probably two-thirds the size of the Yukon proper. It was flowing muddy water at the time, and our surmise that this would spoil our splendid grayling fishing proved to be correct. While the Tahk-heen'-ah noticeably flows less water than the Yukon, and therefore is not entitled to be called the river proper, its bed seems to correspond with the general characteristics of the Yukon from its mouth on. From the Grand Cañon to the Tahk River (*heen'-ah* in Chilkat signifying river) the banks of the Yukon are high and bold, and often broken into perpendicular bluffs of white sandy clay, while from here on the shores are much lower, similar to those of the Tahk-heen'-ah, and wooded to the water's edge.

We reached the last lake about five in the afternoon, and had the misfortune to stick in the apex of an acute-angled sand-bar at the mouth of the river, and this with a fair wind in our favor to help us over the like. Two hours and a half's steady work swung the *Resolute* clear of her sandy anchor, and we went into camp alongside our lightered cargo, wearier, wetter, and wiser men,—certainly wiser in the fact that a sand-bar was a much more formidable obstacle to our peculiar craft than a gravel-bar of equal depth. On the latter it was necessary only to be able to lift the raft by a series

IN THE RINK RAPIDS, UPPER YUKON.

of combined efforts, the swift current carrying it forward over even the widest bars, while with the former the raft would rapidly settle during the short rests that were rendered necessary by such fatiguing work, and could be pried forward only the short distance the current had cut out the sand ahead of the logs. On sandbars a series of laborious swingings of the raft, end for end, even against the current. until the ponderous concern was clear, was generally the quickest solution of the problem, while the raft could be pried over gravel-bars with ten inches of water, although it drew double that amount. The new lake was called by my Indians the Kluk-tas'-si. Like all the lower lakes, it was full of banks, occasioned by the deposition of the glacier-mud brought down by the mountain streams, for their outlets all become clear again until receiving the waters of some muddy river heading among the glaciers. It is a mere matter of geological time when these lakes will be filled by these deposits, and nothing but a river left coursing through bottom-lands. Such ancient lakes are noticeable on the course of the great stream farther on.

The right bank of Lake Kluk-tas'-si is composed of rounded cliffs of gray limestone, the gullies between being filled in with foliage, especially spruce and pine, and from the opposite side of the lake this effect is quite pretty and peculiar. On the west bank of the lake great towering red rocks culminate in what appears to be a picturesque island of this material, but an Indian with us says that these are part of the mainland; and near this comes in a large river whose whole course is flanked by such scenes, from which the Indians give it the name of Red River. Not desiring to add another Red River to the geography of the world, I called these the Richthofen Rocks and River, although the latter we were not able to make out from our position on the lake as we sailed by, and the former from all points seemed strangely like an island. Quite a number of salmon-trout fell victims to our pot-hunting trout-lines, one of which weighed over eight pounds, the limit of the doctor's fish-scales.

The 9th of July saw us sail out of Kluk-tas'-si, the last of the lakes, and as we hauled down the old wall-tent that had done us double duty as a sail and a tent, I think we were all light-hearted enough to make the *Resolute* draw an inch less water. The river was now very shallow, wide, and swift, and we were constantly grating over bars of gravel, and occasionally sticking on one, but so rapid was the current that merely jumping off the raft was sufficient to start it forward and override the most of these. On both sides of the river the forest fires had done considerable damage to the timber, and on every side were stumps of all shades of darkness, from the blackened crisp of this year's conflagration to the light-brown ones covered with moss and rotting to the earth's level. "How closely that one resembles a big grizzly bear!" remarked one of the party, pointing to a huge shaggy brown stump some

GENERAL VIEW OF THE RINK RAPIDS.

six or seven hundred yards ahead of us on the edge of a high clay bank overlooking the river. The likeness to this animal was close, and as we rapidly floated down towards it and it came walking down the edge of the cliff, the resemblance was sufficient to produce two or three guns from their cases. At four hundred yards the "stump" got one good look at the formidable raft, evidently just bursting on his vision, and before we could fully realize how quickly he had done it, he disappeared in a grove of spruce, and we never saw him again. Every living thing avoided us as if we were a known pestilence, and grizzlies, the worst terror of the Indians in all this country, never felt satisfied until they had put a glacier or two between us. Rounding a bend a young lark, sitting on an overhanging bush turned its head, and in its hurry "to do something mighty quick," fell into the water and drowned.

THE RAFT.

LOOKING DOWN THE YUKON (NORTH)
FROM THE VILLAGE OF KITT-AH-GON.

LOOKING UP THE YUKON
(SOUTH) FROM THE VIL-
LAGE OF KITT-AH-GON.

while scraping along had no bad effect, and often slowed our gait to half its usual rate, until a line ashore would complete our stoppage and allow us to go into camp.

On the 9th we passed the mouth of the Newberry River, about one hundred and thirty yards wide, and the Yukon at once became very much deeper, swifter, and the water of a darker hue, showing that the Newberry drained a considerable amount of *tundra* land, or land where the water, saturated with the dyes extracted from dead leaves and mosses, is prevented from percolating through the soil by an impervious substratum of ice, and is carried off superficially directly into the draining rivers. The 10th, forty miles farther on, we passed the mouth of D'Abbadie River, over one hundred and fifty yards wide at this point, and said to be over two hundred and fifty miles long to its head. The D'Abbadie is important in an economical sense as marking the point on the Yukon at which gold in placer deposits commences. From here on nearly to the mouth or mouths of the great Yukon, a panful of dirt taken from almost any bar or bank with any discretion will give several " colors," in miners' parlance. The Yukon, now widening out, was studded with numerous islands. It also became quite tortuous in its windings, and at one place where a grand river came in from the west (which I called Nordenskjöld) a bald prominent butte was seen no less than seven different times, directly ahead of the raft, on different stretches of the river. Tanta-

We were all congratulating ourselves on the swift current which was carrying us so speedily on, until along in the evening, when the subject of camping came up. Then we found the current too rapid to make a landing without possibly tearing a log or two off the shore side of the raft. The river was of a perfectly uniform width that would have done credit to a canal, and consequently not an eddy was to be found in which we could retard our motion; while a rank growth of willows springing from marshy ground, stretching for miles along the river, gave us but little desire to camp, even were it possible. We now instituted a system of "down-brakes" with the *Resolute*, which consisted in keeping the stern of the raft dragging along the shore with the rear oar, while the head was kept well out with the bow oar. Had she been struck bow first in such a current, it would have converted her shape into that of a lozenge at the expense of a log or two;

lus Butte marks the spot on the map. The very few Indians we now saw along the river were of the most abject appearance, living in houses formed of three poles, one of which, being much longer than the rest, was used as a support for a couple of well-ventilated caribou skins; and this dilapidated but simple arrangement was their residence in a country that abounded with good timber for log-cabins. The only use to which this timber was put, besides fuel, was in the construction of small rafts, canoes being almost unknown from the Grand Cañon to old Fort Selkirk. Their winter quarters are just above the latter point, and when in the spring they sally up the river to their hunting and fishing grounds, their household effects are of so simple a nature that they can be readily carried upon their backs. Returning in the fall, they build a small raft to carry the meager addition accumulated by the summer's hunt. Moose, caribou, black bear, and salmon form their principal diet. These rafts are collected from the dry drift-logs that accumulate on the upper end of each island in wooden bastions from ten to fifteen feet high, deposited during the spring (June) freshets. So uniform are these driftwood deposits that, in the many archipelagoes through which we had to pass, the islands would present an entirely different aspect as one looked up or down stream at them, having quite a pretty appearance in the former and looking like tumble-down and abandoned wood-yards in the latter case.

On the 11th one of my Indians told me that the next day we would have to shoot our fourth and last serious rapid; and while he had known Indians to accomplish this with their little rafts of a few small logs, he felt anxious regarding our ponderous craft. There were three channels through the rocks, the middle one being the widest and for most craft the best, but it had the serious disadvantage of having a sharp right-angled turn about half-way through and a projecting rock in its center. The rapids could be heard (on the 12th) quite a while before we reached them, and beaching the raft a few hundred yards above them, they were given an inspection of a hurried nature. This disclosed a most picturesque gorge with perpendicular columns of rocks forty or fifty feet high, standing in three or four groups in the very midst of the narrow rapid. The right-hand channel was the straightest, although quite narrow, and the waves were running high enough to make us fear they might sweep something from the decks. When we did finally essay this passage, it was amongst the greatest clattering of gulls, young and old, that one would care to hear. The summits of the rock islands were splendidly protected from the invasions of any land animals, and hundreds of gulls had selected these fortresses of nature as their breeding-places, and we were saluted as we shot through as intruders of the worst character.

This right channel of the Rink Rapids, as I named them, is situated within a sharp bend of the river; so that a steam-windlass operated from a river steamer's deck could be worked to the very best advantage in ascending these rapids. Counting on such ascent, the Grand Cañon would be the true head of navigation on the Yukon, and thus the great river would be passable for light-draught river boats for eighteen hundred and sixty-six miles from the Aphoon or northern mouth, being the greatest length of uninterrupted navigation in any stream emptying into the Pacific Ocean.

On the 12th our first moose was seen,—a great awkward-looking animal that came rushing through the willows, his palmated horns making the first observer believe that it was an Indian swinging his arms in the air. We occasionally caught sight of these broad antlers and his brown sides, and I saved my reputation as a shot by the gun not going off when the hammer fell. That night we camped on the eastern bank of the river at the first true Indian village we had so far encountered, and even this was deserted, the inhabitants being up the river fishing and hunting, as already explained. It is in a most picturesque position, and is called Kitt-ah-gon, meaning "the town between two cañons." On one side comes in a small creek that drains a conspicuous and beautiful valley among high hills, and one which looks as if it would support a much larger stream than the twenty-yard creek that empties near Kitt-ah-gon. The village itself consists of but one log-house about 18 x 30 and a dozen or more of three-sided camping-places of poles and brush, which are houses to be covered in with skins. The next twenty miles, through an archipelago of islands which hardly gave us a chance to know our distance from the two banks, brought us to old Fort Selkirk, which we found on the left bank, despite the fact that the five or six maps we had consulted placed it at the junction of the Yukon and Pelly, a large stream that here comes in from the east. Its blackened chimneys, three in number, still held out against the elements after a third of a century, and were now almost lost in a little grove of poplars that had taken root since this frontier post of the Hudson's Bay Company had been burned to the ground in 1851. We were now on ground familiar to white men. Our journey to Fort Yukon, five hundred miles farther on, and thence to the river's mouth will be described in another article.

Frederick Schwatka.

The Great River of Alaska
of Alaska
Part 2

THE CENTURY MAGAZINE.

VOL. XXX.   OCTOBER, 1885.   No. 6.

THE GREAT RIVER OF ALASKA. II.

EXPLORING THE MIDDLE AND LOWER YUKON.

OLD Fort Selkirk forms the connecting link between the article which appeared in the September CENTURY, entitled "The Great River of Alaska," and the present paper. (See map with the former article.) The fort had been erected as a trading-post by the Hudson's Bay Company on ground the Chilkat Indians claimed as their own trading ground. The Chilkats received their trading stores from the Russian Fur Company, and, having no use for Fort Selkirk, took the Indian method of weeding out competition.

The scenery around Selkirk is fine, though hardly so grand as the high ramparts a hundred miles below. From the mouth of the Pelly, across the river, a high basaltic bluff runs down the Yukon for nearly twelve miles, and is then lost among the bold hills that crowd upon the river. Beyond this bluff lie high, rolling hills, with their green grass tops contrasting vividly with the red ocherous soil of their steep sides that the land-slides leave bare.

Selkirk was first occupied by traders who came down the Pelly from the tributaries of the Mac-

kenzie. So that the post Fort Yukon, kirk stands an at a civilized The Ayans among the plains. Even white man, in pole, with its flaunt- by the totem that desig- or some other earthly from fifteen to twenty the grave is generally spruce. A little prun-

rough was the way down the Pelly to Selkirk, was finally supplied by the roundabout way of lower down the river. On the site of Sel- Ayan grave, not unlike a very rough attempt one, and is probably borrowed from civilization. formerly buried their dead on rude scaffolds trees, like the Indians of the great Western when adopting the burial methods of the part, they cannot abolish the ever-present ing strips of many-colored rags, surmounted nates the clan, a fish, or a goose, or a bear, thing converted into an idol. As this pole is or twenty-five feet in height, the place for selected near the foot of some healthy young ing and peeling of the bark is, in this case, the

A MEDICINE-MAN.

only labor. The graves are always near the river banks, but I never noticed any number of them together. At Selkirk several Ayan Indians met us and anxiously asked us to visit their village, but a short distance below. They were a far superior race to the abject tribe we had left behind us on the Upper Yukon. A conspicuously Hebrew cast of countenance was noticeable in this tribe, and some of its younger numbers were respectably neat and clean compared with Indians in general. Their canoes, of birch-bark covering and fragile cedar framework, were the smallest and lightest I had ever seen, except the skin canoes of the Eskimo, and they were well made to the smallest detail.

Though the grass was almost luxuriant on the plain about Selkirk, no signs of game were seen. It seemed fair to infer that the dense swarms of the omnipresent mosquito could alone account for the absence. This pest is sufficiently formidable in the summer months to put an end to all ideas of stock-raising as a possible future industry. Shortly after noon on the 15th of July the raft was cast loose, and we started down the picturesque river. So scattering had been the Indian population on the river above Selkirk, that we were greatly surprised, on rounding the lower end of an island, to see nearly two hundred Indians drawn up across the south channel of the river. We worked at our cumbersome oars valiantly, cheered on by the wildly frantic throng, that plainly feared that we, the supposed traders, would pass. Many excited Indians came out to assist us, and placing the prows of their canoes against the outer side of the raft, paddled us furiously towards shore. Our line was run out at last, and, seized by nearly two hundred Indians, who brought us to land with a crash. Shortly after our landing the throng formed a line, from one to three deep, the men on the left and the women and children on the right, and gave us a dance,—

the same old Indian monotonous *Hi-yi-yi* with the well-measured cadence as its only musical part, and with an accompanying swaying of the body from side to side, while their long mop-like hair swung round like a magnificent mosquito-brush.

After I had distributed a few insignificant articles among them, I tried to get a photograph of some attitude that was a part of the dance, and though I am sure my object was understood by the more intelligent, I did not succeed. Often, when ready to take the cap from the camera, we were foiled by some young man starting a low *Hi-yi-yi*. In an instant it ran the whole length of the combustible line, and all were swaying like leaves in the wind. A similar attempt to get a picture of the three head men, Kon-it'l, his son the hereditary chief, and the medicine man, was almost equally futile, until I formed the center to the group. The tube of the camera had a gun-like appearance that made some of them uneasy. My willingness to sit with them was sufficient assurance of no danger. The village proved to be a much ruder affair than the improved appearance of the Indians over the natives of the Upper Yukon gave me to expect. Their houses were mere hovels of brushwood, with here and there a covering of moose-skin or a worn strip of canvas.

Though the slight character of the houses might find excuse in the fact that these were only used during the summer months, while

ALONG THE BANKS.

the inhabitants fed on the salmon that ran up the river to spawn, a closer inspection showed that the household utensils were equally rude. We found a few buckets and pans, ingeniously made of single pieces of birch-bark. We also found a few spoons made of the horn of the mountain sheep or goat, but the carvings on the handles were dismal failures compared with the elaborate work of the Indians on the Pacific coast of Alaska.

The brush houses of the Ayans seem to be constructed so as to accommodate two families, with a common ridge-pole and an aisle, open at both ends, running down between the two compartments. Possibly this style of architecture was necessary where there was no tree for the pole to rest against. In the roofs of the houses strings of salmon were hung up to dry, and the sleeping dogs held the floor below. Though little room was left, the stranger was always welcome.

In drying the salmon they split it, as packers do when salting the fish. In addition they slice the flesh to the skin in longitudinal and transverse cuts an inch apart. They prepare none for winter use, I understand, though the fish are abundant enough, but depend in that season upon moose, bear, and caribou.

In winter they live in mooseskin tents much like the circular tepees, or lodges, of the Sioux, Cheyennes, and other

OLD FORT YUKON.

INDIAN BURIAL GROUND.

whole bank, sinking into the shallow current, presents to one approaching its intact forest of trees, like a body of Polish lancers. Where the current is swiftest the erosion is most marked, and on the swiftest current our raft was always prone to make its onward way.

The morning of the 16th of July we took an early start to avoid much begging, and dropped westward with the current. It was hard that day to imagine, with a blistering heat on the river and thunder-showers often going over us, that we were within a few days' journey of the Arctic circle.

Shortly after one o'clock on the afternoon of the 17th we passed the mouth of the White River. Here the Yukon entirely changes its character. Heretofore a clear, bright mountain river, with now and then a lake-like widening that caught and held the little sediment it might bear, it now becomes the muddiest river on the western coast of North America, and holds this character to its mouth.

This change is caused by the White River. The White is very swift, and is thus enabled to hold in solution the débris that the glaciers pour into its head-waters. Meeting the Yukon, its rapid current carries its silt and sediment nearly across that river, and changes the blue of the greater stream to a chalky white. All our sport with hook and line now disappeared, and we were thereafter dependent upon the nets and weirs of the Indians for our fish.

A few miles below the White a river of nearly equal size comes in from the right. This is the Stewart, or, as the Indians call it, the Nachonde. Years ago the Hudson's Bay Company had a thriving trading-post near its head-waters, but it, too, fell shortly after the fall of old Fort Selkirk. A small party of American miners had found good prospects in placer digging at the mouth of the Stewart, and were preparing their camp. They certainly deserved success. I took our old water-logged canoe, and, with a half-breed native, visited them at their camp.

Returning late in the evening, with the sun in my face and with no knowledge of the resting-place of my party, I found, in the vast spreading network of islands, no assurance of a speedy meeting. We had made an agreement on parting that the advance should burn spruce boughs at reasonable intervals, that I might have a sign on my return. Though spruce was everywhere in sight, there was that night none found on the island where the camp was made. So I had no sign. I never knew until that evening how like an ascending smoke looked the pencil-points of ridges of spruce fading into the water's edge, and tinged with the rays of the setting

Indians of the treeless plains of the West. When one reflects that winter in this region is simply polar in all its aspects, one wonders how life can hold out in such abodes. From a trader's description of the winter tents, I learn that the Indians know the non-conducting powers of a stratum of air, for these tents are made double.

Directly opposite the large Ayan village is another much smaller one, called Kowsk-hoú, and a sketch of it is introduced to show the general tenor of the banks over the larger portion of the Yukon River: — great rolling bluffs, fringed with a footing of spruce, and lower down an almost impenetrable underbrush of deciduous vegetation, make a pleasant contrast in color with the more somber green of the overtopping evergreens. On low alluvial banks, especially those of the islands, this glacis of bright green has been washed away, and the spruce, becoming undermined by the swift eroding current, form a network of ragged boughs, almost impassable to one who would reach the bank.

One may see this in temperate climes, where felled trees still cling to the washed-out roots, but along the Yukon the soil, frozen to the depth of six or eight feet, will not fall until undermined for many feet. When it does fall, it is with a crash that can be heard for miles, reverberating up and down the valley like the report of a distant cannon. The

sun. An occasional shout was at last rewarded with an answering cry.

We met a tribe of Indians calling themselves "Tahk-ong" on the following day. With them we found resting four of our Ayan friends, and both said that a short distance ahead we would come upon a trading-post. It was not until the following day that we drifted past the post, marked on the map as Fort Reliance, and found it deserted, to our great disappointment, for we had there hoped to obtain stores.

That evening at ten o'clock we went into camp at a point where a fine river came in from the east, with water so clear that it

ing by astronomical observations, and waited till noon. Only two rough "sights" rewarded my delay. During this time of the year the prevailing winds, I noticed, were from the south, and always brought fog or light rain, a circumstance easily explained by the theory that the winds, coming off the warm Pacific loaded with moisture, have the moisture precipitated in crossing the glacial summits of the Alaskan coast-range.

At the Indian village of Nuclaco, opposite the site of Fort Reliance, the entire population, with a large number of Indians from the Tanana River, received us with a great banging of guns. From here to the mouth of the

SWEEPERS.

tempted some of our party to get out their fishing gear again, but to no purpose. This the traders call the Deer River, from the large number of caribou that congregate in its valley during certain seasons of the year. Here lies the narrowest part of the Yukon for many hundreds of miles. Though its width here cannot be more than two hundred and fifty yards, the majestic river sweeps by with no added force or haste, showing the great depth it must have to discharge the vast volume of water that a short distance above had spread over a bed two or three miles wide.

Here I tried to "check" my dead-reckon-

river this method of welcoming strangers is universal. We made no stop, however, and the salute died suddenly out as we drifted slowly past.

The Tanana Indians, the visitors at Nuclaco that day, are said to be hostile in their own country, but on their frequent trading excursions are discreetly inclined towards peace. The river from which they take their name, the Tanana, is probably the largest unexplored river of the Western continent. Nearly two miles wide at its junction with the Yukon, it is nearly as long as the latter.

On the 20th of July we drifted a little over

AYANS PULLING THE RAFT.

fifty miles in eleven hours. This was one of the very few days that we were not aground for any appreciable length of time, and the distance traveled was great enough to establish firmly the reputation of the river as probably the swiftest stream of any magnitude in the world. We were aground but once that day, having run upon a submerged rock while the entire party was occupied in using four bears for movable but untouched targets. We came to a halt with a shock that would have dis-

jointed our craft had she been less stanch than a well-nigh solid piece. She swung safely around, however, and in three minutes was again holding her undisturbed way.

About three o'clock a most remarkable rock was seen on the east bank of the river, springing directly out of a level plain, bounded in the distance by a crescent of low hills sweeping around a huge bend in the river. It was probably three hundred feet high, and rose with perpendicular sides from the plain. On

JOHNNY'S VILLAGE, OR KLAT-OL-KLIN.

the other side of the river, directly opposite, stood another rock, the exact counterpart of the first, except that the second fades away into the bluff behind it. The Indians explain the situation by a legend which holds that the rocks were long ago man and wife, but incompatibility of temper led the husband to kick the wife out into the plain and draw the river from its bed, near the distant hills, for a perpetual barrier.

July 21st brought us to the Indian village of Klat-ol-klin, a name we found with difficulty, as even the natives call it "Johnny's village," from the Americanized name of its chief. This was the first permanent village we had seen on the river. There were but six log houses in all, abutting against each other, with their gable-ends turned towards the river. It was perched on a steep bank, so close to the crest that two could not pass between the houses and the river. At the water's edge was a perfect network of birch-bark canoes, and back of these an inclined scaffolding of spruce poles, where salmon hung drying in the sun. Here, for the first time, we found the Indians preparing any considerable number of this fish for winter use. The fish are caught with scoop-nets three or four feet long, fastened on two poles from ten to twelve feet in length. A watcher, generally a squaw, standing in front of the cabins, heralds the approach of

a fish, perhaps a half-mile down the river. Never more than one fisherman starts. Paddling out to the middle of the river, he guides his canoe with his left hand, as the voices from the shore direct, and with his right dips his net to the bottom. Upon the

FISHING ON THE YUKON.

KILLING A MOOSE IN THE WATER.

careful adjustment of this depends his success. Failures are rare. As the fish swim near the bottom, I do not understand how they are detected in the muddy water of the river.

On the 22d the soil appeared thick, black, and loamy, and grass, always good, was now becoming luxuriant, with the mosquitoes increasing in number and the country perceptibly opening. On the 23d we came to "Charley's" village, an exact duplicate of "Johnny's," even to the number of the houses and the side of the river.

The next day we camped at St. Michael's Bar, or Island. From here to Fort Yukon the country is as flat and open as the Pampas, and but five or ten feet above the level of the river. Our Indians, having never been so far, thought we were going out to sea, although we were over a thousand miles from the river's mouth.

As soon as this flat country is entered the channel splits and subdivides every few

miles, until for days we could not tell whether we were on the main stream or on one of the many waterways between the many islands. At Fort Yukon the river is said to be seven miles wide. In spite of the many channels into which the river spreads, the current never decreases, and we went drifting on in the same good old way until Fort Yukon was reached.

At this point, one thousand miles from the river's mouth and about the same distance from its head, the river sweeps with a marked curve into the arctic regions, and then, with less enthusiasm than most polar seekers, turns back into the temperate zone, having been in the arctic for less than a league, and, as the current runs, for less than an hour. The early traders at Fort Yukon supposed their river ran parallel to the Mackenzie; and so it was mapped, its bed being continued north to where its hypothetical waters were poured into the Arctic Sea. The conservative slowness of the English to undo what the English have done had a new illustration as late as 1883, when one of the best of English globe-makers, in a work of art in his line, sent the Yukon with its mighty but unnamed tributaries still into the Arctic. There it will be made to flow until some Englishman shows that it surely flows elsewhere.

For a hundred miles above and two hundred miles below Fort Yukon, the river flows through a region so flat that it seems like the floor of an emptied lake. This area is densely timbered with spruce, and but for this would be nothing but a salient angle of the great flat arctic tundra of the polar coast. The dreariness of unlimited expanse is broken to the northward by the pale-blue outline of the Romantzoff Mountains, so indistinct as to seem a mirage; while to the south arise, in isolated points, the Ratzel Peaks, the outlying spurs of the Alaskan Range, from the Upper Ramparts of which the Yukon flows towards the Lower. Fort Yukon was left behind on the 29th of July, our raft that day drifting by a village where nothing greeted us but a howling troop of dogs. This village would have attracted no attention further up the river, but here, where the river divides itself in many channels, making salmon-catching of but slight importance, villages are very rare.

The 29th was a hot, sweltering day, with the sun and its thousand reflections sending their blistering heat into our faces. In fact, our greatest inconvenience near this short arctic strip of the stream was the tropical heat and the dense swarms of gnats and mosquitoes that met us everywhere when we approached the land. That night none of the party could sleep, despite the mosquito-bars over us. Mosquitoes do not depend for their numbers so much on their latitude as on the superficial extent of stagnant water in which they can breed, and nowhere is this so abundant as in the tundras and timber-flats of the polar coasts. The intense cold of winter sinks its shafts of ice deep into the damp earth, converting it into a thick crust of impervious stone. However warm the short summers may appear to one who judges it from the acclimated standpoint of a rigorous country, it is insufficient to melt more than a superficial portion of this boreal blanket, where only a swampy carpet of moss may flourish upon the frozen stratum below. Through this the stagnant water cannot sink. As the weather is never warm enough to carry it off by evaporation, these marshes extend far and wide, even up the sides of the hills, and give the mosquito ample room to propagate.

We took an early start the next morning, and drifted down the hot river, by low banks that needed nothing but a few breech-clouted negroes to convince us that we were on the Congo. Between six and eight in the evening the thermometer stood about eighty degrees Fahrenheit in the shade, with shade for nothing but the thermometer. Hoisting one of the spare tents for a protection from the sun would have prevented the helmsman from seeing his course and made grounding almost certain, and heat was to be preferred to this, with its attendant labors.

Singularly enough, at this very time a couple of sun-dogs put in an appearance, a phenomenon we usually associate with cold weather, and now sadly out of place. Rain made sleep possible that night and traveling impossible the next day, and left us nothing to do but to sit in the tent and watch nature waste itself in a rainfall of four inches over a vast marsh already six inches deep. Some of our party, wandering over the gravel-bars, through the showers, found the scattered petrified remains of a huge mastodon. All through the valley such remains are numerous.

On the evening of the 2d of August we came in sight of the high hills where the " Lower Ramparts " begin. So closely do the ramparts of the lower river resemble those of the upper that I could not help thinking of them parts of the same range, which bears eastward and westward like a bow-string across the great arc of the Yukon, bending northward into the flat arctic tundra.

Near our camp that night we saw the only family burial-ground we had seen on the river. It contained a dozen graves, perhaps, and was decorated with the usual totems perched on high poles, some of which were fantastically striped in the few simple colors the Indians had at their command.

A gale of wind on the 4th allowed us to drift but twenty-six miles. From here to the mouth of the river strong head-winds are generally raging at this season of the year. On both sides of the river, from this point, the small tributary creeks and rivers bear down clear, transparent water, though deeply colored with a port-wine hue. The streams drain the water from the turfy tundra where the dyes from decaying leaves impart their color. Probably iron-salts are also present.

On the 5th we approached the rapids of the Lower Ramparts, and made all preparations for their stormy passage. Making hasty inquiries at an Indian village concerning them, we found that we had already left them behind us. This part of the river was picturesque, and not unlike the Hudson at West Point. I should have stopped to take some photographs but for the dark lowering clouds and constantly-recurring rain-squalls.

Eighteen miles below the mouth of the

ANVIC INDIANS.

Tanana, we found the trading station of Nuk-lakayet. Here our raft-journey of over thirteen hundred miles came to an end, the longest of its kind in the interest of exploration. As we dragged the raft upon the bank and left it there to burn out its existence as firewood, we felt that we were parting from a true and trusty friend.

We met our first Eskimo dogs here, a finer and larger race than those I had seen farther to the east. They seemed a distinct type of dog in their likeness to each other, and not the vagabond mass of variable mongrels of all sizes and conditions that my previous knowledge of cold-weather canines had led me to consider them.

At Nuklakayet we were furnished with a small decked schooner of eight or ten tons, called, in the rough Russian vernacular of the country, a " barka." It was said to be the fleetest " barka " on the river, when the sails were spread in a good wind. We had good wind in abundance, but there were no sails, so the current was again our motive power. There was, indeed, a palsied jib that we could tie up when the wind was just right, but the wind rarely made its use possible. We got away from Nuklakayet on the 8th, and drifted down the river till camping-time. Then we found that the " barka " drew so much water that we could not get within thirty or forty yards of shore, and were obliged to bring our rubber boots into use.

All the next day we had a heavy head-wind and made but eight miles, our craft standing so high out of water that at times she actually went up-stream against a three-mile current. At night, however, these daily gales fell and left us a prey to the swarms of mosquitoes. All day the 10th we passed Indian villages, with their networks of fish-weirs spread on the river. We passed, too, the mouth of the Newicargut, or Frog River. On this part of the Yukon we pass, in succession, the Sooncargut, Melozicargut, and Tosecargut, which the traders have simplified into Sunday-cargut, Monday-cargut, and Tuesday-cargut, *cargut* being a local Indian termination meaning river or stream. The Newicargut marks the point where explorers from the upper river connected with those of the lower, and established the identity of the Pelly of the English and the Kwichpak of the Russians. Since then the river has been known as the Yukon, the Russian name disappearing, and the name Pelly becoming restricted to the tributary that flows into the Yukon opposite Selkirk.

Near the Indian village of Sakadelontin we saw a number of coffins perched in trees. This was the first time we had seen this method of burial on the river. In all the Indian villages on this part of the river we found the number of women greatly in excess of the men, for at this season all the able-bodied hunters were inland on the tundra north of the river hunting for their winter stock of reindeer clothing and bedding. The Russian or local name for the reindeer coat is " parka," and here we saw the first one made from the spotted or tame reindeer of the native tribes of eastern Siberia. The spottings are great brownish-red and white blotches like those on a "calico" pony. A generous offer to the owner of this particular "parka" was immediately and scornfully refused.

Facing the usual gale, we drifted slowly down the river to Kaltag, where the south bank becomes a simple flat plateau, though the north bank is high and even mountainous for more than four hundred miles farther.

It seemed not improbable that this had been the Yukon's ancient mouth, when the river flowed over all the flat plain down to the sea. Certainly the deposit from the river is now filling in the eastern shores of Bering's Sea. Navigators about the coast say it is dangerous for vessels of any considerable draught to sail within fifty or a hundred miles of land near the Yukon's mouth, and every storm lashes the sea into a muddy froth.

We amused ourselves, late in the evening of the 18th, by drifting far into the dark hours of the night in search of a fair place for a camp, but without avail. Two days later it blew so hard that we could not think of stirring, but lay at our moorings in momentary danger of shipwreck. Anvic, a picturesque little trading-post, was reached on the 22d. The trading-posts become more numerous now, but just beyond Anvic the last Indian village is passed, and forty miles below the Eskimo villages begin.

Myriads of geese were now seen everywhere, mobilizing for the autumn journey to the south. We had a further token of coming autumn on the morning of the 24th, when we found the high grass white with frost, and we were told by the trader at Anvic that ice would sometimes be thick by the 1st of Sep-

tember. The little trading-steamer came down the river the same day, and taking us in tow, brought us down to a mission where an old Greek church of the Russian Company still draws subsidies from Russia. The following day we reached an Eskimo village, and slept for the first time since spring under a roof. Andreavsky was made the next day, where the hills were plainly lowering. The spruce and poplar disappeared now, and low willows took their place, though plenty of wood still abounded in immense drifts on the upstream ends of the numerous islands. Near Andreavsky begins the delta of the Yukon, with its interminable number of channels and islands.

We reached Koatlik, at the mouth of the river, on the 28th, and came to St. Michaels on the afternoon of the 30th, meeting our old acquaintance, the southern gale, outside. We had hoped to take sail on the revenue cutter *Corwin*, but she had been gone already two weeks, and we were forced to turn our hopes to the schooner *Leo*.

It was not until the 8th of September that the *Leo* hove in sight, bearing down upon St. Michaels in a gale of wind. She had on board Lieutenant Ray's party from the international meteorological station at Point Barrow, and, although overcrowded already, we were kindly made welcome. The *Leo* was in a bad way, having "stove in" her bow against the ice while trying to make Point Barrow, and a few doubts were expressed as to her seaworthiness in the choppy seas of the autumn. We got under way on the 11th, however, and, once out of Norton Sound, made a quick passage across to Oonalaska in the Aleutian Islands. Here the *Leo* was beached and repaired. We had grown tired of long strolls and trout-fishing in the mountain-streams at Oonalaska, and were glad at last to take ship and bear away from the last foothold on Alaska.

Frederick Schwatka.

3
Eskimo Whaling

ESKIMO WHALING.

BY HERBERT L. ALDRICH.

CENES of great excitement and danger in chasing whales, which tradition has made us so familiar with, have long since passed so far as the American whalemen are concerned. Modern invention, by the introduction of powerful explosives, has, reduced this once noble sport to a mere slaughtering operation. Now and then exciting scenes occur when the whale is wounded and in the throes of death, but in at least ninety-nine cases out of a hundred the bomb does its terrible work and the whale rolls over dead, with only a quiver, caused by the terrific explosion.

Whales are not as numerous as they formerly were, and as they decrease in numbers they seem to become tenfold more shy. Hence skill of a different sort is requisite in a good whaleman now than in former years. Then it was not a question of manœuvring the boat so as to approach near enough to the whale to kill him, but what was the speediest and safest way when reached to attack him and kill him. Now the killing question is of minor consideration, except to a bungler, while to approach the whale and not "gally" him requires consummate skill and judgment, or, as the whalemen express it, it requires a large amount of "luck."

All danger is, of course, not eliminated, for I once saw an infuriated whale, ago-nized by the wound of a poorly-shot bomb, balance a boat on his back, then "sound" and, rising again, sweep his flukes through the air and smash the stern off the boat with almost the neatness that a buzz saw could cut it off ; and I have been in a boat when the delay of a second or a misjudged movement of the steering oar would have brought the boat directly into the sweep of the whale's tail and resulted in the boat being instantly converted into kindling wood.

Scenes like these are intensely exciting and enjoyable, more especially for future talk, but they are rare occurrences and unlike the whaling scenes of years ago when only harpoons and lances were used, the element of danger to life and limb being now brought to an irreducible minimum.

But the modern scientific appliances have not been introduced into whaling as it is carried on by the Eskimo. The sport with them still possesses all the elements of danger that did whaling in its palmiest days and perhaps more. This is due to the clumsy implements used, lack of cunning and the greatly-increased shyness of the whales.

In witnessing one of these primitive whaling scenes the wonder seems to be

AN UNEXPECTED LANDING.

SATISFACTION.

that every canoe is not swamped and the occupants drowned. To a skilled whaleman there appears to be every reason why the chase should be a failure and every man killed or drowned. But, theories to the contrary, the natives seem to have excellent "luck" in their whaling, and, perhaps on account of their innate timidity, very few casualties.

I doubt if a much more exciting scene was ever witnessed than one I once saw at Indian Point, a native settlement on the coast of Siberia, about five hundred miles below Behring Straits. The point juts boldly out into the ocean for six or eight miles. It is narrow and low, a mere sand bar washed up by conflicting currents and tides. At the extreme end of it is an Eskimo settlement, one of the largest on the coast of Siberia.

The natives have always been great whalemen after their own fashion, and the main supply of their food has been secured by their whaling expeditions. Evidences of their many expeditions are at every hand in the settlement. Many ruins of huts and caches abound, the frameworks of which were made from bones of the massive skeleton of the whale, and there are several extensive scaffoldings the pillars of which are the massive jaw bones of the whale. In one of these scaffoldings there must be at least seventy-five of these great jaw bones. Many caches are walled up with the vertebræ of the whale, and as these caches are below the frost line meat in them remains frozen solid. We saw tons of meat in these caches, and on our return from the Arctic probably added five tons of blubber to their supply.

The whales, always alert and vigilant, work northward toward the Arctic as fast as the main pack of ice in the southern part of the sea breaks up. They seldom venture far from the ice, but skirt along the edge of it. Whalemen "raise" the whales by seeing their spouts along the edge of the pack or the shore ice. The whale comes to the surface to breathe, spouts a few times and then darts back again under the ice. They seldom spout, however, in the open sea.

Frequently the currents sweep the floating ice out of the bight at the south of the point, leaving the sea clear of all except the shore ice, and rather than venture out into the open water to get around the point the whales oftentimes delay a little and sport about along the edge of the ice.

The second day after our vessel dropped anchor off the point two of us went ashore to pay our respects to the leading traders among the natives and to learn what great excitement was going on. We could hear the babel of noises, interspersed with the howling of dogs, and could see that something unusual was transpiring.

On the south shore we found the whalemen hurriedly preparing to launch their canoes, for they had seen several spouts along the edge of the ice. Some of the men were rigging canoes, while others were untangling and straightening out the whaling gear. The women, to do their share of the work, were blowing up the "pokes" — whole skins of the seal transformed into huge air bags as floats. As the work had been going on for some time before our arrival, soon all was ready. One canoe after another was shoved off through the breakers by the women, everybody chattering like so many apes.

This launching was a difficult undertaking, for the canoes were light as cork and the surf was unusually heavy, but the natives were accustomed to such things and were so intent upon catching the whale that they took no notice of getting wet by being soused by a heavy sea or run down by another excited native. Several canoes after being launched were hurled back high and dry on the beach by the waves, but they were promptly shoved off again. One canoe had to be shoved off three times before it finally got beyond the breakers.

During the excitement of the launching

we saw and heard several "blows," and, to add to the excitement and to our own interest in the scene, we shouted and urged the native whalemen into greater haste. The consequence was that as soon as the canoes were fairly afloat their crews were frantic. They paddled wildly, but yelled much more wildly. Every canoe seemed to start off by itself toward the scene of the spouting, but so much time had been consumed that all evidences of the presence of the whales had long disappeared. This only seemed to make the crews all the more frantic. It was their whaling, not ours, so we saw only the amusing side of things, as we were not interested in the whale for our "lay" in case he was killed.

The five canoes launched were soon hovering along the edge of the ice. There they lay to. The Eskimo are models of patience and the crews waited patiently for another blow. The minutes seemed to us like hours, but the natives appeared indifferent to the delay. The men in the boats held close to the edge of the ice, watching their opportunity, while the women and others on shore squatted about in groups, some talking, others eating and not a few sleeping.

The older men, who from infirmities were unable to take part in the sport, by natural force of gravity told themselves off into groups and related some of their early whaling experiences. We could not fully understand what they said, not knowing much of the language; but it was evident from their gestures that they were living over their experiences again. They would dance about as though in a canoe riding over a rough sea, go through the movements of paddling, then suddenly change to darting a harpoon, then haul on lines and perhaps raise a hand to their foreheads to scan the sea. Now and then, in the height of his excitement, a story teller would stop suddenly, break off his narrative, glance out to sea at the canoes for a few moments, then suddenly start in again with his story as vigorously as he had left it off.

Most of their women had their children, many of them unweaned babes, and between caring for the children, smoking an occasional pipe of tobacco, gossiping a little and doing more or less work, with an occasional look to see how the whalemen were prospering, they seemed to enjoy themselves. Nearly every man, woman and child would take an occasional nap, wake up with a start, look out at the sea, then fall off to sleep again or go on talking as though picking up the thread of a story.

The whalemen in the canoes—in spite of the fact that the settlement had its eyes on them, and perhaps part of their own winter's supply of food was at stake —appeared to be indifferent. They lolled about in the canoes, paddled a little, splashed considerably and did many things which the skilled white man would regard as absolutely certain to "gally" the whale, and which we took for granted would end the day's sport, if in fact it was not already ended by the whales stealing a march and going off Arcticward without a spout or breach to indicate their movements.

My companion and I let the noon hour come and go, for what was dinner when

EXPECTATION.

VICTORY.

such excitement was in hand? But when 1 o'clock came, then 2 o'clock, and finally 3 o'clock and no spout we began to think the whales had certainly outwitted us; still we held on to the slight possibility remaining, as the natives did not give it up. So about 4 o'clock we adjourned to the top of an adjoining knoll and called a council of two to decide upon further action. We proceeded to this business without preliminary or ceremony, but before the deliberations had gone far an old man who had been lying for hours flat on his stomach, at the foot of the knoll, jumped to his feet and began to gesticulate and shout:

"He-e-e, he-e-e, he-e-e-e."

Every man in the canoes took up the cry. The women and children took it up. Even sleepers awoke and took it up.

A whale had spouted near one of the canoes.

The men were at their oars. Again the whale spouted and "rounded" to "sound."

In an instant one of the men poised his harpoon and darted it into the bilge of the whale. Attached to the harpoon was a line about sixty feet long and on the end of this line were several "pokes," which acted as buoys or floats to impede the progress of the whale as he headed for the ice. Irritated by the harpoon and hindered by the pokes the whale rose out of the water in a tremendous effort to sound, that he might reach bottom and rub the harpoon from his side.

As he raised his great body out of the water another harpoon with its bunch of pokes was made fast to him. With a sweep of his flukes as he sank out of sight he struck one of the canoes tossed it into the air a complete wreck, and dumped its occupants into the water, but in doing it he entangled his tail in another bunch of pokes.

A volcano under the water could not have created greater commotion than the whale did as he attempted to sound, but the three bunches of pokes harried him and buoyed him up so that he could not reach bottom.

The four canoes rescued the wrecked men, then paddled about the struggling whale, while the men harassed him with long-handled lances and harpoons at his every appearance above the water.

The struggle was terrific and the men stood manfully up to their task, facing every danger. Yet, for lack of bombs,

victory was uncertain. Again and again the whale rose, spouted vigorously, then endeavored to sound. But at each effort the pokes brought him back to the surface again. The natives had cut many deep gashes into the blubber, and even through into the flesh of the whale, but no vital spot had been touched—the death blow was yet to be dealt.

With each rising the whale lashed the water with greater fury. Could he break loose from his entanglements?

At an opportune moment one of the canoes spurted quite near to the monster, and fastened into him another harpoon with its bunch of pokes. An instant later more pokes were entangled into the fast bunches.

The fury of the whale continued to increase, but he was evidently becoming exhausted. He was a prisoner, yet too dangerous to be approached. The men knew their game and knew also that their great hope of success lay in patiently waiting until the whale had exhausted his strength. So they lay to and allowed the monster to struggle it out unopposed. As the wounds made by the harpoons and lances bled copiously, he had already lashed the sea into a bloody foam.

The sight was certainly a grand one, a contest new to my whaleman companion. He was accustomed to seeing boats manœuvre with great skill until within striking distance of the whale, then with one blow end his existence. But here were apparently all the theories of the expert whaleman set at naught and the powerful creature so tangled up by a few crude appliances that he was helpless. His struggles were magnificent exhibitions of strength, but availed him nothing; the natives could sit calmly in their canoes and have the satisfaction of knowing that they now had the monster completely at their mercy. All that they would have to do would be to wait patiently and see the whale hasten his own death, almost literally beat out his own life by his great struggles.

The point of exhaustion gradually approached. Each struggle became weaker than the last and the intervals of quietude lengthened perceptibly. Just after one faint struggle a canoe darted up alongside the great creature. The boat header, with a powerful effort, threw his lance home to a vital spot, and the canoe darted away beyond reach of the whale's tail.

There was a short, vicious flurry, a

stream of blood poured out of the whale's spout holes with a spurt, and he rolled over on his side, dead.

The natives were in a perfect frenzy of joy at their success. Each canoe picked up a line attached to a harpoon and began to tow the carcass close up to the beach opposite the settlement. Long lines were run ashore, and with long, steady pulls, in which every man, woman and child had a part, the whale was soon nearly high and dry. The midnight sun made the day never ending, and when my companion and I returned to the ship we left the natives in high carnival, cutting in the whale and feasting on blubber and black skin as the operation went on. There were no sleepers then, but everyone turned to and made himself useful and came in for a share of the meat. As we passed through the settlement to return to our boat we saw numerous dog teams dragging loads of blubber and flesh, which were carefully stowed down in the caches as part of the food supply for the coming winter.

4
Hunting the Big Game of Alaska

HUNTING THE BIG GAME OF WESTERN ALASKA*

AFTER BEAR ON KADIAK ISLAND

By JAMES H. KIDDER

EARLY in April, 1900, I made my first journey to Alaska for the purpose of searching out for myself the best big game-shooting grounds which were to be found in that territory. Few people who have not traveled in this country have any idea of its vastness. Away from the beaten paths, much of its 700,000 square miles is practically unknown except to the wandering prospector and the Indian hunter. Therefore, since I could obtain but little definite information as to just where to go for the best shooting, I determined to make the primary object of my journey to locate the big game districts of Southern and Western Alaska.

My first two months were spent in the country adjacent to Fort Wrangell. Here one may expect to find black bear, brown bear, goats, and, on almost all of the islands along the coast, great numbers of the small Sitka deer; while grizzlies may be met a short distance back from the coast, and the *Ovis stonei*, or black sheep, on the hills about Glenora and Telegraph Creek. Both of these places are on the Stikine River, some one hundred and fifty miles from its mouth, and so in Canadian territory.

It must be borne in mind that the rivers are the only highways, for the country is very rough and broken, and on account of the almost continuous rainfall (until one has passed beyond the coast range of mountains) the underbrush of Southern Alaska is very dense, offering every obstacle to the progress of the sportsman. All the streams are swift and by no means easy to ascend.

The Hudson's Bay Company has trading posts at Glenora and Telegraph Creek, and during the early summer sends a light draft stern-wheel steamer up the Stikine with a new stock of goods and provisions. It would be well if one intended to make the journey after the Stone sheep to time one's arrival at Fort Wrangell, so as to take advantage of this steamer, thus doing away with the hard river work. †

The game of Alaska which appealed to me especially were the various bears. Large brown bears (varying in species according to the locality) may be found in almost all districts of Alaska. Besides there are the grizzly, and the glacial, or blue bear. It is claimed that one of this species has never fallen to a white man's rifle. It is found on the glaciers from the Lynn Canal to the northern range of the St. Elias Alps, and, as its name implies, is of a bluish color. I should judge from the skins I have seen that in size it is rather smaller than the black bear. What it lives upon in its range of eternal ice and snow is entirely a subject of surmise.

Of all the varieties of brown bears, the one which has probably attracted the most attention is the large bear of the Kadiak Islands, *Ursus middendorffi* (wrongly called a grizzly). Before starting upon my journey I had communicated with Dr. Merriam, Chief of the Biological Survey at Washington, and had learned from him all that he could tell me of this great bear. Mr. Harriman, while on his expedition to the Alaskan Coast in 1899, had by great luck shot a specimen, and in the second volume of "Big Game Shooting," in "The Badminton Library," Mr. Clive Phillipps-Wolley writes of the largest "grizzly" of which he has any trustworthy information as being shot on Kadiak Island by a Mr. J. C. Tolman. These were the only authentic records I could find of bears of this species which had fallen to the rifle of an amateur sportsman.

---

* This is the first of a series of five papers on Alaskan hunting by Mr. Kidder, who has made the first and most extended study of the big bears of this region.—[EDITOR.

† In 1900 this steamer left the last of May, and I believe there was another one the last of July.

After spending two months in southern Alaska, I determined to visit the Kadiak Islands in pursuit of this bear. I reached my destination the latter part of June, and three days later had started on my shooting expedition with native hunters. Unfortunately I had come too late in the season. The grass had shot up until it was shoulder high, making it most difficult to see at any distance the game I was after.

The result of this, my first hunt, was that I actually saw but three bear and got but one shot, which, I am ashamed to record, was a miss. Tracks there were in plenty along the salmon streams, and some of these were so large I concluded that, as a sporting trophy, a good example of the Kadiak bear should equal, if not surpass, in value any other kind of big game to be found on the North American continent. In this opinion I received further confirmation later, when I saw the size of the skins brought in by the natives to the two trading companies.

As I sailed away from Kadiak that fall morning I determined that my hunt was not really over, but only interrupted by the long northern winter, and that the next spring would find me once more in pursuit of this great bear.

It was not only with the hope of shooting a Kadiak bear that I decided to make this second expedition, but I had become greatly interested in the big brute, and, although no naturalist myself, it was now to be my aim to bring back to the scientists at Washington as much definite material about him as possible. Therefore the objects of my second trip were:

Firstly, to obtain a specimen of bear from the Island of Kadiak; secondly, to obtain specimens of the bears found on the Alaska Peninsula; and, lastly, to obtain, if possible, a specimen of bear from one of the other islands of the Kadiak group. With such material I hoped that it could at least be decided definitely if all the bears of the Kadiak Islands are of one species; if all the bears on the Alaska Peninsula are of one species; and, also, if the Kadiak bear is found on the mainland, for there are unquestionably many points of similarity between the bears of the Kadiak Islands and those of the Alaska Peninsula. It was also my plan, if I was successful in all these objects, to spend the fall on the Kenai Peninsula in pursuit of the white sheep and the moose.

Generally I have made it a point to go alone on all big game shooting trips, but I was fortunate in having as a companion on this journey an old college friend, Robert P. Blake.

My experience of the year before was of value in getting our outfit together. At almost all points in Alaska most of the necessary provisions can be bought, but I should rather advise one to take all but the commonest necessities with him, for frequently the stocks at the various trading companies run low. For this reason we took with us from Seattle sufficient provisions to last us six months, and from time to time, as necessity demanded, added to our stores. As the rain falls almost daily in much of the coast country, we made it a point to supply ourselves liberally with rubber boots and rain-proof clothing.

On the 6th of March, 1901, we sailed from Seattle on one of the monthly steamers, and arrived at Kadiak eleven days later. I shall not attempt to describe this beautiful island, but shall merely say that Kadiak is justly termed the "garden spot of Alaska." * It has numerous deep bays which cut into the land many miles. These bays have also in turn arms which branch out in all directions, and the country adjacent to these latter is the natives' favorite hunting ground for bear. In skin canoes (bidarkas) the Aleuts, paddling along the shore, keep a sharp lookout on the near-by hillsides, where the bears feed upon the young and tender grass.

It was our plan to choose the most likely one of these big bays as our shooting grounds, and according to local custom hunt from a bidarka.

It may be well to explain here that the different localities of Alaska are distinctly marked by the difference in the canoes which the natives use. In the southern part, where large trees are readily obtained, you find large dugouts capable of holding five to twenty persons. At Yakutat, where the timber is much smaller, the canoes have decreased proportionately in size, although still dugouts; but from Yakutat westward the timber line becomes lower and lower, until the western half of the island of Kadiak is reached, where the trees disappear altogether, and the dugout gives place to the skin canoe or "bidarka." I have never seen them east of Prince William Sound,

* The only other islands of any size in this group are Afognak and Shuyak.

but from this point on to the west they are in universal use among the Aleuts, a most interesting race of people and a most wonderful boat.

The natives of Kadiak are locally called "Aleuts," but the true Aleuts are not found east of the Aleutian Islands. The cross between the Aleut and white (principally Russian) is known as the "Kreole."

The natives whom I met on the Kadiak Islands seemed to show traces of Japanese descent, for they resembled these people both in size and features. I found them of a docile disposition, remarkable hunters and weather prophets, and most expert in handling their wonderful canoes, with which I always associate them.

The bidarka is made with a light frame of some strong, elastic wood; is covered with seal or sea lion skin; not a nail is used in making the frame, but all the various parts are tied firmly together with sinew or stout twine. This allows a slight give, for the bidarka is expected to give to every wave, and in this lies its strength. There may be one, two, or three round hatches, according to the size of the boat. In these the occupants kneel, and, sitting on their heels, ply their sharp-pointed paddles: all paddling at the same time on the same side, and then all changing in unison to the other side at the will of the bowman, who sets a rapid stroke. In rough water camelinkas (large shirts made principally of stretched and dried bear gut) are worn, and these are securely fastened around the hatches. In this way the Aleuts and the interior of the bidarka remain perfectly dry, no matter how much the sea breaks and passes over the skin deck.

I had used the bidarka the year before, having made a trip with my hunters almost around the Island of Afognak, and believed it to be an ideal boat to hunt from. It is very speedy, easily paddled, floats low in the water, will hold much camp gear, and when well handled is most seaworthy. So it was my purpose this year to again use one in skirting the shores of the deep bays, and in looking for bears, which show themselves in the early spring upon the mountain sides or roam the beach in search of kelp.

The Kadiak bear finds no trouble in getting all the food he wants during the berry season and during the run of the various kinds of salmon, which lasts from June until October. At this period he fattens up, and upon this fat he lives through his long winter sleep. When he wakes in the spring he is very weak and hardly able to move, so his first aim is to recover the use of his legs. This he does by taking short walks when the weather is pleasant, returning to his den every night. This light exercise lasts for a week or so, when he sets out to seek upon the beach kelp, which acts as a purge. He now lives upon roots, principally of the salmon-berry bush, and later nibbles the young grass. These carry him along until the salmon arrive, when he becomes exclusively a fish-eater until the berries are ripe. I have been told by the natives that just before he goes into his den he eats berries only, and his stomach is now so filled with fat that he really eats but little.

The time when the bears go into winter quarters depends upon the severity of the season. Generally speaking, it is in early November, shortly after the cold weather has set in. Most bears sleep uninterruptedly until spring, but occasionally they are found wandering about in midwinter. My natives seemed to think that only those bears which have found uncomfortable quarters are restless, and that they leave their dens at this time of year only for the purpose of finding better ones. They generally choose for their dens caves high up upon the mountain sides among the rocks, and in remote places where they are not likely to be discovered. The same winter quarters are used year after year.

The male, or bull bear, is the first to come out in the spring. As soon as he recovers the use of his muscles he leaves his den for good, and wanders aimlessly about until he comes upon the track of some female. He now persistently follows her, and it is at this time that the rutting season of the Kadiak bear begins, the period lasting generally from the middle of April until July.

In Eagle Harbor (on Kadiak Island) a native, three years ago, during the month of January, saw a female bear which he killed near her den. He then went into the cave and found two very small cubs whose eyes were not yet open. This would lead to the belief that this species of bear brings forth its young about the beginning of the new year. At birth the cubs are very small, and there are from one to four in a litter—two, however, is the usual number. The mother, although in a state of semi-torper, suckles these cubs in the den, and they remain with her all that year, hole up with her the following winter, and continue to follow her until the second fall, when they shift for themselves.

For many years these bears have been so persistently hunted by the natives, who are constantly patrolling the shores in their skin canoes, that their knowledge of man and their senses of smell and hearing are developed to an extreme degree. They have, however, like most bears, but indifferent sight. They range in color from a light tawny lion to a very dark brown; in fact, I have seen some bears that were almost black. Many people have asked me about their size, and how they compare in this respect with other bears. The Kadiak bear is naturally extremely large. His head is very massive, and he stands high at the shoulders. This latter characteristic is emphasized by a thick tuft of hair, which stands erect on the dorsel ridge just over the shoulders. The largest bear of this kind which I shot measured eight feet in a straight line from his nose to the end of the vertebræ, and stood fifty-one and a half inches in a straight line at the shoulders, not including between six and seven inches of hair.

Most people have an exaggerated idea of the number of bears on the Kadiak Islands. Personally I believe that they are too few ever to make this kind of sport popular. In fact, it was only by the hardest kind of careful and constant work that I was finally successful in bagging my first bear on Kadiak. When the salmon come it is not so difficult to get a shot, but this lying in wait at night by a salmon stream cannot compare with seeking out one's game on the hills in the spring and stalking it in a sportsmanlike manner.

It was more than a week after our landing at Kadiak that the weather permitted me to go to Afognak (the next island), where my old hunters lived, to make our final preparations. One winter storm after another came in quick succession, but we did not mind the delay, for we had come early and did not expect the bears would leave their dens before April.

I decided to take with me on my hunt the same two natives whom I had had the year before. My head man's name was Fedor Deerinhoff. He was about forty years of age, and had been a noted sea otter and bear hunter. In size he was rather larger than the average of his race and absolutely fearless. Many stories are told of his hand-to-

hand encounters with these big bears. I think the best one is of a time when he crawled into a den on his hands and knees, and in the dark and at close quarters shot three. He was unable to see, and the bear's heavy breathing was his only guide in taking aim.

Nikolai Pycoon, my other native, was younger and shorter in stature, and also had a great reputation as a hunter (which later I found was fully justified), and furthermore was considered the best bidarka man of Afognak. He was a nice little fellow, always good natured, always keen, always willing, and the only native whom I have ever met with a true sense of gratitude. *

The year before I had made all arrangements to hire for this season a small schooner, which was to take us to our various shooting grounds. I was now much disappointed to find that the owner of this schooner had decided not to charter her. We were, therefore, obliged to engage a very indifferent sloop, but she was fortunately an excellent sea boat. Her owner, Charles Payjaman, a Russian, went with us as my friend's hunter. He was a fisherman and a trapper by profession, and had the reputation of knowing these dangerous island waters well. His knowledge of Russian we expected to be of great use to us in dealing with the natives; Alaska was under Russian control for so many years that that language is the natural local tongue.

It was not until the first of April that we got our entire outfit together, and it was not until four days later that the weather permitted us to hoist our sail and start for the shooting grounds, of which it was of the utmost importance that we should make a good choice. All the natives seemed to agree that Kiliuda Bay, some seventy-five miles below the town of Kadiak, was the most likely place to find bear, so we now headed our boat in that direction. It was a most beautiful day for a start, with the first faint traces of spring in the air. As we skirted the shore that afternoon I sighted, through the glasses on some low hills in the distance, bear tracks in the snow. My Aleuts seemed to think that the bears were probably near, having come down to the shore in search of kelp. It promised a pretty fair chance for a shot, but there was exceedingly

---

* I do not believe that any one making a hunting expedition to the Kadiak Islands could get a better hunter than Nikolai Pycoon.

bad water about, and no harbor for the sloop to lie, so Payjaman and my natives advised me not to make the attempt. As one should take no chances with Alaskan waters, I felt this was wise, and we reluctantly passed on.

The next forenoon we put into a large bay known as Eagle Harbor, to pick up a local hunter who was to accompany us to Kiliuda Bay, for both my Aleuts and the Russian were unacquainted with this locality. Ignati Chowischpack, the native whose services we secured, was quite a character, a man of much importance among the Aleuts of this district, and one who had a thorough knowledge of the country which we had chosen as our hunting grounds.

We expected to remain at Eagle Harbor only part of the day, but unfortunately at this point we were stormbound for a week. Several times we attempted to leave, but each time had to put back, fearing that the heavy seas we encountered outside would crush in the bidarka which was carried lashed to the sloop's deck. Therefore, it was not until early on the morning of April 12, just as the sun was topping the mountains, that we finally arrived at Kiliuda Bay.

Our hunting grounds now stretched before us as far as the eye could see. We had by this time passed the tree area, and it was only here and there in isolated spots that stunted cottonwoods bordered the salmon streams, and scattered patches of alders dotted the mountain sides. In many places the land rolled gradually back from the shore until the mountain bases were reached, while in other parts giant cliffs rose directly from the water's edge, but generally one could, with the glasses, command a grand view of this great, irregular bay, with its long arms cutting into the island in all directions.

We made our permanent camp in a large barabara. The barabara is so often seen in Western Alaska that it deserves a brief description. It is a small, rude, dome-shaped hut, with a frame generally made of driftwood, and thatched with sods and the rank grass of the country. It has no windows, but a large hole in the roof permits the light to enter and serves also as an outlet for the smoke from the fire, which is built on a rough hearth in the middle of the barabara. These crude huts, their doors never locked, offer shelter to any one, and are frequently found in the most remote places. The one which we now occupied was quite large, with ample space to stow away our various belongings, and we made ourselves most comfortable, while our Aleuts occupied the small "banya," or Russian bathhouse, which is also generally found by the side of the barabara. This was to be our base of supplies from which my friend and I were to hunt in different directions.

The morning after reaching our shooting grounds I started with one of my natives and the local hunter in the bidarka to get the lay of the land. Both Blake and I thought it wise to divide up the country, for the reasons that we could thus cover a much greater territory, and that our modes of hunting differed materially. Although at the time I believed from what I had heard that Payjaman was an excellent man, I preferred to hunt in a more careful manner, as is the native custom, in which I had had some experience the year before. I firmly believe that had Payjaman hunted as carefully as my Aleuts did, my friend would have been more successful.

We spent our first day in skirting the shores of the entire bay, paddling up to its very head. Ignati pointed out to Fedor all the most likely places, and explained the local eccentricities of the various winds — a knowledge of these being of the first importance in bear hunting. I was much pleased with the looks of the country, but at the same time was greatly disappointed to find that in the inner bays there was no trace of spring, and that the snow lay deep even on the shores down to the high-water mark. Not a bear's track was to be seen, and it was evident that we were on the grounds ahead of time.

We stopped for tea and lunch about noon at the head of the bay. Near by a long and narrow arm of water extended inland some three miles, and it was the country lying adjacent to this and to the head of the bay that I decided to choose as my hunting grounds.

We had a hard time to reach camp that night, for a severe Alaskan storm suddenly burst upon us, and a fierce wind soon swept down from the hills, kicking up a heavy sea which continually swept over the bidarka's deck, and without camelinkas on we surely should have swamped. It grew bitterly cold, and a blinding snow-storm made it impossible to see any distance ahead, but Ignati knew these waters well, and we reached the main camp, safe, but half frozen, just at dark.

On the Lookout for Bear.

Next day the storm still continued, and it was impossible to venture out. My friend and I passed the time playing piquet and listening to our natives, who talked earnestly together, going over many of their strange and thrilling hunting experiences. We understood but little Russian and Aleut, yet their expressive gestures made it quite possible to catch the drift of what was being said. It seemed that Ignati had a brother killed a few years ago while bear hunting in the small bay which lies between Eagle Harbor and Kiliuda Bay. The man came upon a bear, which he shot and badly wounded. Accompanied by a friend, he followed up the blood trail which led into a thick patch of alders. Suddenly he came upon a large, unwounded male bear, which charged him unprovoked and at such close quarters that he was unable to defend himself. Before his companion, who was but a short distance away, could reach him he was killed. The bear frightfully mangled the body, holding it down with his feet and using his teeth to tear it apart.

Ignati at once started out to avenge his brother, and killed in quick succession six bears, allowing their bodies to remain as a warning to the other bears, not even removing their skins.

During the past few years three men, while hunting, have been killed by bears in the same vicinity as Ignati's brother, two instantly and one living but a short time. I think it is due to these accidents that the natives in this region have a superstitious dread of a "long-tailed bear" which, they declare, roams the hills between Eagle Harbor and Kiliuda Bay.

The storm, which began on the 13th, continued until the 17th, and this was but one of a series. Winter seemed to come back in all its fury, and I believe that whatever bears had left their winter dens went back to them for another sleep. It was not until the middle of May that the snow began to disappear and spring with its green grass came.

All this time I was camped with my natives at the head of the bay, some fifteen miles from our base of supplies. On the 23d of April we first sighted tracks, but it was not until May 15th that I was finally successful in bagging my first bear.

The tracks in the snow indicated that the bears began again to come out of their winter dens the last week in April; and should one wish to make a spring hunt on the Kadiak Islands the first of May would, I should judge, be a good time to arrive upon the shooting grounds.

When the wind was favorable our mode of hunting was to leave camp before daylight, and paddle in our bidarka up to the head of one of these long bays, and leaving our canoe here, trudge over the snow to some commanding elevation, where we constantly used the glasses upon the surrounding hillsides, hoping to see bear. We generally returned to camp a little before noon, but in the afternoon went back again to the lookout, where we remained until it was too dark to see.

When the wind was blowing into these valleys we did not hunt, for we feared that whatever bears might be around would get our scent and quickly leave. New bears might come, but none which had once scented

mountain ridge with rocky sides stretching all across our front; while to the left rose another towering mountain ridge with steep and broken sides. All the surrounding hills, and much of the low country, were covered with deep snow. The mountains on three sides completely hemmed in the valley, and their snowy slopes gaves us an excellent chance to distinguish all tracks. Such were the grounds which I had been watching for over a month, whenever the wind was favorable.

The sun was just topping the long hill to our right as we reached our elevated watch-

Our Permanent Camp Near the Harbor's Mouth on the Alaska Peninsula.

us would remain. For days at a time we were stormbound, and unable to hunt, or even leave our little tent, where frequently we were obliged to remain under blankets both day and night to keep warm.

On May 15th, by 4 o'clock, I had finished a hurried breakfast, and with my two Aleuts had left in the bidarka for our daily watching place. This was a large mound lying in the centre of a valley some three miles from where we were camped. On the right of the mound rose a gently sloping hill, with its sides sparsely covered with alders, and at right angles and before it extended a rugged

ing place. The glasses were at once in use, and soon an exclamation from one of my natives told me that new tracks had been seen. There they were—two long, unbroken lines, leading down from the mountain on our right, across the valley, and up and out of sight over the ridge to our left. It seemed as if two bears had simply wandered across our front, and crossed over the range of mountains into the bay beyond.

As soon as my hunters saw these tracks they turned to me, and with every confidence said, "I guess catch." Now it must be remembered that these tracks led completely over the mountains to our left, and it was the most beautiful bit of hunting on the part of my natives to know that these bears would turn and swing back into the valley ahead. To follow the tracks, which were well up in the heart of our shooting grounds, would drive out all the bears that might be lurking there, and this my hunters knew perfectly well, yet they never hesitated for one moment, but started ahead with every confidence.

We threaded our way through a mass of thick alders to the head of the valley, and then climbing a steep mountain, took

ground, and he was unquestionably a bull of great size. Shortly after I had the satisfaction of seeing a second bear, which the first was evidently following. This was without doubt a female, by no means so large as the first, and much lighter in color. The smaller bear was apparently hungry, and it was interesting to watch her dig through the snow in search of food. Soon she headed down the mountain side, paying absolutely no attention to the big male, which slowly followed some distance in the rear. Shortly she reached a rocky cliff, which it seemed impossible that such a

" The bidarka is made with a light frame of strong, elastic wood, covered with seal or sea-lion skin."

our stand on a rocky ridge, which commanded a wide view ahead and to our left in the direction in which the tracks led. We had only been in our new position half an hour when Nikolai, my head hunter, gripped my arm and pointed high up on the mountain in the direction in which we had been watching. There I made out a small black speck which to the naked eye appeared but a bit of dark rock protruding through the snow. Taking the glasses, I made out a large bear slowly floundering ahead and evidently coming downward. His coat seemed very dark against the white back-

clumsy animal could descend, and I almost despaired of her making the attempt, but without a pause she wound in and out, seemingly traversing the steepest and most difficult places in the easiest manner, and headed for the valley below. When the bull reached this cliff we lost sight of him; nor could we locate him again with even the most careful use of the glasses. He had evidently chosen this secure retreat to lie up in for the rest of the day. If I could have killed the female without alarming him, and then waited on her trail, I should undoubtedly have got another shot as he

"The barabara is a small, dome-shaped hut, thatched with sods and the rude grass of the country."

followed her after his rest. It was 8 o'clock when we first located the bears, and for nearly three hours I had a chance to watch one or both of them through powerful glasses. The sun had come up clear and strong, melting the crust upon the snow, so that as soon as the female bear reached the steep mountain side her downward path was not an easy one. At each step she would sink up to her belly, and at times would slip and fall, turning somersault after somersault; now and again she would be buried so deep in the snow that it seemed impossible for her to go either ahead or backward. Then she would roll over on her back, and, loosening her hold on the steep hillside, would come tumbling and slipping down, turning over and over, sideways and endways, until she caught herself by spreading out all four legs.

In this way she came with each step and turn nearer and nearer. Finally she reached an open patch on the hillside, where she began to feed, digging up the roots of the salmon-berry bushes at the edge of the snow. If now I lost sight of her for a short time it was very difficult to pick her up again, even with the glasses, so did the light tawny yellows and browns of her coat blend in with the dead grass of the place on which she was feeding.

The wind had been blowing in our favor all the morning, and for once continued true and steady. But how closely we watched the clouds to see that no change in its direction threatened us!

We waited until the bear had left the snow and was quietly feeding before we made a move, and then we slowly worked ahead and downward, taking up a new position on a small ridge, which was well to leeward, but still on the opposite side of the valley from the bear. She seemed in an excellent position for a stalk, and had I been alone I should have tried it. But the Aleut mode of hunting is to study the direction in which your game is working, and take up a position which it will approach.

Taking up our stand, we waited, watching with much interest the great, ungainly creature as she kept nibbling the young grass and digging up roots. At times she would seem to be heading in our direction, and then again would turn and slowly feed away. Suddenly something seemed to alarm her, for she made a dash of some fifty yards down the valley, and then, seeming to recover her composure, began to feed again, all the while working nearer and nearer. The bear was now well down in the bottom of the valley, which was at this point covered with alders and intersected by a small stream. There were open patches in the underbrush, and it was my intention to shoot when she passed through one of these, for the ground was covered with over a foot of snow, which would offer a very tempting background.

While all this was passing quickly through my mind, she suddenly made another bolt down the valley, and went directly opposite our position, turned at right angles, crossed the brook, and came straight through the alders into the open not eighty yards away from us. As she made her appearance, I could not help being greatly impressed by the massive head and high shoulders, on which stood the pronounced tuft of hair. I had most carefully seen to my sights long before, for I knew how much would probably depend on my first shot. It surely seemed as if fortune was with me that day, as at last I had a fair chance at the game I had come so far to seek. Aiming with the greatest care for the lungs and heart, I slowly pressed the trigger. The bear gave a deep, angry growl, and bit for the wound, which told me my bullet was well placed.* But she kept her feet, and made a dash for the thicket. I was well above, and so commanded a fairly clear view as she crashed through the leafless alders. Twice more I fired, and each time with the most careful aim. At the last shot she dropped with an angry moan. My hunters shook my hand, and their faces told me how glad they were at my final success after so many long weeks of persistent work.†

I at once started down to look at the bear,

when out upon the mountain opposite the bull was seen. He had heard the shots, and was now once more but a moving black speck on the snow, but it will always be a mystery to me how he could have heard the three reports of my small-bore rifle so far away and against a strong wind. My natives suggested that the shots must have echoed, and in this I think they were right; but even then it shows how abnormally the sense of hearing has been developed in these bears.

I was sorry to find that the small-bore rifle did not give as great a shock as I had expected, for my first two bullets had gone through the bear's lungs and heart without knocking her off her feet.

The bear was a female, as we had supposed, but judging from what my natives said, only of medium size. She measured six feet four inches in a straight line between the nose and the end of the vertebræ, and forty-four and five-eighths inches at the shoulders. The fur was in prime condition, and of an average length of four and a half inches, but over the shoulder the mane was two inches longer. Unfortunately, as in many of the spring skins, there was a large patch over the rump, apparently much rubbed. The general belief is that these worn patches are made by the bears sliding down hill on their haunches on the snow; but my natives have a theory that this is caused by the bear's pelt freezing to their dens and being torn off when they wake from their winter's sleep.

Although this female was not large for a Kadiak bear,* I was much pleased with my final success, and our camp that night was quite a merry one.

Shortly after killing this bear Blake and I returned to the trading post at Wood Island (near the town of Kadiak) to prepare for a hunt on the Alaska Peninsula.

---

* When a bullet strikes a Kadiak bear, he will always bite for the wound, and utter a deep and angry growl; whereas of the eleven bears which my friend and I shot on the Alaska Peninsula, although they, too, bite for the wound, not one uttered a sound.

† Including the time spent last year and this year, this bear represented 87 days of actual hunting.

* As was proved by one I shot later in the season.

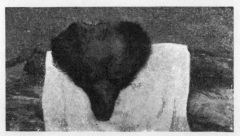

Hunting the Big Game of Alaska
Part 2

HUNTING THE BIG GAME OF ALASKA

BEAR STALKING ON THE ALASKA PENINSULA

By JAMES H. KIDDER

THE year before I had chanced to meet an old pilot who had the reputation of knowing every nook and corner of the Alaskan coast. He told me several times of the great numbers of bears that he had often seen in a certain bay on the Alaska Peninsula, and advised me most strongly to visit this place.

There were numerous delays in getting started, but finally, on May 31, we set sail in a good-sized schooner we had chartered from the North American Commercial Company, and in two days were landed at our new shooting grounds. Rarely, if ever, does it fall to the lot of amateurs in modern days to meet with better sport than we had for the next month.

The schooner landed us with our natives, two bidarkas (native canoes), and all our provisions near the mouth of the harbor. Here we made our base of supplies, and the next morning, in our two canoes, started with our hunters to explore this wonderful bay. At high tide it extends inland some fifteen miles, but at low water is one vast bog of glacial deposit. Rugged mountains rise on all sides, and at the base of these mountains there are long meadows which extend out to the high water mark. In these meadows, during the month of June, the bears come to feed upon the young salt grass.

There was a long swell breaking on the beach as we left our base of supplies, but we passed safely through the line of breakers to the smooth waters beyond, and now headed for the upper bay. The two bidarkas kept side by side, and Blake and I chatted together, but all the while kept the glasses constantly fixed upon the hillsides. We had hardly gone a mile before a small black bear was sighted; but the wind was unfavorable, and he got our scent before we could land. This looked decidedly encouraging, and we continued on in the best of spirits. About midday we went on shore, lunched, and then basked in the sun until the afternoon, when we again got into the bidarkas and paddled farther up the bay, to a place where a wide meadow extends out from the base of the mountains. Here Nikolai, my head hunter, went on shore with the glasses, and, raising himself cautiously above the bank, took a long look at the country beyond. It was at once quite evident that he had seen something, and we all joined him, keeping well hidden from view. There, out upon the marsh, could be seen two large bears feeding upon the young salt grass. They seemed in an almost unapproachable position, so we lay and watched them, hoping that they would move into a more advantageous place. After an hour or so they fed back toward the trees and soon passed out of sight.

We matched to see which part of the meadow each should watch, and it fell to my lot to go farther up the marsh. I had been only a short time in this place when a new bear came into sight. We now made a most beautiful stalk right across the open to within one hundred years. All this while a new dog, which I had bought at Kadiak and called Stereke, had crawled with us flat on his stomach, trembling all over with excitement as he watched the bear. I had plenty of time to take aim, and was in no way excited, but missed clean at one hundred yards. At the report of my rifle Stereke bit himself clear from Nikolai, who was holding him, and at once made for the bear, which he tackled in a most encouraging manner, nipping his heels, and then quickly getting out of the way as the bear charged. But I found that one dog was not enough to hold these bears, and this one got away.

Next day we loafed in the sun until evening, while our natives kept constant watch of the great meadow where we had seen the bears the day before. We had just turned in (although ten o'clock, it was still daylight), when one of the natives came running up to say that a bear was in sight; so Blake with three natives and Stereke made the stalk. I had a beautiful chance to watch it from the high rocks beside our camp. The men were able to approach to within some fifty yards, and Blake, with his first shot, hit, and with his third, killed the bear before it could get into the brush. Stereke, when loosed, tackled the bear savagely.

Unfortunately no measurements were taken, but the bear appeared to be somewhat smaller than the female I killed at

side by side, and pushed up to the extreme head of the bay, where we came upon an old deserted Indian camp of the year before. Numerous stretchers told of their success with bear; but the remains of an old fire in the very heart of our shooting grounds warned us that in this section the bears might have been disturbed; for the Alaskan bear is very wary, and is quick to take alarm at any unusual scent. We came back to our camp on the beach by ten o'clock, and had our first substantial meal of the day; for we had now adopted the Aleutian habit of taking simply a cup of

Drying a Bear Skin in the Field.

Kiliuda Bay, and weighed, I should judge, some four hundred and fifty pounds. It appeared higher in the legs and less massive than the Kadiak bear, and had a shorter mane, but was of much the same tawny lion color on the back, although darker on the legs and belly.

On Friday morning, June 7, we made a three o'clock start from where we had passed the night on the beach. The sun was not over the mountains for another hour, and there was that great charm which comes in the early dawn of a summer's day. Blake in his bidarka and I in mine paddled along,

tea and a piece of bread, in order to make the earliest of starts each morning.

After our midday breakfast we usually took a nap until afternoon: but this day I was not sleepy, and so read for a while; then I loaded my rifle (which I always kept within arm's reach) and was just settling my rugs to turn in, when Stereke gave a sharp bark, and Blake shouted "Bear!" Seizing my rifle I looked up, and, walking toward us on the beach, just one hundred and ten yards away, was a good-sized bull bear. My dog at once made for him, while Blake jumped for his rifle. The bear was just turning when I fired. He bit for the wound, but uttered no sound, and was just disappearing in the brush when I fired a hasty second. Blake and I now rushed into the thick alders after the dog, which was savagely attacking the bear. His barking told us where the bear was, and I arrived just in time to see him make a determined charge at the dog, which avoided him and renewed the attack.

I now forced my way through the alders, and got in two close shots which rolled him over. It appeared that my first shot had broken his shoulder, as well as cut the lower portion of the heart; but this bear had gone some fifty yards, and was still on his feet when I came up and finished him off. He was a fair-sized bull, six feet two inches, in a straight line along the vertebra, and stood exactly three feet at the shoulders. He had evidently been fighting, for one ear was badly torn, and his skin was much scarred with old and recent wounds. After removing the pelt the carcass was thrown into the bay, so that there might be no stench, which my natives declared would be enough to

the rump and nose; and again others were saddle-backed; still others stood with their front feet directly under them, making a regular curve at the shoulders; while others had the front legs wide apart and seemed to form a triangle, the apex of which was at their shoulders.

Their range of color seemed to be from very dark, silver tipped, to a very light dirty yellow, but with dark legs and belly.

This evening, just as we were having our tea, another bear made his appearance. The first, which we had been watching, evidently heard him coming through the woods, and as the second came out into the open the former vanished. The new one was a dirty yellowish white, with a very dark belly and legs, which gave him a most comical appearance.

The wind still continued unfavorable, and my friend and I passed an extremely interesting evening with the glasses, for this watching game, especially bear, gives me almost as much pleasure as making the actual stalk.

spoil any future shooting in this locality. This same afternoon we moved our camp to a new marsh.

The next morning we sighted a bear, which fed into the woods before we had time to come up with him. Shortly after five o'clock the brute made a second appearance; but as the wind had changed and now blew in the wrong direction, a stalk could not be made without their scent being carried into the woods where many bears were apt to be. We made it a great point on this hunt never to make a stalk unless the wind was right, for we were extremely anxious not to spoil the place by diffusing our scent and driving away whatever bears might be lurking near. Therefore, often we could watch bears at only a few hundred yards.

It was most interesting to see how careful these big animals were, and how, from time to time, they would feel the wind with their noses, and again stop feeding and listen. No two bears seemed to be built on quite the same lines. Some were high at the shoulders, and then sloped down towards

We had just finished supper when we saw another bear in a better position, and I proceeded to make the stalk, going part of the way in the bidarka, for the great meadow was intersected by a stream from which small lagoons made off in all directions. The wind was very baffling, and although we successfully reached a clump of brush in the middle of the marsh, the bear for sometime continued to graze in an unapproachable spot. We had almost given up hopes of getting a shot, when he turned and fed slowly some fifty yards in a new direction, which was up-wind. This was our chance. Quickly regaining the bidarka, we paddled as noiselessly and rapidly as possible up the main stream of the marsh to a lagoon.

There was great charm in stalking game in this manner, although we were, in a sense, but passengers in my natives' hands. But it was fascinating to watch their keenness and skill as they guided the frail craft around the sharp turns, the noiseless use of the paddles, the light in their eyes as they constantly stood up in the canoe to keep a hidden gaze upon the game ahead, watching its every movement, as well as the local eddies and currents in the light evening breeze. All was so in keeping with the sombre leaden clouds overhead and the grizzled sides of the ungainly brute, blending in with the background of weather-beaten tree trunks and the dull gray rocks. And so, silently and swiftly (stopping many times when the bear's head was up), we approached nearer and nearer, until my headman whispered, "Boudit" (enough), and I knew that I was to have a fair shot. Stealthily raising my head above the bank, I saw the bear feeding, only seventy-five yards away. Creeping cautiously out of the boat I lay flat upon my stomach, rifle cocked and ready, waiting for a good shot. Soon it came. The bear heard some sound in the forest and raised his head. Now was my chance, and the next second, he dropped without a sound; he struggled to rise, but I could see he was anchored with a broken shoulder. My men were unable to restrain themselves any longer, and, as I shot for the second time, their rifles cracked just after mine. We carried the entire carcass to the bidarka, and even the cartridge shells were taken away to avoid tainting the place with an unusual scent.

Three days afterwards we were back again at our camp behind the rocks. We had wanted rain for some time to wash out all scent. Then again, bears are supposed to move about more freely in such weather. Therefore, we were rather pleased when the wind changed, bringing a northeast storm which continued all the next day. The lofty mountains were rapidly losing the snow on their summits, and the night's rain had wrought marvels in their appearance, seeming to bring out every shade of green on their wooded slopes. One of our natives was kept constantly on the lookout, and a dozen times a day both Blake and I would leave our books and climb to the watching place for a view across the great meadow. By this time we knew the bear trails and the most tempting feeding grounds and the surest approaches to the game when it had once come into the open. Therefore, when I was told this evening that a bear had been sighted I felt pretty sure of getting a shot.

The wind was coming in great gusts across our front, and the corner where the bear was feeding offered a dangerous place for eddies and back-currents against the mountain side. In order to avoid these we kept just inside the woods. Nikolai, going first, showed the greatest skill in knowing just how close to the wind we could go. We quickly reached the place where we expected to sight the bear, but he was hidden in the bed of the river, and it was some minutes before we could make out the top of his head moving above the grass. Then, noiselessly, we crawled up as the bear again fed slowly into view. He was now about one hundred and twenty-five yards away, and offered an excellent shot as he paused and raised his head to scent the breeze; but Nikolai whispered, "no," and we worked nearer, crawling forward when the bear's head was down, and lying flat and close when his head was up.

It is curious to note that often when game is being stalked it becomes suspicious, although it cannot smell, hear, or see the stalker—instinct, perhaps; call it what you will. And now this bear turned and began moving slowly towards cover. For some time he was hidden from view; and then, just before he would finally vanish from sight, he paused a moment, offering a quartering shot. The lower half of his body was concealed by the grass, but it was my last chance, and I took it, aiming for the lungs, and rather high, in order to get a clear shot. I saw, as he bit for the wound, that the bullet was well placed, and as he turned and lumbered across our front I fired two more deliberate shots, one going through the foreleg and one breaking a back leg.

Nikolai also fired, giving the bear a slight skin wound, and hitting the back leg just above where one of my bullets had previously struck. As the bear entered the brush we both ran up, my hunter going to the left while I went a little below to head the bear off. We soon came upon him, and Nikolai, getting the first sight, gave him another bullet through the lungs with my heavy rifle, and in a few moments he rolled over dead.

It was my thought always to keep a wounded bear from getting into the brush, as the blood spoor would have ruined future shooting.

I think it important to point out that when my bullet struck this bear he bit for the wound. As he did so he was turned from his original direction, which would have carried him out of sight among the trees, and galloped across our front, thereby giving

"The largest female we got on the Peninsula, measuring six feet, six and one-half inches along the vertebra."

me an opportunity to fire two more shots. It frequently happened that bears were turned from their original directions to the sides upon which they received the first bullet, and we always took this into consideration when making an approach.

My Aleuts were not permitted to shoot unless we were following up a wounded bear in the thick brush; but I found it most difficult to keep them to this rule. The large hole of the bullet from my fifty calibre which Nikolai carried made it easy to distinguish his hits, and if a bear had received the mortal wound from his rifle I should not have kept the skin.

The pelt of this bear which we had just killed was in excellent condition, and although he was not fat he was of fair size, measuring six feet three and one-eighth inches along the vertebra.

Great care was used, as usual, to pick up the empty cartridge shells, and we pulled up the bloody bits of grass, throwing them into a brook, into which we also put the bear's carcass.

On the morning of the 19th my friend and his hunter went up the shore to investigate a small marsh lying a mile or so from camp. Here they saw that the grass had been recently nibbled, and that there were fresh signs about. They returned to this spot again that evening and sighted a bear. The bear fed quickly up to within sixty-five yards, when Blake rolled him over. This bear was not a large one and was of the usual tawny color.

The next morning a bear was seen by my natives in the big meadow by our camp, but it did not remain long enough for a stalk. At 9:30 it again came out into the open, and Nikolai and I made a quick approach; but the bear, although he was not alarmed, did not wait long enough for us to get within range. We had skirted the marsh, keeping just inside of the thicket, and now when the bear disappeared, we settled ourselves for a long wait should he again come into the open. We were well hidden from view, and the wind blew slanting in our faces and across our front. I had just begun to think that we should not get a shot until the bear came out for his evening feed, when Nikolai caught my arm and pointed ahead. There, slowly leaving the dense edge of the woods, was a new bear; not so large as the first, but we could see at a glance that she had a beautiful coat of a dark, silver tip color.

Removing our boots and stockings and circling around, we came out about seventy-five yards from where we had last seen the bear, but she had moved a short distance ahead, and offered us a grand chance for a close approach. Keeping behind a small point which made out into the open, we were able to crawl up to within fifty yards, and then, waiting until the bear's head was up, I gave her a quartering shot behind the shoulders. She half fell, and bit for the wound, and as she slowly started for the woods I gave her another shot which rolled her over. This bear proved to be a female, the first we had shot upon the mainland, probably the mate of the bear we had originally attempted to stalk. The skin, although small, was the most beautiful I have ever killed.

Upon examining the internal effects of my shots I was disappointed to find that my first bullet, on coming in contact with one of the ribs, had torn away from the metal jacket, and had expanded to such an extent that it lost greatly in penetration. I had of late been forced to the conclusion that the small-bore rifle I was using on such heavy game lacked the stopping force I had credited it with, and that the bullets were not of sufficient weight.

On June 23d we turned our bidarka's bows to the upper bay, at the head of which we ascended a small river that wound through a vast meadow until the stream met the mountains. Here we unloaded our simple camp gear, and, while the men prepared breakfast, Blake and I ascended an elevation which commanded an uninterrupted view of the grassy plain. No bears were in sight, so we had time and undisturbed opportunity to enjoy the beauty of the scene. We lay for some time basking in the sun, talking of books and people, and of many subjects of common interest. Now and then one would take the glasses and scan the outskirts of the vast meadow which stretched before us. All at once Blake gave a low exclamation and pointed to the west. I followed the direction of his gaze, and saw four bears slowly leaving the woods. They were at some distance, and we did not think we had time to reach them before they would probably return to the underbrush for their midday sleep, so for the present we let them go.

After breakfast, as they were still in the same place, we attempted the stalk, going most of the way in our bidarkas, winding in and out through the meadow in the small lagoons which intersected it in all directions. Every little while the men would ascend the banks with the glasses, thus keeping a watchful eye upon the bears' movements. Taking a time when they had fed into the underbrush, we made a quick circle to leeward over the open, then, reaching the edge of the thicket, we approached cautiously to a selected watching place. We reached this spot shortly after one o'clock. The bears had entered the woods, so we settled ourselves for a long wait. It was Blake's turn to shoot, which meant that he was to have an undisturbed first shot at the largest bear, and after he had fired I could take what was left.

Just before three o'clock three bears again made their appearance. Two were yearlings, which would, in the fall, leave their mother and shift for themselves, and one much larger, which lay just at the edge of the underbrush. Had these yearlings not been with the mother she would not have come out so early in the afternoon; and as it was, she kept to the shelter of the alders, while the two smaller ones fed out some distance from the woods.

We now removed our boots, and, with Stereke well in hand (for he smelt the bears and was tugging hard on his collar), noiselessly skirted the woods, keeping some tall grass between the bears and ourselves. In this way we approached to within one hundred yards. Twice one of the smaller animals rose on his hind legs and looked in our direction; but the wind was favorable, and we were well concealed, so they did not take alarm.

My friend decided to shoot the mother, while I was to reserve my fire until after his shot. I expected that at the report of his rifle the bear I had chosen would pause a moment in surprise, and thus offer a good standing shot. As my friend's rifle cracked the bear I had selected made a sudden dash for the woods, and I had to take him on the run. At my first shot he turned a complete somersault, and then, quickly springing up, again made a dash for cover. I fired a second time, and rolled him over for once and all. Stereke was instantly slipped and made at once for my bear. By the time we had run up he was shaking and biting his hind quarters in a most approved style. We at once put him after the larger bear which

Blake had wounded, and his bark in the thick alders told us he had located her. We all rushed and found that the bear, although down, was still alive. Blake gave her a final shot through the lungs.

The third bear got away, but I believe it was wounded by Nikolai. The one that Blake had killed was the largest female we got on the Peninsula, measuring six feet six and one-half inches along the vertebra.

It is interesting to note that the two yearlings differed greatly in color. One was a grizzled brown, like the mother, while the other was very much lighter, of a light dirty yellowish color.

We had watched these bears for some hours in the morning, and I feel positive that the mother had no cubs of this spring with her, yet on examination milk was found in her breasts. My natives told me that frequently yearling cubs continue to suckle, and surely we had positive proof of this with the large female bear.

The mosquitoes had by this time become almost unbearable, and it was late before they permitted us to get to sleep. It began to rain, but I was so tired that I slept on, although my pillow and blankets were soon well soaked. As the rain continued we finally put up our small tent; but everything had become thoroughly wet, and we passed a most uncomfortable day.

In the afternoon a black bear appeared not far from our camping place. My friend went after this with his hunter, who made a most wonderful stalk. The bear was in an almost unapproachable position, and the two men appeared to be going directly down wind; but Ivan insisted that there was a slight eddy in the breeze, and in this he must have been correct, for he brought Blake up to within sixty yards, when my friend killed the bear with a bullet through the brain.

I think it is interesting to note that our shooting grounds were the extreme western range of the black bear. A few years ago they were not found in this locality, but it is quite evident that they are each year working farther and farther to the westward.

The next day the heavy rain still continued. The meadow was now one vast bog, and the small lagoons were swollen into deep and rapid streams. Everything was wet, and we passed a most uncomfortable day. Our two hunters were camped about fifty yards off, under a big rock, and I think must have had a pretty hard time of it, but all the while they kept a sharp lookout!

About one o'clock the men reported that a large bear had been seen some distance off, but that it had remained in sight only a short time. We expected this bear would again make its appearance in the afternoon, and in this surmise we were correct, for he came out into the open three hours later, when Nikolai and I with Stereke made the stalk. We circled well to leeward, fording the many rapid streams with great difficulty. The rain had melted the snow on the hills, and we frequently had to wade almost up to our shoulders in this icy water.

In crossing one of the lagoons Stereke was carried under some fallen trees, and for a while I very much feared that my dog would be drowned. The same thing almost happened to myself, for the swift current twice carried me off my feet.

The bear had fed well into the open, and it was impossible, even with the most careful stalking, to get nearer than a small patch of tall grass, about one hundred and seventy-five yards away. I put up my rifle to shoot, but found that the front sight was most unsteady, for I was wet to the skin and shaking all over with cold. Half expecting to miss, I pressed the trigger, and was not greatly surprised to see my bullet splash in the marsh just over the bear's head. He saw the bullet strike on the other side, and now came in our direction, but Stereke, breaking loose from Nikolai, turned him. He now raced across our front at about one hundred and twenty-five yards, with the dog in close pursuit. This gave me an excellent chance, and I fired three more shots. At my last I saw the bear bite for his shoulder, showing that my bullet was well placed. He continued to dash ahead, when Nikolai fired, also hitting him in the shoulder, with the heavy rifle. He dropped, but gamely tried to rise and face Stereke, who savagely attacked his quarters. Nikolai now fired again, his bullet going in at the chest, raking him the entire length, and lodging under the skin at the hind knee joint. Unfortunately, this bear fell in so much water that it was impossible to take any other accurate measurement than the one along his back. This was the largest bear we shot on the mainland, and the one measurement that I was able to take was six feet ten inches along the vertebra.

On examining the internal effect of his wounds, I found that my bullet had struck the shoulder blade and penetrated one lung, but had gone to pieces upon coming in contact with the bone. Although it would have eventually proved a mortal wound, the shock at the time was not sufficient to knock the bear off his feet.

The next morning the storm broke, and we started back to our camp behind the rocks, for the skins we had recently shot needed to be cleaned and dried. We reached camp that afternoon, where I found my old hunter, Fedor, who was now better and had come to join us. He had arrived the night before, and reported that he had seen three bears on the marsh. He said he had watched them all the evening, and that the next morning two more had made their appearance. He could no longer withstand this temptation, and just before we had arrived had shot a small black bear with an excellent skin.

Two days after a bear was reported in the meadow, and as it was my friend's turn to shoot he started with his hunter to make the stalk. It was raining at the time, and I was almost tempted to lie among my blankets; but my insatiable love of sport was too strong, and, armed with powerful glasses, I joined the men on the rocks to watch the hunters.

The bear had fed well out into the meadow not far from a small clump of trees. In order to reach this clump of trees Blake and Ivan were obliged to wade quite a deep stream, and had removed their clothes. Unfortunately my friend carelessly left his coat, in the pocket of which were all the extra cartridges for his and Ivan's rifles.

I saw them disappear among the trees and then turned my glasses on the bear. At the first shot he sprang back in surprise, while Blake's bullet went high. The bear now located the shot and began a quick retreat to the woods, when one of my friend's bullets struck him, rolling him over. He instantly regained his feet and continued making for cover, walking slowly and looking back over his shoulder all the while. Blake now fired another shot, and again the bear was apparently badly hit. He moved at such a slow pace that I thought he had surely received a mortal wound.

Entirely against orders, Ivan now shot three times in quick succession, hitting the bear with one shot in the hind leg, his other two shots being misses. Blake now rushed after the bear, with his hunter following some fifty yards behind, and approached to within ten steps, when he fired his last cartridge, evidently hitting the bear hard, which fell upon its head, but once more regaining its feet, continued toward the woods. At this point Ivan fired his last cartridge, but missed. The bear continued for several steps, while the two hunters stood with empty rifles watching. Suddenly, quick as a flash, it swung round upon its hind legs and gave one spring after Blake, who, not understanding his Aleut's shouts not to run, started across the marsh with the bear in close pursuit. At every step the bear was gaining, and Ivan, appreciating that unless the bear's attention was detracted my friend would soon be pulled down, began waving his arms, and shouting at the top of his voice in order to attract the bear's attention from Blake. The latter saw that his hunter was standing firm, and, taking in the situation, suddenly stopped. The bear charged to within a few feet of the two hunters; but, when he saw their determined stand, stopped and, swinging his head from side to side, watched them for some seconds, apparently undecided whether to charge home or leave them. Then he turned and, looking back over his shoulder, made slowly for the woods.

This bear, while charging, had his head stretched forward, ears flat, and teeth clinched, with his lips drawn well back, and his eyes glaring. I am strongly convinced it was only Ivan's great presence of mind which prevented a most serious accident.

It is a strange fact that a well-placed bullet will knock the light out of such game; but if they are once thoroughly aroused it takes much more lead to kill them. When they had got more cartridges, my friend with two natives proceeded to follow this bear up; but although they tracked him some miles he was never recovered.

The Aleuts, when they follow up a wounded bear in thick cover, strip to the skin, for they claim in this way they are able to move with greater freedom, and at the same time there are no clothes to catch in the brush and make noise. They go slowly and are most cautious, for frequently, when a bear is wounded, if he thinks that he is being pursued, he will swing around on his own trail and spring out from the side upon the hunters.

The next day I started with my two natives to visit a meadow well up the bay. We had gone but a mile from camp, when I caught an indistinct outline of a bear feeding on the grass at the edge of the timber, about one hundred and twenty-five yards away, and I quickly fired, missing.

At the report the bear jumped sideways unable to locate the sound, and my next bullet struck just above his tail and ranged forward into the lungs. Fedor now fired (missing), while I ran up with Nikolai, firing another shot as I ran, which knocked the bear over. Stereke savagely attacked the bear, biting and shaking him, and, seeing that he was breathing his last, I refrained from firing again, as the skin was excellent.

This bear had had an encounter with a porcupine. One of his paws was filled with quills, and in skinning him we found that some quills had worked well up the leg and lodged by the ankle joint, making a most loathsome wound.

This bear was almost as large as the one I had last shot at the head of the bay, and his pelt made a grand trophy. I was much disgusted with myself that afternoon for missing my first shot. It is not enough simply to get your bear, but one should always endeavor to kill with the first shot; otherwise much game will be lost, for the first is almost always the easiest shot; hence one should kill at that chance.

I had been fortunate in killing seven large brown bears, while Blake had killed three browns and one black, and our natives had killed one brown and one black bear, making a total of thirteen, between the 7th and the 28th of June.

The skulls of these brown bears I sent to Dr. Merriam, Chief of the Biological Survey, at Washington, and they proved to be most interesting from a scientific point of view, for from them the classification of the bears of the Alaska Peninsula has been entirely changed; and it seems that we were fortunate enough to bring out a new species as well as a new sub-species.

The teeth of these two kinds of bears showed a marked and uniform difference, proving conclusively that there is no interbreeding between the species.*

* I was told by Dr. Merriam that the idea which is so commonly believed, that different species of bears interbreed (like dogs) is entirely wrong.

Hunting the Big Game of Alaska
Part 3

HUNTING THE BIG GAME OF WESTERN ALASKA

III.—KILLING MY LARGE KADIAK BEAR

By JAMES H. KIDDER

PHOTOGRAPHS BY THE AUTHOR

AS I had been fortunate in shooting bears upon the island of Kadiak and the Alaska Peninsula, nothing remained but for me to obtain a specimen from one of the outlying islands of the Kadiak group, to render my trip in every way a success.

Therefore, I now determined to take my two natives and hunt from a bidarka the deep bays of the island of Afognak, while Blake, not yet having obtained a bear from Kadiak, went back to hunt there. He had been extremely good to his men, and in settling with them on his return from the Alaska Peninsula, had good naturedly paid the excessive demands they made. The result was that his kindness was mistaken for weakness, and just as he was about to leave his hunters struck for an increase of pay.

He sent them to the right-about, and fortunately succeeded in filling their places.

A sportsman going into a new country owes it to those who follow to resist firmly exorbitant demands, and at the same time to be firm and just in all his dealings.

In my former articles I have described bear hunting in the spring, when we stalked our game upon the snowy hillsides, and again on the Alaska Peninsula, where we hunted across the open on foot, and also in the bidarka. I will now attempt to describe still another form of hunting.

Toward the end of June the red salmon begin to run. These only go up the streams that have their sources in lakes. After the red salmon come the humpbacks, and after the humpbacks the dog salmon. Both of the latter kinds in great numbers force their way

A Cave in Which Our Natives Lived and in Which We Did Our Cooking.

85

Brown Bear (Alaska Peninsula).   Mature Female Grizzly (Wyoming).   Brown Bear (Alaska Peninsula).
Kadiak Bear (Shuyak Island).

A Group of Bear Heads in the Author's Collection.

up all the streams, and are the favorite food of the bears, which come down from the mountains in deep, well-defined trails to catch these fish in the shallow streams. When the salmon have begun to run, the only practical way of hunting these bears is by watching some likely spot on the bank of a stream.

Early in July Blake and I parted, intending to meet again two weeks later. My friend sailed off in a small schooner, while I left with my two Aleuts in the bidarka. In Fedor's place I had engaged a native by the name of Lofka. We three paddled with a will, as we were anxious to reach a deep bay on the north side of the island of Afognak as soon as possible.

This was all familiar country to me, for I had spent over a month in this region the year before, and, as we camped for the night after finally reaching our hunting grounds, I could hardly realize that twelve months had gone by since I left this beautiful spot. For the island of Afognak, with its giant cliffs and deep bays, is to my mind the most picturesque spot I have ever seen.

86

The next morning the wind was unfavorable, but in the afternoon it changed round and we were able to visit one of the salmon streams. The red salmon had come, but it would be another week or more before the humpbacks would begin their run. It was a bleak day, with the rain driving in our faces. We forced our way up the banks of a stream for some miles, following welf-defined bear trails through the tall grass. Some large tracks were seen, but we sighted no game. We returned to camp after ten o'clock that night, wet to the skin and chilled through.

was rather ticklish work, as the sea was rough. Early that afternoon we turned into the narrow straits which lie between the islands of Afognak and Shuyak. Shuyak is uninhabited, but some natives have hunting barabaras there. Formerly this island contained a great number of silver gray foxes. A few years ago some white trappers visited it and put out poison. The result was the extermination of all the foxes upon the island, for not only the foxes which ate the poison died, but the others which ate the poisoned carcasses. The hunters ob-

Our Three Largest Bear Skins.

The following day was a repetition of this, only under worse weather conditions, if that were possible.

I now decided to push on to a large bay on the northeast side of the island. This is locally known as Seal Bay, and is supposed to be without question the best hunting grounds on Afognak.

Unfortunately, a heavy wind detained us in Paramonoff Bay for some days. The morning after the storm broke we made a four-o'clock start. There was a strong favoring breeze, and we made a sail of one of the blankets. The bidarka fairly flew, but it

tained but one skin, as the foxes died in their holes or in the woods, and were not found until their pelts were spoiled. This is a fair example of the need for Alaskan game laws and their rigid enforcement.

At the present time Shuyak is rich in bear and in land otter, and I can imagine no better place for a national game preserve. It has lakes and salmon streams, and would be an ideal place to stock.

The straits between Shuyak and Afognak are extremely dangerous, for the great tides from Cook's Inlet draw through this narrow passage. My nerve was tested a bit as the bidarka swept by the shore, for had it once got well started we should have been drawn into the rapids, and then into a long line of angry breakers beyond. At one point it seemed as if we were heading right into these dangerous waters, and then abruptly turning at a sharp angle we glided around a point into a shallow bay. Circling this shore, we successfully passed around the line of breakers and soon met the long ground swell of the Pacific, while Seal Bay stretched for many miles inland on the other side.

As the wind was favorable we stopped only for a cup of tea and then pushed on to the very head of the bay. Here, at the mouth of a salmon stream, we came upon many fresh bear tracks, and we passed the night watching. As we had seen nothing by four o'clock in the morning we cautiously withdrew and, going some distance down the shore, camped in an old hunting barabara. It had been rather a long stretch, when one considers that we had breakfasted a little over twenty-four hours before and had paddled some thirty miles. It is poor sport this watching a salmon stream by night; but it is the only kind of hunting that one can do at this time of the year.

I slept until seven o'clock that evening, when the men called me; and after a cup of tea we started for the salmon stream, which we followed up beyond where we had watched the night previous. We were very careful to wade, so as not to give our scent to any bears which might approach the stream from below. There were many tracks and deep, well-used trails leading in all directions, while every few yards we came upon places where the tall grass was trampled down, showing where bears had been fishing. These bear trails are quite a feature of the Alaskan country, and some of them are two feet wide and over a foot deep, showing that they have been in constant use for many years.

That night we heard a bear pass within ten yards of us, but could not see it. We returned to camp next morning at five o'clock, and I wrote up my journal, for it is extremely confusing this night work, and one completely loses track of the days unless careful.

My men came to me after their mid-day sleep with very cheerful countenances, and assured me that there was no doubt but that I should surely soon meet with success, for the palm of Nikolai's hand had been itching and he had dreamed of blood and a big dog fighting, while Lofka's eyelid trembled. My hunters told me in all seriousness that these signs never failed.

Next day we made a start about ten o'clock, but after a couple of hours paddling, when we had met a fair tide to help us on, I lit my pipe and allowed my men to do all the work, while I lay back among my rugs half-dreaming in the charm of my surroundings. Myriads of gulls flew overhead uttering their shrill cries, while now and then the black oyster-catchers with their long red bills would circle swiftly around the bidarka, filling the air with their sharp whistles, and seemingly much annoyed at our intrusion. Many different kinds of ducks rose before us, and the ever-present eagles watched us from the lofty rocks.

Nikolai now pointed out one of his favorite hunting grounds for seals, and asked if he might not try for one, so we turned into a big bay, and he soon had the glasses in use. He at once sighted several lying on some rocks, and we had just started in their direction when Nikolai suddenly stopped paddling, again seized the glasses, and looked excitedly across the straits to the Shuyak shore. Following the direction of his gaze I saw upon the beach a black speck which my native at once pronounced to be a bear. He was nosing around among some seaweed and turning over the rocks in search of food. Each one of us now put all his strength into every stroke in order to reach the other side before the bear could wander off. We cautiously landed behind some big rocks, and quickly removing our boots my hunter and I were soon on shore and noiselessly peering through the brush to the place where we had last seen the bear; but he had disappeared.

The wind was favorable, and we knew that he had not been alarmed. It took us some time to hit off his trail, for he had wandered in all directions before leaving this place; but after it was once found his footprints in the thick moss made tracking easy, and we moved rapidly on. We had not expected a long stalk, and our feet were badly punished by the devil clubs, which were here most abundant. We could see by the tracks that the bear had not been alarmed, and knew that we should soon come up with him. After a mile or so the spoor led in the direction of a low marsh where the coast line makes a big bend inward; so apparently we had crossed a long point into a bay beyond.

I at once felt sure that the bear was near, having probably come to this beach to feed, and as Nikolai looked at me and smiled, I knew he too felt that we were on a warm trail.

We had just begun to descend toward the shore, when I thought I heard a slight noise ahead. Keeping my eyes fixed in that direction I whispered to Nikolai, who was standing a few feet in front of me, intently peering to the right. Suddenly I caught just a glimpse of a tawny brownish bit of color through the brush, a short distance ahead. Quickly raising my rifle, I had just a chance for a snap shot, and the next instant a large bear made a dash through some thick underbrush. It was but an indistinct glimpse which I had had, and before I could throw another cartridge into the barrel of my rifle, the bear was out of sight. Keeping my eyes moving at about the rate of speed I judged he was going, I fired again through the trees, and at once a deep and angry growl told me that my bullet had gone home.

Then we raced ahead, my hunter going to the left while I entered the thick brush into which the bear had disappeared. I had gone but a short distance when I heard Nikolai shoot three times in rapid succession, and as quickly as I could force my way I hurried in his direction. It seemed that as we separated, Nikolai had at once caught sight of the bear slowly making away. He immediately fired, but missed; at the report of his rifle the bear turned and came toward him, but was too badly wounded by my first two shots to be dangerous. At close range Nikolai fired two more shots, and it was at this moment that I joined him. The bear was down, but trying hard to get upon his feet and evidently in an angry mood, so I ran up close and gave him another shot, which again knocked him over.

Now for the first time I had a good view of the bear, which proved to be a large one. As my men declared that this was one of the biggest they ever had seen, I think we may safely place it as a fair example of the Kadiak species. Unfortunately I had no scales with me, and could not, therefore, take its weight; but the three of us were unable to budge either end from the ground, and after removing the pelt the carcass appeared to be as large as a fair-sized ox. We had much difficulty in skinning him, for he

fell on his face, and it took some half an hour even to turn him over; we were only able to do this by using his legs as levers. It required over two hours to remove the pelt. Then we had "chi" (tea), and shot the bear all over again many times.

It seemed that at the time when I had first caught sight of this bear, Nikolai had just located the one which we had originally seen and were following; and it was a great piece of luck my taking this snap shot, for the other bear was much smaller.

We took the skin and skull with us, while I made arrangements with my natives to return some months later and collect all the bones, for I at once decided to present the entire skeleton to the National Museum.

It was six o'clock when we again made a start. I had a deep sense of satisfaction as I lay lazily back in the bidarka, with the large skin at my feet, only occasionally taking the paddle; for it had been a hard trip, and I felt unlike exerting myself. We camped that night in a hunting barabara which belonged to Nikolai, and was most picturesquely situated on a small island.

My natives were extremely fond of bear meat, and they sat long into the night gorging themselves. Each one would dig into the kettle with his fork, and bringing out a big chunk would crowd as much as possible into his mouth, and holding it there with his teeth would cut off with his hunting knife a liberal portion, which he would swallow after a munch or two.

I had tried to eat Kadiak bear before, but it has rather a bitter taste, and this one was too tough to be appetizing. The meat of the bears which we had killed on the Alaska Peninsula was excellent, and without this strong gamey flavor.

The next morning we made an early start, for to save this large skin I had decided to push on with all haste to the little settlement of Afognak, where I had arranged to meet my friend some days later. It was a beautiful morning, and once more we had a favoring breeze.

Some forty miles across Shellicoff Straits was the Alaskan shore. The rugged, snow-clad mountains seemed to be softened when seen through the hazy blue atmosphere. One white-capped peak boldly pierced a line of clouds and stood forth against the pale blue of the sky beyond; while the great Douglas Glacier, ever-present, wound its way down—down to the very sea. It was all grandly beautiful, and seemed in keeping with the day.

We paddled steadily, stopping only once for tea, and at six o'clock that evening were back at the little fishing hamlet of Malina Place. Here I was asked to drink tea with a man who, my hunters told me, had killed many bears on these islands. I showed him the skull of my big one, which he declared was as large as he had ever seen; my natives told me that all the Aleuts, who on our arrival had crowded around the bidarka, said the same.

This man also told me that at times there were no bears on Shuyak, and that again they were there in great numbers, showing that they freely swim across the straits from Afognak, which are, at the narrowest point, some three miles wide.

While I was having tea in one of the barabaras I heard much shooting* outside, which announced the return of a sea-otter party that had been hunting for two months at Cape Douglas. It was a beautiful sight, this fleet of twenty-odd bidarkas, the paddles all rising and falling in perfect time and changing sides without a break. There is nothing more graceful than one of these canoes when handled by expert Aleuts. These natives had already come forty miles that day, and were now going to stop only long enough for tea, and then push on to the little settlement of Afognak Place, some twenty-five miles away, where most of them lived. In one of the canoes I saw a small chap of thirteen years. He was the chief's son, and already an expert in hunting and handling the bidarka. So is the Aleut hunter trained.

As it had been a warm day I feared that the large skin might spoil, therefore I concluded to continue to Afognak Place without camping for the night, and so we paddled on and on. As darkness came the mountains

*The natives welcome the return of the sea-otter hunters by a brisk discharge of all their guns.

seemed to rise grander and more majestic from the water on either side of us. At midnight we again stopped for tea, and while we sat by the fire the host of bidarkas of the sea-otter party silently glided by like shadows. We joined them, for my men had much to tell of their four months with the white hunter, and many questions were asked on both sides.

Some miles from Afognak the bidarkas drew up side by side in a long even line, our bidarka joining in. "Drasti" and "Chemi"* came to me from all sides, for I had from time to time met most of the native hunters of these islands, and they seemed to regard me as quite one of them.

When all the straggling bidarkas had caught up and taken their places in the line the chief gave the word "Kedar" (Come on), and we all paddled forward, and just as the sun was rising above the hills we reached our journey's end.

Two days later my friend joined me. He also had been successful and had killed a good-sized male bear in Little Uganuk Bay on Kadiak Island.

Our bear hunting was now over, and we had been fortunate in accomplishing the three most important objects of our trip.

MEASUREMENTS OF MALE BEAR.

Inches.

1. Place.—Shot on island of Shuyak (Kadiak Islands.)
2. Length in straight line from nose to end of vertebræ.................................... 96
3. Height in straight line at shoulders between stakes, and not including hair................ 51½
4. Girth of body just back of shoulders 61⅝
5. Height of body just back of shoulders from ground.................................... 28¾
6. Girth of neck just back of ears 38
7. Girth of head just front of ears................. 37¾
8. Length of head from end of nose to front base of ears..................................... 19¼
9. Length of front paw from back of sole to end of middle claw................................ 14⅛
10. Length of back paw from back of sole to end of middle claw 16
11. Width of front paw across sole of foot 8¼
12. Width of back paw across sole of foot........... 7⅝

In all measurements tape was stretched.

*Russian and Aleut for "How do you do?"

5
The Indian Hunter
of the
Far Northwest

OUTING

VOL. XXXIX   MARCH, 1902   NO. 6

THE INDIAN HUNTER OF THE FAR NORTHWEST

ON THE TRAIL TO THE KLONDIKE

By TAPPAN ADNEY

IT is only one of nearly all impressions of the Yukon country (which includes Klondike) received from the meagre reports of the first miners who gazed from the summit of Chilkoot Pass upon the sources of that river upwards of twenty years ago, that the land is forbidding in every particular, and nearly or quite destitute of game. Had we, who joined the great stampede thither in '97, stopped to consider that the fur-trader had been established on that river for upwards of fifty years, we should have known that the fur-bearing animals, the beaver, otter, sable, mink, fox, and ermine were the basis of a profitable trade, and we might not have conceived a country barren of the larger game. I myself had been further unprepared by hearing a lecture delivered before no less a body than the American Geographical Society, in which the lecturer, basing his opinion no doubt on the reports of those who had merely drifted down the river in summer, gravely stated that the mosquitoes were so numerous and venemous there that the larger animals, such as the reindeer and I believe moose, could not exist. On my may in, that eventful autumn, by way of the head of the Yukon River, I encountered thousands of ducks on the lakes; while bands of wretched and wild-looking Indians at occasional intervals offered for trade skins of moose, mountain-goat, mountain-sheep, and black and grizzly bears. At Pelly River, I saw in a trading post a bunch of thirteen silver-gray and black fox skins, and learned that the proportion of blacks to "reds" was greater than in any known place. Farther on, I took a shot, from my boat, at a distant gray wolf; and while drifting in the ice which bore my little craft helplessly along, just above Klondike, I had the exceeding satisfaction of watching my first and only live wolverine, loping along the bank with arched back and drooping tail—characteristic carriage of the weasel family, of which it is the largest representative. And how my imagination carried me back to the tales of the fur countries; lines of broken sable traps, and exasperated trappers!

I heard white men, returned from the upper Klondike, tell of beaver; of bear "signs," plentiful beyond all past experience; and of moose and caribou, in numbers of which they never before had dreamed; and I knew that the real truth, as of game as of mining, was yet to be told. That winter I accompanied a band of about sixty Indians, comprising an entire village, who were established at their ancient home at the mouth of the Klondike River, to the upper waters of that stream; following with dogs, toboggans and "skin-houses" the trail of moose and "deer," as they had been accustomed to hunt for ages. I was the only white man with them, and the only one excepting a missionary, long ago, who ever thus lived with them, and I acquired a knowledge of the game of the country possible to acquire in no other way; of modern and ancient ways of hunting; and of trapping. In all we killed some eighty moose, and sixty-five caribou or reindeer, the main part of which was hauled by dogs to the starving miners at Dawson. Much game was killed by white hunters; but on the whole the best of them lacked the consummate skill of the Indian, brought up as he is to perfect knowledge of the country and of the habits of the game.

The Klondike River, a swift shallow stream a hundred and fifty miles or more in length, rises in a number of branches at the base of lofty, rugged peaks comprising the northern continuation of the Rocky Mountains. Its valley is generally broad and flat, covered with dense growth of spruce, interspersed with birches, poplars and low willows. On either side there rise rounded hills, frequently thousands of feet in height, bare upon their tops, their sides covered with trees the same as of the valleys, but sparse and stunted—so much so that a spruce of the size of one's arm might be hundreds of years old, with rings of growth as close as the leaves of a book. The climate is dry, but little rain falling in summer, and in winter the sky is as " clear as a bell "; what snow there is seems to come more from the rising mists of the river, which is never frozen over entirely (though the ice goes out in cakes ten feet thick!), and this falls gently from day to day and the air is so still that the snow clings to the limbs where it falls, until they reach the size of barrels, and often on the higher hills so envelopes the vegetation that the landscape appears like some gallery of tall, weird forms chiseled from purest marble. The intense cold (reaching seventy below zero, and more) and the absence of wind in early winter prevent the snow from packing and crusting until the returning spring sun warms the earth back to life. Two or three feet of snow is the utmost, and being light as down makes snow-shoeing exceedingly laborious, while offering no obstacle to the movements of the moose, which never is obliged to " yard " as in more southern latitudes, but wanders at will from valley to mountain top, browsing upon the fragrant buds of the white birch and young shoots of the willow. The native inhabitants of the valley of the Yukon, as far as tidewater (where the Eskimo begin), are pure Indian, belonging to the Athabaska group of the Tinneh and the most northerly of Indian tribes; those upon the middle Yukon being known to the old Hudson's Bay people as Kutchins. There are many villages of them along the streams, but they are not numerous and are becoming yearly less so. Until the advent of the white man, who now supplies them in small quantities with tea, sugar, flour and pork, they subsisted entirely, with the exception of a few roots and berries, upon the abundant salmon of the rivers, and on the flesh of reindeer and moose, which also supply their clothing, and the coverings for their winter camps. In summer they live by the side of the rivers, and in winter move inland, hunting, following the wooded valleys of the water-courses. All who are able to move accompany the hunt, and with household goods loaded upon the light birch-wood toboggans, drawn by dogs (the pups and babies riding on top), they

The Women Take Home the Fresh Meat the Hunters Have Killed.

move by short easy stages, seldom more than six or seven miles at a time.

The men are variously dressed. The older men wear shirts of caribou skin (tanned and made up with hair inside), which reach to the middle, with a curious rounded point at front and back extending lower; or a shirt of rabbit skins, split, plaited and sewn together, making at once the lightest and warmest garment known, which they wear next the skin in the coldest weather, with nothing else! Heavy "duffel" blankets, of the most brilliant colorings, are also made into short, full skirts. A piece of

Visiting the Wolverine Trap.

After the Killing Comes the Feasting.

the same makes a pair of pants, while the remainder of a fourteen-pound "four-point" blanket serves as a covering by night. The better nether garment is made of caribou skin with pants and moccasins in one, gathered around the waist by a draw-string. Mittens made full large are of moose hide lined with blanket or lynx-fur, suspended from the neck by a large cord of variegated yarn. The head covering is a flat cap of sable with ear-flaps. The hair generally falls to the shoulders, and with their prominent cheek bones, capacious mouth, and strong eyebrows (often squinting downward toward the nose), they have been characterized as "extremely ugly"—rather, I should say, fierce-looking. The men wear thin, coarse mustaches, and some of them shave this below the nose, with a curious effect. The "A-C" company supplies them with the best of forty-five-seventy repeating rifles, which they carry in brightly ornamented cases of caribou skin open at one end so as to be instantly drawn off in the presence of game. The older men cling to the long, single barrel trade smooth-bore, and bullets and caps are carried in an ornamented bag suspended in front by a strap around the neck, powder being carried in a horn at the side. A plaited moosehide cord fifteen feet long, slung at the side, for packing in the first meat of the freshly killed animal, a pair of snow-shoes five feet long and a foot wide, made and laced of white birch with fine caribou webbing, except under foot, where an open, old-fashioned bed-cord arrangement of thick rawhide is stretched, and a sheath knife and cartridge belt, complete the equipment of the hunter. The women's principal garment is a voluminous over shirt reaching below the knees, with a large hood, which chiefly serves as a carrying place for the baby; her own head being covered by a silk kerchief. If the village has plenty of dogs the women do all the work of making and breaking camp, and cutting wood; the manner of hunting being this: the hunters start ahead before daybreak, usually in a body, with snow-shoes and rifles; where they wish the next camp to be they turn off toward the hills. The women follow with the camp, and when the hunters return it is all ready for a stop of a day or a week, as circumstances shall determine. If dogs are scarce (we had only

fifty, numbers having been sold to the miners at prices too tempting to resist) the hunters turn in like good fellows and help the women. How easy to say of these people (or Indians in general) "the men are lazy, the women do all the work!" Having done my share with them; having accompanied the hunters fifteen to twenty miles a day up and down the steep mountains, in snow so light that a heavy man goes through at every step, I assert, unhesitatingly, that of camp work and hunting, the hunting is the harder. Indeed, all strive to the limit of endurance, with an energy such as is only begotten of sharp, keen air, and imminence of starvation. It is the dogs that really suffer. Starved, lean, ill kept, snarling, cringing, wolfish brutes, howling from the instant toboggans rattle down from the caches, until unharnessed at night. One would scarcely suppose that a moose would remain in the whole country.

The hunters having marked the new camp site, swing toward the hills, in single file, ten to fifteen in number. Usually within one to three miles a fresh moose track is found, and with unerring skill (remarkable because of the lightness of the snow, which at once obliterates the footprint) they turn in the direction which the animal is taking, and when they are assured by the "sign" of the nearness to the game, they quickly spread out, and, rushing forward with swift strides and surprising the moose at close quarters, one of the band is able to drop him by one or more well directed shots. There is some luck about this, for I knew an Indian to fire eighteen shots without touching the moose, and going back next day over the same ground with ten others, himself get two, the only moose killed. It is a common thing for one hunter to get two while the rest get none. Hence the obvious necessity for the law respecting the division of the meat, which is as follows: the hind-quarters are absolutely the property of the man who shoots the animal, the rest belongs to the community; but he may designate to which persons the fore-shoulders shall go. The recipient of a fore-shoulder, in turn, reciprocates. Thus as long as there is game, each gets his share, while there is also incentive for the skilful hunter to increase his personal wealth to some extent. The surplus meat may be traded for guns and blankets, and

Surprising the Moose at Close Quarters.

these in turn are traded with other Indians. The successful hunter and the shrewd trader becomes the man of wealth, and is chosen chief, and his position is that of patriarch who counsels his people, yet without compulsory authority.

The instant the moose has fallen; the work is finished with sheath knives. The carcass is skinned, quartered, and the head removed, with nothing but the knife. While some are doing this, others are breaking small dead trees with their hands

TAPPAN ADNEY.

Klondike Indian Village—Arrival of a Load of Moose Meat.

and building a large fire on top the snow, on each side of which spruce boughs are laid to kneel upon. Strings of fat and shreds of flesh from inside the carcass are toasted in the flames on the ends of sticks, and greedily swallowed. The brilliant colors in the costumes of the hunters as they crowd around the fire add to the general goriness of snow and hands, and the ferocious vigor with which the half-raw flesh is gorged presents a picture that is seldom witnessed of savage revelry and of manners scarcely better than wolves. In the space of an hour from the first shot a lunch will have been partaken, a piece of the moose slung over the back of every one, and all have started back in single file. On the first day we walked eighteen miles, got two moose, and when we reached camp at dark, two others, old men, hunting alone, each brought in one moose. The best hunters prefer to hunt alone, but it requires much skill. No chances are taken rushing the game blindly. As the trail grows "warm" the hunter moves with great circumspection, peering through the trees and bushes on each side, hoping to find the game lying down resting or asleep. As the trail becomes "hot," snow-shoes are laid off, and the hunter creeps slowly ahead until he sees the head and long ears of the moose as it lies in its bed; with a well-directed shot through the head he secures it. Thus one Indian killed three moose. This man had killed moose in quite recent years with a bow and arrow!

Following the killing the men and women next day take dogs and fetch in the meat. The hide is at once prepared for subsequent tanning. It is laid across a slanting pole inside the skin-house and a squaw scrapes off the hair, and then with a sharpened shin-bone "fleshes" the other side. The edges are slit (for lacing into a frame) and the skin is placed in a pan of hot water with which rotten wood has been boiled; the surplus moisture is then wrung out and the skin hung over an elevated pole outdoors. When the camp moves on, the pelt is hoisted into a tree out of reach of wolverines, to be picked up on the return, and tanned in the summer with a "soup" of liver, worked until soft, then smoked, and made into articles of use.

The head and leg bones are roasted before the camp fire, cracked and eaten, and not even the gristle or the cartilage of the ears is wasted. Whatever an Indian cannot eat, he gives his dogs.

By midwinter the antlers have fallen, and there is no readily distinguishing bulls from cows. A cow, indeed, is much preferred to tough bull—for, as Isaac the chief expressed it in his much broken English, "Mull moose, too much tupp; cow moose, plenty fat stop, he-all-right." So we ate the cows; and the tough meat went to the miners! The capture of a fat moose is celebrated by a grand feast. All the hunters assemble in one house, the host (usually the chief first) levies upon all the tin kettles and pans in camp and a great quantity of meat is boiled, each man receiving a share proportionate to the size of his family. At a signal all sit up, and each eats as much as he can; the rest is handed out to the women and children. No salt is used. The hot fat which rises to the top is skimmed off in an immense wooden spoon and passed around the circle, each taking a sip. Tea with sugar is served, and the pans are filled twice; thus the whole day (the only day of rest known to a hunting people, although missionaries have taught them to keep one day in seven as one on which they shall not hunt, but employ for every other household purpose) is spent in talking, smoking, and general enjoyment.

When the country for a radius of six to ten miles has been scoured, the village moves on another stage; then the same hunting and feasting take place. We took five weeks to travel forty-five miles from Dawson, and in that time we got forty-eight moose. No tracks of caribou were seen. The village continued on thirty miles farther toward the foothills of the Rockies, and there found the caribou and killed sixty-five, the meat of which was dried and, with the skins of the moose and deer, packed to Dawson.

The so-called caribou seems to be the Barren Ground species, which is none other than the native "reindeer" of Alaska. The woodland caribou is found in the mountains to the south of Klondike, but I am informed that it does not occur south of Big Salmon River, where the Indians know it by name and distinguish it from the Barren Ground caribou of the North. The caribou of the Klondike region occurs in small bands over the country on the higher hill tops where it feeds

TAPPAN ADNEY

on the gray moss; but it is generally local in its range, migrating at times in bands so vast as to stagger belief. One such range is on the head of Forty Mile River, and from there they migrate, it is said, across the Yukon in winter to the eastern or Klondike side, and are found on the bald foot-hills of the Rocky range. Once in their migration they passed by the mouth of Forty Mile and 400 were shot by the miners. In the fall of 1897, two or three small parties of white men ascended the Klondike to a point above where the Indians went. They reported the "deer," as the caribou is called, exhausted their ammunition in killing forty-seven, and brought back the almost incredible story that the deer were there in numbers that would easily reach ten or twenty thousand. Another party, a member of which I came to know intimately, and to know him as a perfectly reliable man, said that he, too, found the deer, which seemed to be moving in bands of twenty to thirty in a general direction, and that some of the main roads which they traveled were beaten by their hoofs "as smooth as the trail on Bonanza Creek." Thus they occur on Porcupine River and Birch Creek; yet so variable and uncertain are these eccentric animals that the Indians sometimes altogether fail to strike them, and in two cases while I was in the Yukon, a village, one at Porcupine and one at Tanana, was obliged to flee for very life. In the first instance, the Alaska Commercial Company's agent at Fort Yukon, being advised by courier, met the starving village of fifty souls, who in the previous three days had had to eat but a single weasel; while the miners at Circle City similarly sent relief to the others. Hunters told me that above where we hunted the moose were much more abundant. Passing over, the following summer, some of the ground where we had hunted, I found in a walk of six miles and return the fallen antlers in fair preservation of no less than four moose. The gray or timber wolf is found in occasional bands, following the moose and deer, and on the clear surface of the Klondike I saw the

marks of a tragedy only a few days old, where half a dozen wolves had surrounded a moose, which ran only two hundred yards among the bushes before he was downed. The tracks in the snow plainly told the story, and when I came up the ravens were completing the work of the wolves. A hunter who poisoned one of this band told me that from the carcass he obtained a quart of oil, and that in all his considerable experience it was the first wolf which had any fat at all.

In the days of bows and arrows, when Indians were also more numerous, sometimes as many as one hundred hunters would surround a band of caribou. Leaving the village in the valley, the Indians would mount the hills, and, as they neared the band, one went cautiously ahead until he located the herd slowly feeding, perhaps brought down one, then stole back unobserved, and then the hunters spread out each side, keeping an equal space between them until the unsuspecting herd was entirely surrounded. Then they closed in, and, as they came near, the startled deer would rush off only to meet men. The hunters rushed in with shouts, and the poor creatures, knowing not which way to go, fell easy victims to the arrows. In this way (the old men say), as many as four or five hundred deer have been killed at a single time. The Indians usually do not hunt in summer, but during the summer of 1898 the demand for fresh meat continued so great at Dawson that numbers of white men proceeded to the upper Klondike in canoes and hunted moose with considerable success. They lay in wait at roads leading to ponds or salt-licks where the moose came down to drink. There were not lacking men even here, who forfeited every right to carry a gun by shooting down in pure wantonness numbers of moose which they made no attempt to save. I was never able to learn that "calling" is ever employed in Alaska by Indian or white man to bring moose, by imitating the call of the cow, within reach of the hunter. The favorite method of the Indian is to lie in wait by a trail leading to water.

6
Alaskan Notes
of a
Fly Fisherman

ALASKAN NOTES OF A FLY FISHERMAN.

BY W. T. EMMET.

WHILE Great Britain and the United States were at odds half a century ago about the dividing line of their Western territories, tradition has it that one of England's commissioners, a gentleman of the first rank, patriotic and jealous of his country's rights, and withal a keen sportsman, disposed of the Columbia River by saying :

"Dash the stream ! The Yankees can keep it and welcome. England covets no river where salmon will not rise to the fly."

Did you ever notice how difficult it is to convince yourself of the uselessness of attempting some impossibility which you have set your heart on performing? Over and over again you have been told that such and such a thing cannot be done ; you have read it in a score of works whose veracity on other questions you would not think of impugning, yet you must try it yourself, and, if you fail, try it again until at last the sad truth is forced upon you that your cherished wish cannot be realized. It was so with me last summer. I suppose twenty people who ought to have known, and who did know, in fact, tried to persuade me that the salmon of the Pacific Coast were, as the Englishman had said, of such a low-down vulgar disposition, so uneducated and coarse, as to laugh with derision (figuratively speaking) at a split bamboo and turn up their noses at the daintiest fly that ever issued from the hands of a maker.

Yet, despite their words of warning, I might have been seen one fine summer's afternoon disembarking at Victoria, B. C., with a fixed determination—a determination which was fast developing into being my one aim in life—to fight and conquer in a sportsmanlike way a Western salmon.

If failure met me here, as it did and as it had a few days before on the lower Columbia, I was determined to engage passage on the first vessel bound north and try my luck among the far-famed fiords of the Alaskan coast.

One night I stepped up to the desk of the Diard House and remarked :

"Mr. H., do you know when the next Alaskan steamer starts ? "

"Yes ; the *Elder* is due here to-morrow, on her way up, and will probably not stay in port more than an hour or so. You are not going, though, are you? What's the matter? Don't you like the place ? "

"Oh, to be sure, yes—er—delightful, you know. Do you suppose I could get a berth on that boat ? "

"Why, you're just in time ; I've got the very thing you want. Fellow came in to-day and asked me to sell his for him. Want it ? "

"Hand her over." Which being said, I paid my money and in two days found myself steaming to the northward, bitter in spirit at former failures, yet hopeful for better luck to come, and full of the pleasantest anticipation of grand scenery, interesting features of aboriginal life and the quiet, passive enjoyment which invariably attended a voyage such as the one to Alaska has the reputation of being, and as I found it. I soon discovered that I was by no means the only disciple of St. Isaac on board that ship. There was—whom shall I name first? Why, the Parson, of course, keen hunter after game, both small and great, a lover of the beauties of nature and an enthusiastic disciple of the gentle art. Then there was Mac, more rifleman than fly caster ; "Harvard and Yale" fellow travelers in search of sport, and several others more or less fond of rod and gun—a pleasant little coterie, five of whom have since passed together through experiences which they will never forget, and which have welded the acquaintance formed on the way toward the land of the midnight sun into an undying fellowship.

Oh, what a trip that was ! Day after day, night after night, ever onward and upward the serpentine reaches where at times the great pines on either side leant out and interlaced above our heads ; into little known, unsurveyed passageways, passing now and then some solitary red-skin in his dugout, en route for the trading posts of Victoria. Through scenes like these we steamed, halted often and at all sorts of places, for, be it remembered, there was nothing formal about that voyage, and we, the passengers, did about as we pleased as regards stopping. To me there is something indescribably delicious about this sort of journeying, this leaving behind of civilization with its railroads and telegraph wires — this invasion of the wilderness. In that north land Nature is still supreme, and her rule is pleasant. The limitless expanse of forest is as yet unwounded by the white man's axe ; the mountains have yet to feel the tread of his iron heel ; the birds can twitter without fear and sing their matins and evensong undisturbed ; the beasts of the forests know not as yet dread for mankind. A kindly queen is this Dame Nature. May her dynasty yet stand many years before the inevitable overthrow comes !

Often at night as our good ship sped on past unnamed islands and headlands, beauties of which, far from being hidden in darkness, were enhanced by marvelous combinations of twilight, moonlight and aurora, we saw the camp fires of a wandering band of red men. These aborigines are all fisher folk, and therefore, to a certain extent, brothers of ours, even though our ideas of good fishing do differ slightly. Their villages are all placed near the junction of a mountain stream with the salt water, and many times anchor was dropped off one of these "ranches," while such of the passengers as cared to go were pulled ashore in the ship's boat, or in consideration of "two bits" paddled in one of the Indian dugouts, which as soon as we stopped gathered about the ship like flies about a sugar bowl.

One day, I think it was the fifth from Victoria, our little fishing fraternity was seated together in solemn conclave, plotting to stop the vessel by fair means or foul, in order to whip some one of the enticing streams we had of late been passing so often, when " Tennessee," one of our prominent members, exclaimed :

"Ah there, boys ! here's what we're looking for. That must be the Tongass Narrows, and we're stopping. All hands

get out your tackle, quick !" which we did, for sure enough the ship slowed up, the anchor was run out and the boats were lowered. The first that put off toward the straggling collection of shanties that peeped timidly from the interminable forest, as if ashamed of their boldness in doing so, bore a small but select company of anglers bent on wetting their lines, if nothing more, in the waters of an Alaskan stream.

"Well," says the Parson a few minutes later, " I think this rock will suit me ; " I'll try it here at any rate," and he suits his action to the word, unlimbers and makes his first cast without results. We meanwhile move ahead, until, one by one, all have stationed themselves ; then the sport commences.

While completing the inevitable preparations for fly casting, I had opportunity to scan my surroundings more carefully. Mon Dieu ! what a lovely picture did that little Alaskan burn present as it rushed merrily onward to mingle its waters with the salt sea. A noisy, disorderly current it was, with never a sign of still water until within a few yards of its mouth ; an energetic and war-loving current, judging from the manner in which it fought and buffeted the rocks, and yet a current that, with all its noise and romping, loved solitude, else why did the pines hug it so closely that they all but shut out from it the light of day ?

I looked into the quiet pool below me, pondering a little on the contrast it presented to the roaring and rustling stream above, and the glance told me I would not fish here in vain. Three or four royal trout were fanning themselves lazily in the cool water, and as I eyed them eagerly while fastening on a couple of brown hackles I saw that they changed their position not at all, but kept up continuously that tail movement, as is the trout's wont the world over.

Swish ! Surely that cast ought to rouse one of them ; gently, now coax it along the surface slowly. No use ; try it again. Swish !

Sancho Panza ! I've got you, you beauty ! A pretty strike you made to be sure, but I was ready, thank goodness. steady now ; all right, reel in.

So I fished on that July morning in the cool solitude of the northern forest. Did ever the gentle sport seem so delightful ? Not that I claim for myself or the party any heavy creels ; weight was not what we were after, but a few hours' pleasant fishing. Nor did we take any inordinately large fish ; we saw some regular mammoths, but, for I know not what reason, they refused to be beguiled into sampling the edible qualities of our " coachman," " brown hackles " and " silver doctors."

After landing seven I left my companions violently threshing the stream, shouldered my Winchester, which I had brought ashore with me, and started up the mountain side, following as well as possible the course of the torrent. Attrition with the water had worn the boulders as smooth as billiard balls, and many were the tumbles I took while jumping from rock to rock. Finally I paused and looked about me. I have journeyed in many distant and little visited places, and being endowed with some sense of the beautiful have a habit of noticing beautiful things wherever I may be ; but as I stood there that afternoon balancing myself on a huge boulder, with a rifle butt as my alpenstock, I thought I had never seen so entrancing a picture as that surrounding me. The mountain side up which I had been toiling had suddenly transformed itself into a precipice at least fifty feet in height, over which the burn came tumbling with much noise and spray. At the foot of the cataract was a circular basin of limpid, still water, after which, rushing all about my friendly rock, were the rapids hurrying down to their ocean bourne. And such a forest ! I looked and wondered, and said to myself, " Can this be the Alaska of which I have read so much, the half-mythical home of ice and Esquimo, the land of dreary wastes, and grizzly terrors of the Arctic ? " Here was a forest tropical in its luxuriance ; so thick as to resist all attempts to enter it save by the stream bed ; an undergrowth of every conceivable description, creeper, weed and grass, all matted and jumbled together in an inextricable maze. Above my head the pine boughs were mingled, and the place was very dank and dark. The stillness of the spot came upon me and I looked around in a half-startled way, expecting to see some nymph or river goddess disporting among the rock and mosses, but there was only a little Indian girl tiptoeing her way through the stream carrying a basket of berries.

On rejoining my companions I found them unjointing their rods and starting for where our boat lay. They had all been successful, and we pulled back to the ship with a kindly feeling toward the trout stream of Tongass Narrows.

In this place I saw incredible numbers of salmon. A little bay or cove into which our stream emptied was literally alive with the fish ; they were so plenty there that I am sure a spear thrown haphazard among them would have transfixed one almost every time, and of course we tried them again with rod and reel. And here let me say a last word concerning this excellent fish and my total failure in taking it. At every point our vessel stopped we found them in countless thousands.

I am bound to confess that I did not see any living proof of some stories I had heard—that they frequently impeded navigation, for instance—but in Pyramid Harbor I made a little trip in a tug belonging to the trading post at that point, during which I saw the Chilcat Indian haul in untold numbers with nets. At James' Bay, an indentation on the coast of Baranoff Island, near Sitka, I amused myself while out after bears by popping at the salmon with my rifle (I won't say how many I hit) as they leaped out of the water eight or ten at a time. I cast for them early and late, and can affirm with a clear conscience that no opportunity to hook one was left unused, yet, after all my endeavors, I was forced to return East without having accomplished what I wanted particularly to do—the killing of a salmon with rod and reel and fly in a fair, sportsmanlike manner.

Now what is the reason of this contempt for the cunning handiwork of our Eastern tackle makers ? Ah, there you have me. I have heard several explanations, each one as likely (or unlikely) as the rest, and must leave the solution of the mystery to my readers.

The *G. W. Elder*—may her shadows never grow less !—reached Sitka, the capital of our Arctic province, six days after our trout fishing at Tongass Narrows. A pretty little Russian-American town it is, and, with its population of not more than three hundred whites, contains as many objects of interest to the tourist and general observer as any place of its size in the world. There were a few on board, however, who took less note of the Greek church, etc., than of what one of the marine officers stationed there told them, namely, that Indian River, a stream of some parts, emptying into the bay a mile south of the town, was swarming with trout, both great and small, and only waiting for just such a party as ours to allow themselves to be caught.

Sitka is one of the quaintest little places I have ever seen; it has but one drawback, a superabundance of rain. Were it not for this—and the patriotic citizens of Alaska aver that they never think of it, and do not mind it in the least—I should be tempted to locate there to-morrow. And why not? It is a fact, though on first thought it seems rather strange and contrary to the long-accepted idea of Alaska, that the thermometer rarely, if ever, registers below zero; the winters bring but little snow, the summers are cool and pleasant (except for the above-mentioned objection); the situation is perfect, mountains to the north and east cut off high winds, and an almost surrounded harbor, dotted with innumerable islets, shuts out the ocean swell. Are not these advantages, and weighty ones, too? Yet they are not all. Deer swarm within the very confines of the place; they may be found everywhere. Bear, so the inhabitants told me, roam about like hogs on the berry-laden slope of Vostovia, just back of the town, and—anglers take notice!—the prettiest little trout brook this side of the happy hunting grounds meanders among the Baranoff mountains and finds an entrance into Sitka Harbor, scarce a mile from the old Russian castle.

The Sitkans have built a very good walking road to and along the bank of the Indian River. I say walking road advisedly, for up there they have not progressed as far as wagons, horses or mules. A noble forest clothes the island, containing, by all odds, the finest trees we saw in Alaska. It was through this, on angling bent, that we strolled soon after the ship touched the dock. Overhead the sky was clear and blue, with never a cloud in sight; everything was at its best. A perfect day, truly, for solitary communion with nature and for that gentlest of arts—angling.

I soon separated from my companions, and taking the right bank, with rod ready for action, meandered slowly in the course of the current, resting now and again by the side of likely-looking pools and rifts into which the river was divided. Were I versed in botanical lore, many would be the flowers, plants and shrubs

for me to name and describe. The vegetation was most luxuriant, and its beauty was not wasted on me, though I was ignorant of its scientific character.

Nature's vocalists, the birds, thronged the overhanging limbs that day and sang in the ears of the solitary fisherman many pleasing ditties. The birds are all old friends of mine: in many and diverse sections of the country I have studied them, noting down their goings and comings, and prying into their household affairs. Meeting my old acquaintances here in the far north, they all appeared doubly dear, unless it might be a couple of ravens who shrieked at me from the top of a blasted pine. But the chickadees, the robins and certain brightly-colored little warblers whose names I could not determine—these I watched during the intervals of my fishing with unfeigned pleasure.

Our doings that day with the trout were very similar to those experienced at every place we had wet our lines during the trip. There was, I am sorry to say, a paucity of very large fish; those we caught averaged about eight inches. "Tennessee" landed the biggest, a glistening old boy of nearly two pounds. I arrived on the scene just in time to witness the capture. There stood "Tennessee," perfectly calm and unruffled, on the bank of the beautiful stream, his rod bent tip to butt, his line making wild gyrations through the water. Once the fish jumped and in the second he was above surface I saw a foeman worthy of anyone's bamboo.

A couple of Indian boys who were landing fish after fish nearby, using fresh salmon roe as a bait, stopped for a moment their sport to watch the struggle, and a pretty sight it was, for on both ends of that little rod were masters in their different ways—"Tennessee" as a fisherman and the trout as a fighter. As the former saw me gazing entranced at the exhibition of skill, he remarked in a nonchalant tone, "That fellow down there seems somewhat annoyed, doesn't he?" From his movements, I thought "that fellow" did. A cool chap was "Tennessee," and one of the best fly fishermen I have seen for many a day. He, like all of us, fell completely in love with the beautiful scenes we visited, and his last word on parting was to inform me that if I happened to stray up there again within ten years I would find him on some of the fiords or streams, pursuing his favorite pastime.

It seems a pity that such delightful experiences as that Alaskan voyage, with its freedom from care and worry, cannot last for ever; but one fine morning the boat, which we had almost come to look upon as home, steamed into the harbor of Victoria. And here, brother angler, before saying farewell, let me add a few words to what I have already written, a few condensed sentences on fish in the far Northwest.

In the first place, do not go there expecting to do any salmon fishing. I hope I have made clear enough in the preceding pages the futility of this, and that additional warning is unnecessary. You will see extraordinary sights, in which vast numbers of salmon figure prominently, but to you, as a fly fisherman, they will be worse than useless. Nor would I advise you to make the long, albeit pleasant, journey to that Ultima Thule if fishing of any sort is your sole object. That you will find excellent ground for your favorite sport there is no doubt, but the average trout stream there is no better than, if as good as, many nearer home. The sketches I have given of my own and friends' fishing are but examples of what you will find at every stopping place in the trout streams at Metlakahtla Kasaan, Fort Wrangle, Loring, Pyramid Harbor, Chilcat, Killisnoo, Juneau, in fact anywhere you care to land.

"Nothing so very wonderful; no overflowing creels and all that," do I hear you say? All right, my friend, and all very true. We had no fishing that could be called remarkable, and in truth we were not so greatly disappointed.

But if your object in journeying is that of an "all-round" sportsman and lover of nature, who is rather looking for a fair amount of good fishing, with lots of fine scenery, fine air and healthy, out-of-door life, you will find these requisites one and all along the Alaskan coast; and if constituted like others of the genus homo cannot return from that grand region—whose wonders of ice and snow and glaciers, mountains and a thousand and one other features I have not touched upon at all—without a large stock of bodily benefits and pleasant reminiscences.

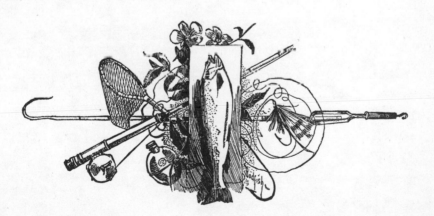

7
Among the Thlinkits
in Alaska

The Century Magazine.

Vol. XXIV.　　　　　　　JULY, 1882.　　　　　　　No. 3.

AMONG THE TLILINKITS IN ALASKA.

We set forth in April, 1877, from Portland, Oregon, in the steamer *California*, and steamed northward till we entered the Straits of Fuca. Our purpose was to climb Mount St. Elias, the highest peak in the world above the snow-line, to explore the Mount St. Elias alps, and to acquire information about the unknown districts lying nearest the coast, with a view to future explorations. For less is known to-day of Central Alaska than of Central Africa. From Cape Flattery to Fort Wrangell—nearly a thousand miles—the passage is entirely inland, excepting short runs across the Gulf of Georgia and Queen Charlotte's Sound. The shores are forest-covered mountains, between which the steamer passed as between the lofty banks of a river. One of these channels, Grenville Strait, is forty-five miles long, perfectly straight, and, in some places, only four hundred yards wide. Cliffs and snow-capped mountains wall it in. Avalanches have mowed bare swaths through the fir-trees from the summits to the water's edge, and the mountain lakes, lying a thousand or fifteen hundred feet above the spectator, pour their waters in foaming cataracts into the sea. Twelve hundred miles from the Columbia River bar we touched at Fort Wrangell, a filthy little town at the mouth of the Stickeen, where the miners from the gold-diggings up the Stickeen River spend the winter in squalor and drunkenness. A native village lies, between high tide and the forest, to the east of the town, along a sweep of the rocky beach. Behind the huts may be seen the graves of some Shamáns, or "medicine-men." Their functions, however, are more spiritual than medicinal, for these savages attribute death and disease to the workings of evil spirits. It is the part of the Shamán to exorcise the evil spirits or to call up the good. His remedies are almost exclusively incantations and frenzied pantomime, accompanied with the wild hubbub of his rattles and drum. The Shamáns alone have tombs. All the other dead are burned on funeral pyres. At Wrangell we first saw the tall ancestral columns, which are carved from the trunks of huge trees, and sometimes are eighty and one hundred feet high. Their colossal symbolic carvings represent the totemic genealogy of the cabin-dweller before whose door they stand. They serve the double purpose of frightening away evil spirits and satisfying family pride. A few sick or bankrupt miners were hanging about the American town. One ragamuffin, almost picturesque in tatters and dirt, was seated on the shoe-box steps of the " Miners' Palace Home and Restrent," playing an asthmatic accordion to an audience of half naked Indians, wearing yellow headkerchiefs and cotton drawers.

After a few hours' stay at Wrangell, we sailed for Sitka by the outside passage around Cape Ommaney and Baranoff Island, as the inside passage is much longer.

As we entered the harbor of Sitka from the sea the general appearance of the place was tropical.* The snowy cone of Edgecumbe first appeared, then the sharp peak of Vostovia— a triangular patch of white against the sky. Everywhere below the snow-line the mountains were green with luxuriant growth. The harbor was protected against the sea by a curved line of reefs, on which grew firs and pines and cedars, with bare trunks and tufts of branches, making them look not unlike palms. The warm, moist atmosphere curtained all the middle distance with a film of

---

* Observations at Sitka during fourteen years give as mean summer temperature, 54.2 Fahr. Mean winter temperature, 31.9 ; average temperature, 42.80.

blue, and, in the foreground, a fleet of very graceful canoes, filled with naked or half-naked Indians, completed the illusion. A line of surf seemed to bar every approach to the town, but suddenly a narrow channel opened. The ship swung sharply to the right and glided into a long, narrow harbor. The Indian village is built upon the beach, and at evening it was covered by the shadow of the adjoining forest. The green spire on the belfry of the Greek church reached up above everything except the former Russian governor's " castle," a huge log structure perched upon a pinnacle of rock near the sea. The church on the lower ground was surrounded by the rambling, dilapidated houses and hovels of the Russian inhabitants, who then numbered about four hundred, their neighbors being two hundred mixed whites and about twelve hundred Sitka Indians. Sitka was abandoned as a military station shortly after our arrival, since which time several efforts have been made to induce Congress to organize some sort of government there.

When we landed at Sitka we forced our way through a crowd of Indians, Russians, half-breeds, Jews, and soldiers, to whom this monthly arrival is life itself, and went directly to the trading-store and post-office. Mr. C. H. Taylor, of Chicago, who supported the expedition, had written to engage Phillips's fur-trading schooner to take us to Yakutat, where we were to begin our exploration. This schooner was the only craft available for rough work in the ice-drifts, so it was with much anxiety that we asked :

" Where is your schooner ? "

" Gone to Behring's Bay for a load of furs," was the disappointing answer.

After fruitless efforts to obtain something better, we decided to risk ourselves in one of the large Indian canoes. The Alaskans, having a superfluity of time on their hands, devote long periods to the most trifling transactions, and, in important bargains, it takes days, and sometimes weeks, to reach an agreement. We found them grasping, shrewd, and unscrupulous.

It was April 16th when we first asked for a large war canoe, or *yahk* (a word which would seem to be related to the yacht of the Germanic tongue), with crew. We negotiated with several of the chiefs, sub-chiefs, and principal men who owned the canoes and slaves to man them. But after wearing ourselves out chaffering with them, we found we could save time by taking the experienced Phillips's advice to " let'm alone." By and by, these aboriginal land-sharks began to offer terms. The winter and spring drizzle set in, and we joined the group of loungers around the trader's stove. We visited " Sitka Jack," an arrant old scoundrel, but one of the wealthiest men of the Sitka tribe. Of course his house stood among the largest, at the fashionable end of the town. These houses were built of planks, three or four inches thick, each one having been hewed from a log, with an adze formed by lashing a metal blade to the short prong of a forked stick. In constructing the native cabin, the planks are set on edge and so nicely fitted that they need no chinking. The shape of the house is square ; a bark roof is laid on, with a central aperture for chimney. The door is a circular opening about two feet in diameter. It is closed with a sheet of bark or a bear-skin or seal-skin. On arriving at Sitka Jack's hut we crawled through the door, and found ourselves in the presence of Jack's wives, children, and slaves, who were lounging on robes and blankets laid on a board flooring which extended along

THLINKIT COVERED BASKET AND SPOON. (CHILKÁHT KWÁHN.)

GOING FISHING.

each side of the room. A dirt floor about seven feet square was left in the center, and on this the fire burned and the pot of halibut boiled merrily. Our arrival was hailed with stolid indifference. The family circle reclined and squatted as usual, and went on with the apparently enjoyable occupation of scooping up handfuls of raw herring-roe, which they munched with great gusto. Sitka Jack was absent on a trading expedition to the Chilkáht kwáhn or tribe. One of his brothers-in-law was chief of this tribe, and being a one-eyed despot of sanguinary principles not only held his tribe under absolute control, but inspired his relatives and connections with wholesome awe. His sister, Mrs. "Sitka Jack," was, therefore, a person of great consequence, and her influence surpassed even the usual wonderful authority of the Alaskan women. Evidently she was the head of the house, and as such she received us haughtily. She weighed at least two hundred pounds. She gave us her terms, pointed coldly at the slaves she would send with us, and told us she was the sister of the terrible Chilkáht chief. As we still hesitated, she threw her weight into the scale, and said she would go with us and protect us. We could not get one of the great canoes holding from sixty to eighty warriors, but finally closed a bargain with Tah-ah-nah-klékh for his canoe, of about four tons burden. He was to act as pilot and steersman. We hired Nah-sach, Klen, and Jack as crew. Jack, our interpreter, was a Sitka Indian who had a smattering of mongrel Russian and English. Myers went with us as prospector and miner.

We had accumulated a cargo that looked fully twice the size of the canoe, which, like all of her kind, was as buoyant as a bladder, as graceful as a gull, and very capacious, so that by skillful stowage we loaded in the entire cargo and left room for ourselves; that is, we could swing our paddles, but we could not change our seats. Jack, or Sam as we had newly named him, was fond of "Hoo-chinoo." This is a native distilled liquor, colorless and vilely odorous. The stills are large tin oil-cans, and the coils are giant kelp. The Sitkans never set forth on an expedition of unusual importance without first getting beastly drunk. Sam had evidently gauged the importance of this expedition as immense. We loaded him in as cargo, and waited for the last man, Myers, who presently appeared, dragging at the end of a rope a half-grown black dog. Myers took his place, his canine friend was put

THE INDIAN VILLAGE AT SITKA.

in the bow, and amid the cheers of idle Sitka we paddled rapidly toward the north. The dog gazed wistfully at the retreating crowd, then suddenly sprang into the water and swam ashore.

For a time we were in mortal terror, lest we should capsize the shell by our awkwardness; an anxiety on our part that was epitomized, at our first landing, in Myers's fervent exclamation:

DOMESTIC BOWL FOR SEAL-OIL. (HOONÁH KWÁHN.)

"Thank Heaven, I kin shift my foot!"

One drowsy evening we saw the peak of Edgecumbe for the last time. The great truncated cone caught the hues of the sunset, and we could note the gloom gathering deeper and deeper in the hollow of the crater. Our Indians were stolidly smoking the tobacco we had given them, and were resting after the labors of the day with bovine contentment. Tah-ah-nah-klékh related to us the Thlinkit legend of Edgecumbe:

"A long time ago the earth sank beneath the water, and the water rose and covered the highest places so that no man could live. It rained so hard that it was as if the sea fell from the sky. All was black, and it became so dark that no man knew another. Then a few people ran here and there and made a raft of cedar logs, but nothing could stand against the white waves, and the raft was broken in two.

"On one part floated the ancestors of the Thlinkits, on the other the parents of all other nations. The waters tore them apart, and they never saw each other again. Now their children are all different, and do not understand each other. In the black tempest Chethl was torn from his sister Ah-gish-áhn-akhon ['The-woman-who-supports-the-earth']. Chethl [symbolized in the osprey] called aloud to her, 'You will never see me again, but you will hear my voice forever!' Then he became an enormous bird, and flew to south-west till no eye could follow him. Ah-gish-áhn-akhon climbed above the waters and reached the summit of Edgecumbe. The mountain opened and received her into the bosom of the earth. That hole [the crater] is where she went down. Ever since that time she has held the earth above the water. The earth is shaped like the back of a turtle and rests on a pillar; Ah-gish-áhn-akhon holds the pillar. Evil spirits that wish to destroy mankind seek to overthrow her or drive her away. The terrible battles are long and fierce in the lower darkness. Often the pillar rocks and

We passed a succession of evergreen islands with steep, rocky shores, and in the distance we could see the jagged alps of the main-land. The trees were principally fir, hemlock, and cedar. The evergreen underbrush was so dense and so matted with ferns and moss as to be almost impenetrable. The accumulation of moss was frequently ten or fifteen feet deep. Peat-bogs and coal-fields were common features of the islands, but the

THE MAIN STREET OF SITKA.

sways in the struggle, and the earth trembles and seems like to fall, but Ah-gish-áhn-akhon is good and strong, so the earth is safe. Chethl lives in the bird Kunna-káht-eth. His nest is in the top of the mountain, in the hole through which his sister disappeared.

"He carries whales in his claws to this eyrie, and there devours them. He swoops from his hiding-place and rides on the edge of the coming storm. The roaring of the tempest is his voice calling to his sister. He claps his wings in the peals of thunder, and its rumbling is the rustling of his pinions. The lightning is the flashing of his eyes." *

* Bishop Veniaminoff, Wrangell, and Dall have given versions of this legend.

coal was found to be sulphurous and bituminous. Clams were abundant and good. The smallest, when opened, were about the size of an orange. The largest shells were used as soup-plates by the natives. The waters of the archipelago at all seasons are alive with halibut. They are caught with a peculiar hook, fastened to a thick line made of twisted cedar-root fiber. Our bill of fare in Alaska included clams, mussels, herring, herring-roe, codfish, salmon, porpoise, seal, ducks, geese, and halibut—eternally halibut. Venison and wild goat and bear's flesh were to be had only occasionally, and the craving for good warm-blooded meats was incessant with us whites. Another intense craving was for sweets. We devoured our supply of sugar, and when it was exhausted we consumed much seal-oil, and chewed the sweet inner bark of a species of cedar, of which bark the Indians dry great quantities for the winter.

On the 27th we sighted the mouth of the Chilkáht. Professor Davidson of the Coast Survey has been up this river a little beyond the upper village. The two villages are governed by the Chilkáht chief before alluded to as " Sitka Jack's " brother-in-law. He is a despot and mostly captives from the tribes of the interior, or from hostile coast tribes. So little distinction is made between the bond and the free that at first a stranger finds it difficult to detect the slaves. They sit around the fire and eat from the same dish with their owners, who joke with them, and place them on a footing of perfect social equality. But the slaves hew the wood and carry the water and paddle the canoe. They cannot marry with-

AN ALASKAN INTERIOR.

does not encourage explorations of his river, though recently he has become so envious of the gold mines on the Stickeen, that it is said he will help gold prospectors to ascend his river. This one-eyed chief is very savage and vindictive, but as he holds a monopoly of the fur trade up and down his river he is very wealthy and influential, and can be of great assistance to any expedition.* He owns many slaves,

* A good plan of exploration would be by two parties coöperating: one to go up the Yukon, the other up the Chilkáht, to meet at a depot of supply previously located on the upper Yukon.

out the consent of their master, and they are unpleasantly liable to be offered as sacrifices on their master's grave.

From Chatham Strait we paddled against head winds into Cross Sound. In a sudden turn the whole vast sound opened to us, and the Mount St. Elias alps appeared like a shadowy host of snowy domes and pinnacles. Chief among them were the twin peaks Fairweather and Crillon. About this time we met a canoe-load of Hoonáhs, who had come ninety miles to dig their spring potatoes. On a sunny slope, sheltered by surrounding forests

THLINKIT WAR CANOE. (HAIDÁH KWÁHN.)

and sentinel peaks, these people had long ago planted some potatoes procured from the Russians at Sitka, and every year they come to dig last year's crop, and sow the ground for the following spring. The tubers were about the size of large marbles. In the gardens of Sitka are grown excellent potatoes, beets, turnips, radishes, lettuce, cabbage, and such hardy vegetables. The soil is not suitable for cereals, neither is the season long enough.

Near Cape Spencer we camped on a little island, where Tsa-tate, a young man of the Hoonáh kwáhn, had his summer hut. Three families lived here with Tsa-tate; and, though he was much younger than the other men of the family, he was the head of his clan. Tsa-tate's cabin was like all the other wooden huts we had seen. The cross poles and rafters were hung with fish and snow-shoes and nets. The sides were covered with traps, bows, spears, paddles, and skins of bear, sable, and silver-fox. The women sat around the fire, weaving baskets of different shapes and colors

THLINKIT BASKET WORK. (HOONÁH KWÁHN.)

THLINKIT CHIEF'S CLOAK. (CHILKÁHT KWÁHN.)

from the fiber of a long, fine root, which they soaked in water and split into threads. One old woman was chewing the seams of a pair

WOMAN'S WOODEN COMB. (CHILKÁHT.)

of seal-skin boots so as to soften them, and another was pounding some tobacco leaves into snuff. A man with a fiery red head was carving a pipe in which to smoke the tobacco we had given him, and a sick baby, tenderly watched by its mother, lay in a cor-

ner, with its mouth and nostrils stuffed full of some chewed-up weed. As darkness came on and the halibut fishermen returned from the sea, we all gathered about the central fire in Tsa-tate's hut, and Mrs. Tsa-tate lighted the pitch-wood candles, and with down and resin dressed an ugly gash in the sole of her husband's foot. The children slept or poked the fire with an immunity from scolding that would have cheered the heart of every civilized five-year-old. A young girl sat demurely in a corner. Until they are of marriageable age, and entitled to wear the silver ornament through the lower lip, the maidens are carefully watched by the elder women of the family. An old woman stirred and skimmed the boiling pot of porpoise flesh. Tsa-tate, reclining comfortably on a divan of bear-skins, answered our questions and repeated tribal legends. He pointed to his son, a boy about five years old, who, he said, would be his successor, as head of the clan. It was difficult to ascertain the exact law of succession among the Thlinkits, but the chiefship seems to follow the direct line, though, as in all other savage nations, this is scarcely a rule, for the lineal heir may be set aside in favor of a more acceptable man. In the inheritance of personal property the collateral is preferred to the lineal relationship. The wives, or more properly the widows, being personal property, pass to the collateral next of kin of their husband's totem, for the marriage of two people of the same totem is considered a kind of incest. The widow, in any event, takes with her such possessions as have always been peculiarly her own. She also takes her own infant children; naturally, then, she would take to her new husband the children's inheritance, which may account for the habit of regarding the male collaterally next of kin as proper heir. If there be no male survivor competent to receive the widow, or if he purchases freedom with goods, she then passes into the open matrimonial market, with her pecuniary attractions. Sometimes the heir rebels and refuses to accept his former sister-in-law, cousin, aunt, or whatever she may be. Then her totemic or family relatives wage war on the insulter and such of his totem as he can rally around him, the object being either to enforce her right or extort a proper recompense. Among the Asónques, further to the north and west, I saw a young fellow of about eighteen years of age who had just fallen heir to his uncle's widow. As I looked upon her mummy-like proportions I thought that here was reasonable cause for war. Sometimes a husband already liberally provided for will come into a misfortune in the shape of one or more widows. The only escape is by purchasing freedom. In fact, there seems to be no hurt to a Thlinkit's honor that money or goods will not heal. The scorning of a widow, the betrayal of a maiden, and murder, all demand blood or pecuniary compensation. If in a feud all negotiations fail, and Kanúkh (symbolized in the wolf), the God of War, be unpropitious, and send private war, then the principal antagonists, with their totemic adherents, don their helmets and coats of paint, and stand facing each other in two lines, each

SHAMÁN'S DRUMSTICK AND WAR KNIVES. 1. CHILKÁHT. 2. HOONÁH KWÁHN.

line holding to a rope with the left hand, and wielding heavy knives with the right. They advance, and hack and hew, with more yells than bloodshed, until one side or the other cries the Thlinkit for *peccavi*. In this duel, any warrior violates the code who lets go the rope with the left hand, unless he be wounded, or torn from it; when he has let go, he is then out of the fight and must retire. If the strife be inter-tribal, or public war, the plan of combat is surprise and sudden capture. The villages, from necessity as well as from choice, are placed always at the edge of high tide. The forces of the aggressive tribe embark in a fleet of war canoes, and by a swift and stealthy voyage strike the village from the sea and endeavor to take it by storm. If they are resisted they generally retire at once. The Chilkáht kwáhn came down suddenly upon the main village of the Sitka kwáhn while I was near by, but succeeded in getting possession of only half the houses, so the opposing forces divided the village between them and kept up a lively but rather harmless combat for three days, at the end of which the invaders were bought off with some loads of furs. A member of the

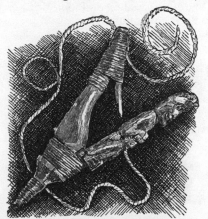

HALIBUT HOOK. (HOONÁH KWÁHN.)

SHAMÁN'S RATTLE. (HOONÁH KWÁHN.)

Sitka kwáhn had murdered his Chilkáht squaw in a fit of passion, and this was the cause of the conflict. The goods paid over as recompense went principally to the relatives of the murdered woman. In these tribal conflicts the captured are enslaved, the dead are scalped, and all property taken is held as booty. Hostages and participants in rope duels do not take food from the right hand for several days, because, figuratively (and literally), it is unclean. A head powdered with down is a sign of truce.

We were now within five days' journey of Yakutat, which is near Icy Bay, at which place one of the Mount St. Elias glaciers

ends in the sea. Threats and bribes were alike useless. Pay or no pay, our crew would not put to sea. Tah-ah-nah-klékh pointed to the mountain, and said:

"One mountain is as good as another. There is a very big one. Go climb that if you want to."

Thus perished our hope of climbing Mount St. Elias. We turned our course directly to the main-land, about thirty miles away, and landed a little below Cape Spencer. A seawind filled the coast-waters with icebergs, and we had great difficulty in picking our way through them. I noticed that, when journeying through the floating ice in good weather, our Indians would carefully avoid striking pieces of ice, lest they should offend the Ice Spirit. But when the Ice Spirit beset us with peril, they did not hesitate to retaliate by banging his subjects. After picking our way through the ice for three days, we came upon a small temporary camp of Hoonáhs, who were sealhunting. We found little camps of a family or two scattered along both shores. One of the largest glaciers from Fairweather comes into the bay, and thus keeps its waters filled with the largest icebergs, even in the summer season, for which reason the bay is a favorite place for seal-hunting. The seal is the natives' meat, drink (the oil is like melted butter), and clothing. I went sealhunting to learn the art, which requires care and patience. The hunter, whether on an ice floe or in a canoe, never moves when the seal is aroused. When the animal is asleep, or has dived, the hunter darts forward. The spear has a barbed detachable head, fastened to the shaft by a plaited line made from sinew. The line has attached to it a marking buoy, which is merely an inflated seal's bladder. The young seals are the victims of the Thlinkit boys, who kill them with bow and arrow. These seal-hunters used a little moss and seal-oil and some driftwood for fuel. In the morning we arose late, and found that our friends of the night before had

1. BROWN WOOD PIPE-BOWL (HOONÁH). 2. PIPE-BOWL MADE FROM DEER ANTLER (CHILKÁHT).
3. WOOD PIPE-BOWL WITH NATIVE COPPER TOP (ASÓNQUE).

silently stolen away, taking with them much of our firewood.

Mr. Taylor decided to return home, and we accompanied him to Sitka. There I reëngaged Sam and Myers, and, obtaining a new crew, returned at once to a bay about twenty miles south-east of Mount Fairweather. My purpose was to explore the bay, cross the coast range, and strike the upper waters of Chilkáht. On the shores of the bay we found hospitality with a band of Hoonáhs. Leaving the crew with our large canoe under the charge of Myers at this place, I took a smaller one and went with Cocheen, the chief of the band, north-westerly up the bay. After about forty miles' travel we came to a small village of Asónques. They received us with great hospitality, and as our canoe had been too small to carry any shelter, the head man gave me a bed in his own cabin. He had a great many wives, who busied themselves making me comfortable. The buckskin reënforcement of my riding trowsers excited childish wonder. I drew pictures of horses and men separate, and then of men mounted on horses. Their astonishment over the wonderful animal was greater than their delight at comprehending the utility of the trowsers. The Alaskan women are childish and pleasant, yet quick-witted and capable of heartless vindictiveness. Their authority in all matters is unquestioned. No bargain is made, no expedition set on foot, without first consulting the women. Their veto is never disregarded. I bought a silver-fox skin from Tsa-tate, but his wife made him return the articles of trade and recover the skin. In the same way I was perpetually being annoyed by having to undo bargains because "his wife said *clekh*," that is, "no." I hired a fellow to take me about thirty miles in his canoe, when my own crew was tired. He agreed. I paid him the tobacco, and we were about to start when his wife came to the beach and stopped him. He quietly unloaded the canoe and handed me back the

THLINKIT WOMAN. (SITKA KWÁHN.)

tobacco. The whole people are curious in the matter of trade. I was never sure that I had done with a bargain, for they claimed and exercised the right to undo a contract at any time, provided they could return the consideration received. This is their code among themselves. For example: I met at the mouth of the Chilkáht a native trader who had been to Fort Simpson, about six hundred miles away, and failing to get as much as he gave in the interior of Alaska for the skins, was now returning to the interior to find the first vender and revoke the whole transaction. Among themselves their currency is a species of wampum, worth about twenty dollars a string, beaver-skins worth about a dollar a skin, and sable or marten worth about two dollars a skin. From the whites they get blankets worth four dollars apiece, and silver dollars; gold they will not touch (except around Sitka and Wrangell), but they accept copper and silver. They are a laughing, good-natured people,

SHAMÁN'S RATTLE. (ASÓNQUE KWÁHN.)

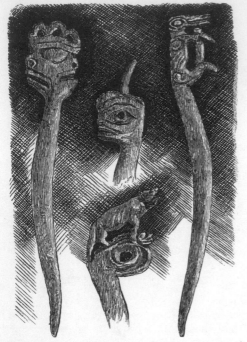

BONE STAKES FOR MARTEN TRAP. (INTERIOR OF ALASKA.)

ordinarily very quiet. Even their large meetings are subdued and orderly. They are undemonstrative. The mothers do not fondle nor play with their children much, but a stranger can win their hearts by kindness to their little ones. They consider corporeal punishment a disgrace, and I did not see a child struck during the time I was among them. A rebuke, a sharp tone, or exclusion from the cabin seemed to be the only punishments. Even the dogs are curiously exempt from punishment and abuse, and a more wolfish, starved, mangy lot of curs it would be hard to find. Good bear-dogs they will not sell at any price. With all their gentleness of voice and manner, and their absolute respect for the rights of the smallest and youngest of the family, their love and affection seemed of the coolest sort. Etiquette required only about forty days of ostensible mourning. The loss of children seemed to cause the greatest grief. They have a curious habit of blacking the face with a mixture of seal-oil and lamp-black, or burnt pitch, but I believe this custom, whatever its origin, is now merely a kind of toilet, to be used according to the whim of the individual.

From this Asónque village I went, with a party of mountain goat-hunters, up into the Mount St. Elias alps back of Mount Fairweather— that is, to the north-east of that mountain. For this trip our party made elaborate preparations. We donned belted shirts made of squirrel skins, fur head-dresses (generally conical), seal-skin bootees fitting very closely, and laced half-way to the knee. We carried spears for alpenstocks, bows and arrows, raw-hide ropes, and one or two old Hudson Bay rifles. The climbing was very laborious work. The mountains, where not covered with ice or snow, were either of a crumbling schistose character or ice-worn limestone, and sometimes granite. The sides were terribly rugged; some of the face walls were about eight hundred feet sheer, with a foot slope of shell-rock or *débris* of two hundred or three hundred feet more. Ptarmigan were seen on the lower levels where the ground was bare, but I saw nothing on which they could feed. The goats kept well up toward the summit, amid the snow-fields, and fed on the grass which sprouted along the edges of melting drifts. They were the wariest, keenest animals I ever hunted. The animal is like a large white goat, with long, coarse hair and a heavy coat of silky underfleece. The horns, out of which the natives carve spoons, are short, sharp, and black.

After crossing this coast range the country seemed much the same—rugged, bleak, and impassable. The Indians with me, so far as I could understand them, said it was an exceedingly rough country all the way over, and that the Chilkáht River had its rise among just such alps as those around us, only it was warmer in the Chilkáht mountains, and there was more grass and plenty of wild goats,

THLINKIT TRAVELING CHEST.

sheep, and bears. We found a bear that, so far as I know, is peculiar to this country. It is a beautiful bluish under color, with the tips of the long hairs silvery white. The traders call it "St. Elias's silver bear." The skins are not common.

Being unable to go further overland I returned to the Asónque camp. There we fitted ice-guards to a small canoe, and with ice-hooks pulled our way through, and carried our canoe over the floes and among the icebergs, to the extreme limit of so-called open water in that direction. The ice-guards were merely wooden false sides hung to a false prow. From this point, also, I found the interior impenetrable, and went to a temporary

Here he paused again, picked up the corner of his squirrel robe and raised it with a sweeping forward gesture, which he maintained till his words had produced their full effect, when the sing-song intonation would begin again.

Coon-nah-nah-thklé, for that was his name, showed me his sorcerer's kit. There was an immense drum of stretched seal-skin or goat-skin, made to accompany him in his incantations, and to terrify the wicked spirits preying

THLINKIT ANCESTRAL SPOONS. (FROM HORNS OF MOUNTAIN GOAT. HOONÁH KWÁHN.)

camp of seal and goat hunters, who were camped on a ledge of rocks above the crunching and grinding icebergs. The head man of this camp was a young fellow of about thirty, who was both Shamán ("medicine-man") and hereditary chief. He was the most thoughtful and entertaining Thlinkit I had met. He told me that within his own life-time this place where we now were had been solid ice. He would listen with breathless attention whenever I spoke, and then reply in low, musical intonations, almost like chanting. His narration of the traditions of his people was pathetic in its solemn earnestness. He said:

"You are the only white man that has ever been here, but I have heard of your people. Before I was born—a long time ago —a ship came to the mouth of this bay, and gave the Thlinkits iron to make knives like this one. Before that they had made knives from copper or from stone, like this."

Then he would pause, fix his eyes on me, and hold up the knife. When he saw I had absorbed his words, he would give a graceful wave of the hand and continue:

"Then the Thlinkits had many furs,—foxes, and bear, and sable,—all the people were warm, all were happy, and lived as Yéhl had set them to live [or after Yéhl's example, I don't know which]. There was plenty to eat, and plenty to wear. Now, sometimes we are hungry and wear ragged robes."

upon the life of the sick person. The drum had formerly belonged to a celebrated Shamán, and his spirit was either in the drum itself or had passed into the possessor of the drum, I could not determine which. I found it to be a common belief that anything that had belonged to a dead wizard possessed some inherent virtue. For this reason it was almost impossible to secure Shamán instruments. These Shamáns claim to be able to see the "life" or soul leaving the body or being dragged from it by spirits, and it is their business to seize the soul with the mouth and breathe or force it back into the body. The dress they wear depends upon what malign spirits they determine are at work. I only saw one Shamán exorcising, and I do not believe he would have continued had he known I was observing him. He kneaded, pounded, yelled, chanted, frothed, swayed to and fro, played tunes all up and down the suffering patient, blew in his mouth and nostrils, and literally worried the life out of him. In general practice the Shamán continues this performance till the wretched patient declares he is better or well. If he cures, the Shamán gets large pay. If he kills, he restores the goods he has previously received on account. If any one who is not a regular Shamán does anything for a patient who dies, the self-constituted doctor is held responsible, and must pay forfeit in life or goods. If the patient is obdurate and will not declare

BODY OF CHIEF "SHAKES" LYING IN STATE, PREPARATORY TO CREMATION.

that the spirits have left him, the Shamán makes that statement for him. The hair is generally worn long by the Alaskan women; always short by the men, except the Shamáns, who never cut or comb the hair, nor are the matted locks benefited any by the habit of powdering and greasing for occasions of ceremony. The hair is kept tied up, except when the Shamán is exercising his peculiar functions. Then it is shaken out in long, snaky ropes, which dance over the shoulders. Some take these ropes of hair and stick them all over with flat scales of pitch, increasing thereby the Medusa-like appearance of the head. I made for myself a fair reputation for sorcery while in Coon-nah-nah-thklé's camp by a judicious use of my repeating-rifle and revolver. The chief and I shot at a mark, and I am afraid he was the better shot. He gave me a little amulet (whale totem), which he said would bring me good luck if I would hang it on my rifle. Then he took the weapon and passed his hands over it, and blew on it, which he said would prevent its ever hurting him.

The spirits of the Thlinkit mythology are classified as Ki-yékh, spirits of the air; Tah-ki-yékh, spirits of the earth; Te-ki-yékh, spirits of the water; and Yékh, subordinate or minor spirits. The spirits of those killed in war become Ki-yékh, and the aurora is the flashing of their lights when they are dancing their war dances. Hence, an auroral display is a sign of war. The chief deity of the Thlinkits, the Bramah, the Creator, is Yehl. One would suppose that he would be the deity of the Tinneh, or interior Indians. Yet among the Thlinkits the raven is held peculiarly sacred for his sake, and the early writers (Veniaminoff and Wrangell) declare the raven to be a foul and ill-omened bird among the Tinneh. Yehl is symbolized in the raven for the reason that one of his chief exploits, the bringing of fresh water to the Thlinkits, was done under the guise of a raven. The sum of Thlinkit philosophy is, "Live as Yehl lived." Their great totem is Yehl's totem or the raven totem, the raven being the symbol. Another scarcely inferior totem is the Kanúkh (wolf), the wolf being the symbol. The third (and, so far as I know, the last) totem is Tset'kh (the whale). Who Tset'kh was before he was a whale and what he did I could not learn.

Their totemic system is the most curious one that ever came to my notice. The totemic relationship is stronger than that of blood. The child follows the totem of the mother, and in family quarrels the opponents must array themselves with their totems; hence, half-brothers are often called on to fight each other. I used to be surprised at having my vagabonds tell me perfect strangers were their "brothers" or "sisters," until I found it meant brother or sister in the totem. The Kanúkh (wolf) totem is the warrior caste. Men of this caste are the soldiers of the whole people, and are led in war only by chiefs of their own caste. Kanúkh is either the older brother of Yehl or an older deity—I don't know which. He is now the god of war and patron saint of the "wolves," but the myths tell of a celebrated encounter between him and Yehl. It is difficult to arrive at the religion of the Thlinkits from the stories of these deities. In my short visit I certainly could not, and Veniaminoff, who lived among them, has left little information on the subject.

A very wise old raven was pointed out to me as the embodied spirit of a defunct Shamán. Suicides are very frequent, because the tired person wishes to enter upon a happier existence; this and the superstition as to the aurora points to a belief in a spirit life. Then again all bodies are cremated (except Shamáns), and whatever may have been the origin of the pyre, the reason given now is that the spirit may not be cold on the journey to the Spirit Land. A Thlinkit, in answer to my questionings, replied:

" Doctors wont burn."

" But why don't you try ? " I persisted.

" Because we know they will not burn."

I once saw a body ready for the funeral pyre. It was lying behind the cabin in a crouching attitude, with a native blanket from the wool of mountain goats thrown over it, and its robes and possessions near by. A hole had been cut through the rear wall of the cabin, for if the corpse had been carried through the entrance, it would have left the dread mystery of death upon the threshold, and the living could not enter. The Shamán attends to the burning. One day a little boy of the Sitká Kwáhn was pointed out to me as a Shamán. He wore the untouched long hair. I asked how they knew so soon that he was to be a Shamán.

" Oh," they answered, " he was alive a long time ago as a Shamán." At the proper time, this boy must take his degree in the college of Shamánism by fasting in solitude in the wilderness. No one must approach him, and his food must be the roots of the earth. When he has become sufficiently spiritualized, the Great Shamán will send to him the otter, to impart the secrets of his order. The novice will meet the animal. They will salute three times. He will fall upon the otter and tear out its tongue and take off its skin. Then in a frenzy he will rush back to his tribe and madly bite whatever comes in his way. These bites are often dangerous, but are sought for as wounds of honor. This frenzy fit among the Haidáhs is called be-

coming " Taamish." If the otter is not forthcoming in due time there are various artifices to compel his presence, such as getting the tooth or finger of a dead Shamán and holding it in the mouth. After the Nawloks, or evil spirits, have thus wrestled with him, the Shamán ever after has his own attendant retinue of Nawloks and Yekhs, or even of higher spirits, whom he summons to his aid. In supernatural matters, therefore, his word is law.

At Coon-nah-nah-thklé's, I found the people using stone-axes, knives, and other implements, some of which I brought away with me. They were made of hypo-chlorite and slate, tempered in oil. The children there were greatly frightened at me, and would not let me approach them. On my return I encountered another Shamán, and purchased from him a finely carved medicine rattle. But a skinny hag snatched it from my hand, just as I had concluded the bargain, and compelled the " Doctor " to return me my tobacco. She said the rattle had been the favorite one of her dead husband, a Shamán, who had left her and his rattles to this nephew, the " Doctor," who certainly did not seem too happy over it. By judicious coaxing and tobacco I succeeded in pacifying her, and renewed my trade with the nephew. The rattle is carved with crane's, owl's, and raven's heads, and has queer long-tongued demons turning back somersaults over it.

From Cocheen's I turned southward and homeward. I had applied for a year's leave with the purpose of exploring the interior of Alaska, and now was anxious to return to Sitka for the reply. In Chatham Strait, near Cross Sound, the old head chief of the Hoonáhs, came and begged me to go to his island to doctor his boy who was very sick. I went but was loath to do any doctoring; for the Thlinkit custom of killing the doctor in case his patient dies, is discouraging to a beginner. The boy was feverish and had a complication of troubles, so I gave him hot-water baths followed with a seidlitz powder. The effervescing of the powder put me at once at the head of the Shamáns. During my stay I built up an extensive practice. I made for the chief some camphorated soap liniment. Eye troubles are common among the Thlinkits, and are due to the glitter of snow and ice and the irritation caused by the smoke in the huts. One feeble old man to whom I had ministered was surely dying, and I was anxious to be off before that event. I visited all my patients preparatory to departing. I gave to some dried onions stewed in sugar, to others cod-liver oil, and diluted alcohol to the feeble old man to keep him up until I could get away. From the father of the sick boy, then nearly well, I took a fee of some finely carved spoons made from horns of the mountain goat.

At this camp I found traces of a custom which prevails to some extent in Central Africa and is said to obtain throughout the interior of Alaska. When a stranger of rank visits a chief, the latter presents his guest with a wife from among the women of his household. In morals the Alaskans are much inferior to most Indian tribes of the plains. Avarice is their ruling passion. They are the most knavish and cunning of traders. Theft, if successful, brings no disgrace. The detected thief is laughed at and ridiculed. I saw old Cocheen look with fond admiration on Kastase-Kúch, his son, when the latter drew from under his robe some articles he had purloined from the village where we had lodged for the night. Their gratitude seemed small and they have no expression for "I thank you." Flaws in gifts were always carefully examined and critically pointed out to the giver. An Alaskan who shot at some decoy ducks near Sitka, went to the owner of the decoys and demanded the return of his wasted amunition. Two Alaskans were driven to sea in a canoe. A schooner picked them up, but would not or could not take their canoe as it was still blowing a gale. The rescued demanded payment for the lost craft. Another fellow came to the doctor of the post at Sitka and begged for medicine for his brother and then asked the doctor to pay him for carrying it to the brother. I lent Tah-ah-nah-klékh a goat-skin robe of mine and at the end of our voyage asked him to clean it. He did so and demanded full payment. We did not lose much by theft, because our crew knew very well the value would be deducted from their wages. Thlinkit virtues are hospitality, good-nature, peaceableness, filial obedience, and, after their own code, a respect for solemn contracts or engagements. Even when very angry they only sulk. They are demonstrative only in the expression of surprise. My host, the old Hoonáh chief, was disinterested kindness itself. At his bountiful board I had a seat between his youngest and prettiest wives. They prepared seal-flipper for me with a celery-like dressing of some plant. We lived in ease and luxury and a little necessary grease and dirt. When the fire was stirred, and the spears and paddles were put away for the evening, my host smoked his pipe and told tales of the land of the Tinneh, where all the best furs were and where the mountains were bleak and merciless. His youngest son, a sturdy little fellow of five, shared the pipe with his father, and they passed it from one to the other with amusing solemnity. I told of a wonderland where the *yahks* were as large as islands and moved against the wind without the help of hands; of great horned animals giving milk; of other great animals on which men rode; of thousands of great stone-houses; of the vast multitude of white people. The Thlinkits received my stories, as they do every statement, with courteous deference. When I rose to go to my own camp the chief selected the handsomest bear-skin from a pile of them, and bade his youngest wife present it to me. When next he came to my camp I gave him, among other things, a fine woollen blanket. He folded it about him and said he would not use it as a hunting blanket. When he went away he would leave it at home, and when he died it should not go with his other effects to his wives and children, but he would be burned in it and it would go with him to the Unknown. A niece of the Chilkáht chief, one of the comeliest of her race, who had married a hideously ugly, but very rich old Hoonáh, the second man in the village, mended my clothes and my sealskin boots, and sang songs or chants for my entertainment that were quite wonderful, I thought, for their flowing measure and rhythm. This is one which I learned to understand the best, called "The Song of the Salmon Fishing":

Why is the young man sorrowful?
Oh why is the young man sad?
Ah-ka. His maiden has left him.
The long suns have come,
The ice now is melting;
Now comes the salmon
He leaps in the river,
In the moon's gentle twilight
He throws up a bow—
A bow of bright silver.
Lusty and strong he darts through the water,
He sports with his mate;
He springs from the water.
All the dark season
He has lain hidden.
Now he comes rushing,
And ripples the river.
Purple and gold, and red and bright silver
Shine on his sides and flash in his sporting,
How he thrashes the net!
How he wrenches the spear!
But the red of his sides
Is stained with a redder;
The maid of the young man leans o'er the salmon
White laugh her teeth,
Clear rings her laughter;
Which passes canoes all busy and happy,
Which outstrips the noise of the many mixed voices
And pierces the heart of her sorrowful lover.
She has forgot him,
She joys with another.
All for another she chases the salmon,
Ah-ka. Your sweetheart has left you.
So do they jeer him,
Ah-ka—your sweetheart is here at the fishing!
Ah-ka—how like you this gay salmon season?

The crabs I saw at this village were wonderful for their size. Two crabs were brought to me, the largest of which measured a little more than six feet on a line joining the extremities of its outstretched mandibles. The body was eighteen inches long. When broken in pieces one crab filled a camp kettle, and four men made a hearty meal off it, and it was all very good. The boy archers of the village who brought me the crabs held their bows horizontally, and strained the bow against the front of the thumb and back of the little fingers, the arrow passing between the fore and middle fingers, a mode of archery peculiar to the Alaskans. Many of the men and boys of the village were making boxes and firkins, and shaping bows and paddles. They used dried dog-fish skin for sand-paper.

In this village were many little bee-hive huts, temporarily constructed of mats or bark, which were due to one of the most universal superstitions, and especially cruel, as influencing these people. These huts were the temporary shelter to which women were driven at certain times when they most needed comfort and attention, that is, at the periods of childbirth, etc.

When a maiden reaches a marriageable age her lover demands his bride from her parents, and if they answer favorably he sends the purchase-money or goods, and on the appointed day seats himself outside her hut with his back to the door. If they are willing to accept him he is invited in. The maiden sits modestly in a corner. The relatives form a circle round the fire and sing and dance. The wedding gifts are displayed and critically examined. They are laid upon the floor, and the girl walks over them to her lover. According to the Russian priest, Veniaminoff and Wrangell, the marriage ceremony is not complete until bride and groom have fasted four days, and lived away from each other for a month. They then live together as man and wife. I had no opportunity of confirming the accuracy of these statements.

A man frequently takes the name of his son, but, before doing so, he gives a festival and announces his intention. He does not give up his former name or names, but assumes a new one as the father of his son; or he takes the name of a dead ancestor, but first gives a festival in honor of that departed progenitor. They call such a ceremony " elevating " (or reverencing) the dead. Another festival is of a political character. It is to gain popularity and influence. To this end the ambitious person will save for years till he has an accumulation of this world's goods. Then he makes a feast of unlimited eating and drinking, and all this store of wealth is distributed to the guests present. Festivals also celebrate the arrival of distinguished guests.

In the gray dawn, as we were about to push from shore, the old chief came to us accompanied by two of his wives. My blanket was wrapped round him. He said I had a good heart. I was a young chief now, but some day I would be a great one. Among the Thlinkits, he said, when a friend was leaving on a long journey, they watched him out of sight, for he might never return. I was his friend. I was going away to my own land. He would never see me again. Therefore he had come to watch me out of sight. He then motioned to his elder wife, who handed me a beautiful sable skin, and he continued : " Wherever you go among Thlinkits, show them this and tell them I gave it to you."

The breeze was freshening. I wrapped my capote about me and stepped aboard. We paddled rapidly out to sea, and it was not long before the three figures were lost to view. We were about three hundred and fifty miles from Sitka. In three days we reached Koutzenóo, a large village opposite the entrance to Peril Strait, where most of the native distilled liquor is made. Here we witnessed a drunken revel of indescribable abandon, during which naked and half-naked men and women dragged themselves about the place.

With a comparatively mild climate throughout the Archipelago, with most valuable shipbuilding timber covering the islands, with a cedar that now sells at one hundred and fifty dollars a thousand feet in Sitka, with splendid harbors, with inexhaustible fisheries, with an abundance of coal, and the probability that veins of copper, lead, silver, and gold await the prospector, with the possibility of raising sufficient garden vegetables, and with wild cranberry swamps on nearly every island ; with all these advantages it is surprising that an industrious, amphibious, ship-building, fishing colony from New England, or other States, has not established itself in Alaska. One drawback is that Congress has not yet organized a territorial government, but when this region shall have been opened up to individual enterprise and settlement, it will then be discovered that Alaska is a valuable possession. There is lacking neither the wealth nor the will to contradict this, but to those who are really interested I will say what the opposition does not say :—Go and see ! The round trip from New York will cost you about six hundred dollars, which does not include hotel expenses.

C. E. S. Wood.

8
On the
Fur Seal Islands

ON THE FUR SEAL ISLANDS.

BY THE FIRST SPECIAL TREASURY AGENT.

HORTLY after the cession of Russian America to the United States, the latter government began to take active measures for the protection of the few fisheries of the islands of the ceded territory, and thus it happened that I, as one who had had eighteen years' experience as a whaler in the North Pacific, became a factor in the plans for protection. My knowledge of the natural history, conditions of life, and currents of the North Pacific had brought me into communication with Professor Louis Agassiz and with Professor Benjamin Peirce, who was at the time Superintendent of the Coast Survey, and at their instance I was appointed by Hon. Hugh McCulloch, Secretary of the Treasury, first to report on the fur-seal fisheries and then to organize a system by which the interest of the islanders could be guarded and the seals protected against unnecessary destruction. The system established by me is still in active force. I reached the Fur Seal, or Pribyloff, Islands early in March, 1869, but it was not until the spring of 1871 that order was finally brought out of the confusion into which the fisheries had been thrown by the change in ownership, and we began operations under the lease granted to the Alaska Commercial Company. I had found the natives disorganized and terrified concerning their future, as the irregularities practiced by the various parties who had raided the islands for seals in the previous year had threatened extermination both to islanders and to seals; and the plan of fishing finally adopted was grafted on the general method which the Russians had observed, and in which the natives, who knew it, would therefore be likely to have confidence.

The Russians had maintained a head agent on the islands, with whom had been associated two creole subordinates who had been sufficiently educated in the counting-houses of Sitka to keep the accounts with the natives and to direct them in killing the seals and preparing the skins. A certain sum was allowed the islanders for compensation. The head agent employed three or four of the most capable men to direct parties at work, and the driving and killing of the seals had been left mainly to these. Their method had been to drive the seals as near as possible to the salting-houses, in order that the labor of carrying the skins might be made as light as possible; and they had become sufficiently expert in their work to understand that by killing the smaller seals the work would be lighter, though no discrimination was made as to the quality of the skins in the animals killed. The number of skins taken annually had varied from forty thousand to sixty thousand.

That the Government agent in charge of the islands might have full power to enforce and supervise all operations, it seemed best to leave to some responsible company the right to take a stated number of seals under restrictions and regulations that would best subserve the interests of the United States and of the natives themselves, who were to have the exclusive right to kill the seals and salt the skins.

When the sealing began in the spring of 1871, it soon became evident that the clumsy methods in vogue were open to very great improvement. To take the necessary number of seals to fill out the annual catch, the whole working force of the islands was kept busy from the 1st of June until September, the women helping, particularly in carrying the skins to the salting-houses. These had been built too far from the landing, and as soon as possible they were moved nearer to the beach, in order to facilitate the transfer of the skins to the boats on shipping. As the skins prepared for shipment, and all the salt necessary for curing them, had to be carried on the backs of the natives across a broad beach of soft sand and through the shallow water to and from boats, a railway of light iron rails was eventually built, to be laid in movable sections, with high-wheeled flat-cars. Mules, carts, and harnesses were brought to the islands, and whenever the skins were to be carried to the salting-houses from the slaughter-grounds the boys and girls, for the sake of the ride back in the empty carts, were ready to load them. This relieved the women of the necessity of all outdoor work in sealing time, except occasional journeys for the necessary supply of seal flesh for food. Later, when we had taught them to make bread and had introduced various articles of food, seal flesh and blubber, which had been formerly almost the sole means of sustenance, were used much less frequently. Under the lease held by the Alaska Commercial Company the number of seals to be killed annually was limited to 100,000; and at 40 cents a skin, the sum allowed the natives for each skin brought in, $40,000 was annually divided among the islanders employed in the killing of seals. We learned when the returns for the first season's catch were made that the skins were assorted into fourteen or fifteen classes. A small number—less than ten per cent.—ranked as first-class, at $14 a skin; about the same per cent. fell to less than $2.50 each, while the general average was about $5.87. This discrepancy in the value of the skins called attention at once to the question of what constituted the difference in quality between a skin worth $14 and one worth only $2.50. An agent of the Company was sent to London to examine the skins as they were classified for the market: the result of his examination revealed the fact that the fur of a seal was most valuable when the animal was three years old, the proportion being that at present prices a two-year-old seal would be worth $15 or $16, a three-year-old $16 or $19, a four-year-old $16, and a five-year-old only $2.50. As the agent had the opportunity of selecting the animals before killing, he aimed to take as many three-year-old seals as possible, making out the one hundred thousand from those two or four years old. This trebled the value of the annual catch at once. Again, it being desirable to secure the quantity with the least possible loss of life, a careful supervision of the manner of driving the seals to the slaughter-ground was instituted. Very fat seals often become overheated in driving, and die from convulsions, rendering their fur valueless for the market. In consequence of this difficulty each driver is required to carry a club and a knife, that any seal showing indications of an overheated condition may be killed immediately and skinned. These skins are collected after the herd is cared for, and are usually equal to eight or ten per cent. of the whole drive.

The cost of maintaining these fisheries is about $10,000 a year; the revenue obtained during the twenty years that the present lease has been running amounts to $365,000 a year. A careful count is made of the number of skins taken, each party through whose hands they pass keeping its own account. First they are counted by the chiefs, that the natives may be paid a proper sum; the Treasury officer in charge of the islands counts them when they are taken from the salting-houses for shipment; when received at the side of the vessel they are counted by the executive officer for his bills of lading; at San Francisco a revenue officer takes charge of them and has them counted; they are counted again at the warehouse in San Francisco, where they are packed in one-hundred-gallon tierces and shipped to New York, and thence to London, where they are counted twice again before they are ready for sale. An important element in the economy of the business is that, by reason of the many improved methods used in capturing and handling the seals, the time required for this work has been materially shortened. Formerly the work was continued from the 1st of June until September, but now the whole time required for taking the one hundred thousand skins and shipping them has been shortened to forty-five days. This gain in time also increases the value of the skins, as the fur is far brighter when the seals first land.

The present lease to the Alaska Commercial Company expires July 1, 1890. When the lease was granted, in 1870, the bids were governed by the average price of sealskins in London, which had never exceeded $6. Under the terms of the lease the Company paid the Government an average price of $3.65 per skin. If the business was profitable at that rate, the Government should now obtain a much larger share, in consideration of the trebled value of the skins in the London market at the present time. As there should be a large increase in the number of seals now available, owing to the improved methods of killing which reserve all the females, a far larger number might now be killed annually—perhaps twice as many. The seals occupy as breeding-grounds about eight miles of coast-line, and at the beginning of my stay on the islands I estimated the number of breeding females to be fully 1,130,000. When I left, eight years later, a similar method of computation gave 1,800,000 breeding females on the ground.

The males come to the islands the 1st of May and remain until about the 20th of July, when they scatter slowly, although a large number of them remain as late as November. The males appear on the ground first, and soon after their arrival they begin to locate about a rod apart, forming a line entire length of the shore. The younger and weaker males, beaten back by the stronger, coast along, entering the bays, and haul up on the hillsides and in the valleys. The greatest number at any one time upon St. Paul, the largest of the islands, is on the 20th of July, when we have estimated the number to be five millions. The seals really walk on four legs, raising their bodies from the ground as they move. Under favorable conditions they travel about a mile and a half an hour, and the longest drive we ever made was eight miles. As England alone has the necessary skilled labor for preparing the skins for final sale, she receives an amount of profit from the fur-seal fisheries equal to the whole profit of the United

States in the islands, and she therefore is equally interested in the question of wanton destruction of the seals. Under such circumstances an international agreement for the protection and regulation of the trade ought not to be difficult to obtain.

The Fur Seal Islands lie nearly in the middle of Behring's Sea, the nearest mainland being three hundred miles away to the north. When discovered in 1789 they were uninhabited, although traces of firebrands gave proof of earlier visitors. The islands are four in number — St. Paul, St. George, Otter, and Walrus, the former being the largest, though but fifteen miles long. It is triangular in shape, and furnishes ninety per cent. of the whole number of seals. The average mean temperature for the year is about the same as that of New England, though it is cooler in summer and warmer in winter. The islands are of volcanic origin, but around the shores accumulations of marine sand have been washed up by the sea, which high winds have driven over the rocky surface, forming a light soil. The moist climate has clothed this with a thick vegetation, and in the valleys and lower plains a wild grass resembling rye abounds, which furnishes excellent feed for horses and sheep. On the hillsides great masses of purple lupine grow, and a thick moss-like plant is found, which bears a delicious berry, and is much used for making wine as well as for cooking purposes.

On the whole group of Aleutian Islands there were 8000 people, and on the Fur Seal Islands about 400. A few of the men from the latter had been to Sitka on Russian vessels, and two or three had been taught enough of the Russian language to allow them to act as clerks in keeping accounts with the natives, but the great body of the people had never been from home. They had no money, and trade was chiefly a barter. The houses were merely turf huts, half underground, and the only fuel was seal blubber, and seal flesh and blubber almost the only food. For lighting their huts they also used seal oil, in small dishes with floating wicks, and of course the ceilings were always sooty. The necessity for improved habitations was evident, and later when the sealing company holding the lease offered to build houses and permit the natives to live in them free of rent, no time was lost in accepting the generous proposal. Before I left St. Paul there had been built small cottages of three rooms sufficient to house every family on the island. The people were so convinced of the necessity of keeping their habitations underground for warmth that at first we could not convince them that houses could be made comfortable in any other way. We passed through various stages of unsatisfactory yieldings to this prejudice, but our last houses were the best, and were built on high ground, uncompromisingly above the earth. A skillful mechanic was brought out by the sealing company, and under his guidance the natives soon became sufficiently expert to assist very materially in building. After a row of foundations, the length of the street, had been made ready, the people were divided into three gangs, who were soon able to put up one of these houses and finish it in a day. One gang laid the sills and floors, another set up the frame and boarded the house laid the day before, and the third shingled the roof and clapboarded the walls of the one framed two days before. We introduced furniture as quickly as possible, and it was not long before the islanders were as comfortably situated as are the average employees in any manufacturing community.

It was interesting to note the difference in character crop out as the community gradually took upon itself civilization. Some were naturally prudent, and easily saved a surplus; others would be in debt at the end of the year. In 1877 a small proportion of their number, perhaps ten per cent., had invested about ten or twelve hundred dollars with the Fur Company; another ten per cent. were always in want; the remainder spent what they received. The best paid class, the ablest workers, received over four hundred dollars each for their season's work, and as they could obtain a large part of their food from the resources of the island without cost, and received their houses furnished, rent free, their needs were few. To foreign ways in clothes and fashion they inclined very naturally. The year before my coming sealing parties had brought to the island considerable quantities of ready-made clothing as an article of trade, and the men were consequently fairly well dressed; but only a small quantity of cloth suitable for dresses had been taken, and the women had not begun to make their clothing in any regular form. But in time, with some assistance, their ready adaptability made them a very well-dressed people. Before I came away the wives of those who had been saving sent their measures to Sitka with orders for silk dresses for church wear, and the young men arrayed themselves in broadcloth, wore gloves and well-blacked boots, and carried perfumed handkerchiefs.

As my time was not fully taken up with my duties, and good fortune brought to me an abiding place of unusual size for St. Paul, I seized the happy chance of making my house a meeting-place for the people, and especially for the children. Later we fitted up a school-room, which we also made a place for social entertainment, and kept the school open eight months in the year. We were greatly assisted in our school duties by illustrated books and papers sent to us; for so unvaried and barren was the scenery of the island, which was all of the world these children had ever seen, that it was well-nigh impossible for them to comprehend physical objects of the simplest nature. What a mountain might be was beyond their understanding, and the difficulty of explaining the appearance of a great forest to children who knew no vegetable growth larger than the purple lupine on their gentle slopes was greater than one can tell. It was necessary, however, to exercise the strictest censorship in our illustrated lessons, as it was difficult for all to comprehend caricature even in its simplest forms; even the most impossible pictures they believed represented facts.

I found the people living in separate families, and, as far as I could see, there was no more immorality among them than would be found in any decent civilized community. The women were modest in deportment, the children obedient and respectful to their parents, and the men always manifested a disposition to assist me in all my efforts.

In character they were mild and gentle, with the expression of settled melancholy habitual to those races which have no amusements. In this respect, however, they changed greatly as opportunity developed the merriment latent in their nature. The children when first taught to speak did so in a serious way, and the utter absence of anything like hearty laughter in a group of them always affected me strangely. It seemed as if their avenues of expression were closed to pleasure, and later, when they had learned the simple games I taught them, it was a great satisfaction to me to hear my rooms ring with their merry voices.

Charles Bryant.

9
Billions
of Treasure

BILLIONS OF TREASURE

SHALL THE MINERAL WEALTH OF ALASKA ENRICH THE GUGGENHEIM TRUST OR THE UNITED STATES TREASURY?

BY

JOHN E. LATHROP AND GEORGE KIBBE TURNER

ILLUSTRATED WITH PHOTOGRAPHS

IN 1901, prospectors for oil found a billion dollars' worth of coal in southern Alaska. They were looking, without much luck, for oil-wells, when the Indians and squaw-men took a few of them back into the glaciers and showed them the mountains of coal along Bering River — known to the local tribes for years. Nowhere else on the face of the earth has anything like these mountains ever been discovered. They are masses of tilted rock from one to four thousand feet high, cut across from one end to the other with seams, from five to fifty feet thick, of the highest class of bituminous and anthracite coal. The people having inside information on this land were naturally anxious to secure title to it away from the United States Government, which owned it.

Just how to do this was a puzzle. The United States has been giving away its coal within its main borders at a nominal price for thirty-five years, as fast as it has been applied for. But, because of pure carelessness on the part of Congress, it was impossible for it to give away this coal land in Alaska. In 1900 Congress had voted to extend the coal-land laws to this district, but no one had taken the trouble to notice that the coal-land laws of the United States only provided for giving away lands that had been surveyed by the Government. As there were no Government-surveyed coal lands in Alaska, and in all human probability would not be for decades to come, this law was useless to any one who wanted to get hold of the Government's coal there. About all that the people who wanted to appropriate these coal mountains at Bering River could do was to take possession of them, hold them physically, and wait till they could get a new law.

The Englishmen Take 200,000,000 Tons

The first people to get their hands on these lands were a syndicate of big English capitalists who in 1901 had an outfit looking for oil in this Bering River district. Being Eng-lishmen, without experience in getting together large sections of American Government lands, they went to work rather baldly. They had a company — the Pacific Oil and Coal Company. This company made a standing offer of one hundred dollars to anybody in the section who would locate a claim on these coal lands for them. Then the company took over the deeds from these people — mostly miners and company workmen — before the locators had any sign of title to the land. This is not a legal way of getting any kind of United States land. The American land laws have never proposed giving public land to corporations or rich individuals. They were intended primarily to help American citizens of small means to settle and develop the great West. It was quite a joke in the district at that time that the Englishmen were getting locations from foreigners, who, not being or intending to be American citizens, had no right to take Government lands at all. But the Englishmen were energetic. Before they got through they were in possession of some fifteen square miles of this Government coal land, with more than 200,-000,000 tons of the finest commercial coal on it. They got it cheap, too; undoubtedly $12,000 or $15,000 would cover all they paid their locators.

The Syndicate of Northwestern Millionaires

The English syndicate used local labor in getting their claims. But just after they had started, the news of the coal bonanza began to filter into Seattle — the business and news center of all Alaskan interests — and the man with the powers-of-attorney arrived in the district from the United States. This individual appears, with absolute certainty, in successful new mining districts, and appropriates all the territory he can file on in the names of an indefinite number of relatives and acquaintances in the home country. No character in mining districts is regarded with a more nervous and eager hatred than this power-of-attorney "stampeder." But, being a creature of our

141

mining laws, his rights are fully protected by our Government.

After the Englishmen, the next group to take a slice of this Bering River coal find was a syndicate of millionaires from Washington and Idaho, operating through a typical power-of-attorney "stampeder" named Clarence Cunningham, from Wallace, Idaho, in the Coeur d'Alêne silver- and lead-mining district. These men were largely bankers, mining operators, and speculators. They were not all millionaires, but they were nearly all rich men, and the group of thirty-three was undoubtedly worth over $20,000,000. This was probably the most remarkable syndicate that has ever filed on United States coal lands. The almost invariable practice of capitalists, in securing lands of this kind, is to take them over from other locators. In this way there is no danger of prosecution for fraud and perjury. But this syndicate of Western millionaires took the chance of filing on this Bering field in their own names. They got together eight square miles of coal lands. Not less than 90,000,000 tons of high-class commercial coal can be taken out of this; and probably a great deal more. It cost perhaps $15,000 to get settled on it.

The Politicians Get the Best

But probably the best territory of all was taken up by a group that came after these two. This, in view of its development, may be called the politicians' syndicate. It was engineered, through a power-of-attorney man named M. A. Green, by Harry White. White was at one time mayor of Seattle, but resigned very suddenly, for reasons that have never entirely been made public. He did not retire from practical politics, however, and was one of the most prominent workers in the West for the Republican party during the last presidential campaign. White's political acquaintance extends throughout the entire Pacific Coast, and Republican politicians and office-holders of both local and national prominence appear in his syndicate. Altogether, this political group acquired fifteen or eighteen square miles of territory. The coal on this is anthracite, the finest quality in the district; there is not less than 200,000,000 tons of it; and probably a great deal more.

The Bartenders and Miscellaneous Groups

But by the time these last people filed — in 1903, 1904, and 1905 — it was a general free-for-all race for mining promoters all over the United States to plaster the map of this Bering River coal district with powers-of-attorney from anybody they could get hold of. These

documents went forward to Alaska from all sections, from the Pacific Coast to Washington, D. C., literally by the hundreds. But the center of the speculation was still Seattle — the natural center of all Alaskan interests, and the present capital of the get-rich-quick belt of this continent. No class of society was exempt from taking a chance at these Government coal lands. It was the greatest project to get something for nothing from the United States Government that had ever been proposed in Seattle.

There was one interesting group — the Christopher-Simmonds — made up quite largely of bartenders, theatrical scene-shifters, and men with similar vocations in life. Bartenders, between selling drinks, signed documents they didn't understand, just to "be a good feller"; and got and expected nothing from it. Another prominent syndicate, headed by a former Y. M. C. A. secretary, formed a company and sold stock by mail before it had title to the land at all. It got together five thousand stockholders. Another stock-selling concern operated out of Portland, Oregon, under the management of a bank officer and an owner of the leading newspaper. One "stampeder," with a strong sense of family obligation, tied up more than half of his three square miles of claims in the family name.

Chicago and Detroit Take Another Great Field

In two or three years this Bering River coal field was practically covered by locators. It lies between glaciers, and its boundaries are very definitely marked out. In the meanwhile, the power-of-attorney men were getting to work on a second coal field of about the same size, about two hundred miles up the coast, at Matanuska River. There were two big groups concerned there — one connected with the projected Alaskan Central Railroad, where locators were very largely in the employ of the road in connection with its Chicago headquarters, in positions from stenographers to attorneys. These generally expected to get nothing personally from the claims. The other aggregation — the largest of the entire crowd of syndicates looking for Government coal lands — was the Michigan-Alaska Development Company. There were 175 claimants in this — about a quarter of them women, and nearly all from Detroit, Michigan; practically all from there, in fact, except the steam-laundrymen — that is, the people gathered up by one of its three active promoters, who just before had been a traveling salesman for steam-laundry supplies, and who put a lot of steam-laundrymen from all over the country into this opportunity.

There were, finally, about 950 of these power-of-attorney claimants who were lined up to get these coal-mines on the two Alaska fields from the United States. About 600 of them held the coal mountains at Bering River. Ninety-five per cent of them had never seen the coal-mines; not more than ten per cent had ever been in Alaska, and most of this ten per cent were the power-of-attorney "stampeders." Over 100 of the prospective coal-miners were women. Altogether they had filed upon about a billion and a half dollars' worth of commercial coal, and a billion dollars' worth of this was in the Bering River district. They were in a very tantalizing position. They had their hands on it, but it wasn't worth one cent to them till they could get it away from the Government. They were in much the same position as the waiting heirs in a great contested will case. But the stakes in the famous will controversies of history were trifling affairs compared to this. Each one of these claimants was asking for shares of the public land whose contents were worth from $500,000 to $1,500,000 apiece.

The Most Wonderful Coal District on Earth

Now, these people were fighting for the most wonderful coal district in the world. All kinds of experts, private and Government, have looked it over; and the more it is examined, the better it looks. Here are certain and definite things about it: It is the only first-class bituminous and anthracite coal on the Pacific Coast; from the Bering River district railroads can be built to the sea, not more than one hundred and ten miles long, over perfectly level country; and, according to a published statement by Alfred H. Brooks, head of the Government's geological survey work in Alaska, there are six billion tons of it in both fields — more than one and a half times all the coal that has ever been taken out of Pennsylvania. Two thirds of this has been filed upon by these claimants—that is, as much coal as has so far come from the mines of Pennsylvania. Mr. Brooks estimates it to be worth a dollar a ton as it lies; that is, he estimates the coal in the two fields at six billion dollars.

Andrew Kennedy, the coal expert of the Land Office, with an experience of twenty-five years as a practical coal-miner, thinks this estimate of value too high for the Bering River field, which he examined carefully last summer. The amount of coal is there; the field will produce two billion tons of coal for sale, he says. But a dollar a ton is a good deal of money to make

mining coal. Besides, labor is rather high in Alaska. And this Bering River coal is very friable. It will produce fifty per cent fine coal, which sells cheap. Everything considered, it ought to give a mining profit of fifty cents a ton. That would put the Bering River coal at a billion dollars. That much can be relied upon. At the same rate, the part of the Matanuska coal field that has been taken up by these claimants would figure half a billion more.

A billion and a half is something of a prize to fight for. It is half the currency now in circulation in the United States; it is considerably more than the whole national debt. What this billion and a half dollars' worth of Alaskan coal has done in the last five years — the men it has bought, directly and indirectly; the big reputations it has smirched; the policies it has changed — makes the greatest business and political story in America to-day. In the first place, it is the greatest single prize ever played for in this country. Incidentally, it threatens to involve a political administration and the whole trend of future national policies.

Alaska Protests Against Power-of-Attorney Man

Now, the first thing that was necessary was to force new coal laws for Alaska. Up to this time it had been almost impossible to secure legislation for Alaska. The residents of the district were unable to get the attention of Congress. For years it was impossible to get a safe title to farm-land; the mining laws were as bad as possible. In 1903 a committee of the United States Senate made a very careful investigation of the needs of that country, holding hearings all the way across it. One of their chief recommendations was for a correction of the abuse of the location of claims in mining districts by powers of attorney.

"From the time the committee reached Dawson," says their report, "at every place they afterward stopped on the Yukon, at St. Michaels and at Nome, almost every person they came on contact with denounced the abuses which are practised in the location of claims under power-of-attorney by people outside the district."

Virtually no results came from the report of this committee. Congress did not find time for Alaskan legislation. In the spring of 1904, however, when the variegated regiment of power-of-attorney coal claimants — bankers, politicians, stenographers, housewives, and bartenders — went after Alaskan legislation, they got it at once. They went at it right. From this time on the Cunningham group took the lead, naturally. They were millionaires, captains of industry, and men of large political influence. They broke the way for the other groups, financially and politically.

"Have Agreed with Mr. W. B. Heyburn"

The general business management of this syndicate was in the hands of its promoter, Clarence Cunningham. He kept a ledger, cash-book, and a careful and detailed journal of its accounts. In the journal, under date of September 19, 1903, this memorandum appears:

"Have agreed with Mr. W. B. Heyburn in consideration for his services as attorney to carry him for one claim of 160 acres in the coal, free of cost to him, and he agrees to do all our legal work in procuring titles, etc., free of expense to us."

This arrangement would bring high compensation to Mr. Heyburn, if the Cunningham claims went through. From the present estimate of the value of the coal in this property, each claim would have a value of $1,500,000 in commercial coal. In 1903 it was perfectly clear that each share would be of great value. It would certainly constitute a great fee, demanding valuable service. In September, 1903, Mr. Heyburn was a United States Senator, having been elected by the Idaho legislature eight months before.

The basic unit in political or legislative oratory concerning Alaska is the "hardy prospector." Everything is done in his name. In the spring of 1904 Mr. Heyburn introduced in the Senate, for the benefit of the "hardy prospector of Alaska," the Alaska coal land bill of April 28, 1904. This broke the circle in which the law of 1900 had placed the Government's coal in that district, and allowed it to be taken over by persons who had surveyed it at their own expense. It was thought at the time that it placed the Alaska coal lands upon exactly the same footing as the Government coal lands in the body of this country.

Mr. Ballinger Describes a National Scandal

The coal-land laws of the United States were passed in 1873. Under modern conditions, they virtually compel everybody taking coal from the Government to commit perjury and fraud. Coal-mining to-day is invariably done by large corporations operating great tracts of land. By this law the Government can turn over its coal only to individuals or small associations. The thing is very simple. As all coal lands taken from the United States are destined to be mined by large corporations,

and as the persons taking them at first hand from the Government must swear that they are for their own use, practically all persons taking them over must, and do, commit actual or virtual perjury. The general principle of the law is this: Every citizen or prospective citizen of the United States is entitled to take one 160-acre tract of coal land at a nominal price, and no more. No association or company of men can take more than 640 acres of this land — a privilege allowed to four or more men who have spent $5,000 in improvements on this square mile of land.

Up to 1904 and 1905 it was the simple and usual process for the corporations of the West to secure their coal from individual claimants. Richard A. Ballinger, the present Secretary of the Interior, in his report as Land Commissioner in 1907, described this process, in sharp and ringing language, as a national scandal.

"In the securing of these lands," he said, "the unscrupulous have not hesitated to resort to perjury and fraud, carrying their schemes of fraud and corruption to such an extent as to amount to national scandal. . . . These lands have almost uniformly passed into the hands of speculators or large combinations, controlling the output or the transportation, so that the consumer is at the mercy of both in the greater part of the West."

Mr. Ballinger in his statement scores the custom of taking over the coal lands in the West rather savagely. But at this time it had become so common that it was practically an unconscious habit. The claimants for the Alaskan coal certainly expected to use this standard method, under the law of 1904.

New Affidavits from Senator Heyburn's Office

Legislative carelessness, however, again caused delay. It was thought that at least it would be possible, under this 1904 Alaska law, for four individuals legally to combine to hold 640 acres, as under the law of 1873 for the United States. Mr. Heyburn's bill, however, was so worded as to make this questionable. In view of this, Mr. Heyburn sent a long telegram from his home office at Wallace, Idaho, to the Land Office at Washington on October 8, 1904, to inquire, for the Cunningham claimants, whether four locators could join in taking 640 acres under this bill, as under the general coal land act of 1873.

Up to this time the Cunningham claimants had spent a considerable sum of money in developing their claims as a whole. Upon the receipt of an adverse ruling against this association of claimants under the Alaskan law,

J. P. Gray, Mr. Heyburn's associate in his law office at Wallace, made out affidavits for the Cunningham claimants, by which they refiled upon the land as individuals.

Senator Mitchell of Oregon Found Guilty

At the time there was every reason to expect that — after the filing of these affidavits — the Alaskan coal claimants would get their land by swearing what the law required, without further difficulty. Then, without the slightest warning, the Government began to turn its attention to

DANIEL GUGGENHEIM
HEAD OF THE AMERICAN SMELTING AND
REFINING COMPANY

the land frauds of the Northwest. Toward the end of 1904 John H. Mitchell, of Oregon, was indicted for being a party to these frauds while a Senator of the United States, under the following United States statute:

No Senator, Representative, or Delegate, after his election and during his continuance in office, and no head of a department, or other officer or clerk in the employ of the Government, shall receive or agree to receive any compensation whatever, directly or indirectly, for any services rendered, or to be rendered, to any person, either by himself or another, in relation to any proceeding, contract, claim, controversy, charge, accusation, arrest, or other matter or thing in which the United States is a party, or directly or indirectly interested, before any department, court martial, bureau, officer, or any civil, military, or naval commission whatever. Every person offending against this section shall be deemed guilty of a misdemeanor, and shall be imprisoned not more than two years, and fined not more than $10,000, and shall, moreover, by conviction therefor, be rendered forever thereafter incapable of holding

any office of honor, trust, or profit under the Government of the United States.

Senator Heyburn Writes a Letter

Senator Mitchell was sentenced to prison, under this statute, for his work for persons engaged in securing land from the United States Government, in the summer of 1905. On October 20, 1905, Senator Heyburn wrote the following letter to Clarence Cunningham:

WALLACE, IDAHO.
October 20, 1905,
CLARENCE CUNNINGHAM, Esq.,
Seattle, Washington.

DEAR SIR: On frequent occasions I have stated to you that I did not desire to be interested in the coal lands in Alaska, which you are proceeding to locate and patent. As I have already informed you, I do not desire to participate in, or be interested in any manner, directly or indirectly, in acquiring public lands. I prefer during my official career to be absolutely free and clear from any possible interest in the subject matter of legislation.

Whatever services I may perform properly within my duty as a public official for yourself or any other constituent, I shall cheerfully perform, but not for any consideration, directly or indirectly.

In order that there may be no mistake about this, I desire to say that I do not desire any interests to be carried for me on my account with a view to any present or future profit to myself.

If I can be of service to you within the proper line of my duty, I shall be glad to do so.

With kind regards and best wishes for your enterprise and success, I am,

Sincerely yours,
W. B. HEYBURN.

This letter was written two years and one month after the record in Clarence Cunningham's journal of Mr. Heyburn's employment. Immediately after it was received, items of cash payments for legal services appear for the first time in this journal.

Roosevelt Holds Up All Coal Claims

The agitation against the taking over of Government lands in 1905 and 1906 made it very difficult for the Alaskan coal claimants to make progress. The millionaire Cunningham syndicate went ahead and spent money on their claims, however. A coal expert, H. L. Hawkins, reported that they could take out 63,000,000 tons of coal from one tunnel. Clarence Cunningham wrote, in transmitting this report to his claim-holders: "I have no doubt the ground not reported on will contain as much more." Both these statements referred alone to the coal lying in the mountain, and took no account of the amount lying below the surface of the valleys, which would add greatly to the total. The expert reported also that a railroad to the coast would be feasible and cheap. All this was encouraging.

But in 1906 the Government began attacking the methods of taking over coal lands in Colorado, Wyoming, and the West generally, which have been characterized in Mr. Ballinger's report. Then suddenly, in the fall of 1906, President Roosevelt withdrew all right to take over coal lands in the United States, on the ground that it was time to make a general revision of the coal-land laws. On November 12, 1906, his order went out holding up all Alaskan coal lands from claimants. The billion-and-a-half-dollar Alaska claims were stopped short.

It was now more than two years since the passage of the Alaskan coal-land act of April 28, 1904, and considerably more than that since many of the claims had been started. The outlook was discouraging. The taking and holding of the coal rights involved considerable expense, and some of the speculative coal-land syndicates had not any great financial backing. By a natural and inevitable process, the coal lands of the Bering River district were beginning to drift toward the ownership of the great Guggenheim syndicate, which was gaining control of Alaska.

The Guggenheim Mining Monopoly

The Guggenheim family had by that time already become — with possibly one exception — the greatest firm of Hebrew financiers in America. Meyer Guggenheim, a Swiss Jew, began his career in Philadelphia, in 1847, as a peddler of glue and shoe-blacking, and later of lace. Through continued success, he be-

came a large lace merchant. In the early eighties he acquired an investment in a Colorado mine, and by the late eighties he and his seven sons had built up a great business in smelting silver and lead ores in that State. By their great business acumen, and the manipulation of railroad privileges, they soon secured a practical monopoly of the smelting business, and, through this, almost absolute control of the product of lead-silver ores throughout the West — the greatest source of these ores in the world. From this they advanced to large control of mining generally, more particularly of copper-mining. By a system of majority control, originating largely with the American Smelting and Refining Company, they built up a pyramid of corporations, with three or four hundred million dollars of capital, all of which are controlled by them. From the West they advanced into Alaska.

Great Syndicates Control New Countries

The control of all newly exploited countries, especially mining countries, in the last twenty years has come inevitably into the hands of great syndicates. For the last ten years, and especially in the last five, the control of Alaska has been drifting steadily into the hands of these Guggenheims — exactly as the diamond and gold fields of South Africa came into the hands of the great diamond speculators, Alfred Beit, Barney Barnato, and their associates. At the present time the Guggenheims' final acquirement of the district seems inevitable. They started there in a small way nearly ten years ago, in the Nome district, through the Northwestern Commercial Company. They now hold the great part of the famous gold district in the Klondike, with their $17,000,000 Yukon Gold Company; and they have a practical control of the ocean transportation to the district. In all, their companies exploiting Alaska represent capital aggregating forty or fifty million dollars. As in the West, they pay especial attention to the question of control of transportation, which is the key to the control of all mining business.

In 1905 the Guggenheims secured control of the Bonanza Copper Mine in southern Alaska. This mine contains, running to the surface of the ground, a great body of ore from five to fifteen times as rich as the ore in the big copper-mines of the United States. The district in which it lies is believed by the experts who have examined it to contain the richest and greatest deposits of copper in the known world. The trouble with it is simply the inconceivable difficulty of ordinary transportation across the mud and snow of Alaska.

The cost of transporting freight to or from this section runs from thirty cents to a dollar a pound. With copper worth from twelve to twenty cents a pound, a mine of solid copper would now be valueless in that country. The Guggenheims, on buying the Bonanza Mine, started at once to control transportation into the upper district.

Defense by Legislation and Manslaughter

The only practical gateway through the mountains from the coast into this section is the deep-cut valley of the Copper River. The Guggenheims, having bought the Bonanza Mine, in 1905 started immediately to occupy the Copper River valley with a railroad. For four years their possession of it has been defended by every method, from legislation in Congress — where they are represented by one of the family, Senator Simon Guggenheim, of Colorado — to manslaughter.

On July 2, 1907, two men were killed, and nine wounded in their successful fight for the right of way out of the harbor of Catalla.

Copyright. Harris and Ewing

RICHARD A. BALLINGER
SECRETARY OF THE INTERIOR

On September 25 of the same year a desperado named Edward Hasey, employed by an agent of their railroad, and one of a party armed with Winchester rifles by this agent, shot and killed one and badly wounded two others of a party of unarmed workmen who were attempting to occupy with another railroad a mountain pass that had been abandoned by the Guggenheims. Great masses of capital will not be denied. The Guggenheims now have, and will continue to have, in all human probability, the only railroad through the Copper River. In this way they have successfully sealed up the great copper district of Alaska.

The interests that control the transportation of the district will eventually obtain their choice of the mines at reasonable prices.

The Guggenheims Begin to Control the Coal

The Guggenheims had scarcely begun their fight for the copper field when their eyes fell upon the billion-dollar coal field of Bering River. The last and greatest contestant immediately came into the great fight. By 1905 the Guggenheims' agent was negotiating to secure some option upon the Christopher group of claims, although it was clear that any option would itself destroy whatever rights there were. By the fall of 1906 they threw away $200,000 or $300,000, which they had expended on a more northerly ocean terminus, and came south to Catalla, locating on the coast twenty-five miles from the Bering River field. The control of this coal field by a railroad depends upon the railway's control of a practical harbor. There is just one such harbor there, experience has now shown — that at Cordova. The Guggenheims started to build at Catalla.

But there were bigger interests concerned in these coal fields than in the copper-mines. The English syndicate, with its claims on 200,000,000 tons of coal, decided to secure a railroad of its own. M. J. Heney, one of these claimants, in the winter of 1906 made a sudden survey, seized a terminus on Cordova Bay, and started building a railroad. The president of the new railroad company was S. H. Graves, president of the Yukon White Pass road, four hundred miles down the coast, for which Mr. Heney had been contractor. The

Cordova road was started with the open purpose of carrying out the English syndicate's coal. Its head, when it was started, naïvely wrote to the authorities at Washington that he and his associates had acquired "thousands and thousands of acres of coal lands" at Bering River.

This English syndicate was too strong to legislate or shoot out of its right of way. In the summer of 1907 the Guggenheims found that their artificial harbor at Catalla was not a success. The great waves, plunging across the sea from the Sandwich Islands, were throwing down its breakwater. The Guggenheims at once threw away a million-dollar investment at Catalla, hurried into Cordova, and bought control of the road of the Englishmen. Mr. Heney is now the contractor for the Guggenheims' Copper River and Northwestern Railroad; E. C. Hawkins, formerly with the White Pass Road, its engineer; and S. H. Graves an associate in the enterprise.

A " Proposal" to Daniel Guggenheim

By this deal in 1907 the Guggenheims could naturally feel that they had the mountains of coal at Bering River cornered in very much the same way as the copper deposits up the Copper River. Whatever rights there were in the "thousands and thousands" of acres controlled by the Englishmen's railroad had come into their hands. They were well along with the negotiations with the Christopher group.

On July 20, 1907, A. B. Campbell, Clarence Cunningham, and M. C. Moore, ex-Governor of Washington, acting as representatives for the Cunningham claimants, signed and delivered to Daniel Guggenheim, the head of the American Smelting and Refining Company, a "representation and proposal" to form a coal company with $5,000,000 capital, give Guggenheim half of the stock on his payment of $250,000 working capital into the company's treasury, and to sell to his railroad the company's output of coal at $1.75 a ton for its own use and $2.25 a ton for general sale. This document recites that:

"A meeting of said entrymen was recently held at the city of Spokane, in which twenty-five out of the thirty-three participated. At said meeting a resolution was unanimously passed authorizing said committee, or a majority of them, to enter into negotiations with parties with a view to the equipment, development, and operation of the consolidated property, and the sale of its product.

"Acting for themselves and as such committee representing their associates, under such resolution, they submit to Mr. Guggenheim, for his consideration, the following proposal."

Members and lawyers for the Cunningham claimants deny that this document is an option. Whatever it is, the Guggenheims still have it in their possession, and the long journal of Clarence Cunningham ends abruptly in September, 1907, with a detailed account of the receipt of some three thousand dollars from Daniel Guggenheim, as payment for the examination of the property called for in the claimants' signed proposal.

It is interesting to note, as a practical illustration of the grip of the Guggenheims on this district, that by this proposal they secure a full half interest in this property without payment, excepting that of $250,000 working capital into its treasury.

Results of the Guggenheim Connection

By December, 1907, the line of the forces moving on these Bering River coal deposits was reinforced by the Guggenheims. They may have had no definite arrangements to secure more than the claims on 300,000,000 or 400,000,000 tons of coal. But the logic of the situation was absolute. A great variety of dead or unborn railroad lines to the coast are sketched in engineers' maps of the district; but they will never go any farther than across the surface of these maps. With possession of the only feasible harbor, that at Cordova, and with their Copper River Railroad already built over a third of the district to the fields, the Guggenheims hold an absolute key to transportation.

Government Land Agents Charge Fraud

As a result of the investigation of the land frauds in the Northwest in 1904 and 1905, there was built up in the United States Land Office a force of special agents to inquire into the question of the validity of claims for Government land, which, for the first time, was both adequate in size and not in collusion with the persons engaged in securing land. In 1905 M. S. Duffield, a resident of Ely, Nevada, wrote a letter to the Land Office, claiming that the Alaska coal lands were being taken up fraudulently. A special service agent, H. K. Love, was detailed to investigate on the ground, and on October 6, 1905, reported a bewildering array of fraudulent schemes that were being practised by the claimants there. The matter then lay dormant in the Land Office until 1907. In June, 1907, a second agent, Horace T. Jones, was detailed to make a further investigation of the facts in the case. He interviewed a large number of persons in Seattle and in the

Pacific Coast States who had knowledge of or interest in the Alaska coal claims. In August he strongly advised a thorough investigation of the matter by a competent man. Among the suspicious claims to which he called especial attention in his report were those of the Cunningham, Christopher, Simmonds, Doughton, and English syndicate groups.

About a week before this report was received, the Land Department had a short report from H. K. Love, the first agent who had looked into the matter. In this he did not retract the detailed charges he had made before, but merely gave a general recommendation that the claims for the coal be allowed by the Land Office. Love had at this time become an active candidate for appointment by the President as marshal in Alaska.

A Land Office from Seattle

When the reports of these men were made, the Land Office was in the hands of men excellently equipped to give intelligent attention to the questions raised; for it was under the management of Seattle men, and the knowledge of this whole matter focussed in Seattle. Richard A. Ballinger, a successful corporation attorney, a former State judge, and ex-mayor of Seattle, was Land Commissioner for the year March, 1907, to March, 1908. His assistant was Fred Dennett, until that time a special service man, who for the previous two years had been stationed in Seattle; Mr. Ballinger's nephew, "Jack" Ballinger, was his confidential secretary. Commissioner Ballinger early directed his attention to the Alaska coal matter. While the investigation of Jones and Love in Seattle was going on, he indicated very definite opinions on the question. These are described by Jones in his letter turning over the work of investigating the Alaska coal claims to another special agent later in the year.

"About this time" (the summer of 1907), he writes, "I met H. K. Love, and I took him to Judge Ballinger's office [in Seattle] and introduced him to the Judge. He and Love seemed to think it would not be right to disturb the title to any of these lands, upon which large sums of money had been spent and various small investors had risked their money. Judge Ballinger then said that if the law is so construed as to prevent a number of men, with the inten-

W. B. HEYBURN
UNITED STATES SENATOR FROM IDAHO

tion, in good faith, of developing this Alaska coal land, from acquiring title to more than 640 acres in cases of corporations or companies that had expended five thousand dollars in improvements, or 160 in cases of ordinary associations of men, he was going to see what Congress could do about it. He said I should get together the laws relating to coal lands in Alaska (see my report on said lands), so as to enable him to speak intelligently before Congress."

Mr. Ballinger in Doubt

Jones' letter proceeds: "Munday [the manager of the English syndicate], Love, and I had a conference with Judge Ballinger in the Judge's office, and Munday made a plain statement of what he intended to do. He said in so many words that he intended to get as much coal land as possible. He admitted that he had other people file on lands for him, and in one or two instances, if I remember correctly, he had supplied the money himself. He said he wanted to go about this thing the proper way, and did not want to get anything illegally, and that he did not think he was getting anything illegally.

"I said that if the procurement of persons who did not have the money to make the payments required by law, and whose rights were merely being used by Munday and his associates for their own gain, was proceeding in a legal manner, then my knowledge of the spirit of all land law was very defective, as I supposed that one could not barter away his rights or give another an interest therein before getting title to the land.

"The Judge was asked by Munday to say whether or not his scheme for getting these lands was legal, but the Judge refused to commit himself."

In December, 1907, Commissioner Ballinger, in his annual report, made his savage attack, already quoted, upon the methods used by the coal speculators and railroads of the West in securing coal. In the same month he decided to investigate further the validity of the similar transactions in the Alaska coal fields. He called in Louis R. Glavis, the chief of the field division of the special agent service, with headquarters at Seattle, and put the whole matter in his hands, saying that Love, being a candidate for the appointment as marshal, was not in a position to make an investigation of these claims. On December 28 he gave his final instructions to Glavis in Washington. Glavis started for Seattle.

What Coal Claimants Must Do

In the meanwhile, the Cunningham claimants, being men of large interests, were restive at the delay that they were meeting in securing their lands. They had pushed their affairs up to the very last action allowed by the Government, showing great energy and acumen in so doing. When President Roosevelt, in November, 1906, had stopped all action in public coal lands, the other groups of claimants were discouraged. But these men kept right on. There are two main actions that must be taken by coal claimants, according to law, each having two parts. The first is the "location and filing" of a claim; the second the "purchase and entry" of the land. The Attorney-General of the United States has defined these terms as follows:

Under the coal-land law, " location," " claims," " purchase," and " entry " have acquired well-defined meanings. A " location " is made by going upon coal land, opening and developing one or more coal-mines thereon, and taking possession of the land. The locator's " claim " is thus initiated. It may be preserved by giving the notice required by law. The " purchase " and " entry " are made at the time of final proof and payment, which in Alaska may be four years after the location is made.

The Cunninghams and the Juneau Land Office

Now, after the Heyburn law of April 28, 1904, and before the President's message stopping all action in Alaska coal lands in November, 1906, virtually all the Alaskan coal claimants had taken the first action required; that is, they had located claims under the new law. After that there seemed, to many of the groups, to be nothing to do. The Cunningham group, however, had associated with themselves, as one of their members, Ignatius Mullen, a young man of small means, but whose father was P. M. Mullen, the Government's receiver at the Land Office for Alaska at Juneau. According to Clarence Cunningham's journal, this young man paid but half the amount due when he took his claim; but Mr. Cunningham adds, "he will pay balance at any time." It was also stated, in the reports of the agents Love and Jones, that his father, the Land Office receiver, said that he himself had advanced the money paid on Ignatius Mullen's claim. This, however, was afterward denied by Mr. Mullen.

In February, 1907, while it was generally believed that the Government would take no money in payment for Alaska coal lands because of President Roosevelt's order, the Cunningham claimants tendered payment for their claims to P. M. Mullen, land receiver at Juneau, with whom they had this close relation, and through him got a special ruling from the Land Office at Washington. Their contention that they could pay their purchase money was right. The Land Office ruled that, while no more coal could be filed upon in Alaska, those who had filed in good faith upon land before the order of November, 1906, could proceed to make "purchase" and "entry" of the land.

Ex-Governor Moore Calls on Mr. Ballinger

The members of the Cunningham group finally swore they made their entries in good faith for their individual benefit; paid in their ten dollars an acre to the Land Office; and received their receipts. One final document remained to be obtained from the Government, the "patent" to the land. During all the summer and fall, while the claims of the Cunningham and other groups were being examined for fraud, these large business men had been held back from completing their enterprise. Finally, in the last of December, 1907, ex-Governor M. C. Moore, of Walla-Walla, one of the claimants, called upon Mr. Ballinger at Washington to see what could be done to expedite matters.

Agent Glavis had been instructed on December 28 to investigate all the Alaska coal cases

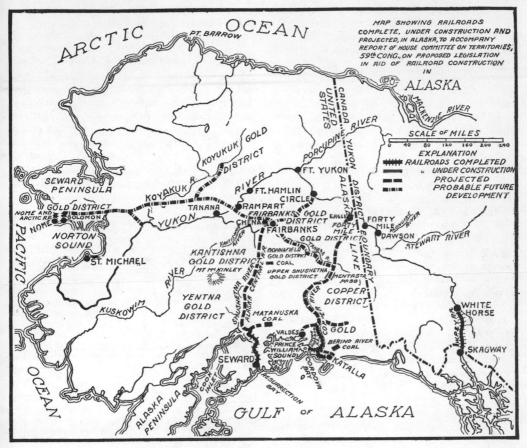

MINERAL LANDS AND RAILROADS OF ALASKA

for fraud. On January 4 a telegram, signed by Commissioner Ballinger, was sent to the discredited agent Love in Alaska, asking him to send the plats of the Cunningham claims required for issuing "patent," the last approval still required from the Government for these claims. On January 7 Assistant Commissioner Dennett notified Glavis that the Cunningham claims had been approved for patent on the Love report of August. Glavis, having some knowledge of the evidence against these claims, protested at once by telegram and letter. Immediately after, the order to "clear-list" the Cunningham claims for "patent" was revoked by the Land Office. The incident was closed and the Cunningham claims were still as far from "patent" as before. The attention of the claimants of all the groups was now centered on securing legislation from Congress.

Congressmen and Governors Claimants

These claimants for Alaska coal were now in a much stronger position to secure favorable legislation from Congress than they had been when the law of 1904 was given them. In the Senate, the friendship of Senators Heyburn and Guggenheim could be counted on.

In the group of politicians managed by Harry White were now included Congressman James McLachlan, and a second Republican Congressman for California; also James N. Gillett, the Republican Governor of California, with his wife. Another Congressman from farther East took an interest in this group of claims at about the time the Alaska coal-land legislation was pending in the spring of 1908. These persons did not appear as original claimants, but took assignments from them. Another Republican Governor, Fred M. Warner of Michigan, had secured an interest in the Michigan-Alaska Development Company. Mr. White was in Washington, looking after his affairs there.

There were two very clear needs for legislation by the Alaska coal claimants in the winter of 1908. The first was the right to wipe off their slate entirely, and secure the ability to take this land regardless of any act committed in the past. The revelations made by the investigations of their conduct up to this time made this absolutely necessary. Then, having been absolved by Congress, they desired a law that would allow their syndicate to take as much coal land as they could get. It was finally decided to ask for the right to take four square miles — that is, four times as much as could then, or can now, be taken under the coal laws for the body of the United States. Three of these bills were introduced. All of them agreed in this feature of the amount of coal to be allowed.

In the other feature these bills differed. All were curative measures, that is, intended to a greater or less degree to relieve the claimants for coal from their having broken the coal laws as they had existed. The fact that they had done this was admitted by all, but excused by the regulation argument that they were "hardy Alaska prospectors" who did not know any better. Of these bills, the one introduced by Frank W. Mondell, Chairman of the House Committee on Public Lands, forgave the "hardy prospector" for having formed companies — after he had found and located his lands — in order to pay for the expense of the survey required before he could make final "entry," but insisted that the first "location" be a valid one.

Heyburn and Ballinger Appear

The two other bills, however, had not this shortcoming, from the claimants' standpoint. Under their provisions Alaska coal claimants, no matter what they had done in the past, could find a way to locate or re-locate their holdings in blocks of four square miles. Senator Heyburn of Idaho introduced one of these bills; the second was introduced by Delegate Cale of Alaska. The Cale bill conformed to Commissioner Ballinger's idea of legislation on the subject. One of his last acts as head of the Land Office was to appear before the House Committee on Public Lands and warmly advocate it.

James R. Garfield, then Secretary of the Interior, agreed with the position taken by Mr. Mondell, that it was not necessary for the "hardy prospector" of Alaska to form a stock company before finding coal and notifying the Government that he had done so. He was willing to have the bill absolve them for having formed associations or companies to get money to pay for surveying the land, after they had located it. After something of a struggle, this view prevailed, and the Heyburn bill was amended so as to make it impossible for persons who had first located the coal land by "dummy entrymen," hired locators, or as

corporations or associations, to get title to them. There was an anti-trust provision in the bill, which it is believed could be easily evaded.

How Much Should the Government Grant?

Up to this time the question of the amount and value of coal to be turned over to the coal claimants in four square miles of the Alaska land does not seem to have engaged serious attention anywhere. It remained for William B. Wilson, from the great coal-mining State of Pennsylvania, to raise this point, when the bill came up on the floor of the House of Representatives on May 25, 1908. The debate over Mr. Wilson's point was as follows:

MR. WILSON of Pennsylvania: Has the [Public Lands] Committee any information as to the numbers of veins of coal there are on these lands?

MR. ROBINSON (speaking for the Committee): No.

MR. WILSON of Pennsylvania: Then how does the gentleman arrive at the conclusion or the determination as to what the limitation should be on the amount of land involved [to be granted to claimants] if the Committee has no means of estimating the amount of coal?

MR. ROBINSON: The only answer to this question is that some arbitrary limitation must be fixed, but it is thought that, by past experience in the operation of coal-mines in the United States, where surveys indicate that the character of coal is similar to that in Alaska, the area of 2,560 acres would be a fair and reasonable limitation.

MR. WILSON of Pennsylvania: Two thousand five hundred and sixty acres of land, with several veins of coal on it from four feet in thickness upward, would produce an enormous amount of coal. Coal usually produces, after allowing for the waste, about 1,000 tons per foot in thickness per acre. If you have a four-foot vein on your acreage of 2,560 acres, you would have over 10,000,000 tons of coal on that acreage alone. If you have several veins of coal, some of them thicker than that, it runs up to an enormous tonnage.

Single Grants Worth Tens of Millions

The basis of 1,000 tons per foot an acre production, quoted by Mr. Wilson, is a matter of primary, commonplace knowledge to all coal-miners. In these Bering River Alaska fields there are veins of the highest-class coal that run fifty feet in thickness; therefore, acres that will produce 50,000 tons of commercial coal. At the Government expert's allowance of fifty cents a ton as it lies, such an acre is worth $25,000. The main vein on the Cunningham claims, the most carefully experted property in the district, is twenty-four feet wide, worth $12,000 an acre, on a basis of fifty cents a ton, without counting the other veins on the land where it appears. The price charged by the Government for this land to the claimants is ten dollars an acre. A tract of 2,560 acres of the Cunningham property would produce at east 45,000,000 tons, worth $22,500,000. The Government price to the claimants, under these former liberal Alaska coal laws, would be $25,600. The coal on it, in other words, will yield a profit, when developed, approximately one thousand times what the Government sells it for.

Mr. Wilson continued his questions as follows:

Mr. Wilson of Pennsylvania: Does the gentleman not think we ought to have some information as to the value of those lands before we determine the limit [of grant]?

Mr. Robinson: I will state to the gentleman that that is a new country. Men who go there, and take their picks on their shoulders, and go into that wild country, take the chances that all explorers take, and you cannot get that information until somebody has gone there and started to develop.

Mr. Humphrey of (Seattle) Washington: And surveyed it.

For the "Hardy Prospector of Alaska"

With the appearance of the phantom form of the "hardy prospector of Alaska" Mr. Wilson of Pennsylvania persisted no further, and his question remained unanswered. Immediately afterward there were cries of "vote," and the Alaska Coal Bill of 1908 passed the House by 147 to 38. Among those voting for the bill was Congressman McLachlan of California, a claim-holder. The other California Congressman interested was recorded as not voting. The bill became a law three days later, May 28, 1908.

It was no longer necessary now for Alaska coal claimants to show — as all other claimants in the United States must do — that they had intended, up to the time of the final "entry" of the land, to take it for their own use. All that was necessary was to prove that they intended to take it for their individual use, when they found it and drove four stakes at its four corners. This permission to abrogate the coal law in part was secured simply by the continued representation that the "hardy prospector of Alaska" was interested in the bill, when, as a matter of fact, not five per cent of those interested in the coal claims had ever seen the mines. The bill meant a gain in the campaign of the coal claimants, but not nearly so much as was hoped. In most instances, it would be difficult to prove that the coal lands were even located in good faith in the interest of the locator. Having lost their fight to secure from Congress legislation that would validate all claims in Alaska regardless of what had been done before, the coal claimants were now primarily interested in one thing — a loose interpretation of the Alaska coal law.

The Two Ballingers, Land Attorneys

In March, 1908, Mr. Ballinger retired from the office of Land Commissioner, and returned to his private practice in Seattle. As the headquarters of the great majority of the Alaska coal enterprises were in that city, he was at once in demand among them as an attorney to further their claims. "Jack" Ballinger, his nephew, and his confidential secretary while he was Land Commissioner, immediately began to build up a practice in cases coming before the Land Office of the United States.

The ex-Commissioner of the Land Office in September, 1908, made a trip across the continent to Washington as attorney for the Cunningham group, to interview the authorities of the Land Office and the Secretary of the Interior, and to rebut by an affidavit from the promoter Cunningham some very damaging evidence that had been secured against this group in the spring. Mr. Ballinger was also consulted by the Hunt or Lippy-Davis group of claimants. But the Ballinger family was perhaps more closely connected with the White political group than any other. Richard A. Ballinger was attorney for the members of this group, among them one of the Congressmen who took an interest in it. "Jack" Ballinger is at the present time its attorney, and Webster Ballinger, a cousin, is a claim-holder in the Morrow group, which is practically a part of the White group.

There is an old Federal law that says:

It shall not be lawful for any person appointed after the first day of June, 1872, as an officer, clerk or employe in any of the departments, to act as counsel, attorney or agent for prosecuting any claim against the United States which was pending in either of said departments while he was such officer, clerk or employe, nor in any manner, nor by any means to aid in the prosecution of any such claim within two years next after he shall have ceased to be such officer, clerk or employe.

Mr. Ballinger and his nephew have been criticized for taking up these Alaska coal cases as attorneys, on the ground that they have violated this act. This criticism is not accurate. It is true that other departments of the Government enforce this law; and it is true that L. Q. C. Lamar, afterward Justice of the Federal Supreme Court, ruled, while Secretary of the Interior, that the statute applied to claims for land in the Land Office, but his ruling was reversed by Hoke Smith when he was Secretary. Mr. Ballinger was clearly within the letter of the law in taking up, as attorney, the cause of the Alaskan coal cases, as his nephew still is in carrying them on before the officials of the Interior Department, of which his uncle is now head.

The New Commissioner

With Mr. Ballinger's retirement as Land Commissioner in March, 1908, the Alaska coal-land laws' interpretation — in which the claimants were now chiefly concerned — fell into the hands of his former assistant, Fred Dennett, who had succeeded him. Mr. Dennett entered political service as secretary to Senator H. C. Hansborough of North Dakota and clerk of the Senate Committee on Public Lands. He then came into the Land Office, and was stationed at Seattle, as chief of the field division, in charge of the special agents to investigate claims for fraud in the Northwest. Mr. Dennett, while in the latter position, made a considerable fortune in land speculation about Seattle, and is still a large real estate holder there.

When Mr. Dennett took office, he found one aggressive force that was directed against the Alaska coal claimants. This was the agent Glavis, whom Mr. Ballinger had set to work on this matter. Mr. Glavis was an active, ambitious, intelligent young man in whom the Land Office had great confidence. Having recently been appointed chief of the field division in the Northwest, he was eager to make a record for himself in these cases. A few days after Mr. Ballinger's retirement, he secured most damaging evidence against the Cunningham group of claims, including the promoter's journal, which has already been quoted. Glavis not only directed agents to get evidence of fraud, but he himself traveled over the entire country and secured testimony and records, now in the Government's possession, showing a great variety of fraud of the most serious character. Indeed, virtually all the evidence of value against the Alaska claimants was secured by this man.

Dennett's Liberal Interpretation

In May Mr. Dennett decided to take Glavis off the work in the Alaska coal-land frauds, for a time at least. Glavis protested strongly against this, on the plea that the ground of the claims in Alaska should be examined to see whether the claims had been occupied in good faith, according to law. This could only be done in the few summer months, because the remainder of the year the claims are buried in snow. Mr. Dennett, however, did not feel that he could do this, but in October ordered Glavis to take up the work again. The snow was then on the ground in Alaska, and so Glavis' idea of examining the claims had to be given up.

It was soon quite clear that Mr. Dennett took a very liberal view of the law, especially of that of 1908. He indicated clearly, for instance, that he thought the Cunningham claims would be given their long-desired "patent" by the Government under this law. About the same time, Glavis, who was always anxious to prosecute the coal claimants, felt that he had an excellent plan by which to prosecute the Lippy-Davis group — whose corporate name was the Alaska Petroleum and Coal Company — for selling stock in the venture before they had final title to their land. Mr. Dennett did not feel that he could do this. He was, in fact, placed in an especially awkward position by this proposal, because one of the members of this group was the agent in charge of his real-estate ventures in Seattle.

Mr. Ballinger's Delicacy

In March, 1909, Mr. Ballinger returned to Washington as the Secretary of the Interior of Mr. Taft's Cabinet, and as such was the final authority in the Department dealing with the Alaska coal cases. Mr. Ballinger expressed a delicacy about making decisions on the various claims for which he had acted as attorney, and turned the whole matter over to Mr. Dennett and others in the Department.

Six days after Mr. Ballinger became Secretary of the Interior, Glavis was asked to make complete reports in his examination of the coal cases, and in the last of April he was instructed by the law office in Washington that the Alaska coal investigation must be concluded by July 1. Glavis still insisted that the evidence against the claimants would be only partial until some one went to Alaska when the snow was off the ground and examined the claims, to see whether they had been worked by individual claimants or companies, or had been opened at all as coal-mines. In May, soon after he received the last order, Glavis went to Washington.

When Glavis arrived in Washington, he, his chief in the field service, H. H. Schwartz, and Commissioner Dennett went into conference. In this a discussion arose between them concerning the interpretation of the Alaska coal-land law of 1908. Mr. Schwartz and Mr. Glavis held that the act validated only those claims in which the first "locations" had been made in good faith and in the individual interest of the locator. Mr. Dennett held a more liberal view. By Secretary Ballinger's direction, Schwartz and Glavis prepared a letter to Attorney-General Wickersham, summarizing the evidence obtained against the Alaska coal claimants, and asking for a ruling on it under the law of 1908. In view of the intimate relations of both the Secretary of the Interior and the head of the Land Office to claim-holders, it was natural that they should determine to do this.

Immediately after this, however, Glavis was

notified that the Interior Department would decide on the law in its own legal department, and on May 19, 1909, Frank Pierce, the First Assistant Secretary of the Interior, gave a decision which ended as follows:

"In passing upon entries sought to be perfected under the act of 1908, where the only objection thereto is an arrangement or agreement of the character specifically described in your letter, the same might and should be accepted and passed to patent."

Various groups of coal claimants had by this time started to consolidate under the law of 1908, the larger ones splitting up into the four-square-mile groups required by law. The rest of the groups were waiting. It was felt now that the way was at last clear for the final "patenting" of and release by the Government of the Cunningham claims, and after them of the claims of the entire regiment of claim-holders. Their natural feeling of satisfaction lasted, however, only about a month, for on June 12, 1909, Attorney-General Wickersham rendered a decision sustaining the position of Schwartz and Glavis, and bringing out the evident intention of the Secretary of the Interior, Congressman Mondell, and others active in the framing of the bill, that, although the bill forgave consolidation before the final act of "entry," the first act — the "location" of the land — must have been made in good faith and in the individual interest of the locator. This opinion was secured by a direct appeal of the agent Glavis on his own responsibility to the Attorney-General over the head of the law office of the Department of the Interior.

A Quick Trial for Cunningham Cases

This indiscreet and unusual act eventually cost Glavis his position. It naturally did not tend to promote smooth relations with his superiors. Friction between him and them was from that time on continuous. The Land Office demanded an immediate trial of the Cunningham group of coal claimants. Glavis responded that it would be wrong to try these cases without having the evidence obtainable on the ground at Alaska, which up to that time there had been no opportunity to get. Mr. Dennett insisted on an immediate trial. Moreover, the Land Office directed that such trial should not be taken according to the hitherto invariable custom of having the claimants for coal appear before the Land Office where the coal land belonged. So long as these claimants for Alaska coal were not in any case Alaskans, but were scattered across the United States, it was deemed proper by the Land Office that it should bring its court to them — thus greatly

conveniencing the Cunningham claimants, most of whom were busy men of large interests.

Matters now moved quickly. Mr. Dennett superseded Glavis with a young lawyer, James M. Sheridan, from the Land Office. Glavis, remembering that a part of this Cunningham claim was located on a forest reserve, called this fact to the attention of the Forestry Department. Gifford Pinchot, the National Forester, on examining Glavis' statements, was of the opinion that the cases should not be heard until fall, so that Government agents from both the Land and Forestry divisions might have the opportunity to examine the ground of the claims in Alaska. Mr. Sheridan, the Land Office lawyer, reported the same view.

President Taft Approves Glavis' Discharge

Finally, Glavis, still eager to convict the coal claimants, committed his final indiscretion by laying the whole case before the President of the United States. Mr. Taft felt, upon examining them, that Glavis' documents reflected upon the Secretary of the Interior, Mr. Ballinger. Concentrating his attention upon this phase of their contents, President Taft at once went over the matter with Mr. Ballinger, and issued a statement exonerating him. Mr. Ballinger then asked for permission to discharge Mr. Glavis, which was given, and Mr. Glavis was discharged.

The eagerness of this young man to prosecute the Cunningham claimants for fraud thus cost him a very promising future in the service of the United States. Incidentally, because of this and other differences between the heads of the Forestry and Land offices, Mr. Ballinger conceived so strong a resentment against Mr. Pinchot that it is a question, while this is being written, which one of them must resign from the Government's service. The case of the Government against the Cunningham claims was, through this action of Glavis, supported by Forester Pinchot, held over until the Government could complete its evidence in the Cunningham cases.

Land Office's Disadvantage in the Trial

The publicity attending the differences of two high Government officials like Mr. Ballinger and Mr. Pinchot for the first time made the question whether this billion and a half dollars' worth of coal should be granted away by the United States to speculative syndicates a matter of national interest. The trials of the Cunningham cases began at Seattle in November, after the testimony desired by Mr. Glavis and Mr. Schwartz had been secured by coal experts sent to Alaska during the summer.

In trying these cases the Land Office was under a considerable disadvantage. In the first place, Glavis, the only man in America who knew the evidence, had been discharged by Secretary Ballinger. The case was put in charge of a young lawyer without a very definite knowledge of the evidence or the coal laws. Against him were pitted two of the most adroit and clever lawyers of the Northwest, one of whom, J. P. Gray, had the advantage of having followed the case since he first made out the affidavits for the Cunningham claimants as Senator Heyburn's law associate in the fall of 1904. And, in addition, members of the Land Office field service, sympathizing with Mr. Glavis, were during the progress of the trial resigning or threatening to resign from the office's employment.

It seems most probable, in view of the evidence, that the Land Office will refuse the Cunningham claimants the patent to their 90,000,000 tons of coal. At the same time, it cannot be certain, even if it does, that the United States will retain this property. This claim is only one of a large number seeking an enormous prize. The organization back of this now includes an array of influential Republican politicians and office-holders of all kinds; and the keen self-interest of one of the greatest single financial powers in the country. The influence exerted in this matter in the Northwest is inconceivable in its variety, subtlety, and strength. That there is no place to which it does not extend socially in a perfectly natural way was shown curiously by the fact that, out of the membership of the Country Club of Seattle, during President Taft's recent visit in that city, it was two Cunningham claimants who came forward as his opponents in his favorite game of golf.

Monopoly from Archaic Laws

If the Cunningham and other coal claimants behind them win their suits and force through their claims, the United States will transfer to private hands, practically as a gift, property worth more by some $200,000,000 than the Federal debt. Of this, sums varying from nothing to three hundred dollars will go into the hands of the men who found the coal; very great profits will go to the speculators who made up the syndicates; and the whole property will almost immediately fall into the hands of one of the ugliest and most dangerous monopolies in the country, which by this means will not only practically complete a monopoly of the mines of Alaska, but have a grip on the whole future development of industry on the Pacific Coast. The process is not new: it is merely the sudden and spectacular exploitation of a new country along the standard lines that have created coal, lumber, and general mineral monopolies in the United States. It is the familiar old double process of the robbing of the American people — by theft of their property, and the re-sale of it at excessive monopoly prices.

The primary reason for this is our mineral and public-land laws. These have been out of date for a generation; they are the ridicule of every other civilized country; and they are founded on entirely wrong principles. The coal, timber, stone, general minerals, and water powers upon the public lands belong to the United States. They must be worked eventually, not by individuals, but by corporations. There are only two essential parties to the transaction — the Government and the corporation. The United States practically refuses to recognize the second party and will deal — because of laws adapted to conditions forty years old — only with the individual. In the meanwhile, sane and modern laws on this subject — such as exist to an extent in Australia and British Columbia — recognize the corporation, deal with it, and get what the Government is entitled to from it. It is time the United States awoke to modern conditions, and did this. When it does, from the resources of Alaska alone it could secure an income aggregating hundreds of millions of dollars. And Alaska is but one part of its present property.

Minnesota now has an arrangement by which it will secure $250,000,000 from operators of its mineral resources. This gives a faint idea of what the United States could secure from the minerals in Government lands. To do this would not delay development; it would merely break monopoly.

The Managers of Our Business

Modern government is more and more devoted to economic questions; it is business, speaking in the largest and best sense of that term. There has been a great deal of sentiment in discussing the conservation of the resources of this country. This is not necessary. The United States now holds property of infinite value. It is in the management of officials who are just as responsible for it as are the officials of a bank to their stockholders. The day of rampant individualism on the political platform and of monopoly control in the committee room is coming to an end. And political parties may well recognize it. If one party or administration will not manage our affairs in our own interests, we will get another management. It may not come to-morrow, or next year. But it will come very soon.

10
Cape Nome's Wonderful Placer Mines

CAPE NOME'S WONDERFUL PLACER MINES

BY GEORGE EDWARD ADAMS

B EFORE the close of this crowning year of the nineteenth century the world's financial and mining interests are to be somewhat rudely awakened and pleasurably surprised when the output of placer gold from America's already famous arctic mining-camp—Cape Nome—is authentically recorded. Surprised? Yes, and more so than when the richness of the Klondike was first telegraphed all over the Union. Wall Street, New York city, and Lombard Street, London, will take cognizance of a new mining district that is to add very materially to the world's supply of gold. Ten millions? The statement smacks somewhat of a mining boomer's advertisement; nevertheless, it is, the minimum figure at which hundreds of well-informed Cape-Nomers place the output for 1900, and Seattle is to witness a repetition of the rather pleasing and exciting spectacle of the mad rush to the Klondike in the summer of 1897. This progonstication is not an ephemeral speculation of a visionary brain, for substantial results have already made a manifest impression upon the mining and financial interests of the United States, and have awakened some inquiry from the busy marts of other nations. The known output of over $2,000,000 the past season from a district not discovered until a year ago, and on which the miner's spade or pick did not break the virgin earth in true mining fashion till in April, 1899, is indeed far in excess of the first season's clean-up in the Klondike, and a most significant augury for the season of 1900. The reader need but give a cursory glance at the illustrations herewith to become informed of what an enterprising American mining-camp can accomplish in *four months* in the face of nature's most severe obstacles. Not a tree or shrub is there to soften the cold and dreary landscape, but notwithstanding the lack of timber, substantial wooden buildings have sprung into existence as if by magic. Stores and shops incident to a mining-town within the shadows of the arctic circle are nearly all well housed to withstand the searching and penetrating elements of such a rigorous climate. This bustling young mining-town of more than six thousand people is indeed one of the present wonders of Uncle Sam's domain, and being the nucleus of one of nature's wonderful and most prolific placer-mining districts, is well worthy some consideration and attention from the reading public.

Every American citizen takes a just and pardonable pride in knowing that the land of the Stars and Stripes produced over $70,000,000 of gold in the calendar year of 1899. This is but a little less than the largest production of any country in the world, and it is indeed possible, and quite probable, that Alaska in general, and the Cape Nome district in particular, will produce sufficient additional gold this year to place our beloved Union first on the list of the gold-producing nations. So surely as the Union is forging to first rank in the world's industrial advance, so surely will it stand first in the production of the standary by which nearly all nations measure their wealth.

It seems like the dream of a dry brain, this washing, rocking, sluicing, and "quicking" gold from sea-beach sand. No old "forty-niner" would have dreamed of such a thing, and, no doubt, would pass along this same Cape Nome beach for years without once deigning to give a serious thought to the sand beneath his feet. Two years ago, if any one had even suggested digging for gold on the ocean beach, he would immediately have been classed as a fit subject for an insane asylum, but within four months after the discovery of gold in paying quantity at Cape Nome, the sea-beach for upwards of fifty miles was prospected, and in most instances with highly satisfactory results. Many thousand claims have been staked, and the season of 1900 will witness a human beehive over a distance of a hundred miles north and south of Cape Nome. The bustle and confusion of jostling humanity on Broadway, New York city, would be but a circumstance to the wild, untamed scramble incident to the short summer season of 1900 at Nome, and if one could but make a trip just off the shore covering the entire range of the beach diggings, he would see thousands of "gold crazy" men working as never before—a sight of a lifetime. Where the neophyte and the skilled placer-miner are

159

equally successful, and where one man with an old-fashioned rocker can clean up $75 to $100 per day, not many of the fourteen hundred and forty minutes will be unemployed. As an evidence that claims at Capt Nome and vicinity are exceedingly valuable, it is but necessary to say that men who have mined for a generation, or who are large investors in placer-mining properties, and who, from years of experience, know the specific difference between rich and poor diggings, have paid as high as $50,000 for a single claim upon which less than thirty days' work had been done. Indeed, capital is seeking investment in the district in large amounts.

Mr. C. D. Lane, of Seattle and San Francisco, who has for years investigated Alaska mining from Ketchikan to the Arctic Ocean, and who is many times a mining millionaire, has invested considerably over $200,000 in the district. Several of his purchases are situated on the rivers and creeks seeking the ocean at and near Cape Nome.. His operations will be conducted on a very large scale, using the latest improved machinery, and by the close of the open season of 1900 it is estimated that his clean-up will approximate a million dollars. He will install a pumping plant this season at a cost of $150,000. Its purpose is to raise the water from Snake River to an ellevation of some seven hundred feet, thus providing, a

water-supply to all the high placer-ground on Dexter, Anvil, Snow, and Dry creeks, adding a very necessary element to these high diggings not supplied by nature. He will also construct about ten miles of railroad from Cape Nome northeast over the tundra, making the tributary river and creek mines easier of access. So far, however, none but crude methods have been employed in the district, but it will be readily seen from the foregoing that this coming season will chronicle a vast change, made possible by the fact that all ocean-going craft can steam within a rifle-shot of the diggings and lighter their cargoes ashore. One of the illustrations herewith will give the reader a fair idea of landing supplies. Fifteen thousand tons were so landed last season. Wharves are practically an impossibility, owing to the winter ice, but, however, a scheme is projected to build a large floating dock. No matter what obstacles prevail, the ingenious and energetic Yankee appears to compass them and thwart ruthless nature even where its power is manifest through the ice-king.

It would be a very easy matter to give the reader a long list of individual fortunes already made in the Cape Nome district, but it is not thought advisable to burden this article with prolixity. The fortunate ones so far believe the district the richest in the world,

UNLOADING FREIGHT AT NOME CITY.

DIGGING ON THE BEACH AT CAPE NOME.

and one and all say that the output for 1900 will treble that of the Klondike at a similar stage of its history. It is known as the poor man's district, as nearly every man who went there last season and would work a claim need not leave without having mined from $25 to $100 per day. Hundreds of destitute miners from Dawson City have recouped themselves at Cape Nome and are now the owners of rich claims.

Seeking the ocean at and near Cape Nome are the Snake, Cripple, Penny, Sinook, Nome, Flambeau, El Doraro, Bonanza, and Salmon rivers, that, with their hundreds of small tributaries, drain thousands of acres of gold-producing tundra. The banks and beds of these rivers and creeks are fairly saturated with flakes of gold somewhat larger than those of the beach diggings. Anvil, Snow, Ruby, and a few other creeks produced many hundred thousand dollars' worth of gold treasure in the short season of 1899, as is amply evidenced by the government Assay Office at seattle, Washington. This institution received upwards of seven hundred thousand dollars' worth of gold dust the past season from the Capr Nome district, and estimates that it will receive $5,000,000 for the season of 1900. The

gold is of superior grade, assaying from $18 25 to $18 50 per ounce after melting. The vast extent of tundra lying to the northeast of Cape Nome has been prospected with very satisfac

ESQUIMAU GIRL.

NOME CITY, FROM THE SNAKE RIVER.

tory results, and it appears that the entire extent carries gold in paying quantities. As the claims on and near the beach are more accessible and productive, but comparatively a small amount of work was accomplished in the tundra district the past season. This coming season, however, will witness an unparalleled activity, and remarkable accomplishments can be expected in these diggings

One would imagine that the earth in prehistoric time became nauseated with such a large quantity of gold, and vomited it forth, permeating its crust and diffusing the small globules over the entire district at Cape Nome and across the strait to the Siberian shore, gold similar to that at Nome having already been mined in paying quantity from the beach sands of the latter shore. It is some thirty miles across from American to Russian territory at the nearest points. One can see the foot-hills on the Siberian side from Nome, and it is quite common in winter for the Esquimau to make the trip across on the ice to trade with his Siberian brothers.

Imagine, if you will, a bustling young mining district producing millions of gold, but with very little, if any, money in circulation. Many of the richest claim-owners will have $20,000 worth of gold dust in their possession, but not a dollar in money. One may go a whole week in this gold-dust-rich metropolis of Bering Strait and not see a single dollar in money. The difficulty is overcome by every store, shop, restaurant, hotel, or other business establishment keeping at hand a set of gold balances, and receiving payment in gold dust as a medium of exchange at $16 per ounce. This unique and rather undesirable condition is to be superseded this coming season by the establishment of two banking institutions. The Canadian Bank of Commerce—capital $6,000,000—one of the pioneer concerns at Dawson City, will open a branch at Nome early in the season of 1900, and the Bank of Cape Nome will open at the same time with a paid-up capital of $200,000, the latter having a directorate and officiary of Seattle, Washington, bankers and mining millionaires. These institutions will be a welcome addition to the district's business enterprises, and will lend stability to its trade relations with the commercial world.

The sanitary condition of the district is most undesirable. Malarial fever was all too common, and nearly every day last summer a death occurred from typhoid fever. This is not to be wondered at, as the digging of cesspools is out of the question and the country for miles around is marshy in summer. With practically no attention given to the proper disposition of garbage, it is a wonder that so few cases of the more malignant fevers were manifest. A proper sewerage and surface-drainage system is a much-mooted subject, and definite action will surely be taken early this coming season, as the town has a Mayor, City Council, health officer, etc., who are all deeply interested in its habitable condition and thoroughly appreciate that work is not possible without nature's greatest gift—health. There are a thousand women in the district, and they have, as usual, taken vigorous action with the sanitary question; brave, noble, energetic, self-sacrificing American women—God bless them!—mothers, wives, daughters, sisters, and sweethearts who will urge upon those near and dear to them the pressing need upon those near and dear to them the pressing need of better sanitation. Life, the breath of God, must not, for lack of pure water and proper sewerage, be left to the domination of the insidious typhoid-fever germ.

At least five thousand people are wintering in the district, and no doubt much winter work is being done under almost insuperable climatic conditions. It must be borne in mind that nature does not permit a tree or even a shrub to grow in this arctic waste to assist man in his strife with the elements, and therefore the only native supply of fuel consists of wood washed ashore by wind and tide. Even this supply is now entirely exhausted, and Cape-Nomers must rely solely upon the importation of fuel. Most of the coal is imported from Seattle, and in October last was worth $75 per ton, the supply being anything but large. However, the fuel and food conditions there this winter are not at all alarming. Many of the Yukon River steam-boats are moored in the river at Nome, and will be used for hotels throughout the long siege of frigid cold, affording much better accommodations than some of the hotels ashore. If one has a rugged constitution, is properly housed, well clothed out-wardly with furs, has a goodly supply of fuel, and sufficient supplies to provide four pounds daily of heat-producing food, he need

not fear to winter at Nome, but God have mercy on the unfortunate "cheated by dissembling Nature," poor in pocket, without proper clothing or sufficient supplies, who is foolhardy enough to try wintering there! His dream of wealth with the coming of the summer warmth is more than likely to end in everlasting sleep.

It is no uncommon happening of a winter night to be wakened by the pitiless cold, and in one's semi-consciousness seem to be at home in the "States," enjoying a bountiful evening dinner with wife and children, and afterward forming a family circle around the cozy fireside, discussing the hardships incident to an arctic winter, and watching with mingled delight the flames in the fireplace form themselves into fantastic shapes as they fill the room with warmth and light. Just as this soul-satisfying fancy is fading from dreamland sight, a devitalizing chill awakens one, and nature makes vigorous demand for a more secure covering of furs or a replenishing of the fading fire. "Yes, the cold and cruel winter, the nipping, biting winter," cares not for human woes. Cape Nome's winter nor'easter, conceived in the home of perpetual ice, cometh forth howling and shrieking, and stinging into numbness the humans encountered in its mad rush across the treeless wilds of Alaska. The poorly housed or illy

GENERAL VIEW OF SKAGWAY.

MAIN STREET, NOME CITY.

CAPE NOME IN JULY, 1899.

nourished man is indeed an easy prey to the penetrating, marrow-destroying, relentless arctic cold, and as the shadows of night are fading, his soul takes flight to its home above, leaving its tenement of clay on the icy waste, far away from friends and loved ones at home.

But after every winter there comes the effulgence of summer. As the sum reaches its summer solstice, a golden flood of sunshine and the gentle invigorating breath of the Bering Sea sou' wester fan into life the dormant rivers and creeks, thaw to a depth of eight or ten inches the moss-covered tundra, an dwhere all seemed as death and stagnation for eight cold, dreary months, there springs into abnormal activity everything of life. With the garish sun shedding its kindly beams nearly every minute of each twenty-four hours, the "land of the midnight sun" is a pleasing and satisfying sight to the seeker after its hidden wealth, and it is no wonder that the Cape Nome miner accomplishes as much in four months as does his brother miner in double that time in a more temperate zone.

Cape Nome is situated on the shore of Bering Sea at the mouth of Snake River, Seward Peninsula, central-western Alaska, U. S. A., 65 degrees north latitude and 166 degrees west longitude, and, by the ocean route, distant from its base of supply, Seattle, some twenty-seven hundred miles. In making the ocean trip from Seattle one steams westward for nineteen hundred miles across the North Pacific Ocean to Dutch Harbor on the Aleutian Archipelago, and thence northward eight hundred miles to the land of gold, passing *en route* the government's seal-rookeries on the Pribyloff Islands. During the ocean voyage of ten days one is encompassing a part of the six hundred thousand miles of Alaskan territory, and on reaching Cape Nome is as far west of Seattle as Chicago is east.

It is fitting to make brief mention of a route to Cape Nome unsurpassed in scenic effect

and enchanting grandeur. The beautiful and enjoyable days immortalized in book and song do not surpass in splendor a day on Puget Sound in early June. The pure ozone, the mildly tempered sunlight, the ethereal blue of the cloudless sky, the prismatic tints of the sparkling water, the cool, invigorating breeze from the north, the pink-tinted, snow-capped Mount Rainier towering heavenward 14,444 feet, the white-topped Cascade and Olympic mountain ranges, respectively to the east and west, and the hum of the city's industry, all hail one with a hearty and refreshing greeting while promenading the deck of a palatial ocean steamer leaving Seattle Harbor of a morning in June. As the steamer feelingly glides along with "a bone in its mouth," there appear to the right the mammoth elevators and locks of the Pacific-coast terminus of the Great Northern Railway, and to the left, ten miles across the sound, the largest saw-mill on the globe. A mile farther on, and one is under the shadow of Fort Lawton, where grim sentinels are trained across, up, and down the sound, ever ready to deal death and destruction to a foreign enemy endeavoring to invest the harbor. Two miles farther, the West Point light-house is passed. A few furlongs farther, and to one's right is the entrance of the projected government waterway to a reserve harbor on a magnificent body of fresh water— Lake Washington. Now, under full speed and steaming head on into the balmy breezy, the mind is refreshed and the soul stirred with ever-changing scenes; now rounding a headlong point, then through a narrow channel between abrupt banks overtopped with towering evergreen-trees, the breeze freighted with the balsam sweetness of exuding pines; now and again passing bustling young, up-to-date towns, and of a sudden rounding Point Wilson into the magnificent Strait of San Juan de Fuca. Looking to the westward, one beholds the broad expanse of the mighty Pacific

Ocean, and to the east the ever-glistening snow-capped Mount Baker rising nearly eleven thousand feet into the sky, a beacon to the mariner. One leaves behind the placid waters and enchanting landscape of the Mediterranean of America, and ploughs the mighty deep for thirty miles across the strait, feeling the steamer tremble in the deep swells from the ocean, and having the monotony of the surroundings relieved with the pleasure of watching, now and then, a school of fin-back whales at play. As the evening shadows gather, the steamer touches at Victoria, British Columbia, but is soon pushing forward in the waters of Queen Charlotte Sound between Vancouver Island and the British Columbia mainland. The moon now adds its reflected light to that of the stars, and one enjoys a cozy nook on deck until late in the evening. For three days more of nature's most delightful weather one is winding among islands that rival in beauty the Thousand Islands of the St. Lawrence River. A few hours after the steamer touches at Juneau, the proposed capital of Alaska, there comes in sight the gateway to the Klondike, and soon one steps from the steamer to the wharf at Skagway, revitalized in mind and body, the eyes sparkling with health and the heart full of he gladness and warmth of summer.

Standing on the station platform watching, with a deal of interest, the hurrying people, the loaded trucks, the ton or more of mail and express matter going aboard the train, the sign of industry on every hand, one is amazed to learn that on this very spot, less than three years ago, white man but seldom ventured. One is soon aboard the train and comfortably seated in a first-class railway coach. The bell rings, the train moves onward, and shortly enters a wild, narrow valley, while, below, the boiling river rushes willingly on its way to the sea, singing the song of summer. With a deal of puffing and throbbing the steel horse begins the ascents of the apparently insuperable barrier between the coast and interior points. Up and up the power of steam takes one, over foaming mountain torrents, under overhanging bowleders, through the solid rock, by Crystal and Black lakes, soon passing immense schists of tessellated rock, the eyes discovering a niche in the rugged slope where the envious vine is 'muffling with verdant ringlet" the rippling water of a mountain rill. With a constant change of delightful scenery the summit of the mountain range is reached. Then a short descending run to Lake Bennett, and one steps upon the wharf at Bennett after

enjoying three and a half hours of scenery surpassing in grandeur and rapidity of change that along the Denver and Rio Grande Railway. A commodious steamboat is waiting at the wharf, and is soon gliding over the crystal waters of Lakes Bennett, Tagish, Le Barge, and Marsh, the surrounding scenery, in the mellow light, equal to if not surpassing in charm that of Switzerland. In a very few hours this beautiful chain of lakes is left to the south, and one is steaming down Fifty Mile River and rapidly approaching the well-known treacherour Miles Canyon. After making a secure landing just above the canyon, one takes a steam-car ride for five miles around this natural barrier to navigation, and is soon aboard another steamboat as handsome and graceful as the better class of those plying on the Mississippi River. It is now but a short distance to the mighty Yukon, and the steamboat is soon rushing along the river's rapid current toward the gold-famous Klondike, and after three days' travel from Skagway one arrives at Dawson City, the commercial headquarters of the Klondike mining district. Nineteenth-century progress has put the city in telephonic touch catch outlying districts and in telegraphic communication with Skagway. After a few hours of sight-seeing one boards a larger steamboat then heretofore, and is shortly passing down on Alaska's majestic waterway to Bering Sea. On the way down the river the steamer touches at many points, among them Circle City, Rampart, Manook (where is mined the highest grade of placer gold in all Alaska), Nulato, Greek and Russian mission posts, after which the delta of the Yukon appears in sight and the steamer takes the Aphoon or north channel into Bering Sea. A few miles on the briny deep, and the steamer's mate heaves a line to the wharf at St. Michaels. Here is located the depots of Alaska's pioneer transportation companies, and of the United States, this point being the government's military headquarters for Alaska.

During the seven day's trip down the Yukon one is more than charmed and delighted with the wild surroundings, for in this rugged land of the far North is repeated the best of the natural wonders of the Yosemite Valley, of the Yellowstone National Park, of the Bad Lands, of the Colorado River, of the Alps, of Switzerland and Scotland, and indeed the most realistic and descriptive words employed by man to present nature's handiwork to the human vision are impotent to fittingly picture the grandeur manifest on every hand.

11
The
Klondike

THE KLONDIKE

EAGLE NEST ROCK ON THE YUKON

BOATS COMING DOWN LAKE TAGISH

THE FIRST SIGHT of Dawson, which one gets after being several weeks on the trail, travelling through wild, rough, and constantly changing scenery, is a surprise to the most immovable of men. Situated as it is on the river bank, and stretching back and up on the shelves of the hillside, its tiers of tents and cabins give it a surrounding which seems theatrical and unreal.

Before arriving at the big bend in the Yukon, just above Dawson, one catches a glimpse, over the islands in the river, of a few tents, high up on the hillside, and back of them still the huge gray slide of rock and gravel called the "Moosehide."

On rounding the bend we come directly on the town itself, and from this minute until one steps on the main street one is going through a continual succession of vague remembrances of something seen before and something dreamed of in the past.

The waters of the Klondike come in at the south end of the town and are a sharp contrast to the yellowish gray waters of the Yukon, by their black transparency. Until safely within this discoloration mark, provided one is in a rowing boat, one has not arrived at Dawson, because the Yukon here is swift and the black waters are sluggish, and it needs quite a struggle to get out of one into the other. In fact, it is a common sight to see large rafts of timber, representing in their size the summer's work of perhaps many men and valued at hundreds of dollars, go by Dawson from up the river, notwithstanding the efforts of their crew to bring them into the slack water. Boats have gone past, too, with the owners gazing open-mouthed at the town, too overcome apparently by the sights to use energy enough to bring them into the banks

During the summer of '98 the whole waterfront was lined with thousands of boats of all sizes and descriptions, from small canoes to large scows containing cattle or merchandise.

Fortunate was the late-comer, at such a time, who could find place for his boat.

Dawson itself runs from the Klondike River for about one and a half miles down the east bank of the Yukon, until it is abruptly stopped by a precipitious hill. Above Dawson and connected to it by a suspension bridge across the Klondike is a suburban town called Klondike City. Opposite Dawson there is also a settlement which bids fair to rival Dawson in point of health if not in enterprise, but which has the disadvantage of being cut off from Dawson for two or three weeks while the ice is running in the river.

To come suddenly from the stillness of the river and the quietness of the weeks of work on the trail into the main street of a town of some twenty thousand to thirty thousand people, and with most of them on the same street, is bewildering in the extreme. To us, perhaps, it was less so than to a vast majority, because we had been prepared in a great measure by friends who had come from Dawson to the

ON THE SUMMIT OF CHILKOOT PASS

Stewart River and described its wonders to us. However, we sat on the board walks, quite the most comfortable seats we had had in weeks, thoroughly filled with amazement, and watched the crowd talking, discussing, and spitting.

The town is most orderly and rows are exceedingly rare. Drunkenness is an exception, perhaps attributable to the high price and quality of the liquor and to the efficiency of the Northwest Mounted Police, who are a fine body of strapping young men, well officered, and deservedly popular among all classes for their justice and zeal.

The main street of the town is lined, in the business portion, by the big trading stores, the saw-mills, small stores of all kinds, and saloons alternating every two to three stores. In nearly every saloon is either a dancehall or a gambling-room, generally both.

The saloon takes the place of a club, and becomes the common meeting-ground of all classes. As it becomes necessary to meet all classes of men in this country, the most fastidious of men finds himself obliged to become a regular visitor of one or two saloons in the course of his mining experience.

The gambling-rooms are generally in the rear of the saloon, and run "wide open." They are usually thronged during the summer all night long, and the best of good-nautre and order prevail. At the dancehalls an evening vaudeville performance (so called) usually precedes the dancing, and in one there is generally a play of some sort, with an extremely good orchestra for such a place. In fact there are two or three small orchestras in the town. One saloon has a café in its rear, which is excellent in point of service and cooking, while during the dinner one listens to playing by one of the viloins of a well-known San Francisco orchestra, and, at times, a very good baritone song by an ex-member of one of our eastern opera companies.

During the summer there is but little work going on on the creeks; the town therefore is filled with men. This summer this crowd was augmented by an enormous number of people who came in over the trail or up the river and hung around the town, either trying to get work or on their way prospecting up the creeks and rivers.

If any one were to ask what the general topic of conversation was, I should say food in all its forms. Instead of asking a man whether he was well or what news he had, the most

A NIGHT'S CAMP ON THE KLONDIKE

A RESCUE AT THE MOUTH OF HERMIT RIVER

PROSPECTORS LEAVING DAWSON

THE SUMMIT OF CHILKOOT PASS

SCALING CHILKOOT PASS

WHITE HORSE RAPIDS   THROUGH MARSH LAKE UNDER SAIL

nautical question would be to ask him if he had any evaporated cream in his cache, or if he knew what the price of butter was that day. This becomes so much the case that you will notice in the newspaper reports of returning Klondikers that they will enumerate long lists of the prices of food instead of giving mining news of any importance. This does not imply that food is scarce, because food is very plentiful, and there is not an article of daily use or form of necessary food that may not be obtained in Dawson at the present writing.

During the summer fresh vegetables and fresh fruit came in on the boats in abundance—at high prices, to be sure—but still they were in Dawson. Fresh meat was plentiful and supplied to the sick in the hospitals at times when it was a great luxury.

There are two or three hospitals in Dawson, the largest the Catholic Hospital, conducted by the Jesuits, the nurses being Sisters of Charity. Father Judge of the Jesuits, who is looked up to by every resident of Dawson, has had charge of this hospital and has successfully managed it in the face of extreme difficulties.

The smaller hospitals, of which I believe one is private, were opened this summer. All were filled to overflowing, owing to the great number of fever cases prevalent. It is perhaps right to say that this large number of fever cases in Dawson is due more to exposure on the trail and poorly prepared and scant food than to the unsanitary condition of the town itself, although there has been little attempt by the government to improve this condition. Only the fact that the stagnant water in what ditches there are is water thawing from the frozen muck under the moss, and therefore at a low temperature, prevents a really enormous amount of ill health. Most of the water used for drinking comes from, springs of glacial character in the hillsides and is very good.

For the moral support of the inhabitants there are three churches—an Episcopalian, a Presbyterian, and a Catholic—the largest being the latter, the building a gift of one of the most prominent of the miners. It is a fair-sized building built of logs, and indeed an example of proportion and good taste in design to many an architect of more accessible regions.

Most of the inhabitants are Americans, a great number Swedes, Canadians, Australians, South Africans, and Englishmen, while there is a fair representation of every nationality.

The men who have been most successful in the country, and who are the pioneers, are for the most part surprisingly young men, men of intelligence and bearing. The old miner of fame and story-book is conspicuous by his absence, as is also the "bad man." The prevailing characteristics of these men engaged in mining is their readiness to adapt themselves to the new conditions of this country, and also their honesty and justice in dealing one with another. To many of them, being of Scandinavian descent, the climate is no particular trial. There are a great many young men here who are men of the world, and one is quite likely to run against a club acquaintance of former days. Most of these are men from the Pacific Coast, or from London, engaged in business or representing London capital in some form. A stranger must be struck with the fact, however, that young men are in the majority.

Notwithstanding the apparent listlessness and apathy of the crowd in the streets, a good deal of business goes on in the town. Buildings going up on every side make a continual clatter, while the sound of the hammers recalking or chinking the big stores with moss

LAKE LINDEMAN   HEAD OF LAKE BENNETT—DEPARTING MINERS' BOATS IN DISTANCE

for the winter months brings one back, as it were, to the busy shipyard scenes in teh East. Above all sounds is the continual buzzing of the saw mills running night and day.

Now and again a pack-train comes into town from the creeks laden with canvas sacks of gold to be deposited either at the big stores, at the bank, or at the police barracks. Auction sales of food, merchandise and clothing go on during day and evening, while from a saloon or a store comes the sound of a phonograph rasping out the last Sousa march.

Dogs of all descriptions lie in the road everywhere, and when they are not being stepped on are busy fighting over an old moose hoof or a bit of caribou hide. In fact, the dogs make Dawson the rival of Constantinople, for in summer they are allowed to roam at large and make the street their home. As soon, however, as the first snow comes the dogs disappear from the streets, as they become in demand at home.

At the hour of midnight on the 3d of July every patriotic American in the town proceeded to fire a gun or a revolver, as long as he could spare his ammunition. As there were many thousands of Americans, the popping lasted for nearly an hour, and the noise was deafening. The dogs became very much frightened, tore up and down the streets, over the hills and into the river, barking, yelping, and colliding. Above the sound of firing came continuous peals of laughter at their flight. It was a curious sight, and an incident that cost many a man the loss of his dog for several days; indeed, some never came back.

There are now several of the big stores in Dawson, the oldest being the North American Transportation Co. and the Alaska Commercial Co., these stores providing the miners and inhabitants with everything from a side of bacon to a pair of white kid dancing gloves.

Until the present season these two stores have been alone, but now there are several new competitors in the field, with their own corresponding line of steamers, in consequence of which there is a much further reduction in prices.

From the main street by the Alaska Commercial Co.'s store runs the main trail to the mines and creeks. This trail takes the form of a wagon road, and is very fair for three or four miles; after that it is a disgrace to the government, when one considers the readiness with which it could be improved.

There is another trail which starts from Klondike City and runs up along the Klondike and meets the first one about two miles from Dawson. Every day may be seen men with packs on their backs, dogs with packs, pack-trains of horses and mules going up or coming down from the creeks. Occasionally information will be brought to town of a new strike on some creek; then the trail will be crowded with stampeders anxious to be the first in the field to stake.

A man has been known to stampede a great part of the town by simply walking into the various saloons and whispering to a few friends in each, with a pack on his back and a general air of satisfaction on his face.

In summer, however, little work is done besides cutting wood, after the general wash up, and men take a well-earned rest, not a few spending more than they make in the winter.

Contrary to one's expectations, there are no mosquitoes in Dawson to amount to anything. Outside, on some of the creeks most worked, there are a few; but away from these places, they are something to wonder at—it is useless to say more. One is obliged to live in the smoke of a "smudge" fire, made fo "punk" or moss and green leaves, most frequently made in a perforated pail, unless one is especially adapted to stand the incessant buzzing, even if provided with mosquito netting.

Occasionally one hears, from away up on the top of the hill back of the town, a faint cry of "Steamer!" which is taken up and repeated again and again from the hill down to the street, as one of the boats from St. Michaels appears in sight far down the river. Everybody in town at leisure then wends his way to the river-front, and waits for the steamer to struggle up to the wharf, panting hoarsely, against the strong current. Over eighty steamers have successfully made their way up to Dawson this summer, and hence there is no shortage of everything desired.

Dawson's first boom is over, but it will now settle down to be the serious mining camp it should be. Its position and the exceeding richness of the diggings in the vicinity demonstrate that it will continue to be the centre of transportation, trade and mining in that far-away part of our continent for years to come.

O. H. P. LA FARGE.

12
Alaska

ALASKA.

I.

WE owe the discovery of Russian America, now called Alaska, to the curiosity of the Czar Peter the Great, who, in 1720, was seized with a longing desire to ascertain whether or not his remote possessions to the eastward were united to the continent of America.

So he issued orders to prepare a vessel in Southern Kamtschatka, whose mission it should be to explore the unknown seas to the northeast of the Okhotsk, and settle the point whether Asia and America were indeed one.

Unfortunately for Peter's curiosity, he died in 1725, before his wishes could be carried into execution; but his widow, the celebrated Catharine I., like a dutiful spouse, pushed on the work so successfully that, in 1728, a little vessel, called the Gabriel, was ready, and placed under the command of one Vitus Behring, a Dane in Catharine's service.

This man had journeyed across the country from St. Petersbury to the Kamtschatka River, enduring great hardships and delays. In fact, nearly three years were consumed in this overland journey, during which Behring and his companions were at times on the verge of starvation.

At last, however, he got away in his little vessel, and, coasting to the northeast, never once losing sight of the coast of Asia, discovered St. Lawrence Island, between which and the main-land he passed, and entered the Northern Ocean. He, however, got no farther north than lat. 67° 18′, when, finding that the coast of Asia trended, as sailors say, to the westward, he turned back, without ever having seen the coast of America at all, and returned in safety to the little port whence he sailed. The next year, he and his lieutenant Tchirikoff made another short voyage; but it yielded no new information. So Behring retraced his steps to St. Petersburg, where, after another long and dreary journey, he arrived in 1730, having been absent over five years.

Now, in these voyages, Behring's attention was attracted to two things. One was the absence of the heavy seas common to the open ocean and the waters he had navigated before; the other was the discovery of huge fir-trees, unknown to the Asiatic coast, which he found floating in the water; and therefore, though the voyages were otherwise meagre in results, they excited such a degree of interest in St. Petersburg, and created such a rage for discovery, that Behring was made a commodore in the Russian Navy, and, in 1732, intrusted with the power to fit out another expedition.

It was eight years, however, before this was ready; but at last, in June, 1741, he sailed with two vessels on his third and last voyage. One of these vessels—the St. Paul—was commanded by Behring himself; the other—the St. Peter—was under the command of Captain Tchirikoff.

For some time they kept well together; but at last a great gale separated them, and then each pursued its voyage alone.

On the 18th day of July, 1741, Behring first saw the western shore of the continent of North America, and two days afterward he anchored in a small bay near a headland which he called Cape St. Elias, for the 20th was that saint's day, the Russians being a very pious people, and having two or three saints at least for every day in the year.

Within sight of this bay, now known as Behring's, is the celebrated Mount St. Elias, the highest land on the North-American Continent.

On landing, Behring found a deserted village of some huts built with hewn logs, in which were rude articles of household furniture, soem copper utensils, bows and arrows, and dried salmon for food. He did not tarry here long, however, and, on getting under way, sailed north, when the trend of the land forced him to diverge to the westward and then to the southward; and now he reached the Aleutian Islands, and they can hardly be numbered for multitude. So, encountering adverse winds, he worked his way cautiously along among the islands, anchoring once at Choumagni. There he saw, for the first time, some of the natives, who seemed to be peaceable fishermen, and wore fur dresses, with caps adorned with hawks'-feathers. They offered the Russians whale's-flesh, and Behring, in return, gave them brandy, which they did not seem to like, though their descendants, having become civilized, have gotten bravely over the innocent prejudice of their ancestors, and now take their liquor "straight" with perfect impassibility.

Meanwhile, the other ship, pursuing her lonely course, made the coast on the 15th July, in lat. 56°, not far from where Sitka now is. Arriving near this bleak and rocky shore, Tchirikoff sent an officer with a boat and ten of his best men, well armed and provided with a small brass cannon, to inquire into the nature of the country, and procure fresh water, of which he stood in need. The boat disappeared in a wooded cove, and was never seen again. Some days elapsed, and a second boat, with crew well armed, was also dispatched, in search of the first; but this too disappeared. At the time, a dense smoke, continually ascending, was observed on shore, and, shortly after, two canoes, filled with warlike-looking and hideously-painted natives, were seen apporaching the vessel. Seeing how large she was, they stopped paddling, hesitated, and finally turned back; and it has ever been believed that the two boats were captured and the crews sacrificed by these Sitkahans, with horrible rites of cruelty and torture.

At all events, Alexis Tchirikoff never saw his men again, and, having lost the only two boats he possessed, he could not land anywhere, and so hastened to return westward to Kamtschatka, where, after encountering terrible weather, and subsisting upon rain-water squeezed from canvas, he arrived in October, 1741, his crew reduced to forty-nine men.

All this time Behring was driven about in these unknown regions by violent gales—one storm having lasted seventeen days, and raged with terrible fury. They lost their reckoning. Scurvy broke out among them, and at last Behring himself broke down. At length, they made an island, where they tried to anchor, but the cables parted; the ship was stranded, and finally went to pieces. The crew, however, succeeded in escaping to the shore; and there the poor old commodore, in a half-decayed state, from that terrible scourge of the voyage—the scurvy—sheltered in a ditch, and half buried in the sand, as a protection against the cold, died, on the 8th December, 1741. His body was scraped out of the hole where he had literally died like a dog, and was buried on the island, which still bears his name. One hundred years afterward, a monument was erected to his memory in Petropaulovski, the place whence he sailed.

The survivors, among whom was Müller, the historian of the expedition, constructed a frail craft from the fragments of the wreck, and, after enduring incredible hardships, finally reached Petropaulovski in August, 1742.

And under such melancholy auspices was Russian America discovered.

Between the period of Behring's discovery and the commencement of this century, Alaska was repeatedly visited by the navigators of different nations—prominent among whom

ALASKA SCENERY.

were the Englishmen Byron, Carteret, Cook, and Vancouver, the Spaniard Bodega, and the unfortunato Frenchman La Pérouse; but the Russians, under Glotoff, Leratcheff, and Baranoff, took the lead, and before the year 1800 had settled some portions of the country; and thus Russia maintained her foothold, and, though sundry fierce disputes took place with Great Britain as to boundaries, the territory became more and more settled, and remained in her possession until the 18th of October, 1867, when the blue Cross of St. Andrew, which floated over the rocky citadel at Sitka, gave place to the Stars and Stripes, amid the cheering of the troops, both Russian and American, and the thundering echoes of two national salutes from the men-of-war in the harbor.

How did we come to get this vast Territory of four hundred and fifty thousand square miles, a tract of country ten times as large as the great State of New York?

Why, Mr. Seward, our late secretary of state, bought it, and Uncle Sam paid the czar seven million two hundred thousand dollars for it—a very considerable sum in these hard times, and one that an economically-disposed individual might eke out life on, if he managed his affairs well. Suppose this amount of money to be placed out at interest for fifty years at seven per cent., will Alaska be worth the result

at the end of that time? The object of these papers is to settle that point in the mind of the reader.

The wits of the time made very merry over Governor Seward's acquisition, just as former generations of wits made merry over the acquisition of Louisiana and Florida. Mr. Seward, however, tells us that Alaska was purchased because of its natural wealth in timber, fisheries, minerals, and fur-bearing animals, and for a political object—to neutralize the power of Great Britain in the North Pacific, and render the annexation of British Columbia but a question of time. "Alaska," said he, "may not be so valuable as we deem it; but you cannot deny the value of the gold-regions of the Cariboo country and Frazer's River, the coal-mines of Vancouver's and Queen Charlotte's Islands, and the unrestricted possession of the magnificent Straits of Fuca. All these, following manifest destiny, will be ours in time. Beside," said he, "we owe a deep debt of gratitude to Russia for her unvarying friendship through long years, and for her kindly sympathy during the sorest of our national trials—the great rebellion."

Perhaps no territory of equal extent on the globe, except Central Africa, is so little known; for even now, although we have been flooded with books from travellers claiming to have explored this country, the interior is yet an

ALASKA INDIANS.

AN ALASKA VILLAGE.

unknown land. The seaboard, and the line of the Yucon, and some other rivers, are the only portions of the Territory we know any thing of.

And, because of the popular ignorance on the subject, much scope has been given to mere invention, and while, on the one hand, the country has been decried as the "fag-end of creation," on the other it has been over-praised. Imagination has been made to supply the place of knowledge, and even poetry has been lugged in to picture the supposed savage desolation of the land and the imagined rigor of the climate.

Now, in the interior of Alaska, the climate is doubtless very severe, and the trappers and gold-miners of the Stachine River report that on the main-land the snow reaches a fabulous depth, and does not disappear until nearly the end of the summer; but in all that part of Alaska and British Columbia which borders on the ocean, and extends from Behring Straits to the Straits of Fuca, the climate is wonderfully soft and mild for the latitude, so much so, indeed, that the temperature in the winter-time is about that of Washington City.

The writer of this passed a winter in Alaska in 60° lat., and the lowest the Fahrenheit thermometer stood at any time was 23° *above* zero, and the average temperature was above 35°, while in the summer the average temperature is about 56°. Certainly not a vey rigorous

climate for such a latitude, and yet some may be inclined to doubt all this unless a reason be given for such an unusual temperature in such high latitudes. "Why is this thus?" as Artemus Ward would say. Well, here is the reason.

Of course, every one has read of the Gulf Stream, which bathes our own shores from Florida to Newfoundland, and then diverging eastward softens the climate of the British Isles, without which influence those islands would be as uninhabitable as the territory of Labrador, which lies between the same parallels of latitude as Great Britain, and is with us a synonyme for every thing that is cold, dreary, and dismal.

Well, in the Pacific Ocean there is also a great current of warm water, resembling our Gulf Stream, which, sweeping along the coasts of Japan and Asia to the northeast, crosses the Pacific, and washes the northwest coast of America as far down as the Bay of Panama, where it again diverges to the westward and forms the great equatorial current of the Pacific.

The average maximum temperature of this singular stream is about 85° Fahr., and it, therefore, fully accounts for the productiveness of the Japan Islands, which, although farther north than Southern Virginia, produce sugar and other crops usually confined to intertropical latitudes. One branch of this current, after striking the Aleutian Islands, is diverted from its course and sweeps away to the north through Behring Straits, and so into the Northern Ocean, which is one reason why no icebergs are ever seen by the whalers to the south of Behring Straits. Off the northern Japan Islands the contact of the warm water of the stream with the colder water of the latitude—for these islands are as far north as Boston—gives rise, as does the Gulf Stream on our northeast coast, to constant fogs.

The evidence in favor of the existence of this great Pacific current is as strong as any thing known to science can be; but, even if there were no other proof, the wrecks of Japanese vessels, which from time to time have been cast ashore upon the coasts of Washington Territory and Oregon, would be evidence enough. Indian tradition says that a number of years ago a junk loaded with beeswax was wrecked at the mouth of the Columbia River, the vessel having been previously disabled and drifted by this current far out of her course. Though the vessel was lost the crew were saved. In proof of this tradition, so late as 1851, pieces of wax, blanched white and covered with sand, were washed up on the beach in this locality after every great gale. Within seven years a Japanese junk was found floating helplessly in this current, the crew saved by one of our vessels, and brought into San Francisco.

The result of this great Pacific stream is to produce a singularly mild climate in the regions under its influence, and in the northern latitudes we hear of a prevalence of much fog, while the moisture deposited upon the lofty mountains of the Alaska coast creates rain.

A cold snap is a godsend at Sitka, for it is no exaggeration to say that there it rains fully two-thirds of the time. May, June, July, and February, are the driest months.

On the sea-coast in the winter the snow seldom falls to the depth of over six inches, and quickly melts away into slush, and the region about Sitka may be said to be one of incessant rain-storms, fierce gales, dripping forests, dank moss, dense mud, and drifting mists. Pluvius reigns with undisputed sway, and renders the country a perfect paradise for ducks and sea-gulls.

The lords of creation may depend that the Sorosis will never emigrate to Sitka, for a woman's right to a dry Monday fails to receive the slighest respect.

The average amount of rain which has fallen yearly, as shown by the records of the past eighteen years, is eighty-six inches! Just think of it! Over seven feet of rain!

Why, if a short man stood still in Sitka for six months, he would be drowned, or else so covered with moss that even Darwin could not place him, or his own mother recognize him! There are but two seasons in Sitka—the long rainy season and the short rainy season. In the long rainy season it rains nine months of the year; in the short rainy season, the other three! Rain, rain, rain!

Occasionally, however, the sun does break through the damp clouds, and then, for two or three days—never longer—there is gorgeous weather. The air becomes soft and balmy, even in midwinter, when the sun rises at nine o'clock and goes down again at three, and the skies become more beautifully blue and cloudless than in any other part of the world. For two or three days there is weather calculated to make men young again, and so all Sitka turns out, including the animals, to seek the brief sunshine and bask in its transient warmth. After which the great floodgates of heaven are opened again, and, by way of variety, it is one continuous rain, rain, rain, for weeks.

Of course, in a country where it rains so constantly, the character of the crops produced on the land must be somewhat peculiar. In point of fact, though the writer of this heard a good deal of crops *before* he went to Alaska, he never saw any there. There were, to be sure, some watery-looking potatoes about the size of a chestnut, and some equally-miserable turnips and cabbages, but they, too, had water in them, and cabbage and water is poor diet.

But yet certain things do grow pretty well in Alaska, among them cranberries and berries of all kinds, though they lack flavor; and, as the population increases, and more land becomes cleared, no doubt some smart Yankee will get out a patent to stop the rain, and then crops may be raised. But the staple productions of the country around Sitka, at least for some years, will, it is thought, be ducks, fish, umbrellas, and gum-shoes!

Notwithstanding the constant rains, Sitka is not an unhealthy place. Prior to our acquisition of it, rheumatism and colds were common, and in the fine, warm weather malignant fevers prevailed to an alarming extent, so much so that, at the period of our occupation of the town, the Russian officials gave a fearful account of the unhealthiness of the place and the fevers incident to warmth and exposure to the sun. It was very soon found that the filthy habits of the people and the filthier condition of the streets and dwellings were, in the main, responsible for this condition of things. The American postsurgeon was looked upon by his Russian brethren in the profession as little less than a lunatic when he announced his intention of improving the ventilation of the hospital by fitting the windows of the building so that they might be opened. Up to his advent upon the ground the windows of all the houses were "built in," so that they were kept at all times tightly closed. A small pane of glass, fitted in a frame on hinges, admitted all the air the Russians needed or allowed—which was not much—and the odor of their apartments baffled description. But all that has been changed, and apparently with the best results, for sickness is now comparatively rare, owing to the improved condition of the dwellings as to cleanliness and ventilation.

And now as to the inhabitants of Alaska.

In October, 1867, just before the occupation by the United States forces, the number of inhabitants throughout Russian America was computed to be, from the best information, about fifty thousand, of which about three thousand were Russians and half-breeds, and the rest Indians. One person to every nine square miles of territory!

These forty-seven thousand Indians are divided into two races and four great branches, namely: Esquimaux, Aleutians, Kenayans, and Koloschians.

1. Of the Esquimaux, which number about eighteen thousand, and inhabit the northern part of the Territory bordering on the Polar Sea, as well as the line of the Yukon River, not much need be said, as most persons are familiar with their principal characteristics from reading works of Arctic travel. Their chief virtues seem to be that they are given to hospitality and are peaceable and domestic. They differ in person very much from the Esquimaux of Greenland, being in stature tall, with copper-colored skin, flat faces, small black eyes, and very white teeth. The women pierce the nostrils, and tobacco, rum, and train-oil, are their special luxuries.

2. The Aleutians, or people who inhabit the islands to the westward of the peninsula of Aliaska, and carry on the seal and other fisheries. They number about five thousand, and are a peaceable, industrious race of beings, who eke out life by hunting the furred seal and seaotter, catching cod and halibut, and attending the Greek Church—for they are all Christians.

Under Russian management they were said to excel as artificers and mechanics when taught, and the Fur Company made use of them largely as sailors.

The native dress is usually a long frock with tight sleeves, called in the Russian language a *parka*. This dress is made from the skins of the bird called the diver, and is almost indispensable to the Aleute, answering for both clothing and blanket, as well as shelter against wind and cold.

The skill of these people in managing their boats is wonderful. In their frail skin-canoes, called *bidarkas*, they venture out to sea and make journeys from island to island in the most tempestuous weather and with the greatest ease and dexterity. Oonalaska, Kodiak, and the seal-islands of St. Paul and St. George, are the principal ones inhabited by this race, though they are scattered throughout the entire chain of islands to the west of Aliaska, and are probably, like the Esquimaux, of Mongolian origin.

3. The Kenayans, numbering about twenty thousand, and taking their name from the peninsula of Kenay, with Cook's Inlet on the west and Prince William's Sound on the east. They inhabit all that part of the country between the Sushina and the Copper Rivers, and belong to the great Indian race of North America; their general characteristics being much the same as those of the northern tribes with which we are most familiar. They are proud, warlike, and exceedingly boastful, their common designation of themselves being that they are "men."

They are more cleanly than the Esquimaux, and less addicted to grease. They are of medium stature, but strong and powerfully built, with large heads, spreading faces, and thick necks. Their hair is straight and coal-black, beard thin, their eyes small and keen, and their teeth very white.

Away from civilization and the traders, they dress in the skins of animals, with the fur outward, over which they sometimes wear a shirt made of skin from the intestines of the whale, as a protection against the wet.

Their canoes are made of common sealskins stretched on frames, and are sometimes, large enough to hold between twenty and thirty persons, but in form they are not so graceful as the canoes of the Aleutes, nor are the Kenayans so dexterous in their management.

As a race, they are thievish, and will steal any thing they can lay their hands on, and their moral character is bad in other respects, for they seem to have acquired, by contact with the traders, all the vices and none of the virtues of the white race.

Small-pox and other diseases have carried them off fearfully within a few years past, and if the modern frontier civilization of rum, obacco, and vice, continues on the increase, hey bid fair to be soon blotted out altogether, and numbered with the lost tribes of Israel.

Lastly, there is the Koloschian race, the most important of all, divided into more than a dozen separate tribes, of which the Tchill-kats Takons, Sitkas, and Kakes, are the most powerful, the whole race numbering, according to Russian accounts, above five thousand, though it is thought that double that number is nearer the mark.

This is the race settlers in Alaska will have most to do with, as they occupy the country between the Copper River and the southern boundary of Alaska on the Portland Channel or canal. The term *Koloschian* is Russian, and signifies Indian, and the tract of country occupied by this race is known as the Alexander Archipelago.

Though numerically inferior to the Kenayans and Esquimaux, these Koloschians occupy far more valuable territory, and are greatly their superiors in habits and character. They subsist almost entirely by hunting and fishing, and, as a race, are intelligent, warlike, proud, treacherous, and exceedingly revengeful, revenge being with them the highest of all virtues.

In appearance they are not prepossessing, and their reputation for morality is rather threadbare. Their houses are shanties on a large scale, with a small entrance, generally circular in form, and reached frequently by a short flight of steps, and the roof has a hole in its centre to let out the smoke.

The dress is commonly a blanket in the summer-time; though the chiefs, when they have any money acquired by the sale of furs to the traders, generally affect the European costume, and dress their squaws in calicoes. These people have a fashion of blacking their faces, and sometimes paint their lovely countenances with red, yellow, and blue, which, when properly done, gives them, as Mark Twain would say, a peculiarly peaceful and lamb-like expression!

All the powerful tribes resort annually to Sitka, the winter being the season chosen.

Now, when one of our fashionable belles resorts to Long Branch or Newport for the summer, she carries with her ten or fifteen trunks, as many bonnets or bandboxes, three or four styles of umbrellas and wrappings, and has one or more young gentlemen to attend her and carry the numerous smaller packages which go to make up a modern belle's outfit; but when a Tchillkat girl goes to Sitka she paddles the whole distance (two hundred miles) by herself in an open canoe, with for

food a bark-box of dried salmon, and for dress a piece of silver or bone stuck though the lower lip, and a blanket thrown over her shoulders.

The canoes are made of huge trees hollowed out, and the war-canoes are sometimes so large as to seat eighty persons with ease. These last are painted with hideous devices in red, black, and yellow, and the sight of one filled with painted natives is enough to give a nervous person the nightmare for a month. The Koloschians are daring navigators, and frequently make voyages of over five hundred miles in these open canoes.

To give an idea of their dauntless courage and intense desire for revenge, it may be interesting at this point to mention an incident concerning the tribe known as the Kakes or Kekons—a tribe which has frequently given the whites much trouble, and has only been perfectly quiet since the Saginaw shelled and destroyed their villages in February, 1869, in retaliation for the murder of two white traders, Messrs. Mauger and Walker.

In 1855 a party of Kakes, on a visit south to Puget Sound, became involved in some trouble there, which caused a United-States vessel to open fire on them, and during the affair one of the Kake chiefs was killed. This took place over eight hundred miles from the Kake settlements on Kuprianoff Island. The very next year the tribe sent a canoe-load of fighting men all the way from Clarence Straits in Russian America, to Whidby's Island, in Washington Territory, and attacked and beheaded an ex-collector—not of internal revenue, for that might have been pardonable—but of customs, and returned safely with his skull and scalp to their villages. Such people are, therefore, not to be despised, and are quite capable of giving much trouble in the future unless wisely and firmly governed.

These Indians are somewhat thrifty, and show some sense of property, and contact with the traders has rendered them exceedingly sharp and cunning in a bargain. They are tolerably honest, and will readily work for wages. Their proud nature, however, disdains corporal punishment even for their children, and a blow is a mortal insult, only to be washed out in the blood of the offender. Their cardinal maxims are as old as the days of Moses, "An eye for an eye, a tooth for a tooth," and they will compass sea and land to retaliate for a supposed injury. Of course, therefore, very few are Christians, and yet the majority can hardly be called idolatrous, since they believe in a Creator, and in the immortality of the soul.

One of their peculiarities is an intense

reverence for the ashes and memory of their ancestors and warriors, who, they believe, are placed in the sky and appear nightly in the Aurora Borealis. They also have a tradition of the deluge, their account of it being that, ages ago, the entire human family was saved from perishing in a great flood by means of a floating vessel. On the subsidence of the water this vessel struck a rock, and broke in halves. One half represents the Koloschian—the other half—the rest of the world!

For generations these Indians have been warriors, and their character has not changed Every male has his sporting-gun and his war-rifle; in some cases this last is of the latest and most improved pattern, and they will give the traders any price for such weapons as the Henry and Spencer arms. Every Indian carries the long knife—quarrels are common, and the duel a recognized institution. "A life for a life" is their maxim, unless the life is at once paid for in blankets, and the loss of a father, brother, sister, or dear relative, can only be atoned for by another death, or else by an equivalent in blankets, every position of relationship having a recognized price. Away from the lines of garrison, slavery still exists quite beyond the reach of amendment to the constitution, or special committees charged with power even to send for persons and papers.

The slave is less in value than a dog, and must implicitly obey his master in all things, even to committing murder, while the master may kill him at any time, and go unquestioned by the tribe. The slave has no rights whatever, and, when dead, is cast into the nearest inlet to feed the fishes.

When a chief dies his slaves are all sacrificed, and his body burned on a funeral-pile, after which his ashes are deposited in the curiously-shaped and grotesquely-wrought posts and boxes which usually stand in front of the chief's lodge in the village. Then the women perform a week or two of dismal howling over the remains thus stored away, and the tribe go in black faces for a year.

These Koloschians have been a perfect terror to the coast for more than a century. It was one of the Koloschian tribes which received the boats from Tchirikoff's vessel, and no survivor ever returned to tell the tale of horror. They were also the actors in another fearfully-bloody drama in 1840, when they surprised and pitilessly massacred, with horrible cruelty, the Russian garrison of old Sitka, a few miles from the present site.

Lisiansky, in 1805, with Baranoff, the founder of Sitka, drove them from the site of the present settlement, and established there a fort upon a rocky eminence dominating the surrounding country. This hill forms a natural fortification, and was, at the period of Lisiansky's visit, in 1805, inhabited by a warlike chief named Katetan. The savages sustained a siege from the Neva and two other men-of-war under Lisiansky and Baranoff, but finally evacuated the hill, after murdering all their comrades that they could not carry off.

After Baranoff had made the fort secure, the necessary houses of a settlement soon sprang up around it, and it became the capital of the Russian-American possessions. The savages long continued to make aggressions on the Russians, who dared not venture beyond the range of their fortifications except when the men-of-war were in the harbor.

Lisiansky describes these Indians as a shrewd, bold, and perfidious people, whose chiefs used very sublime expressions, and swore fearful oaths upon the bones and ashes of their ancestors, calling heaven and earth and the entire solar system to witness—particularly when they wanted to deceive.

They have a way of multiplying suddenly in a place by immense canoe-loads secreted near by, so that although ony a few Indians may apparently be in the village which adjoins every post, many thousands may arrive in a few hours. On one occasion, it is said, over three thousand suddenly made their appearance at Sitka and demanded blankets, which the Russian Company, terribly frightened immediately gave them, when they quietly departed as they came.

It can readily be seen that such a race of people require management of no ordinary kind. Uniform kindness, strict justice, prompt decision, and rigid execution of purpose, are the corner-stones of any policy by which they can be wisely or humanely governed.

Their aggressions have not been unfrequent even in late years. Some five years ago the Kakes captured an English schooner, the Royal Charlie, murdered the crew, and scuttled the vessel after plundering the cargo. In February, 1869, the Saginaw recovered, from the chief's lodge on Kupnauoff Island, some of the equipment of this illfated vessel.

In 1862 a party of the Cross Sound and Hoonah Indians, while trading on board the Hudson Bay Company's steamer, the Labouchère (a vessel of eight hundred tons), suddenly drew their knives, seized the captain on his quarter-deck, and drove the crew forward thus gaining complete possession of the after part of the vessel. Fortunately for the captain his chief officer was a brave and determined fellow, and, getting across the bulkhead, which all these vessels carry for protection athwart the deck, he trained a brass cannon loaded with bags of musket-balls upon the dense mass of Indians on the quarter-deck. These immediately placed the captain in front of his own gun. Finally a parley took place, and the Indians, after robbing the vessel, released the captain, and quitted her. She steamed away at once, and for a long time dared not return to this locality (Suanson's Harbor) to trade.

The only things the Koloschians dread are the men-of-war, which can follow them up rivers and bays, swift to punish any outrage they may commit. Since the punishment the Kake tribe received from the commander of the Saginaw, in February, 1869, the entire race of Indians has been perfectly quiet and suddued.

And now, having disposed of the climate and inhabitants, let us see what the products of this country are.

RICHARD W. MEADE.

II.

TIMBER is the chief vegetable product of Alaska. The forests, which extend from Fort Tongas, on the southern boundary, to Cook's Inlet, where the trees begin to disappear, are boundless in extent, and able to supply for ages to come such countries as California and Northern Mexico, which have a poor supply of timber. There is a large and growing timber-trade carried on from Puget Sound , in Washington Territory, but the timber of Alaska, and especially the yellow cedar of Sitka, is far superior to any thing produced there. The timber is so dense in the wooded portions of Alaska, that it is difficult to make one's way any distance from the beach. Exploring parties from ships have been three and four hours getting half a mile from the beach, and, except where the timber has been cleared away for settlements, this is generally true of the whole sea-board to Cross Sound. One of the curious features of the timbered portion of this country is, that the entire surface of the ground is covered with *sphagnum*, a sort of thick, beautifully-green moss, seldom less than a foot, and sometimes even three feet deep. It forms a soft, marshy surface, into which the foot sinks at every step; and, as it is everlastingly raining here, of course the ground is always soaking wet. If a fire is built in the woods, it is a curious sight to see it sinking down, down, until it comes to "hardpan," when you have the fire burning in a hole a foot deep or more.

Water-power for the saw-mill is everywhere, for the country abounds in running streams; but, even if there were none, the incessant rains would soon supply all the power needed.

Next in order, after the timber, is the fishery question, and here a word or two of preface.

The influence of a great fishery interest can hardly be over-estimated—the herring, for instance, having been described by certain enthusiasts as " a natural product whose use has decided the destiny of nations." This is putting it in rather a forcible way, and yet, without going quite so far, it is easy to see that the fisheries in the North Pacific must eventually exercise a great influence over the population, thus giving a new life to commerce, and enlarging the national resources. The fisheries are the great nurseries for seamen, who, of course, are indispensable for commerce on the ocean. A great commerce gives power to control the sea, and "the nation which controls the sea, controls the world."

Therefore, looking at it in this light, the value of a great fishery interest in the North Pacific cannot be exaggerated, and how soon we may have one the reader may judge for himself, when he is told that there are now between fifty and one hundred vessels (many of which are New-England built and manned, and have doubled Cape Horn within the last three years) engaged in this business. And with all Mexico, Central and South America for a market—for these people must, perforce, have their Friday's fish—the business cannot fail to be a great one.

Our New-England cod and other fisheries bring us over two million dollars annually, and they are far inferior to the French fisheries in value, and still more so to the fisheries of Great Britain.

Now, of fish there is in Alaska an inexhaustible quantity, from the cod and halibut found on the banks, near Oonalaska Island and other places, to the salmon-fisheries of every fresh-water stream in the Territory, and the oolacan or candle fisheries of the Portland Channel and Naas. These last deserve especial mention. The candle-fish is not much larger than the smelt, which it much resembles in appearance, being a beautiful little fish with bright silvery skin and scales. It is caught by the Indians on bright moonlight nights. They use for this purpose a large rake some six or seven feet long, with teeth of bone or sharp-pointed nails. This rake has a handle, and, while one Indian paddles the canoe close to the "shoal of fish," the other sweeps the rake through the dense mass, bringing up generally three or four fish impaled on each tooth of the rake. The canoes are soon filled, and, the contents being taken on shore, the squaws proceed to skewer the fish on long sticks, passing these sticks through the eyes until each one has as many as it will hold, when the whole are suspended in the thick, smoky atmosphere at the top of the hut, which dries and preserves the fish without salt, which is never used by the Indians.

When dry, the candle-fish are carefully packed away in boxes of dried bark. The traders at Fort Simpson catch these fish in nets, salt and dry them in the usual manner practised by the whites; and when this is properly done, no fish are more delicious than the candle-fish, the only trouble being that they are so rich one soon tires of them.

To use them as candles, a piece of wick, or dried pith, is passed through the fish with a bodkin of hard wood, and the tail being inserted in a cleft-stick, or junk-bottle, the wick is lighted. The fish burns with a clear, steady flame.

Of salmon there are myriads. Every fresh-water stream is filled with them during the season, which commences in the latter part of June. At that period the Indians lay in their year's supply of food, by selecting some fresh-water stream about forty feet wide, which has a slight fall of water, say six feet or so, a short distance from where it empties into the sea. Above the fall they either stretch a net or make a weir of twigs and stakes entirely across the stream. When the salmon commence "to run," as the saying is, they make for the streams, and go with a jump clear over the fall into the net, and are scooped out or struck with spears, and thus landed on the river-bank, where they are dried on poles stretched across a frame. The first "run" has the choice fish.

At the bay of Cosaan is a salmon-fishery owned by a Russian named Baronovitch. He informed the writer of this article that he had been the fish so thick in the streams as to impede a canoe, and the same story has been told elsewhere. Baronovitch, with limited means, puts up about one thousand barrels of fish every season, and could put up ten times that number if he had the capital. In Alaska salmon is a drug in the market, and, through-out the length and breadth of the Territory a white man will not touch it if he can get any thing else; but what the Indian would do without it is hard to say; it is his staple of food—he could not exist without it.

A FISHING-VILLAGE IN ALASKA.

FORT YUKON IN ALASKA.

Timber and fish having been disposed of, next in order are the furs.

Prior to our acquisition of the country the trade in furs was in the hands of two great corporations, the Russian-American Fur Company and the Hudson Bay Company, the latter having leased certain localities, and obtained certain rights from the former.

The Hudson Bay Company is much the older of the two, and its original members in 1670, when it was first chartered by the British crown, were such noted characters in history as Prince Rupert, the Duke of Albemarle, and the Earl of Craven. It maintained many ships, and grew rich and powerful by its trade. Its profit in furs was enormous, so much so that half the stories told by the veterans in the trade seem hardly credible,. One is to the effect that, a few years ago, the price of a flint-lock musket in furs was found by standing the musket on its butt-end and piling up marten-furs until they reached the muzzle. Now, these muskets never cost the company over two dollars a piece, and thus several hundred marten-skins, worth from three to thirty dollars a piece, were obtained for a mere song!

But these golden days have passed and gone forever, and the natives know the full value of their furs now.

One may, therefore, gather an idea—a faint one—of the enormous profits formerly realized in this business. The most valuable of all the furs is the sea-otter, which now brings from twenty-five to seventy-five dollars *in Alaska*. It is a beautifully soft purplish-black fur and very heavy, and in Russia is known as the "court fur," only to be worn by certain classes of the nobility. For any plebeian to wear this fur in Russia is an offence punished by fine, imprisonment, or exile to Siberia.

The fur is also extensively sought after by the higher classes in the Chinese empire, hence its very high price. The animal is now scarce, and only to be taken among the Aleutian Islands, the noise of fire-arms having driven it from the Alexander Archipelago.

After the sea-otter, in point of importance to the trader, are the black and silver foxes, also very valuable; then come the furred seal, marten, or Hudson Bay sable, crossed fox, mink, ermine, and red fox; after which come such inferior furs as the bear, lynx, wolverine, mountain-sheep, and many others, the number of fur-bearing animals being very great.

Of all these animals the furred seal is the one most likely to prove valuable for revenue. It is found almost solely on the islands of St. Paul and St. George, to the north of the Aleutian chain, hence known popularly as the Seal Islands, though late accounts now say it resorts to the Commander group. It is different from the common seal, and is one of the most sagacious and intelligent of dumb creatures—in fact, its instinct is almost human. The nervous organization of the animal is peculiar, and so sensitive is he to sharp sounds and noises that the firing of guns or barking of small dogs will cause them to desert their usual haunts, and the keeping of a little dog on St. Paul's Island during a certain year is said to have caused the Russian Fur Company a loss of over one hundred thousand dollars'

AN ALASKA CHIEF.

worth of furs the next year. Consequently, an indiscriminate free trade in these animals would soon cause them to desert the islands now resorted to altogether, and, therefore, a monopoly of this business is essential to its life. Indiscriminate butchery of the seal would also soon glut the market and lower the price so as hardly to pay for transportation. The Russians only allowed a certain number (about eighty thousand) to be killed annually, and this kept the price up, and the seal were not reduced in numbers.

When the season arrives (between May and October), these animals flock to the islands mentioned in incredible numbers and with an organization and system truly wonderful. In one division of a herd are the females with their young; in another division, the young males and females, separated; while the old males preserve order throughout the herd, and act as overseers, constables, and whippers-in generally. If a young male gets in among the females, away goes one of these old chaps for him, and drives him back again with his tail. They have never been known to have any thing resembling the Sorosis among them.

On the arrival of the herd the natives select certain of them for slaughter, quietly drive them into the interior of the island away from the main body, where they are killed with a blow on the nose from a club, the skin stripped off and salted down, and the flesh used to make oil and for many other purposes. The young males and females are the ones selected for slaughter, which is the appreciation the natives set on single blessedness.

The furs when first taken are coarse and have to be sent to Europe to be prepared for the market. In England they are frequently dyed afterward.

But the fur-trade generally throughout the Alexander Archipelago is likely, under the present system, or rather want of system, to die out altogether, since, in course of time, the wholesale slaughter of fur-bearing animals will exterminate them. Under the Russian monopoly the animals were not only protected by statute but in fact, and the natives were not allowed to kill them indiscriminately. This prevented the stock from becoming extinct, and kept the price of furs up. But with all its power—the power of life and death—the company could not prevent an illicit traffic in furs carried on by the English and American whiskey-smugglers from British Columbia and Washington Territory. These scoundrels plied the Indians with liquor of the vilest description, and took their furs from them in exchange.

As a specimen of the manner in which this is done, it may here be mentioned that, in 1868, a fellow named Coffin sailed in a schooner from a port in British Columbia with a cargo of villanously bad alcohol and some common brown sugar. Of course, water costs nothing in this country, and so Captain Coffin was enabled to manufacture a drink which would veritably take a man's scalp off at forty rods! But he knew how to tickle the palate of the Indian, who judges of liquor solely by its fiery taste, and values it in proportion to the amount it takes to produce intoxication—a "cheap drunk" being a great thing in Alaska.

This fellow, by the sale of his infamous decoction, brought on a difficulty between two tribes of Indians before friendly to each other, and seventeen of the Hudson Bay Indians were killed in a fight which subsequently ensued. But he and his vessel shortly after came to grief, being wrecked on Forrester's Island, and Coffin and his companions were found on the beach dead, with their throats so torn and lacerated that for a long time it was thought they had been murdered by the Indians. Subsequently it was ascertained that the sharp rocks on the beach were responsible for the mutilated condition of the bodies.

Of course, if the fur-trade is to fall into the

hands of such fellows as Coffin, in a few years it will be conducted on the whiskey basis unless the United States Government takes the most rigid and inflexible means to suppress it.

The natives themselves give aid and comfort to the whiskey-smuggler by timely warning of approaching danger, by false information to the officers of the law, and by secreting the small vessels of these smugglers when searched for. The myriads of islands and harbors along this coast, which resembles Norway in the character of its fiords; the thick, foggy weather, and the innumerable channels and straits, many of which are not even marked on the charts, give an advantage to the whiskey-trader he is not slow to avail himself of.

Lastly, among the supposed resources of the country is its mineral wealth, and, in regard to this, not much is actually known, for, under the rule of the Russian Fur Company, its employés were so busy in getting furs, and studying the best method of keeping up the supply, that no good mineralogical collection of specimens was made for comparison; while, since the country came into our possession, no regularly-organized expedition for exploration has been sent to Alaska, and the only knowledge we possess is derived from the Indians (generally unreliable), the wandering bands of prospectors, and an occasional account of an excursion from some military post. Yet gold has been discovered on the Stachine River, and the mines have been worked to some extent. Miners from there say that, with ordinary panning, they can make from two to seven dollars per day; but the pleasant season lasts only six months—the rest of the year the weather is too inclement to work in, and the isolated position of the placers renders it difficult to get provisions and stores.

Copper is said to have been discovered on the Copper River, and there is no doubt but that copper utensils were in use among the natives as far back as the days of Behring, though where the copper came from the historian sayeth not.

Silver, iron, and bismuth, are also said to exist, but the writer of this never saw any one in Alaska who could testify to having seen any; and as for diamonds, why, there are quantities—in New York—and sold by the veritable "Original Jacobs!"—so that the mineral wealth of the Territory is uncertain, coal being the only product in that line found there that admits of any discussion as to its probable value. In regard to coal, there is an inexhaustible supply both on Admiralty Island and at Cook's Inlet.

But nothing, as yet, has been said of the scenery—the history, climate, inhabitants, and resources of the country have all been discussed, the useful dwelt upon, the beautiful alone omitted.

Well, the traveller from Alaska may enlarge a good deal on scenery, especially when he can talk of mountain-ranges covered with perpetual snow, huge glaciers awing into silence every beholder with their magnificent sublimity, water-falls, rapid currents, and splendid forests of timber, with the Aurora Borealis thrown in every clear night by way of a make-weight.

The writer of this has no more of the romantic in him than Mark Twain, yet he can say with truth that in twenty-five years' roaming in all quarters of the globe he never saw more magnificent scenery anywhere than in British Columbia and Alaska—the only trouble is, it is so continuously magnificent, it becomes monotonous.

Now let us see if it is possible to convey a faint idea of the voyage through the inland waters from Victoria, in Vancouver's Island, to Sitka, in Alaska, by means of a simile.

Let us suppose the Highlands of the Hudson River (with which we nearly all are familiar) to be stretched out, as it were, for nine hundred miles. We won't widen the river at all, but we will increase the height of the hills from fourteen hundred to three thousand, seven thousand, and in some cases ten thousand feet. We will cover the peaks of the mountains with snow, and the rest with dense forests of timber, except where the mountain-streams come tumbling down in great water-falls of fifty feet or more, and frequently fall over a huge cliff directly into the sea, near which our vessel passes. As we go farther north, imagine great valleys filled with enormous glaciers, or sheets of ice, from one to ten miles wide, and extending back miles into the interior. These huge masses of ice, sometimes twelve hundred feet thick, are of a blue Alpine hue, and, when the bright sunlight falls upon them, their gleaming surface, rich with prismatic color, presents an inconceivably magnificent sight.

Now, if the reader can gather any thing from this imperfect description, he has in his mind's eye the scenery of Alaska. For miles and miles our steamer journeys along through this wilderness, amid these mountains "wooded to the peak." From base to snowy region, nothing mars the uniformity—a dense, dark forest of pines and hemlock, through whose wilds the foot even of the savage has never wandered! The eye fairly wearies of the endless monotony and death-like stillness of these primeval forests, and seeks for more peaceful landscapes; but in vain. Nothing disturbs the dreary loneliness of this wonderful forest-land, except the splash of the paddles, as the steamer speeds swiftly on her way; the shrill note of the eagle, as he circles over some lofty cliff, or the howl of the wolf amid the recesses of the forest.

Everywhere the depth of water is great—two hundred fathoms of line find no bottom. The hundreds of straits and channels help to bewilder the navigator, so that it is difficult sometimes for him to grope his way through the endless labyrinth. Grenville Channel is forty-eight miles long, about a mile wide, is perfectly straight, and has but two anchorages.

On one occasion an English man-of-war lost her way in one of the "*cul-de-sac* channels," near Bella-bella, and was nearly two weeks finding her way back again. As there is only an occasional anchorage here and there, such a predicament is exceedingly unpleasant, not to say hazardous. The line of channel through this myriad of islands is rarely wider than the Hudson at Haverstraw, and is frequently not over a mile, while in some places it is hardly that; and here, through these fearful gorges, less than a mile wide, the tide runs with a terrible rapidity, to which our current of Hell Gate, near New York, is "a mere circumstance."

Imagine such a pass between ranges of lofty mountains, from three thousand to five thousand feet in height, the tide rushing through at the rate of twelve knots an hour, and the reader has some idea of the Yaculta Rapids, at Seymour Narrows, in British Columbia, and Peril Straits, in Alaska.

Several large vessels have attempted these rapids in their strength, and some have only by good fortune escaped destruction with all on board.

At this stage I hear some reader exclaim that nothing has been said about Sitka and the Russians.

Well, Sitka may be briefly described as the dirtiest collection of log-huts on the Pacific slope. Its appearance as a town is far from inviting, and, with the magnificent scenery in the background, its squalor is all the more striking. There is an old saying that "God made the country, and man the town"—it is strikingly exemplified at Sitka.

On the right of the town, looking at it from the anchorage, stand the buildings formerly belonging to the fur company, the citadel being on the rocky eminence once before

spoken of; farther on, the houses of the citizens; finally, the church and hospital. On the left of the town, outside of the stockade, is the Indian village of about sixty houses; still farther to the left, a collection of Indian graves.

The Russian governor's house, or the citadel, now occupied by the commanding officer of the military district, is the only building in Sitka, except the church, that deserves any especial mention. It is perched on Katalan's Rock before mentioned, and is a huge structure of two stories in height, but very long and broad, roofed with sheet-iron, painted red, and capped by the only light-house in Alaska, which, at night, casts a feeble glimmer three or four miles seaward.

The summit of the hill is defended by batteries which command every point in the harbor. The northwest end is approached by a flight of wooden steps, and half-way up sentinels are kept posted day and night; at this point is a sort of military prison, in front of which is displayed a light battery of brass cannon, loaded with canister, and ready for any emergency.

The upper story of the building is divided into one large room in the centre, flanked by drawing-room and billiard-room at one end, and another large room at the other, all well kept, painted in nice style, and hung with old prints of celebrated English sea-fights. The lower story contains dining-room, parlor, study, and sleeping-apartments, all very large, and furnished with the inevitable Russian stove, or furnace. The entire structure is built of huge logs, squared, joined, and painted.

There is really but one decent street in the town, to which Americans have given the high-sounding title of Broadway, and, after passing the church and hospital, the street forms itself into a road along the beach, after following which for about half a mile, you reach the only natural curiosity in Sitka—a huge stone on which old Baranoff, the first governor, used to sit on fine afternoons and drink brandy until he became so much "overcome" that his friends had to take him home.

The Russians kept their houses in a filthy condition, some even keeping poultry in the rooms over the sleeping-chamber, and, as the little windows were never opened, except at long intervals, the odor was not exactly *bouquet de mille fleurs*. And the pigs and goats roamed the streets with unrestricted liberty.

Fortunately most of the Russians have gone home, or to the Amoor River, and probably, aided by the everlasting rains, Sitka may eventually become clean, and the high boardwalks, rendered indispensable in order to keep people out of the deep mud, be finally dispensed with.

The officers of the garrison have a club-house near the church, where, after the manner of frontier posts, they play cards and billiards, and drink commissary whiskey; that is, when the rest of their time is not taken up in lounging in the sutler's store.

The Greek church is a gaudily-decorated affair, painted in green and gold, after the Eastern fashion, with magnificent regalia and appointments for its exceedingly imposing, but rather tiresome services.

In the church was kept a magnificent Bible, presented by the czar, with jewelled cover, said to be worth a fabulous amount, and the progress of American civilization and republican institutions was marked by its being stolen upon the occupation by the Yankees.

The Indians are never allowed inside the stockade after nightfall, while a guard is kept constantly on the alert with rifles loaded, and a field-battery of Parrott guns kept constantly trained on the Indian village adjoining the town, and a man-of-war lies anchored in the harbor, with her guns pointed at the Sitka village.

The population is about fifteen hundred during the winter season, of whom one thousand are Indians, and the rest Jews, Gentiles, hickory Christians, and soldiers.

And this is the principal, and, if we except Kodiak (for Forts Tongas and Urangel are only military posts), the only town or place of any importance in the whole Territory of four hundred and fifty thousand square miles.

And now, if the reader has had the patience and followed us attentively in this sketch, he can draw his own conclusions as to the present and prospective value of Alaska, and whether, on the whole, it is or is not worth the money we paid for it.

RICHARD W. MEADE.

13
The Klondike
Output for 1900

THE KLONDIKE
OUTPUT FOR 1900

WHILE Nome City, the new gold-camp under the arctic circle, one hundred miles north of St. Michael, is absorbing most of the attention of prospectors here and at Seattle, Dawson does not seem to have suffered much from the new attraction on the bleak shore of Bering Sea. The latest advices from the chief city of the Klondike declare that the clean-up will be large and unusually early, as many men who own claims will have a force to work them, while they will depart as soon as possible for Cape Nome, or Cape York, or the Koyukuk country, to make a personal investigation of the new bonanza fields. For every one who leaves Dawson there will be five to come in, as at least half the people on the way to Nome will go by way of Dawson. All the trails leading to the Klondike are reported crowded with prospectors, who are using every variety of vehicle from dog-sledges to bicycles and automobiles. Among recent arrivals at the metropolis of the Klondike were two women who made the journey from Skaguay wihtout male escort. They had a sleigh with one horse,

and though several times they came within an ace of losing their animal through holes in the ice, they managed to arrive all right.

This spring the dumps at the various mines are being worked much earlier than usual. Some companies use a shot-water plant that washes out a large amount of dirt in a day, and the success of this device shows that it will probably be adopted generally in Alaska, wherever there is no lack of fuel. It gives the nimer the great advantage of ascertaining the value of the dirt that he takes out. Under the old system two or four miners working together spent the whole winter taking out pay dirt and piling it up in huge dumps. No one could tell till spring what these dumps would yield, though an occasional pan, washed out in hot water, gave some clew to the richness of the dirt. With the new steam-washers the dumps may be cleared up every week, and then if a prospect hole is found to be yielding poorly it may be abandoned for new ground. Dawson will be helped by the sale at auction on June 1 by Gold-Commissioner Senkler of all the Canadian government's placer-mining claims.

DOG-TEAMS IN DAWSON.

WET BLANKETS AS PROTECTION AGAINST FIRE.

These claims have been tied up for months and no development work has been done on them. They will now pass into the hands of practical miners or mining companies, and work will begin on them as soon as possible. Dawson during the past winter had several narrow escapes from complete destruction by fire. The worst fire was last January, when the big warehouses of the Alaska Commercial Company were saved only by the original device of wetting blankets and spreading them over the roof and sides of the building. All the company's force of officials was kept on duty for several days to guard the premises from looters.

What the Klondike creeks will yield this spring is still a matter of conjecture, but conservative men estimate that the total output of gold will not fall below $30,000,000. This estimate is based on the fact that a large number of claims have been worked by big gangs of men, using all the most improved labor-saving appliances. The steam-thawer enables a man to do more now in one day in sinking a prospect hole to bed-rock than he was able in the old days to accomplish in a week. Wood has also been far more plentiful, and labor much cheaper and more abundant. Stories of rich discoveries have not come out

of the Klondike this winter and spring, but the men who have sent letters declare they are doing well, and all appear to unite in saying that the gold output will be much larger than ever before.

Life in Dawson during the winter just passed was fairly comfortable. Municipal conditions have improved steadily, the food-supply has been adequate, and prices, as prices go in remote or frontier towns have been quite reasonable. Although the place is "wide-open" in the accepted scense of that term when applied to mining communities, the town has become so settled that refining influences are at work. A higher order of amusements is noticeable in the place. Social meetings are not confined exclusively to the gaming-table. When there are so many men of intelligence—even though many of them appear rough—in a town as there are in Dawson, a good deal of intellectual discussion of various topics is going on all the time. These matters, with speculation regarding Cape Nome and the spring clean-up, with the prospect of new arrivals and the departures for the States, have taken away much of the wearisome dulness that existed in the place in its former winter experiences.

14
The Alaska Trip

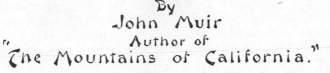

The Alaska Trip

By
John Muir
Author of
"The Mountains of California."

WITH PICTURES BY JOHN A. FRASER.[1]

TO the lover of wildness Alaska offers a glorious field for either work or rest: landscape beauty in a thousand forms, things great and small, novel and familiar, as wild and pure as paradise. Wander where you may, wildness ever fresh and ever beautiful meets you in endless variety: ice-laden mountains, hundreds of miles of them peaked and pinnacled and crowded together like trees in groves, and so high and so divinely clad in clouds and air that they seem to belong more to heaven than to earth; inland plains grassy and flowery, dotted with groves and extending like seas all around to the rim of the sky; lakes and streams shining and singing, outspread in sheets of mazy embroidery in untraceable, measureless abundance, brightening every landscape, and keeping the ground fresh and fruitful forever; forests of evergreens growing close together like leaves of grass, girdling a thousand islands and mountains in glorious array; mountains that are monuments of the work of ice, mountains monuments of volcanic fires; gardens filled with the fairest flowers, giving their fragrance to every wandering wind; and far to the north thousands of miles of ocean ice, now wrapped in fog, now glowing in sunshine through nightless days, and again shining in wintry splendor beneath the beams of the aurora —sea, land, and sky one mass of white radiance like a star. Storms, too, are here as wild and sublime in size and scenery as the landscapes beneath them, displaying the glorious pomp of clouds on the march over mountain and plain, the flight of the snow when all the sky is in bloom, trailing rain-floods, and the booming plunge of avalanches and icebergs and rivers in their rocky glens; while multitudes of wild animals and wild people, clad in feathers and furs, fighting, loving, getting a living, make all the wildness wilder.

[1] With the exception of the pictures on pages 523 and 525, the drawings are based on sketches from nature by the author.

201

All this, and unspeakably more, lies in wait for those who love it, sufficient in kind and quantity for gods and men. And notwithstanding that this vast wilderness with its wealth is in great part inaccessible to the streams of careworn people called «tourists,» who go forth on ships and railroads to seek rest with nature once a year, some of the most interesting scenery in the territory has lately been brought within easy reach even of such travelers as these, especially in southeastern Alaska, where are to be found the finest of the forests, the highest mountains, and the largest glaciers.

During the summer season good steamships carrying passengers leave Tacoma on Puget Sound for Alaska about once a week. After touching at Seattle, Port Townsend, Victoria, and Nanaimo, they go through a wilderness of islands to Wrangel, where the first stop in Alaska is made. Thence a charming, wavering course is pursued still northward through the grandest scenery to Tahkou, Juneau, Chilcat, Glacier Bay, and Sitka, affording fine glimpses of the innumerable evergreen islands, the icy mountain-ranges of the coast, the forests, glaciers, etc. The round trip of two thousand miles is made in about twelve days, and costs about a hundred dollars; and though on ocean waters, there is no seasickness, for all the way lies through a network of sheltered inland channels and sounds that are about as free from heaving waves as rivers are.

No other excursion that I know of can be made into any of the wild portions of America where so much fine and grand and novel scenery is brought to view at so cheap and easy a price. Anybody may make this trip and be blest by it—old or young, sick or well, soft, succulent people whose limbs have never ripened, as well as sinewy mountaineers; for the climate is kindly, and one has only to breathe the exhilarating air and gaze and listen while being carried smoothly onward over the glassy waters. Even the blind may be benefited by laving and bathing in the balmy, velvety atmosphere, and the unjust as well as the just; for I fancy that even sins must be washed away in such a climate, and at the feet of such altars as the Alaska mountains are.

Between Tacoma and Port Townsend you gain a general view of the famous Puget Sound, for you sail down the middle of it. It is an arm and many-fingered hand of the sea reaching a hundred miles into the heart of one of the richest forest-regions on the globe. The scenery in fine weather is en-chanting, the water as smooth and blue as a mountain lake, sweeping in beautiful curves around bays and capes and jutting promontories innumerable, and islands with soft, wavering outlines passing and overlapping one another, richly feathered with tall, spiry spruces, many of the trees 300 feet in height, their beauty doubled in reflections on the shiny waters. The Cascade Mountains bound the view on the right, the Olympic Range on the left, both ranges covered nearly to their summits with dense coniferous woods.

Doubling cape after cape, and passing uncounted islands that stud the shores, so many new and charming views are offered that one begins to feel there is no need of going farther. Sometimes clouds come down, blotting out all the land; then, lifting a little, perhaps a single island will be given back to the landscape, the tops of its trees dipping out of sight in trailing fringes of mist. Then the long ranks of spruce and cedar along the mainland are set free; and when at length the cloud-mantle vanishes, the colossal cone of Mount Rainier, 14,000 feet high, appears in spotless white, looking down over the dark woods like the very god of the landscape. A fine beginning is this for the Alaska trip! Crossing the Strait of Juan de Fuca from Port Townsend, in a few hours you are in Victoria and a foreign land. Victoria is a handsome little town, a section of old England set down nearly unchanged in the western American wilderness. It is situated on the south end of Vancouver Island, which is 280 miles long, the largest and southernmost of the wonderful archipelago that stretches northward along the margin of the continent for nearly a thousand miles. The steamer usually stops a few hours here, and most of the tourists go up town to the stores of the famous Hudson Bay Company to purchase fur or some wild Indian trinket as a memento. At certain seasons of the year, when the hairy harvests from the North have been gathered, immense bales of skins may be seen in the unsavory warehouses, the clothing of bears, wolves, beavers, otters, fishers, martens, lynxes, panthers, wolverenes, reindeer, moose, elk, wild sheep, foxes, seals, muskrats, and many others of « our poor earth-born companions and fellow-mortals.»

The wilderness presses close up to the town, and it is wonderfully rich and luxuriant. The forests almost rival those of Puget Sound; wild roses are three inches in diameter, and ferns ten feet high. And strange to say, all this exuberant vegetation is growing on moraine material that has been scarcely moved or modified in any way by postglacial agents. Rounded masses of hard, resisting rocks rise everywhere along the shore and in the woods, their scored and polished surfaces still unwasted, telling of a time, so lately gone, when the whole region lay in darkness beneath an all-embracing mantle of ice. Even in the streets of the town glaciated bosses are exposed, the telling inscriptions of which have not been effaced by the wear of either weather or travel. And in the orchards fruitful boughs shade the edges of glacial pavements, and drop apples and peaches on them. Nowhere, as far as I have seen, are the beneficent influences of glaciers made manifest in plainer terms or with more strik-ing contrasts. No tale of enchantment is so marvelous, so exciting to the imagination, as the story of the works and ways of snow-flowers banded together as glaciers, and marching forth from their encampments on the mountains to develop the beauty of land-scapes and make them fruitful.

Leaving Victoria, instead of going to sea we go into a shady wilderness that looks as though it might be in the heart of the con-tinent. Most of the channels through which we glide are narrow as compared with their length and with the height of the mountain walls of the islands which bound their shores. But however sheer the walls, they are almost everywhere densely forested from the water's edge to a height of two thousand feet; and almost every tree may be seen as they rise above one another like an audience on a gal-lery—the blue-green, sharply spired Men-zies spruce; the warm, yellow-green Merten spruce, with finger-like tops all pointing in the same direction or gracefully drooping; and the airy, feathery, brownish Alaska cedar. Most of the way we seem to be trac-ing a majestic river with lake-like expan-sions, the tide-currents, the fresh driftwood brought down by avalanches, the inflowing torrents, and the luxuriant foliage of the shores making the likeness complete. The steamer is often so near the shore that we can see the purple cones on the top branches of the trees, and the ferns and bushes at their feet. Then, rounding some bossy cape, the eye perchance is called away into a far-reaching vista, headlands on each side in charming array, one dipping gracefully be-yond the other and growing finer in the dis-tance, while the channel, like a strip of silver, stretches between, stirred here and there by leaping salmon and flocks of gulls and ducks that float like lilies among the sun-spangles.

While we may be gazing into the depths of this leafy ocean lane, the ship, turning suddenly to right or left, enters an open space, a sound decorated with small islands, sprinkled or clustered in forms and composi-tions such as nature alone can invent. The smallest of the islands are mere dots, but how beautiful they are! The trees growing on them seem like handfuls that have been culled from the neighboring woods, nicely sorted and arranged, and then set in the wa-ter to keep them fresh, the fringing trees leaf-ing out like flowers against the rim of a vase.

The variety we find, both as to the contours and collocation of the islands, whether great or small, is chiefly due to differences in the composition and physical structure of the rocks out of which they are made, and the unequal amount of glaciation to which they

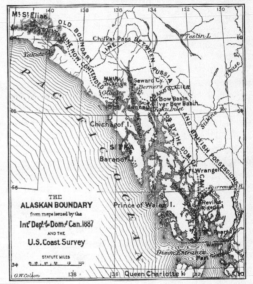

THE
ALASKAN BOUNDARY
from maps issued by the
Int' Dep't & Dom' Can. 1887
AND THE
U.S. Coast Survey
STATUTE MILES

G. W. Colton

have been subjected. All the islands of the archipelago, as well as the headlands and promontories of the mainland, have a rounded, over-rubbed, sandpapered appear-ance, a finish free from angles, which is produced by the grinding of an oversweep-ing, ponderous flood of ice.

FORT WRANGEL.

SEVEN hundred miles of this scenery, and we arrive at Fort Wrangel, on Wrangel Island, near the mouth of the Stickeen River. It is a quiet, rugged, dreamy place of no particu-lar number of inhabitants—a few hundreds of whites and Indians, more or less, sleeping in a bog in the midst of the purest and most delightful scenery on the continent. Baron

Wrangel established a trading-post here about a hundred years ago, and the fort, a quadrangular stockade, was built by the United States shortly after the purchase of the territory; but in a few years it was abandoned and sold to private parties. Indians, mostly of the Stickeen tribe, occupy the two long, draggled ends of the town along the shore; the whites, numbering about fifty, the middle portion. Stumps and logs roughen its two crooked streets, each of these picturesque obstructions mossy and tufted with grass and bushes on account of the dampness of the climate.

On the arrival of the steamer, most of the passengers make haste to go ashore to see the curious totem-poles in front of the massive timber houses of the Indians, and to buy curiosities, chiefly silver bracelets hammered from dollars and half-dollars and tastefully engraved by Indian workmen; blankets better than those of civilization, woven from the wool of wild goats and sheep; carved spoons from the horns of these animals; Shaman rattles, miniature totem-poles, canoes, paddles, stone hatchets, pipes, baskets, etc. The traders in these curious wares are mostly women and children, who gather on the front platforms of the half-dozen stores, sitting in their blankets, seemingly careless whether they sell anything or not, every other face blackened hideously, a naked circle about the eyes and on the tip of the nose, where the smut has been weathered off. The larger girls and the young women are brilliantly arrayed in ribbons and calico, and shine among the blackened and blanketed old crones like scarlet tanagers in a flock of blackbirds. Besides curiosities, most of them have berries to sell, red, yellow and blue, fresh and dewy, and looking wondrous clean as compared with the people. These Indians are proud and intelligent, nevertheless, and maintain an air of self-respect which no amount of raggedness and squalor can wholly subdue.

Many canoes may be seen along the shore, all fashioned alike, with long, beak-like sterns and prows, the largest carrying twenty or thirty persons. What the mustang is to the Mexican vaquero the canoe is to the Indian of the Alaska coast. They skim over the glassy, sheltered waters far and near to fish and hunt and trade, or merely to visit their neighbors. Yonder goes a whole family, grandparents and all, the prow of their canoe blithely decorated with handfuls of the purple epilobium. They are going to gather berries, as the baskets show. No-

where else in my travels, north or south, have I seen so many berries. The woods and meadows and open spaces along the shores are full of them—huckleberries of many species, salmon-berries, raspberries, blackberries, currants, and gooseberries, with fragrant strawberries and service-berries on the drier grounds, and cranberries in the bogs, sufficient for every worm, bird, and human being in the territory, and thousands of tons to spare. The Indians at certain seasons, roving in merry bands, gather large quantities, beat them into paste, and then press the paste into square cakes and dry them for winter use, to be eaten as a kind of bread with their oily salmon. Berries alone, with the lavish bloom that belongs to them, are enough to show how fine and rich this Northern wilderness must be.

ALASKA WEATHER.

THE climate of all that portion of the coast that is bathed by the Japan current, extending from the southern boundary of the territory northward and westward to the island of Atoo, a distance of nearly twenty-five hundred miles, is remarkably bland, and free from extremes of heat and cold throughout the year. It is rainy, however; but the rain is of good quality, gentle in its fall, filling the fountains of the streams, and keeping the whole land fresh and fruitful, while anything more delightful than the shining weather after the rain—the great, round sun-days of June, July, and August—can hardly be found elsewhere. An Alaska midsummer day is a day without night. In the extreme northern portion of the territory the sun does not set for weeks, and even as far south as Sitka and Fort Wrangel it sinks only a few degrees below the horizon, so that the rosy colors of the evening blend with those of the morning, leaving no gap of darkness between. Nevertheless, the full day opens slowly. At midnight, from the middle point between the gloaming and the dawn, a low arc of light is seen stealing along the horizon, with gradual increase of height and span and intensity of tone, accompanied usually by red clouds, which make a striking advertisement of the sun's progress long before he appears above the mountain-tops. For several hours after sunrise everything in the landscape seems dull and uncommunicative. The clouds fade, the islands and the mountains, with ruffs of mist about them, cast ill-defined shadows, and the whole firmament changes to pale pearl-gray with just a trace of purple in it. But toward noon there is a glorious awakening. The cool haziness of the air vanishes, and the richer sunbeams, pouring from on high, make all the bays and channels shine. Brightly now play the round-topped ripples about the edges of the islands, and over many a plume-shaped streak between them, where the water is stirred by some passing breeze. On the mountains of the mainland, and in the highwalled fiords that fringe the coast, still finer is the work of the sunshine. The broad white bosoms of the glaciers glow like silver, and their crystal fronts, and the multitude of icebergs that linger about them, drifting, swirling, turning their myriad angles to the sun, are kindled into a perfect blaze of irised light. The warm air throbs and wavers, and makes itself felt as a life-giving, energizing ocean embracing all the earth. Filled with ozone, our pulses bound, and we are warmed and quickened into sympathy with everything, taken back into the heart of nature, whence we came. We feel the life and motion about us, and the universal beauty: the tides marching back and forth with weariless industry, laving the beautiful shores, and swaying the purple dulse of the broad meadows of the sea where the fishes are fed; the wild streams in rows white with waterfalls, ever in bloom and ever in song, spreading their branches over a thousand mountains; the vast forests feeding on the drenching sunbeams, every cell in a whirl of enjoyment; misty flocks of insects stirring all the air; the wild sheep and goats on the grassy ridges above the woods, bears in the berry-tangles, mink and beaver and otter far back on many a river and lake; Indians and adventurers pursuing their lonely ways; birds tending their young—everywhere, everywhere, beauty and life, and glad, rejoicing action.

Through the afternoon all the way down to the west the air seems to thicken and become soft, without losing its fineness. The breeze dies away, and everything settles into a deep, conscious repose. Then comes the sunset with its purple and gold—not a narrow arch of color, but oftentimes filling more than half the sky. The horizontal clouds that usually bar the horizon are fired on the edges, and the spaces of clear sky between them are filled in with greenish yellow and amber; while the flocks of thin, overlapping cloudlets are mostly touched with crimson, like the outleaning sprays of a maple-grove in the beginning of Indian summer; and a little later a smooth, mellow purple flushes the sky

to the zenith, and fills the air, fairly steeping and transfiguring the islands and mountains, and changing all the water to wine.

According to my own observations, in the year 1879 about one third of the summer weather at Wrangel was cloudy, one third rainy, and one third clear. Rain fell on eighteen days in June, eight in July, and twenty in September. But on some of these days only a light shower fell, scarce enough to count, and even the darkest and most bedraggled of them all had a dash of late or early color to cheer them, or some white illumination about the noon hours, while the lowest temperature was about 50°, and the highest 75°.

It is only in late autumn and winter that grand, roaring storms come down and solidly fill all the hours of day and night. Most of them are steady, all-day rains with high winds. Snow on the lowlands is not uncommon, but it never falls to a great depth, or lies long, and the temperature is seldom more than a few degrees below the freezing-point. On the mountains, however, and back in the interior, the winter months are intensely cold—so cold that mercury may at times be used for bullets by the hunters, instead of lead.

EXCURSIONS ABOUT WRANGEL.

BY stopping over a few weeks at Fort Wrangel, and making excursions into the adjacent region, many near and telling views may be had of the noble forests, glaciers, streams, lakes, wild gardens, Indian villages, etc.; and as the Alaska steamers call here about once a week, you can go on northward and complete your round trip when you like.

THE FORESTS.

GOING into the woods almost anywhere, you have first to force a way through an outer tangle of *Rubus*, huckleberry, dogwood, and elder-bushes, and a strange woody plant, about six feet high, with limber, rope-like stems beset with thorns, and a head of broad, translucent leaves like the crown of a palm. This is the *Echino panax horrida*, or devil's-club. It is used by the Indians for thrashing witches, and, I fear, deserves both of its bad names. Back in the shady deeps of the forest the walking is comparatively free, and you will be charmed with the majestic beauty and grandeur of the trees, as well as with the solemn stillness and the beauty of the elastic carpet of golden mosses flecked and barred with the sunbeams that sift through the leafy ceiling.

The bulk of the forests of southeastern Alaska is made up of three species of conifers —the Menzies and Merten spruces, and the yellow cedar. These trees cover nearly every rod of the thousand islands, and the coast and the slopes of the mountains of the mainland to a height of about 2000 feet above the sea.

The Menzies spruce, or Sitka pine (*Picea Sitchensis*), is the commonest species. In the heaviest portions of the forest it grows to a height of 175 feet or more, with a diameter of from three to six feet, and in habit and general appearance resembles the Douglas spruce, so abundant about Puget Sound. The timber is tough, close-grained, white, and looks like pine. A specimen that I examined back of Fort Wrangel was a little over six feet in diameter inside the bark four feet above the ground, and at the time it was felled was about 500 years old. Another specimen, four feet in diameter, was 385 years old; and a third, a little less than five feet thick, had attained the good old age of 764 years without showing any trace of decay. I saw a raft of this spruce that had been brought to Wrangel from one of the neighboring islands, three of the logs of which were one hundred feet in length, and nearly two feet in diameter at the small ends. Perhaps half of all the trees in southeastern Alaska are of this species. Menzies, whose name is associated with this grand tree, was a Scotch botanist who accompanied Vancouver in his voyage of discovery to this coast a hundred years ago.

The beautiful hemlock-spruce (*Tsuga Mertensiana*) is more slender than its companion, but nearly as tall, and the young trees are more graceful and picturesque in habit. Large numbers of this species used to be cut down by the Indians for the astringent bark, which they pounded into meal for bread to be eaten with oily fish.

The third species of this notable group, *Chamæcyparis Nutkaensis*, called yellow cedar or Alaska cedar, attains a height of 150 feet and a diameter of from three to five feet. The branches are pinnate, drooping, and form beautiful light-green sprays like those of *Libocedrus*, but the foliage is finer and the plumes are more delicate. The wood of this noble tree is the best the country affords, and one of the most valuable of the entire Pacific coast. It is pale yellow, close-grained, tough, durable, and takes a fine polish. The Indians make their paddles and totem-poles of it, and weave matting and coarse cloth from the inner bark. It is also the favorite fire-wood. A yellow-cedar fire is worth going a long way to see. The flames rush up in a multitude of quivering, jagged-edged lances, displaying admirable enthusiasm, while the burning surfaces of the wood snap and crackle and explode and throw off showers of coals with such noise that conversation at such firesides is well-nigh impossible.

The durability of this timber is forcibly illustrated by fallen trunks that are perfectly sound after lying in the damp woods for centuries. Soon after these trees fall they are overgrown with moss, in which seeds lodge and germinate and grow up into vigorous saplings, which stand in a row on the backs of their dead ancestors. Of this company of young trees perhaps three or four will grow to full stature, sending down straddling roots on each side, and establishing themselves in the soil; and after they have reached an age of two or three hundred years, the downtrodden trunk on which they are standing, when cut into, is found as fresh in the heart as when it fell.

The species is found as far south as Oregon, and is sparsely distributed along the coast and through the islands as far north as Chilcat (latitude 59°). The most noteworthy of the other trees found in the southern portion of these forests, but forming only a small portion of the whole, is the giant arbor-vitæ (*Thuja gigantea*). It is distributed all the way up the coast from California to about latitude 56°. It is from this tree that the Indians make their best canoes, some of them being large enough to carry fifty or sixty men. Of pine I have seen only one species (*Pinus contorta*), a few specimens of which, about fifty feet high, may be found on the margins of lakes and bogs. In the interior beyond the mountains it forms extensive forests. So also does *Picea alba*, a slender, spiry tree which attains a height of one hundred feet or more. I saw this species growing bravely on frozen ground on the banks of streams that flow into Kotzebue Sound, forming there the margin of the arctic forest.

In the cool cañons and fiords, and along the banks of the glaciers, a species of silver fir and the beautiful Paton spruce abound. The only hard-wood trees I have found in Alaska are birch, alder, maple, and wild apple, one species of each. They grow mostly about the margins of the main forests and back in the mountain cañons. The lively yellow-green of the birch gives pleasing variety to the colors of the conifers, especially on slopes of river-cañons with a southern exposure. In general views all the coast forests look dark in the middle ground and blue in the distance, while the foreground shows a rich series of gray and brown and yellow trees. In great part these colors are due to lichens which hang in long tresses from the limbs, and to mosses which grow in broad, nest-like beds on the horizontal palmate branches of the Menzies and Merten spruces. Upon these moss-bed gardens high in the air ferns and grasses grow luxuriantly, and even seedling trees five or six feet in height, presenting the curious spectacle of old, venerable trees holding hundreds of their children in their arms.

Seward expected Alaska to become the ship-yard of the world, and so perhaps it may. In the meantime, as good or better timber for every use still abounds in California, Oregon, Washington, and British Columbia; and let us hope that under better management the waste and destruction that have hitherto prevailed in our forests will cease, and the time be long before our Northern reserves need to be touched. In the hands of nature these Alaska tribes of conifers are increasing from century to century as the glaciers are withdrawn. May they be saved until wanted for worthy use—so worthy that we may imagine the trees themselves willing to come down the mountains to their fate!

THE RIVERS.

THE most interesting of the excursions that may be made from Fort Wrangel is the one up the Stickeen River. Perhaps twenty or thirty of the Alaska streams may be called rivers, but not one of them all, from the mighty Yukon, 2000 miles long, to the shortest of the mountain torrents pouring white from the glaciers, has been fully explored. From St. Elias the coast mountains extend in a broad, lofty chain beyond the southern boundary of the territory, gashed by stupendous cañons, each of which carries a stream deep enough and broad enough to be called a river, though comparatively short, as the highest sources of most of them lie in the icy solitudes of the range within forty or fifty miles of the coast. A few, however, of this foaming brotherhood—the Chilcat, Chilcoot, Tahkou, Stickeen, and perhaps others—come from beyond the range, heading with the Mackenzie and Yukon.

The tributary cañons of the main-trunk cañons of all these streams are still occupied by glaciers which descend in glorious ranks, their massy, bulging snouts lying back a little distance in the shadows, or pushed grandly forward among the cottonwoods that line the banks of the rivers, or all the way across the main cañons, compelling the rivers to find a way beneath them through long, arching tunnels.

The Stickeen is perhaps better known than any other river in Alaska, because it is the way to the Cassiar gold-mines. It is about 350 miles long, and is navigable for small steamers 150 miles to Glenora. It first pursues a westerly course through grassy plains darkened here and there with patches of evergreens; then, curving southward, and receiving numerous tributaries from the north, it enters the Coast Range, and sweeps across it to the sea, through a yosemite that is more than a hundred miles long, one to three miles wide, and from 5000 to 8000 feet deep, and marvelously beautiful from end to end. To the appreciative tourist sailing up the river, the cañon is a gallery of sublime pictures, an unbroken series of majestic mountains, glaciers, waterfalls, cascades, groves, gardens, grassy meadows, etc., in endless variety of form and composition; while back of the walls, and thousands of feet above them, innumerable peaks and spires and domes of ice and snow tower grandly into the sky.

Gliding along the swift-flowing river, the views change with bewildering rapidity. Wonderful, too, are the changes dependent on the seasons and the weather. In winter avalanches from the snow-laden heights boom and reverberate from side to side like majestic waterfalls; storm-winds from the arctic highlands, sweeping the cañon like a flood, choke the air with ice-dust; while the rocks, glaciers, and groves are in spotless white. In spring you enjoy the chanting of countless waterfalls; the gentle breathing of warm winds; the opening of leaves and flowers; the humming of bees over beds of honey-bloom; birds building their nests; clouds of fragrance drifting hither and thither from miles of wild roses, clover, and honeysuckle, and tangles of sweet chaparral; swaths of birch and willow on the lower slopes following the melting snow-banks; bossy cumuli swelling in white and purple piles above the highest peaks; gray rain-clouds wreathing the outstanding brows and battlements of the walls; then the breaking forth of the sun after the rain, the shining of the wet leaves and the river and the crystal architecture of the glaciers; the rising of fresh fragrance, the song of the happy birds, the looming of the white domes in the azure, and the serene color-grandeur of the morning and evening. In summer you find the groves and gardens in full dress; glaciers melting rapidly under warm sunshine and rain; waterfalls in all their glory; the river rejoicing in its strength; butterflies wavering and drifting about like ripe flower-bloom in springtime; young birds trying their wings; bears enjoying salmon and berries; all the life of the cañon brimming full like the streams. In autumn comes rest, as if the year's work were done; sunshine, streaming over the cliffs in rich, hazy beams, calls forth the last of the gentians and goldenrods; the groves and tangles and meadows bloom again, every leaf changing to a petal, scarlet and yellow; the rocks also bloom, and the glaciers, in the mellow golden light. And so goes the song, change succeeding change in glorious harmony through all the seasons and years.

Leaving Wrangel, you go up the coast to Juneau. After passing through the picturesque Wrangel Narrows into Souchoi Channel and Prince Frederick Sound, a few icebergs come in sight, the first you have seen on the trip. They are derived from a large, showy glacier, the Leconte, which discharges into a wild fiord near the mouth of the Stickeen River, which the Indians call *Hutli*, or Thunder Bay, on account of the noise made by the discharge of the icebergs. This, so far as I know, is the southernmost of the glaciers that flow into the sea. Gliding northward, you have the mountains of the mainland on one hand, Kuprianof and countless smaller islands on the other. The views extend far into the wilderness, all of them as wild and clean as the sky; but your attention will chiefly be turned to the mountains, now for the first time appreciably near. As the steamer crawls along the coast, the cañons are opened to view and closed again in regular succession, like the leaves of a book, allowing the attentive observer to see far back into their icy depths. About halfway between Wrangel Narrows and Cape Fanshaw, you are opposite a noble group of glaciers which come sweeping down through the woods from their white fountains nearly to the level of the sea, swaying in graceful, river-like curves around the feet of lofty granite mountains and precipices like those of the Yosemite valley. It was at the largest of these, the Paterson glacier, that the ships of the Alaska Ice Company were loaded for San Francisco and the Sandwich Islands. An hour or two farther north another fleet

of icebergs come in sight, which have their sources in Sum Dum or Holkam Bay. This magnificent inlet, with its long, icy arms reaching deep into the mountains, is one of the most interesting of all the Alaska fiords; but the icebergs in it are too closely compacted to allow a passage for any of the excursion-steamers.

About five miles from the mouth the bay divides into two main arms, about eighteen and twenty miles long, in the farthest-hidden recesses of which there are four large glaciers which discharge bergs. Of the smaller glaciers of the second and third class that melt before reaching tide-water, a hundred or more may be seen along the walls from a canoe, and about as many snowy cataracts, which, with the plunging bergs from the main glaciers, keep all the fiord in a roar. The scenery in both of the long arms and their side branches is of the wildest description, especially in their upper reaches, where the granite walls rise in sheer, massive precipices, like those of the Yosemite valley, to a height of from 3000 to 5000 feet. About forty miles farther up the coast another fleet of icebergs come in sight, through the midst of which the steamer passes into the Tahkou Inlet. It is about eighteen miles long, from three to five wide, and extends into the heart of the Coast Mountains, draining many glaciers, great and small, all of which were once tributary branches of one grand glacier that formed and occupied the inlet as its channel. This inlet more plainly than any other that I have examined illustrates the mode of formation of the wonderful system of deep channels extending northward from Puget Sound; for it is a marked portion of that system, a branch of Stephen's Passage still in process of formation at the head; while its trends and sculpture are as distinctly glacial as those of the smaller fiords.

Sailing up the middle of it, you may count some forty-five glaciers. Three of these reach the level of the sea, descending from a group of lofty mountains at the head of the inlet, and making a grand show. Only one, however, the beautiful Tahkou glacier, discharges bergs. It comes sweeping forward in majestic curves, and discharges its bergs through a western branch of the inlet next the one occupied by the Tahkou River. Thus we see here a river of ice and a river of water flowing into the sea side by side, both of them abounding in cascades and rapids; yet how different in their rate of motion, and in the songs they sing, and in their influence on the landscape! A rare object-lesson this, worth coming round the world to see.

Once, while I sat sketching among the icebergs here, two Tahkou Indians, father and son, came gliding toward us in an exceedingly small cottonwood canoe. Coming alongside with a good-natured «Sahgaya,» they inquired who we were, what we were doing, etc., while they in turn gave information concerning the river, their village, and two other large glaciers a few miles up the river-cañon. They were hunting hair-seals, and as they slipped softly away in pursuit of their prey, crouching in their tiny shell of a boat among the bergs, with barbed spear in place, they

ered with glaciers, forests, or a thick blanket of moss. Nevertheless, thousands of hardy miners from the gulches and ledges of California and Arizona are rapidly overrunning the territory in every direction, and making it tell its wealth. And though perhaps not one vein or placer in a hundred has yet been touched, enough has been discovered to warrant the opinion that this icy country holds at least a fair share of the gold of the world. After time has been given for a visit to the mines and a saunter through the streets of Juneau, the steamer passes between Doug-

ENGRAVED BY H. DAVIDSON.

DAVIDSON GLACIER, FROM LYNN CANAL.

formed a picture of icy wildness as telling as any to be found amid the drifts and floes of Greenland.

After allowing the passengers a little time —half an hour or so—to admire the crystal wall of the great glacier and the huge bergs that plunge and rise from it, the steamer goes down the inlet to Juneau. This young town is the mining-center, and, so far as business is concerned, the chief place in the territory. Here, it is claimed, you may see the largest quartz-mill in the world, the two hundred and forty stamps of which keep up a «steady, industrious growl that may be heard a mile away.»

Alaska, generally speaking, is a hard country for the prospector, because most of the ground is either permanently frozen or cov-

lass and Admiralty islands into Lynn Canal, the most beautiful and spacious of all the mountain-walled channels you have yet seen. The Auk and Eagle glaciers appear in one view on the right as you enter the canal, swaying their crystal floods through the woods with grand effect. But it is on the west side of the canal, near the head, that the most striking feature of the landscape is seen—the Davidson glacier. It first appears as an immense ridge of ice thrust forward into the channel; but when you have gained a position directly in front, it presents a broad current issuing from a noble gateway at the foot of the mountains, and spreading out to right and left in a beautiful fan-shaped mass three or four miles in width, the front of which is separated from the water

ENGRAVED BY R. C. COLLINS.

DEASE LAKE, ON THE DIVIDE BETWEEN THE MACKENZIE
AND STICKEEN RIVERS.

areas along the shores and inlets, there are probably not fewer than a thousand salmon streams in Alaska that are crowded with fine salmon for months every year. Their numbers are beyond conception. Oftentimes there seem to be more fish than water in the rapid portions of the streams. On one occasion one of my men waded out into the middle of a crowded run, and amused himself by picking up the fish and throwing them over his head. In a single hour these Indians may capture enough to last a year. Surely in no part of the world may one's daily bread be more easily obtained. Sailing into these streams on dark nights, when the waters are phosphorescent and the salmon are running, is a very beautiful and exciting experience; the myriad fins of the onrushing multitude crowding against one another churn all the water from bank to bank into silver fire, making a glorious glow in the darkness.

From Chilcat we now go down Lynn Canal, through Icy Strait, and into the famous Glacier Bay. All the voyage thus far after leaving Wrangel has been icy, and you have seen hundreds of glaciers great and small; but this bay, and the region about it and beyond it toward Mount St. Elias, are preëminently the Iceland of Alaska, and of all the west coast of the continent.

by the terminal moraine. This is one of the most notable of the large glaciers that are in the first stage of decadence, reaching nearly to tide-water, but failing to enter it and send off bergs. Excepting the Tahkou, all the great glaciers you have yet seen on the trip belong to this class; but this one is perhaps the most beautiful of its kind, and you will not be likely to forget the picture it makes, however icy your after-travels may be. Shortly after passing the Davidson glacier the northernmost point of the trip is reached at the head of the canal, a little above latitude 59°. At the canning-establishments here you may learn something of the inhabitants of these beautiful waters. Whatever may be said of other resources of the territory,—furs, minerals, timber, etc.,—it is hardly possible to overestimate the importance of the fisheries. Besides whales in the far North, and the cod, herring, halibut, and other food fishes that swarm over immense

GLACIERS OF THE PACIFIC COAST.

GLANCING for a moment at the results of a general exploration of the mountain-ranges of the Pacific coast, we find that there are between sixty and seventy small residual glaciers in the California Sierra. Northward through Oregon and Washington, glaciers, some of them of considerable extent, still exist on all the higher volcanic mountains of the Cascade Range,—the Three Sisters, Mounts Jefferson, Hood, St. Helen's, Adams, Rainier, Baker, and others,—though none of them approach the sea. Through British Columbia and southeastern Alaska the broad, sustained chain of coast mountains is generally glacier-bearing. The upper branches of nearly every one of its cañons are still occupied by glaciers, which gradually increase in size and descend lower until the lofty region between Glacier Bay and Mount St. Elias is reached, where a considerable number discharge into the sea. About Prince William's Sound and Cook's Inlet many grand glaciers are displayed; but farther to the west, along the Alaska peninsula and the chain of the Aleutian Islands, though a large number of glaciers occur on the highest peaks, they are mostly small, and melt far above sea-level, while to the north of latitude 62° few, if any, remain in existence, the ground being comparatively low and the snowfall light.

ON THE MUIR GLACIER.

THE largest of the seven glaciers that discharge into Glacier Bay is the Muir; and being also the most accessible, it is the one to which tourists are taken and allowed to go ashore for a few hours, to climb about its crystal cliffs and watch the huge icebergs as with tremendous, thundering roar they plunge and rise from the majestic frontal sea-wall in which the glacier terminates. The front, or snout, of the glacier is about three miles wide, but the central berg-discharging portion, which stretches across from side to side of the inlet like a huge jagged white-and-blue barrier, is only about half as wide. The height of the ice-wall above the water is from 250 to 300 feet, but soundings made by Captain Carroll show that 720 feet of the wall is below the surface, while still a third unmeasured portion is buried beneath the moraine material that is being constantly deposited at the foot of it. Therefore, were the water and rocky detritus removed, there would be presented a sheer precipice of ice a mile and a half wide and more than a thousand feet in height. Seen from the inlet as you approach it, at a distance of a mile or two it seems massive and comparatively regular in form, but it is far from being smooth. Deep rifts and hollows alternate with broad, plain bastions, which are ever changing as the icebergs are discharged, while it is roughened along the top with innumerable spires and pyramids and sharp, hacked blades, leaning and toppling, or cutting straight into the sky.

THE BIRTH OF THE ICEBERGS.

THE number of bergs given off varies somewhat with the weather and the tides. For twelve consecutive hours I counted the number discharged that were large enough to make themselves heard like thunder at a dis-

AFTER A PHOTOGRAPH.   ENGRAVED BY K. C. ATWOOD.

GENERAL VIEW OF MUIR GLACIER, FROM THE EAST SIDE NEAR THE FRONT, LOOKING NORTH.

tance of a mile or two, and found the average rate to be one in five or six minutes. The thunder of the largest may be heard, under favorable circumstances, ten miles or more. When a large mass sinks from the upper fissured portion of the wall, there is first a keen, piercing crash, then a deep, deliberate, long-drawn-out, thundering roar, which slowly subsides into a comparatively low, far-reaching, muttering growl; then come a crowd of grating, clashing sounds from the agitated bergs that dance in the waves about the newcomer as if in welcome; and these, again, are followed by the swash and roar of the berg-waves as they reach the shore and break among the boulders. But the largest and most beautiful of the bergs, instead of falling from the exposed weathered portion of the wall, rise from the submerged portion with a still grander commotion, heaving aloft nearly to the top of the wall with awful roaring, tons of water streaming like hair down their sides, while they heave and plunge again and again before they settle in poise and sail away as blue crystal islands, free at last after being held fast as part of a slow-crawling glacier for centuries. And how wonderful it seems that ice formed from pressed snow on the mountains two or three hundred years ago should, after all its toil and travel in grinding down and fashioning the face of the landscape, still remain pure and fresh and lovely in color! When the sunshine is pouring and sifting in iris colors through the midst of all this wilderness of angular crystal ice, and through the grand, flame-shaped jets and sheets of radiant spray ever rising from the blows of the falling bergs, the effect is indescribably glorious.

GLACIAL NIGHTS.

GLORIOUS, too, are the nights along these crystal cliffs, when the moon and the stars are shining; the projecting buttresses and battlements, seemingly far higher than by day, standing forward in the moonlight, relieved by the shadows of the hollows; the new-born bergs keeping up a perpetual storm of thunder, and the lunar bows displaying faint iris colors in the up-dashing spray. But it is in the darkest nights, when storms are blowing and the waters of the inlet are phosphorescent, that the most terribly impressive show is displayed. Then the long range of crystal bluffs, faintly illumined, is seen stretching away in the stormy gloom in awful, unearthly grandeur, luminous waves dashing beneath in a glowing, seething, wavering fringe of foam, while the

VIEW OF PART OF MUIR GLACIER, LOOKING NORTHWEST FROM TREE MOUNTAIN, SHOWING MEDIAL MORAINES.

ENGRAVED BY PETER AITKEN.

Mount Reid.

ENGRAVED BY C. SCHWARZBURGER.

A MORAINE—STREAKED PORTION OF MUIR GLACIER ON THE EAST SIDE, LOOKING TOWARD HOWLING VALLEY.

new-born bergs, rejoicing in their freedom, plunging, heaving, grating one against another, seem like living creatures of some other world, dancing and roaring with the roaring storm and the glorious surges of auroral light.

CHARACTERISTICS OF THE MUIR GLACIER.

IF you go ashore as soon as the steamer drops anchor, you will have time to push back across the terminal moraine on the east side, and over a mile or so of the margin of the glacier, climb a yellow ridge that comes forward there and is easy of access, and gain a good, comprehensive, telling view of the greater portion of the glacier and its principal tributaries—that is, if you are so fortunate as to have clear weather. Instead of a river of ice winding down a narrow, mountain-walled valley, like the largest of the Swiss glaciers, you will see here a grand lake or sea of ice twenty-five or thirty miles wide, more than two hundred times as large as the celebrated Mer de Glace of the Alps, a broad, gently undulating prairie surrounded by a forest of mountains from the shadowy cañons and amphitheaters of which uncounted tributary glaciers flow into the grand central reservoir. There are seven main tributaries, from two to six miles wide where they enter the trunk, and from twenty to thirty miles long; each of these has many secondary tributaries, so that the whole number, great and small,

pouring from the mountain fountains into the grand central trunk must number at least two hundred, not counting the smallest. The views up the main tributaries in bright weather are exceedingly rich and beautiful; though far off from your standpoint, the broad white floods of ice are clearly seen issuing in graceful lines from the depths of the mysterious solitudes. The area drained by this one grand glacier and its branches can hardly be less than a thousand square miles, and it probably contains more ice than all the eleven hundred glaciers of the Swiss Alps combined. The distance back from the front to the head of the farthest fountain is about fifty miles, and the width of the trunk below the confluence of the tributaries is about twenty-five miles. Though apparently as motionless as the mountains about its basin, the whole glacier flows on like a river, unhalting, unresting, through all the seasons from century to century, with a motion varying in every part with the depth of the current and the declivity, smoothness, and directness of different portions of the channel. The rate of motion in the central cascading portion of the current near the front, as determined by Professor Reid, is from two and a half to five inches an hour, or from five to ten feet a day.

Along the eastern margin of the main trunk the ice is so little broken that a hundred horsemen might ride abreast for miles without encountering much difficulty. But far the greater portion of the vast expanse is torn and crumpled into a bewildering network of ridges and blades, and rough, broken hummocks, separated by yawning gulfs and crevasses unspeakably beautiful and awful. Here and there the adventurous explorer, picking a way in long, patient zigzags through the shining wilderness, comes to spacious hollows, some of them miles in extent, where the ice, closely pressed and welded, presents beautiful blue lakes fed by bands of streams that sing and ring and gurgle, and make sheets of melody as sweet as ever were made by larks in springtime over their nests in the meadows.

Besides the Muir there are here six other noble glaciers which send off fleets of icebergs, and keep the whole bay in a roar. These are the Geikie, Hugh Miller, Pacific, Reid, Carroll, and Hoona glaciers. Of the second class of grand size descending to the level of the sea, but separated from it by mud floats and flood-washed terminal moraines,

there are eight, and the smaller ones are innumerable.

With these views of the ice-world the duty-laden tourist is gladly content, knowing that nowhere else could he have sailed in a comfortable steamer into new-born landscapes and witnessed the birth of icebergs. Returning down the bay in a zigzag course, dodging the drifting bergs, you may see the lofty summits of the Fairweather Range—Mounts Fairweather, Lituya, Crillon, and La Pérouse. Then, leaving Icy Strait, you enter Chatham Strait, and thence pass through the picturesque Peril Strait to Sitka, the capital of the territory. Here the steamer usually stops for a day, giving time to see the interesting old Russian town and its grand surroundings. After leaving Sitka the steamer touches again at Wrangel for the mails. Then, gliding through the green archipelago by the same way that you came, you speedily arrive in civilization, rich in wildness forevermore.

John Muir.

AFTER A PHOTOGRAPH BY REID.   ENGRAVED BY C. A. POWELL.

WHITE GLACIER, A SMALL EASTERN TRIBUTARY OF THE MUIR GLACIER.

15
Moose Hunting
with the
Tro-chu-tin

HARPER'S
NEW MONTHLY MAGAZINE

VOL. C   MARCH, 1900   No. DXCVIII

MOOSE HUNTING

With the

TRO·CHU·TIN

THE Tro-chu-tin are better known as "Klondike Indians." Their village, numbering sixty or seventy souls, was located at the mouth of the Klondike River until white men discovered gold on Bonanza Creek and crowded them away to its present site on the Yukon, two miles below the town of Dawson. One morning early in January three Indians sought an interview with Captain Hansen, agent of the Alaska Commercial Company—"Isaac," the chief; "Silas," a "smart" young man; and "John," a former chief and medicine-doctor, or *shuman*. Silas, having been interpreter for the traders, spoke middling English; Isaac, worse; the old man, none at all. On this occasion Isaac was spokesman. Said he:

"First time, Jack McQuesten all same Injun papa; Yukon Injun all same her children. Just nup, McQuesten he gone; A. C. Company all same Injun papa; her children hungry." The meaning of this was that the Alaska Commercial Company, from the time when it received the lease of the Seal Islands and came into a practical monopoly of the fur trade of Alaska, had

exercised through its various agents, one of whom had been Jack McQuesten, a paternal care over the native tribes, by directing their hunts and feeding them when fish, moose, or caribou were scarce or difficult to obtain. As the Indians had been accustomed during the quarter of a century before the discovery of the Klondike to appeal for aid in time of hunger to McQuesten, it now seemed proper to lay before the visible representative of the company at Dawson the fact that they were on the verge of starvation. This condition was not exceptional. The salmon in the Yukon are abundant; the moose nowhere on the North-American Continent are so large as on the rivers entering the Yukon, or more plentiful; and the Barren Ground caribou, or wild-reindeer, run in bands often numbering thousands; but nowhere does an Indian exert himself until the last pound of "grub" is gone.

Captain Hansen told them in reply that it was true that the "A. C." Company now was "all same Jack McQuesten," but times had changed. It was no longer necessary that they should consider how much fur there was on the beaver's back, but how much *meat* on the moose's bones. He had no food for them, nor for the white men (it is still fresh in mind that starvation stared us all in the face that winter). They must hunt the moose and bring the meat to the white men, and then, but not until then, could he give them food from the store.

Several days after the above conversation a friend introduced me, in the street at Dawson, to a tall, rather angular individual, dressed in a black fur cap of peculiar design, a coat of gorgeous "upholstery"-pattern ed Mackinaw blanket, "store" trousers further encased in leggings of the same fancy material as the coat, moose-hide moccasins with pointed toes and bright scarlet tops. A pair of large caribou-skin mittens hung from his neck by a thick plaited green and white worsted cord, and he was further protected from the dry arctic cold by a knit yarn scarf wrapped once around his neck, the ends being tied behind his back out of the way. In features he was a North-American Indian,

though of the Northern interior "Woods" Indian type; light brown in
color, with prominent cheek-bones, a strong chin, aquiline nose, a large
mouth with a stringy black mustache that drooped at the ends, and a
flashing eye, that gave the impression both of mastery and shrewdness.
Although he carried himself with conscious self-respect, Isaac, as I saw him
that first time and during our subsequent "partnership," would have presented a droll appearance anywhere save in the busy street of a Northern
mining-camp, where every other man wore a shirtlike "parka," and other
articles of native dress appropriate to the place and season.

After an effusive greeting and vigorous hand-shaking, Isaac readily assent-
ed to my proposition to accompany the village on the hunt; first, however,
warily inquiring whether I could snowshoe, and then saying that I should
bring along two sacks of flour, five pounds of tea, I do not know how much
sugar—in fact, a quarter of a year's outfit, including a tent and the usual
miner's sheet-iron stove! Isaac's handling of English was atrocious and
unique, while of course my knowledge of his own language was nil; but by
much repetition, aided by gestures, I gathered that the hunt would last until
the sun rose high above the horizon—three months later ; that he expected
me to "grub-stake" him with provisions, which he would repay out of the
first moose he killed; that the hind quarters belonged to the hunter who
shot the moose, the rest to the village; that he and I were "pudnas"
(partners), and would give each other a fore shoulder; and when the smoke
inside the "skin house" made his eyes "too much sick," he would come
into my tent. The time, however, being more than I could spare for such
an adventure, I cut down the grub-list, and further resolved that if I could
not live in the "skin houses" exactly like one of them, not to go at all.

On the 13th of January the sleepy miners' camp was startled by a wild,
screaming, howling cavalcade of Indians—men, women,
boys, girls, and babies—and dogs of all degrees of leanness,
the dogs hauling birch toboggans, on which were piled
smoke-browned house-poles, skins, and blankets, with

220

babies and pups, the women driving the dogs, and nearly every man hauling a Yukon miner's sled (Isaac had explained that nearly all the dogs had been sold to the miners). The procession, a quarter of a mile long, numbering forty or fifty people and as many dogs, turned up a smooth trail on the frozen surface of the Klondike, the dogs, poor things, howling dismally as the women with shrill voices and long sticks urged them on. Two miles from the Yukon, above the mouth of the Bonanza Creek, the head of the caravan stopped, and Isaac marked the place for the camp at the edge of the river, alongside a dense grove of spruce-trees. As we turned off the smooth miners' trail every person old enough to walk slipped into snow-shoes, as the snow was about two feet deep. The women took long-handled wooden shovels and removed the snow off the ground an elliptical space eighteen feet long by twelve feet wide, banking it all around two feet high. While some covered the exposed river gravel with green spruce boughs and kindled a fire in the centre, others cut sticks three to five feet long and set them upright a foot apart in the bank of snow, the long way of the intended house, leaving an opening at one side two feet wide for the door. The house-poles, an inch thick and ten or twelve feet long, whittled out of spruce and previously bent and seasoned into the form of a curve, were then set up in the snow at the ends of the camp to the number of sixteen or twenty, their upper ends pointing toward the middle in the form of a dome ten feet high. These were strengthened by two arched cross-poles underneath, the ends of which were lashed to the side-stakes with withes of willow twigs thawed out and made pliant over the fire. Over this comparatively stiff frame-work next was drawn a covering of caribou-skin, tanned with the hair on, made in two sections, and shaped and sewed together to fit the dome. The two sections, comprising forty skins, completely covered the house, except in the middle, where a large hole was left for the smoke to escape, and at the doorway, over which was hung a piece of blanket. The toboggans with the balance of the loads were hoisted upon pole scaffolds

221

each side of the house, out of reach of the dogs, who looked and acted as if ready to devour anything from a moccasin to a rawhide toboggan-lashing. Not until the house was done and enough wood stacked before the door to last until morning did any one stop for a moment. In a climate where the temperature remains not higher than thirty degrees below zero, and occasionally drops to fifty or sixty below, it is dangerous to dally, as white men are prone to do under the same conditions.

In our little village there were seven lodges. In the chief's house were nine persons and eleven dogs, divided into two households, each having a side of the fire to itself. On ours were Isaac, his wife, Eliza, with a nursing boy less than a year old, myself, and three native dogs—Chicken (child), Gagul (broken-leg), and John ; also a tawny "white man's dog," Beaber, taken to board, a small black native pup, and an extremely miserable short-haired white man's pup, wrapped in a blanket to keep from freezing, and weighing just fourteen pounds by Isaac's spring scales. On the other side were a middle-aged, stockily built man known as "Billy," or "the missionary's man," and his wife, with two girls respectively about eight and ten years of age, and a boy of the same uncertain age, four large native dogs, and two pups. The human occupants kneeled or reclined before the fire, which was ingeniously built to throw the heat in two directions and to draw well, notwithstanding which latter, I soon discovered that it was often necessary to lie close to the ground, and when the smoke became too thick, to lift the lower edge of the skin covering. We cooked a loaf of baking-powder bread in a frying-pan. A scrap of bacon and a cup of tea completed our meal. The Indians were really near starvation. Isaac himself had the only sack of flour in the village. Each family had its own cooking outfit,

222

consisting of a frying-pan, a tin milk-pan, a tin dish-pan, several tin cups and plates, and a small tin pail for boiling tea, and a larger one, holding two or three gallons, for making soup and boiling meat and washing the children's under-garments.

The following morning before daybreak word was given, "All go." Toboggans were rattled off of caches, and houses taken down and loaded as swiftly as they had been set up. We made ten miles, part way on a miners' trail, the rest on snow-shoes, and camped exactly as before. It was still dark when all hands were awakened, the stars were shining brightly, the white aurora flashed feebly in the northern sky, the black domes of the village were dimly outlined against the snow and the black wall of spruce, and a few sparks and thin smoke were rising from the early fires. Isaac went outside and began to declaim in a loud voice. He spoke not in the smooth, melodious tongue of the Eastern Indian, but slowly and deliberately, in short, crisp, incisive monosyllables. When he was done, he informed me in broken English that we were to hunt on the left-hand side of the river. He buckled on his belt full of "forty-five-seventy" cartridges, and went outside.

Some time afterwards a young man who was warming himself by our fire asked me if I "go hunt moose." Ducking out of the narrow door, and seizing rifle and snow-shoes off the cache, I fell into a trail along with two shadowy figures, with rifles over their shoulders. In half an hour it was light enough to see that my companions were a boy of about twelve, with a large repeating-rifle, and the old *shuman*, John, dressed in a coat of bright orange blanket and nether garments of caribou-skin. He carried a single-barrelled shot-gun in a caribou-leather case handsomely embroidered with beads and red cloth, and a sort of pouch made of black cloth, richly beaded, for holding bullets and caps, hung on his breast, while a leather-covered powder-horn hung at his side. After we had walked seven miles, the river valley, in increasing light, was seen to be several miles across, the white frozen stream winding between low flat banks covered with a growth of scrubby spruce, beyond which rose evenly sloping mountains covered sparsely with small spruce, birch, and cottonwoods. The trail made by several snow-shoes ahead of us turned abruptly to the left. The boy and I turned into the spruce. The old man kept on alone, and we saw no more of him.

We reached the hill and were quite on the crest of the first ridge when the toe of one of my snow-shoes broke off. Motioning Indian fashion for the boy to go ahead, he disappeared among the snow-laden trees, leaving me to limp slowly on. It was just twelve o'clock by the watch when I heard a rifle-shot, followed quickly by another. The next thing I was in a moose's feeding-ground, and saw snow-shoe tracks running hither and thither among the bowed-down birches, in evident pursuit. Plunging on the moose's trail, down the back side of a little hill, I had not gone two hundred yards before I saw smoke among the evergreens, and the familiar

figure of Isaac and several others around a long fire, and two others near by skinning a large moose which lay in the snow. It was a gory sight— the white snow splashed with the blood, the Indians in variegated red, yellow, and green blanket coats, holding portions of the moose's vitals in the flames on sticks, and greedily licking up the fat that dripped into the snow. They were all smiling and happy. They had made the fire without axes, simply breaking off dead limbs with their hands. The two Indians soon had the moose skinned, and proceeded to separate part from part, using only their hunting-knives. After cutting off a chunk of ten to fifteen pounds of meat for each person present, the rest of the meat was covered with snow, and the smaller pieces were wrapped in spruce boughs and made into a pack, a braided rawhide cord, which each carried, being used as a sling. At just one o'clock each of us shouldered a pack, and we started back single file, reaching camp at dark, having travelled about eighteen miles. On the way we passed another moose, which an Indian was skinning. That accounted for the second shot. That night the old *shuman* and Billy, who had gone off separately, returned, each with a piece of moose, making thus *four* moose for the first day's hunt.

No wonder every one was happy! Even the dogs, who had been having nothing but a thin soup of boiled salmon-heads, took a new lease of existence. Our moose was a fat cow. The moose are still too plentiful for the Indians to stop to consider the ultimate consequence of killing cows at this season, when they are heavy with young. Indeed, they much prefer the cow to the bull. "Mull [bull] moose," said Isaac, "too much tup [tough]; cow moose plenty fat; *he* all right." He would eat the cow moose himself, and sell the bull moose to the miners.

The following day we moved camp seven miles, and the morning after that a man went ahead with an axe and cleared a trail for the women and toboggans, who hauled the meat into camp, where it was taken into the several houses and laid over poles at the side of the house, so as to be guarded from the dogs. The hides were brought in-doors, and women at once set to work dressing them. The hair was shaved off; then the skin was turned over, and all the sinew and meat adhering was removed by means of a sort of chisel made of a moose's shin-bone; and finally scraped, a work requiring a whole day of incessant and tiresome labor. The skin was now washed in a pan of hot water, and then wrung dry with the help of a stick as a tourniquet. After which the edges were incised for subsequent lacing into a frame, and then hung out-doors over a pole. The tanning, with a "soup" of liver and brains, is done the next summer. After which the skin is smoked, and made into moccasins, gold-sacks, etc. The various portions of the moose were divided among the village. One family got a head, another a slab of ribs, another the fore shoulders. The shin-bones were roasted and cracked for

224

the marrow; the ears, although nothing but cartilage, were roasted and chewed up; the rubberlike "muffle," or nose, and every particle of flesh, fat, or gristle that could be scraped from head or hoofs, were disposed of. Even the stomach was emptied of its contents and boiled and eaten; but the very choicest delicacy was the unborn moose, which was suspended by a string around the neck and toasted over the fire. With plenty of meat, the village was in no hurry to move. There were no regular meals now. Whenever one wanted anything to eat, he cut off a piece of meat and threw it into a frying-pan. In our house some one was cooking about all the time. No one cared for salt: it is a civilized habit they have not yet acquired. Moose-meat answers all requirements of nature, and one can live on it alone.

The killing of a fat cow moose is celebrated by a feast. Our first was prepared by Isaac. Two or three of the largest tin pails were brought into the house, and an Indian selected by the chief as cook filled them with water from an ice-hole in the river, and hung them over the fire, with all sorts of odds and ends of meat and bone. While the meat was cooking, the hunters gathered inside to the number of twenty-three, lying on their backs with their feet to the fire, completely filling the little room. They laughed, talked, smoked, until about noon, when the cook brought out a large wooden spoon, and skimming the pure grease off the top of the kettles, passed it around the circle. Each took a sip at the fiery-hot, saltless tallow, apparently regardless of considerable moose-hair and wood-ashes. When the meat was done, a number of milk-pans and plates were partly filled, each one's share being apportioned according to the size of his family.

Considerable merriment was caused by Isaac, ever fond of a joke, who inquired how much of my allowance I was going to give to a certain fat, greasy, very muscular, dusky young lady in another lodge, whom they seemed

to have had picked out for me as a "partner," in case I remained in the country. Isaac hastened to explain, however: "Injun no fool; just laugh." A cup or kettle of tea was set before each person, and all hands sat up and pitched in with hunting-knives and fingers. Now I learned the way to eat meat: people who eat nothing but meat surely ought to know the way. You grasp the bone, or roll of fat, tightly in the left hand, and seize the other end firmly in the teeth. Then with the hunting-knife, dagger fashion, in the other hand, keeping both elbows well out, and lifting the lips away so that no accident may happen by a slip of the knife, you bring the keen edge squarely downward, severing as much as you wish for a mouthful. Never have I seen so much energy thrown into eating. Whatever was left in the pans was handed out to the women and children, and eaten in their respective houses. Then we lay back for more smoking and talking until another batch of meat was ready. At 3 P.M. pans and plates were again filled, and again disposed of, to the accompaniment of the same fierce arm and elbow movements. Thus ended a day of feasting, which, come when it may, is really the "Sunday" of a hunting people. Several sleds took meat to town, where it readily sold to the miners for $1 25 to $1 50 per pound. When all the meat had been cared for, the hides were hoisted on poles into trees out of reach of wolverenes, to be picked up at the end of the hunt. We journeyed leisurely on, making six or seven miles each day, and hunting both sides of the river. By the time we reached the Forks of Klondike, forty miles from Dawson, nearly four weeks had elapsed; just thirty-two moose had been killed, and eaten, sold, or "cached" until the final homeward trip.

The broad valley and mountainous banks of the Klondike are an admirable feeding-ground for the moose. The temperature in winter is exceedingly cold and crisp, but the snowfall is light, and by reason of the intense cold the snow does not settle or pack. There is so little wind, especially during the early part of the winter, that the snow accumulates on the trees in strange and often fantastic masses, giving the landscape, especially on the mountain-tops, the appearance of having been chiselled out of pure white marble. On

account of its lightness, the snow is no impediment to the long-legged, gaunt moose, which is not obliged to "yard," as in southern deep-snow regions, but wanders at will from valley to mountain-top in search of the tender twigs of willow, white birch, and cottonwood. The Indians surround the moose in its feeding-ground, and as it runs, one or more of them is tolerably sure of a quick shot. Their skill with the modern repeating-rifle is remarkable, especially in view of the fact that comparatively few years ago they had no guns at all, but stalked and killed the moose with bow and arrow alone. The "old-time" way of hunting the caribou was for a band of Indians, number of sometimes fifty and more, to surround the unsuspecting herd and run in upon them at a given signal. The frightened animals were easily shot down, and sometimes out of a herd of several hundred not a single one escaped. Billy, who asserted that he himself had killed moose with a bow and arrow, preferred to leave the round-up and hunt alone. Three of the moose that fell to his rifle he shot through the head as they lay in their beds in the snow.

Not many years ago the Tro-chu-tin dressed entirely in the skins of animals. The sable, mink, otter, and beaver of the Yukon are of great fineness and value, the sable especially being considered second only to the Russian sable. In exchange for furs, they received from the traders guns, ammunition, tea, tobacco, sugar, flour; also extremely thick blankets, which often weigh twelve pounds, and are made expressly for the Northern trade. Out of these, as well as of fancy cottons and bright flannels, they made garments that have now to some extent supplanted the old. The younger men affect a bright Mackinaw coat that vies with the spectrum in brilliancy and variety of color. One fellow was the proud possessor of a coat striped in brown, pink, yellow, blue, and green; and another of a coat checked in large squares of pink, green, blue, yellow, and lilac. With these are worn blanket trousers stuffed into the tops of moccasins. The old men, who cling tenaciously to old customs, wear a garment, comprising trousers and moccasins in one, made of caribou-skin, with the hair inside. These are worn next the skin. One old man wore, in addition, a "parka," or shirt, made of white rabbit-skins cut into strips and plaited, leaving openings through which one could thrust the fingers; and yet in the coldest weather he wore positively nothing else, except a blanket hood and mittens of rabbit-skin. The mittens are generally made of caribou-skin, with the hair inside, and are very warm. The women, when in-doors, wear a dress of light cloth fashioned on civilized lines, but when travelling they don either a blanket coat over a shortish skirt of the same, or a voluminous over-dress of caribou-skin, having a hood, which upon occasion may be hauled over the head, but in which commonly reposes the baby. The women's head-gear is invariably a large fancy silk or cotton kerchief knotted under the chin. The skin dress reaches half-

"Gagul"

way from the knees to the ground, deer-skin legging-moccasins protecting the lower extremities. The little girls wear garments similar to their mothers, while the boys wear a shirt of caribou-skin, with fur outside, made with a hood for pulling over the head. Their legs are encased in diminutive skin trousers with feet, while the mittens of the very smallest children are sewed fast to their sleeves. When a small boy gets ready to go out-doors, he lies on his back and sticks his legs into the air, while the mother draws on his "pants."

The children, dressed in their warm thick furs, have as happy a time as children anywhere. Most of their play is out-of-doors, where 'they make play-houses in imitation of the large ones, and roll about in the snow like little polar bears. Sometimes they take papa's snow-shoes and slide down some little bank, but they did not use the toboggans for that purpose. A favorite game was "kli-so-kot," or "throwing-the-stick." A row of five or six small stakes is set up in the hard-packed snow of the village street, and another row thirty or forty feet distant. Each contestant provides himself with two clubs, and taking turns, they throw these at first one, then the other, of the group of upright stakes, the one who knocks down the greatest number of stakes being the winner. Although these Indian children are so tough, they are great cry-babies. One of the things the women particularly wanted to know was whether white babies cried very much. Isaac's "hope of posterity" was a fearful nuisance. He was crying about a third of the time. Not a regular cry, but a nasal, monotonous drone, punctuated at intervals by three or four inward catches of the breath. He would keep this up for perhaps half an hour without the slightest diminution, until humored or petted. Often Billy's boy would imitate him, with the result only of increasing and prolonging the distressful performance. I rarely saw a child punished, and never one whipped.

The grown people in their own amusements were as simple-minded as the children. They had learned what a camera was, but they had never seen any one make pictures "by hand." I drew everything I saw, and it amused them to recognize the various members of the village and the different dogs. They never tired looking at the sheets and passing them around the circle, screaming with laughter as they recognized some person or dog. I was given the name "picture-man." Some of the old men and women objected to having their pictures made, but it was more from fear of ridicule than superstition. Isaac himself had objections to "hand pictures" of himself, as he called them. He asked me privately, as a favor, not to make any. "Machine picture, *he* all right." He evidently thought it did not befit the dignity of chief to become an object of even harmless merriment.

The dogs are a feature of every Northwest Indian village. Ours were a ragged, wolfish, scrawny, poor, miserable lot, the best, with few exceptions, having been sold to the miners for twenty times what they were worth a few years ago. That dogs could be treated so and live, or not fly in des-peration at the throats of their human, or inhuman, owners, was a constant wonder to me. Like wolves, they are able to go for days at a time with next to nothing to eat. Even when we were revelling in moose-meat the dogs received only what no one could eat, namely, bones, gristle, the scrapings of the moose-hides, and whatever else they could pick up. A "Siwash" dog, under such conditions, grows up a natural thief. He is proud of it. I have watched one sit blinking before the fire, apparently oblivious of everything but the warmth, but when a morsel of food fell to the ground, like a flash he would cut it out, and if it proved sizable,

he would spring for the door, yelling to the sound of a stream of whacks of the poker-stick. One time he failed to locate the coveted morsel, which had been thrown to a puppy. As the woman laid the stout stick soundly over his back the dog yelled as if he was being murdered, but he would not run, and between the yelps I saw him, with an agonized expression that was ludicrous in spite of the cruelty, trying with his eye to find the meat. At length he found it and made for the door. I have seen a little pup, by nature kind and playful as a kitten, beaten with the fire-poker by a child a year old.

"Four-Bits."

Another time I undertook to deliver, with a toboggan and one dog, a shoulder of meat Isaac had sold to a miner on Hunker Creek. I asked Isaac's wife what I should take to feed the dog. She replied, nonchalantly, "Nawthin'." "But," I replied, "I may be gone two days. What shall I take?" "Nawthin'." Sometimes they go to the other extreme. "Patsy" could not stand "Siwash" dog-fare, and grew steadily thinner. Isaac had set great store by the pup, for which he had paid, I believe, two dollars, and was expecting in the course of a year to get two hundred dollars for him from some miner. The dog was now so weak he could barely stand. In the distribution of shreds from a moose-hide, Patsy's leanness attracted the notice of an Indian woman. She tried to see how much he could hold, so she filled him up. He grew as big around as a stove-pipe, and the hair, not being very thick anyhow, his sides had much the same shiny appearance. He still looked up for more, and finally got so full he could not lift himself, which amused us all.

Soon after the first day's hunt Isaac had conveyed word to me that one or two of the Indians were nervous about my hunting with them in the bunch, lest when the moose ran I should shoot an Indian instead of the moose. He stated that although he himself did not share that fear, he thought it best I should hunt alone in future, as they now had few Indians, and could not afford to lose any. It was a rather hard compliment, but as the camp life of the people themselves was so interesting, it really mattered little whether I hunted at all. At the Forks we remained upwards of a week, the Indians securing in that time twelve more moose. Here I made long excursions, in some cases ten miles from camp, hunting alone on the sides and tops of the high mountains. But in the first place I had misjudged the ease with which a moose could be picked up; in the next place I was not acquainted with the country, nor was I able to learn from the Indians' well-meant directions just what ground they were hunting over. So that at the end of a week of the hardest and most persistent hunting of which I was capable I found myself without a moose to call my own.

One day after an unusually long tramp, wherein I had resolved to get beyond the snow-shoe tracks of the Indians, I had remained overnight at a new miner's cabin, returning to camp next day. Being unable to dry the perspiration and frost from my clothes thoroughly as by the direct blaze of the skin house, a cold set in that took a sudden and serious turn. I followed the Indians another stage up the "North Fork," but realizing the danger, I started back, and leaving the sled behind, succeeded in reaching a miner's cabin, where for six days I lay unable to eat or sleep. Isaac and his people had cared for me as one of themselves, but now their solicitude, expressed in language I could not understand, but in looks that left no doubt, could be of no assistance. Isaac reported in Dawson: "Picture-man too much sick. Mebbe two days he all right, mebbe two days he dead." My partner came after me with a basket-sleigh and four stout dogs. Meanwhile I was up and on my way home, and passed him in a bend of the Klondike River. The Indians killed in all about eighty moose and sixty-five caribou, much of which they sold to the miners in Dawson, as Captain Dansen advised them, and invested the proceeds in finery and repeating-rifles.

16
An
Explorer-Naturalist
in the Arctic

AN EXPLORER-NATURALIST IN THE ARCTIC

By Andrew J. Stone

ILLUSTRATIONS FROM THE AUTHOR'S PHOTOGRAPHS

SUMMER-LAND OF ALASKA

THE Kenai Peninsula was the summer-land of the early Russian settlers in Alaska. A Russian settlement, or colony, was established there some years before the famous expedition of Lewis and Clark visited what is now the Northwest States of the Pacific coast, and on the south shores of the peninsula, some of the first ships ever constructed on the Pacific coast of America were built.

One who knows the country can readily understand its many attractions for the early Russian comers to the generally desolate shores of the north. For it is very unlike any other country in the north, and, at the time of their coming, was the best suited to the many needs of such a colony.

It is a land of magnificent, rugged mountains, and of beautiful, rolling meadow-lands ; a land of eternal fields of glistening snow and ice, and of everlasting fires of burning lignite ; of frozen moss and lichen-covered plains, and of vegetation that is tropical in its luxuriance ; a land of extensive coal-fields, smoking volcanoes, and of earthquakes so frequent as to fail to excite comment among its native residents ; of charming, quiet bays and harbors, and of tides and tide-rips, among the greatest in the world ; of almost endless days of sunshine in summer, and of long, dismal winter-nights ; of an abundant animal-life, both in the water and on the land, every feature of which is of great interest to zoölogists. Nowhere else in the world does Nature exert itself in so many ways as in the Kenai Peninsula. The very earth itself seems to be in constant motion, shifting and changing position. The waters, the mountains, the great rivers of ice, the vegetable and animal life, all vie with each other in the production of something unusual and wonderful ; nor does this activity exist on the surface only ; down deep in the soil numerous layers of coal are forming. Almost every stage of carbonization is taking place, from that of beds of peat, at the very moss-roots, to that of an exceedingly clean and excellent lignite coal, down deep in the earth. And yet, very much farther down in the depths, burn the fires that keep alive Chinabora, Iliamna, Redoubt, and other volcanoes.

When the first Russian colonies were established here, in 1793, they found a congenial climate, a romantically picturesque country, teeming with rich furs, wild meats and fruits, and tall grasses ; whose shores were peopled with numerous and populous tribes of hardy, happy natives, that lived in villages, or communities, and whose kungas (houses) everywhere dotted its rich, green shores.

The waters abounded in the sea-otter, whose royal fur has been a valuable thing of commerce for many years. But they possessed no unusual value to these simple people, who parted with them for the merest trifles. Delareff, a Russian trader, obtained in one year more than three thousand of these beautiful skins. The sea provided the natives with the greater portion of their food, and with many of their other requirements. The waters abounded in the finest salmon, halibut, and other varieties of food-fishes. Porpoise, seal, sea-lion, white and black whale were plentiful, and were not only a source of food in abundance, but furnished skins for clothing, lashings, bidarkas (canoes), and for the covering of their kungas. Although the natives of the Kenai were never made slaves to the Russian-American Company, they were obliged to pay an annual tribute of furs. When Russian America was transferred to the United States and Fort

Kenai, the old Redoubt St. Nicholas, near the mouth of the Kenai River, was garrisoned by United States troops, natives and sea-otter were still plentiful, but the white hunter soon exterminated them both. He was better equipped for the capture of the otter, and he could drink more bad whiskey, and live, than could the native. To-day the sea-otter is a stranger in these waters, the kunga is but a mass of mould, mingled with decaying vegetation, the bones of this once happy race are buried among the sands of the beautiful, pine-clad shores, and the baraboras (houses) of the early Russians are things of the past. Hardly a trace of old Redoubt St. Nicholas remains as it was. The one thing least alive on all the peninsula, to-day, is the small remnant of natives—they are a stolid, wretched, miserable, heart-broken people—utterly degraded, and entirely worthless, even in the one capacity to which they were best adapted—that of the hunter.

The eastern shores of the peninsula are washed by the waters of the beautiful Prince William Sound, and its southern shores by the broad Pacific, where it receives the full benefit of the warming influence of the Japan current. The Cook Inlet, with its mighty, rushing tides, sweeps its west and north coasts.

The most prominent features of geographical interest on the west coast of the inlet are Cape Douglass and the mountains of Chinabora, Iliamna, and Redoubt, all of which are active volcanoes. Redoubt volcano is an almost perfect symmetrical cone, rising to the height of 11,270 feet; Iliamna is the highest of a group of very high mountains, its own height, of 12,066 feet, towering but slightly above its neighbors. Although these giant-smokestacks pour forth volumes of black smoke, often visible for a hundred miles, yet, to all appearances, their covering of snow remains perfectly white to the top. Earthquakes are evidently caused by eruptions or explosions that take place deep down in the earth. I can find no more reasonable theory for those earthquakes, so frequent in western Alaska, than that the high-reaching tides of Cook Inlet, or the damming from some other source, must cause water to pour over into, and down through, great caverns, that lead to the mighty furnaces below, creating steam of such awful pressure as to shake the earth for hundreds of miles in every direction, in its mad effort to escape. At such times Nature's great smokestacks are utilized by it, and the usual volume of smoke gives way to steam, that carries with it every sort of thing that its powerful force dislodges from the interior of these great furnaces.

I shall long remember my first experience with an earthquake. Early in October of 1900, I was at Homer Spit, that lies between Chugachik and Kachemak bays. I was very anxious to get some men to go with me into the mountains, and, hearing there were four living in a cabin at Anchor Point, twenty-five miles north of Homer Spit, whose services I might secure, I started out a-foot to find the place. I did not leave Homer until one P.M., and night then came very early in these latitudes. I felt sure, however, that I should reach the place before it became very dark, and I might have done so, but the only route was along the beach, and in many places it was extremely rocky, affording very uncertain footing; then, at short intervals, small streams poured over the high seawalls, and spread out over the sands of the beach, where I was compelled to wade them, and my footwear was soon full of water. I had not gone far when a cold rain commenced to pour down upon me in torrents, and I was soon thoroughly soaked, and my clothing, much increased in weight, clung to me, and greatly retarded my progress. After many trying adventures, I arrived at the cabin late at night, so tired that I lost no time in stretching myself in a pair of blankets, on the floor, and was soon asleep. I had slept several hours, when I was awakened by a very peculiar and unusual sensation. The cabin was rocking and creaking and performing all sorts of strange evolutions, and everything loose on the floor and walls was playing hide-and-seek, in and out of its dark corners. My first impression was that our hillside was sliding into Kachemak Bay. I hurriedly staggered to the door, very much after the style of walking in a rapidly moving express-train while running over a rough roadbed. When I opened the door, I could see by the coming light of day that our hillside was yet intact, and then I realized what was taking place. I was really delighted, for I had often wished for the experience, and, unlike almost all other experiences in the north, it came to me without any effort on my part. From that time, during my stay of several months on the peninsula, the shocks were frequent. The most violent ones were nearly always preceded by a rumbling sound, very much like that of heavy truck-wheels, rolling over cobble-stones in the distance. So really distinct were these sounds, that I soon learned to recognize them as unmistakable evidence of a coming shake. Slight tremblings and shakings of the earth were of such frequent occurrence as to fail to arouse any special comment.

The greatest feature of the Kenai Peninsula is the mountain-range, running the full length of the peninsula, a distance of more than one hundred and seventy-five miles. Next in importance are the enormous rivers of glacial ice that plough their way down through the scores of rugged cañons and break off into the great, salt seas. The most enthusiastic admirer of nature, in its wildest forms, could not picture a lovelier sight. From every point of the compass they present the same high and rugged outlines, always clothed in perfect white.

The climate is equable but humid. The humidity results in very heavy snow-falls in the higher mountains, that slide down the steep mountain-sides by the millions of tons, packing into solid masses that form into glacial ice. Where the pressure of this yearly creation is sufficiently great to keep the whole field of ice ahead of it moving—the term "live glacier" is applied.

The glaciers are extensive in both numbers and size. The beautiful college glaciers, Wellesley, Vassar, Bryn Mawr, Smith, Radcliffe, Harvard, and Yale, discovered and named by the Harriman expedition, are among the most easterly in the mountains. The one farthest west extends from Port Dick, on the south, completely across the mountains to Tutka Bay, on the north, a distance of about twenty-five miles. Throughout the entire length of the eastern and southern coast of the peninsula are many others as yet unexplored, several of which are very large. On the north are the beautiful twin glaciers, Doroshon, and Wossnessenski, and yet a little farther east the Gremingk and the Sud, all descending to Chugachik Bay.

The rolling meadow-lands to the north of Kachemak and Chugachik bays are beautifully dotted with spruce, cottonwood, and alder, and studded with numerous lakes, some of which are of considerable size.

Numerous coal-veins crop out all along the high sea-walls to the east of Kachemak and north of Chugachik bays, and many fires of burning lignite are found along the coast and among the high hills inland. Everywhere on the peninsula the wonderful beauty of the country is apparent. No park-lake ever grew pondlilies to greater perfection than I have seen them in the shallow lakes, high up in the meadows. From the summit of the mountains I have overlooked the Pacific Ocean, Cook Inlet, and the mountains beyond the latter—from one position.

Both the water and land are abundant in animal life. Clams and crabs are of good quality and plentiful—the largest kelp I ever saw floating was in Kachemak Bay; and near Anchor Point grow large quantities of sponges, though of inferior quality; birds of many varieties are numerous in the summer months and some of the land-animals, especially the moose, seem to reach their greatest state of perfection in size and in the growth of their antlers.

To undertake to give people a correct conception of Arctic America, or of any part of it, is difficult. Although they know that the country is much larger than the United States, they look upon it as being all alike—a country of long, dark winters, fields of ice and snow, and barren wastes. In truth, within Arctic and sub-Arctic America there is much diversity of climate. And in this beautiful summerland of Alaska, there are, in midsummer, endless fields of beautiful plant-life. Many times I have left my camp at the foot of the mountains, and, passing through a little meadow where a variety of wild grasses waved their tops above my head, I would commence to climb among the dense, tangled, and almost tropical jungle of alders, where grew several varieties of

Lupinus (Lupine). *

the most beautiful ferns. Reaching the upper limits of the alders, great, waving fields of the purple lupine and dainty red columbine covered acres and acres of the high, rolling hills. Among them, wild celery and wild parsnip grew many feet high, and other luxuriant foliage-plants gave my surroundings an almost tropical appearance. A little farther, many little ponds grew beautiful, yellow lilies, with their great leaves resting on the surface of the water, and the purple iris bordered the shores.

Still higher came the yellow sun-flowers, white and purple daisies in endless fields, and, higher yet, violets, pinks, forget-me-n o t s, buttercups, and blue bells, and dozens and dozens of dainty, blossom-ing plants in many colors.

Purple is the pre-dominating color, then white and yel-low and blue and

Achillea (Northern Yarrow).

pink dividing honors. But few red flowers were seen. I have travelled many miles where every foot of my way was one grand profusion of beautiful flowers in many varieties.

WHERE EAST AND WEST JOIN

" CAST off the lines there ! " shouted the ruddy, robust, good-natured captain of the little Newport, and we steamed away from the long sand-spit that divided Chugachik and Ka-chimak bays. In a few hours the beau-tiful shores of the Kenai Peninsula in southwestern Alas-ka, with their dark fringe of spruce and the rugged, snow-clad moun-tains above them, faded behind us.

It was now the middle of Octo-ber, and I had

* This and the following flower pictures were taken on the Kenai Peninsula in July.

236

been hunting on the Kenai since early summer.

I had often wanted to visit the land where join the East and West. *The land beyond the setting sun.* The land too far west and too young for trees to grow. The land of the Aleut and of smoking volcanoes. The land that had been made for us after the rest of the world was moulded into shape.

I would surely find there many new and interesting things; and in the thought of this my sombre feelings took on a more rosy hue.

The next day broke clear and bright, and a beautiful, rugged mountain - range, white to the sea, stood out in silhouette against the perfect blue of a northern sky; and I could actually breathe hope from the pure, cold, stimulating air.

During the day we left behind us the last of the tree-growth in western America, and all day the mountains of the Alaska Peninsula descended to the sea quite bare of everything but snow. The higher peaks, all dressed in the newest white, glared like huge diamonds in the brilliancy of a perfect sun. The day was wonderfully inviting, and the wind was not so strong as to prevent our being on deck. After this, however, followed typical western-coast winter weather. Storm, and cold, and fog, and cloud, and wild seas; and when we finally anchored in a little bay off the shore of Popoff Island, past the middle of a bleak, stormy night, the wind howled through the rigging of the ship in a manner that made the night ghostly hideous. After my baggage was lowered into one of the small boats, myself and the one man I had with me felt our way through the dark, down the ladder, and were rowed ashore at Sand Point, on Popoff Island, a little cod-fishing station. Popoff Island is one of the

Bringing Fuel to Camp at Chicago Bay.

Shumagin group, far to the west. The Shumagins were named after a sailor from the St. Peter, Vitus Behring's ship—the first to ever touch these shores—who died while being carried ashore in August, 1741. The islands are barren of timber, but picturesquely diversified in topography; in places sloping gently down to the water, in others breaking abruptly into the sea from great heights, forming bold, rocky headlands. Gently rolling hills and rugged mountains complete the landscape. The climate is equable for such latitudes, but the winds blow almost constantly, and often with such terrific force as to compel even the traveller on land to seek shelter.

From Popoff Island I proposed to go in small boats across Unga Straits, about twelve miles to the mainland, and skirt the shores until I reached a favorable locality for hunting. I was a week occupied in securing two more men and two boats, and it was the very last of Kimadgin tugid (October—the hunting-month of the Aleuts) before I left Sand Point. All the time I was preparing for the trip to the hunting-grounds, the winds were terrific, and the seas running high. I began to have some fear as to whether I might find an opportunity to cross the straits; and I was delighted when Andrew Golovin, a Russian Aleut who was to travel with me, waked me early one morning, and reported that he thought it possible for us to cross.

I dressed and hurried through breakfast, and our boats were soon ready. There were four of us, and we were to travel in two codfisher's dories, a very light craft about eighteen feet in length.

The sea was high and breaking everywhere, but we hugged the lee-shore of Unga Island for about three miles, and then headed straight across the channel, under sail in a strong beam-wind. Our

Chicago Bay Point, Alaska Peninsula, opposite Shumagin Islands. Our Camp in Foreground.

Iris.

little boats were slow sailers, but as sea-worthy as it is possible to make such small craft, and we shipped very little

Delphinium (Larkspur).

water. It did not seem possible that small craft could live in the sea that was running in Unga Straits that day, and I should indeed have been nervous, only for the reassurance that came from my native's countenance. He knew the straits perfectly, and was a splendid sail-or, and very strong.

Reaching the mainland, we found smooth water in the lee of a high, rugged shore-wall, along which we travelled until late in the afternoon, when we put ashore at the head of Santiago Bay. The night was perfect, clear, and beautiful, and we slept in an old, deserted barabara on a bed of dry grass, and cooked our supper on an open camp-fire made from drift-wood gathered from the beach.

The following day we were driven ashore by storm, and were compelled to remain for two days. The winds blew a perfect gale and threatened to sweep our tent from over us, but calmed suffi-ciently for us to travel on the third day.

Most of the mainland was very high, even to the water's edge, and the irreg-ular coast was slashed with narrow fiords that extend inland to the very base of the mountains; and the winds poured over the mountains and came whirling down these narrow water-ways as though under

Nymphæa (Yellow Pond Lily).

force of some great pressure, producing what is known as woolies.

The last of these we had to cross before reaching the hunting-ground was Doinay Bay, a strip of water about four miles in width, and running inland a great distance between high and abrupt mountains. As we rounded a high point, before starting across, the water promised fair, with a light, favorable wind just tossing a few scattering white-caps; but we had not gone half-way across when we were caught in a squall that blew a living gale, driving before it blinding masses of snow, that beat in our faces with such fury as to almost blind us. The sea became very rough, and the wind carried immense sheets of water through the air, drenching us to the skin with the icy stuff, and every moment I thought our boat would either capsize or fill. But Andrew was equal to his task, and he handled the boat while I kept bailing out the water as fast as the waves boarded us.

My salt-water bath was cold, but I was so completely engaged in my work to save the boat that I felt no discomfort, and the excitement became so great that I began rather to enjoy than to fear our position.

We were almost surrounded by heavy breakers, any one of which might crush our boat to atoms, but in a few minutes, that seemed hours, our position was so changed as to show us a break in the

Veratrum (False Hellebore).

reef that was producing the heavy surf, and our boat glided through without accident, and we were inside a beautiful little bay about a mile in extent, nearly surrounded by low, rolling, grass-covered hills, with rugged snow-covered mountains in the back-ground.

240

Chicago Bay and the Mountains beyond Alaska Peninsula.

As we crossed the little sheet of water, the clouds gave way to sunshine, and the wind calmed. On landing, we pitched our tents just above a pretty, sloping beach at the foot of the sea-wall, and prepared a hurried lunch with hot coffee that we enjoyed very much after our cold soaking.

Then we cut a lot of coarse grass with our skinning-knives, and put it in the bottom of our tents to put our beds on and to sit on. Next, we lashed down our tents with heavy ropes, made fast to stakes, and dragged up our boats and filled them half full with rocks, to keep them from blowing away. Then we made a trip across a high point to another small bay, where we collected firewood along the beach, which we carried to camp on our backs ; and our temporary home was in order.

A change to dry clothing made me comfortable, and I climbed to the top of a high hill, back of camp. The day was nearly spent and I wanted to be alone for a short while, that I might better study and more perfectly understand my wonderful surroundings.

Here I was in the newest and strangest

of all the lands of America. Ages upon ages after the rest of our continent came into existence, this land lay buried beneath the sea—when some mighty power below heaved with awful force, and a few of the heads of what are now the lofty snow-capped mountain-peaks in the background, peered above the surface of the water, huge masses of sharp and jagged rocks. Centuries passed, and the same forces again exerted themselves with renewed energy, and these great, black rocks were lifted higher above the water, and many new ones came to the surface, and in many places continuous ridges were formed. Even then the very country where I was sitting was deep down beneath the sea. Throughout other ages this great internal force lived and developed power, shoving again and again, until all this vast, picturesque, mountainous country came from beneath the sea. The winds and waters carried seeds, and grasses and mosses grew, and finally people came. In fact, people came when this strip of land was not yet finished, for high up the mountain-sides, just above where the rocks are smooth from the wash

In Camp, Oisenoy Bay, Alaska Peninsula, where we were Storm-bound in October.

of the sea in ages past, are yet to be found reliable indications of the habitations of a people who once lived there, a people who obtained their living largely from the sea, and who always lived near the shore.

Back of me, and very near, rose the beautiful mountains upon whose sides once lived the first people to inhabit this country.

To the south of me stretched the broad Pacific and in the foreground the beautiful Shumagin Islands. It is but a century and a half since the first white man set foot on these islands; but the Aleut, who, perhaps, fled with his family from persecution on the eastern coast of Siberia, is to-day sleeping beneath the moss, the result of the coming of a cruel and stronger people.

Few countries ever possessed such valuable and interesting animal-life as the one that lay before me—the very centre of the greatest wealth of furs the world has ever produced. In the sea once lived vast herds of the sea-cow (Rhytini Stelleri), the only species of the Sirenia ever found north of the equator. These magnificent animals lived along the shores, feeding on seaweed, kelp, and marsh-grasses, and would have continued to live for ages, only for the coming of the white man, who succeeded in exterminating them in less than thirty years after his first arrival. The valuable fur-seals are being persecuted beyond endurance. The still more valuable sea-otter has been driven from the shores everywhere, and the miserable, scattered fragments of the most valuable of all fur-producing animals can no longer find either peace or safety near land. How inhuman and heartless is the destruction of such beautiful and valuable life.

As I looked on the scene around me—a land so strange—so full of interest—*the land where joins the East and the West*—I felt as though I had been transplanted to a new world.

The low-lying sun shed a gleam of red on the gold of the hills and the white of the mountains, and glistened on the waters below me. The little, Aleutian sparrow flitted from rock to rock and sang. The water ouzel fluttered from cañon-wall to cañon-wall of the mountain-streams,

242

and bathed his dark, lead-colored plumage in the icy waters of its cataracts.

Falling shadows suggested camp ; and as I turned toward the shore, I looked back once more over the hills, and there, on the crest of a little knoll, almost within gun-shot, sat a beautiful red fox, his magnificent bushy tail curled round his forefeet, eying me intently. Farther down the hill, on my way to camp, I flushed streams back into the hunting-ground. These would usually wind back and forth across a narrow cañon, from the base of the cañon-wall on one side, to that on the other, but they were rarely so deep that I could not wade them with my high boots. It was very cold one morning as I proceeded up one of these for several miles, and the ice was forming along the edges, and there was slush-ice everywhere and

Profile of the Nose of Rangifer Granti.
New species of caribou discovered by Mr. Stone in Autumn, 1901.

a small covey of snow-white ptarmigan, that flew but a short way, chattering and scolding at being disturbed.

A camp, lighted with candles—clean, dry hay to sit upon, and a smoking-hot supper, were real luxury, and I enjoyed them all, and looked forward to another day, and the coming hunt.

We were nearly two weeks in camp, during which time we secured a magnificent series of caribou (the *Rangifer Granti*, named in honor of the Secretary of the New York Zoölogical Society), and a monster bear (the *Ursus Merriami*, one of the largest species of bears in the world), both of which proved new to science—a splendid addition to my year's work, and repaying me many times for the extra travel and effort they had cost.

I generally followed the course of small the stream was somewhat deeper than usual. Andrew was with me, and, after several miles of travel, we were successful in securing a magnificent bull-caribou, the measuring and skinning of which occupied considerable time ; and I also noted the markings of its beautiful coat, and studied its anatomy.

I was not much surprised, on starting to camp, to find the stream damming with ice at short intervals, causing the water to back to a greater depth. The skin, and head, and bones were a heavy carry, but they must go to camp, and I wanted Andrew to carry meat. I glanced at the swollen stream, and then at the hills, that were everywhere cut into deep gulches, and I decided to try the course of the stream. Picking up my load, and pulling up my boots as far as I could stretch them,

I started for camp. I was very careful in making the first two or three crossings, and succeeded in landing dry; but with every crossing the stream evidently grew deeper. In a very short time my high boots were full of ice and water, and every succeeding crossing poured in a fresh supply. At first, the warmth of my flesh succeeded in warding off any serious results from my repeated, ice-cold baths; but gradually my feet and legs began to suffer severely from the cold, and a little later to grow numb. I had intended to brave it out, but I soon began to suffer extremely, and my legs so rapidly became benumbed, that, at last, in trying to climb out of the stream, up one of the little, low banks, I fell, and my legs were so lifeless that I could not regain my feet. Andrew was taller and stronger, and had suffered less, and he hurried to my assistance. He removed my boots and emptied the water from them. Then he set to work pounding my feet and legs with his hands until I could feel the circulation in them once more. I did not suffer so seriously afterward, but when I finally left the stream, to climb the one high hill between us and camp, benumbed, cold, and fatigued, I thought I should surely never reach the top; and I was never more thankful than when I did finally reach the last rise on that long, steep climb. But the prize I carried with me was fully worth the effort, as such prizes always are to the naturalist. The species of caribou found here range high up in the mountains in summer, de-scending to the lower levels, even to the very sea-shore, in winter. They are a large variety of the barren-ground type, and are very uniformly marked, and grow magnificent heads of delicate antlers. The country ranged by them is generally quite accessible, and they are secured by the experienced hunter with but little difficulty.

Aleut tradition says that when their people first came to the country it was much warmer, and was blessed with more sunshine than it is now; that storms were not so frequent, and that the seas were calmer and easier of navigation by small craft. The most beautiful basket-work produced by any native people in the world is made by these Aleuts, from grasses that grow along the borders of the salt marshes.

The whole of the country is more or less mountainous, though the mountains of the peninsula do not form a continuous chain, but are separated, in many places, by low passes, that extend from the shores of the Pacific to those of Bering Sea. These were at one time channels connecting the two great bodies of water, and what is now the peninsula was then but a continuous chain of islands. The summits of the higher mountains are clothed in perpetual snow, below which, in summer, wild flowers and berries grow in magnificent variety.

Many of the volcanoes have become extinct, but Davlof, Shishaldin, Pogrumnof, Makushin, Tulik, and a few others, are still active.

17
Hunting Alaskan White Sheep with Rifle and Camera

MY CAMP ABOVE TIMBER-LINE.

HUNTING ALASKAN WHITE SHEEP WITH RIFLE AND CAMERA.

BY DALL DE WEESE.

IN the fall of 1897 I hunted the moose, the rare white sheep, and the huge brown bear in the Kenai Mountains of Alaska, and with my own gun secured a fine specimen of each. I returned to Alaska again last fall (1898) to procure specimens of large mammals for the Smithsonian Institute. On this trip I had provided myself with cameras suitable to photograph some of this wild game in their native haunts, which would give me more pleasure than shooting the animals. Never before had the *Ovis dalli* been caught in a sportsman's camera.

After a six weeks' trip of four thousand miles, August ninth found me in camp (with two packers, one white man and one Indian) on the Kenai Mountains, at timber-line, some ninety miles back of Cook's Inlet. At the start I had had three white men and five Indians in my party to assist me in getting my outfit up the rapids of the Kussiloff River and to the head of Lake Tuslumena. This consumed eight days of arduous labor, as we were compelled to pull the boat at the end of a one-hundred-foot line, wading the ice-cold water, passing the line under and around leaning timber; and many times it consumed three hours to make one mile, while the bloodthirsty mosquitoes sapped the life out of us and almost drove us frantic.

Mr. H. E. Lee, of Chicago, had accompanied me as far as Cook's Inlet and intended to continue, but while I was preparing for our trip to the interior he changed his mind, saying: "I would not go up that Kussiloff River and endure the hardships and dangers and suffering from the infernal mosquitoes for all the game and gold in Alaska." I told him he could return to Homer and get good hunting within twenty-five miles of the beach. He so decided, and was very successful.

Mr. Berg, who was with me in 1897, also started with me, but the first night out from salt water he was taken with rheumatism in the limbs so severely that it was necessary for him to stay in the boat. His condition grew worse from day to day, and on reaching the lake I made camp for him, and detailed Mr. Singer to remain with him and do everything possible for his comfort, while I pushed on to the mountains. I kept two packers constantly on the trail between this camp and my line of camps to the summit of the range, so that I could get supplies, send meat down, and learn the condition of my unfortunate companion.

The next ten days I spent in making a map and collecting topographical data of the country, killing one white sheep for our larder. I now set about to get photos and the desired specimens, as the season had advanced to the proper time when the pelage of the sheep was in good condition, the old coat having been entirely shed and the new one out about an inch in length.

This rare wild white sheep is found nowhere in the world but Alaska, and few specimens for mounting whole have ever been obtained. This species, named *Ovis dalli* by Professor Dall, differs from his cousin, the Rocky Mountain big horn (*Ovis montana*), in color, *O. montana* being a dull brown in midsummer, changing to a grayish drab in winter, with a light ashy colored patch over the rump all the year, while the *O. dalli* is snow-white at all seasons ; in fact, there is not a colored hair on any part of his body. He is not quite so stockily built as our " big horn," yet more trim and shapely. Two of my specimens stood forty-two inches at the shoulder. His limbs are not quite so heavy, and his horns will not average as large at the base, although quite as long. The horns of my largest specimen of 1897 measured 41¼ inches in length and 14½ inches in circumference at the base.

The flesh is the most delicious of all wild game. In the summer this sheep lives chiefly on the rich succulent growth of the *Asplenium septentrionale*, which grows in the crevices of the rock on the sunny slopes of this rugged range. This beautiful animal must endure great hardships to survive the winters of this icy North. Many of the higher peaks are snow-capped all the year, while on

A CAMP BELOW THE TIMBER-LINE.

the lower hills, that range in altitude from four to five thousand feet, there is a period of some six to eight weeks of partially open ground. The home of the *Ovis dalli* in this section of Alaska is on the high range where its frowning sides break into deep gashy cañons and precipitous walls to a mighty nameless glacier from ten to twenty miles long.

I had now made a side camp above timber-line and on a range of peaks never before visited by white men or Indians (so my Indians claimed). We had nothing to burn but a scrubby willow brush which we pulled up by the roots. The weather was very changeable at this altitude; rain, heavy fog and spitting snow, with an occasional day of sunshine, and cold, frosty nights.

Early morning found me moving toward the glacier, intent on getting a photo of the sheep. I had pointed out a mountain about six miles to the east, and instructed my two packers to meet me at its base about noon, and to approach cautiously and watch out for me on their right, for it was a photo I more desired as I could get the animal later. I had traveled some two or three miles, stopping occasionally to scan the mountain sides closely with my field glass for a band of sheep. From the summit of a very broken ridge, I sighted a bunch of some thirty to forty quietly feeding and slowly moving toward a glacier. They were some three or four miles away and a little to the left of my course. I carefully took in the country and outlined my route.

The blood now began to quicken as I followed the ridge into the gulch and commenced the stalk to a favorable position where I could get an exposure that, as yet, had never been the privilege of man. When under the cover of a hillside, I ran up hill and down, then climbed out of a cañon from eight hundred to a thousand feet, with the perspiration saturating every stitch of clothing, yes, even through my moccasins. Upon rounding a ledge of rock, I caught sight of three sheep within a hundred yards, on my lee. I drew back quickly and circled to my left to cut them off from the bunch. This took me considerably out of my course and caused me to travel an extra two miles. Another climb of some six or eight hundred feet I thought would put me on a bench level with my quarry.

I now had the wind in my favor and cautiously approached a ledge of rock for a look. Oh, what a sight! Through my glasses, it seemed but a hundred feet to the picture I would give five hundred dollars to have on the plate of my camera at a hundred-foot snap. About half of the bunch had gone out on the edge of the glacier while the rest were nipping the *Asplenium*. Occasionally an old ewe would start on a seemingly educating tour with her one or two half-grown lambs, rush about in a short circle, then back into the bunch again; while the great horned "fellows" seemed to gaze on the proceedings with delight, for the season had come when *they* leave their more lofty and secluded locality to visit the mothers and young.

I had fears that my two men would come in sight and alarm them; then I thought they would surely be on the lookout. On and upward I climbed among the rocks, with weary limbs, breathless and the perspiration dropping from my face like rain. A half hour more had passed, and I was within one hundred yards of the ridge between me and the band that I felt would soon make an impression on the film of my 5x7 camera.

I paused for breath in which to adjust my camera and climb to the spot for position that I had selected with my glasses an hour before. I suddenly cast a glance up the mountain on my left in line where I felt sure the boys would naturally pass. For some reason I had doubted what would be their tactics. Lo! and behold, there they were about five hundred yards up and moving along that comparatively smooth mountain side. Cæsar's ghost! Reader, can you imagine my disgust and wrath? No, you cannot, unless you have had similar experiences. I was at the first glance paralyzed; I chilled, the sweat seemed to run cold, and I felt my features contract and my jaws set. I gave the hat signal to drop down—I repeated it. I stared and clutched my rifle. Should I take a shot at them? On they tramped as if going to a corn-shucking. In my wrath and despair I tore the grass from its bed and turned my finger-nails back clutching at the rocks. I gave the hat signal again and again. Finally to my intense relief they dropped.

I climbed along feeling convinced that the sheep had sighted my men at different times as they passed along the breast of the opposite mountain and had now disappeared over the glacier, and probably the only chance of my life to get a photo of a band of wild white sheep on a glacier had been foiled. With a spark of hope still left, I reached a higher point, thinking they had traveled upward. I peered over the rocks and I was not disappointed, for sure enough they were just moving out of sight near the crest of a low ridge. I was sick. I had noticed higher and to my right two rams seemingly taking in the situation, from a point among the rocks where they felt safe and whence they had watched the men making their way for the last half mile. Now, they had sighted me some three hundred yards from them and had commenced to move. They stopped, to pose for their pictures, of course, at that long range. Well, it was a fatal stop for the larger one, for in an instant I sent a ball through him and he rolled over dead. I took a running shot at the other ram, but missed.

My two packers came over to me. I will not write our conversation. Indian no sa ba, and I forgive them. I took photo, then measurements, dressed the noble game, then ate a cold lunch, and sent my men back with the head, skin and meat, instructing them to go to the camp at timber-line and care for the skin; for the Indian to take a pack of meat down to camp number one to my sick man, and for Hobert, my white man, to bake bread the second day at camp number two, and for them both to meet me with bread and bedding for all at camp number three (above timber-line) on the evening of the fourth day.

My good Mr. Hobert did not like the idea of leaving me alone, but I assured him that I had often done this and would be careful, so we shook hands for a four-days separation. They slipped into their pack-straps and rose up with their heavy loads; and as they picked their way down the mountain homeward I started northward determined on getting another chance for the much-desired photo. Two hours of hard climbing brought me to the summit of this spur. Then a snowsquall set in. Soon the wind grew fierce, and the clouds of snow and mist surrounded me and sent a chill to the bone. I commenced descending on the opposite side and began prospecting the

mountain for mineral, as it was now evident that I could do nothing with my camera. I reached timber-line camp (number three) at nine o'clock in the evening, soaked to the skin with rain, which had changed from snow after I had reached a lower altitude. My faithful Hobert had placed my outfit under my rubber blanket and weighted it down with stones. He had also pulled some scrub willow and piled it near by. I added an extra sweater and a heavy coat to my wet body, and soon had a supper of boiled rice and raisins, broiled mutton chops, bread and tea.

The scrub willow was so scarce that I did not dare to use it in quantities for a fire sufficient to dry my clothing. My bed consisted of two caribou skins (undressed, which are the best thing on earth, for they really seem to generate heat), one camel's-hair blanket and rubber spread. I was soon snugly tucked in and at peace with all the world.

Next day at 2 P. M. I was far from camp and on a broken side of a rugged mountain. I now sighted a bunch of sheep some two miles away on my left, on a table of another mountain. Hope kindled anew, as the day was favorable, and being entirely alone on these grand old peaks I felt confident of success. To get in proper position it was necessary for me to make a long detour, on account of the wind and the lay of the country. I traveled rapidly, and soon reached a point from which I expected to lay out my line for the final approach. I reached the top of a break in the slide rock, and, looking over the ledge, I saw a fine old ram sitting (they will sit on their haunches like a dog) on the next ledge in front of me.

It is unusual for a ram to post as sentinel unless he takes a position from one to three hundred yards above his flock. An old barren ewe is invariably on guard. A careful survey of the country convinced me that the bunch was quite near him on a shelf immediately below. I retreated a few yards, divested myself of every superfluous article, including my old hat, drew my camera from its heavy case and adjusted it for a sixty-foot snap. I used a sixteenth stop, and set the time for a twenty-fifth of a second, in case of a running shot. I crept to the ledge for another look. The old fellow had now lain down from his sitting position. No other sheep were in sight. I again retreated, and crept cautiously up the slope for a short distance, then to the edge and looked again. Over the back of the old guard I could now see the bunch about thirty yards below him. There were some fifteen to twenty; some lying down while others were feeding. I saw it was impossible for me to approach nearer from this point. I retreated below my first position. I now took another look; the old ram was again in a sitting attitude, and some twenty yards above was the ever-watchful ewe that I had not been able to see.

My approach was now cut off from this direction also, and the situation became perplexing. I finally decided on a plan. I moved down the mountain until entirely out of sight of the old ram, but still where I could get a view of the ewe. I hammered some rocks together to attract her attention, and waved my red handkerchief over the ledge. She was up in an instant facing me. I did not repeat this, but watched. This was an anxious period.

After five minutes or so she slowly descended to the bunch. I now returned to my first position. The old ram was standing and turning his head in all directions. Not seeing anything, he seemed unwilling to leave his post, although his faithful mate had warned him and had returned to her charge. They certainly had decided to wait an alarm from him; they had not moved off, for I could see them as there was only one way for them to retreat without passing me.

Ten minutes passed and still he stood with all the wary instincts of his nature aroused. What a picture, with his snow-white, graceful form, his head erect and crowned with massive, wax-colored horns that curved to a full circle. He seemed to have convinced himself that it was a false alarm, for he became more composed, and I felt that the flock had again quieted as their lordly sentinel still held his ground. Now was my time for the final effort.

My heart beat violently, almost loud enough for him to hear. I quickly stole to where I had left my rifle and cautiously returned to my position. He now stood facing me. To drop him dead on the spot was my desire, for as he lay there, I could make a dash to his ridge and get a snap at the flock before

it became aware of his fate. I knew that the report of my rifle would be so light that the flock would not be alarmed at that distance; besides I had the ridge and wind in my favor. I took careful aim and fired. He dropped as if stone-dead. I quickly laid down my gun, snatched my camera, rushed quietly as possible down the ridge and up the next, aiming to reach a position a little below him. Out of breath I reached the point and looking over, I saw that the old fellow had regained his feet, and was staggering into the flock, which had just begun to move away and was now about thirty yards distant. I raised my camera in position and pressed the bulb. I wound the film and made another exposure. I believe these to be the first negatives ever obtained of wild sheep alive on the mountains.

The flock were now fully alarmed, and it was marvelous to witness the agility they displayed in making their ascent among the crags and ledges. I went back for my rifle and returned to hunt the wounded ram, which I felt certain could not go far. I followed the trail across rocks and snow-drifts. Suddenly I saw a white object ahead and high on the cliffs. I adjusted my glasses and discovered it was a big ram, although I could not see the horns with the naked eye. It was a four-hundred-yard shot.

Bang—I missed. Bang—he started. Bang—he dropped and commenced rolling down, then getting up and rolling again. It was a hard climb to reach him, but on doing so, I found to my surprise it was not my wounded ram, although a very fine specimen.

It was now too late in the day to look for the lost one. I then took measurements and dressed my noble prize. I had my pack-straps with me, and started to my lonely camp, which I did not reach until eleven o'clock P. M., for I carried the whole skin, head and saddles of this sheep. Hunters, you have an idea of my load.

The next day it was necessary for me to repair my moccasins and climbing shoes, which I had worn through in several places. In the afternoon I made a trip to a glacier and saw sheep, but will not go into detail regarding them. The next day I started for a long, hard trip and to return where I expected to find my wounded ram, for I

Painted for OUTING by Jas. L. Weston.

IN CLOUD-SWEPT PASTURES.

could not leave him there. After a long prospecting trip to the head of an enormous glacier, I reached a place where the precipitous cliffs joined the yawning crevasses of the walls of living ice. I saw several sheep out, crossed over the divide, and commenced the semicircular return to camp, yet keeping in mind the locality where I hoped to end the suffering of my quarry.

My route brought me to a very rough, steep slope on which a narrow arm of a glacier extended from the summit of the range down at an angle of about fifty degrees for some twelve to fifteen hundred feet below me. To go around this, either above or below, meant the loss of my course and the day as well. It was frightful; however, I put on my ice irons and slowly worked my way across, but solemnly promise I will never do so again.

Another hour of hard climbing brought me around this mountain, where I felt confident my game had hidden. I was yet a mile or more from it, but I noticed a suspicious looking, small white spot on a shelf of rocks and a little below me. I focused my glasses and found it to be a sheep lying down with head erect. I felt this must be my ram, for there were no others in sight and he was wounded. He had hunted seclusion among the rocks to die alone. I steadily advanced in open view for at least half a mile, when I noticed him get up. I stopped and adjusted my glasses. There he stood, looking in my direction. I sat down and watched for him to move. Presently he slowly turned around and began picking his way around the mountain, in the direction he had come two days before. I could plainly see him limp. When he came to the last ridge where he would disappear behind the mountain, he stopped for another look. I still remained quiet and watched his every move through my glasses. Finally he passed out of sight.

It was now eight P. M., and I knew I must act quickly. I scaled the mountain to its summit, crossed over and down the other side on a noiseless run, knowing about where I should get to head him off. I had traveled about half a mile and was watching on my right for his shapely horns, when suddenly on my left, and within sixty yards, on a low bench, I saw two fine old rams. We looked at each other a full minute. It would have been easy work to kill them both, but I passed on, for I felt that a shot might turn my unfortunate from his course.

A heavy mist or fog was now settling down over the peaks, and while descending through it, I caught sight of his head over the swell of a smooth, sloping ridge. He saw me at the same instant and bounded forward on a more level footing, running quartering from me and to my left. The distance was some two hundred yards. I quickly brought my rifle to place. Bang—he turned a little more to my left and increased his speed (overshot). Bang—I noticed him jerk his head backward (shot in front of him). Bang—and with the report he rolled over and over. I approached him and found that my shot of two days before had entered his breast and passed between the shoulder-blade and the ribs and made its exit at the loin, not having broken a bone or touched a vital spot. How he lived I knew not. My last shot was through the shoulders.

It was now nearly nine P. M., and the sun had just sunk behind Mt. Illimana. While I was glad of the prize, I was truly sorry for this beautiful animal. He was my last *Ovis dalli*.

18
A Woman's Experience at Cape Nome

NOME CITY FROM SNAKE RIVER.

A WOMAN'S EXPERIENCE AT CAPE NOME.

BY ELEANOR B. CALDWELL.

A NOME HOSTELRY.

WE left Washington, D. C.—my daughter and I —on May 11, 1900, our destination Cape Nome, our object a fortune. We started with brave feelings, yet I read in my diary: "Washington looked like a paradise as I passed along the streets."

Practical preparations for the trip were not made until Seattle was reached, thirteen days before the departure of the "Tacoma" for the latest Mecca of the fortune-hunter. Of course, we had to take our own roof-tree, household gods and food. Our purpose was firm to start as little burdened as possible. A tent, a stove, some chairs and a couple of tables seemed oppressive possessions indeed when all was collected and measured for disposal in the too limited space of the steamer's interior. It was not easy to procure anything in the overtaxed and tired city, but the acquisition of a stove was a special and difficult problem of itself. A discouraging sign was conspicuously displayed in the shops, "No more orders taken for Alaska." The process by which I became the owner of the coveted article was a lengthy one; feminine arts and cajolery were not entirely left out of consideration; failure seemed imminent, when, lo! my pressing needs above all other Nome travelers were recognized, and I had the satisfaction of seeing my treasure, filled with nuts, safely stowed in the "Tacoma's" hold. The order for grocer's supplies was not large, as I should have no place for storage.

At four in the morning of May 31st, the steamer glided from the Seattle wharf. The passenger-list was unique in the history of Arctic travel, for one hundred of the gentler sex were betaking themselves, for one reason or another—one was a professional gambler—to the City of the Golden Sands. The best-represented profession was that of the sick-nurse—young women starting out to relieve suffering in a cold-ridden, congested community, where

257

A "SAMPLE-ROOM."

as a matter of course the most unsanitary conditions must prevail. It must be confessed that few had come to strike claims.

There were some women, tempted by the comfortable journey, accompanying husbands just for fun, and some to open restaurants and hotels. They were there, however, and the steamship officers didn't seem to know quite what to do with them. No stewardess had been provided, and all service was rendered by the hashers—translated, the men working their way as waiters.

In a week we were cutting the smooth gray waters of Bering Sea. Many of the passengers were now laid up with terrific colds. Starland had been left behind; even through the heavy fog that had settled around us the clear daylight filtered at every hour of the twenty-four. Huge icebergs became our compagnons de voyage, monsters looming up on all quarters. Sunday, June 10th, dawned bright and beautiful after a snow-storm the day before. We found ourselves in other company than the icebergs. There was a boat ahead—the "Aberdeen," as she proved—black with passengers and heavy-laden. Then together the "Aberdeen" and the

"Tacoma" struggled for an entrance into Norton Sound. Thicker and thicker pressed the floes as we struck shallow water. Every one was on the qui vive and expected something to happen, and perhaps this is why when it did come there was not much excitement. But that evening signals of distress were flying from our vessel—we had struck, and remained on bottom.

For three days we stayed on the Yukon flats. On the second, passengers and crew found diversion in heaving overboard coal worth seventy dollars a ton at Nome. Three hundred tons of the precious carbon went to lighten ship for the highest tide of six months, which was due the next day. With the rising tide next morning the passengers were gathered in the bow. They had an important duty to perform—to rush from side to side to help the motion of the boat. That they were equal to the occasion was soon evident, for with steady motion the ship churned its way into deep water.

At 6 P.M. that lucky June 13th, Nome was sighted, and eight hours later we dropped anchor a mile and a half from shore. In the west the orange-hued full moon was just leaving the horizon, and back of the thickly tented stretch of beach to the eastward were snow-capped peaks

TYPICAL NOME CABIN.

from behind which the sun, gone too short a while to let darkness fall on the land, was just peeping.

The scene beckoned us, but the captain spoke of ''light-ers'' that must be awaited. This situation when once understood was not an agreeable one for impatient folk to face. Every day, steamers, cargo-laden and bearing from three to eight hundred people, came to anchor in front of the town, and to await one's turn for lighterage meant an unendurable delay, so by four o'clock a party had chartered a boat and were put on shore for two dollars and a half a head.

One street ran the length of the curious canvas metropolis, but even its communal rights were not respected, for at one point, quite in the center, an enterprising merchant had pitched a tent and was offering his wares. Naturally we first looked for a spot which we could call our own. The prospect appeared hopeless. There seemed not a square inch on which we could put the little tent that would come ashore that afternoon. The beach for five miles was completely covered. Back of this, a plain of spongy tundra stretching to the base of the mountains presented a uniform and thick floor of mud.

A DOG-TEAM

It was quite uninhabitable, but even so, impossible, for it was all somebody's ''claim.'' Legally or illegally, every foot of the land had an owner. Most of the original claims had been jumped. For this there was no redress. Possession was nine points of the law, the tenth had resolved itself into a question of skill in pistol practice. Many an original claimant has returned from the States with an outfit to find his land in other hands, and no use for his expensive machinery but to let it rust upon the beach. There was no court to settle claim disputes. And still, penniless but hopeful, men were digging holes ten feet deep that brought but ''a fraction'' for their pains; for the truth is—the sands contain very little gold. Even as long ago as last spring the more hopeful and stout-hearted had turned their eyes to Port Clarence, thirty miles to the north. Truth about Nome is just now coming out.

HARD AT WORK.

From our impression of Nome City, we looked to our first meal with apprehension. We sought it in a restaurant, and were served with a thin, tough steak, potatoes, poor bread and poor coffee, for two dollars apiece. We soon learned that all the money was being made in saloons,

UNLOADING A FREIGHT LIGHTER.

restaurants and lodging-houses. Contrary to usual conditions, the presence of a drinking-saloon raised the value of all property around it. One small eating-house, twelve by twenty feet, rented for seventy-five dollars a day, a large element in this rent being the fact of its juxtaposition to the finest saloon in town.

The gambling-houses, as is unusual in such places, were not flourishing. The reason—there was little cash in circulation. Gold-dust, too, was scarce, and what there was had been brought from Dawson.

The industrial class was undoubtedly making money. Labor brought one to two dollars per hour. Good cooks could command ten dollars a day. A freight lighter made a thousand dollars a day easily. Provisions, of course, were very high—bread twenty-five cents a loaf and poor at that; butter one dollar a pound; chickens four dollars each. Eggs at fifty cents a dozen seemed remarkably cheap. It may be noticed here that ham and eggs three times a day was the average fare of the Nomite.

The street was alive with people; there was a din of traffic, and loud cries of "Mushon!" ("Go ahead!")

were constantly addressed to the Eskimo dogs, while "Gangway!" was hurled at the loitering pedestrian. Such "chu-cha-ka" (tenderfeet) as we, held by the strange sights and novelty of the scene, became a serious obstacle to progress, and we accepted the name as gracefully as possible.

I was walking a little in the rear of the party at one point, when suddenly I was seized and drawn between two tents. Surprise had not had time to give way to stronger feeling when, "Ping!" a bullet

ALASKAN DOGS USED FOR HAULING.

ROCKING OUT GOLD.

went past the spot where I had been standing. I saw that a strange man had hold of me, and he lifted his hat. "I saved you from that," he explained. "The settling of a little dispute," he continued, in response to my questioning. "But you are as safe here as on Fifth Avenue, New York; any man would come forward to the protection of a lady."

Still, one's presence out of the trajectory

of a bullet is not always a matter that can be arranged for on the spur of the moment. "Going gunning," as they term it, was a popular diversion at Nome. One might see the results of this sport at any turn.

But all this time the consciousness was becoming more pressing that we had no roof for our heads, and it was well along in the afternoon. We repaired to the beach to watch for our freight. Every conceivable article, from huge mining machinery to hen-coops, was strewn pellmell upon the sands; yet the freight agents worked wonders in getting order from chaos. Most of the material was simply stored there, in danger of destruction by the sea if a storm should come.

Perched on trunks, we watched in vain until ten o'clock, when we were directed to the Hotel Casco, a small frame building of one full story and a sloping roof for a second. Here, in a large room under the roof, slowly filling with rough men and negroes, we were, in company with two other women, given a shake-down—a skin thrown upon the floor—for one dollar a head. Yet we thankfully rolled our wraps into pillows and lay down. We had no sense of fear, for the white light of day was

MAIN STREET.

always there. The room was never quiet; men were constantly tramping through to the proprietor's office boarded off at the front. The constant daylight had disarranged any methodical apportionment of the twenty-four hours. Men worked, slept and ate as fancy dictated.

On our rising in the morning, true hospitality was shown us in the gift of some water in which to wash. Water sells at Nome three buckets for twenty-five cents.

Now came days of anxious watching for the possessions that the lighters failed to yield up. They were, in fact, quite the

prepared for any of the hardships we saw around us. None of these could dampen the hope and expectation that had drawn us hither. But there are some things that even the most careful of calculators is apt to neglect. The variety of possibilities is infinite. No one ever realized this better than I did when it was known that small-pox had broken out in camp. Some forty passengers of a plague-stricken ship, condemned to quarantine, had escaped to the shore, bringing the pestilence with them. By the next morning the danger had grown. There were more serious problems for me

FREIGHT PILED UPON THE BEACH.

last things taken from the "Tacoma." A second night was spent upon the skins of the Hotel Casco. Then two nurses, fellow voyagers, offered a part of their tent. Here we stayed for one night, when the steamship agents, in pity, curtained a portion of their own large tent for our use.

In a week we had our things, but they were never taken from the beach. For ten days we sought one little spot that had been overlooked, but none could be discovered. We had not the slightest idea of giving up. Accustomed as we had become to the rough state of affairs, we were

to face than the mere risk of taking the disease, of which I had little fear; the prospect of being quarantined all winter at Nome was fast becoming a certainty. This I could not afford. That day the "Tacoma" was reported returned from Penny River. By night my mind was made up. We took passage, sold our outfit at a slight loss, and within twenty-four hours had left that wild life with its perils, and its prospects which, as the world now knows, have nearly reached the vanishing-point. As we sailed south into the Pacific, dearly familiar seemed the night and the stars.

19
Hunting Sheep in
Western Alaska

HUNTING SHEEP IN WESTERN ALASKA

By JAMES H. KIDDER

TOWARD the last of July, Blake and I left the Kadiak Islands in a schooner which we chartered to take us to the Kenai Peninsula, where we were going for the white sheep which range on the mountains lying back from the coast some thirty miles. The hills may be reached by one of several rivers. It takes only two days of hard river work to ascend some of these streams, but we determined to select a country more difficult to enter, thinking it would be less often visited by the local native hunters. We therefore chose the mountains lying adjacent to one of the large inland lakes—a district which took from a week to ten days to penetrate.

When we reached the lake which was to be our base of supplies, we decided that each should take a light outfit and push on until we came upon rams, and there to make our shooting-camp, the natives taking the trophies out to the permanent camp on the lake and packing back needed provisions.

At noon of August 22d Blake and his outfit started for his shooting-grounds at the eastern end of the sheep range, and shortly after my outfit was under way. My head man and the natives each carried packs of some sixty pounds, while I carried about fifty pounds besides my rifle, field-glasses and cartridges; even my dog Stercke had some thirty pounds of canned goods in a pack-saddle.

After two days' hard tramping, mostly above timber, and with few good camping places, we were among the sheep, and as hunting in these hills is at best hard work I decided to keep the camp as high up as we could find wood and water. The next morning as we started on our first real hunt the day was dull and the wind was fortunately light, for it generally sweeps over these rugged, barren summits with great velocity.

We had been gone from camp but little over an hour when, on approaching a small knoll, I caught sight of the white coat of a sheep just beyond. At once dropping upon my hands and knees, I crawled up and carefully peered over to the other side. We had unconsciously worked into the midst of a big band of ewes, lambs and small rams. I counted twenty-seven on my left and twenty-five on my right, but among them all there was not a head worth shooting.

This was the first great band of white sheep I had seen, and I watched them at this close range with much interest. Soon a telltale eddy in the breeze gave them our scent, and they slowly made away, not hurriedly nor in great alarm, but reminding me much of tame sheep or deer in a park. Man was rather an unfamiliar animal to them, and his scent brought but little dread.

From this time on until darkness hid them, sheep were in plain view the entire day. In a short while I counted over one hundred ewes and lambs.

We worked over one range and around another, with the great valley of the river lying at our feet, while beyond were chain upon chain of bleak and rugged mountains. Finally we came to a vast gulch supposed to be the home of the large rams. My men had hunted in this section two years before, and had never failed to find good heads here, but we now saw nothing worth stalking. By degrees we worked to the top of the gulch, and coming to the summit of the ridge paused, for at our feet was what at first appeared but a perpendicular precipice of jagged rock falling hundreds of feet.

We seated ourselves on the brink of this great gulch, and the glasses were at once in use. Soon Hunter—my head man—saw rams, but they were so far below that even with my powerful binoculars it was impossible to tell more than that they carried larger heads than some other sheep near them.

It was impossible to descend the cliff at the point where we then were, so we moved around, looking for a spot where we might work our way down, and finally found one where it was possible to descend some fifty yards to a sort of chute. Moving with the greatest caution, we finally reached the chute, and after a bit of bad climbing found the slide rock at the lower end, as we had expected, but it took us a good two hours to get low enough to tell with the glasses how big were the horns the sheep carried.

There were eight rams in all. A bunch of three small ones about half a mile away, and just beyond them four with better heads, but still not good enough to shoot; and apart from these, a short distance up the mountain side, was a solitary ram which carried a really good head. The bunch of three was unfortunately between us and the big sheep, and it required careful stalking to get within distance of the ones we sought. When we were still a long way off we showed ourselves to this bunch of sheep, and they took the hint and went slowly up the crags.

Although the four had become suspicious from seeing the three go slowly up the cliff on our approach, still they had not made us out, and the wind remained favorable. Lying close long enough for them to get over their suspicions, we cautiously stalked up to within some two hundred yards. Again we used the glasses most carefully, but could not see the big ram, which had come down toward the others from his solitary position. Suddenly the sheep became alarmed and started up the mountain. I expected each second to see the large ram come out from behind the boulders, and therefore withheld from shooting. But when he did not appear, I turned my attention to the four which had paused and were looking down upon us from a rocky ridge about four hundred yards above. As they stood in bold relief against the black crags, I saw that one carried horns much larger than the others, which proved to be the big sheep our carelessness had allowed to get so far away. My only chance was to take this long shot. We had been crossing a snow-bank at the time, and I settled myself, dug my heels well in, and with elbows resting on my knees took a steady aim. I was fortunate in judging the correct distance, for at the report of my rifle the big ram dropped, gave a few spasmodic kicks, and the next minute came rolling down the mountain side, tumbling over and over, and bringing with him a great shower of broken rocks. I much feared that his head and horns would be ruined, but fortunately found them not only uninjured, but a most beautiful trophy. The horns taped a good thirty-four inches along the curve and thirteen and one-half inches around the butts.

That night the weather changed, and thenceforth the mountains were constantly enveloped in mist, while it rained almost daily. These were most difficult conditions under which to hunt, for sheep have wonderful vision, and can see a hunter through the mist long before they can be seen.

A week after killing the big ram we visited again this great basin, but found nothing in sight, and cautiously moved a little higher to a sheltered position. From here we carefully scanned the bottom of this large gulch, and soon spied a bunch of ewes and lambs, and shortly afterwards three medium-sized rams. When we first saw them, one had become suspicious and was looking intently in our direction, so we crouched low against the rocks, keeping perfectly still until they once more began to feed. When they had gradually worked over a slight knoll, we made a quick approach, cautiously stalking up to the ridge over which the sheep had gone. I had expected to get a fair shot at two hundred yards or under, but when I peered over, nothing was in sight. I concluded they had not gone up the mountain side, for their white coats against the black rocks would have rendered them easily seen. I therefore started to walk boldly in the direction in which we had seen them go, thinking they had probably taken shelter from the gale behind some rocks, and that I should suddenly come upon them.

I had only gone some paces when we located them standing on a snow patch, which had made them indistinguishable. I sat down and tried to shoot from my knees, but the wind was so fierce that I could not hold my rifle steady, so I ran as hard as I could in their direction, looking hastily about for some rock which would protect me from the gale.

The sheep made up the mountain side for some three hundred yards, when they paused to look back. I had by this time found a sheltered position behind a large boulder, and soon had one of the rams wounded, but, although I fired several shots, I seemed unable to knock him off his feet. Fearing that I might lose him after all, I aimed for the second ram, which was now on the move some distance farther up the mountain, and at my fourth shot he stopped. Climbing up to within one hundred and fifty yards, I found that both the sheep were badly wounded and were unable to go farther, so I finished them off. What was my surprise to find that the larger ram had seven bullets in him, while the smaller one had three.

The weather continued unfavorable for hill shooting until the 3d of September, but that day opened bright and clear, and fearing lest the good weather might not last, we made an early start, and traveled some distance before we saw sheep; but having once reached their feeding-ground, I had the satisfaction of watching more wild game than on any previous day. But though we saw a multitude—one band of no less than forty-eight—we failed to get a single shot. Late in the afternoon, on the return trip to camp, we paused for a brief rest and a smoke, and here Hunter sighted two lone rams in a gulch at the top of the mountain above us. By this time we were both pretty well used up, but the glasses showed that they carried good heads, and I determined to stalk them even if it meant passing the night on the hills. So we worked our way up to the top of a ridge which commanded a view of the gulch in which the sheep were grazing, but they had fled some distance away by the time we reached the place where I had expected to shoot, and were at too long a range to make my aim certain. However, I could count on several shots before they ran out of sight, and even at such a distance I hoped to get one, and possibly the pair. Both sheep carried good heads, but I aimed at the one which stood broadside to me. Hunter, who had the glasses, told me afterward that the ram with the more massive horns got away, but I succeeded in wounding the other so that he was unable to move. Knowing he would shortly die, and that I could find him the next morning, we at once started at our best pace for camp.

The following day we were literally wind-bound in camp. It was not until the day after that we could set out for the wounded sheep, which eventually we found not fifty yards from where we had last seen him. It was a long and hard climb to reach him, but he carried a very pretty head with massive horns of over a full turn. I found that two shots of the seven which I had fired had taken effect.

Two days later the native arrived from the main camp with more provisions, and brought a rather interesting letter from Blake, from which it was clear that I had been hunting at a great disadvantage in my district, and that there were proportionately more big heads among the sheep at his end of the range. I at once determined to retrace my steps to the main camp and follow up his trail.

Therefore, the next morning (September 7th), we shouldered our packs and went over the mountains to our main camp.

Starting out from the main camp, we soon found the tracks of Blake's party, which led up a moraine, and carried us over much quicksand and through many glacial streams, icy cold. Finally we came to where Blake had started up the mountain side, and with all due regard to my friend, his trail was not an easy one. About noon it began to rain, but we pushed upward, although soon soaked to the skin, and came out above timber just at dark. The next morning broke dismally, with the floodgates of the heavens open and the rain coming down on our camp in torrents. Later in the afternoon we succeeded in getting some wood to burn, and had a square meal. While we were crouched around the fire the natives saw sheep on the hills just above us, but it was raining so hard that it was impossible to tell if they were rams. In fact, when sheep's coats are saturated with water they do not show up plainly, and might easily be mistaken for wet rocks when seen at any distance.

The next day opened just as dismally, with the storm raging harder than ever, but by eleven o'clock it began to let up, and we soon had our things drying in the wind, for the clouds looked threatening, and we feared the rain would begin again at any time.

As we were short of provisions and depended almost entirely upon meat, my head man and I started at once for the hills. Climbing to the crest of the mountains on which we had seen the sheep the evening before, and following the summit, we soon saw a large and two small rams feeding on a sheltered ledge before us. We much feared that they would get our scent, but by circling well around we succeeded in making a fair approach. I should have had an excellent shot at the big ram had not one of the smaller ones given the alarm. The gale was coming in such gusts that it was difficult to take a steady aim, and at my first shot the bullet was carried to one side. I fired again just as the sheep were passing from view, and succeeded in breaking the leg of the big ram. Hunter and I now raced after him, but the hillside was so broken that it was impossible to locate him, so my man went to the valley below, where he could get a good view and signal me.

It is always well in hill shooting to have an understood code of signals between your man and yourself. The one which I used and found most satisfactory provided that if my man walked to the right or left it meant that the wounded game was in either of these directions; if he walked away from the mountain, it was lower down; if he approached the mountain, it was higher up.

As Hunter, after reaching the valley and taking a look with the glasses, began to walk away, I knew that the sheep was below me, and I suddenly came close upon the three which had taken shelter from the gale behind a large rock. Very frequently sheep will remain behind with a wounded companion; especially is this so when it is a large ram. Now, unfortunately, one of the smaller rams got between me and the big one, and as I did not want to kill the little fellow the big ram was soon out of range. But he was too badly wounded to go far over such grounds, and I soon stalked up near, when I fired, breaking another leg, and then, racing up, finished him off. This ram carried a very pretty head, thirteen and one-quarter inches around the butts and thirty-six and three-quarters inches along the curve; but, unfortunately, the left horn was slightly broken at the tip. It was undoubtedly an old sheep, as his teeth worn to the gums and the ten rings around his horns indicated.

When a ram's constitution has been undermined by the rutting season, the horns cease to grow, nor do they begin again until the spring of the year, with its green vegetation brings nourishing food, and this is the cause of the rings, which, therefore, indicate the number of winters old a sheep is. This was my head man's theory, and is, I believe, a correct one, for in the smaller heads which I have examined these rings coincided with the age of the sheep as told by the teeth. Up to five years the age of a sheep can always be determined by the teeth; a yearling has but two teeth, a two-year-old four teeth, a three-year-old six teeth, and a four-year-old or over, eight teeth, or a full set.

The next day, the 13th, and Friday opened dismally enough, but by the time we had finished breakfast the mountains were clear of clouds, and there was no wind to mar one's shooting. Such conditions were to be taken advantage of, and Hunter and I were soon working up the ridge well to leeward of the place where we had seen the sheep the night before. The white coats of these sheep against the dark background of black moss-covered rocks render them easily seen, but we now failed to sight any even on the distant hills. Therefore we pushed ahead, going stealthily up wind and keeping a careful watch on all sides. We had crossed over the ridge and worked our way just below the sky line on the other side of the mountain from our camp, never expecting that the sheep would work back, for they had seen our camp-fire on the night before. We had traveled nearly to the end of the ridge and were just about to cross and work down to a sheltered place where we expected to find our game, when Hunter chanced to look back, and instantly signaled me to drop out of sight.

While we had been working around one side of the summit the sheep had been working back on the other side, and we had passed them with the mountain ridge between. Fortunately, they were all feeding with their heads away, or they must have seen us as we came out on the sky line. My man had the glasses, and assured me that there were two excellent heads. We now felt quite certain that these were part of a band of sheep I had seen at a distance a week before and had been trying to locate ever since.

We cautiously dropped out of sight and worked back, keeping the mountain ridge between us. We were well above and had a favorable wind and the entire day before us. It was the first and only time upon these hills that the conditions had all been favorable for a fair stalk and good shooting. Hunter did his part well, and brought me up to within one hundred and twenty-five yards of the rams, which were almost directly below us. They had stopped feeding and were lying down. Only one of the smaller sheep was visible, and my man advised me to take a shot at him, and then take the two large ones as they showed themselves. Aiming low, I fired; and then, as one of the big rams jumped up, I fired again, killing him instantly. The smaller one that I had first shot at went to the left, while the one remaining large ram and the second smaller one went to the right. The latter were instantly hidden from view, for the mountain side was very rough and broken, and covered with large slide rock. I raced in the same direction, knowing well that they would work up hill. But hurrying over such ground is rather dangerous work. Soon the two sheep came into view, offering a pretty quartering shot at a little under a hundred yards. The old ram fell to my first bullet, and I allowed the smaller one to go and grow up, and, I hope, offer good sport to some persevering sportsman five years hence.

While Hunter climbed down and skinned out the heads I turned in pursuit of the one which I had first fired at, for we both thought he had been hit, having seen hair fly. I soon located him in the distance, but he showed no signs of a bad wound, and as his head was small I was glad that my shot had only grazed him.

The larger ram measured thirteen and one-quarter inches around the base of the horns, and thirty-seven and five-eighths inches and thirty-seven and seven-eighths inches along the outer curves. These were the longest horns of the *Ovis dalli* that I killed. The other ram measured thirteen inches around the horns, and thirty-four and one-half inches along the outer curve.

While we were having tea that afternoon we chanced to look upon the hills, and there, near the crest of the ridge, was one of the small rams from the bunch we had stalked that morning. He offered a very easy chance had I wanted his head.

It is worthy of note that these sheep seem to have no fear of the smell of blood or dead comrades, and on several occasions I have observed them near the carcass of some ram which I had shot.

The next day opened perceptibly cooler, and the angry clouds overhead told us to beware of a coming storm. As I now had seven heads, five of which were very handsome trophies, I concluded to take Hunter's advice and leave the high hills.

Our hill shooting for the year was now practically over. Had the weather been fine it would have been an ideal trip; but with the exception of the 3d and 13th of September every day passed upon the mountains was not only disagreeable, but with conditions so unfavorable that it had been almost impossible to stalk our game properly; for when I had been once wet to the skin the cold wind from the glaciers soon chilled me to such a degree that I was unable to remain quietly in one place and allow the game to get in a favorable position for a stalk. I had been obliged to keep constantly going, and this frequently meant shooting at long range. With the exception of the rams shot on the 13th of September I had killed nothing under three hundred yards. Therefore, much of the sport in making a careful and proper stalk had been lost.

My success with the white sheep had come only with the hardest kind of work, but I now had five really fine heads, which I later increased to six my limit. I was quite satisfied with the measurements of these horns along the curve, but had hoped to have shot at least one which would tape over fourteen inches around the butts, which would be extreme, for the horns of the white sheep do not grow so large as those of the common Rocky Mountain variety. They are also much lighter in color. I believe that large and perfect heads will be most difficult to find a few years hence in this section, and the sportsman who has ambitions in this direction would do well not to delay his trip too long; for this range of hills is not over large, and unless these sheep have some protection, it is only a question of time before they will be almost entirely killed off.

20
The Fish
of the
Alaska Coast

THE FISH OF THE ALASKA COAST

BY CHARLES HALLOCK

THE great salt ocean which washes the Pacific side of this continent is far more prolific of fish and other marine forms than the North Atlantic, or even the Gulf of Mexico. For not only do we find (or did find until recently) the sea lion, the sea otter, the sea elephant, the walrus, the manatee, the fur seal, and other exceptional forms in vast numbers, but we discover a great many genera and species unknown to Atlantic waters, and of especial economic value. Principal among the latter are the sculpins, the scorpænids and the embiotocids, or viviparous fishes, which comprise a great number of species.

The viviparous fish may be said to be somewhat intermediate in external appearance, as they are in structure, between the Labrids and the Sparids, but they are readily recognizable and distinguished from all others by ichthyologists. In reproduction they develop a uterus-like envelope which encloses the young fish to the number of from seven or eight to forty and these are hatched out at maturity just like a litter of kittens or mice. The family is characteristic of the Western coast, only two or three species being known to occur beyond the limits of the Pacific Coast of temperate North America, and these few only on the opposite coast of the Pacific in the northern temperate region and in the opposite hemisphere in the temperate seas of New Zealand and Australia.

There are no less than seventeen varieties of the family Embiotocidæ on the Pacific Coast, with a sub-relative fresh water species in the Sacramento River, Cal. This family is collectively known as surf-fish, which is a proper enough name for them. None of them, it is said, is very good for the table, being more or less insipid and watery, but they are all marketable fishes. There is one very large, handsome fish called *Tæniotoca lateralis* in accepted nomenclature, which is olive-colored, marked with longitudinal stripes. It is found abundantly on the California coast and is known simply as "perch" by the San Franciscans. None of the number, however, are at all related to the true perch, or any of the so-called species elsewhere.

The scorpænids are locally known as "rock cod," but they have not the remotest relation to the family Gadidæ. They are very closely allied to the snappers and groupers of the Gulf of Mexico and the South Atlantic, and I am unable to discover any structural difference, or difference in color, between the red snapper of Alaska and the *Lutjanus blackfordii* of Florida. As long ago as the summer of 1885 I helped to catch them by the boatload and to eat them and was so fortunate as to secure portraits in oil of this and other leading fishes, by the kind assistance of Mrs. Fanny Storkbridge of Baltimore. These were sent to the Smithsonian Institute at Washington.

Other varieties differ in coloration as well as in the armature of the bones of the head and the minor structural characteristics. These fish and the black cod (a true gadus locally known as coalfish) have not disappointed the great expectations commercially which were then based upon them. Its flesh is highly regarded wherever eaten and is considered far superior to that of the Newfoundland cod, being richer and of finer fiber. The color of the salted fish when cooked is a bright yellow. There are a number of banks off the Alaska coast where fisheries are carried on by men from San Francisco and the Atlantic side, who salt many thousand tons annually. Deep sea fishing has been also followed for some time with profit. The sculpin is not esteemed as an edible or handsome fish, but he is very numerous and a great scavenger. He looks very much like a rutabaga turnip covered with warts with a slit entirely across the big end for a mouth. He is so ugly that old fishermen torture him just for his ugliness. Of the groupers or snappers (*scorpenidæ*) there are no less than fifteen known varieties, four of which I took from the same locality at one sitting. We fished a rocky ledge in about two hundred feet depth of water, some quarter of a mile off shore, using hard clams and fresh meat for bait, and it was very easy to determine whenever we swung off the ledge, for the fish stopped biting— a fact which shows how important it is to ascertain and keep the precise location of their feeding grounds.

While there are many Atlantic fishes like the tautog, cunner, striped bass, orgy, sheepshead, bluefish, etc., which have no correspondents on the Pacific side, there are many varieties, three of which are unknown to Atlantic waters. I find the range of the true cod, the halibut, the salmon, the sea trout, and some other fish, to be the same on both sides of the continent. The cod ranges between the fiftieth and sixtieth parallels of latitude. In the East the principal food of the shore cod is the caplin, the fishermen not only use the caplin chiefly for bait, but they follow their movements to ascertain the whereabouts of the cod. On the west side (the Pacific) the eulachon, or candle fish, is the correspondent of the caplin, and is almost identical with it. It is smoked, salted, and dried on the rocks in the same way, and is largely used for food by the Indians, but it is much more oily, and will burn like a candle. Eulachon oil is considered superior to cod liver oil or any other fish oil known. It is of a whitish tint, about the consistency of thin lard, and is a staple article of barter between the coast Indians and the interior tribes. The fish begin running about the first of March and swarm into the river and estuaries by the million for several weeks. This period should be the cod-fishing season. They are caught in purse nets by the canoe load. In the province of British Columbia where the manufacture of the oil is prosecuted to some extent, the fish are boiled in water about four hours, in five-barrel wooden tanks with iron bottoms, and then strained through baskets made from willow roots into red cedar boxes of about fifteen gallon capacity each. When the run of fish is good, each tribe will put up about twenty boxes of oil.

Herring swarm in the bays and rivulets during the spawning season in the spring, but are not at that time of as good quality as when taken in nets from their permanent banks and feeding grounds. They are somewhat smaller than the herring of Europe, though fully equal in quality when taken in their prime. There are several factories along the coast where herring oil is pressed out and fertilizers made from the scraps. Halibut are taken in great numbers in deep water, frequently five hundred pounds in weight. The Indians are adepts in taking halibut, and use hooks of native manufacture, made of bone or of wood and iron, which are far more efficient than any shop rig. White fishermen who have tried them will use no other, for a fish who once bites seldom gets away. Some of them are beautifully carved. Halibut fishing long ago became a regular industry. The fish are salted, smoked or marketed fresh. Sturgeon also exist in great numbers, as well as anchovies, haddock, flounder, sole, tomcod, and whiting or kingfish (*Menticirrus undulatus*). The sole has no correspondent in the Atlantic. He is specifically and structurally different from his relative, the flounder, and has reached a more advanced stage of development, for he has two pectoral fins, while the flounder has but one. There is a fish caught in salt water along shore where weeds and kelp grow, which is the exact counterpart in color and structure of the black bass of eastern inland fresh waters and affords equally good sport for the trolling spoon. He belongs to the family Serranidæ, of which there are said to be four varieties on the Pacific coast. A very beautiful fish of fine flavor was taken with a fly off the rocks of Calvert Island, lat. 51 deg. 30 min., a portrait of which I send you. To my eye it is handsomer than any brook trout, which is a hard thing to say of a lifelong acquaintance. Indeed, the fish of the Pacific are all more highly colored than their congeners of the Atlantic, a characteristic which is true of all marine forms found there, as well as of plants, fruits, vegetables, trees and flowers; and they are larger as well, and generally of higher flavor. And the Pacific ocean, like the adjacent land, is more prolific than the Atlantic. I have seen a tideway so crowded with incoming jellyfish (*Medusæ*) that a man had no room to swim. Notoriously, the salmon jam the streams in the spawning season so that they cannot move! In the coves at low tide, starfish of many patterns pave the bottom like cobble stones—starfish of five, eight, ten, eighteen, and twenty-two fingers, or points, and of bright crimson, pink, dark red, yellow, drab and gray hues; all of the crabs and prawns, left by the ebb, climb and skip over their motionless bodies, seldom provoking them to stir the least bit out of position. On all the piles of the wharves, and wherever there are sunken logs or trees, anemones of pink and purest white grow in clusters, shaped like lilies, but more mysteriously beautiful in their composite character and instinct of animal and vegetable forms. And there are many kinds of repulsive octopus, with decapods and cephlapods, and all tribes of sepia, squid, and inkfish. The sea cucumber (*holothuria*) is abundant also. When cured and dried it makes the article of commerce known as "bèche-de-mer," highly prized in China for food, where it is called "trepang." A valuable industry might be built up by preparing this commodity for market. Indeed, attention needs only to be directed to the opportunities to prompt new efforts in this new and unprospected region.

In Alaska there are few sandy beaches or gravelly shores. The margins of the mainland and islands drop plump into many fathoms of water, so that the tide never goes out—it merely recedes; and when it is lowest it exposes the rank yellow and green weeds which cling to the damp crags and slippery masses of rock, and the mussels and barnacles which crackle and hiss when the lapping waves recede. In some places there are little bights, a few yards wide, between the rocks, where there is a sort of beach formed entirely of comminuted shells, and one can pick up cockles and abelones by the peck—clams of all sizes, some large and tough, weighing eight pounds, and some small and sweet. By digging, a bushel of the big ones can be gathered in no time. After noticing the conformation of the coast it is easily understood why there are no oysters in Alaska. I cannot learn that any person has ever seen an Alaska oyster; but there are a good many beds farther south, in British Columbia, and I have eaten lots of bivalves and enjoyed them. However, alongside of regulation "saddle rocks" they look insignificant, inasmuch as seven stewed oysters go to the tablespoonful, by actual count!

To me it is a great pleasure to see what the ebb tide uncovers, and to watch the career of the counter currents, as they surge to and fro in the narrow channels betwixt sunken rocks, awash now at low water and eloquent with the dangers of Peril Strait or Seymour Rapids, which are invisible when the flood is full. At flood or slack water the surface is as placid as the morn, but whenever the tide turns and the ebb or flow begins it is strange to observe the tide-rips in what seems to be an interior land-locked lake. One can hardly grapple with the phenomenon. Immediately on the flood all the trash and floating trees, chunks of ice, dead fish, loose seaweed and what not, which have been floating about on the slack, begin to set in with the tide; great kelps with stems three hundred feet long buoyed up by bulbs or bladders, and broad streamers sprawling in all directions and half under water, like the hair of a drowned woman, lift their weird forms as they drift by; jellyfish and medusæ come in countless myriads, steadfastly following the inexorable stream of fate; schools of herring and small fish of all sorts swarm in all directions, fretting the surface like flaws of wind; and last of all, predatory and with fell intent, follow the whales and porpoises and thresher sharks, tumbling, spouting, diving and feasting with appetites never cloyed by repletion. Here and there along the shore, where some little bight makes into the land, herds of seals bob up serenely out of the water and gaze with large and solemn eyes. All the atmosphere is filled with the softened light of a summer haze, and the air aloft and around about is noisy with the screams of gulls quartering the azure field on the wings of the warm southwest wind.

This is a summer picture of Alaska. Occasionally there are nights when the sea is luminous with phosphorescence, and all the crests of the flowing waves break in cascades of silver and gold; every dip of the oar stirs up pyrotechnics of sparks and glistening stars, and the revolving wheels of the steamer throw off streams of evanescent light. The lustrous glow piles up in front of the prow and trails off in the receding wake. Whenever the vessel chances to overhaul a school of struggling fish their every movement can be distinctly traced in scintillations and curves of fire, as they dart aside and deviate to avoid the inexorable advance. Even the size and shape of the fish are seen. I have observed such marine phenomena in many seas, but nowhere as vivid or prevalent as in the Northern Pacific Ocean.

Who can say that the fecundity of these shores in all their forms of animal and vegetable life is not due to this abnormal profusion of phosphorescence in the ocean?

Now as regards the anadromous and inland fresh water fishes of Alaska, there are the salmon and the sea trout, the lake trout, two kinds of stream trout (S. *irrideus* and S. *pleuriticus*), pike, sturgeon, perch, eels, and a very superior whitefish. Of salmon there are five recognized species, to wit:

Species	Range
Dog Salmon (*Oncorhynchus keta*)	Sacramento River to Bering Strait.
Humpback (*O. gorbuscha*)	Sacramento River to Kotzebue Sound.
Silver Salmon (*O. kisutch*)	Sacramento River to Kotzebue Sound.
Blueback (*O. nerka*)	Columbia River to Kotzebue Sound.
Quinnat (*O. chouicha*)	Monterey to the Arctic Ocean.

Their specific characteristics differ very materially from those of the Atlantic coast. The quinnat, or King Salmon, is the most comely and commercially valuable of his class and may be justly called its rival representative. He is a good deal heavier than his Atlantic congener and in the rivers of Western Alaska will average fifty pounds, individuals often running up to one hundred pounds in weight. His range is even more remarkable than that of any of his related species wherever found, for they not only swarm in Sacramento River in Southern California, but are found crowding the upper waters of the Yukon and the channels of the Back's Great Fish River and its tributaries in the Arctic Ocean. The canned commodity is known all over the world where commerce extends. The steelhead trout (*Salmo gardneri*) which was supposed to be a true salmon until ten years ago, is the best game fish of them all, taking the artificial fly in fine style, the red ibis and royal coachman being favorites. It spawns on the feeders of the main streams and returns to the sea, whereas the oncorhynchus salmon deposit their spawn and die. With the steelhead it often occurs that before spawning is accomplished the streams fall so low as to prevent the fish passing out so that they remain in the deep pools until the streams flush again. This, it is claimed, will account for what is known as land-locked salmon on the Pacific coast.

A lake trout of the Dolly Varden type (*S. carinatus*), with red spots as large as a pea, is found in the lakes on the small islands as well as the mainland. The sea trout, closely resembling the Canadian sea trout, and spotted in the same way with blue and crimson spots much like the eastern brook trout, makes its appearance in the streams at stated intervals, like its Atlantic brothers. All the trout take bait and fly. The sea trout takes the trolling spoon readily in the bays. It is found all the way from Victoria, B. C., northward to Bering Strait, and in Hudson's Bay replaces the salmon which is not found there at all. Its range on the west coast corresponds very nearly with its range on the eastern coast, where it is often a nuisance to salmon anglers, being apt to rise to the fly during the period of its stated runs.

The canning of salmon has become an important industry in Alaska and establishments have been located at principal points along the southeastern coast and as far north as Norton Sound in Bering Sea, the services of native Indians and Chinese being enlisted as auxiliaries. Notable among these is the Chilcat cannery situated in 59 deg. 13 min., north latitude, which is well up toward the frigid zone, but warmed, like the rest of the Alaskan coast by the Japan current, or Kuro-Siwo, which corresponds to the Gulf Stream of the Atlantic. I dare say that no commercial company in the world ever found its way to a nook of earth so ineffably romantic; for the grandeur of the surrounding scenery is supreme. Parallel ranges of snow-capped mountains of majestic height inclose a narrow strait whose waters are deep and green, and seldom disturbed by the storms which beat the outer wall. High up in the bluest

empyrean the glittering peaks flash to each other the reflections of the noonday sun, and where the silvery summer clouds rest upon the summits, the eye can scarcely distinguish the fleecy vapors from the spectral snow. Below the snow line their sides are covered with fir and hemlock, and in the dark waters under the shadow of their confronting abutments, the salmon are continually tossing the spray so that the surface fairly boils. Through one of the clefts of the mountains the sparkling Chilcat River leaps over the obstructing rocks in a succession of pools and rapids, and upon the point of rocks at its mouth the cannery is situated. Perched upon a ledge so narrow that the wharves and fishing stages can scarcely keep a foothold above the tide, it looks out toward a long vista of headlands whose clear-cut outlines are set against the sky in graduated shades of blue as they recede and overlap each other. And out of another great rift the famous Davidson glacier presses toward the sea, filling the valley four miles wide; and the masses of ice which are successively pushed to the front and break off, float away with the recurring tides, and chases up and down the land-locked channels until they finally melt away or drift out into the ocean. On a beach opposite the cannery is a village of Indian employees with the usual adjuncts of half-dried salmon spread about the rocks, wolfish dogs, and log canoes drawn up on shore and carefully protected from the weather by boughs and blankets when not in use. Gray and white gulls fill the upper air or sit on the drifting icebergs and scream, while large wisps of sandpeeps flit constantly from point to point, feeding on the landwash. The foreground is active with the movements of canoes and boats hauling seines.

Dr. Tarleton H. Bean, of the U. S. Fish Commission, who has devoted many years to the study of fishes and fishing grounds of Alaska, enumerates one hundred and thirty-five species, one hundred and eight of which live in the sea and twenty-seven permanently or temporarily in fresh waters. The number of kinds of food and bait fishes is about seventy. Among the fresh water fishes are the burbot, pike, trout and long-nosed sucker, all of them larger and heavier than their eastern congeners, the burbot attaining sixty pounds. In the sea we recognize the cod (*gadus*), and polar cod, the halibut, capelin, spined dogfish, and eleven other species common to the Atlantic coast. There are eleven species of flounder, five of cod; five blennies, five rock cods, three sword-bearers, two wolf-fish or lancet mouths (*alepido sanrus*), tomcod, three rock eels, pollock, wachna, three eelpouts, cusk, lumpfish, four species of suck fish or sea snails, five species of alligator fish, sculpins two feet long, etc., etc.

The catalogue of the National Museum

gives the scientific classification of all
known fishes to the present date. Nature
has certainly provided amply for coming
use of mankind affording the Alaska
fisherman a superabundance of fish in
remarkable variety, conveniently located
with reference to good harbors, where
ample supplies of fuel, water and game
may be obtained; spreading out for his
occupation tens of thousands of square
miles of soundings inhabited by the valuable food creatures which attract the fish.

21
Over the Chilkoot Pass to the Yukon

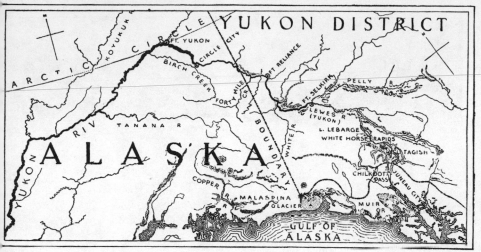

OVER THE CHILKOOT PASS TO THE YUKON

By Frederick Funston

THE tourists who every summer crowd the excursion steamers that sail up the long stretches of the inland passage to Alaska find their view to the north and east everywhere limited by a range of snowy peaks silhouetted like card-board against a sky as clear and blue as that of California. On the one side is a narrow strip of main-land and on the other a thousand islands, large and small, that constitute southeastern Alaska, where are the busy mining town of Juneau, and Sitka, the sleepy old capital. This is the Alaska of the tourist, famous for its great glaciers, its beautiful fiords, and its Thlinket Indians and their totem poles. But beyond the big white range is another and a totally different country, the valley of the Yukon, a great, lone land where winter reigns supreme for nine months of every year, and whose inhabitants are roving bands of fur-clad savages. Over in the British Northwest Territory, just across the coast range from Dyea Inlet, Alaska, is a chain of lakes surrounded by snowy

mountains and drained by a small stream, which, now roaring between gloomy cañon-walls and now gliding among birch-covered hills, bears away to the northwest. On either hand it receives numerous tributaries, some of them of great size, and seven hundred miles from its source leaves the British possessions and enters Alaska. After winding for 1,400 miles across this territory it pours its huge flood into Behring Sea. On the lower half of its course the river receives the waters of the Porcupine, Tanana, Koyukuk, and numerous smaller streams, until the little brook, less than ten feet wide, draining Lake Linderman, has in the 2,100 miles of its course become one of the mightiest rivers on the face of the earth —three miles from bank to bank, thirty feet deep, and with a current of five miles an hour.

Four of us were landed with our effects at the head of Dyea Inlet, a hundred miles north of Juneau, at daybreak on April 10, 1893. My three companions were McConnell, a grizzly old Canadian, Thompson, a miner from Idaho, and Mattern, a good-natured German, who had mined in half a dozen Western States. I was the only one of

the party who had had any previous Alaskan experience, but all had roughed it in other countries, and we felt equal to the much-vaunted terrors of Chilkoot Pass, Miles Cañon, and the White Horse Rapids. McConnell, Thompson, and Mattern were bound for the placer gold-mining camp of Forty Mile Creek, at that time the only one on the Yukon, while I had a sort of roving commission from the United States Department of Agriculture to make a botanical collection, take weather observations, and obtain any other scientific information possible, and eventually extended my journey to the Mackenzie River and the Arctic Ocean, and thence down the Yukon to its mouth, which I reached after a journey on foot and in rowboat of more than 3,500 miles. Our outfit consisted of two small tents, a couple of hand-sleds, each eight feet long, with steel-shod runners; blankets, guns, ammunition ; a six-weeks' supply of flour, bacon, and coffee ; a whip-saw, axes, and other tools for boat-building, and my collecting material and two small cameras, the whole weighing about a thousand pounds. Our plan was to take the usual route of miners bound for the Yukon — to cross the Chilkoot Pass and descend to the frozen lakes on the other side—dragging our outfit on the hand-sleds across these lakes until we reached a point where there were trees sufficiently large to build a small boat in which to continue

the journey. Near our landing-place was a small Thlinket Indian village of Dyea, whose inhabitants turn an honest penny every spring by assisting miners bound for the interior in packing their supplies to the summit of the pass. We divided our goods into seven packs and engaged five men and two women to carry these loads to the summit of the pass, a distance of fifteen miles, where they were to leave us to our own devices. The start from the village was made on the morning of the second day after our arrival. The Indians supported the loads on their backs by the aid of deerskin bands, passing across the forehead. Several children carried on their backs light loads, consisting of food and cooking utensils for the use of the Indians, while two of the dogs also wore packs.

Our route lay up the valley of the Dyea River, a small creek which heads near the foot of Chilkoot Pass, and which we were compelled to wade a number of times. Near sea-level the snow had nearly all disappeared, but a couple of miles up the cañon the ground was covered, and from here on our progress was much impeded by it. Every two or three hundred yards the entire party stopped to rest. At one o'clock we reached the forks of the river, seven miles from our starting-point, and the Indians, throwing off their loads, said we would camp for the night. They were completely exhausted by

floundering through the soft snow under their heavy packs. The snow at this camp was about two feet deep, and much more fell during the night. Half of the next day was spent in wading through snow from three to six feet deep to the place known as Sheep Camp, only five miles beyond. Our camp for the second night was at the upper limit of timber, at the foot of the dreaded pass, and only twelve miles from the coast that we had left two days before. Snow had been falling and did not cease until the morning of the next day. Roused before daybreak, we found the sky clear and the air frosty. Below us was the scattering growth of stunted spruce-trees and above the great slopes of snow and ice. Looking for a couple of miles up a large gorge flanked by precipitous snow-covered mountains, we could see at the summit, thousands of feet above, the little notch known as the Chilkoot Pass, the gate to the Yukon land. The seriousness of the work at hand was now apparent. Our picturesque retinue of children and dogs was left in camp to await the return of the Indians, and having had breakfast at eight o'clock, the seven Indians and ourselves began the toilsome climb upward. On either hand were the huge masses of the coast range, buried in perpetual snow and ice, nobody knows how deep. The Indians, struggling under their heavy loads, stopped for breath every few moments. We four white men had the exasperating task of dragging along the two empty sleds.

As we ascended, the snow, which at lower altitudes had been soft, was found to be hard and crusted, being on the last part of the ascent more like ice than snow. At eleven o'clock we had reached the foot of the last and hardest part of the ascent. From here to the summit is only half a mile, but the angle of the slope is about forty-five degrees, and as we looked up that long trough of glistening ice and hard-crusted snow, as steep as the roof of a house, there was not one of us that did not dread the remainder of the day's work. As soon as the Indians ascertained that the crust of the snow was hard and unyielding they divided the packs, leaving nearly half of their loads at the foot of the ascent, intending to make a second trip for them. The two women who had accompanied us thus far now returned to Sheep Camp, and one of the men, producing a strong plaited line of rawhide, about one hundred feet long, which he had brought with him, passed it under every man's belt, lashing the nine of us together about ten feet apart. The man at the head of the line carried in his hands one of our hatchets, and as we advanced cut footholds in the ice and hard-packed snow. The slope being too steep for direct ascent, we resorted to "zigzagging"—that is, moving obliquely across the bottom of the trough for about sixty

feet and then turning at right angles in the opposite direction. Our progress was painfully slow, as every step had to be cut. It was no place to indulge in conversation. There was no use in stopping, as there was no opportunity to stretch one's limbs and nothing to sit down on, so that we kept pegging away, and the hours seemed endless before we stood on the narrow crest of snow and ice that divides the valley of the Yukon from the sea. It was six and a half hours since we had left Sheep Camp and three since we had lashed ourselves together at the foot of the last ascent. On the summit all threw themselves down on the snow and remained motionless for half an hour, when the Indians started down to get the remainder of their packs that had been left at the foot of the last portion of the ascent. The trail having already been cut and not being hampered with the sleds, they were with us again in less than two hours. We had by this time taken in our surroundings. Behind us and to the right and to the left was a jumble of icy peaks, and below the zigzag trail up which we had labored so breathlessly. But these things were now of small interest, and our gaze was fixed ahead, where, stretching away in billows of spotless white,

was the valley of the great river of the north. There was neither rock, nor tree, nor shrub, nor any living thing to break the monotony of that huge blanket of snow, the wooded shores of the lakes being concealed by a range of low hills. The use of the two sleds that had been brought along empty was now apparent, and on to them was loaded and securely strapped down the thousand pounds of stuff that the Indians had carried to the summit. And down grade we started on the northern side of the range. For the first half mile down the glassy slope it was a wild ride. All efforts to control the sleds were fruitless, and we concluded to simplify matters by getting on board and taking "pot luck" with whatever rocks or other obstructions might be at the bottom. The route lay down the bottom of a wide gorge, so that we could not well get far out of the way. The sleds, each with two men in addition to its load of five hundred pounds, flew down grade with the speed of an express train. It was well that they were of oak and the runners shod with steel, for sometimes they would clear the snow for thirty feet at a bound. No sooner had we got started than we began to wonder how we were to stop. We found out. The sled ahead of the one I was on struck an uneven

place and went over ; its lashings broke, and for a few brief seconds the air was filled with rolls of blankets, sides of bacon, mining tools, and earnest, soulful profanity. Our sled coming on to a gentler slope and softer snow, was eventually stopped without disaster. In half an hour Thompson and Mattern got their sled reloaded and joined us. We were now out of the gorge and on a sort of bench or flat covered with soft snow. We got into the harness and, pushing and pulling, struggled on in the hope of reaching Lake Linderman before night. For several hours the wind had been rising and was now coming down from the north at a furious rate, and before darkness set in the air was so full of flying snow that one could not see fifty feet. When night came we were so exhausted and so weakened by hunger that we decided to abandon the sleds until the next day. In order to mark the location a long-handled shovel was stood on end in the snow, and draped with a spare blanket. Then taking each a blanket, we struck out through the gathering darkness, down a ravine which we correctly judged was the tributary of Lake Linderman. After what seemed an endless struggle through the howling storm we reached, at about eleven o'clock, a little clump of dwarfed spruce - trees, the upper limit of timber. Collecting some dry branches, we got on the lee side of a cliff, and after many fruitless efforts started a small fire, which smoked and spluttered a great deal, but was singularly devoid of warmth. Wrapped in blankets, we huddled together all night, while the wind roared up the cañon walls and piled the snow about us. When we stretched ourselves out at daybreak the next morning the storm had almost died away. We were weak and ravenous from hunger and thirst, for we had not had a mouthful of food nor water since leaving Sheep Camp. After a weary tramp of about four miles, which had taken us five hours, we found the sleds entirely buried, nothing but the blanket tied to the shovel being visible above the surface. We got out the one which contained the cooking utensils and part of the provisions, and all four taking hold, dragged it slowly, a hundred yards at a time, toward our camp of the night before. It was exasperating to have with us provisions that were of no use, as it was out of the question to eat raw beans and flour. Thompson, in a frenzy of hunger, insisted on eating a raw piece of bacon, with disastrous results. Dozens of times during the afternoon we threw ourselves down on the snow from sheer exhaustion, but toward evening reached the remains of the camp at the foot of the cañon-wall. As soon as another fire could be built we melted snow for water and prepared a meal of flapjacks, bacon, and coffee, breaking a fast of thirty-seven hours,

during which we had had not a wink of sleep. Without troubling to put up a tent or make any sort of camp, we drew our blankets about us and lay back in the snow for ten hours of glorious sleep. The next day we brought down the remaining sled, a comparatively easy task, as the trail had been opened the day before. Our worst hardships for the time being were now over. The sky was clear and the air cold enough to make exercise comfortable. On this day, only one hundred yards below camp, I found a spring feeding a small stream a few inches deep, which was soon lost to sight in the snow. It was the very beginning of the mighty Yukon. Most of the sixth day from the coast was spent in recuperating our physical selves, but before evening we dragged the two sleds for a couple of miles down the ravine to Lake Linderman, the first of the chain of six lakes of the Upper Yukon. Lake Linderman is six miles long and half a mile wide, and is shut in by glacier-worn granite hills. Here and there along its shores are a few small spruce and black-pine trees. All of these lakes remain frozen until early in June. An examination proved that the surface of the lake was in very good condition, and hitching ourselves again in the sleds, we covered the entire length of Lake Linderman and crossed the short portage on to Lake Bennett, twenty-six miles long, going into camp

for the night in a clump of spruce on the west shore, six miles from its head, having dragged our half-ton of stuff twelve miles. The following day was marked by a unique and successful experiment. A strong wind was blowing from the south, and in order to utilize it we put on to the front of each of the sleds a sort of V-shaped mast, on to which was rigged a tent-fly. Then, with a good wind astern, we went down the lake at a lively trot. It was not necessary to pull a pound. One man merely held on to the tongue of each sled to guide it and keep it from going too fast. In that day we covered the remaining twenty miles of Lake Bennett and followed the bank of a short river connecting it with Lake Nares, where we went into camp. Lake Nares is the smallest of this system, being about three miles long and two miles wide. The general surface of the country was quite broken, and to the east were lofty mountains. Wherever there was soil there were trees, mostly spruce, pine, and poplar, but the largest not more than a foot in diameter. The snow throughout this region was about three feet deep on the level. On going into camp for the night on this journey down the frozen lakes we would pull off from the ice to a grove of trees on the lake shore, and after collecting a quantity of dry wood build a fire, and then, preparing the usual rough, but appetizing, camp-meal, would lie down

286

to sleep. The tents were not put up, and usually the only attempt at a bed was a quantity of spruce-boughs strewn on the snow. Two days of hard work, in which there was no wind to aid us, took our little party over Lake Tagish to the short river connecting it with Lake Marsh. The weather had been quite warm for two days and the snow had begun to melt perceptibly, but we were much surprised to find this stream open in mid-channel. Following the left-hand, or west, bank of this stream for about four miles, we went into camp a mile above Lake Marsh.

On the other bank, directly opposite, were the Tagish Houses. These buildings, two log structures of the Thlinket type, have no permanent occupants, but are the yearly rendezvous of bands of natives who meet on neutral ground to trade and indulge in their great annual drunk, with the accompanying feasts and dances. Here come not only the Tagish Indians, who live in the immediate vicinity, but Thlinkets from Chilkat, Dyea, and Taku River, and Tinneh or Stick from as far away as the mouth of Pelly River. The fact that the snow was melting rapidly, making sledding extremely difficult, impelled us to establish a camp here for the purpose of building a boat in which to continue the journey. There was plenty of timber, some of the trees being of fair size. The first day was spent in constructing a "saw-pit," a

scaffolding about eight feet high. Two good, straight spruce-trees were then felled and a twenty-foot log cut from each. These logs were about sixteen inches in diameter, and after being rolled by means of skids on to the pit, were squared with the whip-saw and gradually and laboriously worked up into boards. We had barely settled down into this new camp before we were overtaken by a party of a dozen men bound for Forty Mile Creek, who had crossed the Chilkoot Pass three days after we did. These men went into camp near us for the purpose of building boats, and every day, from sunrise until dark, the woods rang with the sounds of whipsaws, axes, and hammers. As several of these new arrivals expected to prospect along the bars of the upper river before going to Forty Mile Creek, and Thompson wished to join them, our party was now reduced to three—McConnell, Mattern, and myself. The two weeks spent in this camp were not at all unpleasant. We were up every morning at daybreak, and after breakfast went to work in the saw-pit, and, with the exception of an hour at midday, kept at it until nearly dark. The whip-saw is an instrument with a blade eight feet long and with a handle at either end. One man on top of the scaffolding drew the saw up, while one standing on the ground pulled it down. The extra man busied himself planing the boards and doing odd jobs about

287

the camp. Small game was plentiful, and in an hour's walk with the gun one could always bring in a day's supply of grouse, ducks, and rabbits. The air was alive with geese and cranes on their northward migration. Near us were camped a couple of families of Tagish Indians, and a boy about ten years old spent most of his time loafing about our camp and eating such scraps of bacon and flapjacks as were thrown to him. On account of this weakness for the leavings of a rich man's table he was christened Lazarus. At the end of a week we had a pile of clean, straight boards, 20 feet long, 10 inches wide, and ¾ of an inch thick. A week later the boat was completed. She was a flat-bottomed skiff, 18 feet long, 26 inches wide at the bottom and 4 feet at the top, and had two pairs of oars and a mast which could be rigged with a square sail made from a tent-fly. She was very carefully put together, the seams being filled with wicking and well pitched. Although built of green lumber, this boat stood the long portage of the frozen lakes and around the White Horse Rapids, ran Miles Cañon, and collided with blocks of ice innumerable. The next year she carried me on my long, lonely journey down the big river to the sea, 2,000 miles from the camp on Tagish River, where she was built, and is now the property of a Jesuit missionary, to whom I gave her. There was no champagne at hand, so,

as the boat slid over the blocks of ice on her initial plunge into the river, a pailful of Yukon water was dashed over her bow and she was christened Nancy Hanks, in honor of the little trotter that had acquired fame the preceding year. The miners who had stopped there for the purpose of building boats completed their work at the same time, so that we left in company. Our outfit and provisions, the latter materially reduced in bulk, we stowed away in the boat, and on top were put the two sleds, that would be needed in the portages over Lakes Marsh and Lebarge.

The little fleet of boats, seven in all, dropped down the river to the head of Lake Marsh, which was still frozen, and here the boats were dragged out of the water on to the ice of the lake. Two sleds were put underneath each boat, one under the bow and one under the stern, and our companions rigged large blankets as sails on to their boats in order to lighten the work of the twenty-mile portage. Then, one pulling the forward sled and one pushing behind, the six boats started out down the lake. The small sails aided very materially, there being a strong breeze astern. Before leaving

camp, McConnell, who was an ingenious fellow, had rigged up a contrivance to enable us to avoid this draft-horse work, and with astounding success. This was merely a light pole, the middle of which was fastened to the bow of the boat and one end to the tongue of the forward sled, the other extending back nearly to the mast. A man standing at the bow of the boat could, by moving this pole to the left or right, control the forward sled perfectly. Two spars had been attached to the mast, one at the top and the other near the gunwale of the boat, and between them was stretched a tent-fly ten feet square. By means of a halyard the upper spar could be lowered instantly, thus shortening sail at will.

By the time that these elaborate preparations were completed the miners with their six boats had got two miles out on the ice, and now looked like a few dark spots on the white surface. Before leaving they had good-naturedly jeered at our "winged chariot," and offered, if we were not over the lake in a couple of days, to come back for us; but our time had come now. As the sail filled with the strong wind we gave the Nancy Hanks a shove and jumped on board. McConnell took the steering pole in the bow and away she went. The novelty of the situation made it a most exciting ride. Gradually we crept up on the file of men trudging along, dragging and pushing their heavy loads,

and passed them, fairly skimming over the ice. They threw their hats in the air and yelled, while a wild-eyed individual, who called himself "Missouri Bill," grasped his Winchester and proceeded to puncture the atmosphere in all directions. But even this was not glory enough. No sooner had we passed these men than we determined to make improvements. The sail was lowered and we came to a stop; the mast was taken out and lengthened six feet by lashing on to it an extra spar that we had in the boat. Across the end of this was lashed one of the boat's oars, making a spar eighteen feet above the ice. From this there was suspended a large double blanket fourteen feet long, the lower end fastened to the boat. Our speed was materially increased, at one time doubtless reaching twelve miles an hour—not half bad when one considers that the boat and its load weighed more than a ton. The great height of the blanket sail above the surface made our novel iceboat top heavy, however, and more than once we came near going over. As we approached the northern end of the lake the ice became more uneven, with occasional drifts of hard-packed snow. Crossing several of these successfully gave us overmuch confidence and brought us to grief at last. I was steering at the time, and sighted ahead of us a drift that extended entirely across the lake. As we approached it seemed but little worse

than some that we had already crossed. Mattern wanted to take in sail and examine it, but was voted down two to one, and we went at the obstruction full tilt. Just before striking I saw that the ice on the other side had a big sag, and shouted to McConnell to cut the halyards. It was too late; the sleds struck the drift and went over it beautifully, but as we went down on the other side the boat turned quartering to the wind, and over we went. I landed on all fours a dozen feet ahead of the boat; McConnell and Mattern were thrown against the sail, while bags of flour, boxes, guns, and tools flew in every direction. The bolster of the forward sled and all the spars and the mast were broken, while the boat itself was badly wrenched. It required an hour to overturn the boat and reload it. We got up what nautical men would call a "jury rig," and limped over the remaining mile to the foot of the lake. It had taken three hours and forty-two minutes to run the twenty miles from the head of the lake to where we were wrecked, exclusive of the half-hour lost in putting up the additional sail. The men whom we had distanced did not overtake us, and but two of them reached the foot of the lake before dark. Between Lake Marsh and Lake Lebarge, which is the last and largest of the chain of lakes, there are fifty-five miles of river, but in this short space are the two greatest obstructions to navi-

gation in the whole Yukon system—Miles Cañon and the White Horse Rapids.

The stream was about three hundred feet wide, from two to six feet deep, and very swift. Great quantities of ice were piled up along the banks and in some places large blocks were grounded on shallow bars. These, with occasional bowlders, made navigation exciting work. Spring had now so far advanced that the snow had nearly all disappeared and the weather was superb. On arriving at the foot of Lake Marsh the boat was relaunched and the sleds placed on board instead of underneath, and the next morning we were under way down the river. At two o'clock we passed the mouth of the Tahkeena River, coming in from the left, and at five went into camp for the night. We knew that we must now be near Miles Cañon, and the next morning kept a sharp lookout. We had gone scarcely a mile when we whirled around a bend and saw ahead a low brown rocky ridge, divided by a slit less than thirty feet wide, and at the same time heard the roar of the river in its wild rush through the cañon. With one impulse we pulled frantically for the bank and got a line ashore and around a tree just in the nick of time. Landing, we found in camp seven men with their boats. These men had crossed the pass a week before we did and had built their boats at the foot of Lake Marsh, and were now engaged in portaging

them around the cañon. This cañon was named by the late Lieutenant Frederick Schwatka in honor of General Nelson A. Miles, who had been instrumental in sending him on his trip to the Yukon in 1883. The river, which has been about three hundred feet wide, suddenly contracts to about a tenth of that width, and increasing its velocity to twenty miles an hour, rushes with terrific force through a cañon with absolutely perpendicular walls a hundred feet high. The cañon is only three-quarters of a mile long, and at its lower end the river spreads out into a series of rapids, culminating three miles below in the White Horse. There are two ways of passing this cañon, one by portaging over the hill on the east bank and the other by boldly running through. Some of the men whom we found encamped there were utilizing the former method. The boats were unloaded and dragged out of the water, and by means of a windlass hauled up the hill-slope a hundred feet high, and then pulled on wooden rollers for three-quarters of a mile, being finally slid down another hill to the river. The contents of the boats were carried over by the men on their backs. It is the most slavish work imaginable, and uses up the better part of four days.

Among the party in camp here was a man who had formerly been a Wisconsin lumberman and who announced in lurid language that he was going to run the cañon. He had set this morning for the attempt, so that we were just in time to witness the feat. The men, dragging their boats up the hillside, stopped work and joined us on the cliff a short distance below the head of the cañon. The old man steered his little boat into the entrance of the gorge, where it was caught by the swift current, thrown up and down like a cork, and in a few seconds was out of sight around the first bend. As he passed underneath we gave him a great cheer, and in a couple of minutes heard a rifle-shot, the prearranged signal that he had passed through in safety. In the meantime a couple of young fellows from Colorado, whom we left on Lake Marsh, came up, and after a half-hour discussion made the attempt. They narrowly escaped destruction, but got control of their boat again, and in a short time we heard another faint rifle-shot down the river. We had seen both ways of passing Miles Cañon, one requiring four days and the other two minutes. We three looked at each other in an inquiring sort of way, and then without a word walked down to where the Nancy Hanks was moored against the bank. All took their places, kneeling and facing the bow, McConnell in the stern, Mattern amidships, and I forward. The oars were placed on board and each of us used an ordinary canoe paddle. I must confess that I never felt sicker in my life than as we shoved

291

away from shore and steered for the entrance. It was all over so quickly that we hardly knew how it happened. Barely missing the big rock at the mouth of the cañon, the boat started on its wild ride. The walls seemed to fairly fly past us, and after starting we heard a cheer from the rocks above, but did not dare look up. By frantic paddling we kept in the middle and off from the cañon walls. The sensation was akin to that of riding a bucking broncho. There was not a dry spot on one of us when we got through, and the boat had taken on so much water that she nearly foundered before we could bail her out. But a great weight was off our minds, for Miles Cañon, more than all other things, is dreaded by Yukon travellers. Including those lost in 1894, an even dozen of men have had their boats swamped or crushed like eggshells against the cañon walls, and not one of them has come alive out of that wild maelstrom of water. Below the cañon the river spreads out to its normal width, but is shallow and a succession of rapids. We ran through these for a mile, but after colliding with bowlders and ice-cakes a dozen times found it altogether too interesting, and so "lined" the boat the remaining two miles down to the White Horse. Fastening a line to the bow and one to the stern, we waded in shallow water near shore, and so could control the speed of the boat, as we could not otherwise do,

and prevent its being crushed. Arriving at the head of the White Horse, we went into camp, landed all of our effects and spread them out in the sun to dry, and remained idle until the next morning. These rapids are half a mile long, and the river has its usual width of three hundred feet except in the lower part, where the stream contracts to about thirty feet, and drops through a chute for forty yards. We looked the ground over carefully and spent all of the day after our arrival in carrying the contents of the boat through the woods, depositing them at the foot of the rapids. We determined to run the now empty boat through the rapids as far as the chute, instead of lining it. Realizing that it would be very difficult to stop where we wanted to, McConnell took his station on the bank near the head of the chute in order to take a line, which we were to throw to him as we passed. Everything worked smoothly. Mattern and I steered the boat through the rapids, and as we neared McConnell I threw a line, which he caught, and taking a hitch around the bowlder, brought us to a rather sensational stop. In this ride I seated myself in the stern of the boat with the kodak and tried to make a snap shot of the rapids as we ran them, but was so excited that three of the four exposures were on the sky, the surrounding scenery, and the bottom of the boat; but of the successful one I am not a

little proud. The boat was dragged out of the water on to the rock, around the dangerous narrows, and we went into camp at the foot of the White Horse. The next day we drifted down the river twenty-five miles to the head of Lake Lebarge, which was still frozen, although the ice was becoming quite soft. This lake is thirty-two miles long and eight wide. Here we found in camp Mark Russell, a well-known Alaskan prospecter, and three other men, with two boats. After a delay of a day, caused by a severe storm, we began our last and longest portage, Russell and his party accompanying us. The three boats were placed on sleds, as at Lake Marsh, but no sail was raised, as there was almost a dead calm. For three long days we pushed and pulled over the sloppy ice of the lake, and finally, worn out, wet and bedraggled, again reached open water. It was thirty-three days since we had left the coast at Dyea and we had covered but two hundred of the seven hundred miles to Forty Mile Creek. But we had left behind Chilkoot Pass, the six frozen lakes, Miles Cañon, and the White Horse ; and from here to its mouth, 1,900 miles, the Yukon is unobstructed save by a few unimportant rapids, and the remainder of our trip was to be a delightful excursion. The next morning we again took our seats in the much-buffeted Nancy.

For nine beautiful, cloudless days we drifted down the river to the northwest,

rowing only enough to break the monotony of lounging about in the boat. This part of the stream from Lake Lebarge to the mouth of Pelly River is often called by the miners Lewes River, although it is, as a matter of fact, a part of the Yukon. Great quantities of ice remained along the river-banks, and as the current was strong, there was sure to be an exciting time whenever we attempted to stop to go into camp. The surface of the country was rolling and hilly, backed by low mountains, and was generally wooded in the valleys, the uplands being bare. Caribou and moose were occasionally seen, but we did not succeed in killing any. We passed the mouth of the Teslin or Hotalinqua, and reached the mouth of Little Salmon River, where we found a small camp of Tinneh Indians, the first of these people we had met. They were a fine-looking lot of savages, dressed in skins and guiltless of any knowledge of English. In four days we reached the mouth of Pelly River, the site of old Fort Selkirk, burned and looted by Indians from the coast in 1850. It is a telling commentary on the intelligence of makers of maps that this obscure fur-trading post, abandoned nearly half a century ago and whose only remains are a blackened chimney, should still be marked on every map of that region. The same may be said of Fort Reliance and Fort Yukon, farther down the river.

The river was now much larger, and

293

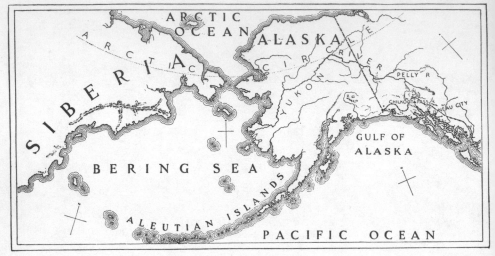

for some distance below the mouth of the Pelly islands were numerous. We passed the mouth of White River, the great unexplored stream coming in from the west, which, with its milky flood, discolors the Yukon for five hundred miles, and a short distance below, Stewart River, a large eastern tributary. The Yukon was now from half to three quarters of a mile wide, deep and swift, the banks in some places huge cliffs or palisades 1,000 feet high. On the morning of May 23d we passed the big Indian village of Klonjek, but, despite a vociferous greeting from the natives, declined to stop. All day we were swept along between towering cliffs of red and brown rock, and at five o'clock, rounding a bend, saw below us a group of cabins, surrounding a big storehouse, and in half an hour more were ashore at Forty Mile Creek, the loneliest mining camp on the face of the earth, where it is midnight all winter and daylight all summer, and where the mail comes but once a year. We were the first arrivals from the outside for that spring, and brought the year's budget of news to the three hundred white men who, in addition to the Indians, at that time formed the population of this placer gold-mining camp of the far north.

The village is situated on the left hand or west bank of the Yukon, at the mouth of Forty Mile Creek. There were all sorts of men among the min-

ers, who spent their summers in washing gold out of the gulches, and their winters in playing poker and spinning yarns.

Gold was discovered in the bars along the creek in 1884, and subsequently in the gulches, and placer mining has been successfully carried on ever since. New discoveries made in 1893 caused a considerable increase in the population, so that there are now more than a thousand men in the camp, in addition to those at Circle City, the recently discovered diggings two hundred miles farther down the Yukon, where that stream is intersected by the Arctic circle.

We had been just forty-two days in the journey from the coast. McConnell and Mattern went prospecting for gold, and I never saw them again. The Nancy Hanks had an easy time during the summer, and later in the season did good service, when I pushed on farther to the north.

294

22
From the Coast
to the Golden Klondike

☉UTING.

VOL. XXX.   SEPTEMBER, 1897.

DRIVING A BARGAIN WITH THE NATIVES.

FROM THE COAST TO THE GOLDEN KLONDIKE.

THE RECORD OF AN OFFICIAL JOURNEY.

By Edward Spurr.

THE question of the veracity of the rumors from time to time reaching the Government as to the mineral wealth, especially in gold, of the upper Yukon district of Alaska, and the conditions under and means by and times of the year at which the district could best be reached, were in the early part of last year subjects of departmental consideration.

In order to gather reliable information on the geological questions involved, and, incidentally, of course, some others, I, in the spring of 1896, as a member of the United States Geological Survey, was officially requested to undertake a journey into the interior of Alaska.

I had never been west of Utah, and, judging from the few accounts of travelers who have written concerning this remote region of central and northern Alaska, the difficulties were considerable. Only one season was possible, and that was the near-approaching one of high summer, and only two routes are available. One must either go to St. Michael, in the Behring Sea, and thence

Painted for OUTING by J. L. Weston. From a photo by the author.   HIGH SUMMER IN THE CHILKOOT PASS.

up the River Yukon, from its outlet to the beginning of its headwaters, some fifteen hundred miles; or land at some point on the Pacific, cross the head of land, and tap the headwaters of the Yukon at their source.

In either event the journey must be completed before September, when the Yukon freezes, and Alaska's arctic winter of the utmost rigor sets in and grips its vise.

Yet the possible novelties which the country offered, both from a scientific and from a personal standpoint, were so great that the opportunity was quickly accepted.

river as a highway, making such excursions from it as became necessary.

Alaska is a most difficult country for traveling, even in the only available short season of its arctic summer, there being no roads; and even Indian trails, on account of the small number of natives, are very rare. The surface is rough, being traversed by many ranges of mountains. Even in the more level portions travel is hindered in the summer by the wet moss which grows knee-deep, and by the insect pests; in the winter it is made impossible by the intense cold. In view of all these difficulties, the peculiar relation of the

TAGISH LAKE.

The time for preparation was very short, but when we left Washington at the end of May we carried with us so many good wishes that our spirits rose accordingly—for such good wishes from such good hearts carry with them actual influence over evil material things, I hope and half believe.

From Seattle we took passage on a steamer for the southern coast of Alaska.

At the little town of Juneau we left the steamer, and made preparations to turn our backs for good upon civilization. Our proposed route lay across the coast mountains to the headwaters of the Yukon, and thence down that

Yukon River to the coast is such that one might fancy Nature had arranged it especially for a highway through this inaccessible interior, in partial compensation to man for the obstacles she has put in his way.

The headwaters of the network of streams that ultimately drain into the Yukon River fortunately lie within about thirty miles of the sea, just on the northern or inland side of a range of mountains which runs along the southern coast of Alaska. From this point the river flows north, away from the sea, far toward the Arctic Ocean; then, suddenly changing its mind, turns west ; and finally, after traversing the whole width of Alaska, arrives at the Behring Sea, its entire course being considerably over two thousand miles. For a considerable distance it is a broad and deep stream, so that one may go quite through the center of Alaska, from sea to sea, by crossing only thirty miles or so of land. This little geographical explanation has been made so that the plan of our trip may be clearly understood. There are various routes across the coast mountains to the various heads of this river. Of these we chose that over the Chilkoot Pass, which is the shortest, although the mountains which must be thereby crossed are higher than on any of the other routes.

After a few days in Juneau, making the necessary preparations, we bade good-bye to civilization for good, and engaged passage on a little tug for Dyea, a more eastward point on the coast, where we were to begin our inland journey. The *Scrambler*, as the boat was called, had been originally designed for freight, but had been pressed into the passenger service without the formality of making alterations. A dozen men might have made themselves comfortable in her, but our load comprised fifty or sixty. They were mostly miners and prospectors, with pick, gold-pan, and flour-sacks, striking out for the rumored Golden Land in the interior. With one of these miners, who had prospected and mined in Alaska for many years, we entered into an agreement to travel together as far as he was going. De Windt's party of three were on the same boat. Among the other passengers were two men who had undertaken to carry the first regular mail into the Yukon district, and a Catholic priest bound for his mission among the Esquimaux on the lower river. We were huddled together so closely that we perforce became speedily acquainted, for although the space on the floor was large enough for all of us to sit down, there was hardly room to stretch out. When we grew weary of chatting, however, and of listening to the sound of the water as the boat threshed its way onward, we were forced by drowsiness to sleep where we could, and soon sleepers were scattered around in the most grotesque and uncomfortable attitudes. I had coveted a space

on or under the little table used for eating purposes, but found that choice position fully occupied before I made up my mind to retire ; but I finally wedged myself into a narrow space between the boiler and the pilot-house, where, throughout the night, passers continually stepped on my head. However, I slept several hours.

The system of eating is worthy of note. The table accommodated about six at a time, whereas, as I have mentioned, we were fifty or sixty in all. At each meal one or two, or sometimes three, sets of passengers would be fed ; then the captain, the sailor, the Chinese cook, and the dish-washer, after which the rest of us got our rations, in good time. As we grew very hungry during this process, we would stand around patiently waiting our chance to slip in ; but sometimes before we had tasted the tempting liver and coffee (to say nothing of the beans), we would be summarily ejected by the dish-washer, who was a very young man of dashing exterior and peculiar vocabulary, and who would disperse us with the assertion that "By——, the crew is going to eat now."

The day was foggy and rainy, and the sea quite rough. The Lynn Canal, up which we were steaming, is a long, deep, narrow fjord, from which the cold, snowy mountains to the north rise steeply to lonely heights. On this day the fog hid the precipices partly from view, giving us mostly half-veiled glimpses, strangely distorted. At times we saw a slim waterfall leaping down ; and here and there stood great broad glaciers, stretching from the clouds nearly down to the sea. These glaciers, like all that I have seen in Alaska, have wonderful purity of color. The predominating tint is a beautiful robin's-egg blue, which changes into pure white in the upper part, where the solid ice grades into the less compact frozen snow. Their surfaces are fantastically carved—pinnacled and turreted ; and irregular masses stand out in relief, which the imagination can transform into strange groups of figures. These surroundings produced upon me an uncanny sensation, which I think was shared by others on board. It seemed a gigantic, gloomy country, a fit abode for wild beasts and wild men, but, as one of the miners expressed it, "no place for a white man to live."

When, toward night, we approached our destined landing-place, the surf on the beach was too heavy to attempt getting ashore, so we lay anchored during the night. About noon the next day, the captain made the first trial at landing, in a small boat, and was capsized. Then the dish-washer made himself conspicuous by his presence of mind.

"Man the life-boat!" he cried in such stentorian tones that one might shut his eyes and imagine himself at home in a theatre. "Man the life-boat; the captain's overboard!" There was, unfortunately, no life-boat to man; and the sailor, having but just come from driving a milk-wagon in San Francisco, did not know how to row well enough to venture out. Meanwhile the captain drifted ashore, righted his boat, and pulled out to the *Scrambler* again.

Shortly afterward we all debarked, and that night we pitched our tent on land. The place is called Dyea; there is a small trading-post, kept by a white man, around which is gathered a village of Indians or Siwash, belonging to the Chilkoot tribe. They are by no means ill-looking people. The men are strong and well-formed; the women (naturally, when one considers their mode of life) are inferior to the men in good looks. These women have a habit of painting their faces uniformly black with a mixture of soot and grease, a covering which is said to prevent snow-blindness in the winter and to be a protection in summer against the mosquitoes. Some have only the upper part of their faces painted, and the black part terminates in a straight line, giving the effect of a half-mask. At the time of our arrival the Indians were engaged very busily in catching and drying small fish. These fish are very oily, and when dried can be lighted at one end and used as candles; and for this purpose they are stored away against the long winter night.

Early next morning we were on the trail for the pass. The trip from salt water to the head of the navigable waters of the Yukon is usually made in two stages, each of about fifteen miles. The trader at Dyea had brought in a few horses, and we engaged him to transport our camp-outfit and provisions over the first stage, where the trail, though rough, can be gone over by pack-animals. Some of the miners, however, engaged Indians immediately at Dyea to pack the whole distance; and, as it afterward proved, this was the wiser plan. We could also have obtained saddle-animals, but our party preferred to walk for the sake of getting toughened for the harder journeys.

The trip turned out to be exceptionally fatiguing, a large part of the distance being through sand and loose gravels in the bed of a stream, where it was impossible to find a firm footing; several times also we had to wade the stream. The valley along whose bottom we were thus traveling was narrow and canyon-like, with steep bare mountains rising high on either side. The tops of these mountains, so far as we could see, were capped with ice; and this great glacier stretched out long fingers down into the valley along each of the gulches or recesses in the mountain-wall. Finally, crossing the river a last time on a fallen tree, we followed the trail up into the more rocky and difficult portion of the valley; and some miles of this brought us, thoroughly tired, to our halting-place. A few miles before reaching this place I overtook one of the miners, who, with his two companions or "pardners," had started to pack over a part of their outfit themselves. He was a stalwart young Irishman, but the load of seventy-five pounds or thereabouts and the difficulties of the road had exhausted him, although he had outstripped by several miles his less robust companions. After a rest, however, he was able to get to the camp, where we ate together a supper proportioned in amount to the trials we had undergone.

We had brought with us from Juneau lumber for the purpose of building a boat when we should get across the pass into the Yukon waters, but the Indians demanded such high wages for carrying it over that it was left at Dyea, the more readily since there was a rumor that some white men had taken a small saw-mill across the pass in the winter and were now engaged in sawing lumber at one of the lakes on the other side. In order to make sure, however, Wiborg, the miner who accompanied us, started in advance across the pass early the next morning, taking with him an Indian, while we lay in camp till he should send the Indian back with news from the other side.

We profited by the delay to climb up to the face of the glacier which over-hung the camp. The climb up the mountain side was difficult, there being a constant succession of cliffs, the rocks of which had been so severely wrenched by glacial action that it was not safe to trust to them for handhold or foothold ; so that we depended mainly on the stout bushes or young saplings which grew in the crevices and on the benches. These trees averaged fifteen or twenty feet in length—I say length, for most of them grew straight out horizontally, and some even had a down-hill inclination ; this was evidently the result of the weight of snow and ice moving down hill over them for a large part of the year.

We were well paid for our trouble on reaching the glacier, which expanded before our eyes as we drew nearer. It was of pure blue ice, extremely beautiful; and its front rose perpendicularly for several hundred feet. A deep chasm separated it from us as we stood on the summit of a pinnacle of bare rock, a few hundred feet away ; and as we looked across we saw great irregular clefts and caverns of the deepest blue, guarded by slender towers. Further up the great blue-white field stretched till lost to sight in the mists of the mountain, its surface seamed and cracked and obstructed by huge, irregular mounds, so as to be apparently impassable. I have seen few things more awe-inspiring than this great ice-field, this vast, pure, chaotic silence.

As we sat we noticed a very slender spire of ice quite near which seemed as if it must topple. After awhile it began to aggravate us that it would not, so we began shooting at it with the repeating rifle which we had brought along, firing a number of shots in rapid succession for the purpose of knocking it over. This we did not succeed in doing, but when we got back to camp we found that our shots had greatly excited the Indians who were camped near by, and who imagined that we were quarreling with one of the great bears found in these mountains. The idea of a sensible being shooting at a piece of ice is not readily grasped by the savage mind.

From Sheep Camp, where we were, the only way to get our supplies over the pass was to get Indians to carry them. Although these Indians are no stronger than average white men, yet they greatly excel them in point of endurance; and they willingly undergo extreme fatigue for any limited period. At this time, however, the trail was so bad, on account of the softening of the snows in the hot June sun, that they concluded to strike for higher wages. This was the cause of some little delay for us, for most of the men in camp were opposed to yielding, especially the miners, who represented that the increased cost would inconvenience them considerably. So began a siege on both sides ; we announced our intention to the Indians of staying in this pleasant place for a month or two, and both in our camp and in that of the Siwashes the most ostentatious carelessness prevailed. Late in the day this state of affairs was interrupted by the action of one small party of miners, who were anxious to get at the gold which they imagined lying around thickly in some interior gulch, waiting for the first comer to pick it up, and so went secretly to the other camp and compromised

LAKE BENNETT.

LOOKING UP LAKE LINDERMAN.

with them. We were informed of this by a series of wild whoops from the Siwashes, as they poured over the hill and into our camp. Our first thought was that it was a hostile attack, but we were reassured when we saw them begin to parcel out the goods belonging to the miners. It happened that these men were the very ones who had so strongly urged holding out against the increased price; and as it took all the available Indians to carry their outfit over, we were delayed a couple of days by this. Finally, however, we secured packers,

LOOKING DOWN DYEA INLET.

and one afternoon they announced their intention of starting across the pass— for they are very independent about such matters, and will wait indefinite periods till the weather or their humor is satisfactory. Unlike the civilized man, the Indian has plenty of time ; he is never in a hurry.

Once we saw the Siwash safely started with their packs, we set out ourselves, at about six o'clock in the afternoon. At this time of year the trip is usually timed by the Indians so that the deepest snow will be crossed between twelve o'clock at midnight and three in the morning ; for in these hours a crust forms, which in daytime is softened by the warm sun. Our way soon led us on to a glacier-like field of snow, which often sounded hollow to our feet as we trod, and at intervals we could hear the water rushing beneath. The grade became steep, and the fog closed around us thickly, joining with the twilight of the Alaska June night to make a peculiar obscurity which gave things a weird, ghostly appearance. As we toiled up the steep incline of hardened snow, those ahead of us looked like huge giants ; while those on whom we looked down were ugly, sprawling dwarfs, toiling up the mountain side like Hendrik Hudson's sailor, whom luckless Rip Van Winkle met. As we drew near to one another, our faces seemed a pale blue color, though very clearly seen ; and we left bright blue footprints on the pale snow.

Presently we saw a fire a little way above the trail, and climbing up to it found a deaf-and-dumb Indian and his squaw or "klutchman," who were drying their moccasins before a fire made out of a few stunted bushes. He explained to us by signs that the trail was dangerous, aud that it was too dark to see clearly. So we waited till midnight, when another Indian, one of our packers, came up, and we started out on the trail again.

All the rest of the climb was over snow, the ascent being very steep, with cliffs on all sides, which loomed up gigantic and ghostly. It is impossible to describe the effect produced by these bare, jagged rocks rising out of the snow-field, in the silence, the fog, and the twilight. We were forcibly reminded of some of Doré's imaginative drawings. In the course of the ascent

Goodrich and myself found ourselves ahead of the party, who followed the Indian, toiling along under his pack.

After a while the well-beaten trail faded to almost nothing, and at the same time the snow-slope became of excessive steepness. We were obliged to kick footholds for every step on a surface so smooth and steep that a slip would have sent us sliding into depths which we could not see. Looking down, it seemed a bottomless pit, shapeless and fathomless, in the eddying fog. After a while we gained the top, and waited till the rest should come up. When they appeared, we were surprised to find that they came from a somewhat different direction ; and we found on inquiry that we had neglected to turn off with the regular trail, which led in a roundabout way through the rocks, with a rope for handhold and safety, and had instead kept straight up the mountain to the top.

On the other side of the summit a short but steep declivity led down to a small frozen lake, named by the miners Crater Lake, on account of the steep crater-like walls which surround it on three sides. On one side, however, this wall opens out into a valley, through which a small stream runs ; the lake is, therefore, one of the ultimate sources of the Yukon, and it was with a feeling of relief that we stepped upon its frozen surface.

From here our way lay down the stream-valley and across little lakes into which the stream broadened out at intervals. Sometimes we walked over the stream on an archway of snow and ice, and again trod cautiously along its banks, while the river, broken loose from its covering, ran turbulently between its icy banks. The upper lakes were frozen, but further down we had to wade knee-deep in slush for miles, putting occasionally a foot through the rotten ice beneath ; and finally we were obliged to skirt along the shore, which was precipitous. During the last few miles it rained and snowed alternately. Finally, at nine o'clock at night, we reached the shore of Lake Linderman, the first of the Yukon's navigable waters.

Linderman is a pretty little lake several miles in length, and partly shut in by the high, snow-capped mountains over which we had come. Here we found Wiborg waiting for us under a shelter made of trees, and presently the Indian who was carrying our tent came along, and we proceeded to make ourselves as comfortable as possible, after some time spent in settling affairs with our packers. The endurance of these people is shown by the fact that they made this very fatiguing trip, with loads averaging over a hundred pounds each, in the same time as ourselves who carried little or nothing.

These Indians all have some English name, which they have got from the mission, where they hang around when there is anything to be got by it. I find in my notes "Tom" credited with carrying one hundred and ten pounds of meat, and "Jim" with one hundred and sixty-one pounds of sundries. Tom's original name was Kuk-shon, and he claimed to be a chief of the interior, or Stick, Indians. He spent his spare time during the short space of my acquaintance with him in daubing vermilion around his left eye. Before starting across the pass he painted the rest of his face black with soot and grease, but carefully left the red around his eye; and this ornamentation, together with a smile, which I think he meant to be engaging, and which he offered on all occasions as a substitute for conversation, made him a particularly villainous-looking personage. Among the packers were also a number of women. These were mostly ugly old hags, and many of them plainly suffered greatly from fatigue; yet their patient endurance was remarkable. It seems to fall to the lot of the old women, among these people, to do the hardest work; but men, women and children are schooled to carry heavy burdens. We met on the trail a whole family packing, carrying out a sort of contract with some of the miners. The man carried one hundred and twenty-seven pounds, a boy of thirteen carried one hundred pounds, and the squaw and little girls had heavy loads. Even the dog, about the size of a setter, carried forty pounds, with which he waddled along patiently enough.

We had some very slight perplexity in settling accounts. One woman, who started across the pass as Jenny, turned up as Sally at Lake Linderman, having evidently made up her mind to change her name on the way; and as she understood no word of English we had a momentary difficulty in identifying her. She and her friends seemed to have some inkling of political principles, for they all wanted to be paid in silver, and distrusted gold, while it was with difficulty that they could be induced to accept bills. Nearly all of these people on being paid started immediately back over the trail, without resting, intending to travel all night, and be in Sheep Camp in the morning; and this after they had already been twenty-four hours on the road.

Wiborg had succeeded in obtaining for us a boat already built, which saved a great deal of time, as it takes about two weeks to whipsaw lumber and build a boat, as miners usually do.

The next morning, therefore, we loaded our outfit and sailed down Lake Linderman with a fair wind. The boat was a small, double-ender, flat-bottomed craft, fifteen feet or so in length, and open to sun and rain alike. For a sail we used our tent-fly, an article which was put to many important uses in the course of our trip, but never to that for which it was originally intended.

De Windt's party followed us in a similar boat; and with De Windt came the priest whom we had encountered on the *Scrambler*—a genial and cultured gentleman, whose light heart kept him from being long affected by the physical discomforts we were all obliged to undergo. To complete the flotilla, there was a small scow, of rather shaky construction, which had just been completed by a party bound for the American mining camp of Circle City; this party was remarkable for containing one of the fair sex, who seemed as well fitted as the men to make the journey successfully. In after days we met the party repeatedly as we all floated down the river, the lady always sitting in the front of the scow and six or seven men behind, all wearing flowing veils as defence against the mosquitoes, and waving branches for the same purpose; and we likened her to Cleopatra, in her barge. Just after starting, Cooper, a frontiersman who was with De Windt's party, sighted a mountain-goat close to the shore, and shot at it, but failed to bring it down.

The lake down which we sailed is only a few miles long; at its foot it connects with a larger body of water, called Lake Bennett, by a short but rapid and danger-

CLEOPATRA'S BARGE.

ous channel. For such places as this we had brought along a hundred and fifty feet of strong line ; and after unloading our outfit at the head of the rapids, leaving only a few light things which would not be damaged by water, we attached the line to the bow of the boat, and let it drop down with the current. Wiborg remained on board to steer, for if a boat sheers or yaws when going over rapids, she is likely to careen and capsize. We three greenhorn geologists held the line, with which we waded in the shallower parts of the current, and scampered over

EMBARKING, LAKE LINDERMAN.

the rocks and cliffs where the water was deep and swift, letting run or holding firm, as Wiborg signaled. These rapids are among the most difficult to pass of all those on the Yukon, and it is customary for miners to go below them before building their boats; so the process of lining our boat down was not devoid of excitement. Any tendency to overheating as a consequence of exertion was, however, counteracted by our having to wade in ice-water up to the waist. We had unwisely put on rubber boots reaching to the hips, and strapped to the belt ; these soon got full of water, the weight of which was so great that it was hardly possible to walk, so I was obliged to take advantage of a lull in the proceedings to stagger ashore and make frantic attempts to stand on my head, till most of the water ran out of my boots down my back, and so made me capable of freer movement. We were finally successful, however, and the boat shipped very little water, thanks to Wiborg's manœuvring. Afterward we named our craft the *Skookum Pete,* as a compliment to the cool and determined Norwegian—*skookum* being a Chinook word signifying strength and daring, together with other qualities necessary to a man who lives in the woods. Pete's modesty, however, made him erase his own name from the legend, so that the boat was, and is, if she still exist in the possession of the Indian who finally obtained her, simply the *Skookum,* and as such she must go down in history.

The weather was cool, and our bath in ice-water none of the most agreeable; we were thoroughly dried, however, before we finished the remainder of our task, which was to carry the outfit, we

AT SHEEP CAMP.

had unloaded at the head of the rapids, across the portage, which was three-quarters of a mile in length. We had about twelve hundred pounds in all.

For this work I had brought specially made packsacks from Minnesota, where I had used and thoroughly tested them; they consisted of a canvas bag with broad shoulder-straps of leather, and a still broader one to go across the forehead or the top of the head. This latter band, called the "tump-strap" in Minnesota, is mostly used to sustain the weight of the articles carried in the sack, the shoulder-straps being mainly for steadying the load, and occasionally relieving the strain upon the neck. The Alaskan Indians carry packs in much the same way, but use straps which they fasten to the article to be carried; with our packsacks, however, they were much pleased, and all anxious to be allowed to carry them, in preference to more difficult bundles, in the trip across the pass. With this apparatus a man can carry for half a mile or more a weight far greater than he can lift to his back unaided.

When we had finished packing, we lighted a fire on the beach and cooked supper ; and presently we rolled ourselves in our blankets, lay down in the sand under the clear sky, and slept soundly. As the wind was blowing smartly, we piled some of our provisions up as a wind-break ; toward morning the wind freshened and toppled over a portion of this wall. I was awakened rudely by a bag of flour falling upon my stomach ; and it took me fully five minutes to recall where I was, and how and why I came there.

There was a fresh breeze blowing fair down the lake, so we soon got under way, and with our little tent-fly as a sail we went merrily skimming along. The further we went, however, the harder the wind blew, and the rougher became the water, so that when about half-way down the lake we made a landing to escape a heavy squall. After dinner, it seemed from our snug little cove as if the wind and waves had abated, and so we put out again. On getting well away from the sheltering shore we found it rougher than ever; but while we were eating dinner we had seen Cleopatra's barge go past, its square bows nearly buried in foaming water, and had seen it apparently run ashore on the opposite side of the lake, some miles further down. Once out, therefore, we steered for the place where the scow had been beached, for the purpose of giving aid if any were necessary. On the run over we shipped water repeatedly over both bow and stern, and sometimes were in imminent danger of swamping, but by skillful handling we gained the shelter of a little nook about half a mile from the open beach on which the scow was lying, and landed. We then walked along the shore to the scow, and we found them all right, they having beached their craft voluntarily, on account of the roughness of the water. However, we had had about enough navigation for one day, so we did not again venture out. Presently another little boat came scudding down the lake through the white water, and shot in alongside of the *Skookum*. It was a party of miners—the young Irishman whom I had overtaken on the trail to Sheep Camp, and his three "pardners."

It was not an ideal spot where we all camped, being simply a steep rocky slope at the foot of cliffs. When the time came to sleep we had some difficulty in finding places smooth and level enough to lie down comfortably, but finally all were scattered around here and there in various places of concealment among the rocks. I had cleared a space close under a big bowlder, of exactly my length and breadth (which does not imply any great labor), and with my head muffled in my blankets, was beginning to doze, when I heard stealthy footsteps creeping toward me. As I lay, these sounds were muffled and magnified in the marvelous quiet of the Alaskan night (although the sun was

still shining), so that I could not judge of the size or distance of the animal. Soon it got quite close to me, and I could hear it scratching at something; then it seemed to be investigating my matches, knife and compass. Finally wide-awake, and somewhat startled, I sat up suddenly and threw the blanket from my face, and looked for the marauding animal. I found him—in the shape of a saucy little gray mouse, that stared at me in amazement for a moment, and then scampered into his hole under a bowlder. As I had no desire to have the impudent little fellow lunching on me as I slept, I plugged the hole with stones before I lay down again. Some of the same animals came to visit Schrader in his bedchamber, and nibbled his ears so that they were sore for some time.

As the gale continued all the next day without abatement, we profited by the enforced delay to climb the high mountain which rose precipitously above us, for this lake is shut in on all sides by a rock wall. And apropos of this climb, it is remarkable what difference one finds in the appearance of a bit of country when simply surveyed from a single point and when actually traveled over. Especially is this true in the mountains. Broad slopes which appear to be perfectly easy to traverse are in reality cut up by narrow and deep canyons, impossible to cross; what seems to be a trifling bench of rock, half a mile up the mountain, grows into a perpendicular cliff a hundred feet high before one reaches it; and pretty gray streaks become gulches filled with great angular rock fragments, so loosely laid one over the other that at each careful step one is in fear of starting the whole mighty avalanche, and of being buried under rock enough to build a city. Owing to difficulties like these, it was near supper-time when we gained the top of the main mountain-range. As far as the eye could see, in all directions, there rose a wilderness of barren peaks, covered with snow; while in one direction lay a desolate, lifeless table-land, shut in by higher mountains. Below and near us lay gulches and canyons of magnificent depth, and the blue waters of one of the arms of Lake Bennett appeared, just lately free from ice. Above us rose a still higher peak, covered with deep snow, steep, and difficult of access; and this the lateness of the hour prevented us from attempting.

Next day and the next the wind was as high as ever; but the enforced waiting became finally too tedious, and we started out, the four miners having preceded us by about half an hour. Once out of the shelter of the projecting point, we found the gale very strong and the chop disagreeable. We squared off and ran before the wind for the opposite side of the lake, driving ahead at a good rate under our little rag of a sail. Although the boat was balanced as evenly as possible, every minute or two we would take in water, sometimes over the bow, sometimes the stern, sometimes amidships. I have in my mind a very vivid picture of that scene: Wiborg in the stern, steering intently and carefully; Goodrich and Schrader forward, sheets in hand, attending the sail, and myself stretched flat on my face across the provision sacks, in order not to make the boat top-heavy, and bailing with the frying-pan. On nearing the lower shore we noticed that the boat containing the miners had run into the breakers, and presently one of the men came running along the beach, signaling to us. Fearing that they were in trouble, we made shift to land, although it was no easy task on this exposed shore; and we then learned that they had kept too near the beach, had drifted into the breakers and been swamped, but had all safely landed. Three of our party went to give assistance in hauling the boat out of the water, while I remained behind and fried the bacon for dinner. After dinner we concluded to wait again before attempting the next stage, picked out soft places in the sand and slumbered. When we awoke we found the lake perfectly calm and smooth, and lost no time in getting under way. On this day we depended for our motive power solely on the oars, and we found the results so satisfactory that we kept up the practice steadily hundreds of miles.

Below Lake Bennett came Tagish Lake, beautiful and calm, and walled in by mountains. Its largest arm is fjord-like, and is famous for heavy gales, whence it has been given the name of Windy Arm; but as we passed it we could scarcely distinguish the line of division between the mountains in the air and those reflected in the sea, so completely at rest was the water. At the lower part of the lake, where we camped, we found the first habitation since leaving the coast. Here was a party of natives, belonging to the Tagish tribe; a handful of wretched, half-starved creatures, who scatter in the summer season for hunting and fishing, but return always to this place, where they have constructed rude habitations of wood for winter use. We bought from these people a large pike, which formed a very agreeable change from bacon, beans and slap-jacks.

After passing out of this lake we entered another, appropriately called by the miners, Mud Lake; it is very shallow, with muddy bottom and shores. On this lake we found camping disagreeable, for on account of the shallowness we could not bring our rather heavily laden boat quite up to the shore; but were obliged to wade knee-deep in soft mud for a rod or two before finding even moderately solid ground.

About this time also we experienced the first sharp taste of the terrible Alaskan mosquito—or it might be more correct to reverse the statement, and say that the mosquitoes experienced their first taste of us. At the lower end of Tagish Lake they suddenly attacked us in swarms, and remained with us steadily till near the time of our departure from the Territory. We had heard several times of the various difficulties and hardships to be encountered in Alaska, before venturing on this trip; but, as is often the case, we found that these accounts had left a rather unduly magnified image of the difficulties in our imaginations, as compared with our actual experiences. In this generalization the mosquito must be excepted. I do not think any description or adjectives can exaggerate the discomfort and even torture produced by these pests, at their worst, for they stand peerless among their kind, so far as my experience goes, and that of others with whom I have talked, for wickedness unalloyed.

Out of Mud Lake we floated into the river again, and slipped easily down between sand-banks. Ducks and geese were very plentiful along here, and we practiced incessantly on them with the rifle, without, however, doing any noticeable execution. On the second day we knew we must be near the famous canyon and rapids of the Lewes; and one of our party was put on watch, in order that we might know of its whereabouts before the swift current should sweep us into it, all heavily loaded as we were. The rest of us rowed, steered, and admired the beautiful tints of the hills, now receding from the river, now coming close. Presently we heard a gentle snore from the lookout, who was comfortably settled among the flour-sacks in the bow; this proved to us that our confidence had been misplaced, and all hands immediately became alert. Soon after we noticed a bit of red flannel fluttering from a tree projecting over the bank, doubtless a part of some traveler's shirt sacrificed in the cause of humanity; and by the time we had pulled into the shore we could see the waters of the river go swirling and roaring into a sudden narrow canyon, with high, perpendicular walls.

We found the party of miners already landed, and presently, as we waited on the bank and reconnoitred, De Windt's

INDIAN GRAVE AT PELLY POST.

the water was very high and turbulent; and they thought best to run the boats through themselves. Our own boat was selected to be experimented with; most of the articles which were easily damageable by water were taken out, leaving perhaps eight hundred pounds. I went as passenger sitting in the bow, while the two old frontiersmen managed paddles and oars. Rowing out from the shore we were sucked immediately into the gorge, and went dashing through at a rate which I thought could not be less than twenty miles an hour. So great is the body of water confined between these perpendicular walls, and so swift is the stream, that its surface becomes convex, being considerably higher in the center of the channel than on the sides. Waves rushing in every direction are also generated, forming a very puzzling chop. Two or three of these waves presently boarded us, so that I was thoroughly wet, and then came a broad glare of sunlight as we emerged from the first half of the

party came up, and not long after Cleopatra, with her barge and retinue; so that we were about twenty in all. Wiborg and De Windt's guide, Cooper, were the only ones who had had experience in this matter, so all depended on their judgment, and waited to see the results of their efforts before risking anything themselves.

In former years all travelers made a portage around this very difficult place, hauling their boats over the hill with a rude kind of windlass; but a man having been accidentally sucked into the canyon came out of the other end all right, which emboldened others. In this case Wiborg and Cooper decided that the canyon could be run, although

canyon into a sort of cauldron which lies about in its center. Here we were twisted about by eddying currents for a few seconds, and then precipitated, half sidewise, into the canyon again. This latter half turned out to be the rougher part, and our bow dipped repeatedly into the waves, till I found myself sitting in water, and the bow, where most of the water remained, sagging alarmingly. It seemed as if another ducking would sink us. This fortunately we did not get, but steered safely through the final swirl to smooth water. During all this trip I had not looked up once, although as we shot by we heard faintly a cheer from the rocks above, where our companions were.

Painted for OUTING by J. L. Weston.

"SOMETIMES THEY SAW ONLY THE BOTTOM OF THE SCOW."

Next day, after a night rendered almost unbearable by mosquitoes, we arose to face the difficulties of the White Horse Rapids, which lie below the canyon proper, and are still more formidable. Here the river contracts again, and is confined between perpendicular cliffs of basalt. The channel is full of projecting rocks, so that the whole surface is broken, foaming and tossing, and there are many strong conflicting currents and eddies. At the end of these rapids, which extend for a quarter of a mile or so, is a narrow gorge in the rocks, through which the whole volume of water is forced. This is said to be only twenty or thirty feet wide, although at the time of our passing the water was sufficiently high to flow over the top of the enclosing walls, thus concealing the actual width of the chute. Through this the water plunges at a tremendous velocity — probably thirty miles an hour—forming roaring, foaming, tossing, lashing waves which somehow make the name White Horse seem appropriate.

Above the beginning of the rapids we unloaded our boat, and carefully lowered it down by ropes, keeping it close to the shore, and out of the resistless main current. After having safely landed it, with considerable trouble, below the chute, we carried our outfit (about twelve hundred pounds) to the same point. De Windt's boat, and that belonging to the miners, were safely gotten through in the same way, all hands helping in turn.

When it came to Cleopatra's barge, it was the general opinion that it would be impossible to lower it safely, for its square shape gave the current such a grip that it seemed as if no available strength of rope or man could hold out against it. As carrying the boat was out of the question, the only alternative was to boldly run it through the rapids, in the middle of the channel; and this naturally hazardous undertaking was rendered more difficult by the frail construction of the scow, which had been built of thin lumber by unskilled hands. The royal retinue did not care to make the venture themselves, but finally prevailed upon Wiborg and Cooper to make the trial.

Reflecting that at any future time I might be placed in similar difficulties, in this unknown country, and thrown upon my own resources, I resolved to accompany them, for the sake of finding out how the thing was done; but I was ruled out of active service by Wiborg, who, however, consented finally to my going along as a passenger. Two of the scow's own crew were drafted to act as oarsmen, and we pushed out, Cooper steering, and Wiborg in the bow, iron-shod pole in hand, fending off from threatening rocks; and in a second we were dancing down the boiling rapids, tossed hither and thither like a cork. I sat facing the bow, opposite the oarsman, who tugged frantically away, white as death; behind me Cooper's paddle flashed and twisted rapidly, as we dodged by rocks projecting from the water, sometimes escaping them by only a few inches, where a collision would have smashed us to chips. The rest of the party, waiting below at the chute, said that sometimes they saw only the bottom of the scow, and sometimes looked down on it as if from above. As we neared the end, Cooper's skillful paddle drove us straight for the center, where the water formed an actual fall; this was the most turbulent spot, but the safest, for on either side, a few feet away, there was danger of grazing the shallow underlying rocks. As we trembled on the brink, I looked up and saw our friends standing close by, looking much concerned.

A moment later there was a dizzying plunge, a blinding shower of water, a sudden dashing, too swift for observation, past rock walls; and then Wiborg let out an exultant yell; we were safe. At that instant one of the oarsmen snapped his oar, an accident which would have been serious a moment before. On the shore below the rapids we found flour-sacks, valises, boxes and splintered boards, mementoes of poor fellows less lucky than ourselves.

We camped at the mouth of the Tahkeena River that night, and arrived the next day at Lake Labarge, the last and longest of the series. When we reached it at one o'clock its water was calm and still; and although it is nearly forty miles in length, we decided to keep on without stopping till we reached the other side, for fear of strong winds such as had delayed us on Lake Bennett. De Windt's party concluded to do the same, and so we rowed steadily all night, after having rowed all day. About two o'clock in the morning a favorable wind sprung up suddenly, and increased to a gale. At this time we became separated from the other boats, which kept somewhat close to the shore, while we, with a rag of a sail, stood straight across the lake for the outlet. As soon as we stopped rowing I could not help falling asleep, although much against my will, for our position was neither comfortable nor secure; and thus I dozed and woke half a dozen times before landing. After landing, we found difficulty in sleeping, on account of the swarms of hungry mosquitoes, and so we soon loaded up again.

Below Lake Labarge the journey was comparatively easy. The skies were always clear and blue, and the stream had by this time increased to a lordly river, growing larger by continual accessions of new tributaries. It is dotted with many small islands, which are covered with a dense growth of evergreen trees. On the sides of the valley are often long, smooth terraces, perfectly carved, and smoothly grassed, so as to present almost an artificial aspect. From this sort of country are sudden changes to a more bold and picturesque type, so that at one time the river flows swiftly through high gates of purple rock rising steeply for hundreds of feet, and in a moment more emerges into a wide low valley. The cliffs are sometimes carved into buttresses or pinnacles, which overlook the walls, and appear to form part of a gigantic and impregnable castle, on the top of which the dead spruces stand out against the sky-like spires and flag-staves. Usually on one side or the other of the river is low, fertile land, where is a profusion of shrubs, vines, and flowers. In the mellow twilight, which lasts for two or three hours in the middle of the night, one can see nearly as far and as distinctly as by day, but everything takes on an unreal air. This is something like a beautiful sunset effect further south, but is evenly distributed over all objects in the landscape. At about ten o'clock the coloring becomes exquisite, when the half-light brings out the violets, the purples, and exquisite shades of yellow and brown in the rock, in contrast with the green of the vegetation.

We had some difficulty in finding suitable camping-places in this country One night, I remember we ran fifteen miles after our usual camping-hour,

with cliffs on one side of the river and low thickets on the other. Three times we landed on small islands, in a tangle of vines and roses; and as many times were driven off by the innumerable mosquitoes. Finally, we found a strip of shore about ten feet wide, between the water and the thickets, sloping at a considerable angle, and there made shift to spend the night.

There are two places below the White Horse Rapids, where the channel is so narrowed or shallowed that rapids are formed. At the first of these, called the Five Finger Rapids, the river is partially blocked by high islets of conglomerate, which cut up the stream into five chief portions. Although the current in each of these "fingers" is rapid, and the water rough, yet we found no difficulty in running through without removing any part of the loads, although one of the boats shipped a little water. When we arrived at the second rapids, which are called the Rink Rapids, and are not far below the Five Fingers, we were relieved to find that, owing to the fullness of the river, the rough water, which in this case is caused by a shallowing of the stream, was smoothed down, and we passed through, close to the shore, with no more trouble than if we had been floating down a lake.

During our whole trip the country through which we passed was singularly lonely and uninhabited. After leaving the few huts on Tagish Lake, which I have mentioned, we saw a few Indians in a summer camp on Lake Labarge; and this was all till we got to the junction of the Lewes and Pelly Rivers, over three hundred miles from Tagish Lake. At Pelly we found a log trading-post, with a single white man in charge, and a few Indians. There were also three miners, who had met with a misfortune, and were disconsolate enough. They had started up the Pelly River with a two years' outfit, intending to remain and prospect for that period, but at some rapid water their boat had been swamped and all their provisions lost. They had managed to burn off logs enough to make a raft, and in that way had floated down the river to the post, living in the meantime on some flour which they had been lucky enough to pick up after the wreck.

Although there are very few people in the country, one is continually surprised at first by perceiving a solitary white tent standing on some prominent point or cliff which overlooks the river. At first this looks very cheerful, and we sent many a hearty hail across the water to such habitations; but our calls were never answered, for these are not the dwellings of the living, but of the dead. Inside each of these tents, which are ordinarily made of white cloth, though sometimes of woven matting, is a dead Indian, and near him are laid his rifle, snow-shoes, ornaments and other personal effects. I do not think the custom of leaving these articles at the grave implies any belief that they will be used by the dead man in another world, but simply signifies that he will have no more use for the things which were so dear and necessary to him in life—just as, among ourselves, articles which have been used by some dead friend are henceforth laid aside and used no longer. These dwellings of the dead are always put in prominent positions, commanding as broad and fair a view as can be obtained. At Pelly we saw several Indian graves which were surrounded by hewn palings, rudely and fantastically painted, and some by poles.

Below Pelly we found no settled habitations till we reached a considerable village of the Klundek or Clondike Indians. These people were watching very eagerly for the appearance of the salmon that came up the river every year from the sea to spawn; and at the time of their coming the Indian lays in a large part of his year's food-supply, hunting them with spear and club from a birch canoe, so narrow and so light that the operation seems a marvel of skill. On account of the swift current of the river, the canoes used by these natives are very narrow and shallow, having some suggestion of a racing shell in their lines, and they are difficult to manœuvre.

The day after passing the Klundek village we arrived at the mining-camp of Forty Mile. We had reached the edge of the Klondike. Our next effort would be to see the gold producing country about which we had heard so much.

AN ARM OF THE DYEA GLACIER.

23
An Ethnologist in the Arctic

TENTS AND FISH-DRYING HOUSE, SHINGLE POINT

An Ethnologist in the Arctic

BY VILHJÁLMR STEFÁNSSON

Formerly of the Peabody Museum of American Ethnology, Harvard University, and the Ethnologist of the recent Anglo-American Polar Expedition

IN the last days of January the sun came back to my Eskimos and me, after an absence of about eleven weeks. The period of darkness had not been at all tedious; neither the natives nor I had felt the depression that the want of sunlight is supposed to bring. Nevertheless we were all glad to see the red disk showing a third of its surface at noon over the hills to the south. I climbed the highest knoll within reach, with the result that I saw two-thirds of the new sun.

By the first week in February I felt myself growing a little restless; two months of fresh air and stale fish had accumulated more surplus energy than could be gotten rid of in the rather tame occupation of fishing through a hole in the ice, or in taking short runs ahead of the dog teams to visit our neighbors twenty or forty miles away. In December I had, it is true, taken a three days' trip inland to where the only other white

man in the country, Mr. Harrison, the English geographer, was living with his hired native families. At his kind invitation I might have stayed there a considerable while had not food been running rather low with him. He had flour, tea, coffee, sugar, and some other civilized edibles, but his stock was running so low that it evidently could not last till spring. Though his pancakes tasted good, I never feasted on one without seeing in my mind's eye the little store of twenty-five-dollar sacks of flour growing smaller at my every bite. It was with almost as good an appetite and a much better conscience that I returned to the raw fish diet of Tuktuyaktok. About this time a travelling Eskimo gave me half a pound of salt to eat with my fish, but I found I had quite gotten over the salt-eating habit so far as raw or cooked fish was concerned. A carnivorous man seems to have no more need for salt than does the carnivorous dog.

This little trip to the Eskimo lakes had not satisfied the desire to move about, so I was much rejoiced when my host Ovayuak announced his intention of going to Herschel Island to visit his daughter and see his grandson, of whose recent arrival a visitor had told us the previous week. I at once asked to be allowed to accompany the sled westward, but at first Ovayuak demurred. He was, he said, going to take his younger wife, Illerok, and her little boy, Kakhilik, who was only four. February, he told me, is the worst month of the year, and white men are like babies when they have to travel in bad weather. He had once travelled in February with a white sailor and at another time with a missionary, and they were worse than children, because they were bigger and therefore harder to take care of. A baby may cry, but he does not argue, but white men are continually giving directions about things they don't understand. He knew I was a better traveller than most white men (Eskimos are always polite), but when the sun comes back he brings with him a cold that is twice as keen as the bitterest weather of the dark days. Anyway, he would be glad to take me along if it were not for the child Kakhilik. It would be much more difficult to take care of both of us than of either alone.

The upshot of the matter was, however, that he finally agreed he would take me along on my representing it was almost a matter of life and death for me to get to Herschel and see if there were any news of my ship. As a matter of fact, my chief desire was to be moving, and to undertake a journey in difficult weather for the purpose of trying myself out and (if possible) impressing the Eskimos and the police at Herschel with my ability as a traveller.

To partly compensate him for the many inferiorities of his outfit to that of an Eskimo, the ordinary polar explorer has this one advantage—that he has light condensed food, such as pemmican and malted milk. A five days' ration of condensed food for men and dogs weighs no more than a one day's ration of the fish or seal meat an Eskimo must carry. Our sled in this case was loaded with about six hundred pounds of fresh fish, and was, for the first few days, heavy for the six

dogs and the two of us who hauled on the ropes. Ordinarily Ovayuak and I did the pulling, while Illerok walked ahead of the team, and little Kakhilik slept on top of the load, bundled up in furs. On an average we made about ten miles per day, starting before daylight in the morning so as to be able to camp by the noonday sunlight.

The first day out we slept at a neighbor's house at Kangianik, and during the night there blew up the worst blizzard of the year, continuing for three days. Although the house was so crowded that it was a serious problem to find sleeping-room on the floor even after some of the household articles had been suspended from the ceiling or carried out into the passage, still we passed the time very pleasantly in singing and telling stories.

It was the third evening of the blizzard and the storm had abated a trifle, when, about eleven o'clock, the dogs in the outside passage began barking. As customary, most of the people were sitting stripped to the waist. The moment the barking was heard every man jumped for his gun and, taking his coat in one hand, ran out of the house, without stopping to put the garment on till he got outside. I had seen similar occurrences, but never in bad weather, and had therefore attributed the hurry in rushing out to the eagerness for catching sight of a possible polar bear at which the dogs were barking. I had never asked any questions before, but this evening I did, and found out the reason.

As is well known from various sources, including Franklin's travels and the records of the Hudson's Bay Company, the Mackenzie Eskimos have always been a warlike people, dreaded alike by neighbors of their own blood and by the Indians to the south. In the fights with the Indians the Eskimos were usually the aggressors, and made warlike expeditions far up the Mackenzie even in the memory of white traders still living. Occasionally, however, the Indians attempted reprisals, and not infrequently attacked an Eskimo house in the night, burning the people, or killing them as they came out through the door; but often the barking of the Eskimos' dogs gave warning of the enemy's approach, and if the inmates once got into the open before the Indians reached the door, the latter frequently took to flight, or at least the Eskimos thus got a chance for their lives. For this reason it was always the custom that everybody should run out of the house whenever a dog barked. Even now, although it is some eighteen years since the last bloodshed took place (and since the Hudson's Bay Company purchased peace between the peoples by blankets and copper kettles given the Indian relatives of those then recently killed in battle with the Eskimos), the custom is maintained. The practice seems to be more a habit, a matter of good form, than any indication of present distrust of the Indians, for the two groups are now on excellent terms.

The fourth day at Kangianik dawned clear, and we started on our uneventful way, to reach Herschel Island in seventeen days. Unfortunately for narrative purposes, an Eskimo knows so well how to travel safely and comfortably under the worst conditions of cold and storm that nothing extraordinary happens. Your face may freeze, but all there is to do is to pull your hand out of the warm mitten, rub whatever portion of your face happens to be getting stiff, and put the hand back in the mitten again before the fingers have had time to freeze—for freezing a finger is serious, though a frost-bitten nose is little worse than a sunburnt one. One gets pretty thirsty, but this can be alleviated by the eating of a little snow—or that has been my own experience, though many travellers consider the practice unsafe. At night the snow-house is dry, warm, and comfortable, and too substantial to be blown away by the wind, as tents sometimes are. Nothing happens except that a few miles of trail are left behind each day. A competently managed journey is as uninteresting as the history of a country at peace with its neighbors; and of all travellers in the world none adapts means to an end better than the Eskimo. We reached Herschel Island toward the end of February with our store of fish a trifle low, but with nothing to tell of the trip except the number of days it had taken.

At the island there was, sure enough, news of the *Duchess of Bedford*. In November, while I was still at Shingle Point, a sled had arrived at the police station from the expedition, which was wintering at Flaxman Island, about two hundred miles to the westward. It was known at Herschel that I was then only sixty miles (or three days' journey) away, but Mr. Leffingwell, Mr. Storkerson, and their team of dogs were so worn out by the trip down from Flaxman that they did not make the attempt to reach me—especially as Eskimo report reached them that I was well off and likely to continue so. They had spent Thanksgiving with Captain Leavitt aboard his ship *Narwhal*, which was the only whaler wintering at Herschel (or anywhere in the western Arctic), and had then gone back to Flaxman Island, merely leaving word for me as to the whereabouts of the ship.

Now that the location of the *Duchess* was known, it seemed to me an interesting thing to make a trip to her and back; besides, I was out of writing materials and photographic supplies. Although the whaler was short of provisions and the police had little to spare, both Captain Leavitt and Sergeant Fitzgerald assisted me in securing dogs and supplies for the trip. This was the first journey of the winter on which I used white men's food. The travelling conditions were so much better than they had been in the fall that the trip which had taken Mr. Leffingwell thirty-five days we made in nine. My fellow traveller this time was an immigrant from Bering Strait, and proved a good companion. He was the first Christianized native I travelled with. He used to say his prayers before going to bed and at meal-times. In this he differed markedly from most of the Eskimos, as he did also in being a thief and a liar. But he was energetic, resourceful, and good-tempered, and those are the things that matter on a long journey.

At Flaxman Island we found the two commanders of the expedition, Captain Mikkelsen and Mr. Leffingwell, off on an ice-exploring trip to the northward, and with them the ship's mate, Mr. Storkerson. The *Duchess of Bedford* had been crushed by the ice the previous March (this was April), and the crew were living on shore under the command of the expedition's surgeon, Dr. Howe.

That the ship was lost immediately

changed my plans for the remainder of the year, for it was now impossible to proceed to the eastward in the summer, as had been planned. I therefore determined to devote the rest of my time in the north to investigating ethnological and archæological conditions on the north coast of Alaska. I therefore made a hasty trip to Herschel Island to return my borrowed sled and dogs. The ship's quartermaster, Mr. William Hickey, made this trip with me, and we accomplished it in a trifle less than a month, getting back on the 17th of May, or two days before the return of the ice - exploring party.

As the general story of the expedition has already been told, it is not necessary to give much space to the period from my joining it in May till I separated from it again in July. The chief activity in the mean time was the excavating on Flaxman Island of a number of ancient ruins and the recovery from them of various specimens of more or less scientific value. The first week of July I accompanied a party under Captain Mikkelsen's command to the mouth of the Colville River, at which point I separated from them for the purpose of a scientific exploration of the Jones and other islands near Beecher Point. The expedition at this time had no other work on hand, so Captain Mikkelsen detailed two of the sailors, William Hickey and Max Fiedler, to assist me. We had an Eskimo skin-boat (umiak), owned and commanded by our Flaxman Island friend Sakhawanna, so there were altogether four of us to voyage along the string of coast islands in search of ruins, relics, and dead men's bones—for of such things are the data of archæology.

Our longest stay was on that one of

AN INLAND ESKIMO WOMAN

the Jones Islands known to the natives as Pingok, or the Island of Little Hills. Here we found ruins of unknown age left by people who built their houses largely with the bones of whales to take the place of timbers. The present Eskimos tell that before the time when their grandfathers were boys (and that is as far as Eskimo chronology ever goes) this island was already deserted, though their grandfathers had the tradition that there once lived here a people who hunted exclusively the monstrous bowhead whale, and who were men of prowess and remarkable seamanship. In a measure our excavations confirmed this tradition, as does even a walk along the beach, which may be said to be strewn with the bones of the bowhead whale. Of course many a student of folklore will say that it is not unlikely that the story of ancient whalehunters may have been deduced from the presence of the bones, and that they rather explain the origin than prove the truth of the yarn.

Perhaps the most interesting archæological discovery made on the north coast of Alaska has a relation to the present methods of personal decoration now used by the natives of Alaska, the most significant feature of which is the wearing of lip-buttons, or labrets, by the men. The present custom is that when a boy is fourteen or sixteen years of age holes are pierced in his lower lip, one below each corner of the mouth. A small wooden plug is at first inserted to keep the hole from growing together, and month by month a bigger and bigger plug is used, till finally the openings are half an inch in diameter. At this point the young man begins to wear stone or ivory plugs. These ornaments are put in from the inside ordinarily as one might insert a button into a shirt front. Usually the two buttons worn are each of a different sort, while sometimes only one of the holes is filled, and in summer men are occasionally met with who wear no buttons at all. When a visitor is seen approaching, however, the ornaments are always inserted, for one does not feel dressed without them. In preparing for sleep they are usually removed.

It seems probable to ethnologists that this custom of wearing labrets is borrowed by the Eskimo from the Indians of southern Alaska. But these Indians wear one labret only, and that in the centre of the lower lip, while the Eskimos as far east as Cape Bathurst wear two uniformly, and east of the Coppermine River the practice of piercing the lips is unknown. Murdock, however, in 1882 found some traditions at Point Barrow that pointed to the wearing long ago by the Eskimos of labrets of the single Indian type, and he also secured three specimens that looked as if they were centre-lip labrets. In one of our excavations some two hundred and fifty miles east of Point Barrow we found five centre labrets, thus showing that they were probably worn in former days along the north coast, and showing further that

among the Eskimos, as elsewhere, fashions change in dress and ornament.

It had been my intention on separating from Captain Mikkelsen in the Colville delta to remain there till the first whaling-ships should pass eastbound for the Beaufort Sea fishing-grounds. Unfortunately for our work among the islands, but fortunately for the whalers, ice conditions to the west of us at Point Barrow were that summer the best in years, and the *Belvedere*, first of the Arctic fleet, hove in sight at three o'clock in the morning on July 26th, two weeks before we had expected her. Greatly to the delight of the sailors and our Eskimo friend, we succeeded in paddling our boat far enough seaward to be seen and picked up. We received a warm welcome on board from Captain Cottle, his wife, and his officers, whom I had met the previous summer at Herschel Island. By noon we reached Flaxman Island, and sent Max Fiedler and Sakhawanna ashore, while Mr. Hickey and I proceeded to Herschel to continue our archæological work at that point, intending to remain there till fall and then take passage for San Francisco by one of the outbound whalers.

We had been at the island only a few days, however, when disturbing news

A SPRUCE BARK SUMMER HOUSE OF THE ARCTIC INDIANS

reached us from Macpherson up the Mackenzie. Major Arthur Jarvis, the new commander of the Mounted Police in the north, arrived from there August 4th, bringing the report that a definite statement had been sent up the Mackenzie by the Hudson's Bay Company's mail steamer to the effect that Captain Mikkelsen, Mr. Leffingwell, and Mr. Storkerson were all dead—lost on the ice-exploring expedition. The story had been told in great detail and was given on my authority, who was supposed to have reported the tragedy on my visit to Herschel in April. Almost simultaneously with Major Jarvis, Captain Mikkelsen arrived on a whaler he had boarded at Flaxman Island. The news of his own and his comrades' supposed death disturbed him greatly, for unless special efforts were made to overtake and contradict these reports that were now on their way up the Mackenzie, the relatives and friends of all three concerned would believe them dead, till the whalers should reach port in November. On account of my being somewhat familiar with overland and river travel, Captain Mikkelsen consulted me as to the practicability of forestalling these up-river despatches. As they had been sent from Macpherson July 24th and were already half-way to their destination at Athabasca Landing, Alberta, the first week in September, there was evidently but one hope—that of crossing the coast ranges of the Rockies and descending the Bell and Porcupine rivers to the telegraph offices and settlements on the Yukon. This I volunteered to do, partly because Captain Mikkelsen was very anxious that the safety of his party should become known, and partly because the trip looked in perspective difficult enough to be interesting. Twelve hours from the final reaching of this decision, Captain Porter's engines were whistling us their farewell salute as we sailed our little whale-boat from the harbor, bound for the mouth of the Mackenzie sixty miles away.

On the way east nothing happened beyond the sudden springing up of a gale that made our boat dangerous in the incapable hands of its Indian steersman —for I was taking passage back to Fort Macpherson in the boat that had brought

Major Jarvis down, and this was manned by Indians, who are (the best of them) poor sailors as compared with the Eskimos. When once the river mouth was attained we had favoring northerly winds, and reached Macpherson in six days, thus establishing, by travelling day and night, a new record for either summer or winter travel between Herschel and Macpherson, an estimated distance of 260 miles.

At Macpherson guides had to be hired and supplies bought for the hundred-mile portage to the Bell River. The police stationed at the fort, Mr. Firth of the Hudson's Bay Company, and (especially) Mr. Harvey for Hyslop & Nagle, all did their utmost to see that I was well provided. But this was a time when no Indians were at the fort, and, although one of them was sick, I had to take with me two of the Indians with whom I had come in the boat from Herschel. Carrying seventy pounds each and with two dogs carrying forty-pound packs, we set off. The sick Indian, William, soon had to be lightened up, so that for the first three days both Joseph and I carried more than our seventy pounds.

A great deal of reading may fail to impress the stay-at-home with the fact that the arctic summer is a much worse season for travel than the arctic winter, but a very little actual experience puts the matter beyond debate. The good three weeks that now separated me from Rampart House on the Porcupine were the least like fun of any trip I have so far undertaken.

To begin with, the journey was to be so long that we could carry no tent, nor anything much but food and the axe and rope for constructing a raft on the Bell. Crossing the mountains it rained every day and every night—except one night, when it snowed. I had an oilskin coat that had been waterproof the year before; the Indians, with their sore chests and racking cough, had not even a make-believe waterproof. But one thing we did have was our mosquito-nets. Under these we slept soaking wet on the sponge-soaked moss, but safe at least from the buzzing fog of mosquitoes that hung over us as thick as the drizzling rain.

It took a bit over five days to reach

RAMPART HOUSE

the Bell. Here the building of a sixteen-foot raft of green spruces was not a serious task, and took less than half a day. When this was finished no delay was made in pushing it off. Five minutes later my Indians waved me a last "good luck" as I drifted around a bend on my fifteen-day journey southward to the Yukon.

The journey is summed up in the statement that it was monotonous, cold, and wet. Of the eleven days spent in reaching Rampart House, ten were rainy. It may be guessed that sitting soaking wet on a waterlogged raft drifting a mile or mile and a half per hour is not a cheerful occupation. The first night I slept on the raft, floating ahead most of the time, but occasionally waking to find myself on a mud bank, in which case there was nothing to do but push the raft afloat and go to sleep again.

Much as I object to such things, I did on this trip have some small "adventures"—but fortunately they illustrate a favorite thesis: that most ad-

ventures are a sign of incompetence, which may consist either in bad craftsmanship or an insufficient knowledge of local conditions. My first adventure happened in this wise:

It was the second night of my river journey and I was sleeping on the raft. It may have been twelve o'clock—it was certainly pitch dark—when I awoke with a roar in my ears that I first took for the sound of a high wind up in the tree tops. I was near one bank of the river, and the spinning around of my raft and its motion past the trees on shore showed that it was in a rapid and uneven current. As soon as I got over the half-stupor of waking from an uncomfortable sleep I knew that I was in a rapid; the increasing noise of the water showed the worst part was still ahead.

It was a trifle fortunate I had not been aroused sooner, for I could not have gotten the unwieldy raft ashore (it usually took half an hour to do that), and being gradually pulled through pitch darkness into a rapid you recognize as

323

STEAMING DOWN THE YUKON RIVER

stony by its roar is, on the whole, a trying experience. Of course the Hudson's Bay men had told me there were no "impossible" rapids in the Porcupine "if one used ordinary care." But was this using ordinary care—drifting in the dark into what might as easily be the unsafe as the safe side of a "possible" rapid?

I believe I did the thinking outlined in the above paragraph—at least I might have done so if I had had the time. As it was, I was no more than fully awake when I was in the swirl. I threw myself flat on my little heap of mail and other belongings on the centre of the raft, to protect them from loss in case the raft held out. Then there followed a series of bumps upon what were apparently rounded boulders. A moment later the raft stuck fast by its front end, swung side on, and stuck also with its back end; then it began to rise on edge as if to tip over. When, however, I threw myself and my armful of mail parcels and food upon the rising side of the raft it paused in its tilt as if thinking what to do. At that moment the front end

of the raft loosened again and swung down stream; then the rear end was freed also, and the raft floated into quiet water. The "adventure" was over, and I worked the raft landward to sleep the rest of the night on shore.

This experience netted me a little river wisdom, and made me temper my impatience to drifting eighteen instead of twenty-four hours per day. Those eighteen-hour days were even longer than the watch indicated. The occasional sight of such animals along the river bank as deer, moose, and wolves was rather diverting if they appeared in one of the odd half-hours of sunlight, but I found it hard to be interested in anything when shivering in the drizzling rains. I did not carry a rifle, and could not have afforded time for hunting if I had, though I might have shot with ease a moose that first watched me from the bank and then swam to within a few feet of my raft to investigate me. This happened, too, at a time when my food was getting rather low. The following day, however (my sixth day on the river), I came to the first signs of human habitations—a *cache* of dry moose-meat on a platform of poles at the mouth of a little river. I took a few pounds of meat and left in payment a silk handkerchief.

The days following the finding of the moose-meat *caches* I watched sharply and rather eagerly for people or the traces of them along the banks. Every curve that brought a new reach of the river into view held the promise of cabin or camp. Several times, near dawn or dusk especially, the fog films on the hillsides simulated the wreaths of smoke from wigwam fires and were sources of cheer for a moment. At last, late on the evening of August 28th, a group of huts appeared on the right bank, and I paddled the raft ashore. But the village was deserted, its inhabitants off somewhere hunting or fishing. All the houses were locked except one that was building and had as yet no roof; in that I took up my lodging nevertheless.

The next morning I made a great fire —not to cook, but to sit beside while I ate my breakfast of dried moose-meat. The building of a fire proved a fortunate thing for me, for it brought the most welcome sight of my travelling experience—an Indian running along the beach to catch me just as I was pushing my raft from shore. He was from a fishing-village of tents half a mile away and so situated that I should probably have missed it had they not seen my smoke and sent this messenger. When I got to the village every one of twenty men, women, and children seemed overjoyed to see me, but none of them were half so glad as I was.

After half a day of gorging on fresh fish and berries I emerged sufficiently from the stupor of pure joy into which I was fallen, to remember that the Yukon was still some distance away, and announced my intention of proceeding forthwith on my raft to Rampart House, which was now not far distant. But one of the Indians, who spoke good English, told me that I could not safely go any farther on so small a raft as I had, but must have one twice as big to pass without capsizing in the Boiling Tea Kettle rapid just below. The whole camp professed their willingness to help me enlarge the raft, but said that at best rafting through the "Tea Kettle" was serious

business, while a canoe can keep out of the current and pass safely. I therefore hired a bark canoe built for one man, and in it its owner and I proceeded down the river. It felt more dangerous, but doubtless was safer than the old raft. There was scarcely an inch of freeboard, and the thing was so crazy that sitting in it is best compared to a tight-rope performance, while its birch-bark sides were so fragile that it sprang a leak every time the boat was subjected to the strain of going through even a slight rapid. But where the river twists like a rope through the elbow-shaped gorge of the "Tea Kettle" everything went well, for we hugged the inside shore and were in quiet water, while a raft would inevitably be drawn into the centre of the current. When I had seen the rapid and the cañon that leads to it I felt that through no merit of my own I had escaped an adventure whose value for narrative purposes would have become vested exclusively in my literary executor.

Just above Rampart House we fell in with Harry Linklater, an old Hudson's Bay man, who, with his family, joined us for the rest of the way to the trading post—some six miles. Here Daniel Cadzow—whose generous hospitality is the brightest spot in every journey into the Porcupine—met us at the water's edge.

Although there were still two hundred miles to the Yukon, all the difficulties of the trip were over. The journey had so far covered six or seven hundred miles and lasted twenty-four days, eleven of which had been spent on the raft between the farewell to the Indian guides on the Bell and the meeting with people on the Porcupine. From Rampart House I travelled comfortably in Mr. Linklater's boat, for he was going to Fort Yukon anyway, and hastened his departure for my sake. The morning of September 4th I was on board the magnificent river steamer *Hanna* going up-stream toward Dawson, while my most urgent despatches were going down-stream with the *Koyukuk* to be cabled over the government's telegraph lines from Fort Gibson. As I found out later, the news of the safety of our ice party was wired from Gibson thirty-six hours after the sending out from Athabasca Landing the report of their supposed death.

24
Finding a Volcano and Wiping a 16,000 Feet Mountain from the Map of Alaska

Valdes Is a Typical Village of the Far Northwest.

FINDING A VOLCANO AND WIPING A 16,000 FEET MOUNTAIN FROM THE MAP OF ALASKA

By ROBERT DUNN

AMATEUR exploring, as Jack and I do it, is hard to justify. In June, 1898, while in college, we heard that the last herd of bison roamed the Arctic Basin of North America; that it was a country full of gold; that a thousand Argonauts were dying off and going mad up there on the way from the Hudson's Bay slope to the Yukon. We left college. By November we had covered 1500 miles of the Mackenzie River Valley. We hadn't found any gold or bison—had shot only seven bears and a lynx—but we had crossed the Rocky Mountains up underneath the Arctic Circle by a trail which men said all who had taken had died upon, and we had seen brave men sink with their raw-backed cayeuses through the terrible muskeg swamp of the North.

That sort of thing changes a man queerly. After we reached civilization we wanted to go right back north again. We didn't care for gold or game now. We simply wanted to travel in the North, beyond all horizons, among unexplored mountains. Our friends couldn't understand it — and we didn't altogether, either.

But we had to suffer civilization for two years. In 1900, we were free again, and got out our maps of the North. Right where Alaska starts out to reach Siberia we saw that the mountains which follow the Pacific from Oregon north ended abruptly. Here two new chains began. First, the St. Elias-Chugatch range, which borders the Pacific from Muir Glacier to Cook's Inlet. Second, the Alaskan range, which also starts and ends at about the same two points, but is bowed further to the north, reaching two hundred miles inland. Between these two systems, near their eastern ends, five separate peaks were mapped, forming a sort of circle; and in turn were themselves almost completely surrounded on the west by the Copper River. The mountains were: Mt. Tillman 16,600 feet, Mt. Drum 13,700 feet, Mt. Sanford 13,500 feet, Mt. Blackburn 12,500 feet, and Mt. Wrangell 17,500 feet. We read that they had been dis-

329

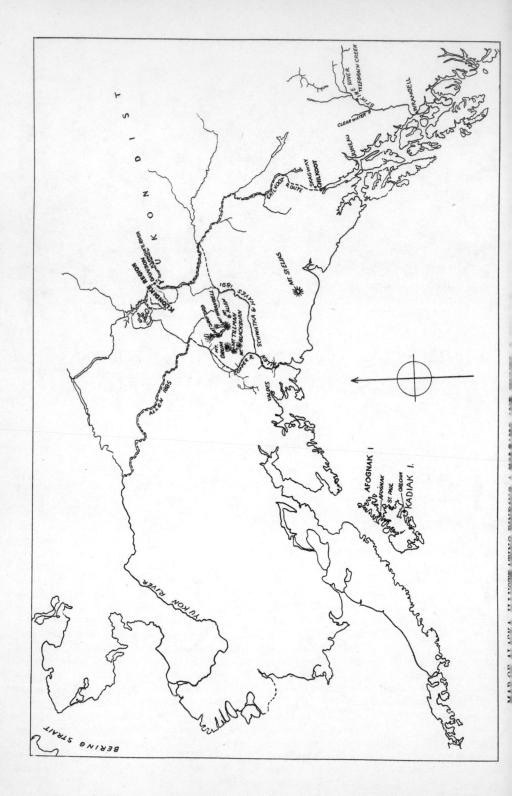

Snyder's Peak, as It Looked from the Crater of Mt. Drum.

covered in 1819, but that up to 1884 every one who had tried to reach them had failed, because the Copper River natives were hostile. One party had been massacred. In 1885, however, Lieut. (now Capt.) H. T. Allen, Second Cavalry, passed safely up Copper River along their eastern base. In 1891, Lieut. Schwatka and Dr. Hayes passed along the southern edge of the group. In 1898, the Copper River Valley was full of tenderfeet trying to reach the Klondike. A few of them got to the base of the mountains, but they told nothing new. All maps of the country were Allen's.

But what stirred us in all we read of the region was this: Mt. Wrangell, the highest peak of the group, was constantly referred to as a volcano, and Allen had drawn a fantastic picture of it—a cornucopia of snow with a stream of smoke coming out of the top. But he wouldn't say flat that Wrangell was active; no one seemed sure about it; no one would commit himself. Yet we found records of terrible eruptions in the region, of smoke and fire seen " far inland " by Russian archimandrites, which blackened the whole Alaskan Peninsula. Lots of geographical problems seemed to hang on Wrangell's being an active cone. George Dawson reported a thick layer of white volcanic ash covering thousands of square miles in the Upper Yukon Valley. It fell in the last few centuries, he said — and could it have come from Wrangell?

A question mark had been hung over Wrangell — "Volcano?" That seemed to us enough to stir any one. Could we rub it out? It led us to make a rash resolution, — to smoke a pipe upon the snows of Wrangell, to make sure if it would smoke with us or not, though we had never seen a glacier, nor been on a snow mountain. Simply, the whole region inspired us; it was our country, God's country, no matter what the scurvied gold-seekers said. We dreamed of it as an enchanted land,

after sliding for eight days on tide-rips among snowy islands, past Mt. Crillion's three miles of snow pitched up from mid-Pacific, stuck on the mud-flats of an ice-hung fjord, where the cabins of Valdes stood in a strip of woods between glacier and sea.

Valdes lies west of the mouth of Copper River, and is the only point of entry into interior Alaska across the Coast, or Chugatch Mountains. Here we found the War Department trail to the Yukon, 500 miles away,

"We rested from our packing on the gravel-covered ice."

where earthquakes and tidal waves wrecked Siwashes' villages; where glaciers sixty miles broad miraged cities of the other hemisphere—men said—and islands—as Bogoslof did— popped up from the sea, smoked awhile, and dived down again.

In June Jack and I took the train for Seattle and there bought flour, beans, sowbelly, sugar, tea, nine unbroken cayeuses, —and nothing else. We sailed for Port Valdes, the northermost settlement on the Pacific Coast of Alaska, on July 1st, and

had been marked out as far as Copper Centre, a deserted prospectors' camp 110 miles to the northeast, in the interior, on Copper River, and southwest of Wrangell but had only been completed over the coast pass, thirty miles from Valdes. Trail-building isn't easy in a sub-Arctic land, where grub is worth its weight in gold (which no one had found about there yet) and the land is mostly a frozen swamp, which thaws down to Hades when you strip it.

Day after day we ran a circus on Valdes beach, breaking bronchos and remembering how to throw the diamond pack hitch. Regularly as we cinched up the five pack-horses with two hundred pounds apiece in the panniers, they careered off across the mud-flats, backs humped, heels together, and sacks of flour, sugar, beans, soaring through the air, while the townsfolk—whom the Angel Gabriel couldn't have made try a mount—shouted advice from the corral.

"There's the thing to do, boys, I tell yer," went on Bill—"climb Wrangell. There ain't no one but's only been to the bottom of him. She must be twenty miles from where snow begins to the top."

And they told how Siwashes had gone to its base never to return; how in September, '99, from Copper Centre fiery lava was seen at nights brimming over distant snows; how the forest shook like a quilt for two Sundays, and men cast themselves to the

A Prospector's Pack Train Outfitting for a Journey to the Klondike.

The townsfolk told weird tales of Wrangell. One morning, Bill Rhodes, head government packer, drawled, Montana fashion:

"Some yere outfit of dudes came in last year, sayin' they was going to climb Wrangell. I'd as soon walk alone to the North Pole. That mountain's as big on top as Coyote County, and as flat."

Jack wanted to know what became of the dudes, but I wouldn't let him ask, because any one who doesn't come north for gold is a "dude"; and it's a stigma, and— we were novel enough, as it was, for Valdes.

ground and were seasick; and the two-story "hotel" at Valdes was wrecked.

We asked no more questions, but the next day we set out for Copper Centre. We started inland on the half-built government trail. By night we had gone twenty miles up Lowe River—its bed a strip of Arizona in the exotic forest—and then through Keystone Canyon by a five-foot trail cut in the cliff's face a thousand feet above the stream. In the canyon were two waterfalls, each 700 feet high; Jack was thrown and his horse stamped over him, as he clung to the

An Indian's Cabin, on Copper River.

precipice. Another day among ptarmigan and ice and blue morainal tarns took us over the misty pass into the great valley of Copper River.

Traveling now a hundred miles to Copper River itself, where it bounds the Wrangell group on the east, we endured what only they who have suffered in this cursed country can conceive; the musquito plague, sleepless nights, endless swamps where the horses mire, rain (we had no tent), getting lost, hunting strayed horses, and fording glacial streams, where you drop if once the water reaches over your waist. We were always wet and cold and tired and profane. That is life in Alaska. Now we came to a trail cutter's camp; now we met two grizzled partners, bowed under pack-backs, still searching for an eldorado. A handful of argonauts, who had not died or quit the country, still "stayed" with it, roaming across the great distances, swallowed up in the wilderness. We crossed fifteen-mile muskegs, and were twenty hours without eating; and the horses stampeded on the back trail, and rolled off their packs, and Jack's saddle-horse — Rosinante — foundered in the forest and was left to die. At last, from the inland foot-hills of the Coast Range we first saw the great peaks of the Wrangell Alps. That never-to-be-forgotten dawn we were hunting horses — life was a horse-hunt — over moss-covered ice in a dead spruce forest. Eastward, suddenly, across Copper River, between the horizon of its boundless purple valley, and the sky of a midnight dawn, the sun flashed bar after bar of light across glistening snows.

When our eyes were used to it we saw four great mountains. There must be some mistake, we thought. Five mountains, Allen's map said, lay east of Copper River. We got out the map, on which the five peaks were ranged in a rough circle. According to it, Mt. Tillman might hide Mt. Wrangell from here. The third mountain from the North was surely the highest of all — an enormous plateau of snow, like forty miles of the polar regions, close under the sky. It might be Tillman, according to Allen. But the immense area it covered, and its flat top — "big as Coyote County" — tallied with the packer's description of Wrangell. We could see no sign of steam, smoke, or ash. We were puzzled. The two northernmost peaks, according to Allen's map, were clearly Mts. Drum and

Sanford. They were extraordinary; the whole southern face of each was a sheer, lace-white, amphitheatrical precipice.

The next day we reached Copper Centre's line of gaping cabins, and its yard of wooden gravestones among aspens on a silty river-flat. Most of the prospectors who had wintered here in 1898, had died of scurvy. And here we lost all our horses, for in Alaska feed's too scarce to picket them. Four days later, when we found a few, they were bronchos again; and their withers, galled by the villainous "saw-buck" pack-saddle, were fly-blown and maggoty. We tied up their legs, threw them, cut out the rotting flesh; and life changed from treading down swamps on the horse-hunt, to bandaging and poulticing the kicking brutes with liniments found in a drug-outfit left by the dead argonauts.

On August first the clouds lifted, and we got a second glimpse of the great peaks. And only two — besides Blackburn, far to the south — were visible now. According to Allen's map, Mt. Sanford from here should be masked by Mt. Drum. It was, clearly. Next to the south Tillman might still hide Wrangell from here, according to Allen's map; but the remaining mountain was the same enormous, flat plateau of snow we had seen before. It had a queer peak, like a tusk, on its smooth northern quarter. One evening, as we were looking at it, we thought we saw dark globes of vapor rise at minute intervals — and vanish; but we were too far away to be sure it was steam.

That night two prospectors wandered into camp, and said this peak we had seen steaming was Wrangell. "There's no Mt. Tillman," they said. "Mt. Tillman is a myth." A mountain 16,600 feet high, and a myth! Impossible! Why, just like the two Lop-Nor Lakes in the Tarim desert in the heart of Asia, we thought. Were Tillman and Wrangell the same?

We steered for the great mountain, whatever it was. We scooped the horses off a gravel bar into the foam of Copper River, and stoned them across. Then we crossed the burned plains of Drum, miring the beasts to their noses, unpacking and dragging them out by their fore-legs. At last we came to a river heading into the big glacier that filled the amphitheatre on the south face of Mt. Drum, followed it up to tree line, and camped.

"Let's climb Drum," said Jack, that

The Summit of Mt. Wrangell, Alaska's Live Volcano.

night. "Maybe we can see if there is a Mt. Tillman or not from the top." The left-hand wall of the peak seemed to give a continuous ridge to the summit, but it was badly corniced and looked perpendicular in places. We started on foot, leaving the horses at camp, and packed four days' grub and our cameras eight miles up the gravel-covered ice. As it wound into the mountain, the glacier was splashed with scarlet and purple, and held bluish ponds in cone-shaped basins; and it sent one crinkled arm to a basin of steely ice upon a sheer peak, sharp as the Matterhorn; another to a tower of violet snow blocks. At last it all hung upon the lace-white walls. We packed over a cross-ridge, and made camp deep in the bowels of the mountain.

Down there, in what we called the dead crater of Mt. Drum — for that the eroded pit may once have been — I made these unpleasant notes on a photograph film wrapper:

August 8th — Packed firewood up to camp 2 on Drum. To-night, at the bottom of a fis-

sure in this lava mountain. We have dug out boulders for a place to sleep in. We must shout to be heard above the roar of the torrent. Jack seems depressed. He says we can never get up the arête. The gloom is ghastly.

August 9th — Not a wink all night. Oh how we ache! It is dark, windy, with an icy drizzle. Jack still depressed. Sometimes I think he is out of his head. He sits around, shivers, hides his face. I'm depressed, too. We avoid each other.

(Later) — After a lot of talk Jack has left me. I don't know what he said. He went suddenly. He climbed over the wall of the pit with the sleeping bag.

So, all alone, I wandered up into cloud and snow among the scarlet pinnacles, over another ridge into the farthest corner of the crater, by a heap of rose-colored ice, and the paths of a last night's avalanche. Then I, too, climbed out of the pit and down for miles again into the world. I found Jack by the horses. He had come to, and was starting back to find me.

The next day the gray horse grew another tumor, which delayed us till August 12th, when we kept on east across the southern slopes of Mt. Drum, toward the big mountain seen from the Coast Range and Copper Centre. We dragged the horses up through strangling brush out of the valley, and camped between two gnarled spruces by a pond. Northeast the great peak appeared over our treeless slopes. We saw no steam. That night the glacial stream far below caught the sunset and turned to veins of blood. Drum's red lava, sugared with snow, shone like chased gold. Out over Copper River Valley Tazlina Lake gleamed in a stream of fire, and beyond the coast range rose dim and greenish, guarding the sea beneath a sky of brass. We were beyond all trails, beyond where men had been.

How we made sure that Mt. Tillman positively does not exist where it is mapped my diary for this day tells:

August 12th — To-night is absolutely clear. We have studied Allen's map and taken compass directions. Did Tillman exist where he has mapped it, we should now be between it and Drum, actually upon Tillman's northern slopes. Drum is due north, and due south of us, where Tillman should be, the country is absolutely flat for fifty miles, to the Coast Range. There can be no doubt of this. One thing is cer-

tain, we have wiped a 16,600-foot mountain from the position where it has been accepted to lie for fifteen years. Jack says we have done a geographical stunt.

The entry for August 14 tells how we found Allen did not reduplicate Wrangell, as we then supposed, to make his Tillman.

August 14— At five o'clock it cleared. Straight up the valley, towered the Mt. Sanford of Allen's map, its whole southern face a sheer precipice. It lay almost due north. Drum is now northwest of us, the big mountain northeast. We have found that no mountain lies where Tillman is mapped. Now, the *outline sketch of Mt. Tillman is identical with the sky-line of the mountain we can see up this valley,* which lies *exactly where the map has placed Mt. Sanford.*

So Allen reduplicated, not the great mountain northeast of us — which, therefore, is Wrangell — but the peak we see due north up this valley. Tillman and Wrangell, then, are not the same, but Tillman and Sanford are*

On August 15th we floundered through the river quicksands for eight miles or more, and strung our tarpaulins for camp on the Drum side of the valley, in a clump of cottonwoods

*Careful study proves this correct. Full explanation of the reason for the triple disagreement of Allen's outlines, maps, and existing conditions I have worked out, and it is too complicated to detail. It is clear that what Allen called Santford on his map, he first named Tillman.

" We scooped the horses off a gravel bar into Copper River, and stoned them across."

at tree-line. Then, tired as we were, we kept on a-foot up the stream which we could see came from a glacier, falling in a mighty serac from the great mountain. We climbed its ice fall, 2,000 feet high, and crept along an undercut ledge in the pulpit-like cliff high over it. A sudden storm broke over us, and we shivered alone in the gloom high over the northern world as slides roared in the distance, and the glacier-ice groaned, and we caught the smell of brimstone.

From this day's diary:

Jack is cooking a pie of red berries that grow on a kind of strawberry vine. We have eaten two toadstools and are waiting for results. Jack says the gray horse's swelling is coming to a head, and that the sorrel is spavined. It's a big job three times a day poulticing horse sores with hot rags, then washing with corrosive, then smearing on vaseline, *then* bacon-grease.

August 16th—Fifth day of rain. My birthday. This morning the gray beast's abscess broke. Later it cleared, and again we climbed the serac. This time the blizzard broke in snow. We lay beside the hoofs and skeleton of a mountain lamb. Soon came the ptarmigan — flocks of them — driven from the heights, shrieking what sounds like "Fire! Fire!" How white and graceful they were, how gently they fell, like forms of snow!

August 17th — Sixth day of rain. Among the moraines we found bear prints ten inches long. Weird tales are told of Alaskan bears — of the fierce St. Elias beast, of Kadiak bears as big as horses, of terrible blue-nosed glacier bears. Plainly he thinks he owns this valley. We stalked him — and he still owns the valley.

Our Hudson's Bay knife is put to queer uses. It cuts bacon, tobacco, and my toe-nails; lets pus from the gray's abscess, halves pie-crusts, digs bannock-holes, chops wood, and turns pancakes. We ate two pies to-day — blueberry and currant. Jack says this high living will give us gout.

August 18th — Seventh day of rain. Will it never clear? Are we never to see the huge sloping summit of Wrangell again?

The tusk-like spur over the glacier which we saw from Copper Centre we've named Zanetti's peak—after the Count.* Jack says it's appropriate to name part of a volcano after a Spaniard — though the Count's a Cuban.

August 20th — Clear! Our day at last. To-day it is, "See those high Wrangell snow-fields smoke — or quit."

The sun scarce stood above Zanetti Peak, colorless, as we started up the old ice-fall. From the top we could look in along the level

*Some one we knew at college, not really a count.

glacier, and then eastward up the illimitable snow-fields of Wrangell, folded, foreshortened on the high sky line. Then an orange ring circled the sun. Storm! But we steered out into the middle of the glacier, keeping straight on, zig-zagging among crevasses, creeping across ice-bridges where the roar of streams issued faintly from the depths. It was hot, like an April day on a New England pond, and cone-shaped heaps of morainal sand wasted over the wet ice.

At ten o'clock we could see the "smoke" of blizzards. That settled our day. When men see that on Valdes Glacier, they creep under their sleds for days — or forever. Climb Wrangell? "It's twenty miles if it's an inch over those snowfields. Let's not be d—d fools, Bobbie," said Jack. Jack was right. What knew we of snow-climbing? We had no tinned grub, no alcohol. And then I thought of Israel C. Russell, and his fruitless years on St. Elias. Wrangell is all Greenland beside St. Elias.

We said we'd see how high we could get to-day. We started north across the snowy plateau of overlapped lava ridges. By noon we had reached the base of a steep-faced dome. We shinned straight up the lava needles, grasped their tops, let ourselves down blindly on the other side. We weren't roped. How we did it, I don't know, but there's no such thing as danger when the fret for great heights is in the blood. Digging foot-holes in the lava, hugging the needles, swinging by our arms from ledge to ledge, we scaled at last up a rock chimney, to a lofty place where it was bare and flat.

We lit our pipes. The wind was bellowing through the pinnacles. It was beginning to rain. We smoked on — alone. Alas! Hidden were the endless snows piled up beyond Zanetti. How could we tell if Wrangell smoked, since its summit was invisible?

And then the storm veiled all, and we groped down to the talus, its ponds and sandy creeks; and in the dark all but pitched over its edge with the stream we followed, reached the valley of strange boulders, passed the river boiling from its glacier, crept under our tarpaulin. We hadn't seen Wrangell steam; we'd failed.

All the next morning, as we chopped spongy cottonwood, blew out our lungs over the fire, and flipped water from the blankets, a dull roar, which we thought the river

"An Indian passed down stream in a stick canoe."

swelled by the rain, was growing louder, louder. I said, "I guess a moraine-choked pond on the glacier has broken through," and just then Jack stepped out from under the soaked tarpaulin.

"Look at that, Bobbie, look at that!" I heard him shouting. Outside, he was pointing across the stream. A landslide was roaring down a gulley from the very top of the Rainbow Hills. It was a stupendous sight. We looked at it silently, and then said both at once, "I thought an avalanche was sudden." This thing wriggled like a huge snake down a sheer three thousand feet of rock. The roar seemed forever to increase. Dust—or smoke—trailed from this thing, and enormous boulders skipped solemnly from side to side of its path like pebbles. Water mingled with it, and when it reached the terrace, it was a black stream, viscous and heavy.

Jack bet it wouldn't cross the half mile of flat to the river. But in a moment we saw boulders shooting out over the terrace, and aspen groves fall as if laid with a scythe. A cancerous fan ate out to the bank, and gravely slopped over like lumpy paint, cutting deep channels down to the river. This lasted twenty minutes, when behold! down the talus on the Drum side, our side of the valley, and right behind camp, burst another avalanche.

The diary for this day says:

August 21st—The roar of slides is incessant, increasing, and now it is dark. Cataracts have been twisting straight down from the talus right overhead. It's a fearful sight. When I went out for water a minute ago, I found our stream had dried in its bed. That means one thing—a slide is coming down our ravine. We keep our eyes fixed on the cottonwoods, and if we see them wavering, are ready to move to the morainal hills. We're sleepy, and if we drop off—well—

August 22d—"Hello," said Jack this morning from his blanket bag, "We're here, eh?" And our stream had come back, too.

By the time the beanpot was boiling to-day, and the currant pie crust was brown, a queer blue was reflected by the glacier in the sky over Wrangell, and the Ravine of Needles suddenly lit up with golden light.

We started to climb back over the spurs of Drum. As we went up, up, up, Zanetti Peak and the great snow fields seemed to grow higher, higher, higher. At last they topped Mt. Tillman. We went far back over the lava talus. Yes, certainly, there towered Wrangell, across our valley — the same big mountain we'd seen from Copper Centre. There couldn't be any doubt of it, no doubt but that from the valley and its own slopes we'd seen Wrangell much foreshortened. Then, all of a sudden, as we were getting out our cameras, from the left of a little nubble in the middle of the great snow slope rose a little black wall of vapor. *Steam—there could be no doubt of that, either.* There wasn't a cloud in the sky, and we were so near, so very near. It seemed like a tiny thunder-cloud. It rose, and in a second, vanished; and then — rose another, and another, and another. They came at about minute intervals. We watched them, fascinated. We laughed, we hugged ourselves. We lit our pipes to old Wrangell. We'd won.

We left the valley next day as we had entered it, and got back to Copper Centre. I started alone on September 27th for Forty Mile on the Yukon, a five-hundred-mile journey, on which I didn't see a white man for fifteen days, and my one horse petered out, when I had to guess the way every time the snow-covered trail forked, and live on Siwash charity—moose tallow and cranberries—and swim rivers in zero weather, with all I owned in the world packed on a white wolf-dog I bought for seven dollars and a razor — it was then that I saw what looked mightily like an eruption of Mt. Wrangell. On October 3, when I was north of the Wrangell group, following up Slahna River from the Copper to Mentasta Pass in the Alaskan range, a black column rose from the summit of Wrangell, pierced a layer of cloud, and bulged into a huge mushroom-shaped thing over all. The next morning the whole mountain was black.

When we left the States in 1900 we had no way of being sure Wrangell was active. But the matter had then been settled. Mr. Oscar Rohn, Lieut. W. C. Babcock, 8th United States Cavalry, and others in Copper River Valley, in 1899, saw Wrangell steaming from a distance, were convinced it was active, and reported it so to the Government. In June, 1900, these reports had not been published. The same men in 1899 noted the absence of the so-called Mt. Tillman.

25
Matters in Alaska

Matters in Alaska

By A. G. KINGSBURY

Nome, Alaska, August 5, 1905.

BI-CENTENNIALS and centennials have become common in the United States, but in these rapid days there are some people who cannot wait for even half a hundred years before they want to organize a ceebration. The latest development of taking time by the forelock, indeed of reaching for his whole scalp, is seen in a plan which is already fairly under way for an Exposition to celebrate the fortieth anniversary of the acquisition of Alaska by the United States, which occurs in 1907. Eastern people, who naturally have but little idea of the rapidity of "the march of progress" in this unpromising section of the world where natural conditions are especially unfavorable for material development, will perhaps rub their eyes when they read such an announcement, but a second look will convince them of the fact.

Another surprise comes in the announcement that the plan for the celebration of the acquisition of Alaska contemplates the location of the affair outside the territorial limits directly concerned. The Alaska Club of Seattle, Washington, is sponsor for the enterprise, and the celebration is under arrangement in that city. Alaska is a country of such magnificent distances, and its conspicuous business centres are so widely scattered, that while there is "room enough" in the territory there is no centre available. The narrow coast-strip along the Canadian border in the southern section, of which Juneau and Skagway are the leading points, the vast area about the upper waters of the Yukon and the Tanana rivers, and the Seward Peninsula with Nome as its heart, might each aspire to the honor of a local celebration, but they are far, far apart, and with no means of extensive intercommunication, while all three districts have their best outlet and inlet through Seattle, which while geographically an outsider is. practically the only available location for a general assembly of Alaskan products.

Mr. Godfrey Chealander, of Skagway is credited with the original conception of the idea, and he has so stimulated the patriotism of the Alaskans in Seattle that they have taken hold with the energy and enthusiasm which is characteristic of this twentieth century. He is now on a tour which will cover the upper Yukon and the Tanana, and down the former river to the Seward Peninsula and Nome, to secure cooperation of the various mining, trading and transportation companies, and to collect material illustrating the resources and the present development of the country.

In my letter in the August number of the New England Magazine I told in outline the prospects of tin mining in Alaska. This spring's developments fully justify my conception of the importance of this new mineral wealth of the peninsula. A group of tin placer claims covering over two thousand acres in the York region of Seward Peninsula where the first discoveries were made, has just been bonded to an English syndicate for $5,000,000, and other smaller but important enterprises in this line are also under way. Discoveries of gold in this tin district are quite frequent and several very promising ventures are under way. The competition of tin and gold for popular interest here promises to be quite a prominent factor in the development of the near future.

The Congresional party headed by Speaker Cannon, which came to the Pacific coast for the opening of the Portland, Oregon, Exposition extended their trip to southern Alaska, visiting Juneau, Skagway, and several other interesting points. They did not come so far north as Nome, nor did they get a glimpse of the Yukon district, and their area of observation was accordingly greatly limited. They might as well "observe" the Atlantic states by a brief stop on Long Island. They were evidently impressed by this fact, for, while they were dignified and reticent in expressions of opinion there was manifest a sentiment that the country deserves well of the general government, and that they would favor the sending of a special committee next season to make an exhaustive inspection of the territory. Congressional aid, for the construction of the harbors and docks, and for highways, is considered necessary and equitable by all the people here, and if such a committee should come it will be generously enlightened.

A new wrinkle in the Alaskan salmon fishery has been inaugurated. An enterprising Minneapolis merchant has contracted to deliver two thousand and four hundred tons of salmon to parties in Japan, and to save the expense of canning he has secured an ocean tug and a ship in which he proposes to pack the fish with a moderate quantity of salt, "just like cord-wood." The fish are not yet caught, but their fate is certain, for, if reports are true the purchaser has so much faith in the new venture that he has adavnced a considerable portion of the purchase money. To get the fish is easy; to get them to Japan by the new method—well, that's another story.

That the authorities here have full faith in the permanence of Nome as a commercial point is shown by their plan, already under way, for the improvement of the harbor. Up to the present time all shipping has to anchor a mile or two from shore, and all freight is lightered through the shallow water. Half a million dollars is already in hand with which to begin the work of dredging and the construction of jetties and piers. A ship channel two thousand feet long will thus be secured, and commerce will be greatly facilitated thereby. This work is understood to be only the initial enterprise, the full scheme, which will take years to complete, contemplating much more extended dredging and construction.

A considerable delay in the work of the open season will follow a terrific storm which covered this district the last week in June. Heavy rains fell for several days, and much of the work on the numerous water-courses in this district—bridges, dams, sluice-boxes, etc.,—will have to be replaced, before advanced work can be begun. Thousands of dollars worth of construction and machinery has gone down stream, and a larger sum will be lost through the delay of reconstruction before the real work of the season, all too short at the best, can be resumed.

Water courses are abundant all through Alaska and the Klondike region, and in the short summer season there is little difficulty in securing adequate supply for sluicing and other mining purposes, but winter work is sadly handicapped because all surface water is hopelessly congealed. Nome people are therefore watching with much interest the progress of an experiment now going on at Dawson, to find a water supply from below the frost line, by artesian wells. Eastern people, who are annoyed when their water-mains, four feet under ground, are frozen in winter, can hardly appreciate the conditions when a bore of one hundred and eighty feet in depth is still in frozen earth and rock, and no indication that anything else is farther down. This is, however, the condition at Dawson. The projectors of the enterprise have already expended about three thousand dollars, and are prepared with machinery to go to the depth of five hundred feet if necessary. After going through about sixty feet of alluvial and glacial drift, the drill encountered solid mica schist rock, which with the exception of two belts, each of about three feet in depth, of iron and sulphurets has proved continuous to the present depth of the well. If they ever get through the frost and strike a fissure in the rock containing water, similar enterprises will be in order here.

There was considerable excitement and wrath here, just before the close of navigation last fall, by a combination of the steamship lines to Seattle to raise passenger rates from fifty dollars to one hundred dollars for the trip. The matter went to the courts and was declared to be a violation of the inter-state commerce law by an unlawful "trust." The companies receded from their position, and rates are back again at the old figure. Now the same companies have doubled their charges for the transportation of gold, and there is another excitement but a similar result to that in the raise in passenger rates is looked for, as soon as the question can be adjudicated. Meanwhile there is considerable uneasiness among the producers, as the banks cannot advance on shipmeats until the cost of transportation is settled.

When the mine owners started in to clean up their winter dumps, early in April, the banks agreed to accept the gold dust at the same low margin that they had always taken it. This they did under the belief that the rate of transporting it to Seattle would be the same as in former years. Although the cable was in working order, no advices were received in Nome during the spring of the advanced rate. In fact, not until the first boats arrived, about the middle of June, did they know of the raise.

One man who left on the steamer due at Seattle June 27th, ignored the transportation company and packed $400,000 in his state-room rather than pay the exorbitant charges. He took a risk, but I hear that he landed his "baggage" at Seattle all right.

The situation became so serious here that the Nome Chamber of Commerce took up the matter in the interests of the miners and mine owners, and sent a delegate to interview the steamship companies at Seattle, with a view to having the old rate of one-eighth of one per cent. re-established. Although every pressure available was brought to bear, they were unable to break the combination. The companies stated that they were bound by an agreement to enforce the increased rate on gold shipped out. This action is a great injustice to the mining and commercial interests of the camp, and the people generally at Nome feel justly indignant. At this time it is hard to predict what the outcome will be if the steamship companies refuse to recognize the rights of the people. One thing is certain, however, and that is that Seattle will be the loser, although the city itself is undoubtedly an innocent party in the transaction, for the steamers direct to San Francisco will get the business.

The first steamer from Nome, due at Seattle July 10, carried about a third of the winter's output of gold from this district. It was in rough bars and was valued at $1,250,000. Such a "pile" displayed in the window of a Seattle banking house was well calculated to excite the wonder and ambition of the hundreds who were there securing outfits for the season's work in this district. The "pile" was the outcome of the winter work by Nels Peterson, who, with two associates, secured a "lay" or privelege of working the claim of the Pioneer Mining Company on the Portland Bench, a short distance back of Nome, with five assistants and a cook. The company was astounded at the result, but their "rake off" of forty per cent. with no expenses, is not so bad. Besides, they have the assurance, from this result under the difficulties of winter work, that with the opening of the season work under their own auspices will give a profitable return.

Mr. Peterson's experience is the typical one of this country. He was one of the pioneers in the Klondike region and made a fortune near Dawson. Then he was attracted to transportation on the Yukon river, and inaugurated a big enterprise, which proved disastrous and he was reduced to poverty. He has "made good" again, however, and is ready for other ventures.

The richness of the Portland Bench district is further illustrated by the luck of "Joe" Brown, last winter, on a claim adjoining that of the Pioneer Company. In a single day's work of twelve hours he cleaned up $15,000.

Later shipments to Seattle, as the result of the winter in Alaska swell the total to $2,786,000, including a $25,000 "brick" destined for the Portland, Oregon, Exposition . This winter output has given a great impetus to plans for next winter's mining, and the indication are that especially in the Little Creek district where rich deposits are so fully demonstrated, the Arctic winter will not be an insuperable obstacle to systematic work. Extensive ditch excavation in this district is well under way, and the wise ones are eager to secure claims, while the gossips are already forecasting the results of this summer's work. Already "sluicing" has begun, and the steamer "Senator," which sailed from here for Seattle, June 14th, took $400,000 as the first instalment of this season's harvest. Water is not yet plenty and the work is hindered, but every one is confident of an exceptionally successful summer's work.

26
The Sun-dog Trail

The Sun-dog Trail

BY JACK LONDON

SITKA CHARLEY smoked his pipe and gazed thoughtfully at the newspaper illustration on the wall. For half an hour he had been steadily regarding it, and for half an hour I had been slyly watching him. Something was going on in that mind of his, and, whatever it was, I knew it was well worth knowing. He had lived life, and seen things, and performed that prodigy of prodigies, namely, the turning of his back upon his own people, and, in so far as it was possible for an Indian, becoming a white man even in his mental processes. As he phrased it himself, he had come into the warm, sat among us, by our fires, and become one of us.

We had struck this deserted cabin after a hard day on trail. The dogs had been fed, the supper dishes washed, the beds made, and we were now enjoying that most delicious hour that comes each day, on the Alaskan trail, when nothing intervenes between the tired body and bed save the smoking of the evening pipe.

"Well?" I finally broke the silence.

He took the pipe from his mouth and said, simply, "I do not understand."

He smoked on again, and again removed the pipe, using it to point at the illustration.

"That picture—what does it mean? I do not understand."

I looked at the picture. A man, with a preposterously wicked face, his right hand pressed dramatically to his heart, was falling backward to the floor. Confronting him, with a face that was a composite of destroying angel and Adonis, was a man holding a smoking revolver.

"One man is killing the other man," I said, aware of a distinct bepuzzlement of my own and of failure to explain.

"Why?" asked Sitka Charley.

"I do not know," I confessed.

"That picture is all end," he said. "It has no beginning."

"It is life," I said.

"Life has beginning," he objected.

"Look at that picture," I commanded, pointing to another decoration. "It means something. Tell me what it means to you."

He studied it for several minutes.

"The little girl is sick," he said, finally. "That is the doctor looking at her. They have been up all night—see, the oil is low in the lamp, the first morning light is coming in at the window. It is a great sickness; maybe she will die; that is why the doctor looks so hard. That is the mother. It is a great sickness, because the mother's head is on the table and she is crying."

"And now you understand the picture," I cried.

He shook his head, and asked, "The little girl—does it die?"

It was my turn for silence.

"Does it die?" he reiterated. "You are a painter-man. Maybe you know."

"No, I do not know," I confessed.

"It is not life," he delivered himself, dogmatically. "In life little girl die or get well. Something happen in life. In picture nothing happen. No, I do not understand pictures."

"Pictures are bits of life," I said. "We paint life as we see it. For instance, Charley, you are coming along the trail. It is night. You see a cabin. The window is lighted. You look through the window for one second, or for two seconds; you see something, and you go on your way. You see maybe a man writing a letter. You saw something without beginning or end. Nothing happened. Yet it was a bit of life you saw. You remember it afterward. It is like a picture in your memory. The window is the frame of the picture."

For a long time he smoked in silence. He nodded his head several times, and grunted once or twice. Then he knocked the ashes from his pipe, carefully refilled it, and, after a thoughtful pause, he lighted it again.

"Then have I, too, seen many pictures of life," he began; "pictures not painted but seen with the eyes. I have looked at them like through the window at the man writing the letter. I have seen many pieces of life, without beginning, without end, without understanding."

With a sudden change of position he turned his eyes full upon me and regarded me thoughtfully.

"Look you," he said; "you are a painter-man. How would you paint this which I saw, a picture without beginning, the ending of which I do not understand, a piece of life with the northern lights for a candle and Alaska for a frame?"

"It is a large canvas," I murmured.

"There are many names for this picture," he said. "But in the picture there are many sun-dogs, and it comes into my mind to call it 'The Sun-dog Trail.' It was seven years ago, the fall of '97, when I saw the woman first time. At Lake Linderman I had one canoe. I came over Chilcoot Pass with two thousand letters for Dawson. Everybody rush to Klondike at that time. Many people on trail. Many people chop down trees and make boats. Last water, snow in the air, snow on the ground, ice on the lake, on the river. Every day more snow, more ice, any day maybe freeze-up come; then no more water, all ice, everybody walk; Dawson six hundred miles; long time walk. Boat go very quick. Everybody want to go boat. Everybody say, 'Charley, two hundred dollars you take me in canoe,' 'Charley, three hundred dollars,' 'Charley, four hundred dollars.' I say no; all the time I say no. I am letter-carrier.

"In the morning I get to Lake Linderman; I walk all night and am much tired. I cook breakfast, I eat, then I sleep on the beach three hours. I wake up. It is ten o'clock. Snow is falling. There is wind, much wind that blows fair. Also, there is a woman who sits in the snow alongside. She is white woman, she is young, very pretty; maybe she is twenty years old, maybe twenty-five years old. She look at me. I look at her. She is very tired. She is no dance-woman. I see that right away. She is good woman, and she is very tired.

"'You are Sitka Charley,' she says. 'I go to Dawson,' she says. 'I go in your canoe—how much?'

"I do not want anybody in my canoe. I do not like to say no. So I say, 'One thousand dollars.' She look at me very hard, then she says, 'When you start?' I say right away. Then she says all right, she will give me one thousand dollars.

"What can I say? I do not want the woman, yet have I given my word that for one thousand dollars she can come. And that woman, that young woman, all alone on the trail, there in the snow, she take out one thousand dollars in greenbacks, and she put them in my hand. I look at money, I look at her. What can I say? I say: 'No; my canoe very small. There is no room for outfit.' She laugh. She says: 'I am great traveller. This is my outfit.' She kick one small pack in the snow. It is two fur robes, canvas outside, some woman's clothes inside. I pick it up. Maybe thirty-five pounds. I am surprised. She take it away from me. She says, 'Come, let us start.' She carries pack into canoe. What can I say? I put my blankets into canoe. We start.

"And that is the way I saw the woman first time. The wind was fair. I put up small sail. The canoe went very fast. The woman was much afraid. 'What for you come Klondike much afraid?' I ask. She laugh at me, a hard laugh, but she is still much afraid. Also she is very tired. I run canoe through rapids to Lake Bennett. Water very bad, and woman cry out because she is afraid. We go down Lake Bennett. Snow, ice, wind like a gale, but woman is very tired and go to sleep.

"That night we make camp at Windy Arm. Woman sit by fire and eat supper. I look at her. She is pretty. She fix hair. There is much hair, and it is brown; also sometimes it is like gold in the firelight when she turn her head, so, and flashes come from it like golden fire. The eyes are large and brown. When she smile—how can I say?—when she smile I know white man like to kiss her, just like that, when she smile. She never do hard work. Her hands are soft like a baby's hand. She is not thin, but round like a baby; her arm, her leg, her

"'I GO TO DAWSON IN YOUR CANOE,' SHE SAYS"

muscles, all soft and round like baby. Her waist is small, and when she stand up, when she walk, or move her head or arm, it is—I do not know the word—but it is nice to look at, like—maybe I say she is built on lines like the lines of a good canoe, just like that,—and when she move she is like the movement of the good canoe sliding through still water or leaping through water when it is white and fast and angry. It is very good to see.

"I ask her what is her name. She laugh, then she says, 'Mary Jones; that is my name.' But I know all the time that Mary Jones is not her name.

"It is very cold in canoe, and because of cold sometimes she not feel good. Sometimes she feel good and she sing. Her voice is like a silver bell, and I feel good all over like when I go into church at Holy Cross Mission, and when she sing I feel strong and paddle like hell. Then she laugh and says, 'You think we get to Dawson before freeze-up, Charley?' Sometimes she sit in canoe and is thinking far away, her eyes like that, all empty. She does not see Sitka Charley, nor the ice, nor the snow. She is far away. Sometimes, when she is thinking far away, her face is not good to see. It looks like a face that is angry, like the face of one man when he want to kill another man.

"Last day to Dawson very bad. Shore-ice in all the eddies, mush-ice in the stream. I cannot paddle. The canoe freeze to ice. All the time we go down Yukon in the ice. Then ice stop, canoe stop, everything stop. 'Let us go to shore,' the woman says. I say no; better wait. By and by everything start down-stream again. At eleven o'clock at night everything stop. At one o'clock everything start again. At three o'clock everything stop. Canoe is smashed like egg-shell, but it is on top of ice and cannot sink. I hear dogs howling. We wait; we sleep. By and by morning come. There is no more snow. It is the freeze-up, and there is Dawson. Canoe smash and stop right at Dawson. Sitka Charley has come in with two thousand letters on very last water.

"The woman rent a cabin on the hill, and for one week I see her no more.

Then, one day, she come to me. 'Charley,' she says, 'how do you like to work for me? You drive dogs, make camp, travel with me.' I say that I make too much money carrying letters. She says, 'Charley, I will pay you more money.' I tell her that pick-and-shovel man get fifteen dollars a day in the mines. She says, 'That is four hundred and fifty dollars a month.' And I say, 'Sitka Charley is no pick-and-shovel man.' Then she says: 'I understand, Charley. I will give you seven hundred and fifty dollars each month.' It is a good price, and I go to work for her. I buy for her dogs and sled. We travel up Klondike, up Bonanza and Eldorado, over to Indian River, to Sulphur Creek, to Dominion, back across divide to Gold Bottom and to Too Much Gold, and back to Dawson. All the time she look for something; I do not know what.

"She has a small revolver, which she carries in her belt. Sometimes, on trail, she makes practice with revolver.

"At Dawson comes the man. Which way he come I do not know. Only do I know he is che-cha-quo—what you call tenderfoot. His hands are soft. He never do hard work. At first I think maybe he is her husband. But he is too young. He is maybe twenty years old. His eyes blue, his hair yellow; he has a little mustache which is yellow. His name is John Jones. Maybe he is her brother. I do not know.

"One night I am asleep at Dawson. He wake me up. He says, 'Get the dogs ready; we start.' No more do I ask questions, so I get the dogs ready and we start. We go down the Yukon. It is night-time, it is November, and it is very cold—sixty-five below. She is soft. He is soft. The cold bites. They get tired. They cry under their breaths to themselves. By and by I say better we stop and make camp. But they say that they will go on. After that I say nothing. All the time, day after day, it is that way. They are very soft. They get stiff and sore. They do not understand moccasins, and their feet hurt very much. They limp, they stagger like drunken people, they cry under their breaths; and all the time they say: 'On! on! We will go on!'

"We make Circle City. That for

which they look is not there. I think now that we will rest, and rest the dogs. But we do not rest; not for one day do we rest. 'Come,' says the woman to the man, 'let us go on.' And we go on. We leave the Yukon. We cross the divide to the west and swing down into the Tanana Country. There are new diggings there. But that for which they look is not there, and we take the back trail to Circle City.

"It is a hard journey. December is 'most gone. The days are short. It is very cold.

"We limp into Circle City. It is Christmas eve. I dance, drink, make a good time, for to-morrow is Christmas day and we will rest. But no. It is five o'clock in the morning—Christmas morning. I am two hours asleep. The man stand by my bed. 'Come, Charley,' he says; 'harness the dogs. We start.' I harness the dogs, and we start down the Yukon.

"They are very weary. They have travelled many hundreds of miles, and they do not understand the way of the trail. Besides, their cough is very bad—the dry cough that makes strong men swear and weak men cry. Every day they go on. Never do they rest the dogs. Always do they buy new dogs. At every camp, at every post, at every Indian village, do they cut out the tired dogs and put in fresh dogs. They have much money, money without end, and like water they spend it. They are crazy? Sometimes I think so, for there is a devil in them that drives them. They cry aloud in their sleep at night. And in the day, as they stagger along the trail, they cry under their breaths.

"We pass Fort Yukon. We pass Fort Hamilton. We pass Minook. January has come and nearly gone. The days are very short. At nine o'clock comes daylight. At three o'clock comes night. And it is cold. And even I, Sitka Charley, am tired. Will we go on forever this way without end? I do not know. But always do I look along the trail for that which they try to find. There are few people on the trail. Sometimes we travel one hundred miles and never see a sign of life. The northern lights flame in the sky, and the sun-dogs dance, and the air is filled with frost-dust.

"I am Sitka Charley, a strong man. I was born on the trail, and all my days have I lived on the trail. And yet have these two baby wolves made me tired. Their eyes are sunk deep in their heads, bright sometimes as with fever, dim and cloudy sometimes like the eyes of the dead. Their cheeks are black and raw from many freezings. Sometimes it is the woman in the morning who says: 'I cannot get up. I cannot move. Let me die.' And it is the man who stands beside her and says, 'Come, let us go on.'

"Sometimes, at the trading-posts, the man and woman get letters. I do not know what is in the letters. But it is the scent that they follow; these letters themselves are the scent. One time an Indian gives them a letter. I talk with him privately. He says it is a man with one eye who gives him the letter—a man who travels fast down the Yukon. That is all. But I know that the baby wolves are after the man with the one eye.

"It is February, and we have travelled fifteen hundred miles. We are getting near Bering Sea, and there are storms and blizzards. The going is hard. We come to Anvig. I do not know, but I think sure they get a letter at Anvig, for they are much excited, and they say, 'Come, hurry; let us go on.' But I say we must buy grub, and they say we must travel light and fast. Also, they say that we can get grub at Charley McKeon's cabin. Then do I know that they take the big cut-off, for it is there that Charley McKeon lives where the Black Rock stands by the trail.

"Before we start I talk maybe two minutes with the priest at Anvig. Yes, there is a man with one eye who has gone by and who travels fast. And I know that for which they look is the man with the one eye. We leave Anvig with little grub, and travel light and fast. We take the big cut-off, and the trail is fresh. The baby wolves have their noses down to the trail, and they say, 'Hurry!' All the time do they say: 'Hurry! Faster! Faster!' It is hard on the dogs. We have not much food and we cannot give them enough to eat, and they grow weak. Also, they must work hard. The woman has true sorrow for them, and often, because of them, the tears are in her eyes. But the devil in her that drives her on will not let her stop and rest the dogs.

"And then we come upon the man with the one eye. He is in the snow by the trail and his leg is broken. Because of the leg he has made a poor camp, and has been lying on his blankets for three days and keeping a fire going. When we find him he is swearing. Never have I heard a man swear like that man. I am glad. Now that they have found that for which they look, we will have a rest. But the woman says: 'Let us start. Hurry!'

"I am surprised. But the man with the one eye says: 'Never mind me. Give me your grub. You will get more grub at McKeon's cabin to-morrow. Send McKeon back for me. But do you go on.' So we give him our grub, which is not much, and we chop wood for his fire, and we take his strongest dogs and go on. We left the man with one eye there in the snow, and he died there in the snow, for McKeon never went back for him.

"That day and that night we had nothing to eat, and all next day we travelled fast, and we were weak with hunger. Then we came to the Black Rock, which rose five hundred feet above the trail. It was at the end of the day. Darkness was coming, and we could not find the cabin of McKeon. We slept hungry, and in the morning looked for the cabin. It was not there, which was a strange thing, for everybody knew that McKeon lived in a cabin at Black Rock. We were near to the coast, where the wind blows hard and there is much snow. Everywhere were there small hills of snow where the wind had piled it up. I have a thought, and I dig in one and another of the hills of snow. Soon I find the walls of the cabin, and I dig down to the door. I go inside. McKeon is dead. Maybe two or three weeks he is dead. A sickness had come upon him so that he could not leave the cabin. He had eaten his grub and died. I looked for his cache, but there was no grub in it.

"'Let us go on,' said the woman. Her eyes were hungry, and her hand was upon her heart, as with the hurt of something inside. She swayed back and forth like a tree in the wind as she stood there.

"'Yes, let us go on,' said the man. His voice was hollow, like the *klonk* of an old raven, and he was hunger-mad. His eyes were like live coals of fire, and as his body rocked to and fro, so rocked his soul inside. And I, too, said, 'Let us go on.' For that one thought, laid upon me like a lash for every mile of fifteen hundred miles, had burned itself into my soul, and I think that I, too, was mad. Besides, we could only go on, for there was no grub. And we went on, giving no thought to the man with the one eye in the snow.

"The snow had covered the trail, and there was no sign that men had ever come or gone that way. All day the wind blew and the snow fell, and all day we travelled. Then the woman began to fall. Then the man. I did not fall, but my feet were heavy, and I caught my toes and stumbled many times.

"That night is the end of February. I kill three ptarmigan with the woman's revolver, and we are made somewhat strong again. But the dogs have nothing to eat. They try to eat their harness, which is of leather and walrus-hide, and I must fight them off with a club and hang all the harness in a tree. And all night they howl and fight around that tree. But we do not mind. We sleep like dead people, and in the morning get up like dead people out of our graves and go on along the trail.

"That morning is the 1st of March, and on that morning I see the first sign of that after which the baby wolves are in search. It is clear weather, and cold. The sun stay longer in the sky, and there are sun-dogs flashing on either side, and the air is bright with frost-dust. The snow falls no more upon the trail, and I see the fresh sign of dogs and sled. There is one man with that outfit, and I see in the snow that he is not strong. He, too, has not enough to eat. The young wolves see the fresh sign, too, and they are much excited. 'Hurry!' they say. All the time they say: 'Hurry! Faster, Charley, faster!'

"We make hurry very slow. All the time the man and the woman fall down. When they try to ride on sled, the dogs are too weak, and the dogs fall down. Besides, it is so cold that if they ride on the sled they will freeze. It is very easy for a hungry man to freeze. When the woman fall down, the man help her up. Sometimes the woman help the man up. By and by both fall down and cannot get up, and I must help them up all the time, else they will not get up and will die there in the snow. This is very hard work, for I am greatly weary, and as well I must drive the dogs, and the man and woman are very heavy, with no strength in their bodies. So, by and by, I, too, fall down in the snow, and there is no one to help me up. I must get up by myself. And always do I get up by myself, and help them up, and make the dogs go on.

"That night I get one ptarmigan, and we are very hungry. And that night the man says to me, 'What time start to-morrow, Charley?' It is like the voice of a ghost. I say, 'All the time you make start at five o'clock.' 'To-morrow,' he says, 'we will start at three o'clock.'

"And we start at three o'clock. It is clear and cold, and there is no wind. When daylight comes we can see a long way off. And it is very quiet. We can hear no sound but the beat of our hearts, and in the silence that is a very loud sound. We are like sleep-walkers, and we walk in dreams until we fall down; and then we know we must get up, and we see the trail once more and hear the beating of our hearts.

"In the morning we come upon the last-night camp of the man who is before us. It is a poor camp, the kind a man makes who is hungry and without strength. On the snow there are pieces of blanket and of canvas, and I know what has happened. His dogs have eaten their harness, and he has made new harness out of his blankets. The man and woman stare hard at what is to be seen. Their eyes are toil-mad and hunger-mad, and burn like fire deep in their heads. Their faces are like the faces of people who have died of hunger, and their cheeks are black with the dead flesh of many freezings. We come to where we can see a long way over the snow, and that for which they look is before them. A mile away there are black spots upon the snow. The black spots move. My eyes are dim, and I must stiffen my soul to see. And I see one man with dogs and a sled. The baby wolves see, too. They can no longer talk, but they whisper: 'On, on! Let us hurry!'

"And they fall down, but they go on. The man who is before us, his blanket harness breaks often and he must stop and mend it. Our harness is good, for I have hung it in trees each night. At eleven o'clock the man is half a mile away. At one o'clock he is a quarter of a mile away. He is very weak. We see him fall down many times in the snow.

"Now we are three hundred yards away. We go very slow. Maybe in two, three hours we go one mile. We do not walk. All the time we fall down. We stand up and stagger two steps, maybe three steps, then we fall down again. And all the time I must help up the man and woman. Sometimes they rise to their knees and fall forward, maybe four or five times before they can get to their feet again, and stagger two or three steps and fall. But always do they fall forward. Standing or kneeling, always do they fall forward, gaining on the trail each time by the length of their bodies.

"Sometimes they crawl on hands and knees like animals that live in the forest. We go like snails—like snails that are dying we go so slow. And yet we go faster than the man who is before us. For he, too, falls all the time, and there is no Sitka Charley to lift him up. Now he is two hundred yards away. After a long time he is one hundred yards away.

"It is a funny sight. I want to laugh out loud, Ha! ha! just like that, it is so funny. It is a race of dead men and dead dogs. It is like in a dream when you have a nightmare and run away very fast for your life and go very slow. The man who is with me is mad. The woman is mad. I am mad. All the world is mad. And I want to laugh, it is so funny.

"The stranger man who is before us leaves his dogs behind and goes on alone across the snow. After a long time we come to the dogs. They lie helpless in the snow, their harness of blanket and canvas on them, the sled behind them, and as we pass them they whine to us and cry like babies that are hungry.

"Then we, too, leave our dogs and go on alone across the snow. The man and the woman are nearly gone, and they moan and groan and sob, but they go on. I, too, go on. I have but the one thought. It is to come up to the stranger man. Then it is that I shall rest, and not until

Half-tone plate engraved by A. Hayman

"AND THUS I, SITKA CHARLEY, SAW THE BABY WOLVES MAKE THEIR KILL"

then shall I rest, and it seems that I must lie down and sleep for a thousand years, I am so tired.

"The stranger man is fifty yards away, all alone in the white snow. He falls and crawls, staggers, and falls and crawls again. By and by he crawls on hands and knees. He no longer stands up. And the man and woman no longer stand up. They, too, crawl after him on hands and knees. But I stand up. Sometimes I fall, but always do I stand up again.

"On either side the sun are sun-dogs, so that there are three suns in the sky.

"After a long time the stranger man crawls no more. He stands slowly upon his feet and rocks back and forth. Also does he take off one mitten and wait with revolver in his hand, rocking back and forth as he waits. His face is skin and bones, and frozen black. It is a hungry face. The eyes are deep-sunk in his head, and the lips are snarling. The man and woman, too, get upon their feet, and they go toward him very slowly. And all about is the snow and the silence. And in the sky are three suns, and all the air is flashing with the dust of diamonds.

"And thus it was that I, Sitka Charley, saw the baby wolves make their kill. No word is spoken. Only does the stranger man snarl with his hungry face. Also does he rock to and fro, his shoulders drooping, his knees bent, and his legs wide apart so that he does not fall down. The man and the woman stop maybe fifty feet away. Their legs, too, are wide apart so that they do not fall down, and their bodies rock to and fro. The stranger man is very weak. His arm shakes, so that when he shoots at the man his bullet strikes in the snow. The man cannot take off his mitten. The stranger man shoots at him again, and this time the bullet goes by in the air. Then the man takes the mitten in his teeth and pulls it off. But his hand is frozen and he cannot hold the revolver, and it falls in the snow. I look at the woman. Her mitten is off, and the revolver is in her hand. Three times she shoot, quick, just like that. The hungry face of the stranger man is still snarling as he falls forward in the snow.

"They did not look at the dead man.

'Let us go on,' they said. And we went on. But now that they have found that for which they look, they are like dead. The last strength has gone out of them. They can stand no more upon their feet. They will not crawl, but desire only to close their eyes and sleep. I see not far away a place for camp. I kick them. I have my dog-whip, and I give them the lash of it. They cry aloud, but they must crawl. And they do crawl to the place for camp. I build fire so that they will not freeze. Then I go back for sled. Also, I kill the dogs of the stranger man so that we may have food and not die. I put the man and woman in blankets and they sleep. Sometimes I wake them up and give them little bit of food. They are not awake, but they take the food. The woman sleep one day and a half. Then she wake up and go to sleep again. The man sleep two days and wake up and go to sleep again. After that we go down to the coast at St. Michaels. And when the ice goes out of Bering Sea the man and woman go away on a steamship. But first they pay me my seven hundred and fifty dollars a month."

"But why did they kill the man?" I asked.

Sitka Charley delayed reply until he had lighted his pipe. He glanced at the illustration on the wall and nodded his head at it familiarly. Then he said, speaking slowly and ponderingly:

"I have thought much. I do not know. It is something that happened. It is a picture I remember. It is like looking in at the window and seeing the man writing a letter. They came into my life and they went out of my life, and the picture is, as I have said, without beginning, the end without understanding."

"You have painted many pictures in the telling," I said.

"Ay,"—he nodded his head. "But they were without beginning and without end."

"The last picture of all had an end," I said.

"Ay," he answered. "But what end?"

"It was a piece of life," I said.

"Ay," he answered. "It was a piece of life."

27
The Sea Horse

THE SEA-HORSE.

No CREATURE is so repulsive in appearance as an old male walrus, or morse *(rosmarus);* the head, large in itself, seems ridiculously small set upon the immense neck, and the ungainly body is all swollen and tremulous with the excessive deposit of flabby fat and blubber, distending the coarse, hairless, wrinkled hide into the shape and semblance of a wool-sack. No wonder that the eyes of the early Christian navigators opened wide in amazement as the sinister head of this brute amphibian rose unexpectedly from the cold green waters of the north, and then as suddenly disappeared beneath the

the one genus, and it in turn alone represents but two species. Curiously, too, while this animal is found in great numbers here and there within the waters of the Arctic Ocean, Baffin's Bay, and Behring Sea, no one has ever seen or even heard of the existence of a sea-horse in the equally frigid Antarctic seas and Southern circumpolar zone. The variation existing between the walrus of Spitzbergen and that of Behring Sea is a very sensible one, owing to the much greater size and almost hairless skin of the Alaskan adults; this difference may be due to the fact that our walrus has nothing to do

ESQUIMAUX HUNTERS CRUISING.

waves with its peculiar snort and hog-like grunt. However, soon after that, some hardy sailor put a harpoon into a "sea-horse," and its ivory teeth, and the oil found under its tough skin, at once stimulated a grand general hunting of this brute by all the seamen of northern Europe. It was a walrus-hunter who first beheld the frozen coasts of Spitzbergen and Nova Zembla, and it was a walrus-hunter also who first passed from Asia to this continent across the Straits of Behring.

Though doubt exists even now among scientific men as to the true character and appearance of the walrus, yet there is but

but to grow in comparative peace and seclusion, while the annual raids made upon the Spitzbergen branch of the family may tend to dwarf it by inculcating fearful anticipation.

From the peculiar, wicked-looking tusks that hang down over the chin from the massive upper jaw, one instinctively jumps to the conclusion that the walrus must be a terrible fighter—that these enormous dental weapons are used for tearing, cutting, and striking in conflict among themselves and with their enemies; as a matter of fact, the walrus is among the most peaceable and inoffensive of animals, and these savage-looking teeth are used almost exclusively in

ESQUIMAUX TAKING WALRUS.

the quiet service of prodding up and digging out clams and other shell-fish from their sand and mud beds in the shallow marine waters and estuaries of the north, and to grub the bulbous roots of the wild celery, and to tear juicy sea-weed fronds from their strong hold upon the rocky bottoms of rugged coasts and reefs. The walrus does not subsist upon any animal food or fish : he is a good vegetarian and has a decided taste for mollusks; he is far too clumsy as a swimmer to capture fish, and he seems to be too much oppressed with his own unwieldy bulk to fight either by land or sea, even in self-defense. Still, in some directions, awkward as he is on shore, he is capable of exerting immense muscular power and displaying unwonted agility. To give an illustration : the size and strength of a polar bear are well known, but the largest of its kind cannot knock down and drag out a full-grown walrus bull, while it could easily destroy and dispose of one of our heaviest oxen in that manner. An incident occurred under the eye of the writer, while surveying on St. Matthew's Island, in 1874, that very clearly presents the decidedly different natures of the two animals. At the base of a series of bold, high bluffs

on the north side of the island, quite a' large herd of walrus were lying out from the surf on the rocks, stretching themselves comfortably in all sorts of positions, as they basked with great pleasure in the clear rays of an August sun. An old male walrus was hauled up, a little aloof from the herd, all alone, only a few hundred yards away, and enjoying himself, also, after the fashion of his kind when they come out for an air-bath. Lurking in the background, I observed a very large polar bear, as he took the scent of this old sea-horse, and watched him as he made a stealthy approach. Crouching and flattened to the ground, the bear rapidly came up to within a dozen yards of the dozing morse, when he sprang into a lumbering gallop, closed at once with him, and attempted, bear-like, to break in and crush his skull by dealing the astonished walrus a swift succession of thumping blows over the head with his heavy, powerful fore paws. The massive occipital of the walrus was, however, too thick to give way, even under the force of Bruin's immense feet; and, after the first shock of surprise, the clumsy amphibian righted himself, and, without striking back a single blow, turned and started for the water. The bear tried to head him off; but the strength of the walrus and the momentum of his bulky body, when started down grade to the surf, was more than his great white foe could overcome. So, instinctively realizing that his quarry was to escape, the infuriated bear leaped upon his broad, flabby back, buried his claws in the tough hide and his teeth in the neck of the unhappy walrus, and actually hung on and rode down in this manner fifteen or twenty yards to the sea, where he quickly dismounted when the first wave combed over the flanks of his victim. This surf-bath, undoubtedly, cooled the bear's passion; but it did not destroy his interest, for he retreated, turned, squatted upon his haunches, and regarded the wake of the fleeing morse with great attention.

But when Bruin selects a young walrus, or a sick or feeble adult, then there is no satisfactory; were it not for the subsistence furnished so largely by the flesh and oil of the morse, it is exceedingly doubtful whether the Esquimaux of North America, from Behring Straits clear around to Labrador, could manage to live. It is not to be inferred that walrus-meat is the sole diet of these simple people, for that is very wide of the truth; but there are several months of every year when the exigencies of the climate render it absolutely impossible for the hardiest native to go out and procure

A ROUGH RIDER.

such failure; the skull is crushed by quick, repeated blows; then, when the stunned and quivering body of his prey lies extended, he fastens his ugly fangs upon the throat, tearing the hide and flesh until an artery is reached, when he settles down and fairly drinks out the life of the unfortunate walrus.

In looking at this uncouth animal, the most natural question at once arises—What earthly service can such an ungainly, stupid beast render? What, indeed, is the use of its existence? But the answer is swift and food, and then the value of the *cache* of walrus-meat is appreciated, when for weeks and weeks it forms the beginning and the end of every meal. The walrus responds to as many demands of the Innuit as the camel of the Arab, or the cocoa-palm of the South Sea islander. Its flesh feeds him; its oil illuminates and warms his dark hut; its sinews make his bird-nets; its tough skin, skillfully stretched over the light wooden frame, constitutes his famous kayak, and the serviceable oomiak, or bidarrah; its intestines

ESQUIMAUX SORTING AND STRINGING
WALRUS IVORY.

are converted into water-proof clothing, while the soles to its flippers are transferred to his feet; and, finally, its ivory is a source of endless utility to him in domestic use and in trade and barter.

Walrus famines among the Esquimaux have been recorded in pathetic legends by almost all of the savage settlements in the Arctic. Even now, as I write (November, 1880), comes the authentic corroboration of the harsh rumor of the starvation of the inhabitants of St. Lawrence Island—those people who live just midway between the Old World and the New, in Alaskan waters. The winter of 1879–80 was one of exceptional rigor in the Arctic, though in this country it was unusually mild and open. The ice closed in solid around St. Lawrence Island —so firm and unshaken by the mighty powers of wind and tide that the walrus were driven far to the southward and eastward, out of reach of the unhappy inhabitants of that island, who, thus unexpectedly deprived of their mainstay and support, seem to have miserably starved to death, with the exception of one small village on the north shore. The residents of the Poonook, Poogovell-yak, and Kagallegak settlements perished, to a soul, from hunger—nearly three hundred men, women, and children. I was among these people in 1874, during the month of August, and remarked their manifold superiority over the savages of the northwest coast and the great plains. They seemed then to live, during nine months of the year, almost wholly upon the flesh and oil of the walrus. Clean-limbed, bright-eyed, and jovial, they profoundly impressed one

with their happy subsistence and reliance upon the walrus-herds of Behring Sea; and it was remarked then that these people had never been subjected to the temptation— and subsequent sorrow—of putting their trust in princes; hence their independence and good heart. But now it appears that it will not suffice, either, to put your trust in walrus.

Walrus naturally occupy a large place in the spiritual horizon of the Esquimaux; his whole idea of paradise is bound up in finding walrus by countless herds in the spirit land, which in itself, however, does not differ at all from the one he now lives on, except that there he will be uniformly successful in the chase, and always sure of meat to eat day in and day out. When the writer attempted to argue with one of these people that we could get along very well in the next world without these unsavory animals, the emphatic response was: "Without walrus there is no heaven!"

In view of the unremitting warfare waged upon the walrus-herds of northern Europe, it is most likely that the sandy shoals and muddy bars of Bristol Bay, Behring Sea, are now the chosen resort of the largest congregations of these animals. When the ice-pack closes in solid above the straits between Asia and America, then the great mass of the walrus, which have been spending the summer on the broken ice-floes, engaged principally in breeding, return to the open waters of Bristol Bay and Norton Sound, where they spend the winter, scattered in herds from a dozen or so in number up to bodies of thousands; living in perfect peace among themselves, and almost unmolested, though several districts are carefully hunted over by the Esquimaux of Nushagak for oil and ivory.

The shoal waters of this region and the eccentric tides have alone preserved these bands of *rosmarus* from extinction. Years ago, when the North Pacific was the rendezvous of the greatest whaling fleet that ever floated, vessels could not, nor can they now, approach nearer than sixty or even eighty miles of them.

The walrus is born upon the floating ice-fields of the Arctic Ocean, and during the whole of the summer remains there, carefully suckled and guarded by its mother, with whom it instinctively retires to the south as the packs begin to close over the

top of the square, flat head; the nostrils open directly above the muzzle, and are vertically oval and about an inch in diameter. Like the seal, the walrus, when traveling, swims entirely submerged, rising at prolonged intervals to breathe, when it "blows" with little jets of vapor and a noise not unlike a whale; on a cool, quiet day, the progress of these creatures as they swim may be traced by the succeeding tiny white columns of vapor thrown up. As the nostrils are scarcely raised above water, nothing is seen of the animal itself, unless it pauses in the act of swimming and rises up, head and shoulders, for a survey.

The chief glory of the *rosmarus*, however, must be embodied in its long white tusks, or canine teeth of the upper jaw, that

ESQUIMAUX DRESSING WALRUS-HIDES.

sea. Following the example of its elders, it soon begins to dig clams with its tiny tushes, to pull sea-grass and celery roots, and to tear up the tender sea-weed streamers, upon all of which it fairly thrives, until it reaches maturity in its eighth or ninth year, when it will measure twelve to thirteen feet in length from the nostrils to the root of its almost imperceptible tail, and possess a girth of twelve to fourteen feet around its blubber-loaded neck and shoulders. The immense accumulation of fat in the region of the neck and shoulders makes the head and posteriors look small in proportion and attenuated. The singularly flattened head and massive, abrupt, square muzzle strongly resemble those of the African river-horse. The nostrils, eyes, and ear-spots are planted nearly on

are set firmly beneath the nostrils in deep, massive, bony sockets, which cause the distinguishing breadth and square cut front of the muzzle. These ivory teeth grow down, sometimes spreading a little as they descend; then again the tips of the tusks will nearly meet, varying in size from the six or seven inch tushes of youth to the average of two feet at maturity; the writer has seen examples over three feet in length, so large, indeed, that they might have belonged to a young mastodon. The usual weight of a good full-grown tusk is about eight pounds, but such teeth are rare: out of a herd of a hundred adult walrus, it will be very difficult to select an example which shall possess a perfect pair of tusks, because in rooting around for food they are almost invariably broken off by their owners at the tips or even up as high as the jaw itself; when walrus ivory is perfectly white and free from cracks, it rates as high as the best elephant-teeth; but most of it has a yellow, porous core, and is badly cracked from the tips to the base.

The upper lips are thick and gristly, completely overhanging and shadowing the lower; they are set full of short, stout, gray-ish-white and horn-colored bristles, varying in length from a half to three and four inches; this mustache is decidedly the most sinister and peculiar in the whole animal kingdom.

A dull, wooden expression is given by the eyes of the walrus. These are small, and protrude from their sockets like those of a lobster; the iris and pupil form less than one-

the nostrils of the morse, and instantly the clumsy brute would snort in fright, and push, roll, and slide its huge bulk back into the sheltering sea. Most emphatically does the walrus aver that seeing is not believing, but smelling is!

After all, the crowning peculiarity of this creature comes with age. When an Alaskan *rosmarus* has wintered and summered for eighteen or twenty years in the chilly, desolate regions of its choice, it becomes bald, and, more than that, all of its hair, from head to tail, falls out, with the trifling exception of little sparse tufts here and there, rooted in the deep wrinkles and plications of its hide, giving a raw and naked appearance to the old veteran. The skin, bare of hair, is covered with a multitude of un-wholesome, pustular-looking warts and pim-

A WALRUS BREEDING-GROUND, BEHRING STRAITS.

quarter of the exposed surface. The sclerotic bulges out from the lids, which are tinged a coffee-yellow and brown, with an occasional admixture of white in tiny spots When the walrus is aroused, the eyes are rolled about in every direction,—forward, backward, up, down, and around,—while the head itself seldom turns, the animal only moving it, more or less stiffly, as it rears up. These odd, lobster-like optics, however, render their owners but little service out of water, and perhaps as little in. The natives have repeatedly amused the writer by going up gently to a walrus bull from the leeward, almost to within striking distance, causing that animal to make no other sign than a stupid stare and low grunts of curiosity; but did the man move a trifle to windward, so that the faintest whiff of his individuality reached

ples, deeply wrinkled and traversed with a coarse net-work of dark red venous lines, that show out in bold contrast through the thick, yellowish-brown cuticle, which in turn seems to be scaling off in places, as if from leprosy. A herd of these old stagers (they always keep together) strikes the eye of the observer in a most unpleasant manner.

This thick, tough hide of the walrus gives a strong superficial resemblance to the pachydermata; its weight alone, divested of blubber, is more than three hundred and fifty pounds! Naturally, its grain is very coarse, especially where it is three inches in depth, as it is found to be over the shoulders and around the neck, and nowhere is the skin of an adult less than half an inch in thickness; when young, however, it is thor-oughly covered with short, moderately fine

WALRUS-HERDS ON THE CLAM SHOALS AT BRISTOL BAY.

brown hair, growing coarser, thinner, and finally falling out with age.

In landing and crawling over low, rocky beaches, shelves, and bowlders, or in dragging themselves out on sand-bars, the walrus is as ungainly and as indolent as the sloth; they crowd up from the water in slow, labored movements, accompanied by low, swine-like grunts and then by a stifled bellowing, like that of oxen. The first walrus out from the water no sooner gets composed upon the ground to bask and sleep than the second one comes along, prodding and poking with its blunted tusks, demanding room, and causing the first to change its position a little farther on and up from the surf; then the second is in turn treated similarly by the third arrival, and so on; in this way, a piece of beach or shingle will be packed in the course of a day or two with hundreds and thousands as thickly as they can lie, their heads or posteriors being frequently pillowed upon the bodies of one another; and throughout the whole congregation there is nothing like ill-humor evinced. As they pass all the time when on land in sluggish basking or deep sleep, they seem to have an instinctive appreciation of the necessity of keeping watch, and guarding themselves from attack, and this is done satisfactorily by resorting to a somewhat singular though effective method; whenever a dozing herd of walrus is approached, there are always one or two stirring with their heads high up, snorting and grunting; these remain on duty only a very brief period,

usually a few minutes, when they lie down to sleep, but before doing so, they strike and poke the drowsy forms of their nearest companions with their tusks, causing them to rouse up suddenly; these stand on the alert in turn for a few minutes also, again pass the blow to the next, and resume their pleasant siesta: and thus the signal of danger is incessantly transmitted throughout the whole herd; this disturbance, evidently preconcerted among themselves, has the effect of always keeping some four or five of their number more vigilant than their drowsy fellows.

In moving on land, the walrus has no power in its hind limbs, which are always dragged and hitched up in the rear as the animal slowly and tediously progresses by a succession of short, trembling steps on the stubby fore-flippers. If in good condition and undisturbed, the herds will remain out of the water, in the summer season, and fast in great apparent comfort for a month or six weeks at a time. The *rosmarus* is monogamous, and the difference between the sexes in size, color, and shape is inconsiderable, save in respect to the teeth; the female is never found to possess as long or as heavy tusks as the male, but her ivory is generally harder and whiter. The walrus mother is devoted to her offspring, caring for and nursing it nearly a year, but her action in protecting it, as well as herself, is always passive. The writer finds it exceedingly difficult to reconcile the stories so frequently told of the attacks made by sea-horses upon boats and their crews, with the timid and rapid dispersion which always attended the appearance of his boat among a swimming herd. Under no provocation whatever could either males or females be persuaded to show fight.

Occasionally, if you are coasting in Behring Sea, running along before a light breeze, your vessel will silently glide upon a small band of walrus sound asleep in the water; and, unless the sail flaps or the keel strikes a sleeper's form, you will pass on and leave them entirely unconscious of their dreaded visitor. They sleep grotesquely enough at sea, just like so many water-logged sticks, one end down and the other up. Nothing but the muzzle, with a few inches of the gleaming white tusks, appears to mark the position of a sleeping morse; its huge body rests vertically extended to a depth of twelve or thirteen feet below the surface of the rippling wavelets. You arouse a sleeper, and, with one short snort of surprise, it instantly tips itself back into a horizontal position and swims off, steering with its hind flippers; if not badly frightened it will re-appear, head and shoulders, after a lapse of ten or fifteen minutes, to resurvey and grunt its amazement; but if thoroughly alarmed, it disappears entirely.

Much amusing speculation has been indulged in by various writers as to what particular animal gave rise in olden time to the weird idea of the merman and mermaid: some authorities, and one of them encyclopedic, declare it is the "human expression" of the *rosmarus!* Evidently that man has never seen the beast, for no matter how harshly he may feel toward mankind, he never for a moment would make this charge, could he only see his type; however, several species of the common hair seals (*Phoca vitulina*) and the dugong, as they rise from the water, have a decided suggestion in their eyes of the famous girl-fish, and these are probably the source of the suggestion. No amount of imagination can invest the uncouth head of the sea-horse with this pleasant fancy, for when the gristled muzzle of a walrus rises above the sea an observer cannot see the creature's eyes; those small, skin-colored organs are wholly undistinguishable at the distance one is compelled to keep by reason of the excessive timidity of the snorting pachyderm.

ARCTIC FOG-HORNS.

28
The Discovery
of
Glacier Bay

THE DISCOVERY OF GLACIER BAY.

BY ITS DISCOVERER.

Y first visit to the now famous Glacier Bay of Alaska was made toward the end of October, 1879, when young ice was beginning to form in the branch inlets occupied by the glaciers, and the mountains were mantled with fresh snow all the way down from the highest peaks and ridges of the Fairweather Range nearly to the level of the sea.

I had spent most of the season exploring the cañon of the Stickeen River and its glaciers, and a small portion of the interior region beyond the Coast Mountains, on the divide of some of the southerly tributaries of the Yukon and Mackenzie rivers. When I got back to my headquarters at Fort Wrangel, about the beginning of October, it seemed too late for new undertakings in this icy northland. The days were growing short, and winter, with its heavy storms, was drawing nigh, when avalanches would be booming down the long white slopes of the peaks, and all the land would be buried. But, on the other hand, though this white wilderness was new to me, I was familiar with storms, and enjoyed them, knowing well that in right relations with them they are ever kindly. The main inland channels, extending in every direction along the coast, remain open all winter; and their shores being well forested, it would be easy to keep warm in camp, while in a large canoe abundance of provisions could be carried. I determined, therefore, to go ahead as far north as possible, with or without companions, to see and learn what I could, especially with reference to future work. When I made known my plans to Mr. Young, the Wrangel missionary, he offered to go with me, and with his assistance I procured a good canoe and a crew of Indians, gathered a large stock of provisions, blankets, etc., and on October 14 set forth, eager to welcome whatever wildness might offer, so long as food and firewood should last.

Our crew numbered four: Toyatte, a grand old Stickeen nobleman, who was elected captain, not only because he owned the canoe, but for his skill in woodcraft and seamanship; Kadechan, the son of a Chilcat chief; John, a Stickeen who acted as interpreter; and Sitka Charlie. Mr. Young is one of those fearless and adventurous evangelists who in seeking to save others save themselves, and it was the opportunities the trip might afford to meet the Indians of the different tribes along our route that induced him to join me.

After all our bundles were stowed aboard, and we were about to cast loose from the wharf, Kadechan's mother, a woman of great natural dignity and force of character, came down the steps alongside the canoe, oppressed with anxious fears for the safety of her son. Standing silent for a few moments, she held the missionary with her dark, bodeful eyes, and at length, with great solemnity of speech and gesture, accused him of using undue influence in gaining her son's consent to go on a dangerous voyage among tribes that were unfriendly to the Stickeens. Then, like an ancient sibyl, she foretold a long train of disasters from storm-winds and ice, and in awful majesty of mother-love finished by saying: "If my son comes not back, on you will be his blood, and you shall pay. I say it." Mr. Young tried in vain to calm her fears, promising Heaven's care as well as his own for her precious son, assuring her that he would faithfully share every danger that might assail him, and, if need be, willingly die in his defense. "We shall see whether or not you die," she said as she turned away.

Toyatte also encountered domestic difficulties in getting away. When he stepped into the canoe I noticed a cloud on his grand old face, as if his sad doom, now drawing near, was already beginning to overshadow him. When he took leave of his wife she wept bitterly, saying that the Chilcat chiefs would surely kill him in case he should escape the winter storms. But it was not on this trip that the old hero was to meet his fate, and when we were fairly free in the wilderness these gloomy forebodings vanished, and a gentle breeze pressed us joyfully onward over the shining waters.

We first pursued a westerly course through Sumner Strait, between Kupreanof and Prince of Wales islands; then, turning northward, we sailed up the charming Kiku Strait, through the midst of innumerable picturesque islets, across Prince Frederick Sound, up Chatham Strait, and thence northwestward through Icy Strait and around Glacier Bay. Thence, returning through Icy Strait, we urged our way up the grand Lynn Canal to the Davidson Glacier and Chilcat, and

371

returned to Wrangel along the coast of the mainland, visiting the icy Sum Dum Bay and the Le Conte Glacier on our route. Thus we made a journey more than eight hundred miles long; and though hardships were encountered, and a few dangers, the wild wonderland made compensation beyond our most extravagant hopes.

The first stages of our journey were mostly enjoyment. The weather was about half bright, and we glided along the green and yellow shores in comfort, the lovely islands passing in harmonious succession, like ideas in a fine poem. The rain did not hinder us, but when the wind was too wild we stayed in camp, the Indians usually improving such storm times in deer-hunting, while I examined the rocks and woods. Most of our camps were made in nooks that were charmingly embowered, and fringed with bushes and late flowers. After supper we sat long around the fire, listening to the stories of the Indians about the wild animals they were acquainted with, their hunting adventures, wars, traditions, religion, and customs. Every Indian party we met we interviewed, and every village we came to we visited. Thus passed our days and nights until we reached the west coast of Admiralty Island, intending to make a straight course thence up Lynn Canal, when we learned from a party of traveling Hoonas that the Chilcats had been drinking and quarreling, that Kadechan's father had been shot, and that we could not go safely into their country before these whisky quarrels were settled. My Indians evidently believed this news, and dreaded the consequences; therefore I decided to turn to the westward through Icy Strait, and to go in search of the wonderful ice-mountains to which Sitka Charlie, the youngest of my crew, had frequently referred. Having noticed my interest in glaciers, he told me that when he was a boy he had gone with his father to hunt seals in a large bay full of ice, and that he thought he could find it if I cared to have him try. I was rejoiced to find all the crew now willing to go on this adventure, judging, perhaps, that ice-mountains under the present circumstances might prove less dangerous than Chilcats.

On the 24th, about noon, as we came near a small island in Icy Strait, Charlie said that we must procure some dry wood there, for in the ice-mountain country which we were now approaching not a single tree of any kind could be found. This seemed strange news to the rest of the crew, and I had to make haste to end an angry dispute that was rising by ordering as much wood to be taken aboard as we could carry. Then we set sail direct for the ice-country, holding a northwesterly course until long after dark, when we reached a small inlet that sets in near the mouth of Glacier Bay, on the west side. Here we made a cold camp on a desolate snow-covered beach in stormy sleet and darkness. At daybreak I looked eagerly in every direction to learn what kind of place we were in; but gloomy rain-clouds covered the mountains, and I could see nothing that could give me a clue, while Vancouver's chart, hitherto a faithful guide, here failed us altogether. Nevertheless, we made haste to be off; and fortunately, just as we were leaving the shore, a faint smoke was seen across the inlet, toward which Charlie, who now seemed lost, gladly steered. Our sudden appearance so early that gray morning had evidently alarmed our neighbors, for as soon as we were within hailing distance an Indian with his face blackened fired a shot over our heads, and in a blunt, bellowing voice roared, "Who are you?" Our interpreter shouted, "Friends and the Fort Wrangel missionary." Then men, women, and children swarmed out of the hut, and awaited our approach on the beach. One of the hunters having brought his gun with him, Kadechan sternly rebuked him, asking with superb indignation whether he was not ashamed to bring a gun in his hand to meet a missionary. Friendly relations, however, were speedily established, and as a cold rain was falling, they invited us into their hut. It seemed small for two persons; nevertheless, twenty-one managed to find shelter in it about a smoky fire. Our hosts proved to be Hoona seal-hunters laying in their winter stores of meat and skins. The packed hut was passably well ventilated, but its oily, meaty smells were not the same to our noses as those of the briny, sprucy nooks we were accustomed to, and the circle of black eyes peering at us through a fog of reek and smoke made a novel picture. We were glad, however, to get within reach of information, and of course asked many questions concerning the ice-mountains and the strange bay, to most of which our inquisitive Hoona friends replied with counter-questions as to our object in coming to such a place, especially so late in the year. They had heard of Mr. Young and his work at Fort Wrangel, but could not understand how a missionary could be doing in such a place as this. Was he going to preach to seals and gulls, they asked, or to the ice-mountains? and could they take his word? Then John explained that only the friend of the missionary was seeking ice-mountains; that Mr. Young had already preached many good words in the villages we had visited on our way, in their own among the rest; that our hearts were good; and that every Indian was our friend. Then we gave them a little rice, sugar, tea, and tobacco, after which they began to gain confidence and to speak freely. They told us that the main bay was called by them Sit-a-da-kay, or Ice Bay; that there were many large ice-mountains in it, but no gold-

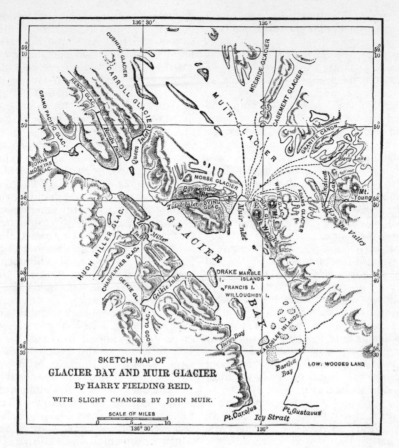

SKETCH MAP OF
GLACIER BAY AND MUIR GLACIER
By HARRY FIELDING REID.
WITH SLIGHT CHANGES BY JOHN MUIR.
SCALE OF MILES
0   5   10

mines; and that the ice-mountain they knew best was at the head of the bay, where most of the seals were found.

Notwithstanding the rain, I was anxious that we should push and grope our way beneath the clouds as best we could, in case worse weather should come; but Charlie was ill at ease, and wanted one of the seal-hunters to go with us, for the place was much changed. I promised to pay well for a guide, and in order to lighten the canoe proposed to leave most of our heavy stores with our friends until our return. After a long consultation one of them consented to go. His wife got ready his blanket and a piece of cedar matting for his bed, and some provisions — mostly dried salmon, and seal sausage made of strips of lean meat plaited around a core of fat. She followed us to the beach, and just as we were pushing off said with a pretty smile: "It is my husband that you are taking away. See that you bring him back." We got under way about 10 A. M. The wind was in our favor, but a cold rain pelted us, and we could see but little of the dreary, treeless wilderness which we had now fairly entered. The bitter blast, however, gave us good speed; our bedraggled canoe rose and fell on the icy waves,

solemnly bowing to them, and mimicking the gestures of a big ship. Our course was northwestward, up the southwest side of the bay, near the shore of what seemed to be the mainland, some smooth marble islands being on our right. About noon we discovered the first of the great glaciers — the one I afterward named for Geikie, the noted Scotch geologist. Its lofty blue cliffs, looming up through the draggled skirts of the clouds, gave a tremendous impression of savage power, while the roar of the new-born icebergs thickened and emphasized the general roar of the storm. An hour and a half beyond the Geikie Glacier we ran into a slight harbor where the shore is low, dragged the canoe beyond the reach of drifting icebergs, and, much against my desire to push ahead, encamped, the guide insisting that the big ice-mountain at the head of the bay could not be reached before dark, that the landing there was dangerous even in daylight, and that this was the only safe harbor on the way to it. While camp was being made I strolled along the shore to examine the rocks and the fossil timber that abound here. All the rocks are freshly glaciated even below the sea-level, nor have the waves as yet worn off the surface polish, much less the heavy scratches and grooves and lines of glacial contour.

The next day being Sunday, the minister wished to stay in camp; and so, on account of the weather, did the Indians. I therefore set out on an excursion, and spent the day alone on the mountain slopes above the camp, and to the north of it, to see what I might learn. Pushing on through rain and mud and sludgy snow, crossing many brown, boulder-choked torrents, wading, jumping, wallowing in snow to my shoulders, I had a desperately hard and dangerous time. After crouching cramped and benumbed in the canoe, poulticed in wet clothes and blankets night and day, my limbs had been long asleep. This day they were awake, and in the hour of trial proved that they had not lost the cunning learned on many a mountain peak of the high Sierra. I reached a height of 1500 feet, on the ridge that bounds the second of the great glaciers on the south. All the landscape was smothered in clouds, and I began to fear that I had climbed in vain, as far as wide views were concerned. But at length the clouds lifted a little, and beneath their gray fringes I saw the berg-filled expanse of the bay, and the feet of the mountains that stand about it, and the imposing fronts of five of the huge glaciers, the nearest being immediately beneath me. This was my first general view of Glacier Bay, a solitude of ice and snow and new-born rocks, dim, dreary, mysterious. I held the ground I had so dearly won for an hour or two, sheltering myself as best I could from the blast, while with benumbed fingers I sketched what I could see of the landscape, and wrote a few lines in my note-book. Then I breasted the snow again, crossed the muffled, shifting avalanche tali, forded the torrents in safety, and reached camp about dark, wet and weary, but rich in a notable experience.

While I was getting some coffee, Mr. Young told me that the Indians were discouraged, and had been talking about turning back, fearing that I would be lost, or that in some way the expedition would come to grief if I persisted in going farther. They had been asking him what possible motive I could have in climbing dangerous mountains when blinding storms were blowing; and when he replied that I was only seeking knowledge, Toyatte said, " Muir must be a witch to seek knowledge in such a place as this, and in such miserable weather." After supper, crouching about a dull fire of fossil wood, they became still more doleful, and talked in tones that accorded well with the growling torrents about us, and with the wind and rain among the rocks, telling sad old stories of crushed canoes and drowned Indians, and of hunters lost and frozen in snow-storms.

Toyatte, dreading the treeless, forlorn appearance of the region, said that his heart was not strong, and that he feared his canoe, on the safety of which our lives depended, might be entering a skookum-house (jail) of ice, from which there might be no escape; while the Hoona guide said bluntly that if I was so fond of danger, and meant to go close up to the noses of the ice-mountains, he would not consent to go any farther : for we should all be lost, as many of his tribe had been, by the sudden rising of bergs from the bottom. They seemed to be losing heart with every howl of the storm, and fearing that they might fail me now that I was in the midst of so grand a congregation of glaciers, which possibly I might not see again, I made haste to reassure them, telling them that for ten years I had wandered alone among mountains and storms, and that good luck always followed me; that with me, therefore, they need fear nothing; that the storm would soon cease, and the sun would shine; and that Heaven cared for us, and guided us all the time, whether we knew it or not : but that only brave men had a right to look for Heaven's care, therefore all childish fear must be put away. This little speech did good. Kadechan, with some show of enthusiasm, said he liked to travel with good-luck people; and dignified old Toyatte declared that now his heart was strong again, and he would venture on with me as far as I liked, for my " wawa " was " delait " (my talk was very good). The old warrior even became a little sentimental, and said that if the canoe were crushed he would not greatly care, because on the way to the other world he would have pleasant companions.

Next morning it was still raining and snowing, but the wind was from the south, and swept us bravely forward, while the bergs were cleared from our course. In about an hour we reached the second of the big glaciers, which I afterward named for Hugh Miller. We rowed up its fiord, and landed to make a slight examination of its grand frontal wall. The berg-producing portion we found to be about a mile and a half wide. It presents an imposing array of jagged spires and pyramids, and flat-topped towers and battlements, of many shades of blue, from pale, shimmering, limpid tones in the crevasses and hollows, to the most startling, chilling, almost shrieking vitriol blue on the plain mural spaces from which bergs had just been discharged. Back from the front for a few miles the surface is rendered inaccessible by a series of wide, weathered crevasses, with the spaces between them rising like steps, as if the entire mass of this portion of the glacier had sunk in successive sections as it reached deep water, and the sea had found its way beneath it. Beyond this the glacier extends indefinitely in a gently rising prairie-like expanse, and branches among the slopes and cañons of the Fairweather Range.

From here a run of two hours brought us to the head of the bay, and to the mouth of the northwest fiord, at the head of which lie the Hoona sealing-grounds, and the great glacier now called the Pacific, and another called the Hoona. The fiord is about five miles long, and is two miles wide at the mouth. Here the Hoona guide had a store of dry wood, which we took aboard. Then, setting sail, we were driven wildly up the fiord, as if the storm-wind were saying: "Go, then, if you will, into my icy chamber; but you shall stay until I am ready to let you out." All this time sleety rain was falling on the bay, and snow on the mountains; but soon after we landed the sky began to open. The camp was made on a rocky bench near the front of the Pacific Glacier, and the canoe was carried beyond reach of the bergs and berg-waves. The bergs were now crowded in a dense pack against the ice-wall, as if the storm-wind had determined to make the glacier take back her crystal offspring and keep them at home.

While camp affairs were being attended to, I set out to climb a mountain for comprehensive views; and before I had reached a height of a thousand feet the rain ceased, and the clouds began to rise from the lower altitudes, slowly lifting their white skirts, and lingering in majestic, wing-shaped masses about the mountains that rise out of the broad, icy sea. These were the highest and whitest of all the white mountains, and the greatest of all the glaciers I had yet seen. Climbing higher for a still broader outlook, I made notes and sketched, improving the precious time while sunshine streamed through the luminous fringes of the clouds, and fell on the green waters of the fiord, the glittering bergs, the crystal bluffs of the two vast glaciers, the intensely white, far-spreading fields of ice, and the ineffably chaste and spiritual heights of the Fairweather Range, which were now hidden, now partly revealed, the whole making a picture of icy wildness unspeakably pure and sublime.

Looking southward, a broad ice-sheet was seen extending in a gently undulating plain from the Pacific Fiord in the foreground to the horizon, dotted and ridged here and there with mountains which were as white as the snow-covered ice in which they were half, or more than half, submerged. Several of the great glaciers flow from this one grand fountain. It is an instructive example of a general glacier covering the hills and dales of a country that is not yet ready to be brought to the light of day — not only covering, but creating, a land-

scape with all the features it is destined to have when, in the fullness of time, the fashioning ice-sheet shall be lifted by the sun, and the land shall become warm and fruitful. The view to the westward is bounded and almost filled by the glorious Fairweather Mountains, the highest of them springing aloft in sublime beauty to a height of nearly 16,000 feet, while from base to summit every peak and spire and dividing ridge of all the mighty host was of a spotless, solid white, as if painted. It would seem that snow could never be made to lie on the steepest slopes and precipices unless plastered on when wet, and then frozen. But this snow could not have been wet. It must have been fixed by being driven and set in small particles like the storm-dust of drifts, which, when in this condition, is fixed not only on sheer cliffs, but in massive overcurling cornices. Along the base of this majestic range sweeps the Pacific Glacier, fed by innumerable cascading tributaries, and discharging into the head of the fiord by two mouths, each nearly a mile wide. This is the largest of all the Glacier Bay glaciers that are at all river-like, the trunk of the larger Muir Glacier being more like a lake than a river. After the continuous rainy or snowy weather which we had had since leaving Wrangel, the clear weather was most welcome. Dancing down the mountain to camp, my mind glowing like the sun-beaten glaciers, I found the Indians seated around a good fire, entirely happy now that the farthest·point of the journey had been reached. How keenly bright were the stars that night in the frosty sky, and how impressive was the thunder of the icebergs, rolling, swelling, reverberating through the solemn stillness! I was too happy to sleep.

About daylight next morning we crossed the fiord, and landed on the south side of the island that divides the front wall of the Pacific Glacier. The whiskered faces of seals dotted the water between the bergs, and I could not prevent John and Charlie and Kadechan from shooting at them. Fortunately, they were not skilled in this kind of hunting, and few, if any, were hurt. Leaving the Indians in charge of the canoe, I climbed the island, and gained a good general view of the glacier. At one favorable place I descended about fifty feet below the side of the glacier, where its denuding, fashioning action was clearly shown. Pushing back from here, I found the surface crevassed and sunken in steps, like the Hugh Miller Glacier, as if it were being undermined by the action of the tide-waters. For a distance of fifteen or twenty miles the river-like ice-flood is nearly level, and when it recedes the ocean water will follow it, and thus form a long extension of the fiord, with features essentially the same as those now extending into the continent farther south, where many great glaciers once poured into the sea, though scarce a vestige of them now exists. Thus the domain of the sea has been, and is being, extended in these ice-sculptured lands, and the scenery of the shores is enriched. The dividing island is about a thousand feet high, and is hard beset by the glacier, which still crushes heavily against and around it. A short time ago its summit was at least two thousand feet below the surface of the over-sweeping ice; now three hundred feet of the top is free, and under present climatic conditions it will soon be wholly free from the ice, and will take its place as a glacier-polished island in the middle of the fiord, like a thousand others in this magnificent archipelago. Emerging from its icy sepulcher, it gives a most telling illustration of the birth of a marked feature of a landscape. In this instance it is not the mountain, but the glacier, that is in labor, and the mountain itself is being brought forth.

The Hoona Glacier enters the fiord on the south side, a short distance below the Pacific, displaying a broad and far-reaching expanse, over which many of the lofty peaks of the Fairweather Range are seen; but the front wall, thrust into the fiord, is not nearly so interesting as that of the Pacific, and I did not observe any bergs discharged from it.

After we had seen the unveiling of the majestic peaks and glaciers that evening, and their baptism in the down-pouring sunbeams, it was inconceivable that nature could have anything finer to show us. Nevertheless, compared with what was coming the next morning, all that was as nothing. As far as we could see, the lovely dawn gave no promise of anything uncommon. Its most impressive features were the frosty clearness of the sky, and a deep, brooding calm, made all the more striking by the intermittent thunder of the bergs. The sunrise we did not see at all, for we were beneath the shadows of the fiord cliffs; but in the midst of our studies we were startled by the sudden appearance of a red light burning with a strange, unearthly splendor on the topmost peak of the Fairweather Mountains. Instead of vanishing as suddenly as it had appeared, it spread and spread until the whole range down to the level of the glaciers was filled with the celestial fire. In color it was at first a vivid crimson, with a thick, furred appearance, as fine as the alpenglow, yet indescribably rich and deep — not in the least like a garment or mere external flush or bloom through which one might expect to see the rocks or snow, but every mountain apparently glowing from the heart like molten metal fresh from a furnace. Beneath the frosty shadows of the fiord we stood hushed and awe-stricken, gazing at the holy vision; and had we seen the heavens open and God made manifest, our attention could not have been more tremendously strained. When the highest peak began to burn, it did not seem to be steeped in sunshine, however glorious, but rather as if it had been thrust into the body of the sun itself. Then the supernal fire slowly descending, with a sharp line of demarkation separating it from the cold, shaded region beneath, peak after peak, with their spires and ridges and cascading glaciers, caught the heavenly glow, until all the mighty host stood transfigured, hushed, and thoughtful, as if awaiting the coming of the Lord. The white, rayless light of the morning, seen when I was alone amid the silent peaks of the Sierra, had always seemed to me the most telling of the terrestrial manifestations of God. But here the mountains themselves were made divine, and declared his glory in terms still more impressive. How long we gazed I never knew. The glorious vision passed away in a gradual, fading change through a thousand tones of color to pale yellow and white, and then the work of the ice-world went on again in every-day beauty. The green waters of the fiord were filled with sun-spangles; with the upspringing breeze the fleet of icebergs set forth on their voyages; and on the innumerable mirrors and prisms of these bergs, and on those of the shattered crystal walls of the glaciers, common white light and rainbow light began to glow, while the mountains, changing to stone, put on their frosty jewelry, and loomed again in the thin azure in serene terrestrial majesty. We turned and sailed away, joining the outgoing bergs, while "Gloria in excelsis" still seemed to be sounding over all the white landscape, and our burning hearts were ready for any fate, feeling that whatever the future might have in store, the treasures we had gained would enrich our lives forever.

When we arrived at the mouth of the fiord, and rounded the massive granite headland that stands guard at the entrance on the north side, another large glacier, now named the Reid, was discovered at the head of one of the northern branches of the bay. Pushing ahead into this new fiord, we found that it was not only packed with bergs, but that the spaces between the bergs were crusted with new ice, compelling us to turn back while we were yet several miles from the discharging frontal wall. But though we were not then allowed to set foot on this magnificent glacier, we obtained a fine view of it, and I made the Indians cease rowing while I sketched its principal features. Thence, after steering northeastward a few miles, we discovered still another great glacier, now named the Carroll. But the fiord into which this glacier flows was, like the last, utterly inaccessible on account of ice, and we had to be content with a general view and a sketch of it, gained as we rowed slowly past at a distance of three or four miles. The mountains back of it and on each side of its inlet are sculptured in a singularly rich and striking style of architecture, in which subordinate peaks and gables appear in wonderful profusion, and an imposing conical mountain with a wide, smooth base stands out in the main current of the glacier, a mile or two back from the great ice-wall.

We now turned southward down the eastern shore of the bay, and in an hour or two discovered a large glacier of the second class, at the head of a comparatively short fiord that winter had not yet closed. Here we landed, and climbed across a mile or so of rough boulder-beds, and back upon the wildly broken receding snout of the glacier, which, though it descends to the level of the sea, no longer sends off bergs. Many large masses were detached from the wasting snout by irregular melting, and were buried beneath the mud, sand, gravel, and boulders of the terminal moraine. Thus protected, these fossil icebergs remain unmelted for many years, some of them for a century or more, as shown by the age of trees growing above them, though there are no trees here as yet. At length melting, a pit with sloping sides is formed by the falling of the overlying moraine material into the space at first occupied by the buried ice. In this way are formed the curious depressions in drift-covered regions called kettles, or sinks. On these decaying glaciers we may also find many interesting lessons on the formation of boulders and boulder-beds, which in all glaciated countries exert a marked influence on scenery, health, and fruitfulness.

Three or four miles farther down the bay we came to another fiord, up which we sailed in quest of more glaciers, discovering one in each of the two branches into which the fiord divides. Neither of these glaciers quite reaches tide-water. Notwithstanding their great size and the apparent fruitfulness of their fountains, they are in the first stage of decadence, the waste from melting and evaporation being greater now than the supply of new ice from the snow. We reached the one in the north branch after a comfortable scramble, and climbed over its huge, wrinkled brow, from the top of which we gained a good view of the trunk and some of the tributaries, and also of the sublime gray cliffs that tower on each hand above the ice.

Then we sailed up the south branch of the inlet, but failed to reach the glacier there, on account of a thin sheet of new ice. With the tent-poles we broke a lane for the canoe for a little distance; but it was slow, hard work, and

we soon saw that we could not reach the glacier before dark. Nevertheless, we gained a fair view of it as it came sweeping down through its gigantic gateway of massive Yosemite rocks three and four thousand feet high. Here we lingered until sundown, gazing and sketching; then we turned back, and encamped on a bed of cobblestones between the forks of the fiord.

Our fire was made of fossil wood gathered on the beach. This wood is found scattered or in wave-washed windrows all about the bay where the shores are low enough for it to rest. It also occurs in abundance in many of the ravines and gorges, and in roughly stratified beds of moraine material, some of which are more than a thousand feet in thickness. The bed-rocks on which these deposits rest are scored and polished by glacial action, like all the rocks hereabouts up to at least three thousand feet above the sea. The timber is mostly in the form of broken trunks of the Merten, Paton, and Menzies spruce, the largest sections being twenty to thirty feet long, and from one to three feet in diameter, some of them, with the bark on, sound and tough. It appears, therefore, that these shores were, a century or so ago, as generously forested as those of the adjacent bays and inlets are to-day; though, strange to say, not one tree is left standing, with the exception of a few on mountain-tops near the mouth of the bay and on the east side of the Muir Glacier. How this disforestment was effected I have not space to tell here. I will only say that all I have seen goes to show that the moraine soil on which the forests were growing was held in place on the steep mountain slopes by the grand trunk glacier that recently filled the entire bay as its channel, and that when it melted the soil and forests were sloughed off together.

As we sat by the camp-fire the brightness of the sky brought on a long talk with the Indians about the stars; and their eager, childlike attention was refreshing to see as compared with the decent, deathlike apathy of weary civilized people, in whom natural curiosity has been quenched in toil and care and poor, shallow comfort.

After sleeping a few hours, I stole quietly out of the camp, and climbed the mountain that stands guard between the two glaciers. The ground was frozen, making the climbing difficult in the steepest places; but the views over the icy bay, sparkling beneath the glorious effulgence of the sky, were enchanting. It seemed then a sad thing that any part of so precious a night had been lost in sleep. The starlight was so full that I distinctly saw not only the bay with its multitude of glittering bergs, but most of the lower portions of the glaciers, lying pale and spirit-like amid the huge silent mountains. The nearest glacier in particular was so distinct that it seemed to be glowing with light that came from within itself. Not even in dark nights have I ever found any difficulty in seeing large glaciers; but on this mountain-top, amid so much ice, in the heart of so clear and frosty a night,

crossed over to our Sunday storm-camp, cautiously boring a way through the bergs. We found the shore lavishly adorned with a fresh arrival of assorted bergs that had been left stranded at high tide. They were arranged in a broad, curving row, looking intensely clear and pure on the gray sand, and, with the sun-

DRAWN BY J. A. FRASER, FROM A SKETCH MADE BY THE AUTHOR IN 1879.   ENGRAVED BY C. A. POWELL.

THE HUGH MILLER GLACIER.

everything was luminous, and I seemed to be poised in a vast hollow between two skies of equal brightness. How strong I felt after my exhilarating scramble, and how glad I was that my good angel had called me before the glorious night succeeding so glorious a morning had been spent!

I got back to camp in time for an early breakfast, and by daylight we had everything packed and were again under way. The fiord was frozen nearly to its mouth, and though the ice was so thin that it gave us but little trouble in breaking a way, yet it showed us that the season for exploration in these waters was well-nigh over. We were in danger of being imprisoned in a jam of icebergs, for the water-spaces between them freeze rapidly, binding the floes into one mass. Across such floes it would be almost impossible to drag a canoe, however industriously we might ply the ax, as our Hoona guide took great pains to warn us. I would have kept straight down the bay from here, but the guide had to be taken home, and the provisions we left at the bark hut had to be got on board. We therefore

beams pouring through them, suggested the jewel-paved streets of the New Jerusalem.

On our way down the coast, after examining the front of the beautiful Geikie Glacier, we obtained our first broad view of the Muir Glacier, the last of all the grand company to be seen, the stormy weather having hidden it when we first entered the bay. It was now perfectly clear, and the spacious, prairie-like glacier, with its many tributaries extending far back into the snowy recesses of the mountains, made a magnificent display of its wealth, and I was strongly tempted to go and explore it at all hazards. But winter had come, and the freezing of its fiord was an insurmountable obstacle. I had, therefore, to be content for the present with sketching and studying its main features at a distance. When we arrived at the Hoona hunting-camp, the men, women, and children came swarming out to welcome us. In the neighborhood of this camp I carefully noted the lines of demarkation between the forested and disforested regions. Several mountains here are only in part disforested, and the lines separating the bare and the forested portions are

Mount Lituya.   Mount Fairweather.

DRAWN BY J. A. FRASER, FROM A SKETCH MADE BY THE AUTHOR IN 1890.   ENGRAVED BY R. C. COLLINS.

FAIRWEATHER RANGE, FROM GLACIER BAY.

well defined. The soil, as well as the trees, had slid off the steep slopes, leaving the edges of the woods raw-looking and rugged.

At the mouth of the bay a series of moraine islands shows that the trunk glacier that occupied the bay halted here for some time, and deposited this island material as a terminal moraine; that more of the bay was not filled in shows that, after lingering here, it receded comparatively fast. All the level portions of trunks of glaciers occupying ocean fiords, instead of melting back gradually in times of general shrinking and recession, as inland glaciers with sloping channels do, melt almost uniformly over all the surface until they become thin enough to float. Then, of course, with each rise and fall of the tide the sea-water, with a temperature usually considerably above the freezing-point, rushes in and out beneath them, causing rapid waste of the nether surface, while the upper is being wasted by the weather, until at length the fiord portions of these great glaciers become comparatively thin and weak, and are broken up, and vanish almost simultaneously from the mouths of their fiords to the heads of them.

Glacier Bay is undoubtedly young as yet. Vancouver's chart, made only a century ago, shows no trace of it, though found admirably faithful in general. It seems probable, therefore, that even then the entire bay was occupied by a glacier of which all those described

above, great though they are, were only tributaries. Nearly as great a change has taken place in Sum Dum Bay since Vancouver's visit, the main trunk glacier there having receded from eighteen to twenty-five miles from the line marked on his chart.

The next season (1880), on September 1, I again entered Glacier Bay, and steered direct for the Muir Glacier. I was anxious to make my main camp as near the ice-wall as possible, to watch the discharge of the bergs. Toyatte, the grandest Indian I ever knew, had been killed soon after our return to Fort Wrangel; and my new captain, Tyeen, was inclined to keep at a safe distance from the "big ice-mountain," the threatening cliffs of which rose to a height of 300 feet above the water. After a good deal of urging he ventured within half a mile of them, on the east side of the fiord, where with Mr. Young I went ashore to seek a camp-ground on the moraine, leaving the Indians in the canoe. In a few minutes after we landed a huge berg sprung aloft with tremendous commotion, and the frightened Indians incontinently fled, plying their paddles in the tossing waves with admirable energy until they reached a safe shelter around the south end of the moraine, a mile down the inlet. I found a good place for a camp in a slight hollow where a few spruce stumps afforded abundance of firewood. But all efforts to get Tyeen out of his harbor failed. Nobody knew, he said, how far the ice-mountain could dash waves up the beach, and his canoe would be broken. Therefore I had my bedding and some provision carried to a high camp, and enjoyed the wildness alone.

Next morning at daybreak I pushed eagerly back over the snout and along the eastern margin of the glacier, to see as much as possible of the upper fountain region. About five miles back from the front I climbed a mountain 2500 feet high, from the flowery summit of which, the day being clear, the vast glacier and all of its principal branches were displayed in one magnificent view. Instead of a stream of ice winding down a mountain-walled valley, like the largest of the Swiss glaciers, the Muir is a

confluence of the large tributaries is about twenty-five miles. Though apparently as motionless as the mountains, it flows on forever, the speed varying in every part with the seasons, but mostly with the depth of the current, and the declivity, smoothness, and directness of the different portions of the basin. The flow of the central cascading portion near the front, as recently determined by Professor Reid, is at the rate of from two and a half to five inches an hour, or from five to ten feet a day. A strip of the main trunk about a mile in width, extending along the eastern margin about fourteen miles to a large lake filled with bergs, has but little motion, and is so little broken by crevasses that

DRAWN BY J. A. FRASER, FROM A SKETCH MADE BY THE AUTHOR IN 1879.   ENGRAVED BY CHARLES STATE.

THE PACIFIC GLACIER.
View of the front of Pacific Glacier from the head of Pacific Fiord, head of Glacier Bay.

broad, gently undulating prairie surrounded by innumerable icy mountains, from the far, shadowy depths of which flow the many tributary glaciers that form the great central trunk. There are seven large tributaries, from two to six miles wide where they enter the trunk, and from ten to twenty miles long, each of them fed by many secondary tributaries; so that the whole number of branches, great and small, pouring from the mountain fountains must number upward of two hundred, not counting the smallest. The area drained by this one grand glacier can hardly be less than 1000 square miles, and it probably contains as much ice as all the 1100 Swiss glaciers combined. The length of the glacier from the frontal wall back to the head of the farthest fountain is estimated at fifty miles, and the width of the main trunk just below the

one hundred horsemen might ride abreast over it without encountering much difficulty.

But far the greater portion of the vast expanse is torn and crumpled into a bewildering network of hummocky ridges and blades, separated by yawning gulfs and crevasses, so that the explorer, crossing the glacier from shore to shore, must always have a hard time. Here and there in the heart of the icy wilderness are spacious hollows containing beautiful lakes, fed by bands of quick-glancing streams that flow without friction in blue crystal channels, making most delightful melody, singing and ringing in silvery tones of peculiar sweetness, sun-filled crystals being the only flowers on their banks. Few, however, will be likely to enjoy them. Fortunately, to most travelers the thundering ice-wall, while comfortably accessible, is also by far the most interesting portion of the glacier.

The mountains about the great glacier were also seen from this standpoint in exceedingly grand and telling views, peaked and spired in endless variety of forms, and ranged and grouped in glorious array. Along the valleys of the main tributaries to the northwestward I saw far into their shadowy depths, one noble peak appearing beyond the other in its snowy robes in long, fading perspective. One of the most remarkable, fashioned like a superb crown with delicately fluted sides, stands in the middle of the second main tributary, counting from right to left. To the westward the majestic Fairweather Range lifted its peaks and

nearly 16,000 feet high), presents no well-marked features. Its ponderous glaciers have ground it away into long, curling ridges until, from this point of view, it resembles a huge twisted shell. The lower summits about the Muir Glacier, like this one, the first that I climbed, are richly adorned and enlivened with beautiful flowers, though they make but a faint show in a general view. Lines and flashes of bright green appear on the lower slopes as one approaches them from the glacier, and a fainter green tinge may be noticed on the subordinate summits at a height of 2000 or 3000 feet. The lower are made mostly by alder bushes, and the topmost by a lavish profusion of flowering plants, chiefly cassiope, vaccinium, pyrola, erigeron, gentiana,

DRAWN BY J. A. FRASER, FROM A PHOTOGRAPH BY REID.

ENGRAVED BY C. SCHWARZBURGER.

FRONT OF MUIR GLACIER, FROM MOUNT WRIGHT.

glaciers into the blue sky in all its glory. Mount Fairweather, though not the highest, is by far the noblest of all the sky-dwelling company, the most majestic in port and architecture of all the mountains I have ever seen. It is a mountain of mountains. La Pérouse, at the south end of the range, is also a magnificent mountain, symmetrically peaked and sculptured, and wears its robes of snow and glaciers in noble style. Lituya, as seen from here, is an immense double tower, severely plain and massive. Crillon, though the loftiest of all (being

campanula, anemone, larkspur, and columbine, with a few grasses and ferns. Of these cassiope is at once the commonest and the most beautiful and influential. In some places its delicate stems make mattresses on the mountain-tops two feet thick over several acres, while the bloom is so abundant that a single handful plucked at random will contain hundreds of its pale pink bells. The very thought of this, my first Alaskan glacier garden, is an exhilaration. Though it is 2500 feet high, the glacier flowed over its ground as a river flows over a boulder;

DRAWN BY J. A. FRASER, FROM A PHOTOGRAPH.   ENGRAVED BY ROBERT VARLEY.

VIEW OF FOSSIL FOREST NEAR THE FRONT OF MUIR GLACIER, ON THE WEST SIDE.

and since it emerged from the icy sea as from a sepulcher it has been sorely beaten with storms; but from all those deadly, crushing, bitter experiences comes this delicate life and beauty, to teach us that what we in our faithless ignorance and fear call destruction is creation.

As I lingered here night was approaching, so I reluctantly scrambled down out of my blessed garden to the glacier, and returned to my lonely camp, and, getting some coffee and bread, again went up the moraine close to the end of the great ice-wall. The front of the glacier is about three miles wide, but the sheer middle, berg-producing portion that stretches across the inlet from side to side, like a huge green-and-blue barrier, is only about two miles wide, and its height above the water is from 250 to 300 feet. But soundings made by Captain Carroll show that 720 feet of the wall is below the surface, while a third unmeasured portion is buried beneath the moraine detritus that is constantly deposited at the foot of it. Therefore, were the water and rocky detritus cleared away, a sheer precipice

of ice would be presented nearly two miles long and more than a thousand feet high. Seen from a distance, as you come up the fiord, it seems comparatively regular in form; but it is far otherwise: bold, jagged capes jut forward into the fiord, alternating with deep reëntering angles and sharp, craggy hollows with plain bastions, while the top is roughened with innumerable spires and pyramids and sharp, hacked blades leaning and toppling, or cutting straight into the sky.

The number of bergs given off varies somewhat with the weather and the tides, the average being about one every five or six minutes, counting only those large enough to thunder loudly, and make themselves heard at a distance of two or three miles. The very largest, however, may, under favorable conditions, be heard ten miles, or even farther. When a large mass sinks from the upper fissured portion of the wall, there is first a keen, piercing crash, then a deep, deliberate, prolonged, thundering roar, which slowly subsides into a low, muttering growl, followed by numerous smaller, grating, clashing sounds from the

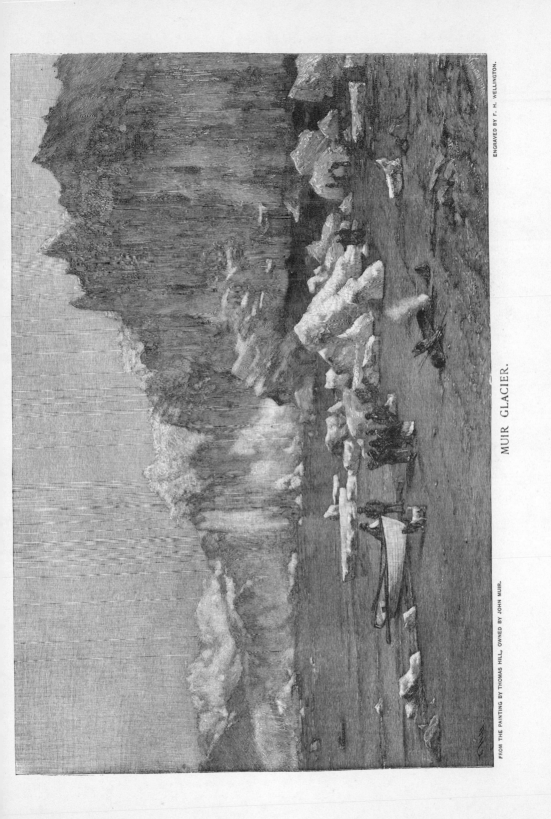

MUIR GLACIER.

FROM THE PAINTING BY THOMAS HILL, OWNED BY JOHN MUIR.

ENGRAVED BY F. H. WELLINGTON.

agitated bergs that dance in the waves about the newcomer as if in welcome; and these again are followed by the swash and roar of the waves that are raised and hurled against the moraines. But the largest and most beautiful of the bergs, instead of thus falling from the upper weathered portion of the wall, rise from the submerged portion with a still grander commotion, springing with tremendous voice and gestures nearly to the top of the wall, tons of water streaming like hair down their sides, plunging and rising again and again before they finally settle in perfect poise, free at last, after having formed part of a slow-crawling glacier for centuries. And as we contemplate their history, as we see them sailing past in their charming crystal beauty, how wonderful it seems that ice formed from pressed snow on the far-off mountains two or three hundred years ago should still be pure and lovely in color, after all its travel and toil in the rough mountain quarries in grinding and fashioning the face of the coming landscape! When the sunshine is sifting through the midst of this multitude of icebergs, and through the jets of radiant spray ever plashing from the blows of the falling and rising bergs, the effect is indescribably glorious. Glorious, too, are the nights along these crystal cliffs when the moon and stars are shining. Then the ice-thunder seems far louder than by day, and the projecting buttresses seem higher, as they stand forward in the pale light, relieved by the gloomy hollows, while the new bergs are dimly seen, crowned with faint lunar bows in the midst of the dashing spray. But it is in the darkest nights, when storms are blowing and the agitated waves are phosphorescent, that the most impressive displays are made. Then the long range of ice-bluffs, faintly illumined, is seen stretching through the gloom in weird, unearthly splendor, luminous foam dashing against it, and against every drifting berg; and amid all this wild, auroral splendor ever and anon some huge new-born berg dashes the living water into a yet brighter foam, and the streaming torrents pouring from its sides are worn as robes of light, while they roar in awful accord with the roaring winds, deep calling unto deep, glacier to glacier, from fiord to fiord.

John Muir.

29
Mount Saint Elias
Revisited

MOUNT SAINT ELIAS REVISITED.[1]

THE National Geographic Society, in connection with the United States Geological Survey, sent a small exploring party to Mount St. Elias, Alaska, in the summer of 1890.[2] The country visited during that expedition proved to be so interesting that a second expedition to the same region was decided on. The object of the second expedition was the extension of the surveys previously begun, and the ascent of Mount St. Elias. Like the first, it was placed in my charge. My party consisted of six camp hands, but did not include any scientific assistants. The camp hands were Thomas P. Stamy, J. H. Crumback, Thomas White, Neil McCarty, Frank G. Warner, and Will C. Moore. The first three were also members of the expedition of 1890. The necessary preparations for camp life were made at Seattle, Washington, late in May, 1891. We sailed from Port Townsend early on the morning of May 30, on the United States revenue steamer *Bear*, in command of Captain M. A. Healy, and after a pleasant voyage reached Yakutat, Alaska, on June 4. Arrangements were made there with the Rev. Karl J. Hendricksen, in charge of the Swedish Mission, to meet us on our return at the head of Yakutat Bay on September 25, with a boat and some provisions which we left at the Mission.

The weather on June 5 being thick and stormy, the *Bear* remained at her anchorage until early the next morning, when she started toward Icy Bay, fifty miles west of Yakutat, the locality chosen for beginning our work. At nine o'clock we were about a mile off shore at the place designated on the charts as Icy Bay, although, as previously known, no bay now exists there. The weather was calm. Scarcely a ripple disturbed the surface of the sea, but the usual ocean swell was breaking in long lines of foam on the low sandy beach. A boat was lowered, and Lieutenant D. H. Jarvis went shoreward to examine the surf and choose a place for landing. He returned in about an hour, and reported that landing seemed practicable at a point which we found afterward was about a mile east of the principal mouth of the Yahtse River. Owing to the unfavorable

condition of the surf, except at high tide, the landing of our party with its stores, instruments, etc., was not completed until early on the morning of June 8. As our landing was accompanied by a sad accident, in which the lives of six brave men were lost, I shall pass briefly over the painful incident. The boats that took us ashore were in command of Lieutenants G. McConnell, H. M. Broadbent, D. H. Jarvis, and L. L. Robinson. Three of the boats capsized, one of which was in charge of Lieutenant Robinson, and from that boat only one man reached shore alive. Lieutenant Robinson, four of his boat's crew, and Will C. Moore of my party were drowned. I cannot speak too highly of the kindness we received from Captain Healy and from the officers associated with him, or of the bravery with which the lieutenants I have mentioned, and the men under their command, faced imminent danger and suffered no small hardships in order to facilitate the work of our expedition. Lieutenant Robinson's body was recovered by his comrades and taken to Sitka for interment. The remainder of the men lost were buried near where their bodies were washed ashore.

The *Bear* steamed away to the southwest about three o'clock in the morning of June 8, leaving my party to begin the work which was to occupy us for several months. Our first effort after landing was to remove our "outfit" from the low sand-bar, where it was liable to be washed away should a high tide be accompanied by a shoreward-blowing gale, to a place of safety in the edge of the forest to the eastward. There we established a camp in a delightful spot, about a mile from the sea, and on the border of an open meadow, which was white with strawberry blossoms. West of the Yahtse, and beyond a plateau of broken ice ten or fifteen miles broad, formed by a lobe of the Malaspina glacier, rises a range of "hills," as we called them, in contrast with the greater mountains near at hand, which present abrupt precipices between three and four thousand feet high, to the south. Their northern slopes are more gentle, and are deeply buried beneath snow-fields which contribute to swell the flood of the great Guyot glacier. This splendid range has been named the Robinson Hills, in memory of Lieutenant L. L. Robinson. Our general line of march from Icy Bay was almost due north. For about five miles we traversed broad, barren openings through the forest, formed by the flood-plains of swift glacial streams. The conditions of travel were very favorable, except where the streams were too swift and too deep

[1] The pictures in this article have been drawn from photographs taken by the expedition.

[2] A brief account of the expedition of 1890 appeared in THE CENTURY MAGAZINE for April, 1891, and more fully in the National Geographic Magazine for May, 1891.

to wade, or the sand in their bottoms so soft that it approached the condition of quicksand. Once while returning from a camp at the Chaix Hills to Icy Bay, not being able to find logs with which to make a raft, we had to swim one swift icy stream, and wade another that was considerably more than waist deep. A plunge into ice-water on a chilly, rainy day is far from pleasant, but can be endured if one takes it boldly. To wade slowly out from shore until deep water is reached is a torture that few can withstand. The best way is to take a heroic plunge where the bank is steep, and make the change from air to water as nearly instantaneous as possible.

From a camp at the foot of the Malaspina glacier we cut a trail, about four miles long, through the exceedingly dense vegetation growing on the moraines which cover the outer margin of the ice-sheet. This vegetation is a continuation of the forest covering the flat lands to the south, and extends without a break up over the steep face of the glacier, and thence inland in many places to a distance of from four to five miles. North of the belt of vegetation covering the border of the glacier, we crossed twelve or fifteen miles of exceedingly rough moraine-covered ice and reached the Chaix Hills, which we climbed. Their southern slope is bare of vegetation except at the base, and is buttressed by many sharp ridges, too steep to climb, which unite to form pinnacles above. Joining the pinnacles are graceful curves formed by the exceedingly sharp crest. Their topographic forms alone are sufficient to show the geologist that they have resulted from a very recent uplift. We are told that the architects of India placed outstanding pavilions from which to view the beauties of their " dreams in marble "; so in Alaska, on an infinitely grander scale, the Chaix Hills, situated ten miles in front of the vast southward-facing precipice of the St. Elias range, afford a point of observation that can not be surpassed.

The Chaix Hills rise through a sea of ice, the limits of which can not be determined from their summits. Looking east, and south, there is nothing in sight but an apparently limitless plateau of ice, forming the Malaspina glacier. To the north there is a belt of irregular hilly ground covered by snow-fields and glaciers, and bristling with peaks, which are barren and naked during the summer season. Looking over these, the entire southern slope of Mount St. Elias is in full view. A seemingly level field of ice, forming the Libbey glacier, stretches up to the immediate base of the vast precipice leading to the top of the range. The elevation of the actual base of the mountain is about 2000 feet. The precipitous slope rising above it is 16,000 feet high. The snow breaking away near the top of the mountain rushes down in great avalanches to its very base, and is precipitated upon the surface of the glacier below. Mount St. Elias terminates at the top in a massive pyramid, from the base of which, as seen from the south, a prominent shoulder rises on each side. The eastern shoulder has an elevation of 14,600 feet at its extremity; it then falls off abruptly, and the range terminates about six miles to the east of the main summit. The west shoulder is 16,400 feet high, and beyond it to the west there is a steep descent in the crest line, but the range is continued indefinitely toward the northwest, and bristles with magnificent peaks and sharp crests as far as the eye can reach. Northeast from the Chaix Hills, across a portion of the Malaspina glacier, are the Samovar Hills, which are also, at least in part, formed of stratified morainal deposits, and, like the Chaix Hills, have been sculptured into a multitude of picturesque tent-like forms. Beyond the Samovar Hills rise the sharp peaks of the Hitchcock range, and the white pinnacles and domes of Mount Cook and Mount Irving. They are among the most attractive mountains in the entire Mount St. Elias region. Between Mounts Irving and St. Elias is the Augusta range, on which rise Mounts Augusta, Malaspina, Jeannette, Newton, and several other prominent snow-clad peaks. Far away to the southeast, beyond the Malaspina glacier, is a host of marvelous mountains, lessening in perspective, until the commanding summit of Mount Fairweather terminates the magnificent panorama. On perfectly clear days, when there is not a vapor wreath anywhere about the mountains, it is difficult to realize their full magnificence, owing to the absence of shadows and an apparent flattening of the rugged slopes. On such rare, perfect days there frequently comes a change. The cold winds from the vast ice-fields north of the mountains are beaten back by warm, moist winds from the south, and cloud-wreaths appear in horizontal bands far below the gleaming summits. Under such conditions the mountains lose their flatness, and buttresses and amphitheaters appear where before were expressionless walls. The mountains seem to awaken, and to become aware of their own dignity and sublimity. Usually the first sign of a coming change, when the weather is clear, is a small cloud-banner on the extreme summit of St. Elias. This signal is a warning that can be seen for a hundred and fifty miles in every direction and should not be ignored. Soon other peaks repeat the alarm, like bale-fires in time of invasion, and Mounts Augusta, Cook, and far-away Fairweather fling out their beacons to show that a storm is nigh.

Repairing to a cache that had been left on the border of the clearing southeast of the

Chaix Hills, we made a camp on the glacier, having the luxury, however, of a thin layer of broken slate beneath our blankets; and on the next day, July 8, advanced about five miles northward, when we again encamped on a thin moraine composed of black slate, and the day following brought up the remainder of our supplies. On July 10 we had breakfast at midnight, and began a weary tramp through soft snow to the Samovar Hills. Strange mirage effects appeared on the vast ice-fields when the sun arose. A white mist gathered about us when the warm sunlight touched the glacier, but we traveled on, guiding our course by compass. The light shining through the mist made white halos of remarkable beauty, which lessened the monotony of traveling through the fog. The snow became very soft and every step was wearisome, but still we pressed on, hour after hour, as there was no halting-place. We finally reached the extreme west end of the Samovar Hills, and pitched our tents on a little hillock of mosses and flowers, from which the snow had recently retreated. At our camping-place the Agassiz glacier emerges from a deep cañon about three miles broad, and descending a steep slope, which is a continuation of the precipitous southern face of the Samovar Hills, forms a splendid ice-fall that bristles with pinnacles and ice-blades separated by deep blue crevasses. Late in the afternoon of July 12 we worked our way, with the sled lightly loaded, up the border of the ice-fall near camp, and, after reaching its summit and threading the maze of crevasses just above, gained the center of the glacier. The snow ahead seeming smooth and unobstructed, we left the sled and returned to camp, where each man shouldered a heavy pack and started up the ice-fall once more, while I remained in camp, having enough to occupy my attention during the next day in the neighboring hills. The plan was for the men to advance with the sled as far up the Agassiz glacier as they could during the cold hours of the night when the snow was hard; then to make a cache and return the next day.

The men regained the sled in safety, and, after packing their loads upon it, began the weary tramp; but they had scarcely gone a hundred yards when Stamy and White, who were in the lead, felt the snow give way, and fell about twenty feet into a crevasse. The snow covering the crevasse had previously fallen in, leaving a thin, unbroken dome, but had caught in the fissure and formed a kind of bridge on which the men alighted; except for this they would have gone down to unknown depths. The snow that fell in with them fortunately prevented their moving until McCarty, with great promptness and presence of mind, lowered a rope, and they were assisted to the surface. This accident came nearer being serious than any other we had while on the ice, and served as a warning. After its occurrence we did not begin our night marches until an hour or two past midnight, when the twilight had increased in brightness sufficiently to make traveling safe. On our return, in passing the same ice-fall, we had another accident similar to the one just described. We were marching in single file, and, feeling perhaps over-confident after living for weeks on the glaciers, did not attach ourselves to a life-line, as was our custom in marching over snow which might conceal dangerous crevasses. I was in the lead, and just after passing safely over a snow-covered crevasse heard an exclamation from White, who followed a few steps in my rear, and on looking back saw that he had disappeared, leaving only a hole in the snow to indicate the direction of his departure. Returning quickly, I looked down the hole but saw only the walls of a blue crevasse; a curve in the opening had carried my companion out of sight. He replied to my shout, however, and with the aid of a line was soon on the surface again, uninjured. On the night when Stamy and White came so near losing their lives, several efforts were made by the men to continue their march, but crevasses thinly covered with snow were found to bar their way in every direction but the one by which they arrived. At last they abandoned the attempt to advance, and returned to camp. Early the following day we all returned to the sled, and by skirting along the side of the glacier, and in places climbing along the steep, snow-covered hillside, managed to get around the difficult tract and make a long march ahead.

The Agassiz glacier above the fall at the Samovar Hills is remarkably smooth, and but little crevassed, except along its immediate borders. Its principal tributary is the Newton glacier, which occupies an exceedingly wild valley between the east end of the St. Elias range and the west end of the Augusta range. These two ranges overlap *en échelon*, and each is exceedingly steep and rugged. The walls overlooking the glacier on either side are seldom less than 10,000 feet high, while the peaks that bristle along their crests rise to elevations of from 12,000 to 14,000 feet. At the foot of the ice-fall over which the Newton glacier descends and becomes a part of the Agassiz glacier, the elevation is 3000 feet above the sea. The amphitheater where the glacier has its principal source, between Mount St. Elias and Mount Newton, has an elevation of a little over 8000 feet. The glacier makes this descent of about 5000 feet principally at four localities where ice-falls occur. Between the falls the slope is quite gentle, and in some places the grade is reversed; that is, the ice rises bodily to some extent when pass-

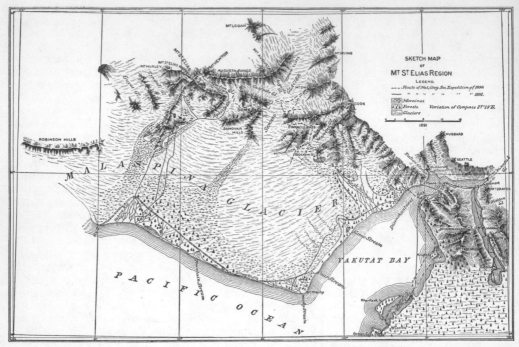

SKETCH MAP OF THE MOUNT SAINT ELIAS REGION, PREPARED BY THE U. S. GEOLOGICAL SURVEY.

ing over obstructions. We made two camps on the broad, undulating surface of the Agassiz glacier, each of them at the margin of a lake of the most wonderful blue. At the higher of these camps we abandoned our sled, which had done good service, and resumed "packing" our outfit. The first ice-fall above was passed by scaling the steep rock-cliff where it emerges from beneath the ice on the west. The actual vertical descent is about five hundred feet. The ice in plunging over the precipice is broken into tables and columns of great beauty. This fall differs in character from the fall in the Agassiz glacier at the end of the Samovar Hills, owing to the fact that it is well above the snow-line and in the névé region. The columns on the steepest part of the fall are not thin spires and blades of ice, as in similar situations lower down, but prisms and pilasters of homogeneous snow, which breaks like granular marble and is without structure, excepting lines of horizontal stratification. Above the fall the glacier is broken from side to side into rudely rectangular tables, and as these are carried over the steep descent they become separated, and frequently stand as isolated columns a hundred feet high, supporting massive capitals. The architectural resemblances of these columns, all of the purest white with deep blue chasms between, are often very striking, especially in the twilight of the short summer nights, when they appear like the ruins of marble temples. Above the first fall we traversed a great area where the crevasses were

long and wide, and separated level-topped tables of snow as large as blocks of city houses, many of which were tilted in various directions. We then came to a second fall, less grand than the first, but more difficult to scale, owing to the fact that we could not climb the cliff at the side, but had to work our way up through partially filled crevasses in the fall itself, and to cut steps in the sides of vertical snow-cliffs. Once, after an hour of hard work in cutting steps up an overhanging snow-cliff and gaining the top, we found ourselves on a broad table separated from its neighbors on all sides by profound crevasses, and had to retreat and try another way. At length we gained the snow-slope on the mountain-side overlooking the broken region below, and found an open way, although exposed to avalanches, up to Rope Cliff, which had given us some trouble the year before. Knowing the conditions at Rope Cliff, however, it did not cause delay. One of us climbed the rock-face and fastened a rope around a large stone at the top, which made future ascents and descents easy. Fragments of the rope left at this place the year before were found. This was the only trace of our former trail that we saw; all else had been obliterated by the deep snows of winter.

About two miles above Rope Cliff we entered a region of huge crevasses, near the place where we had to cut steps up a precipice of snow the year previous. The breaks in the snow were not only numerous, but broad and deep, extending clear across the glacier. On the south there was a big wall of snow parallel with the course of the glacier, and connecting with the cliffs above in such a manner that we could not pass around it. We encamped on a table of snow surrounded on all sides by cre-

DRAWN BY JOHN A. FRASER.

A CAÑON IN THE CHAIX HILLS.

vasses, but inclined so that we could cross to a neighboring table, and there spent the night. An examination of the broken snow ahead from the upturned edge of a fallen snow-block of great dimensions failed to show any practicable way to advance. From our elevated station we could see entirely across the glacier, but, in attempting to pick out a way through the maze of crevasses, always came to a yawning blue gulf or to an impassable wall of snow. At last, almost in desperation, we decided to cut steps up the great wall that ran parallel with the glacier, trusting that the surface above would be connected with the less broken region above the fall. This cliff of snow, which we called White Cliff, was the upper side of a great crevasse, the lower lip of which had fallen and partially filled the gulf at its base. To reach its foot we had to cut steps down a cliff of snow about fifty feet high, and work our way across a partially filled crevasse of profound depth to a table of snow forming a terrace on the opposite side. From this terrace we could cross another small crevasse on broken, angular snow-blocks which partially filled it, and gain the base of the cliff. Above us rose a wall of snow 200 feet high, with an overhanging cornice-like ridge midway up, which projected five or six feet from the face of the cliff and was eight feet thick. McCarty and Stamy were with me, and we began to cut steps, taking advantage of a diagonal crack in the cliff which assisted considerably in the task. All the way up to the cornice we had to hold on by alpenstocks while we used our ice-axes. Reaching the cornice, an opening was cut through it, McCarty and Stamy doing the

greater part of the work. Once above the cornice, the slope was less steep, and McCarty, by using two alpenstocks, was able to ascend the rest of the way without using an ice-ax. Placing an alpenstock firmly in the snow at the top, and making a rope fast to it, our packs were hauled up and we were all soon at the top.

Other great crevasses occurred above White Cliff, but they were in the bordering snow-field and not in the glacier proper, and ran in the direction we wished to travel. By following the broad surface between two of the great gorges we advanced to the point where we had our highest camp the year previous, and then began the ascent of the last ice-fall in the Newton glacier. This fall was higher than any previously encountered, but not so steep, and the blocks of snow were larger. The ascent to the amphitheater above is over 1000 feet. The day we made the climb we reached the foot of the fall about six in the morning, and found the snow soft and traveling difficult. The day was hot, and the elevation being considerable our task proved a fatiguing one. At length we reached the vast amphitheater in which the Newton glacier has its source, and pitched our tent as far within the entrance as safety from avalanches would permit. This proved to be our highest camp, its elevation being a little over 8000 feet.

During the ascent of the Newton glacier the weather had become more unsettled than in the earlier part of the season, which was due in great measure to our increased elevation. While enjoying fair weather near the coast, we did not appreciate the fact that every cloud which wrapped its soft sunlit folds about the higher mountains was accompanied by a local snow-storm. We soon learned, however, that not every cloud has a silver lining. Mist and rain delayed our progress and made our camps on the snow wretchedly uncomfortable, yet they added variety and beauty to the wonderful scenery of the snow-covered mountains, and brought out a world of beauty that would never be suspected if the air always retained its transparency and the sun always shone with blinding intensity. As we ascended the Newton glacier, and gained the summit of one ice-fall after another, the panorama of mighty snow-covered peaks and broad, crevassed glaciers became more and more unfolded, and more and more magnificent. The view eastward down the glacier is one of the most impressive pictures that even Alaskan mountains can furnish. The cliffs of the St. Elias range on the south, and of the Augusta range on the north, rise near at hand to great heights, and are as rugged and angular as it is possible for mountains to be. The snow-covered slopes are utterly bare of vegetation; not even a lichen tints the isolated outcrops of rock. Looking eastward between the two lines of precipices towering over a mile in height, and rising above into pinnacles and crests, the eye follows the descending slope of the glacier, which expands as new ice-streams pour in flood after flood of ice. The surface of the glacier appears rugged in the foreground, but is softened in the distance until only the broadest of the blue gashes that break its surface are visible. Five or six miles

the clustered domes and pinnacles of Mount Cook and Mount Irving, two sister peaks of equal grandeur. Beyond these, glimpses may be had at certain stations of Mount Vancouver, and of still other shining summits which are not named, and perhaps were never before seen by human eyes.

The view down the glacier is a winter landscape. In the full noontide the scene is of dazzling whiteness, except where cliffs cast their

DRAWN BY A. CASTAIGNE   ENGRAVED BY J. W. EVANS.

CUTTING STEPS AT WHITE CLIFF.

away is a heavily snow-covered group of hills, a spur of the Augusta range, which deflects the glacier to the south and causes it to disappear beyond a rugged headland of rocks and snow. Rising above the foot-hills that turn the frozen current are magnificent peaks, the like of which are seldom seen, and are utterly unknown to all who have not ventured into the frozen solitudes of lofty mountains. Mount Malaspina and Mount Augusta, cathedrals more sublime than ever human architect dreamed of, limit the view on the northeast. To the right of these, and forming the background of the picture, rise

shadows or clouds screen the sunlight. The snow-fields and the snow-curtained precipices, when in shadow, have a delicate blue tint that seems almost a phosphorescence. Except on rare occasions, the only colors are white and many shades of blue, with dark relief here and there where the cliffs are too precipitous to retain a covering. Sometimes the sunlight, shining through delicate clouds of ice-spicules, spreads a halo of brilliant colors around some shining summit, or, striking the surface of a snow-field at the proper angle, spreads over it a web of rainbow tints as delicate and change-

DRAWN BY JOHN A. FRASER.   MOUNT SAINT ELIAS FROM THE NEWTON GLACIER.

able as the pearly lining of a sea-shell. The sheen on the surface of the frosted snow suggests the fancy that there the spirits of the Alpine flowers have their paradise.

Beautiful as were the every-day scenes about our camps in the snow, there came at length one rare evening when the mountains assumed a superlative grandeur. We had retired to our tent early in the evening, but on looking out a few hours afterward to see if the conditions were favorable for making a night march, I was surprised to see the change that had taken place in the usually pale-blue night landscape. The sun had long since gone down behind the great peaks to the northwest, but an afterglow of unusual brightness was shining through the deep clefts in the Augusta range, and illuminating a few mountain-slopes here and there which chanced to be so placed as to catch the level shafts of rosy light. The contrast between the peaks and snow-fields of delicate blue faintly illuminated by the light of the moon, and the massive mountains of flame, made one of the most striking scenes that can be imagined. The boldness and strength of the picture, the wonderful detail of every illuminated precipice and glittering ice-field, in contrast with the uncertain, shadowy forms of half-revealed pinnacles and spires, together with the absence of light in the sky and the absolute stillness of the mighty encampment of snowy mountains, was something so strange and unreal that it bordered on the supernatural.

But the great mountains are not always beautiful or always inspiring. When the clouds thickened about us and enshrouded our lonely tent,

which always seemed lost in the vast wilderness of snow and ice, and when the snow fell in fine crystals hour after hour and day after day with unvarying monotony, burying our tent and blotting out the trail which was our only connection with the land of verdure and flowers in the region below, our life was dreary enough. Camp-fires, the ingleside of tent life, were impossible, as we were over 6000 feet above the timber-line, and fully 30 miles distant from the nearest trees. During storms there was nothing to be seen from our tent but the white snow immediately around us, and the vapor- and snow-filled air above. The only evidence of the near presence of lofty mountains was the frequent crash and prolonged, rumbling roar of avalanches, which shook the glacier beneath and seemed to threaten us with annihilation. We occupied our camp at the entrance of the amphitheater at the head of the Newton glacier for twelve days, and during that time, owing to the prevalence of clouds and snow-storms, were able to advance only once.

On the morning of July 24, McCarty, Stamy, and I were early astir, and, having had our breakfast, left the tent at two o'clock and started to climb to the divide between Mount Newton and Mount St. Elias, and as much higher as possible. The morning was clear and cold, but the snow, owing to its extreme dryness, was scarcely firm enough to sustain our weight. On account of the advance of the season, we now had about four hours each night during which the light was not sufficient, even during clear weather, to allow us to travel over crevassed ice in safety. When we started, the twilight was sufficiently bright to reveal the outlines of the great peaks about us, but every detail in their rugged sides was lost. All within the vast amphitheater was dark and shadowy. On our right rose Mount Newton in almost vertical precipices a mile in height, with great glaciers pouring down like frozen cataracts from unseen regions above. On the left stood the crowning pyramid of Mount St. Elias, its roof-like slope rising nearly two miles in vertical height above the even snow-field we were crossing. The saddle between these two giant summits is the lowest point in the wall of the amphitheater, but even that was 4000 feet above us.

During the earlier portion of our stay in our highest camp, when the weather was warm and

On the morning of July 24, however, all was still. Jack Frost, working stealthily throughout the night, had silenced the music of the rills, and fettered the mighty avalanches with chains of crystal. As we advanced, the soft twilight grew stronger, and just as we reached the base of the icy precipices we were to scale, on looking up, I saw the summit of Mount St. Elias aflame with the first ruddy light of morning,

An Apennine, touched singly by the sun,
Dyed rose-red by some earliest shaft of dawn,
While all the other peaks were dark, and slept.

In front of us rose steep cliffs, the height and ruggedness of which appeared to increase as we approached. Across the slope from side to

DRAWN BY A. CASTAIGNE.   ENGRAVED BY J. W. EVANS.

MOUNT NEWTON FROM THE GLACIER.

the peaks surrounded by clouds or shut out from view by snow-storms, the roar of avalanches was frequent both day and night. Sometimes three great snow-slides would come thundering down the cliff at one time, and pour hundreds of tons of snow and ice into the valley. Avalanches of great size were frequent, both from the slopes of Mount Newton and Mount St. Elias, and from the precipices beneath the saddle. To venture into the valley when the south winds were blowing, and the lower ice-slopes were trickling with water, would have been rash in the extreme.

side ran blue walls of ice, marking the upper sides of crevasses. In several places avalanches had broken away, leaving pinnacles and buttresses of stratified snow, 200 or 300 feet high, ready to topple over in their turn as soon as the sun touched them. Trails of rough, broken snow, below the cliffs, marked the paths avalanches had taken during the day previous. On the right of the slope leading to the divide rose the frowning wall of Mount Newton, and on the left the still greater slope of Mount St. Elias. From each of these we had seen magnificent avalanches descend upon the slope we

DRAWN BY JOHN A. FRASER.   ENGRAVED BY F. W. SUTHERLAND.

A SMALL GLACIER ON THE SIDE OF MOUNT NEWTON.

were to climb, and then, turning, rush down into the valley below. The grooved and ice-sheathed paths of these great snow-slides were plainly visible, and were to be avoided if possible. At first the slope was not so steep but that we could climb by digging in the long spikes with which our shoes were provided, and with the constant aid of our alpenstocks; but soon we came to a broad crevasse which we had to follow for several rods before finding a bridge by which to cross. Owing to the steepness of the slope on which the snow rested, the crevasses were really faults, their upper edges rising high above the lower. This made them especially troublesome in ascending. The bridges spanning the chasms were usually poor, and in crossing them we had to exercise the greatest precautions. In some instances, where the slivers of ice crossing a crevasse diagonally seemed too weak to hold the weight of a man, should he try to walk across, we would place two alpenstocks from the lower lip out on the central portion of the bridge, and then one of us would crawl out, and lying flat on the bridge, so as to distribute his weight, advance the alpenstock to the other side and so gain the opposite brink. In one place, where the hanging wall of the crevasse offered no ledge or foot-hold of any kind, we pushed the sharp end of the alpenstock well into it, and one of us, standing on the poles, cut a step in the cliff, and then, making a hand-hold with another alpenstock, cut steps to the top. Some of the way we climbed in the paths of small avalanches that had left rough snow on the slope and saved us the trouble of cutting steps. But for half the way probably to the divide we had to cut our trail up slopes that were too steep and too smooth to climb. In this way we slowly advanced, varying our course now toward the base of the cliff leading up to Mount Newton, and again toward the great pyramid forming the summit of Mount St. Elias, according as the ascent was more gentle, or the crevasses less difficult, on one side or the other. In two or three instances our progress seemed barred by impassable crevasses, but a search always revealed a bridge or a place where the openings were narrow, and we were able to advance.

At length we could see that only one crevasse intervened between us and the smooth slope leading to the divide. This crossed diagonally downward from the south side of the slope to near the base of Mount Newton. Beyond where it ended on the right there was an exceedingly steep slope, sheathed with ice, that led to the divide. This seemed the only way we could expect to advance. The upper wall of the crevasse rose about fifty feet above its lower edge, and was hung with icicles. At the east end a curtain of ice, starting from the top of the upper wall, arched over and joined the lower brink, leaving a hollow chamber within hung with thousands of icicles. In spite of my anxiety to press on, I could not but admire the beauty of the glittering mass of fluted columns, arranged like the pipes of a great organ and fully exposed to the morning sun at the top, while their tapering ends were lost in the obscurity of the blue gulf below. Each icicle was frosted on one side with snow-flakes that had been blown against it and frozen to its surface. The play of rainbow tints among these millions of flashing crystals and burnished pendants made a scene of unusual beauty, even in a region whose wonders multiply as one advances. The lower lip of the crevasse had been built up with snow blown from the heights above, and formed a sharp-crested drift, along which we worked our way to the north end of the crevasse. I then fastened the end of a life-line about my waist, while Stamy and McCarty, placing an alpenstock deep in the snow and taking a half-turn with the line around it, slowly paid out the slack as I advanced. Where the dome of ice curved down and met the lower edge of the crevasse, there was a little ledge about six inches broad, and where this ended only the overhanging shoulder formed by the dome remained. Once around the shoulder we would be able to reach the ice-slope leading to the divide. Cutting holes through the ice-dome a little below the height of my shoulder, I thrust my left arm through, and thus had a sure hold while cutting steps for my feet. Progressing in this way, I was soon around the curve, out of sight of my companions, and in a short time gained the foot of the slope leading upward. But I found that the ascent was so steep, and composed of such smooth ice, that it would require several hours of hard work for us to cut a way to the top, and before undertaking such a severe task I concluded to search for a more practicable route. Being no longer engaged in cutting steps, I became aware that I was in a somewhat dangerous position. The dome which I had passed around curved inward just below me, leaving a sheer descent of several hundred feet to the steep slope beneath, which fell away almost perpendicularly into the valley 3000 feet below. Had I fallen, I should have gone to the bottom of the cliffs before stopping, if some yawning crevasse had not received me. I worked my way slowly back to my companions, and we then followed the crevasse in the opposite direction. Near its highest portion there was a narrow space, where the snow blown from above had built up the snow-bank on the lower lip of the crevasse until it touched the top of the cliff of ice formed by the upper wall. The snow had also bridged a deep crevasse that ran at right angles to the main one, thus rendering us double assistance. These bridges were of light snow, and were so thin that we had to exercise great caution in crossing them lest we should break through. McCarty was now in the lead on the line to which we were all fastened, and, slowly making steps up the curtain of snow that descended from the top of the ice-cliff, he made his way upward out of sight of Stamy and myself who waited below. When he had progressed about 100 feet, the length of our line, he planted his alpenstock deep in the snow and shouted for us to come up. With the aid of the line and the steps that had been made, I was soon beside him, and, detaching myself from the line, continued up the slope, leaving the men to coil up the rope and follow.

I was now so near the crest of the divide that only a few yards remained before I should be able to see the country to the north; a vast region which no one had yet beheld. Pressing on, I pictured in fancy the character of the land beyond. Having crossed this same mountain-belt at the head of Lynn Canal, and traversed the country to the north of it, I fancied that I should behold a similar region north of Mount St. Elias. I expected to see a comparatively low, wooded country stretching away to the north, with lakes and rivers and perhaps some signs of human habitation, but I was entirely mistaken. What did meet my eager gaze was a vast snow-covered region, limitless in its expanse, through which hundreds, and perhaps thousands, of barren angular mountain-peaks projected. There was not a stream, not a lake, and not a trace of vegetation of any

LOOKING UP THE NEWTON GLACIER, MOUNT SAINT ELIAS ON THE LEFT.

The * on the upper border of the picture is placed over the highest point on the mountain-side reached by the explorers.—EDITOR.

kind in sight. A more desolate or a more utterly lifeless land one never beheld. Vast, smooth snow-surfaces, without crevasses or breaks, so far as I could judge, stretched away to unknown distances, broken only by jagged and angular mountain-peaks. The general elevation of the snow-surface is about 8000 feet, and the mountains piercing it are from 10,000 to 12,000 feet, or more, in altitude above the sea. To the northward I could see every detail in the forbidding landscape for miles and miles. The most distant peaks in view in that direction were thirty or forty miles away. One flat-topped mountain, due north by compass from my station, and an exception in its form to all the other peaks, I have called Mount Bear, in memory of the good ship which took us to Icy Bay. The other peaks were too numerous to name. To the southeast rose Mount Fairweather, plainly distinguishable although 200 miles away. At an equal distance to the northwest are two prominent mountain-ranges, the highest peaks of which appeared as lofty as Mount Fairweather. These must be in the vicinity of Mount Wrangle, but their summits were unclouded and gave no token of volcanic activity. I could look down upon the coast about Yakutat Bay, and distinguish each familiar island and headland. The dark shade on the shore, too distant to reveal its nature, was due to the dense forests on the lowlands between the mountains and the sea. This was the only indication of vegetation in all the vast landscape that lay spread out beneath my feet. The few rocks near at hand, which projected above the snow, were without the familiar tints of mosses and lichens. Even the ravens, which sometimes haunt the higher mountains, were nowhere to be seen. Utter desolation claimed the entire land. The view to the north called to mind the pictures given by Arctic explorers of the borders of the great Greenland ice-sheet, where rocky islands, known as "nunataks," alone break the monotony of the boundless sea of ice. The region before me was a land of nunataks.

The divide which we had reached was a narrow crest at the north end, but broadened to about fifty yards at the south. Along each side were snow-banks facing each other, and inclosing a V-shaped area some ten feet lower than the bordering crests of snow. We excavated a little chamber near the base of one of the steep snow-banks, in which to place a small lamp that we had brought with us, and melted some snow to obtain drinking-water. Owing to the lightness of the snow it required some time to get water enough to quench our intolerable thirst. This allowed us an opportunity to rest and eat a light lunch, while we studied the strange scene before us.

The day of our climb was unusually beautiful. Not a cloud obscured the sky. In the lower world it must have been an exceedingly warm summer day. In the rarer atmosphere with which we were surrounded the sun's rays poured down with dazzling splendor and scorching intensity. We wore deeply colored glasses to protect our eyes, but our faces, although tanned and weather-beaten by nearly two months' constant exposure, were blistered by the heat. Those of my readers who have not climbed high mountains will be surprised, perhaps, when I say that while our faces were actually blistering beneath the intensity of the sun's heat, our shoes immersed in the light snow were frozen stiff. At noon the temperature in the shade was 16° Fahr. The snow was light and dry, and showed no indications of softening, even at the surface. The white cliffs about us glittered like hoar-frost in the intense light.

Having finished our lunch, we passed on up the steep ridge leading from the divide to the summit of Mount St. Elias. We slowly cut our way up the slope, having a sheer descent of from 5000 to 6000 feet below us all the time. The breaking away of a foothold, or the loss of an alpenstock, might at any time have precipitated us down those fearful cliffs, where not even the crevasses would have stopped us before reaching the bottom of the amphitheater in which our tent was placed, fully a mile in vertical descent below. We were now above the region of avalanches, but an occasional roar came faintly through the rarified air, telling that large bodies of snow had broken away somewhere on the slopes below. With these exceptions the only sounds that broke the stillness were from the blows of our ice-ax and the beating of our own hearts. There is no stillness more profound than the silence of the mountains. As we slowly climbed up above the divide we could see more of the country to the northeast of Mount Newton, but in other directions the great panorama remained the same, or became less distinct. A change in the atmosphere, which obscured distant objects while it slightly lessened the painful intensity of the sunlight on the cliffs about us, told that an atmospheric disturbance was in progress, and that a storm was gathering. We pressed on, although the work of cutting steps at the altitude we had reached was exceedingly laborious, and gained a second outcrop of rock. At four o'clock we had attained an elevation of somewhat more than 14,500 feet, as determined by measurements made with two aneroid barometers. The great snow-slope continued to tower far above us, and we saw with deep regret that we had not the strength to reach the summit and return to our camp, already 6500 feet below us. Concluding that the only practicable plan would be for us to advance our camp on to the divide between Mount St. Elias and Mount Newton, and from there to attempt to reach the summit, we reluctantly turned back.

The descent began at five o'clock, and we experienced but little difficulty in regaining the divide, but had to be exceedingly careful in crossing the snow-bridge on the ice-slope below. In three places the steps cut during the ascent had been swept away by avalanches. At one locality where the trail went down the face of a steep bluff for about a hundred feet, and then ran diagonally along beneath an overhanging precipice of snow, we found that the cliff had broken away, carrying with it the steps cut on our way up. Below where the cliff had been, the avalanche caused by its fall had cut across a loop in our own trail in two places, but had filled a crevasse that had been troublesome to cross on our way up, and thus proved of some assistance. On reaching the top of the cliff where our steps had been we were at a loss to tell what had become of them, until we noticed the trail of the avalanche below. Had the shadows of evening been a little more dense, our return to camp would have been delayed until the next morning. As it was, however, McCarty scrambled down the slope with a rope fastened about his waist, and cut new steps. As we neared the bottom of the valley the light faded, and we had to find our way as best we could, since it was impossible to see the trail. The slopes were less steep than above, however, and we gained the level floor of the amphitheater without mishap. We reached our tent at ten o'clock, just twenty hours after leaving it. Allowing one hour for the cooking of our breakfast and another for preparing supper, but two hours out of twenty-four remained unaccounted for. The deficiency in the number of hours for sleep was compensated, however, by the fact that it was approaching noon the next day before we awoke.

A heavy cloud gathered about the summit of Mount St. Elias on the afternoon of July 25, and on the following day a snow-storm was in full force and continued until the evening of the next day. At one o'clock in the morning of July 27, I looked out of our tent and found a dense fog filling the valley; but at three o'clock the air was clear, and the absence of cloud banners on the high peaks assured us that the day would be fine. We immediately began preparations for climbing to the divide between Mount Newton and Mount St. Elias. Our plan was to make a cache of rations on the divide, and to advance our camp during the next favorable day. Owing to the delay at the start, we did not reach the foot of the ice-cliffs leading to the divide until the sun was shining full upon them. We began the ascent, but soon the snow, softened by the sun, began to fall in avalanches, which warned us that it was dangerous to proceed. A great avalanche starting far above us on the side of Mount St. Elias came rushing down the roof-like slope with the speed of an express-train. From the foot of the descending mass, tongue-like protrusions of snow shot out in advance, while all above was one vast rolling cloud of snow-spray. Blue crevasses which seemed wide enough to engulf the falling snow were crossed without making the slightest change in its course. On reaching the upper lip of such a gulf the base of the moving mass would shoot out into the air, and seemingly not curve downward at all until it struck the slope below and rushed on with accelerated speed. The rushing, roaring mass was irresistible. Heavy clouds of spray rolling onward, or blown back by the wind that the avalanche generated, became so dense that all beneath was concealed from view. Only a roar like thunder, and the trembling of the glacier on which we stood, told that many tons of ice and snow were involved in the catastrophe. The rushing monster, starting a mile above, came directly toward us until it poured down upon the border of the slope we were ascending; then, changing its course, it thundered on until it reached the floor of the amphitheater far below. The cloud of spray rolled on down the valley, and hung in the air long after the roar of the avalanche had ceased. When it did drift away we saw the fan-shaped mass of broken snow, in which the avalanche ended, looking like the delta of a stream, extending out half a mile into the valley.

With avalanches threatening us from the precipices on either hand, and from the slope up which we wished to ascend, it seemed foolhardy to persist in the attempt to reach the divide that day; so we left our packs in as sheltered a spot as we could find and beat a retreat. The next morning another snow-storm swept over the mountains, and the weather continued stormy for several days.

While Stamy, McCarty, and I were living in the snow, we had a single tent of light cotton cloth, seven feet square at the bottom and five feet high. Our bedding consisted of two sheets of light canvas, used for protecting our blankets, one double woolen blanket, and one light feather-quilt. Our cooking was done over a small coal-oil stove, and our food consisted almost entirely of corn griddle-cakes, bacon or corned beef, and coffee. To live under these conditions at an altitude of 8000 feet, during snow-storms and dense fogs, and

especially when the snow was melting so as to wet our blankets through and through, was very trying. Fearing that if we held on too long we should not have the strength and steadiness of nerve requisite to reach the summit, should the weather permit, I decided, although with great reluctance, to abandon the undertaking and return to Icy Bay. Whether we could advance or not depended on the direction of the wind; should it blow from the north across the broad ice-fields we had seen from the divide, it would bring clear, cold weather, the clouds would vanish from the mountains, and the avalanches be silenced; should it come from the south, it would be warm and moist, the clouds would thicken, and snow-storms and avalanches would render mountain-climbing impossible. The north side of St. Elias is not too steep to climb and offers no insurmountable obstacles, but the climate is very changeable, and clouds and snow-storms are the rule. Reaching the summit depends more upon the chance of getting clear weather at the proper time than on skill in Alpine work.

We began the descent on August 1. The trail leading back had been snowed over and could scarcely be traced; but the fog had lifted, although heavy storm-clouds still enveloped the higher peaks, and we were able to descend without much difficulty. We slowly worked our way through the great crevasses in the fall just below our highest camp, and thence over a comparatively even surface to White Cliff, which we descended with some little difficulty, the steps previously cut having melted away so as to be almost useless. The next day we rejoined the remainder of the party and reached "Sled Camp" on the Agassiz glacier. During our journey down the mountain until reaching the Samovar Hills rain fell almost continuously. At the Samovar Hills we reoccupied our old camp-ground. The flowers were still in bloom, and the air had that delightful fragrance one notices when first venturing into the woods in early spring. The change from the region of eternal snow and ice to an oasis of verdure and of flowers was welcome indeed. From the Samovar Hills we crossed the broad, gently sloping snow-field extending southwest, and made our next camp on a small island in the glacier separated from the northeast end of the Chaix Hills by about two miles of rugged ice. This bright little garden of flowers and ferns we named Moore's Nunatak, in memory of our comrade who was drowned at Icy Bay.

With McCarty and Warner for companions, I again entered the snow-covered region to the north, and made a side trip to the hills intermediate between Mount St. Elias and the Chaix Hills. During this trip, which lasted three days, we had one perfect day of uninterrupted sunshine, the beauty of which was enhanced to us by heavy clouds along the mountain-sides, thus furnishing the contrast necessary to bring out the full magnificence of the frozen heights that towered above us. The lakes to the north of the Chaix Hills were still heavily encumbered with ice, and on the hills bare of snow the earliest of spring-flowers were just awakening. It was springtime to us also, after having been in the wintry mountains for several weeks. We enjoyed the warmth of the glad sunshine, the fresh odors that filled the air, and the delicate tints on the flower-covered slopes around us, far more than we did the stern magnificence of the snow-covered precipices of the great mountains. The storms that had recently passed had left the mountains covered with a fresh mantle of brilliant white down to a level of 4000 feet above the sea. The new snow had not yet been torn from the precipices by avalanches, but was clinging to many of the steepest slopes. In the full splendor of a blazing sun the great ranges seemed mountains of light.

Returning to Moore's Nunatak we passed a night, and then rejoined the rest of our party below at our old camp on the south side of the Chaix Hills. A day or two later we crossed the extreme western end of the Malaspina glacier, just at its junction with another vast plateau of ice stretching westward. Where these two ice-fields join there is a depression which marks the subglacial course of the Yahtse River. We encamped near the spot where this strange river emerges in a roaring, rushing torrent of intensely muddy water, and divides into hundreds of branches as it rushes toward the sea. Another short march took us into the dead forest bordering the river on the east, and partially buried by its sediments, and the following day we occupied the site of our first camp at Icy Bay. After reaching Icy Bay we measured a base-line about three miles long on the beach, and from its extremities obtained the angles necessary to determine the height of Mount St. Elias and neighboring peaks. These measurements were repeated many times in order to obtain an accuracy as great as was possible with the method employed. The height

of Mount St. Elias, thus obtained, is 18,100 feet, plus or minus a probable error of less than 100 feet. From this elevation and certain observations made at Port Mulgrave by the United States Coast Survey in 1874, the position of Mount St. Elias is computed to be approximately, lat. 60° 17′ 51″, long. 140° 55′ 30″. This result is of considerable interest in connection with the position of the eastern boundary of Alaska.

In the convention between Great Britain and Russia, wherein the boundaries of Alaska are agreed upon, it is stated that the eastern boundary shall begin at the south at Portland Channel, and from there follow the summit of the mountains situated parallel to the coast as far as the intersection of the 141st degree of west longitude. From that point north, the said degree of longitude shall form the boundary to the frozen ocean. Wherever the mountains parallel to the coast to the east of the 141st meridian are "more than ten marine leagues from the ocean, the limit between the British possessions and the line of coast which is to belong to Russia, as above mentioned, shall be formed by a line parallel to the windings of the coast, and which shall never exceed the distance of ten marine leagues therefrom." The distance of Mount St. Elias from the nearest point on the coast is 33 statute miles. As 10 marine leagues are equal to 34½ statute miles, the mountain-peak is a mile and a half south of the boundary, and therefore in United States territory. It is also 4′ 30″ longitude, or 2½ miles east of the 141st meridian. The mountain is thus practically at the intersection of the boundary of southeastern Alaska with the 141st meridian, and is one of the corner monuments of our national boundary.

Our return from Mount St. Elias was no less interesting than the journey up the mountain, but space has not permitted me to linger over its details. Nor can I give at this time a sketch of our long tramp along the margin of the Malaspina glacier from Icy Bay to Yakutat Bay, or of the exploration of Disenchantment Bay, which was fully as novel and instructive as our life above the snow-line.

Israel C. Russel.

30
Romances of the World's Great Mines: The Klondike

ROMANCES of the WORLD'S GREAT MINES

V.—The Klondike

By

Samuel E. Moffett

THE gold-miner is the one human being who refuses to recognize the impossible. For three hundred years the nations have been sending their boldest and most resourceful explorers to discover the Pole, and the secret of the North remains a mystery yet. But if it were known that the Pole was surrounded by placer gold-fields, its site would be a hustling mining-camp within a year. The obstacles that have defeated the explorer would not daunt the prospector. He would scramble over the ice-floes, on his hands and knees, if necessary, and he would have his claim staked out before the first summer sun surrendered to the winter night. He has proved it in the Klondike.

The basin of the Upper Yukon has been known for at least a quarter of a century to be more or less abundantly sprinkled with gold. George Holt had crossed the Chilcoot, and prospected through the interior, in the seventies. Before that time the Chilcat Indians had objected to the presence of white men in their country, wishing to preserve a monopoly of the trade with the Indians of the interior, but, in 1879, Captain Beardslee, of the United States ship "Jamestown," induced them to raise the embargo, and a stream of miners began to trickle in. They made good wages, but few sensational strikes. Little mining-camps sprang up here and there—Forty Mile, Circle City, Eagle City and others. A few hundred men were patiently combing the country. And now came the usual perversity of fortune. The great discovery was at hand, and, as at the Comstock and so many other bonanzas, luck passed by the intelligent, hard-working, discerning prospectors and hit a shiftless drifter in the face. The Klondike River had been prospected from time to time, but had not created a good impression, and had been left to the Indian salmon-fishers to whom it owed its name. In 1894, as Mr. Tappan Adney's investigations showed, Robert Henderson, of Scotch breed, Nova

CLEANING UP A DAY'S SLUICING.

INDIANS FREIGHTING ON DYEA RIVER.

eight cents to the pan. Delighted with this promise, Henderson named the stream Gold Bottom Creek. He induced three men to go with him and take up a claim together. They built sluices, and washed out seven hundred and fifty dollars—the first gold extracted from the Klondike basin. Henderson went to Sixty Mile for provisions, and spread the news of his discovery. Returning by way of the Klondike, he passed the Indian fishing-village at its mouth. On the other side of the Yukon River was encamped George Washington Carmack. Henderson went over and told Carmack of his discovery, and urged him to take

Scotia birth and Colorado training, found himself at Joe Ladue's post at Sixty Mile, with a cash capital of ten cents. Ladue had been booming the outlook on Indian River, a few miles above the Klondike. Henderson offered to prospect for him for a "grub-stake," and Ladue accepted the proposition. Henderson explored the tributaries of Indian River during the next two years, making fair wages, with a reasonable propect of something more. In the summer of 1896 he crossed the divide that separated the waters of the Indian from those of the Klondike. Prospecting in the valley of an unknown stream, he washed out

up a claim on Gold Bottom Creek. He went on, and Carmack followed him soon after with two Indian bucks, taking a short cut by way of another stream, called Rabbit Creek. On this trip he found some colors of gold, which he showed to Henderson. Carmack and the two Indians took up three claims on Gold Bottom Creek, and then started back to the fishing-village. The party went down Rabbit Creek, and, after traveling a few miles, stopped to rest. One of the miners filled a pan with dirt. In that pan was the key to the richest gold-deposits ever uncovered on earth—a hoard that was to yield a hundred million

STEAMERS ARRIVING AT HEALY STATION.

A SLEEPING-TENT.

dollars within six years, with nobody knows how much behind. Carmack staked off a thousand-foot "discovery" claim for himself, with two adjoining five-hundred-foot claims, one above and one below, for the two Indians. Then the party hurried to the recorder's office at Forty Mile, recorded their claims, renamed Rabbit Creek "Bonanza," and boasted of their discovery. Forty Mile disgorged its idle population. The news spread up and down the Yukon, and, before long, Bonanza was staked for its entire length, as well as a tributary creek, which turned out to be still more heavily charged with gold, and was named Eldorado.

Meanwhile, Henderson was cheerfully pegging away at Gold Bottom. One day he saw some men coming over the ridge. They told him they were from Bonanza Creek, where they had the richest thing in the world. He asked them where this wonderful creek was located, and when they pointed toward his old Rabbit Creek, he knew that he had missed his future.

Henderson made a succession of plucky attempts to catch the receding tide whose flood should have led him on to fortune, but he met with an extraordinary series of

BLOWING SAND FROM GOLD-DUST.

A CLAIM ON BONANZA CREEK, VALUED AT $750,000.

mishaps, including a change in the law, which deprived him of a valuable claim between the time he staked it out and the time he reached the recorder's office to record it. At last he gave up, and returned penniless to Colorado—robbed of his last dollar on the steamer—to his old job in the Aspen mines.

Carmack made his strike on August 16, or 17, 1896. It happened that Joe Ladue was already on his way to the Klondike in the wake of his "grub-staker," Hen-

derson. It occurred to him that there would be a good opening for a branch trading-post there. When he heard of the sensational discoveries on Bonanza Creek, he expanded the post into a town. He built a store and cabin, and staked out a town site of two hundred acres, of which he secured title to one hundred and seventy-eight, the other twenty-two remaining in the possession of the Government. The Dominion surveyor, Mr. Ogilvie, named the infant metropolis Dawson City, after

CHILCOOT SUMMIT, SHOWING CRATER LAKE.

A MINER'S HUT.

Dr. George M. Dawson, Director of the Geological Survey of Canada, who had established the astronomical boundary between Alaska and the British possessions.

In that first year Luck shut her eyes and scattered her favors with superb abandon. She lifted up the lowly and cast down the exalted. She took special delight in enriching the tenderfoot and humbling the pride of the old-timer. The veteran, who knew barren ground when he saw it, contemptuously passed by the "moose-pastures" of the Eldorado, and the dry-goods clerk, to whom all creeks looked alike, washed in the despised dirt and struck it rich.

A minister's son from Chicago wound up a spectacular career at home by an enforced trip to Alaska for reformatory purposes. He took up a claim that proved a bonanza, and divided his time with equal diligence between shoveling out gold and throwing it at the birds—mostly of scarlet plumage. His father heard of his success, and hurried to Dawson to save the fortune. The news of the rescue expedition traveled ahead, and when it reached the prodigal,

GOVERNMENTAL RELIEF.

he gave his claim and what money he had left to a dance-hall siren and drifted down the Yukon in a skiff.

Clarence Berry was raising fruit in Fresno County, California, some years before the Klondike discovery. He resolved to hunt for gold in Alaska. He had forty dollars of his own, and borrowed sixty more at extravagant interest. In 1894 he set out with forty others, of whom two lasted as far as Lake Bennett. Those two died on the way to Forty Mile, which Berry reached alone. He sent to California for his fiancée, who made the journey by the all-water route to Forty Mile City, and there was a wedding. When the Indian made his find

for eight hundred dollars. In the cold, gray dawn of the morning after, he knew that he had been swindled, but he would not go back on his word. He paid the money, and by the time he had worked a third of the claim, he had taken out two hundred and fifty thousand dollars.

The land in which these incidents happened was one to which no magnet but gold would have drawn any civilized settler. There were three or four months in which hot weather and mosquitoes were prevalent, but, even in those, winter was always growling at the door. The mercury dropped below freezing-point at some time in every month of the year, and there were months

A BENCH CLAIM.

on Bonanza Creek, it did not take the Berrys long to get there. They secured several good claims, from one of which Mrs. Berry picked out fifty thousand dollars to amuse her idle moments. Berry made a trip to San Francisco soon after, and exhibited in a hotel window one hundred and thirty thousand dollars, taken from a single claim. His brother stayed behind, but lived in luxury befitting a millionaire, on canned tomatoes, beans and real beefsteak, cooked by his own hands in his palatial twelve-by-sixteen-foot cabin.

Charles Anderson was plied with drink by two gamblers, and induced to promise to buy an unknown claim on Eldorado

in which it never once went as high as the freezing-point.

At midwinter there was only two hours of sunshine in the day. The ground never thawed except in a shallow layer on top. Below that layer there was solid ice all the year round. The early miners used to dig off the top stratum and expose another layer to the sun, and so gradually work downward toward the bed-rock. Of course, this method confined operations to a few months in summer. Some time before the Klondike discoveries a new scheme had been devised. The miner built fires on the frozen ground, and so bored through the ice in shafts and lateral drifts where the

MACHINE-MINING ON THE BEACH.

sun never could have penetrated. In this way he was able to work all the year round. This device enabled the Klondike to turn out several times as much gold in a year as it could have produced by the old methods. Later, still further improvements were invented, such as the plan of drilling with great hollow augers, through which steam was driven to thaw the ground ahead.

The news of the great find in the north came upon the world with dramatic suddenness. On June 16, 1897, the steamer "Excelsior" tied up to her dock in San Francisco, and a procession of weather-beaten passengers filed gravely ashore. They were loaded down with small baggage —valises, jam-cans, boxes, oil-cans, and packages done up in old newspapers—which they seemed strangely reluctant to entrust to any hands but their own. They were returning miners from the Klondike, and they had with them a trifle of three-quarters of a million dollars' worth of gold. The next day the "Portland" reached Seattle with another batch of miners and eight hundred thousand dollars more in gold, and, like a flood bursting through a broken dam, the maddest rush in the history of mining was under way.

Now, the curious thing is—and it is a remarkable illustration of the power of the press—that this revelation was not really new. The great strike had been made on August 16, 1896, nearly a year before, the tributaries of the Klondike had been staked out in the fall of that year, and letters, sent out by the miners during

the winter, had told their friends outside of the wonderful discovery. These letters were delivered in January and February, and their recipients had headed for the Klondike, and actually reached Dawson, by the time the "Excelsior," with her sensational news, reached San Francisco. Yet the world did not become excited, or even conscious that anything unusual was going on in the north, until the dramatic advent of the "Excelsior" and the "Portland" stirred the newspaper instinct for sensations.

Mr. Ogilvie, the Canadian Commissioner for the Upper Yukon, and the best authority on the mineral resources of the region, had estimated that there was room on the Klondike and its tributaries for about a thousand claims. There were more than this number of miners already on the ground —yet a hundred thousand men started for the new Ophir with no prospect that one in a hundred of them would be able to find a paying location. But there was a graver matter ahead than the mere certainty of financial disappointment. The Klondike region was one of those countries in which "a crow would have to carry his rations with him." It was locked in ice for seven months in the year. Those who knew it were horrified by the apparently certain prospect of an awful tragedy. Here were a hundred thousand men, mostly ignorant and poorly supplied, rushing into a land that was normally stocked for a couple of thousand, and into which all the existing means of transportation could not possibly carry provisions during the short summer for more than a small number. They started with amazing irresponsibility. One observer noticed a traveler assaulting the passes with thirty-two pairs of moccasins, a case of pipes, a case of shoes, two Irish setters, a bull pup and a lawn-tennis set. He was going "just for a jolly good time, you know."

Fortunately, the trap did not lie open to all comers. Its approaches were so guarded by natural difficulties that it was impossible for the crowds to reach it at once. It was necessary first to take a steamer from Seattle or Victoria to the head of the Lynn Canal, or from San Francisco to St. Michaels, and the available steamers would hold only so many. There were two main routes—one by way of the Yukon from St. Michaels, and the other by way of the passes from Dyea or Skagway. The Yukon route was the easier, but it took the little stern-wheel tubs then in service forty days to go up the river out of the five months of open water, and they would not hold more than a minute fraction of the people who wanted to go. Only fifteen

lars to one hundred and twenty dollars per sack for flour, a dollar a pound for beef, and one dollar and fifty cents a pound for mutton. The stores of the great trading-corporations did not raise their regular prices of six dollars per sack for flour, forty cents a pound for bacon, and other things in proportion, but their supplies were limited, and they would sell only a little to each person. The United States Government started a reindeer relief expedition, but through mismanagement most of the deer died, and the attempt was abandoned.

A GROUP OF MINERS AT WORK.

hundred men managed to push through to Dawson before the close of navigation in 1897. Of the eighteen hundred who tried the all-water route by way of St. Michaels and the Yukon steamers, only forty-three got through, and thirty-five of those had to go back, for lack of provisions to carry them through the winter. Even as it was, famine at Dawson was averted only by shipping the people who were without provisions down the river before the ice barred the way.

Six thousand persons took their chances in Dawson, and at one time they were paying speculators from one hundred dol-

There were two possible ways of getting over the coast mountains—by the Chilcoot Pass from Dyea and by the White Pass from Skagway. The Chilcoot was high, steep and terrifying; the White Pass, long, muddy and heart-breaking. As you toiled up the trail from Dyea, you saw a gigantic gray wall, seven hundred feet high, barring your progress. But when you reached it, you found you could crawl up its face, and even lead a loaded horse—the latter discovery, like so many others in that region, was made by a tenderfoot. By the White Pass route you did not have the precipitous ascent of the Chilcoot, but you had to go twice as far, and you struggled through bogs in which you were likely to leave your horse and, perhaps, your entire outfit as well. The whole trail was blazed by the carcases of dead horses.

Starting at the head of Lynn Canal, within four miles of each other, both trails converged on the other side of the mountains at Lake Lindeman, from which there was a single all-water route to the mines. The little Alpine lake, with its next neighbor Lake Bennett, suddenly became the busiest boat-building center in the world. Every man had to have a boat, or a share

sold boards to the prospectors at two hundred and fifty dollars per thousand feet, was worth more than most Klondike claims, and some expert builders found it worth their while to settle on the lake and sell ready-made boats at from two hundred and fifty dollars to six hundred dollars apiece.

Thirty or forty thousand men endured the hardships of this journey within the first year, and then civilization took possession of the country, and made the trip to Dawson a simple summer-excursion tour. An aerial steel tramway dispelled the terrors of the Chilcoot, and that in turn was super-

SLUICING ON ANVIL CREEK.

in one, and, at first, he had to build it himself. There was no labor to be hired. Moreover, he had, not only to build the boat, but to cut down the trees and saw them into boards for the purpose, sometimes bringing the logs several miles. The work was generally done in partnership, and, when a craft was finished, the neighbors would knock off and help launch it. In the spring of 1898 three thousand boats were set afloat on Lake Bennett within two months. Of course, the opportunities for money-making at this point were not long left unimproved. A little saw-mill, which

seded by the White Pass & Yukon Railroad, one hundred and eleven miles long, from Skagway to White Horse, connecting with daily steamers for Dawson in summer, and with stages in winter. You can have your baggage checked through now from Seattle to the capital of the Klondike, and be tied to the world by telegraph and daily mails when you get there. One more of Nature's fastnesses has been stormed, and the route that was strewn six years ago with the bones of men and horses has no more hardships than the line between New York and Chicago.

31
A Moose Hunt
on the
Yukon, Alaska

A MOOSE HUNT ON THE YUKON, ALASKA.

By the late V. Wilson.

WE had left the coast three hundred miles behind, the last snow-capped range was fading into distant blue, and in their place were grassy slopes, skirting the shores of the first navigable waters of the Yukon. It was a pleasant land of rolling, timbered hills; backed yet again on the hither side by other ranges of high mountains, standing sharp and clear in the never absent light. The many water holes along the river were thronged with geese and duck, and in the rapids fishes were abundant; but we were after bigger game. Moose was our objective, and we were not yet in his country, nor were we likely to be unless we could supersede our present mode of locomotion afoot for one more rapid. Anent this subject, we held many councils, and at last we determined to build a boat, and in ten days we did. We sawed the wood with a whip saw, calked her with an old suit of underwear cut in strips, made her water tight with pitch gathered from the Norway pine, and launched her in triumph. She was not a beauty to look at, and might have raised a smile at Morrisania or Clayton, but she was strong, and carried us and twelve hundred pounds of outfit down a thousand miles of river, and through canyons and rapids that would have wrecked many a smarter craft.

The day of our start in our new ark was a day of triumph in more senses than one, for not only did she carry us forty-five miles before sunset, but those miles disclosed the first sign of the game we were in quest of—moose— and from her stern on this first day out we succeeded in bringing down a fine, large caribou, besides a few duck as they passed over in the morning, and a brace of grouse, which were considered only in the light of a culinary necessity; good sport though they were.

The least sound from our boat sent echoes and re-echoes resounding among the hills in a way actually weird. Sometimes we experimented with our voices, and the distinctness always made one feel that, if these wilds had no ears, they surely had voices.

For thirty days there had been almost perpetual sunshine, with only an occasional thunder shower, and at such times rainbows of the most brilliant hues were ever in sight, sometimes coming just at the boat's end. I tried to photograph some of these, but the motion of the boat made the attempt a failure.

Our first river-side camp was all that a sportsman could desire. A wooded knoll at the junction of the river and a tributary from the hills, covered with rich moss, and timbered with spruce and balm of Gilead trees.

There was still time, after putting the camp ship-shape and overhauling the boat, which had escaped the bad riffles we had passed with the loss of a thole pin, to try my luck with the line, and to add some lively grayling to our larder and gather in sufficient Yukon onions to flavor our grouse, which my camp-mate, Arthur, could fry in butter to a turn. Nor were the arts of making coffee fit for a Turk, and hot biscuits fit for a Yankee, beyond his skill. We lived well in those Yukon solitudes.

A morning's inspection showed signs of moose in abundance, and, although we did not see any, we soon became satisfied that we should do well, before proceeding further down-stream, to try the range some ten miles inland. We began at once preparing food for the trip. I gave the boat's line an extra turn, hung the bacon high in the trees, snugged things about the tent, and, just as the last shadows were drawing into a beautiful Alaskan evening, we shouldered our rifles and an extra pair of stick moccasins and wound our way up the table-land overlooking the canyon formed by the stream which passed our door.

The walking up the canyon was fairly

good for four or five miles, when suddenly it narrowed and terminated in a sheer wall, over which poured our little rivulet, striking the rocky bottom of the canyon some three or four hundred feet below, in clouds of spray, gathering force again and rushing on to the mighty Yukon, and thence, thousands of miles, to the Northern Sea, where a single night and day come once each year, where the babies never cry and the women dress in Mary Walker costume. We found it necessary to retrace our footsteps some distance, when we noticed the deep, fresh tracks of a huge moose. This we followed, well knowing he would take us over the best walking and, possibly, just where we wanted to go. We had little difficulty in following the track, for he sank several inches into the soft moss at every step.

Once above the waterfall the walking became good again, and when we at length reached the summit and looked away to the east, the warm rays of the morning sun were dancing on the smooth surface of a small lake, stretching away some two miles. At its farthest end a pretty, ribbon-like little meadow wound up among the mountains and out of sight, dotted with clumps of trees and small water holes.

On the south side of the lake a thick forest came down quite to the water's edge, while on the north, grassy, terraced hills and open, wooded slopes stretched away to the meadow beyond, making an ideal moose country.

We separated here, Arthur taking the open, while I took to the woods, which seemed alive with flocks of young grouse; and how so many rabbits could live on the same piece of ground seemed incredible. In fact the whole upper river fairly swarms with them. There were scarcely any signs of moose about these woods, but many signs of caribou, all of which were old, and I began to believe we were getting out of the moose country instead of into it. But, as I reached the upper end of the lake, signs began to appear again and the meadow looked like a cattle corral. One track showed, by its size and the depth it sank into the mud, to be just what I was looking for. I could already imagine the giant who made it lording it about

here, monarch of all he surveyed. He little knew how I longed to dispute it with him. What worried me most was whether Arthur or I would see him first; but I felt sure the time could not be long before I should test my 40-65 Winchester, and on noble game.

The morning was one of those typical to Alaska's great interior. Not a breath stirred the leaves of the birch and balm of Gilead, and, as I cautiously crept along the meadow, flocks of water fowl rose from the water holes, and their hoarse croaking was a great source of annoyance; for would not my game take warning and vacate? I had yet to learn that the moose here will stand any amount of noise, but the scent of man sends him off in a hurry.

I crept farther away from the meadow and up the hills, finally emerging on the crest of a small hill which runs well out into the meadow. There I espied a brown bear nosing along the hill-side, some three hundred yards up the meadow. I seated myself on a fallen tree and watched bruin's actions, at the same time carefully scrutinizing the clumps of trees about the meadow bottom. I had no intention of trying to reach him with a shot. He was of the common brown species, and we had wasted quite cartridges enough on them many a day. It was interesting to watch the uneasy gait of bruin, as he worked along, picking berries, but he did not draw my fire.

I was just becoming inspired with that lazy feeling of wonderment and uncertainty which steals over one in such places, where the beauty and stillness of a virgin country have never been disturbed by white men, when the sharp report of a rifle from across the meadow sent its vibrations echoing and re-echoing up the mountains. With the first vibrations that broke the stillness, my heart sank with that heavy feeling so prone to human nature, when some other man has accomplished just what we have been striving for; but only for a moment. The sound was yet lingering up the side gulches, when I became aware of large game nearer than bruin.

I heard the smashing and snapping of brush, saw the trees down in the meadow thicket bend and sway, and the next moment the huge and ungainly

Painted for OUTING by Hermann Simon.

"WITH ONE LAST MIGHTY EFFORT HE REARED."

looking head of a bull moose hove in sight. His mane stood erect, his nose was straight out, and as he made up the meadow with a long, swinging stride, I took aim just back of the shoulder and pulled. I saw the dust rise from his side, saw him stagger once only, then regain his footing, as though he had made an extra effort in some mud-hole. I fired again, and his unsteady gait became quite visible; then he slackened his speed, and finally stopped, the huge body swayed for a moment and, with one last mighty effort, he reared high in the air and fell upon his side, dead

My heart was trying to keep time with the vibrations of wave sound my rifle had sent chasing each other up the mountain sides, as I hurried down; but in my excitement I was delayed some time in crossing a bog hole, and when at length I reached there I slipped. Black muck was soon oozing from the pistol pockets of my corduroys. I am good six feet tall, besides a liberal percentage turned up : pedestrian purposes, and I went down straight, toes first, but never a bottom did I find: I think, however, I should have found it and stayed there, had it not been for a black alder growing near by, which I grasped, and drew myself up slowly. How many times I had showered anything but blessings on those sin-inspiring hectors of the fisherman's life! I never could see what they grew for, except to shelter the enemy and tangle our best flies, by surrounding all the likely fishing holes, everywhere; but at last I had put one to good use, and felt thankful to look down upon that hole instead of being on a level with it. As I came up to the dead moose, quite out of breath, there sat Arthur on the great, dark carcass.

"A good head," was his greeting. Then he looked at me and burst out laughing, asking if shooting such a moose was not quite enough to satisfy an ordinary man in one day, without trying to fathom the bottomless pit. The remark was lost, for I felt like no ordinary man; besides, I was very busy examining the head and trying to act like a man who had killed plenty of moose in his day. I am afraid it was a failure, for Arthur looked at me with a look of pity, then came suddenly to my relief by asking: "What on earth are we to do with him, now we have him ?" and true enough, there was more than a thousand pounds of meat and we were ten miles from camp. To be sure, the head was an ideal one, the horns spread more than five feet. It would make my long ist of photos more complete, make one nore camp-fire yarn, and, in fact, was just the relic I wanted.

32
A Summer Tour
of Alaska

MOUNT EDGECUMBE FROM SITKA BAY.

A SUMMER TOUR IN ALASKA.

By Lucy M. Washburn.

IT is the union of inspiration and rest that makes the Alaska summer tour unique. Nature offers no other such open rift into those majestic scenes that she usually reserves as rewards of heroic exertion. Elsewhere the grandest mountains and glaciers draw themselves up in their fastnesses, cordoned by heights or moated by stretches of ocean. But the lace-like edge bordering the American continent on the northwest for a thousand miles, an interwoven network of mountain and sea, affords a marvellous island-sheltered passage free from rocking ocean swells. There is the clear, deep salt water, untroubled as inland lake. From his reclining chair on the steamer deck, the traveller has only to gaze and gaze, while the long panorama unfolds ever nobler scenes, crowned at last by visions of Titanic glaciers in their arctic majesty.

The Inland channel begins as stately Puget sound, framed in forests, with outlooks upon the snowy Cascade and Olympian ranges. Towering over all, is the hoary giant, Mt. Ranier, leading the line of those lofty extinct volcanoes that signal to one another from northern California to Puget sound. The "sound cities," Tacoma, Seattle, Port Townsend, and staid British Victoria, are soon left behind, and the long, unbroken wilderness entered, that calls itself, first, British Columbia, and then, Alaska.

The mountains rise sheer from the water's edge, their bold curves, glacier-carved, now arrayed in living green, of spruce and fir, above which, untamed peaks of bare rock lift aloft those eternal snows that at one touch change a landscape from the beautiful to the sublime. The contours are ever changing as the steamer sweeps by. Sometimes the channel is scarce wider than a river, and the tide swirls through with such force, that even ocean steamers must wait slack water for their passage. Again it widens into a broad, quiet sea, dotted with tree-covered islands, the distant white mountain ranges melt-

421

auk Bay?

INDIAN VILLAGE AND TOTEM-POLES.

ing into the sky; perhaps glorified by one of the long summer sunsets of that northern region, the colors of sky and water, and that purest roseate flush on snowy mountain tops lingering, as if you had reached the haven where beauty is no longer fleeting. Care and distraction slip from your tired spirit; a subtle renewing goes on within ; this noble, free, large nature is no greater than your soul, that leaps to meet it in joyful recognition.

Nothing can try your spirit but rains and low-hanging clouds, shutting out those views you have come so far to see; but your experience of the rainiest part of the world would be very unfair if you saw it only in its vacation spells of sunshine, and when the clouds begin to break, floating in exquisite white mists about the green mountain sides, and fluttering like delicate banners from the higher peaks, you feel that you would have only half known these mountains without their ethereal companions. And then come days of such transparent sunshine, such pure, bracing atmosphere, that you appreciate the words of a veteran resident, " When Alaska weather is good, it is just as good as gold."

It is nature that you came to see. But when, at long intervals, you come upon human life, it has a special interest. In-

dian and Russian, trader and miner, each furnishes a fresh study. Those graceful canoes, with dusky faces looking up from them, seem but a feature of the wild scenery, their silent, sweeping motions akin to those of the circling eagles overhead. Even in Glacier bay we met one or two adventurous canoes. As before, their soft, unobtrusive coloring had harmonized with every scene, the canoe, a tree from the surrounding forest, so now, whitened for creeping unperceived upon stray seals, they seemed tiny ice-cakes among the larger bergs. The seal-hunter sat poised and alert behind his screen of white cloth, while the eyes of his wife and baby looked up pathetically from that cold, floating home. A thrill deeper than all sense of the picturesque comes with the thought of what life must have been to the Alaskan to make the canoe almost his larger body, so that the child, scarce able to peer over the rim, adjusts himself in every muscle to keep the swaying balance true. The canoes, the finest in the world, speak of a long course of evolution, and the natives' Japanese cast of features sets you thinking how many ages would be needed to differentiate the two types.

As you approach one of the rare settlements in the wilderness, uncanny "totem-poles" stand looking out upon you,—huge logs, carved into rude but often forcible figures of bears, eagles, whales, and other animals. Here is a field for the student of folk-lore and race origins: totemism as a system is wide-spread, and this passion for grotesque carving reminds you again of the Japanese. Mr. Duncan, who knows the Alaska Indians better than any one else, writes that these totems are emblems representing mythical genii of ancient clans ; that members of the same clan are counted as blood relations, even though they belong to hostile tribes, speak a different language, or live a thousand miles apart, the Alaskans relating traditions of a flood by which the clans were scattered. On the "totem-pole," before the house, were carved the totem of the owner and those of his ancestors. It was literally a "family-tree," whose genealogical record can be read, while within repose the ashes of the one it honors. The most typical examples usually seen by tourists are at Fort Wrangel, which is now little more than a stranded collection of Indian huts ; its interest lies in these native relics, and the decaying Russian fortifications against the Hudson's Bay company.

But the totems are seen in their original force only at a primitive village. A stop at a little fishery, far off the usual route, allowed such an excursion. As, in the stillness, broken only by the light dip of oars, we rounded the last headland, some fifty weird, ancient totem - poles stood guarding the deserted village in a solemn line. Ferns feathered their tops ; even a large fir-tree was growing in the rain-hollowed bowl at the top of one aged totem. Men, women, and children were away on one of their summer fishing and berrying tours. We were left to wander at will, and enter the ancient council - house crowning the promontory, its central fire-square, now grassy, surrounded by a ruined dais carved in totem-emblems. Outlined against the forest stood other totems guarding graves—how much older who shall say? Even the most thoughtless felt the spell ; as our boats receded, that last sunset-flushed gaze of the totems was like a glance quickened into life out of the remote past.

Tourists gain their main impressions of the natives from those at white settlements, reaping their sole harvest of coin for a long year by selling totem-marked articles, especially graceful spoons of translucent horn, bracelets beaten out of silver coin, and baskets woven of cedar rootlets, so fine and firm that they will hold water. A glance into a native house shows picturesque elements—the fire on the central gravelled square, with blue smoke strug-

From a photo by Partridge, Boston.

INDIANS AND CANOES. NEAR JUNEAU.

gling upward to the great roof-opening, the older Indians crouched about it, the baby swinging in a hammock, the walls hung with furs and accoutrements. But the dirt, the disorder, and the smell of fish, hung over the fire for curing, offend the senses. It is more pathetic, because this disease and degradation are not mere primitive savagery, but its reaction under contact with more developed races. The wrongs of Alaskan natives burn upon the pages of all impartial historians of the century and a half of exploration, trading, and monopoly. "Heaven is high," ran the proverb, "and the czar distant." The worst injury was not the sweeping depopulation,—eighty-five per cent. among the Aleuts,—but the immorality inherited by the survivors. And of this last, America cannot wash its hands. Why must the hem of civilization touch rather for infection than for healing?

The contrasting picture of what may be done to lift a race to higher levels can nowhere be seen more strikingly than at the unique settlement of Metlahkatlan. Thirty-five years ago William Duncan, a young English missionary, began work at Fort Simpson, B. C. Such were the evil influences of the trading post, that he persuaded those Indians wishing to lead a better life to start a fresh settlement, where he taught them the arts of civilization and the practice of Christianity. Natives from near and far were attracted by the new order; the village throve, in spite of interested traders, until it roused the jealousy of officials, and the now improved lands were to be wrested from the Indians. Mr. Duncan, appealing to our government, received the grant of an island in Alaska; and the Indians, leaving their homes, established by thirty years of effort, followed him with what they could carry in their canoes. In the rains and snows of an Alaskan winter, these new Pilgrims landed on a forest-covered shore. Despite poverty, remoteness, and climate, with only a little pecuniary help, they have in five years, under their inspiring leader, built neat homes, church and school buildings, a saw-mill, a general store, and a salmon-cannery, each family encouraged to own a share in these coöperative industries.

The "Declaration of Residents" may well be studied. "We, the people of Metlahkatlan, Alaska, in order to secure to ourselves and our posterity the blessings of a Christian home, do severally subscribe to the following rules: To reverence the Sabbath, to attend divine wor-

VIEW ON INDIAN RIVER, SITKA.

ship, to take the Bible for our rule of faith, to regard all true Christians as our brethren, and to be truthful, honest, and industrious; to be faithful to the government of the United States; to render our votes for the election of the town council, and to obey the orders of said council; to attend to the education of our children; to totally abstain from intoxicants, gambling, and heathen customs; to strictly carry out all sanitary regulations necessary for the health of the town; to utilize the land we hold, and identify ourselves with the progress of the settlement."

Striking, indeed, is the impression made by the neat, orderly village, and by the dusky countenances lit with new intelli

the quaint, foreign-looking little town of some twelve hundred inhabitants, mostly Indians and Russian Creoles, is the capital of one-sixth of the United States area. The headquarters of the governor and other officials are in the old buildings of the Russian régime—massive log structures that speak the rule of force as plainly as the remains of the stockade and block-houses. Within, there are traces of a finer finish, and tales of luxury and revelry haunt the great bare rooms. But it is about the Greek church, with its oriental domes, that the living Russian interest centers. Within its plain wooden walls all is glitter: one looks upon costly pictures of saints in robes of beaten silver and

From a photo by Partridge, Boston.

SITKA AND MOUNT VOSTOVIA.

gence and character. The town now numbers about a thousand. "Are any people going away from Metlahkatlan?" I asked a young Indian returning thither from his further schooling at Sitka. "Oh, no!" "Are any new settlers going in?" "Oh, yes." "Why?" Gathering up his English, he slowly replied: "Because it's all right; no whisky, no saloon, no dance-house. Before Mr. Duncan came to us there was blood shed every day, but now it's all right." "Don't you have a good many laws?" "We make our own laws!" was the proud reply.

Sitka is an epitome of Alaska's past and present. It is difficult to realize that

gold, upon the costly Book that is kissed, but not read, and upon the glittering vestments of the priest who intones the service in ancient Slavonic, an unknown tongue to Russians as well as Indians.

In strong contrast stands the only addition of note to Sitka since it came into American hands: the industrial training school, sustained partly by American churches, and partly by the government, and based on the principle that Christianity, intelligence, and work combined constitute the force for elevating a race. The visitor who sees these bright boys and girls so apt in the kitchen, the laundry, the sewing-room, the little printing-office,

From a photo by Partridge, Boston.

IN THE INLAND CHANNEL.

the smithy, the carpenter, and shoe-shops, recognizes that this is the true system of training. But it requires a going in and out, day by day, with sympathetic insight, to realize the deep needs of these people, and all that is being done by the patient enthusiasm of their teachers. Crowded, dirty, and promiscuous as the Indian quarter of Sitka still is, it shows results of these labors and the vigorous sanitation of former naval commanders. Progress would be more rapid but for the scarcity of paying work; the development of industries must be a main element in solving the problem of making the Alaska Indians good citizens.

As a lovely afternoon was deepening into sunset glory, a suggestive little procession roused me from the beauty of external nature to that something which outlives it. A tiny coffin was borne by stalwart Indians; women and girls, neatly dressed, brought up the rear; the only white face was that of the kindly missionary. Following the silent line to a partially cleared upland, the sunset touched a scene I shall not forget. The grave had been made broad, and the men stepped down into it and received in their arms the little coffin, which they arranged in its place as carefully as if laying the babe to sleep. The women sat on the ground, their backs to the grave, their heads bowed in silent tribute to the great mystery—all but the mother sitting at the head of the grave, who watched her little treasure laid in its last bed while the simple words were spoken that make the whole human family akin: "Earth to earth; and the spirit to God, who gave it."

Steamer passengers never see the normal Sitka; the approaching whistle draws the population to the wharves and along the one street, now turned into a bazaar of "curios." But scarcely has the steamer disappeared when the lingerer seems sole survivor in some dream-village. Then begins for him a dolce far niente as of the tropics, with no offsets of swarming pests and depressing heat. As he strolls along the main street of a morning, he may meet an Indian with a deer over his shoulder, and another flaying his game. He may visit a whale-ship and stand in an improvised archway of two great whalebone fringes. He may persuade the general trader to open his safe and show him precious sea-otter furs; or in some resident's home he may see easy chairs upholstered in spotted hair-seal, or a lady's cloak lined with two hundred skins of little white ermines. In the afternoon there will be a row of Indian women crouching along the walk, with their baskets of salmon-berries that no artist could

From a photo by Partridge, Boston.

AUK GLACIER.

From a photo by Partridge, Boston.
VIEW ACROSS THE FRONT WALL OF THE MUIR GLACIER.

pass without a kindling eye. It is probable that tourists will find out the attractions of Sitka for a summer's stay; then, good-by to Sitka's charm of quaintness.

But nothing can ever do away with its noble natural features. No one view can do Sitka justice ; every turn gives a new picture. Mt. Vostovia lifts its sharp "arrowhead" three thousand feet directly above ; the "Three Sisters" rival it to the left ; just beyond is a loftier, serrated ridge, cool with unmelting snows. Turn seaward,— the bay is crowded with an archipelago of islets, forested greenly above their bold, gray, rocky bases, and fringed with a line of red-gold kelp, vivid against the blue water, while above that variety of form and glow of color the eye centers on the perfect cone of the volcano Edgecumbe, holding aloft an enormous bowl-like crater filled with snow, that seems to overflow in radiating lines down its sides, as if a great eruption had congealed.

Juneau boasts itself, if not the capital, the metropolis of Alaska, for it can number some three thousand souls. It is a center for expeditions into the far Yukon mining territory, while within sight is the gaping pit of the famous Treadwell gold mine, with the largest stamp-mill in the world. Two hundred and forty stamps, required for crushing immense quantities of low-grade ore, make such a din that the chatter of the tourist dies out in hopelessness of a hearing. Right alongside,

to the uninitiated eye part of the same group, are other extensive buildings, but these mark only a great fiasco in which three-quarters of a million have been sunk, —so near is failure to success in mining enterprise, so narrow are those terra-firma "pockets," that the whole world would fain have a hand in. Furs in every shop speak of another great unexhausted interest. Juneau has its fringe of Indian houses and canoes ; its schools and wholesome, helpful mission home. Then it could hardly be Alaskan without a picturesque situation ; the town occupies a narrow ledge, overhung by a snow-seamed precipice. And Juneau, outstripping even its rival Sitka, is the rainiest town in America, rain or snow falling from two hundred to even three hundred days in a year.

The first sight of a salmon-cannery is a new experience,—the gleaming fish heaped upon the floor, Indian canoes unloading their fresh "catch" at the door, Chinamen wielding the knife with a celerity as machine-like as the whirring wheels. It was a thirty-pound salmon five minutes ago ; now it is a row of deftly packed cans that go spinning along a tramway to the soldering. A can is covered, is whirling on a spindle against a hot soldering iron, is working its way onward, by an endless chain, under jets of water that wash it as it goes,—and in a twinkling it is in the boiling bath. Night after night the steamer-loading goes on: the first wonder

INSPECTING THE GLACIER.

land-travel, and spiced by not only the variety of tourists, but by characters from these wilds — the Hudson's Bay company trader, from his lonely post; the Russian bishop, striding moodily to and fro, his six-and-a-half feet of height exaggerated by cloak and tall fur cap; the frontiersman, bringing in eagles whose wings and claws are enviously measured by amateur hunters; the good woman, who tells you, with pardonable pride, that her child's name is Juneau Alaska Brown.

is, how the world can consume so much salmon, the second, how long Alaska can furnish it; for surely no waters can long supply such marvellous quantities of fish.

Wise is that traveller who, instead of being swept back and forth through Alaska's great Inland channel upon the swift excursion steamship, has chosen the smaller steamers that go to these far-away canneries and fisheries, affording a winding course of three thousand miles, and many stops where one may touch, if not explore, the fascinating wilderness. Charming, too, is the social life of the long voyage, unhaunted by sea-sickness, unfretted by the heat, dust, and cares of

The crowning interest of the journey is that it leads into one of the world's greatest glacier regions. The northward route presents the magnificent series in the most instructive and effective order, on an ascending scale of grandeur. It is with a thrill that you recognize your first glacier. You are watching a range of mountains, heavily snow-clad on their upper heights. As you draw nearer, suddenly, in the center of some broad, snowy slope, hollowed like an amphitheater, as if in the heart of some vast shell, your field-glass shows you a pale green color, gleaming through parallel chasms in the dazzling whiteness. It is crystal ice that you see, tinged with that inherent color that becomes perceptible in ice or water only when massed, as when we look through great unbroken sea-waves, or upward toward the sun across the deep current of Niagara, curving smoothly over the brink. This glimpse into the heart of a glacier has been given you by its deep crevasses.

Travelling northward, you see how a larger glacier is formed by the union of such as you saw first, the body of ice now resembling a river. It has plowed itself a mountain furrow, and edged itself with a moraine of rocks torn from the adjacent wall. You

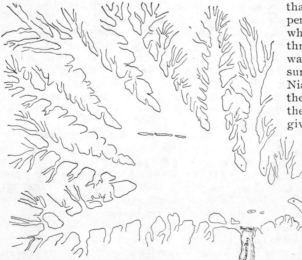

MAP OF THE MUIR GLACIER.

The length of the front wall is a mile and a half. The small circles on the points to the right show where observations were taken. This map is reproduced from a tracing of Mr. Muir's original map.

VIEW OF THE SURFACE OF THE MUIR GLACIER.

see its tributaries, you mark its course until it descends far below the present snow-line, and makes its way between bare rocky mountain flanks. The glaciers of the first rank reach the sea, as all did in a colder geological period, and there are broken up into icebergs. Those of the second rank no longer reach the water, and their rocky débris, not transported away on icebergs, has accumulated as a terminal moraine.

At the Taku inlet, the eye takes in at a sweep the terminations of two great glaciers, one of each class. The climax of this stupendous series is a vast amphitheater of iceberg forming glaciers about the head of Glacier bay, the end of the long Inland channel. The largest glacier of all has been fitly named for John Muir, the intrepid exploring geologist of the Pacific coast, who, with Mr. S. H. Young, in a canoe, with only trembling Indians as helpers, pushed his way to it, through storms and icebergs, in October, 1879.

The morning our steamer enters Glacier bay, the passengers, on tip-toe of expectation, take advantage of the early dawn of that northern latitude, and watch the icebergs all about, weird in the dim light and mists. It seems as if the green islets that have strewn our course had passed under the transmuting and castle-building of some white enchanter. Gradually the icebergs increase in number, until the

steamer is threading its way by short turns. The captain's eye is fixed on the labyrinth; these are no stationary islands, but a fleet of crushing monsters bearing down along the tide with untold momentum. His short, sharp commands, the responses of the man at the wheel, the rattle of the rudder-chains, recall to nervous passengers that on the preceding trip this steamer had its bow torn off.

It was my good fortune to go into Glacier bay twice. On one occasion there was no difficulty; but on the other, winds and currents had combined to keep the ice from floating out of the bay, until there was not enough open water to reflect the bergs. Finally, the captain was obliged to turn back; the disappointed colony of passengers could only dimly descry the glacier they had come so far to see. But they had encountered its great effects; they had had some experience of an arctic ice-pack.

The broad, white expanse toward which the steamer works its way is the Muir glacier. How shall one convey any idea of what so transcends description? Photographs can give but a section here and there. But from the steamer you see that it is a vast, nearly level slope from white mountains beyond, and so buttressed in by nearer mountains that it reaches the bay only by a compressed outlet. Yet that outlet is a mile and a

From a photo by J. W. Taber, San Francisco.
THE EDGE OF THE MUIR GLACIER, SHOWING MORAINE.

half across; the ice-filled amphitheater is over thirty miles in each diameter. It requires hours to train the eye to some realization of this vastness. By and by, we are near enough to see the perpendicular cliff in which it faces the water. At first a mere thread across the front, as we draw nearer it towers above us, cutting off all view of the mass behind it.

The upper surface of the ice is white from disintegration, and sprinkled with débris, forming moraine lines. But the ice below is of that clear, dense structure that we have seen in the icebergs broken off from it, the faint green taking bluer shades farther down, to intensest deep blue. It is St. John's vision in the Apocalypse: "The foundations of the wall were beryl, and sapphire, and amethyst." The glittering front, three hundred feet high, is buttressed, and arched, and crowned with myriads of towers and spires. Milan cathedral, with its white marble fretwork of pinnacles, is the only human structure suggested, but it would look a toy, indeed, before this mile of solid ice. And the visible part is but a fraction of the wall. Soundings, venturously near, show that the submerged portion is seven hundred feet deep, making a sheer front of one thousand feet.

We are landed in boats below cliffs at the side, part of the immense lateral moraine. Eagerly we make our way upward over a mile or two of stones and ooze. Cracks begin to occur, then wider seams, through which we get glimpses of ice underneath. Finally, we step out upon the uncovered ice itself. Surprise is often expressed that guides are not supplied. But there is no danger in this mere edge of the glacier to any person not venturing too near the crevasses in the desire to peer down their depths. The climb is not too difficult for ladies accustomed to walking, if they go equipped in light, strong dress, the present available reforms of under-clothing and foot-gear, and a stout alpenstock. It is not danger that is the fascination, but the overwhelming sight that breaks upon the traveller's eye as he gains this vantage point. The eye sweeps over the vast amphitheater of ice, with its many tributaries, each in itself a great glacier, crowding to the front as a bewildering chaos of lofty crevasse-formed pinnacles, thick as grass-blades on a lawn, and as separate. Alpine glaciers may be crossed, but there is no hope that any human being will ever cross the Muir, except far back from its front.

Thunder-like reverberations of cleaving and falling ice-masses fill up the measure of sublimity. Retracing our steps to the end of the moraine, we face the ice-wall. Which of all those towers will fall first?

How can anything so massive ever give way? How can anything so toppling hold its place? Suddenly a break, a gliding,— then the sharp detonation of the cleavage, —a rush downward, a disappearance in the water,—then the thunder of that mighty blow, and a splash of water and spray two hundred feet up the ice-cliff,— then the boiling below,—and you keep on watching, watching, it seems a long time, till the berg that has plunged rises again out of all this turmoil and rides away on the great wave itself has made.

The most unimpressionable tourist yields to the excitement, springing to his feet and joining in the chorus of long-breathed exclamations. Finally, in one of the quiet intervals of this tremendous bombardment, lo! at the base of the ice wall, a mighty seething began from some unseen force below, and like an enormous whale, rose the largest iceberg of all, broken off at unknown depths. Over and over it turned, starting wave after wave, until, its center of gravity finally adjusted, it rested in the water apparently as immovable as the other great ice-islands. Its darkly intense blue showed that it came from the very depths of the glacier.

The captain must make his way out of Glacier bay by daylight, so sorrowfully we return to the steamer and settle ourselves on deck to fill our eyes and memories as we slowly recede. Once more that lofty wall becomes but a rim of the vast ice-slope. The cold morning mists half veiled it as we approached; as our lingering backward look rests upon it, the sunset bathes it in new, softened glory. The great companion glaciers on the left complete the arc, while faint and far, seen only by those fortunate travellers favored by the clearest weather, a new vision crowns the whole and reveals its true relations. The great Fairweather range of the St. Elias Alps, more than Alpine in loftiness and majestic weight of snows, is outlined against the sunset sky,—peak after peak, their shadows of palest blue, their lights of tenderest rose, lifted into the heavens, and from those heights the mighty glaciers creeping down to the sea.

After this supreme hour there is but one thing more to realize, and that is no single vision, but the new interpretation throughout our long homeward voyage of the marvellous inland passage. The imagination now can strip off these forests from the mountains that show their rounded glacier carving; it can fill these intricate channels of quiet sea with their gigantic ice-streams; and the mind reels thinking how long it took them to grind out these fiords that the ship's line will not fathom—three thousand miles of such fiords, just the fringe of the continental ice-sheet. So God has plowed his earth-farm with glaciers to make it ready for the home of His children.

GLACIER IN TAKU INLET.

33
The Development of
Nome, Alaska

BELLES OF THE DIOMEDE ISLANDS, IN BERING STRAIT

THE DEVELOPMENT OF NOME

By ALFRED H. DUNHAM, Chief Game Warden of Alaska

WHILE Panama, as the site of the great waterway being built to connect the Atlantic and the Pacific, has been attracting so increasingly the interest of the world, there has grown up almost unheralded on the Seward Peninsula of Alaska a city and a civilization destined, there can be no doubt, to form the eastern terminus of a tunnel which will connect the railroad systems of the eastern and western hemispheres.

The development of Nome has been less rapid absolutely than that of a score of American cities in regions more naturally favored. But viewed in the light of the obstacles of transportation, geographical location and isolation from other centers, Nome's rise in five years from a barren strip of beach fronting a frozen marsh, to a city of twenty-five

thousand inhabitants, with banks and schools and theaters, paved streets and electrically lighted thoroughfares, telegraph and telephone systems, and with three separate lines of railroad entering it, stands alone in city-building.

The growth of Nome and the establishment on Seward Peninsula of a permanent civilization which is not dependent wholly upon the mineral wealth of the soil, has brought suddenly from the realm of dreams to the world of fact and probability the project, long mooted, of all-rail communication between Asia and America by way of Bering Sea. Already Seward Peninsula itself is "gridironed" with railroads built and under construction; a central Alaskan railroad is partially completed from Cook Inlet north to the Yukon River, and as

PLACER-MINING ON THE BEACH AT
NOME, TWO YEARS AGO

from her present trans-Siberian line to the Kamchatka peninsula. From East Cape, in Siberia, to Cape Prince of Wales, in Alaska, is but thirty miles.

All the popular conceptions of an Alaskan mining-town are belied by Nome. Every facility or convenience of modern society which is enjoyed by places of its size in other parts of the United States is enjoyed equally by the citizens of Nome. Not only are such utilitarian marks of progress as the telegraph, the telephone, both local and long-distance, electric lights and bicycles everywhere noticeable, but the esthetic side of life is also not neglected, and lectures, musical entertainments and balls are as frequent as in cities farther south. Three daily newspapers are published in Nome; twelve public schools are maintained there, with sixteen teachers and a thousand pupils, and the Alaska Academy of

soon as her affairs in the East are settled, Russia will lay a spur north

HYDRAULIC MINING AT GLACIER CREEK, TO-DAY

RUSSIAN SETTLEMENT ON BARANOFF ISLAND

Sciences provides lectures for higher classes and maintains a library. Besides, there are good hotels, an excellent theater, a high school, a large greenhouse and many fine stores.

During the fiscal year ending June 30, 1904, the commerce of Alaska aggregated more than thirty million dollars, a large amount of it passing through Nome. More than two and a quarter million dollars' worth of manufactures in iron and steel was sent to Alaska from the United States during the same period, and twenty million pounds of tin-plate, valued at a million dollars, and half a million dollars' worth of manufactured tinware. Yet in 1867 the amount which the United States paid to Russia for

A VIEW OF THE PRINCIPAL BUSINESS STREET OF NOME

GROUP OF WALRUSES ALONG THE
SHORE

all Alaska—a territory as large as the whole of the United States east of the Mississippi river, exclusive of the four states of Florida, Georgia, Alabama and Mississippi—was only seven million dollars.

In the spring of 1899, the spot now marked as Nome on the map was as dismal a beach as might be found the world over. By June of the same year a tent-city, sheltering five thousand persons, occupied the site. By the following September the tent-city had vanished and in its place was a town of substantial frame buildings. In the mean time a city government had been formed, a mayor elected, a police force organized, a fire department equipped and a court established.

The bad man with the revolver, who used to "shoot up" the old camps, is a picturesque character that has never appeared in Nome. There were two or three shooting-affairs the first summer, but they were of the character that might occur in New York, London or Paris, not the mining-camp variety at all.

The most remarkable thing about Nome is the rapidity with which it acquired the luxuries of civilization. Its electric-lighting system and its telephone service are excellent. Its large greenhouse supplies fresh vegetables and flowers the year round at reasonable prices. There are numerous clubs, the most important of which is a secret society, the Arctic Brotherhood, whose clubhouse is in every particular all that a clubhouse should be, from the bowling-alleys to the café. The three churches are the largest buildings in Nome.

The first winter of Nome was characterized by what might be called high finance, truly a commentary on the mental trend of the day. Everybody tried to corner something. To corner things was in every particular legitimate, and to neglect an opportunity was to court ruin.

The price of coal under artificial stimulus went to one hundred and fifty dollars a ton, lumber commanded five hundred dollars a thousand feet before the winter

HEADS OF WALRUSES CAPTURED ON THE ICE NEAR NOME

broke. Castor-oil could be had in large quantities for fifty cents an ounce; eggs brought fifty cents each. The most successful corner was that of fresh milk. There was only one cow in the city; the owner thereof cleared one thousand dollars on milk, and sold the cow in the spring for beef, realizing five hundred more. Beer brought unheard-of prices. To take advantage of the high prices expected the following winter, poultry-yards and dairies were established, and a brewery built, and thus prices found their natural level.

The social life of the town during the first two winters would have furnished the student of sociology an interesting chapter, comprising as it did the formation of a "four hundred," a "fast set," and the like. At a charity-ball held early the second season, I wore the first dress-suit ever exposed to public view in Nome. Needless to add, I was the uncomfortable center of all eyes. Judge Clark finally broke the ice by shaking hands with the "man who had nerve enough to wear a dress-suit in Nome."

It was a most amusing thing to see the dress-suits appear after that. Before the winter was over, it was rare indeed to see a man at a function in anything but evening-clothes. Where they came from has never been satisfactorily explained to this day.

Of all sources of amusement in this arctic metropolis, dancing is the first. Everybody from two and a half years to seventy dances. Those who didn't know how when they arrived, soon learned. And to-day it is no exaggeration to say that every man, woman and

CATHOLIC CHURCH. THE LARGEST STRUCTURE IN NOME

child in Nome attends at least one dance a night. I picture them now, old and young, vigorous and happy, dancing under a hundred roofs.

"It seems to me—indeed it do—I mebbe mout be wrong—
That people raly *ought* to dance, when winter comes along:
Des dance bekase dey's happy—like de birds hops in de trees;
De pine-top fiddle soundin' to de blowin' ob de breeze."

And the thing that brought this all about is gold. Nature hides her treasure in strange places, and puts through strange paces us that seek for it. Everybody in Nome has a claim; everybody expects to strike it rich sooner or later. Enough enthusiasm, optimism and ambition are generated in Nome each year to supply the earth—aye, the universe—could they be bottled or dried. The first mining was done by placer methods, right on the sea-beach. At first one man could make as much as fifty dollars a day by the simplest methods. Each inch of beach, one might say, has been worked over by the hand-methods and now the whole beach is being systematically sifted again; this time gasoline-engines and mercury are assisting.

Farther back in the tundra, within three miles of the town, where no one

INTERIOR OF GREENHOUSE AT NOME

FREIGHT, LANDED FROM LIGHTERS, ON THE BEACH AT NOME

suspected that there was gold at all, there has been found a deposit richer than ever has been discovered in Alaska. From five to ten thousand dollars' worth a day has been taken out here. This discovery was made two weeks before the last boat came out in the fall, and will undoubtedly add new stimulus to Alaskan travel in the spring.

A railroad now under course of construction in this immediate district—the Council City and Solomon River—promises to make accessible a district that it is impossible to work successfully at the present time, owing to the difficulty of receiving supplies.

The construction of this railroad, the first of standard gage in operation in Alaska, has demonstrated the possibility of building in the Far North a road-bed practically as solid as that of any of the best-

LANDING STEAMER PASSENGERS AT NOME

equipped systems in the United States. The tundra, or arctic bog-lands, have been conquered by a system of thorough drainage, and the ties planted on gravel brought from a distance for ballasting purposes, reenforced by a top layer of rock from the foot-hills.

The first railroad built in northwestern Alaska was called by the expressive name of the "Wild Goose Railroad." It was constructed during the summer of 1900, and was a financial success from the outset. Recently this line has been acquired by the Nome-Arctic Railroad Company, which has extended its tracks north to Dexter Creek, and, securing a franchise to enter Nome city, has built there a large station and added three spurs to facilitate the handling of freight.

A part of the plan for railroad development on

PURCHASING SUPPLIES WITH GOLD-DUST

Seward Peninsula embraces the furnishing to the mining-camps along the roads a cheap and efficient telephone service. More than three hundred miles of copper wire were used during last summer for this purpose.

A favorite expression in Nome is "lucky Swedes," as most of the big strikes have been made by Swedes. A Swede will stake a claim and dig a hole down to bed-rock, sometimes forty or fifty feet; if he finds nothing, he will dig a second

CHRISTMAS-PARTY OF THE ANVIL MASONIC CLUB, NOME

HERD OF REINDEER, USED FOR TRANSPORTATION PURPOSES IN ALASKA

on another part of the claim. If this proves unsatisfactory, another is dug. Frequently he will dig as many as twelve holes before he will give up a claim. The same determination is absolutely essential to the successful gold-seeker.

I might say, further, that determination alone is not sufficient; no one should think of going to Alaska to hunt gold with less than fifteen hundred dollars capital, and as much more as he can get.

The time is not far distant when Alaska is going to take its place as a great agricultural section. There are at the present moment one million square miles available for cultivation, and with a climate not so severe as that of British Columbia or Manitoba.

The country's canneries and fisheries are rapidly gaining a world-wide reputation, and the time is almost at hand when Nome will make Gloucester, Massachusetts, look to its laurels as the fishing-port of America.

Alaska has the largest game in the world—if we except the elephant—in its great Kadiak bears, and has moose, caribou, goats and mountain-sheep. Herds of caribou that have taken two days to pass a given point are to be seen. These will soon go the way of the buffalo, however, unless some action is taken, for the white man has taught the Indian the value of certain parts of these animals, and they are slaughtered literally by the thousands each year.

Since Alaska was purchased from Russia, in 1867, for seven million two hundred thousand dollars, it has brought to the people of the United States, from its furs, fisheries and mines, over ten billions of dollars. It is interesting to wonder what Alaska would be if it had remained in Russia's hands to the present day. Would Japanese fleets now be bombarding Sitka, Nome, and other Alaskan ports, or would they exist at all?

PHOTOGRAPH OF A MIRAGE, SUPPOSED TO BE OF BRISTOL,
ENGLAND, SEEN AT NOME, FOUR YEARS AGO

34
A Railway
to the
Klondike

A RAILWAY TO THE KLONDIKE.

BY W. M. SHEFFIELD.

FOR less than three years streams of humanity have been pouring into the interior of Alaska. The soil of that country, with that of the adjacent northern portions of British Columbia and the Northwest Territory, is now considered as among the most precious of the earth, and its sections are in eager demand on the exchanges of New York, London and Paris, bought and sold with greater facility than has ever been the case with the mines of South Africa and Australia. Up to the time that gold was discovered in the now famous Klondike valley, little was known of Alaska, even by the government authorities at Washington. Official information was obtained through the revenue cutter service, and with inadequate means at its disposal, its reports were known to be inaccurate, and the government maps to show an incorrect coast-line.

When it came to the interior, it may be said that the topography was largely a matter of the map-maker's imagination, but there was no one to challenge it. Several men penetrated the territory in the early years of our occupation, but their reports told little that could be used as a basis of accurate statement. In later years a few adventurous individuals ascended the Yukon from St. Michaels, others crossed Chilkoot pass and descended the river by the chain of lakes. Most of these pioneers sought the solitude of the north as a result of failure and disappointment, or were driven from civilization because they were no longer useful members of society. What white men they found in Alaska were descendants of the hardy Hudson Bay trappers and hunters, who had formed a chain of settlements throughout the country at the time of Russian occupation or immediately after the purchase by the United States. But these men cared little for and contributed nothing to a knowledge of our great possession in the north. We did not learn to know Alaska until it became worth while, until its secret was wrested from the soil, and it became the great magnet for the world's unstable population.

There are large sections of Alaska, on the mainland, in the interior and on its many islands, suitable for agricultural pursuits—an economic fact upon whose appreciation the proper development of the country depends. Alaska must not be simply stripped of its mineral treasure; this must help to enrich the settler, and afford him opportunities of molding the country in ways that will soonest bring it the joys of civilization.

The soil of the country is rich and its valleys are luxuriant every summer with waving acres of wild hay. Experiments have demonstrated that the hardier cereals and all manner of vegetables can be raised with profit. A government agricultural station has been established at Sitka for experiment, and its reports have been most encouraging. The long days of summer sunshine—when the sun is below the horizon only an hour out of the twenty-four—cause vegetation and cereals to develop with great rapidity. It is not a question of days or weeks with their growth, but simply a matter of sunshine and light. The hundreds of islands of the Aleutian peninsula will some day be dotted with farms and stock-ranges, while the interior is capable of supporting an affluent population. There will come

FIRST SLUICE-BOX ON PINE CREEK.

a time when Alaska will be one of the wealthiest possessions of the American domain.

On July 19, 1897, a steamer arrived from the north with about a hundred and fifty Klondikers on board, their great buckskin sacks almost bursting with gold dust and nuggets. All had money, and several of them had each over a hundred thousand dollars' worth of the precious yellow stuff. Within twenty-four hours the news had spread all over the world, and the rush to the new Eldorado set in immediately. Miners came from England, France, Germany and Spain, while South Africa and Australia gave up their prospectors by the thousand. The mining regions of the United States were threatened with depopulation. Chilkoot pass and Dyea, the route selected by the Indians for

ARRIVAL OF THE FIRST PASSENGER-TRAIN AT THE SUMMIT OF WHITE PASS, FEB. 20, 1899.

THE ROAD-BED NEAR THE SUMMIT.

years in their journeys from the coast to the interior, were finally abandoned by the majority of the immigrants; White pass, with Skagway as the port of entry, became the favorite route. This was seen to be the logical path for the iron horse to make his entry into the Yukon valley, getting over the range at the lowest altitude. English and American capitalists soon had their engineers on the spot, and the work of building the White Pass and Yukon railway followed close upon the preliminary surveys.

The route starts from Skagway, traverses White pass, descends into the Yukon valley by way of the chain of lakes and ends at Fort Selkirk, on the Yukon, over three hundred miles from Skagway. The twenty miles between tide-water and the top of the pass presented a problem of great difficulty. In this there is a rise of two thousand eight hundred and fifty feet, nearly all of which must be overcome in one part. The distinguishing feature in accomplishing this is the employment of many sharp curves, built with great skill on shelves in the face of the rock. By this means a maximum grade of 3.9 per cent., or two hundred and six feet to the mile, has been obtained. Few railroads not depending on the cog can boast of such a steep gradient.

Begun in the spring of 1898, the work steadily advanced under a force of one thousand five hundred workmen, and in days twenty-two hours in length. On the 20th of last February the first train

arrived at the top of the pass, and the terminus at Fort Selkirk will probably be reached before the close of this year. The road is a single-track narrow-gage, and its equipment is light, but its mission is a merciful one, and puts an end to the terrible discomfort and danger of the overland route to the new Eldorado. So far the cost has been excessive, something like sixty thousand dollars a mile, but the very difficult conditions met with in the beginning will disappear in the descent to Fort Selkirk, and the construction consequently will be much cheaper.

There have been many who have predicted an extension of our railway systems along the western shores of this continent to confront a similar extension of the Trans-Siberian on the opposite shores of Bering strait. All things considered, it is quite safe to say that through trains from San Francisco to St. Petersburg are not of the near future. The White Pass and Yukon is not to be thought of as the first link of a scheme at present impracticable. For some time to come it will be a modest affair, and would fail for lack of sustenance were it not for excessive passenger and freight rates. One may ride on its cars for twenty cents a mile, or ship freight at charges equivalent to one hundred dollars per ton between Chicago and New York. The development of the country through which the road will pass will soon reduce these high rates. At all events, they are so reasonable in comparison with those of the Indian packers, who have been asking from fifteen to forty cents per pound to get

MESSENGER ON THE TRAIL BEYOND THE SUMMIT, WITH NEWS OF THE ALIEN EXCLUSION ACT.

FIRST PASSENGER-TRAIN EN ROUTE TO THE SUMMIT.

merchandise over the pass, that no one is likely to complain at the company's getting back in this manner some of its outlay.

The northward traveler landing at Skagway is now met at the wharf by hotel vans, and the ubiquitous hotel runner makes the occasion hideous just as he does in other cities. The town has a population of about eight thousand, resident and transient, and boasts upward of twenty hotels. It has a telephone system, electric lights, water-works, a fire department, a company of National Guardsmen, schools and churches. But the most important of all is the railroad, and next comes a telegraph line soon to run far into the interior as a result of Canadian enterprise.

When the future fortune-seeker arrives at Fort Selkirk after a comfortable railway journey, as he will do after a few months, there will be many directions in which he may strike out, for the thousands of prospectors entering Alaska have brought news of rich gold-fields in other localities.

For a time all roads led to Dawson, but the word Klondike has since been in danger several times of being superseded as a synonym of the miners' paradise. Last August the Atlin district, eighty-three miles north of Skagway, was discovered and developed by Americans. Upward of fifteen thousand claims were staked during the fall, and then the miners were driven to tide-water by the snow and cold weather.

WAITING FOR A TRAIN TO PASS.

While these men were preparing to return to their holdings and work them, the British Columbia Parliament, in session at Victoria, passed an alien exclusion act, depriving Americans from holding or acquiring, by purchase or otherwise, any claims in the province. Very few of the Atlin miners succeeded in getting their claims recorded, and under the operation of the alien act all such claims reverted to the crown. Thus the work of the vast majority of the American miners in the district has been lost. There is a strong impression that the

ects and crossed over into American possessions. The Porcupine mining district on the Dalton trail drew many, and several rich strikes are reported, but this, unfortunately, is still too near the indefinite border for the men to feel sure of the protection of the American mining laws.

The boundary question is one that should be settled at the earliest possible moment. The British Columbia mounted police have not been free from suspicion of maintaining a somewhat elastic border line that has been more than once stretched

AT THE MOUTH OF THE TUNNEL.

passage of the act is a part of a scheme to consolidate the interests of the whole region under the management of a syndicate—a Cecil Rhodes mining trust transferred from South Africa to northern British Columbia. The exclusion act was passed early in January, and proved a great surprise, not only to the Americans, but to the mass of the residents of British Columbia.

When the news of the exclusion act reached the Atlin miners, many became disheartened or threatened fight, but others more wise abandoned their Canadian proj-

to include districts of great mineral wealth. Such a charge has, indeed, been definitely made by the miners driven from the Atlin to the Porcupine claims. The fact is that the dividing line is by no means accurately known, and must be settled by a joint commission of England and the United States. It is to be hoped that Governor Brady's present visit to Washington will result in some definite steps being soon taken in this matter, which becomes of great importance as the surprising wealth and resources of the land are fully realized.

35
The Orphan of Sourdough City

THE ORPHAN OF SOURDOUGH CITY

BY ROBERT DUNN

ILLUSTRATED BY E. L. BLUMENSCHEIN

OURDOUGH CITY nicked the great glaciers of the Alaskan Peninsula. Spring gazed upon its boom, broken; beheld gaping saloons, vacant dance-halls, empty cabins straggling among the lean cottonwoods of the sandbar. Lust of riches had turned to ash in the mouths of a thousand criminals and dreamers. Then to the camp had come—scurvy; yet the two hundred graves in the swamp back of town were pitifully mute of its winter tragedies. The survivors had fled. June saw but four human beings on the beach, each with a particular reason for lingering there. Three of them sat before Bill Silas' trading store. The other, a woman, was auctioning blue overalls to Siwashes at the far end of the spit.

Mrs. Fred Smith was believed to remain because her spell of scurvy had kept her from selling the stock of the clothing store which she had conducted in every stampede camp since the Klondike strike. Most springs she spent in the states, speaking from the lecture platform on the sufferings of the Alaskan aboriginee. Elderly ladies dowered her with cash and garments—and no Siwash was ever made warmer or less hungry by her charity.

Tom Yandaw, gambler, clung to Sourdough because property convertible into cash might have been buried with some scurvy corpses. But he was too "nifty" with his gun to be taxed with ghoulishness, and jealous of life as the North is, its empty shell is too common to be held sacred to a possible Hereafter.

Bill Silas hugged the camp for a more

sentimental reason. Eighty years had not in the least marred his vitality, and he was now openly a candidate for partnership with Mrs. Fred—a profitable job just vacant.

Charles Amy's delay alone was not reasonable. Before the stampede, this Maine-born fisherman had dully followed the traditions of his youth as a salmon-stream prospector for the big canneries, and his seamed red neck and thin hair, the hue of rust, were familiar to the Chinamen at a dozen of the clanking hells of fish-guts and solder in the wilderness. Stranger that he was among the outcasts of Sourdough, his frail young wife, whom he had loved with the simple passion of less feverish lands and fortunes, had been yet more alien to the lost creatures of the camp. She was the child of a whaling captain who had put into Afgonak two winters before while Amy was there. She had died of scurvy this last December, falling ill the day after the theft from Bill Silas' store of the crate of citric acid, with which the dozen scurvy cases then in town were being treated. At first her death seemed to have unseated Amy's mind, and gave him a dazed listlessness, more than pitiful in this lank, Herculean being, always clad in the gray homespun made by the too-beloved little woman on their former lonely exiles. Christmas night Amy had burned her body over a pyre on the beach. The ragged circle of derelicts, who laughed or trembled as they watched in the snow-lit cold, saw his eyes flash from their whitish brows, and heard his oath to run down and kill the acid thieves, if it took all his life.

But he should have believed that re-

453

venge was now futile, unless the guilty were among his fellow-outcasts, for hardly a native or squawman remained on the hill behind Sourdough. The first spring steamship from Seattle, which brought potatoes and curbed the scurvy, carried also measles, which spread like wildfire through the native village, for measles among Esquimaux and Indians is as deadly as plague among whitemen. Half the Siwashes died of it, fate with customary discretion thus levying on the innocent aboriginee the curse of the whiteman's avarice. All the rest fled to the lakes behind the Iliamna volcano, which overshadows Sourdough. Two beings only remained on the hill: Larkin Weed, a whiteman, and his Siwash wife. He, having violated native no less than whitemen's laws by marrying an Indian, had ever been exiled, alike from Siwash hut and boom cabin. Having no money and no dogs, he could not carry his woman from the infection. Measles entered his shack, attacking him also, a week after his wife gave birth to a child, a boy.

"The squawman and his klootch is dead," said Amy to Silas and Yandaw on the beach. "Drawed in their nets about midnight, so I jedge."

"So you ben down to their shack, hev you?" demanded the gambler. "I wouldn't dirty myself so, and I don't fear no measles. Where a squawman lives is no place fer honest whitemen."

The fisherman's blue eyes avoided the little fellow's glance of disgust. "No," hesitated Amy, "I—I ain't been down to Weed's," but his hearers swore under their breath.

Thus the trio sat, discussing the dead squawman, the dead squaw, and the living orphan. Old Silas marveled that Weed could have, "took the rash." After the acid theft, Bill had nursed most of the camp, and was encouraged to pose as a Galen of the North. "But the body of a whiteman hitched to a squaw rots, too, I guess, like his nature," said he, stroking his snowy beard.

"Is the kid down with measles yet?" asked the old man at last.

Amy shook his head. "He's waiting for your healing hand," he sneered.

"He kin wait," snapped the savior of Sourdough. "I don't nurse *him*. White-

men's measles is one thing, but when the pizen's passed through a Siwash *and* a squawman—" he paused, not shocked by his brutality toward the little being whose primordial innocence already was cursed by the sins or a father, but to kill a mosquito on his crinkled forehead. "Some squawmen you might chuck sour beans to if he's a-starvin'," he continued. "But this Weed was a thief. And he beat his woman."

Yandaw favored letting all squawmen and their off-spring starve. "They've cashed in all rights to be called white," said he. "Strong men hes got to civilize this country, and we can't afford to hev our pioneers git soft and lazy in a Siwash shack, eatin' fish-guts, breedin' mongrels. Ain't fair to our own blood, and the refinements we bring after."

To which final casting into outer darkness off all miscegenators, only Charles Amy failed to spit acquiescence. "I suppose you think this orphan kid ain't made of flesh and blood," said he simply, whittling a tiny spruce paddle. "He has no eyes and feet and hands like us. Jab a knife into him, and it don't hurt, I suppose."

"Do it," chuckled Silas. "Knife his heart out. We won't string you up for it. Means one less dirty breed in Alaska," at which Yandaw rubbed his unshaven square chin, laughing softly.

"If you don't, mebbe one of us will," said the gambler. "He'll never pay in my business, nor yours, up here."

Amy sprang to his feet, shaking a bony fist. "You lay one hand on that innocent kid," he cried, "and you answer for it with your lives. Is it his fault he come into this world lower nor a dog. God's give him no soul. Oh, no. We quacks and gamblers have the pre-emption claims to souls here in Alasky. Over yonder he lies pure and naked, but he must learn that all over the North he was born to git nothin' but a kick and oath from every crook in the country, and the dirtiest Siwash. Is it his fault? No! But life is goin' to pound it into his eyes, and mash it into his skull that it *is* his fault, till he believes it, and he'll be the crawlin' beast you hold him now."

Silas whistled and the gambler burst into a nervous laugh. They turned their eyes guiltily toward the sea. South, the tremendous glaciers clothing Cape Douglas, dipped glittering, sepulchral folds into the satin ocean. The reddish cone of the Augustine volcano, rising from the strait without shore-line, buoyed its vague curl of steam in the pure summer sky. Never before had natural scenery so diverted any one at Sourdough.

"Can't you take a josh?" said Yandaw, winking at Silas. "You know we wouldn't murder the kid, even if the' is no hangin' quorum in town."

"Mebbe he's gettin' the measles now," soothed Silas. "Easiest way out from the hard luck Amy here mentions."

"I dare you to go to Weed's shack and see," flashed out the fisherman. "You're afraid, you are, you cowards."

"Afraid, hell!" swore the old man uneasily. "Who fears the rash? But we don't like squawmen's dirt the same as you."

A large figure moving up the beach averted hostilities by seizing the trio's gaze. "Here's Mrs. Fred," observed the gambler. "Doped again, I see. Where does she get her cocaine now? Pity, for she's fine set up with good action to her legs for a musher on the trail, and we need the strong ones to open up this country. I believe she was a good woman once. Bears marks of it yet. Ain't half as foulmouthed as you'd think."

"Mebbe she was a mother once," said Amy, as if to himself.

"You bet, and ain't forgotten all the tricks," jeered Yandaw.

It was then that the idea came to them all together, whether from the fisherman's guess, Yandaw's slur, or simply the grotesque presence of Mrs. Fred. The gambler suggested it with a chuckle, and Silas seconded with guffaws. The plan was for Mrs. Fred to adopt the half-breed orphan of Sourdough. "I ken see her fittin' rubber tubes and condensed milk into pint flasks fer him. But it's understood," said Silas with mock severity, "if me and the woman draw up a partnership, he has no claim on me or mine."

"Poor little gaffer!" sighed Amy. "But worse is that he should die. Give him, and the woman, too, a chance to start again, I say."

"We'll get the little cuss and hand it to her. Hev a surprise party," laughed Yandaw. "We got to bury them corpses, anyhow, ain't we Silas? Health of our city demands it. Say,"—he winked—"but do you think it's fair, even to a rounder like Mrs. Fred, to cast in her lot with a squawman's bastard? Come on."

Amy dug his knife into the bit of spruce, his fingers into his palms, and followed.

Weed's shack crouched in dank grass and slippery clay at the end of the ruined string of huts beginning on the hillock-top. The strange decay that follows plague and sudden flight in the wilderness marked each as the lair of a death unknown to peace. Sometimes a scarlet fish gnawed by ravens hung by a grisly fin from salmon-drying frames all askew. Wolfish dogs, too old to travel, or lamed by frost-bite, slinked among empty cans in the bleached refuse; or their eyes bright with the sadness of starvation, sparkled in the dark of little holes cut for them by the cabin doors.

The trio stooped, entering the squawman's home. Fish-oil reeked predominant in the all but tangible fester of death and filth. Side by side upon an oblong of the earth floor marked off by an angle of sawed boards placed on edge, the father and mother made angular, motionless lumps under a red blanket. Yandaw put out an arm to lift it, but old Silas almost reverently restrained him. Each log of the walls exhaled a poisonous, fetid cold. The rusted stove aimed a pipe badly at a ragged hole in the roof, under which a big, damp circle of earth was edged with mildew; water had washed apart the charred logs of a fire, heaping rusted cups and plates together.

"Was Weed converted to the Siwash Rooshian faith?" growled Yandaw gently, pointing where the gold of a tiny ikon gleamed on the wall.

"Whiteman's candles, by crotch!" breathed Silas, touching the two bits of tallow before the sacred painting. "You make no strike with the Siwash God burning *these*. Must hev the little pink ones you buy to Kenai church. . . . Who's ben here lately?" and he fingered the dust on the shelf.

"Only one man in camp hes candles with braided wicks like them," charged the gambler. "And that's you, Charles Amy. . . . When you said you ain't been down here, then you lied."

"What's it to you if I have, Jim Yandaw?" blazed out the fisherman. "So has others."

"Amy, he wanted them to go to heaven on his own mileage," Silas calmed. "You're a Cath'lic, ain't you, Charles? . . . Why shouldn't he, Tom?"

Yandaw stopped grinning. Under the image or crucifixion, framed with its gothic arch and muscovite traceries, a large baking-powder box lay open on the earth. Its pine boards were curiously fresh and new, but a square of old sacking hid the contents. This suddenly stirred, and from under it was thrust a small brown fist tightly clenched. The creature began to cry. Involuntarily, the three men caught their breaths, and each found a separate spot on the rafters of absorbing interest.

"Quit it, quit it," growled Yandaw, at last. "It ain't right. Can't you stop him yellin', Amy' What hurts him, anyhow?"

He wailed, like all infants, first awakening to the discomfort of existence, groping under its lash, maddened and baffled, to place responsibility for pain. The gambler bravely faced Silas, but turned quickly away. He saw moisture in the old man's eyes, whom he guiltily knew saw the flush that warmed under Yandaw's own stubby beard. Amy knelt, and raising the sacking revealed a bright blue quilt.

"Who'd they steal that from, I wonder?" blurted the gambler. "Or is it yours, Amy?"

"I tell you it ain't mine," said the fisherman doggedly, removing the silk. "But the kid had to be clean. Else he'd 'a' been dead—and so satisfied you."

"Hell, we never meant," began Yandaw, and stopped, seeing the russet sheen of the naked child's skin. It lay amid the wreckage like a precious carved image. The broad cheeks and slant eyes of the Siwash were welded with an alluring neatness to the high forehead and delicate chin of the whiteman. "Fat, ain't he?" said old Bill, glancing to the outline of the two corpses. "Believe they starved themselves to feed him."

Yandaw's voice came subdued from a corner. He had unearthed a square box from the rubbish, and was taking off the loose top boards. "Look here," he said, lifting from within one of two dozen condensed milk cans.

"That's mine, mine, by God!" exclaimed Silas. "They stole them from me, the sneakin' thieves!" and he ground his teeth at the corpses.

"Yes, the mother stole milk fer the little cuss," said Amy. "Meant to feed it to him, knowing she couldn't wean him."

"You ain't missed it till now, did you?" demanded Yandaw. "What you so hot over that for?"

"No, no," said the old man weakly. "But if they'd only asked me, I'd have given them milk. And Pansy brand, perhaps, which is better for kids."

For the first time, the eyes of Amy and the gambler met squarely. At the same moment the baby opened his eyes, gazing with wide, wonderless amusement from one rough face to the other. He caught up Amy's chuckle in a hearty child's crow. The gambler and Silas joined in.

"Laughing seems infectious, eh?" said Bill, "same as measles." The child relaxed his tiny puckered mouth, and opening and clutching his little hands waved them as if they should hold a rattle. Yandaw shyly held out a finger, and the kid grasped it with the uncertain, releasing touch, which explores the first sensations of living.

"I guess you ain't never touched one before, hev you?" said Silas.

"Never mongrels," smiled the gambler. . . . "Where does he get the nerve to be so familiar with white people. Darn the little cuss!"

"How do you read his hand?" asked the old man. "Is he goin' to be smarter with the faro-box, or twirlin' the marble?" And for once no laugh greeted this pleasantry.

Yandaw was again rummaging at the foot of the cradle, when his foot struck against a tin box. "I reckon the crap outfit I lost must be in here," said he. "No" —he turned it over, and read—"'Larkin Weed, Alaska-Pacific Express, Seattle.'"

"Come by this spring's boat," said Silas. "Wouldn't that beat you. Freight fer this squawman here, and not one newspaper fer us."

Yandaw put his hand into the tin, and drew forth—a horse; not a packed cayeuse, but a small painted and varnished toy, glued to a board and running on four gilt wheels. Then a pink celluloid rattle; a dozen lead soldiers in a box with a glass cover; a small engine with a train of tiny cars.

"Toys fer the little monkey, eh?" said the gambler, balancing them on the side of his box. "Sent fer them all the way to the States before the little shaver arrived. There's the father for you, though he be a squawman. You wouldn't think they could love like other beings. But how'd he know it was goin' to be a boy, Silas?"

"What father doesn't always know that beforehand?" laughed the old man. "Ain't you never been one yourself? I hev. So hev you, or we wouldn't be foolin' about here, like three idiots."

A comfortless silence failed to disclaim this sweeping charge. "Well, if we ain't 'a' been fathers, we got to be now, ain't we?" asked the little gambler. "That's agreed, I guess. And damn Mrs. Fred. We can't trust him to a rounder like her."

All three found relief in laughter. Thus the resistless spur of instinct, so guiltily cherished, surrendered its sting. A mad warmth flooded their hearts, now revealed as all one. So adoption was tenderly to seal the orphan's fate, and Amy's tearful eyes, as he tore aside the faded piece of calico that hid the shelf let into the wall over the ikon, met the gambler's without wincing. But the next moment, fatherhood was remoter than murder from these three beings.

His whitish eye-lids half-closed, the fisherman pointed to a wide-necked glass druggist's jar upon that shelf. "Citric Acid," said its yellowed label.

Silas was the first to break out. "You —you—murderers of two hundred white-men, you devils from the Siwash hell!" he cried, gritting his teeth at the corpses. "Stole, and never used the stuff. My acid!"

He seized the jar, and held it at arm's length. The bitter hate peculiar to old age and the instincts of race burned in his eyes. Yandaw, stiffening, muttered with clenched fists. All the despair of the pitiful dark winter past, of friends and partners in pain and death, blotted charity and fatherhood from their rough minds, as it were a perversion. They felt only the eye-and-tooth justice, taught by the hard life of the North. It further goaded them that death prevented direct revenge in warm blood, since equity now lay in mutilation.

At length Amy lowered his yellow head, spoke the name of his dead wife three times quite clearly and stumbled to the box where the naked child lay. He kicked it. The infant burst into wailing crescendoes.

"We fools to come down here!" spoke out Yandaw. "And put ourselves so this d—d kid could cheat our hearts with his spulin' innocence. *Innocence! He* knew, too. *he* did."

"What 'll we do?" asked Silas simply, as the child stopped sobbing, and began to cough.

"Do?" jeered the gambler. "Leave the young devil here to starve. Hear that cough? He's got the measles now. Let him twist himself into knots while he dies of it. His flesh and blood hes murdered our flesh and blood, and it's only God's justice he should pay for it."

Amy gently laid an arm on the little man's shoulder. "No, no, no," he pleaded. "Ain't there an easier way, a *neater* way, Tom? Let's still be charitable, and save him all that pain. 'Taint his fault—not his fault—no. . . . Say, Tom, ain't you still got that knife? Out on the beach you were going to use it on his heart. Give it here, give it, give it. . . . He has a heart, I guess. He cries out of it. . . . You needn't. I'll do the trick." He felt behind the gambler's coat, and drew out his long dirk.

His lined cheeks were scarlet, his blue eyes dancing with light. Clumsily he was reaching toward the infant's box with the steel, when two violent blows sounded on the coop-like door of the cabin. "Hold a holt there," warned Silas, grasping Amy's hand. "Keep yer head. See who it is, Tom. Come in, there!" he shouted.

A couple of black ostrich plumes dipped under the low lintel, and Mrs. Fred Smith stumbled over the charred logs by the stove. In the dim squalor, with her straw-colored hair and powered red cheeks, she might herself have been a corpse just arisen. She held her black silk skirt hitched up by a sort of cable, as you see in dance-halls, and on her feet were high-heeled shoes which once had been white.

The gambler broke the tension. "We hev a job fer you, Mrs. Fred. Ever hired out as a wet nurse?"

"You lay one hand on that innocent kid"—he cried, " and you answer for it with your lives."

Drawing by E. L. Blumenschein.

The woman glared at the three a moment. Then she burst into long, loud laughter. "You'll be askin' me next if I was ever a mother, Jim," she cried in falsetto. "*I* a mother, *me* a mother. Oh. No, no, no!"

"Don't boys," warned Silas. "I don't like her laugh. You never can tell with these dope-fiends whether they take you serious or not. She's gettin' ironic now. Look out!"

Mrs. Fred fumbled in the pocket of her shiny skirt, and drew out a glass pint flask. Milk replaced whisky inside, and a rubber tube hung from the mouth. This the child reached for as she leaned over his box.

"Watch out it ain't your dope bottle, Mrs. Fred," suggested the gambler.

"Get out of here, you cradle-thieves, get out!" she challenged, squaring her shoulders at Amy, who stood with the knife still poised. "I know what you're up to. Give me that knife. I heard you from outside there, every word, you skunk-hearts. Kill the kid, would you, jest because his mother swiped that truck?" and she kicked the glass acid jar, so the white powder rose with the crash from the dirt where Silas had put it. . . . "Citric acid! Hell! It's no damned use in scurvy. Your chiney doll wife would 'a' died anyhow, Charley. . . . Kill the kid, would you, after his melting your coward hearts, so you're all to be his father, and he's too good fer a rounder like Mrs. Fred. . . . Mebbe you think I haven't been a mother in my time, and wasn't straight once. Mebbe you think that once being a mother, the lowest of us ain't a-goin' to fight dogs like *you*. Half-breed and squawman, I hate all, but this kid ain't either one yet. Plain infant he is in this brazen word of ourn, kicked out alone. . . . Did I stay on here at Sourdough to sell jumpers? Not on your wood license. Perhaps you think I ain't been down here regular, and he ain't got his bottle every day, that them blankets over the stiffs ain't mine. . . . Drop yer toad-sticker, *drop it I say*," and the woman struck Amy's arm which held the knife. Then, reaching again to her pocket, she drew out a clumsy .44 pistol, and pointed it at the fisherman's forehead.

He let his weapon fall. Instantly, Mrs. Fred burst into sobs, and fell forward over the infant's box. The men breathed long and heavily, like suffocating creatures reaching air.

"Let her lay, let her be," said Silas at last. "I told ye. She don't mean it. The dope was talking. Her fit 'll be over soon. But we'd better git away. They're likely to be worse when they come to." . . . And the three men wandered from the cabin quite as unsteadily as Mrs. Fred Smith had entered it.

When the *Excelsior* from Kodiak Island appeared off the Cape Douglas ice-foot, crawling like a black sunspot across its glare, the three men of Sourdough again sat before old Silas' store. Three weeks had passed. Still on the beach waited the cherry-wood piano. Still the blue jig-sawing of Mrs. Fred's cottage peeped from under the discouraged cottonwoods of the sandbar.

Glancing thither, Yandaw said, "Funny we ain't heard the kid tune up yet. Must be sleeping late." It was the custom of the three to wait here every morning until the orphan of Sourdough waked; then to proceed to his step-mother's with old Bill on his daily professional visit, and hear him speak authoritatively on the progress of the disease.

Not a word had been spoken for ten minutes when Amy announced his discovery of the vessel, which was to bear the companions another stage, in their old, barren dream of riches, on their endless journey through the desolate, uncertain North.

"The old tub might 'a' waited a week," growled Silas. "Measles leaves the eyes tender, and the kid's can't bear these glaciers. We'll hev to keep them covered."

"New fathers takes their duties very solemn, these days," smiled Amy. "Is it Kenai church, or the Salvation Army Barracks up to Valdez where you and Mrs. Fred get hitched?"

36
The Caribou of
British Columbia
and Alaska

THE CARIBOU OF BRITISH COLUMBIA AND ALASKA

By Dr. J. A. ALLEN

Of the American Museum of Natural History

OUR knowledge of the mammals of North America has necessarily progressed slowly, and only in proportion to the accumulation of material for their investigation. Twenty-five years ago they were supposed by even the experts to be fairly well known; it was thought that very few, if any, new forms remained to be discovered, although it was recognized that there were lacunæ to be filled in respect to their distribution and much to be learned to complete our knowledge of their habits. The continent had been overrun by explorers and collectors, and there were few regions of any great extent that had not been examined, at least superficially. Our larger museums contained considerable series of many species, the study of which seemed to indicate that too many rather than too few species had been recognized. The fact that the existing material was of poor quality, as regards preparation and field data, and altogether too scanty for final results, was not duly appreciated. That this was, however, the true condition of the case became evident some years later, when, through new methods of field work, the accumulation of large collections of carefully prepared specimens, gathered from a wide range of localities, became available for the critical comparison of allied forms from different physiographic areas. Then mammalogists began to realize that we were only on the threshold, as it were, of a satisfactory knowledge of the mammalian fauna of North America. Each year new forms, startlingly distinct from anything previously known, were discovered—not only new species, but even new generic types, not to mention the hosts of lesser forms, or subspecies, to ignore which is to fail to recognize some of the most important facts in the evolution of the varied forms of animal life, and the influence of environment in their development.

It is a comparatively easy matter to bring together material for the study of the smaller forms, as the rodents, bats, insectivores, and smaller carnivores, but a very different and far more difficult thing to secure proper series of the larger game animals. The setting of a few score of small traps, which can be easily transported, and the liberal use of a small collecting gun, will secure an abundant supply of field mice, rats, shrews, gophers, and squirrels, which can be quickly prepared, and shipped with

Osborn's Caribou.

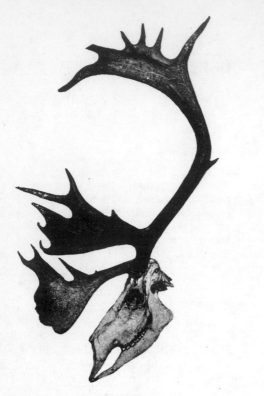

Newfoundland Caribou.   Stone's Caribou.

little trouble or expense. It is needless to say that the conditions are totally different with respect to large game, in obtaining which days and weeks may be required to locate and kill a few specimens; then follows the arduous labor of their preparation, and the long, wearisome "packing" to get them to the nearest place of shipment. This is especially true of the remote and almost limitless regions of the far North, the home of the caribou, which noble animal forms the subject of the present paper.

Caribou (including the domesticated reindeer) range over the greater part of the northern third of the northern hemisphere, from Norway eastward across Siberia and northern North America to Greenland, and southward in North America, roughly speaking to about latitude 48 degrees. Up to within a few years they have been generally regarded as forming a single species, with perhaps two or three varieties, the Old World reindeer (*Rangifer tarandus*), and the Barren Ground, Greenland, and Woodland caribou

(*R. tarandus arcticus, R. tarandus grœnlandicus,* and *R. tarandus caribou*). Even to this day some naturalists claim that there is but one kind of caribou, and that this is doubtfully distinguishable from the reindeer of the Old World.

Caribou vary greatly in color with season and age, and there is also a wide range of variations in the size and form of the antlers, as is the case with all antlered beasts. Yet, despite a large amount of variation in these respects, even among members of the same herd, a little serious attention to the subject soon develops convincing evidence that caribou from different areas within the common habitat of the group present strikingly different characteristics. Our ignorance in the matter has been due to lack of material for comparison, just as was the case twenty years ago with the smaller mammals, when so-called seasonal and individual variations, misunderstood through lack of material, covered numberless then unrecognized species and subspecies. In reality seasonal and individual variation is

Osborn's Caribou.

Newfoundland Caribou.

doubtless no greater than in the spermophiles, ground squirrels, shrews, and scores of other small mammals, and will prove as clearly distinguishable when sufficient material is available for examination.

As already said, three forms of North American caribou were commonly recognized ten years ago, and some were bold enough to regard the Barren Ground and Woodland forms as distinct species. In 1896 a fourth was described from Newfoundland, and since then four others, inhabiting different parts of British Columbia and Alaska have been separated as follows:

Rangifer montanus, Seton-Thompson, August, 1899. Selkirk Range, British Columbia.

Rangifer stonei, Allen, May, 1901. Kenai Peninsula, Alaska.

Rangifer granti, Allen, March, 1902. Alaska Peninsula.

Rangifer osborni, Allen, April, 1902, Cassiar Mountains, northern British Columbia.

Three of these forms are now represented in the American Museum of Natural History by a small series of from four to a dozen specimens each, and the other by a single example. They are, fortunately, strictly comparable as to season. One, and the chief, element of uncertainty in such investigations is thus eliminated. These forms differ notably in size, coloration, character of the antlers, and in certain features of cranial structure. These four forms may be briefly passed in review, beginning with the most southern.

MOUNTAIN CARIBOU (*Rangifer montanus*). —This, as in the case of the other forms, is represented by late September specimens, practically topotypes of the species. At this season of the year the mountain caribou may be described in general terms as a *black* caribou, in contradistinction from the woodland caribou, of eastern Canada, and the Osborn caribou, of the Cassiar district, of northern British Columbia, both of which are brown. The neck and shoulders, especially in the males, are much lighter than the body and limbs, which are deep blackish brown, with a decided lustre. In the short, heavy, much-branched antlers this species strongly recalls the Newfoundland species, which presents the opposite extreme in

465

coloration, being at this season light yellowish gray, with the head, neck, and shoulders nearly white.

The mountain caribou was described from the Illicillewact watershed, near Revelstoke, in the Selkirks of southeastern British Columbia, where it probably attains its extreme of differentiation. It is, so far as known, the caribou of southern British Columbia, and ranges southward doubtless to the northern border of Montana. How far it extends northward is unknown, but it is certainly replaced by

At present this caribou is known only from the Cassiar region of northern British Columbia, but it doubtless has a considerable range to the northward.

STONE CARIBOU (*Rangifer stonei*).—This form was described from a single specimen collected by Mr. Andrew J. Stone on the Kenai Penisula, Alaska, September 24, 1900. It is also a dark caribou, in general features of coloration resembling *Rangifer osborni* of the Cassiar region, as it does also in the general style of the antlers. It differs from this form in the

Grant's Caribou.

Mountain Caribou.

a very different animal in the Cassiar region of northern British Columbia.

OSBORN CARIBOU (*Rangifer osborni*).— This is also a very dark colored animal, the males in late September being dark brown, with the head, neck, and shoulders much lighter than the body and limbs. Although of dark coloration, it contrasts strikingly in this respect with the mountain caribou, differing too widely from it to require further comparison. It also differs radically in the character of the antlers, as may be readily seen by comparing the illustrations which were all photographed to the same scale.

obsolescence of the white rump patch, and in several important cranial details, especially in the shortness of the nasals and the narrowness of the rostral portion of the skull. Further specimens are necessary to show its exact relationship to the Cassiar form, with which its affinities are naturally closest. Unfortunately, it has been almost wholly exterminated by hunters on the Kenai Peninsula, but it doubtless occurs to the northward and eastward —a point yet to be determined.

GRANT CARIBOU (*Rangifer granti*).—A large series of the caribou of the western end of Alaska Peninsula, which represents a form surprisingly unlike any of those already mentioned, was collected by Mr. Andrew J. Stone during the last days of October, 1901. It differs from its big neighbor of the Kenai Peninsula through its small size, pale coloration, and very different style of antlers, which are light and slender, with a long backward sweep. It is a member of the Barren Ground group of caribou, of which there are evidently several quite distinct forms as yet practically unknown. The Grant caribou inhabits the treeless portions of the Alaska Peninsula and some of the islands immediately adjoining its western end, and is thus geographically isolated from the Barren Ground caribou of the Arctic coast. This is the lightest colored caribou thus far known, the young of the year being nearly as white as the Dall sheep in summer coat, while the adults range from clove to broccoli brown, with the head neck and shoulders light gray or creamy white, and a large white rump patch.

Such, in brief, are the characters of the four recognized forms of caribou from British Columbia and Alaska. We know them as yet only by specimens taken in autumn, in a coat corresponding to what is known as the "blue coat" in the deer. What they are like in summer, or in the full winter dress, remains still to be made known. Nor do we know very much in respect to the boundaries of their respec-

Stone's Caribou.

tive ranges, nor what light may be thrown upon their relationships by material gathered at intervening points between the type localities of these several forms. In fact, we are only beginning to acquire a little definite knowledge about the different forms of caribou that inhabit the northern points of North America. What is necessary to satisfactorily complete our knowledge of the group is a series of specimens from at least a dozen to fifty localities, sufficiently large to show the variations in color and other features due to age, season, and locality; in other words, series in some degree comparable to the material we are able to use in the study of the smaller mammals. This is perhaps too much to hope for, in view of the rapid extermination of the caribou over many parts of their ranges, the remoteness and difficulty of access of the haunts of many of the forms, and the expense and privation attending the collection and shipment of such large animals in series.

For the little we do know of these exceedingly interesting animals of Subarctic America we are mainly indebted to the enthusiasm, energy, endurance, and intelligence of Mr. Andrew J. Stone, backed by

Mountain Caribou.

a little financial aid on the part of friends of the American Museum of Natural History, especially the late Mr. James M. Constable, formerly vice-president of the Museum, and Mr. Madison Grant, the indefatigable secretary of the New York Zoölogical Society, who has successfully undertaken the task of raising funds for the Andrew J. Stone Expedition.

The purpose of Mr. Stone's work is primarily to secure for exhibition and for scientific research the larger forms of the mammalian life of Arctic and Subarctic America, and secondarily, as full a representation of the smaller mammals and birds of this region as time and circumstances will permit. His expeditions, considering the small amount of money available for the work, have been eminently successful, and have added a large amount of exceedingly valuable material to the resources of the Museum. These include, besides three new forms of caribou, a new mountain sheep (Ovis stonei), a new bear (Ursus merriami), and a number of new species of small mammals, besides supplying the Museum with its first representatives of many other northern mammals, including some sixteen Alaskan bears and a fine series of the big Alaskan moose.

Mr. Stone's first trip was made in 1896, to the head of the Stickine River, where he obtained the sheep that now bears his name. He started on this second trip in July, 1897, again ascending the Stickine River to the head of navigation, and after an expedition to the Cheonnee Mountains, crossed the divide to Dease Lake, and made an extended trip into the Cassiar Mountains, where he obtained a series of the caribou that has since been named Rangifer osborni. The following winter was spent in the Rocky Mountains near Hell Gate Cañon, and the journey down the Liard River was resumed in the spring. About one hundred miles below Fort Liard a side trip was made to the Nahanni Mountains, where a large series of the Dall sheep was procured. Fort Simpson, on the Mackenzie, was reached in June, 1898, and the head of the delta of the Mackenzie about the middle of October. From Fort McPherson a dogsled trip was made westward into the Rockies in an unsuccessful hunt for caribou. The journey down the Mackenzie delta was completed late in November, and he then turned westward,

following the Arctic coast for 250 miles to Herschel Island. From Herschel Island a thousand mile sled trip was made to the eastward, during March, April, May, and June, 1899, in a vain search for musk oxen; although signs were discovered in the region south and east of Fort Lyon, the animals themselves had migrated.

On the return trip Fort McPherson was again reached June 16; the Rocky Mountains were crossed in July, and the Yukon reached in August. He descended this river to St. Michaels, and thence proceeded to Seattle, the original starting point, where he arrived after an absence of twenty-six months and four days.

Such is an outline of a trip without parallel in the annals of Arctic travel, performed in part alone, and generally with only one or two native assistants.

Mr. Stone's third trip was to the Kenai Peninsula, Alaska, late in the season of 1900. It resulted in the discovery of a new caribou (Rangifer stonei), and the acquisition of a good series of bear and moose; a number of which have been mounted and placed on exhibition in the American Museum of Natural History. His fourth trip occupied the season of 1901, during which about four months were spent on Kenai Peninsula, and one month at Popof Island and the adjoining part of the Alaska Peninsula. This trip resulted in the acquisition of more bear and moose from the Kenai Peninsula, a large series of white sheep, representing a form (Ovis dalli kenaiensis) from the same region; a new, strikingly distinct caribou (Rangifer granti), and a new bear* from the Alaska Peninsula, besides some three hundred small mammals, all new to the New York Museum, and nearly all recently new to science.

In April of the present year Mr. Stone left Seattle on his fifth trip. He will first visit the western part of the Alaska Peninsula to complete the work begun there late in the season of 1901, and later will work at points further east and south in Alaska and northern British Columbia.

Mr. Stone's first interest is in the caribou, whose ranges and local forms he has made a special subject of investigation. As early as April, 1897, before starting on

*This bear has been named Ursus merriami, but may prove to be the same as Dr. Merriam's Ursus dalli gyas, of a few days earlier date.

his long trip to the Arctic, he expressed his belief in the existence of a peculiar form of caribou in the Northwest, and when later in the same year he secured the Cassiar specimens, he wrote enthusiastically of his new find, which he recognized as completely vindicating his prediction of a new form in the Northwest. In his paper, "Some Results of a Natural History Journey to Northern British Columbia, Alaska, and the Northwest Territory, in the Interest of the American Museum of Natural History" (Bull. Am. Mus. Nat. His., Vol. XIII., 1900, pp. 31-62), he devotes eight pages to the caribou, defining these two animals being known respectively as *Rangifer montanus* and *Rangifer osborni*. So thoroughly convinced was he of the distinctness of the Alaska Peninsula form that, on completing his work last fall on the Kenai Peninsula, and fearing another such opportunity for securing it might not be available, he took the risk of a trip of nearly a thousand miles, when the season was far advanced and navigation dangerous, to secure a series of what has proved to be one of the most strongly differentiated forms of the group. There is good reason to believe that other forms he has located in the far North will demonstrate

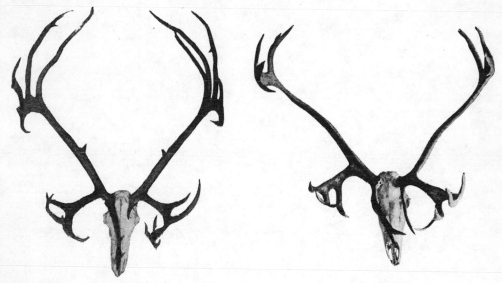

Stone's Caribou.   Grant's Caribou.

the boundaries of the various caribou areas in the great Northwest, indicating some of the characters of several local forms, and lamenting that, owing to their reckless destruction in recent years, "the caribou, the grandest of all land animals, is doomed." He thinks it possible that one well-marked form, which once inhabited the mountains north of Fort Yukon, and referred to by Hudson's Bay traders and the Loucheux Indians as a *red* caribou, may be wholly extinct. He was certainly quite right in distinguishing the caribou of southeastern British Columbia (from the Peace River southward to Montana) as different from the Cassiar form, his sagacity regarding the caribou question, as soon as specimens of them can be procured for examination.

The caribou group is an eminently plastic type, and its numerous phases of development are as yet very imperfectly known. From Maine, Minnesota, and Montana, northward to the Arctic Sea, and from Greenland to the Behring Straits, is a vast extent of country, diversified by forest, mountain ranges, and tundra, throughout which the caribou range, more or less discontinuously, and, thus broken up into bands having divers surroundings, find favorable scope for differentiation through environmental influences.